Demystifying the Darknet:

Technologies, Threats, and Trends

Qasem Abu Al-Haija
https://orcid.org/0000-0003-2422-0297
Jordan University of Science and Technology, Jordan

IGI Global
Scientific Publishing
Publishing Tomorrow's Research Today

Vice President of Editorial	Melissa Wagner
Director of Acquisitions	Mikaela Felty
Director of Book Development	Jocelynn Hessler
Production Manager	Mike Brehm
Cover Design	Jose Rosado

Published in the United States of America by
IGI Global Scientific Publishing
701 East Chocolate Avenue
Hershey, PA, 17033, USA
Tel: 717-533-8845 | Fax: 717-533-7115
Website: https://www.igi-global.com E-mail: cust@igi-global.com

Library of Congress Cataloging-in-Publication Data

LCCN: 2026021809 (CIP Data Pending)
ISBN13: 9798337397559
Isbn13Softcover: 9798337397566
EISBN13: 9798337397573

British Cataloguing in Publication Data
A Cataloguing in Publication record for this book is available from the British Library.

All praises are due to Allah for His countless blessings and the strength He granted us to complete this work. Then, this book, *Demystifying the Darknet: Technologies, Threats, and Trends*, is lovingly dedicated to the memory of my late father, Saleh Abu Al-Haija, and my late mother, Fawzeyah Abu Al-Haija. I also honor my beloved wife, Noor Jebril, and my dear children, Jory, Aysha, Zainab, and Omar, whose steady support, patience, and invaluable contributions have been a constant source of inspiration throughout this journey.

Editorial Advisory Board

Table of Contents

Detailed Table of Contents

The need for privacy, freedom of speech and protection from surveillance online has increased, and many are purchasing darknet technologies that provide these services in an anonymous manner and are hard to censor. This chapter covers the concepts of architecture, routing techniques, encryption protocols, and security mechanisms that underlie these networks. The onion routing of Tor, the garlic routing of I2P and Freenet's decentralized content storage models are analyzed to determine their respective anonymous and privacy-preserving approaches. The chapter provides a comparison of the technologies with respect to performance, scalability, usability, and threat resistance. The legal, ethical, and societal aspects of the darknet usage along with the latest challenges like AI-driven deanonymization and post-quantum security have been discussed. The chapter provides an excellent resource for researchers, practitioners and policy makers to gain in-depth understanding of the evolving nature of anonymity technologies and secure communication systems

This chapter explores advanced techniques and frameworks for crawling, monitoring, and extracting actionable intelligence from the Darknet. As cybercriminal activities increasingly migrate to anonymized platforms such as Tor-based services and decentralized networks, traditional data collection methods are insufficient for effective threat detection. This chapter examines specialized Darknet crawling mechanisms designed to operate within hidden services, addressing challenges such as dynamic content, access restrictions, and anti-crawling defenses. The chapter further examines continuous monitoring strategies for tracking illicit marketplaces, forums, and communication channels, enabling the generation of real-time cyber threat intelligence (CTI). Emphasis is placed on integrating machine learning and natural language processing techniques to analyze unstructured Darknet data, identify emerging threats, and detect patterns of cybercriminal behavior. Additionally, the chapter discusses ethical, legal, and operational considerations, including privacy concerns, data reliability....

Tor signature to be the TCP initial window sizes. The methodology aims to fill gaps in the literature on prior darknet detection in terms of operational gaps in interpretability, robustness and reproducibility.

The darknet, or dark web, is an encrypted overlay network reachable only through specialized software and invisible to standard browsers. Once used mainly to conceal communications, it has evolved into an operational backbone for cybercrime, now supporting the sale of stolen data, ransomware deployment, and money laundering. This chapter frames darknet cybercrime not as a set of isolated attacks but as a service-oriented criminal supply chain, in which ransomware acts as one coordinating layer. It maps the actors and services of this illicit ecosystem, then explains the ransomware lifecycle and the ransomware-as-a-service (RaaS) business model. It compares empirical studies measuring how this economy behaves and reviews the technologies—anonymity networks, cryptocurrency, and AI—that have lowered the cost and time of launching large-scale, high-impact attacks. It further examines defensive mechanisms, including darknet monitoring, cyber threat intelligence, incident response, ecosystem disruption, and policy coordination, before closing with a research agenda.

This chapter explores the role of blockchain and cryptocurrency forensics in investigating Darknet-enabled cybercrime. Cryptocurrencies such as Bitcoin and privacy-focused coins are widely used in Darknet marketplaces because they support pseudonymous transactions that complicate tracing and attribution. The chapter examines forensic techniques for blockchain analysis, including address clustering, transaction graph analysis, and heuristic-based tracing. It also explains how illicit financial flows are concealed through mixers, tumblers, and chain-hopping strategies. In addition, the chapter reviews analytics tools used by law enforcement and cybersecurity professionals to detect suspicious patterns and link wallets to entities. Challenges related to privacy-enhancing cryptocurrencies, blockchain scalability, and legal considerations are discussed. Finally, emerging threats involving decentralized finance (DeFi) and cross-chain transactions are explored to provide researchers, forensic analysts, and policymakers with insights into illicit financial activity in the Darknet ecosystem.

This chapter examines the role of the Darknet as a platform for disseminating extremist and illegal content, including propaganda, recruitment materials, hate speech, and illicit media. The anonymity, resilience, and censorship resistance provided by Darknet technologies have enabled extremist groups and criminal actors to distribute content at scale while evading detection and takedown efforts. This chapter analyzes the structure, channels, and techniques used for content dissemination, including encrypted forums, hidden services, and decentralized platforms. A key focus is placed on understanding how such

There is an urgent need for secure authentication mechanisms considering the rise in cybercrime and illegal activities carried out in secret internet locations. Conventional authentication techniques such as passwords, cryptographic credentials, and others face limitations such as credential theft, weak password handling, among others. This project proposes a novel method called the "Secure Biometric Authentication Framework for Demystifying the Darknet" to be used in accessing darknet websites. The technique incorporates fingerprint-based authentication mechanism complemented by advanced cryptographic systems. It enhances security and ensures that confidential personal information is protected against any kind of identity theft and other threats. Each session is assigned a different encryption key, ensuring perfect forward secrecy as well as prevention of any replay attack and compromise of credentials. It has been tested in a laboratory setting using FVC2002 and NIST databases, showing successful implementation with authentication rates of up to 99.83%, and 0% false negatives.

Generative AI now operates on both sides of darknet conflict. Underground markets sell specialized models for malware authoring and social engineering, while threat-intelligence teams use similar technology to crawl, classify, and disrupt the same infrastructure. This chapter argues that the offensive and defensive uses of generative AI must be understood as one coupled system, where each advance reshapes strategies available to the other. The argument develops across five parts: generative architectures relevant to darknet operations; a taxonomy of offensive capabilities mapped to the cybercrime kill chain; a survey of defensive deployments including hidden-service crawling, jargon-tolerant NLP, traffic classification, and blockchain forensics; an arms-race framework tracing offense-defense feedback episodes; and a discussion of ethical, jurisdictional, and structural questions, including agentic AI within hidden services. This chapter supports researchers, practitioners, and law-enforcement readers analyzing a landscape changing faster than existing surveys acknowledge.

In this book chapter, we have discussed the darknet threat landscape and its criminal ecosystems, where the structure of darknet criminal networks is analyzed, and different illicit activities are classified with their typical actors and supporting technologies. On the other hand, counter-operations in the darknet are examined, from intelligence gathering and the use of emerging technologies such as artificial intelligence to evidence acquisition and chain of custody requirements for court admissibility. Challenges in implementing counter-operations are also explained, showing that collaboration between public and private entities at both national and international levels is now a necessity, not an option, for effective

Preface

INTRODUCTION

The Darknet remains one of the most misunderstood and complex dimensions of the modern digital ecosystem. While often associated with cybercrime, illicit marketplaces, and anonymous communications, the Darknet also represents a technological response to growing concerns regarding privacy, surveillance, censorship, and digital freedom. Over the past decade, rapid advancements in anonymity networks, cryptographic protocols, decentralized platforms, artificial intelligence, and blockchain technologies have transformed the Darknet into a multifaceted environment that presents both opportunities and risks for governments, businesses, researchers, and society at large. Understanding this evolving landscape requires a multidisciplinary perspective that integrates technical, legal, social, ethical, and security perspectives.

The motivation behind this book, *Demystifying the Darknet: Technologies, Threats, and Trends*, stems from the growing need for comprehensive, evidence-based knowledge about hidden networks and their increasing influence on cyberspace. The Darknet has evolved beyond its early perception as merely a repository of illicit activities. Today, it functions as a sophisticated ecosystem where anonymity technologies, cybercriminal enterprises, privacy advocates, political activists, threat actors, law enforcement agencies, and cybersecurity professionals continuously interact. Consequently, understanding the Darknet has become essential for cybersecurity practitioners, intelligence analysts, policymakers, academics, and technology developers seeking to address contemporary digital challenges.

This edited volume brings together contributions from an international group of scholars and practitioners who provide diverse perspectives on the technologies, threats, investigative methodologies, and future directions shaping the Darknet ecosystem. The chapters examine foundational anonymity architectures, advanced threat intelligence techniques, artificial intelligence applications, cryptocurrency forensics, ransomware economies, extremist content dissemination, law enforcement strategies, and post-quantum security considerations. Collectively, these contributions offer a balanced exploration of both the enabling technologies that support anonymity and the security concerns arising from their misuse.

The primary objective of this book is not merely to describe the Darknet but to demystify it. Through rigorous analysis and practical insights, the contributors explore how hidden networks operate, how cybercriminal activities are conducted and investigated, how emerging technologies influence both offensive and defensive capabilities, and how future developments may reshape digital anonymity. By combining theoretical foundations with real-world applications, this volume seeks to serve as a valuable reference for researchers, students, cybersecurity professionals, law enforcement agencies, policymakers, and anyone interested in understanding one of the most challenging domains of cyberspace.

OVERVIEW OF THE CHAPTERS

The book is organized into 15 chapters that examine the technological foundations, operational mechanisms, threat landscape, investigative approaches, and future developments of the Darknet.

Chapter 1, *Darknet Architecture and Anonymity Technologies*, introduces the fundamental architectures that underpin anonymous communication systems, including Tor, I2P, and Freenet. The chapter explains routing mechanisms, encryption protocols, and privacy-preserving designs while discussing emerging challenges such as AI-driven deanonymization and post-quantum threats.

Chapter 2, *Darknet Crawling and Threat Intelligence Analysis*, explores specialized techniques for collecting and analyzing information from hidden services. The authors discuss advanced crawling frameworks, the generation of cyber threat intelligence, machine learning-assisted monitoring, and the ethical and operational considerations involved in Darknet intelligence gathering.

Chapter 3, *Automated Models for Darknet Monitoring and Criminal Attribution*, examines how machine learning, deep learning, graph analytics, and transformer-based natural language processing can be used to automate surveillance activities and identify criminal actors across multiple darknet marketplaces and platforms.

Chapter 4, *Hybrid Metaheuristic Crawlers for Adaptive Darknet Marketplace Intelligence*, introduces an innovative hybrid optimization framework that combines Genetic Algorithms, Particle Swarm Optimization, and Ant Colony Optimization to improve intelligence-collection efficiency and adaptability in dynamic darknet environments.

Chapter 5, *AI-Driven Darknet Threat Detection*, presents advanced artificial intelligence methodologies for identifying darknet-related threats. By integrating supervised and unsupervised learning techniques, interpretability frameworks, and adversarial robustness mechanisms, the chapter demonstrates practical approaches to threat detection and classification.

Chapter 6, *Darknet Cybercrime and Ransomware*, investigates the darknet-enabled cybercrime economy and ransomware ecosystem. The chapter explores ransomware-as-a-service business models, criminal supply chains, cryptocurrency-enabled operations, and strategies for disruption and defense.

Chapter 7, *Blockchain and Cryptocurrency Forensics for the Darknet*, focuses on tracing illicit financial transactions within darknet ecosystems. It discusses blockchain analytics, transaction graph analysis, wallet attribution, privacy-enhancing cryptocurrencies, and emerging forensic challenges associated with decentralized finance platforms.

Chapter 8, *Extremist and Illegal Content Dissemination in the Darknet Ecosystem*, analyzes how extremist organizations and criminal groups exploit anonymous platforms to distribute propaganda, recruit members, and disseminate illicit content. The chapter also examines detection and mitigation approaches supported by machine learning technologies.

Chapter 9, *Darknet Implications in IoT, 5G/6G, and Emerging Infrastructures*, extends the discussion to next-generation technologies and critical infrastructures. The authors investigate how darknet-enabled threats intersect with IoT environments, smart cities, cyber-physical systems, and advanced telecommunications networks.

Chapter 10, *Securing Darknet Web Applications*, examines web application security challenges within darknet environments, with particular attention to SQL injection attacks and advanced detection frameworks that combine static and dynamic analysis techniques.

Chapter 11, *Darknet Authentication and Key Management*, explores secure authentication mechanisms for anonymous systems. The chapter proposes a biometric-based framework supported by advanced cryptographic techniques to enhance identity protection, confidentiality, and secure access control.

Chapter 12, *Weaponized and Defensive Generative AI-Darknet Applications*, investigates the rapidly emerging role of generative artificial intelligence in darknet operations. The chapter highlights both offensive applications, such as malware development and social engineering, and defensive applications, including threat intelligence, content classification, and forensic analysis.

Chapter 13, *Darknet Counter-Operations and Law Enforcement*, discusses investigative methodologies, evidence-collection procedures, legal challenges, and collaborative frameworks used by law enforcement agencies to combat darknet-enabled criminal activities while respecting legal and privacy constraints.

Chapter 14, *Cybersecurity Awareness and Resilience Against Darknet Threats*, emphasizes the human and organizational dimensions of cybersecurity. The chapter presents awareness strategies, resilience frameworks, risk assessment models, and emerging technologies that can strengthen societal defenses against darknet-related threats.

Chapter 15, *Darknet Futures and Post-Quantum Security*, concludes the technical journey by examining future trends in darknet evolution. The authors explore decentralized anonymity platforms, the implications of quantum computing, and post-quantum cryptographic approaches that may shape the next generation of secure and anonymous communication systems.

Together, these chapters provide a comprehensive and multidisciplinary examination of the Darknet, bridging foundational concepts, technological innovations, operational realities, and future challenges.

CONCLUSION

The Darknet represents one of the most dynamic and consequential domains within contemporary cyberspace. As anonymity technologies continue to evolve and digital infrastructures become increasingly interconnected, the significance of hidden networks will likely expand rather than diminish. The chapters in this volume demonstrate that the Darknet cannot be understood solely through the lens of cybercrime; it is also a technological environment shaped by legitimate concerns about privacy, freedom of expression, surveillance resistance, and secure communication. Consequently, effective engagement with the Darknet requires a nuanced understanding rather than a simplistic characterization.

A recurring theme throughout this book is the continuous interaction between technological innovation and security challenges. Advances in artificial intelligence, blockchain technologies, decentralized architectures, and cryptographic systems are simultaneously strengthening privacy protections and enabling more sophisticated cyber threats. This dual-use nature of emerging technologies creates complex challenges for researchers, cybersecurity practitioners, policymakers, and law enforcement agencies. Addressing these challenges demands collaborative approaches that integrate technical expertise, legal frameworks, ethical considerations, and international cooperation.

The contributors to this volume have highlighted numerous opportunities for future research and development. Areas such as AI-assisted threat intelligence, criminal attribution, decentralized platforms, blockchain analytics, critical infrastructure protection, and post-quantum security remain active and rapidly evolving fields of investigation. As cyber adversaries continue to adapt their tactics and technologies, defenders must likewise embrace innovation and interdisciplinary collaboration to remain effective. The future of darknet research will increasingly depend on integrating advances from cybersecurity, artificial intelligence, data science, cryptography, and digital governance.

As editors, we hope that this volume contributes meaningfully to the growing body of knowledge surrounding the Darknet and serves as a valuable resource for researchers, students, practitioners, policymakers, and law enforcement professionals. By bringing together diverse perspectives and emerging research directions, this book seeks to foster informed discussion, encourage further investigation, and support the development of effective strategies to understand and address the challenges and opportunities posed by anonymous digital ecosystems. Ultimately, demystifying the Darknet is not only a technical endeavor but also an essential step toward building a safer, more resilient, and more informed digital society.

Qasem Abu Al-Haija
Jordan University of Science and Technology, Jordan

Acknowledgment

We want to express our heartfelt gratitude to all authors whose chapters have significantly enriched this book. Your insightful contributions and tireless dedication have advanced the development of intelligent and secure software systems and inspired fresh perspectives in this domain. Your work stands as great evidence of the power of interdisciplinary collaboration and serves as the foundation of the invaluable knowledge compiled in this book.

We are equally grateful to the active reviewers whose thoughtful critiques and great commitment to quality have elevated the standard of this publication. A special thank you goes to the IGI-Global, whose exceptional support and professionalism have been instrumental in bringing this project to fruition. Your collective efforts have shaped a resource that we believe will be a cornerstone for future advancements in our field.

Introduction

The rapid evolution of cyberspace has fundamentally transformed the way societies communicate, conduct business, exchange information, and protect digital assets. Alongside these remarkable technological advances, an increasingly sophisticated hidden ecosystem, commonly known as the Darknet, has emerged. Although frequently portrayed solely as a haven for cybercriminals and illicit activities, the Darknet is, in reality, a far more complex technological environment. It embodies both legitimate innovations in privacy-preserving communication and significant cybersecurity challenges that continue to reshape the global digital landscape.

In this context, *Demystifying the Darknet: Technologies, Threats, and Trends* arrives at a particularly important moment. As governments, enterprises, researchers, and law enforcement agencies confront increasingly sophisticated cyber threats, there is an urgent need for comprehensive resources that examine the Darknet from balanced, evidence-based, and multidisciplinary perspectives. This volume successfully addresses that need by moving beyond popular misconceptions and providing readers with a technically rigorous exploration of the technologies, security implications, investigative methodologies, and emerging trends that define hidden digital ecosystems.

One of the greatest strengths of this book lies in its breadth and interdisciplinary vision. Rather than focusing exclusively on cybercrime, the contributors examine the technological foundations that enable anonymous communications while simultaneously exploring their security, legal, ethical, and societal implications. The integration of cybersecurity, artificial intelligence, blockchain analytics, digital forensics, cryptography, cyber threat intelligence, and privacy-enhancing technologies offers readers a comprehensive understanding of one of the most challenging domains in modern cyberspace.

The editors have assembled an outstanding collection of contributions from international researchers and practitioners whose expertise spans both academia and industry. Throughout the volume, readers encounter thoughtful discussions of anonymity architectures, intelligent threat detection, automated Darknet intelligence gathering, ransomware ecosystems, cryptocurrency forensics, extremist content analysis, secure authentication mechanisms, generative artificial intelligence, law enforcement operations, critical infrastructure protection, and post-quantum security. Together, these topics illustrate not only the complexity of the Darknet but also the diverse technological innovations required to understand, investigate, and defend against evolving cyber threats.

Particularly noteworthy is the book's emphasis on emerging technologies. Artificial intelligence is transforming both offensive and defensive cybersecurity capabilities, while blockchain technologies, decentralized platforms, advanced cryptographic protocols, and quantum computing continue to reshape the future of digital anonymity. By examining these rapidly evolving developments alongside practical investigative techniques and real-world applications, this volume bridges the gap between theoretical research and operational cybersecurity practice.

Another distinguishing feature of this work is its balanced perspective. The contributors acknowledge that technologies that support anonymity are not inherently malicious; rather, they are powerful tools whose impact depends on how they are employed. This nuanced treatment encourages readers to appreciate the legitimate roles of privacy, freedom of expression, and secure communication while recognizing the equally important need to combat cybercrime, financial fraud, ransomware operations, illicit marketplaces, and other malicious activity that exploit hidden networks.

This book will undoubtedly serve a wide and diverse audience. Researchers and graduate students will find a valuable foundation for future investigations into Darknet technologies and cybersecurity. Cybersecurity professionals and threat intelligence analysts will benefit from the practical methodologies and emerging defensive strategies presented throughout the chapters. Policymakers and law enforcement agencies will gain meaningful insights into the evolving technical and regulatory challenges associated with anonymous digital ecosystems. Likewise, educators will appreciate the book as a comprehensive reference that captures both the current state of the field and the research directions shaping its future.

As cyberspace continues to evolve, understanding the Darknet is no longer optional—it has become an essential component of modern cybersecurity knowledge. Addressing the challenges posed by hidden networks requires not only technological innovation but also interdisciplinary collaboration among computer scientists, cybersecurity specialists, legal experts, policymakers, and international organizations. This volume provides exactly such an integrated perspective.

I am confident that *Demystifying the Darknet: Technologies, Threats, and Trends* will become a valuable reference for academics, practitioners, students, cybersecurity professionals, and decision-makers worldwide. More importantly, it will encourage informed discussion, inspire future research, and contribute meaningfully to the development of safer, more resilient, and more secure digital societies.

I congratulate the editors and contributing authors for producing an outstanding scholarly work that illuminates one of the most fascinating and strategically important frontiers of cybersecurity. I invite readers to explore the chapters that follow and to engage with the ideas, innovations, and challenges presented throughout this timely and highly relevant volume.

Chapter 1
Darknet Architecture and Anonymity Technologies (Tor, I2P, Freenet)

Karthic Sundaram
http://orcid.org/0000-0002-0968-8468
SRM Institute of Science and Technology, India

Yuvaraj Natarajan
Vellore Institute of Technology, India

S. Vinu
SRM Institute of Science and Technology, India

P. Jessie
Dr. Mahalingam College of Engineering and Technology, India

ABSTRACT

The need for privacy, freedom of speech and protection from surveillance online has increased, and many are purchasing darknet technologies that provide these services in an anonymous manner and are hard to censor. This chapter covers the concepts of architecture, routing techniques, encryption protocols, and security mechanisms that underlie these networks. The onion routing of Tor, the garlic routing of I2P and Freenet's decentralized content storage models are analyzed to determine their respective anonymous and privacy-preserving approaches. The chapter provides a comparison of the technologies with respect to performance, scalability, usability, and threat resistance. The legal, ethical, and societal aspects of the darknet usage along with the latest challenges like AI-driven deanonymization and post-quantum security have been discussed. The chapter provides an excellent resource for researchers, practitioners and policy makers to gain in-depth understanding of the evolving nature of anonymity technologies and secure communication systems

DOI: 10.4018/979-8-3373-9755-9.ch001

1. INTRODUCTION

The internet has been growing rapidly and has completely transformed how people communicate, access information, and conduct transactions. Although the surface web remains the most visible and most accessed aspect of cyberspace, much of the web usage is not visible to common search engines. The darknet is a unique network environment that provides greater privacy, anonymity, and resistance to censorship than the internet, and it exists within this hidden ecosystem. Darknet technologies are a response to the growing threats of surveillance, data collection, cyber-attacks, and restrictions on information flow. As threats from surveillance, data collection, cyberattacks, and restrictions on information flow have increased, darknet technologies have been developed (Muntaka & Bou Abdo, 2026).

Anonymity is a basic requirement for most Internet users. This group encompasses journalists, researchers, activists, whistleblowers, and those residing in oppressive countries. These users are seeking ways to communicate privately and remain anonymous online without being discovered by governments, organizations or criminals. In response to these issues, some anonymity-preserving technologies have been developed, equipping users with the ability to obtain information securely and to hide their identities, tracks, or traces from others (Saleem et al., 2022; Jayapradha et al., 2022).

The three famous anonymity tools are Tor (The Onion Router), Invisible Internet Project (I2P), and Freenet. Even though the goal of each of these three systems is to guarantee user privacy, they differ in target applications, security models, routing methods, and even architectural structures. Tor is mainly geared towards anonymous web surfing through onion routing; on the other hand, I2P is mainly geared towards secure peer-to-peer communication and internal services. While Freenet is mainly geared towards decentralized, censorship-resistant content storage and distribution. Knowledge of how these technologies work is a prerequisite for recognizing their strengths, limitations, and potential for practical use. This chapter explains the darknet architecture and the anonymity of Tor, I2P, and Freenet. It also discusses how they work, their advantages and disadvantages, some real-world applications, and the current challenges and future directions of anonymous communication systems.

2. DARKNET ARCHITECTURE

The darknet is a network of networks that exists on top of the internet and is intended to provide enhanced privacy and anonymity, as well as help users circumvent censorship. Only with special software, setups, and protocols, usually which disguise the user's identity and communication, can access be gained to these networks. Unlike traditional Internet services, darknet systems are more concerned with protecting the content of communication, and they appeal to users willing to sacrifice their content from surveillance, traffic monitoring, and content restrictions. Darknet technologies have, to a great extent, adapted to the new challenges of digital privacy and information control. Their designs focus on making it impossible for an unauthorized party to even catch a glimpse of the user's activities while at the same time operating in a way that guarantees the user's communication under conditions of a hostile network environment (Fachkha & Debbabi, 2016; Kavitha et al., 2023).

Figure 1. Overview of darknet architecture

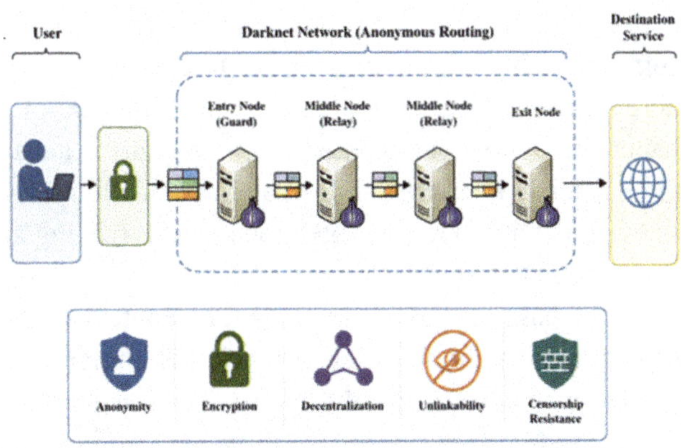

2.1 Surface Web, Deep Web, and Darknet

The Internet is often divided into three main layers: the surface web, the deep web, and the darknet. The surface web comprises publicly available webpages that are indexed by regular search engines. Meanwhile, the deep web contains content not indexed by search engines, including private databases, university libraries, corporate intranets, and subscription-based services. The darknet is a highly specialized segment of the deep web that deliberately uses anonymity-preserving technologies. Darknet networks, unlike the deep web, are made to hide the identification of users, service providers, and communication endpoints. Accessing darknet resources, also called the black net or hidden net, typically requires specialized software such as Tor, I2P, or Freenet, which provide secure, anonymous communication channels (Hatta, 2020).

Table 1. Comparison of surface web, beep web, and darknet

Feature	Surface Web	Deep Web	Darknet
Search Engine Indexed	Yes	No	No
Public Accessibility	Yes	Limited	Restricted
Special Software Required	No	No	Yes
Anonymity Support	Low	Moderate	High
Typical Content	Public Websites	Databases, Portals	Anonymous Services
Privacy Focus	Low	Medium	High

2.2 Core Architectural Characteristics of Darknet Systems

Decentralization: One of the main features of darknet systems is decentralization. Rather than relying on a single authority and centralized infrastructure, the network is operated by distributing the tasks to different nodes. This type of design helps to avoid censorship, it is less prone to single point of failure and it increases the overall availability of the network. Also, it becomes quite difficult for the enemy to disrupt network services or detect communication participants (Jangale, 2025).

Pseudonymity and Anonymity: In fact, the dark net structures are designed to keep users' identities hidden by offering different levels of pseudonymity and anonymity. Anonymity means that the real identity of the participant cannot be figured out, whereas pseudonymity is a condition under which users operate through persistent identifiers which are not directly linked with their real-world identities. The use of these methods provides users with privacy protection against tracking and profiling while, at the same time, enabling safe (Bancroft, 2019).

Encryption: Encryption is the base of darknet security. The content of data sent over darknet networks is protected with cryptographic technologies that block unauthorized users from gaining access or intercepting the data. Encryption not only keeps the communication private but also besides ensuring the authenticity of data, it assists in hiding the users' sensitive data from potential eavesdroppers. Usually, networks implement several layers of encryption to make it harder for outsiders to conduct traffic analysis or surveillance (Moore & Rid, 2016).

Peer-to-Peer Network Design: Darknet systems mostly use peer-to-peer (P2P) models, in which each participating node serves as both a client and a service provider. This distributed approach does away with central servers and leads to better fault tolerance. Besides this, P2P networking also helps in achieving anonymity since the responsibility of the network is shared by many participants, making it very difficult to figure out the sources and destinations of communication.

2.3 Anonymity Requirements in Darknet Networks

The main goal of darknet architecture is to ensure very strong anonymity but also to keep the communication secure and reliable. To fulfill this goal, darknet systems have to meet quite a few important requirements.

Security: Darknet networks are expected to shield their users against various types of threats coming from the cyber world such as eavesdropping, analyzing the traffic, nodes get compromised, and unauthorized data access. Strong cryptographic methods and secure protocols for routing are some of the critical components of network security.

Privacy Protection: Privacy protection means keeping secret the identities of users, the communication patterns, and the browsing activities. Good privacy techniques make it impossible for the attacker to connect the network traffic to one or more individuals or organizations (Adewopo et al., 2019).

Censorship Resistance: Darknet systems are created in such a way that they do not surrender to the restriction of the flow of information set by some bodies. By spreading the services over many different nodes and by using anonymous routing, these networks assist the users in accessing the information even when the conditions are so restrictive that it is not easy to get the information at all (Jardine, 2018).

Reliability and Resilience: The anonymity technologies should not just break down when there is a failure of the network or when there is a situation that is aimed at the disruption of the network. Such resilient architectures make it possible for communication to continue without the least break and they maintain the availability of services even when things are really bad.

2.4 Applications of Darknet Technologies

Privacy Preservation: Protecting personal privacy is probably the most widespread use of darknet technologies. More people are using anonymity networks to secure their private interactions, avoid being tracked, and keep their digital identities under their control.

Whistleblowing and Activism: Darknet platforms are supplying a safe and secure means of communication to whistleblowers, journalists, and activists who might be at risk for revealing sensitive information. The use of anonymity tools helps protect sources and securely exchange information without fear of retaliation (Davis & Arrigo, 2021).

Secure Communication in Restrictive Environments: Using darknet tools, people living in countries where the government controls the Internet can communicate freely and access information without revealing their identities. This not only helps the individual express themselves but also allows them to share information without restrictions.

Cybersecurity Research and Threat Intelligence: Those who work in the field of testing and securing computer systems make use of darknet networks, for instance, to make themselves familiar with newly arisen threats, deciphering the patterns of the criminals' acts, and undertaking studies of the underground digital ecosystems. Such an investigation helps in the enhancement of detecting harmful things and in being ready for attacks in cyberspace.

3. INTRODUCTION TO THE ONION ROUTER (TOR)

TOR is the most widely adopted anonymity network designed to protect user privacy and enable anonymous communication over the Internet. Originally developed in the mid-1990s by researchers at the United States Naval Research Laboratory, Tor was created to secure government communications by concealing the identities and locations of users. Eventually, it transformed into a community-driven open-source project with contributors including researchers, developers and volunteers worldwide (Kareem, 2024).

Tor's main purpose is to mask user's identity by not letting the observers connect the users to their online activities. It does this by a decentralized network of the relays operated by the volunteers that pass the Internet traffic through several layers of encryption. Nowadays, Tor is being used largely by journalists, human rights defenders, students, and other privacy-minded individuals who are looking to guard against surveillance, traffic analysis, and censorship.

3.2 TOR Architecture

TOR uses a layered routing technique called onion routing, where data messages are doubly or triply encrypted and sent through a chain of intermediary nodes before arriving at the destination, figure 2 illustrates this process. Hence, the system is designed in such a way that no single node can know both the sender and the destination.

3.2.1 Onion Routing

Onion routing is the core principle of the Tor network. Prior to being sent, a message is encrypted in several layers, with each layer matching a different relay on the communication path. When a message goes through the network, each relay decrypts one layer, gets the necessary routing information to reach the next hop and the source and final destination of the message remain hidden (Bidv & Waghmare 2024).

This multi-level encryption strategy makes sure that neither the intermediate nodes receive the full path of the communication nor the content of the data being transmitted. To that end, onion routing not only enhances user anonymity but also safeguards users against traffic analysis (Bhuvaneswari et al., 2024).

Figure 2. Outline of TOR architecture

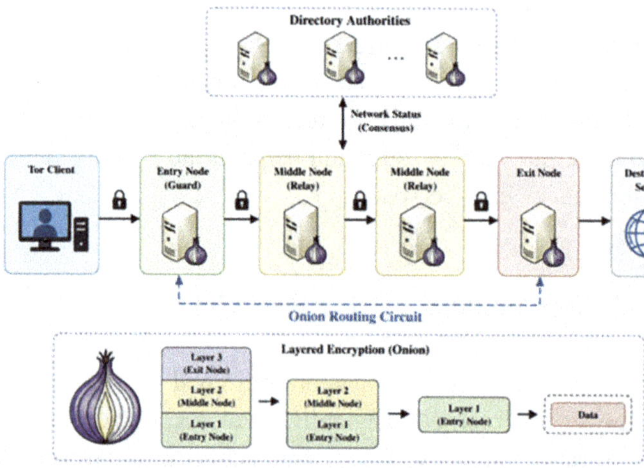

3.2.2 Tor Network Components

The Tor network comprises specialized components that work together to enable anonymous communication, as illustrated in Figure 3.

Directory Authorities: Directory authorities are responsible for keeping track of the Tor relays that are available, as well as their status. The trusted servers gather the information about the network and produce a consensus document which helps clients in choosing appropriate relays for making communication circuits (Döpmann, 2025).

Entry Nodes: Entry nodes or guard nodes act as a user's first contact with the Tor network. These nodes are aware of the user's IP address but do not know the final destination of the communication. To lessen the risk of encountering malicious relays, Tor generally assigns a few guarded nodes that the user trusts.

Middle Relays: Middle relays are responsible for sending encrypted traffic from the entry node to the exit node and vice versa. As they are unaware of the original sender or the final destination, this helps in anonymity and making the route difficult to trace (Swan, 2016).

Exit Nodes: Exit nodes are the last relay in a Tor circuit. They decrypt the last layer of encryption and send the traffic onto the intended destination on the public Internet. Although they can see outgoing traffic which is not secured with end-to-end encryption, they are unaware of the identity of the original user.

Figure 3. Onion routing mechanism

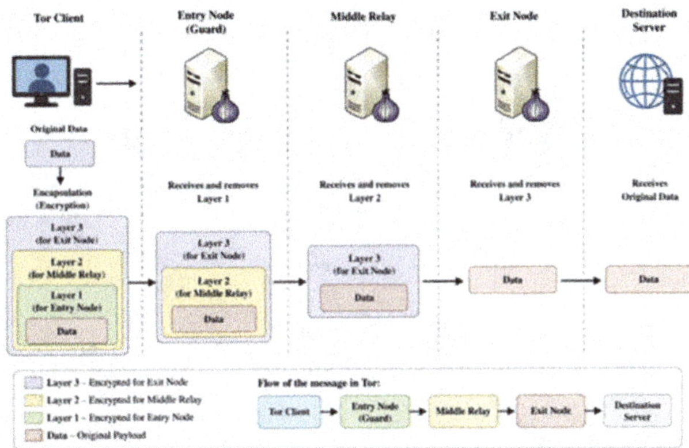

3.2.3 Circuit Creation and Path Selection

Before sending data, Tor creates a virtual communication path called a circuit. Usually, a circuit involves three relays: a guard node, a middle relay, and an exit node (Kate & Goldberg, 2010). The client selects these relays using information from directory authorities and establishes encrypted session keys with each node, as depicted in Figure 4. After the circuit has been established, all communication will be sent through the chosen path. For greater anonymity, Tor changes circuits from time to time, thereby making it harder for someone to do traffic correlation over long periods. The changing nature of circuit formation is a major factor why Tor can still remain hidden even under intense surveillance and tracking (Panchenko & Renner, 2009).

3.3 Advantages of Tor

Tor gives strong anonymity by hiding the link between a user and their online actions. Using multiple relays and encryption at different layers makes it very difficult for an adversary to trace a communication path. Tor allows users to access blocked pages or services that are censored by governments, institutions, or network administrators. Through anonymous routing and bridge relays, Tor helps users evade network restrictions and censorship. Tor Project has a public-source model of its development which helps in keeping the project transparent and receptive to security audits by independent bodies as well as improvement on a continual basis. The network has become more secure and reliable through time as a result of contributions of researchers and volunteers. Tor also includes support of onion services, which lets websites and services to function in an anonymous way without disclosing their physical location or IP address.

This feature allows for communication and content hosting to be securely carried out at the same time as protecting both the hosting party and the users.

Figure 4. TOR Circuit creation process

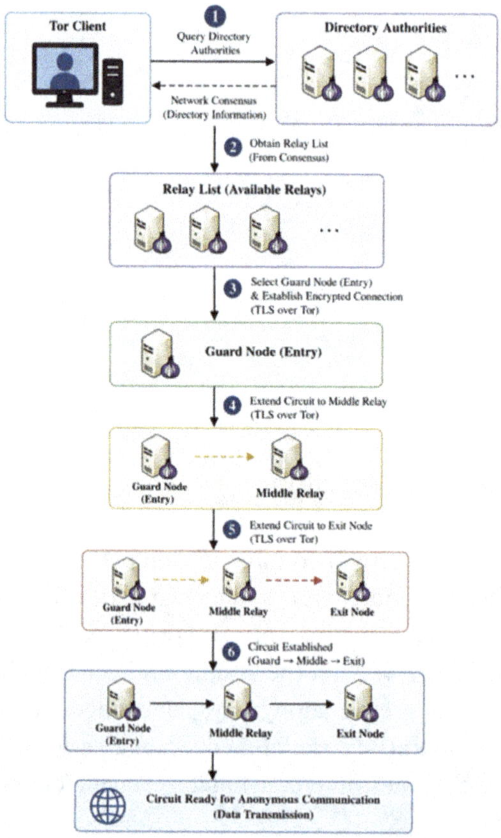

3.4 Limitations and Challenges of Tor

Performance and Latency: Because traffic is routed through multiple geographically distributed relays and encrypted several times, Tor generally experiences higher latency and lower throughput compared to conventional Internet connections. These performance limitations can affect bandwidth-intensive applications (Chauhan et al., 2019).

Traffic Correlation Attacks: Although Tor provides strong anonymity, sophisticated adversaries capable of observing both ends of a communication channel may perform traffic correlation attacks. By analyzing timing patterns and traffic characteristics, attackers may infer communication relationships under certain conditions (Nasr et al., 2018; Basyoni et al., 2020).

Malicious Exit Nodes: Exit nodes represent a potential security concern because they handle traffic leaving the Tor network. Unencrypted data transmitted through an exit node may be observed or manipulated by malicious operators. Consequently, the use of end-to-end encryption protocols such as HTTPS remains essential.

Misuse of the Network: Like many privacy-enhancing technologies, Tor has occasionally been associated with illicit activities. While the technology itself serves legitimate privacy and freedom-of-expression purposes, its misuse has contributed to public misconceptions and regulatory concerns.

3.5 Applications of Tor

Tor is a network that helps people reach special websites and services that use onion addresses to be an anonymous. These sites will give their users and service providers anonymity. The Tor browser allows people the capability of surfing the net while against being tracked, profiled, and having their location disclosed. This feature is extremely helpful to users who run their affairs under surveillance at a very high level. Besides email systems Tor can be put together with messaging applications and other means of communication so that one can gain additional privacy and security against the exposure of highly confidential information coming from unauthorized surveillance. Tor is also a tool that researchers and cybersecurity professionals resort to so that they may be in a position not only to investigate security risks, but also to identify malicious infrastructures and do security analyses without disclosing their identities and locations.

4. I2P (INVISIBLE INTERNET PROJECT)

I2P is a decentralised anonymity network allowing users to have secure and private communications inside a closed overlay network. Compared to Tor that primarily grants users anonymous Internet access, I2P provides a platform where completely anonymous communication, content sharing, and service hosting can be done within its own environment. Initially released as an open-source project, I2P still operates as a highly resilient anonymity network which is not only censorship resistant but also enables secure peer-to-peer communication by using a distributed network architecture (Abdo & Hossain, 2023).

Besides helping to raise public consciousness about online surveillance, traffic analysis and the restriction of digital communication, I2P was also introduced as a weapon to counter these threats. Over the years, it has become a full-fledged platform of anonymity that offers support for myriad applications such as anonymous browsing, messaging, file sharing, and website hosting. By combining sophisticated routing and encryption, I2P allows users to communicate confidentially while hiding their identities and network activity.

4.1 I2P Architecture

I2P operates as an overlay network that routes traffic through multiple participating nodes, known as routers. The architecture is designed to protect both communication content and routing information, making traffic analysis and user identification significantly more difficult as given in Figure 5.

Figure 5. Architecture of I2P model

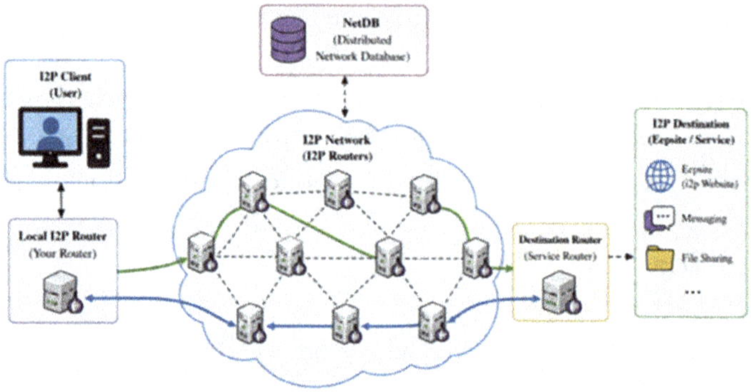

4.1.1 Anonymous Communication Model

The I2P communication model differs from the typical Internet in that in a traditional network, a direct connection is established between a sender and a receiver, while in I2P, data is routed through several other peers. Communication is conducted through a system of inbound and outbound tunnels, which means that not even one person knows the full path of communication. This separation of channels has the double effect of enhancing anonymity and lessening the possibility of traffic correlation attacks (Liu et al., 2019).

Most of the time, the I2P network is used for internal services and destinations marked by cryptographic keys rather than traditional IP addresses. Consequently, users can communicate and access services without revealing their network locations.

4.1.2 Garlic Routing

Garlic routing is the fundamental anonymity tool of I2P. It is a development of the idea of onion routing in that it permits multiple encrypted messages to be combined into one single transmission, which is called a garlic message (Jadav et al., 2023). Each message can have several pieces of information for different recipients or different purposes, as shown in Figure 6.

Besides that, bundling messages also makes it hard for an outsider to analyze the communication by masking the patterns of communication. Moreover, garlic routing allows the network to be more flexible and at the same time provides a secure environment where the control messages and the data can be transferred together. Layers upon layers of encryption guarantee that intermediate nodes only have access to the information about the route that is necessary for forwarding traffic (Maalavika et al., 2023).

Figure 6. Garlic routing mechanism in I2P

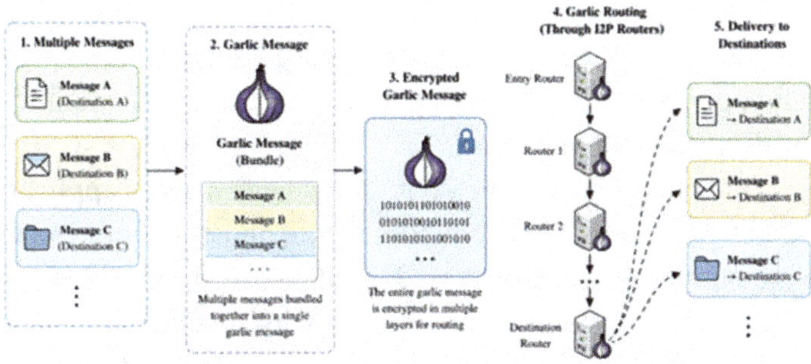

4.1.3 Inbound and Outbound Tunnels

One of the most distinctive aspects of I2P is its communication scheme of using separate inbound and outbound tunnels. Outbound tunnels are the means of a user sending messages to the network; on the contrary, inbound tunnels are the user's way of receiving responses. This back-to-back tunnel system loopholes anonymity boosts because different communication paths are used for outgoing and incoming traffic. Therefore, even if adversaries catch a glimpse of the network, they won't be able to easily match message sources and destinations. Moreover, continuously creating and changing tunnels enhances privacy by preventing long-term exposure to specific network routes (Muntaka & Bou Abdo, 2025).

4.1.4 Distributed Network Database

I2P uses a decentralized network directory called NetDB to keep track of routers running the network and to find services. Rather than relying on centralized directory authorities like Tor, NetDB is fully decentralized and uses a distributed hash table (DHT) as its mechanism. This decentralized architecture increases the system's resistance to censorship and also reduces the risk of single points of failure. The network information is shared among multiple participants; therefore combating adversaries who try to manipulate routing information or disrupt network operations becomes more challenging.

4.1.5 Internal Services and E-Sites

The I2P network can be used to run anonymous services called eepsites which are totally self-contained, hosted websites within the I2P network. Only through I2P-compatible tools can a user access these services which rely on cryptographic destination addresses as a unique identifier. Eepsites enable users to publish information, host forums, share content, and provide services while at the same time achieving anonymity. In the network both clients and servers are hidden; as a result, eepsites are strongly protected both camouflage-wise and against censorship (Gehl, 2018).

4.2 Advantages of I2P

I2P is a product that is highly focused on keeping the identity of the internal anonymous services hidden. Due to its system design, I2P can consolidate the providers of the services as well as the users with strong confidentiality, given this it is highly attractive for those who want to run anonymous sites, messaging platforms, or distributed applications.

The network has been intentionally architected to allow peer-to-peer applications to function in an efficient manner. File sharing, decentralized communication, and collaborative applications can be run securely even without a centralized infrastructure. Not having central directory servers enhances the overall vitality of the system and also lessens the need for trusted authorities. The distributed management is a further step towards making the system more censorship resistant and also contributes to its robustness. Garlic routing, split of tunnels, and constantly changing routes altogether raise the difficulty level for anyone trying to perform a traffic analysis attack. Thanks to these methods it is very hard for adversaries to identify the communication relations between users.

4.3 Limitations of I2P

Compared with Tor, I2P has a smaller user base and a less developed ecosystem. The lower number of users could negatively impact network diversity and also the range of available services and applications. Also, using multiple tunnels, encryption layers, and distributed routing naturally generates extra latency. As a result, some applications might be slower than usual Internet communication. Because I2P mainly concentrates on internal services, the access to resources outside the network is not as straightforward as in the case of Tor. Besides that, new users will have a learning curve to use and set up I2P applications effectively. Running an I2P router demands some work and network resources. Although these are usually very small, they can still be a limiting factor if the device is very low-spec.

4.4 Applications of I2P

Users can visit websites and use services hosted on the I2P network without revealing who they are and also stopping anyone from watching their identities and what they communicate. Being used as a private messaging system, it also includes a discussion forum and other communication platforms which keep the user completely anonymous and confidential. The I2P network is an environment that allows secure and anonymous file distribution without the use of centralized servers. This capability not only enables collaborative information sharing but also ensures that the privacy of the users is maintained. Both organizations and individual persons can set up their websites, blogs, forums, and other digital services inside the I2P network while keeping their actual and network locations hidden.

5. FREENET

Freenet is a decentralized peer-to-peer platform that aims at providing anonymous communication, publication that is resistant to censorship, and secure distribution of content. Ian Clarke developed it in 1999 as a means for users to be able to store and retrieve information without exposing their identities or the locations of the content being hosted. It is different from Tor and I2P that focus mainly on anonymous communication and service access, whereas Freenet is mainly about persistent and distributed information storage (Clarke et al., 2001).

5.1 Freenet Architecture

Freenet is a decentralized distributed storage system in which participating nodes share their storage space and bandwidth with the network. The content gets cut, encoded, and spread through several nodes, so no one can easily identify the content owner or the storage location as shown in Figure 7.

Figure 7. Architecture of freenet

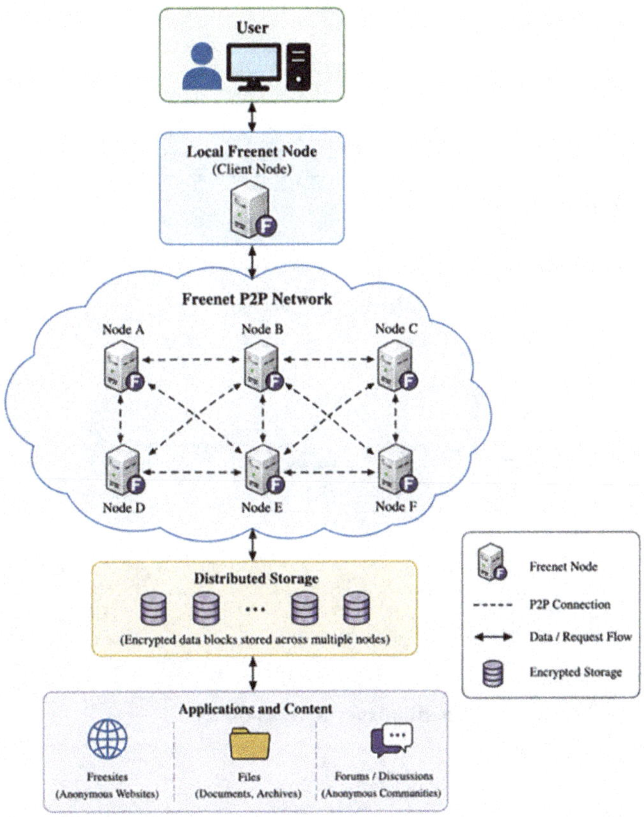

Distributed Data Storage: The essential building block of Freenet is its distributed data storage system. When content is put online, the data is chopped into small pieces and encrypted before these pieces are spread to different nodes in the network. To make sure the content is always available and to tolerate faults, the blocks are redundantly stored (Graham, & Pitman, 2020). Unlike the conventional client-server model, Freenet does not depend on special hosting servers. On the contrary, each node taking part in the system grants its resources for content storage and retrieval. Being decentralized in this way makes the network less vulnerable to censorship and failures and at the same time, it keeps the users' privacy.

Figure 8. Distributed data storage in freenet

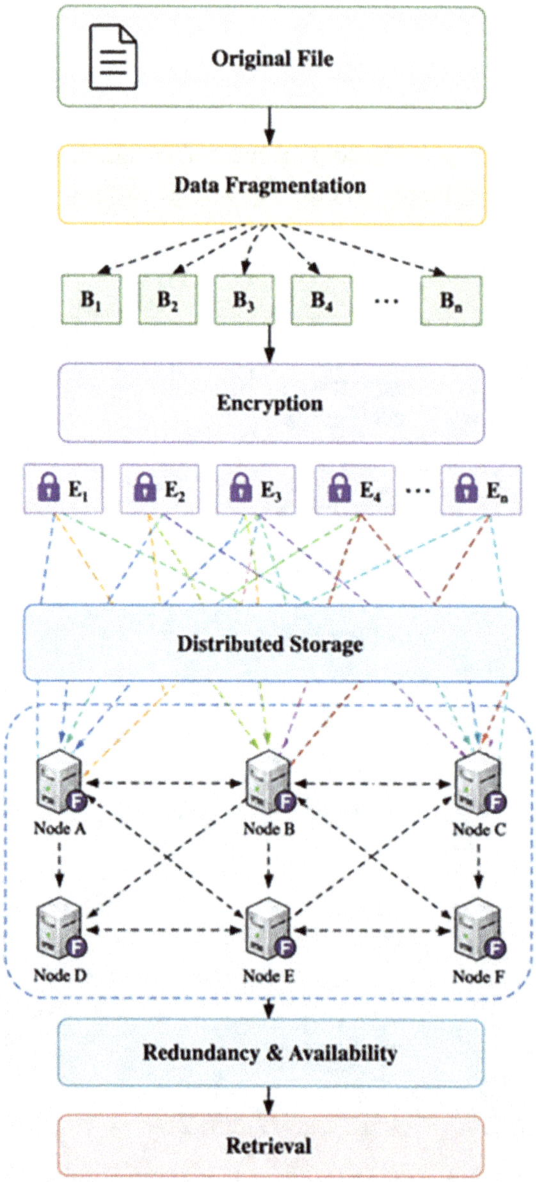

Peer-to-Peer Network Structure: Freenet uses a peer-to-peer system: each computer not only operates as a client but also provides storage. Nodes directly communicate with their neighbors and work together to find and return the desired content. The network can function in two different ways. Opennet mode will automatically link users to random peers, this method is less complicated for users and results in network expansion. Darknet mode is stricter, users can only connect with trusted peers, this provides more security and is more resistant to attacks. The users' choice of a model is based on their privacy and security needs.

Data Encryption and Privacy Preservation: Encryption plays a crucial part in the privacy system of Freenet. Every piece of information that is to be stored in the network gets encrypted before it is sent out so that the intermediate nodes have no idea about the information or its owner. Besides, as nodes generally carry pieces of encrypted files rather than the complete files, the participants usually do not know what information is present on their systems. This approach greatly diminishes the chances of being monitored or getting unauthorized access while at the same time it helps to make content-based censorship and monitoring less effective.

Content Routing and Retrieval

When the user is looking for some content, Freenet uses a distributed routing system that helps find the encrypted data blocks that match their request. Locating the content is a process of passing the request from one node to another along the way. Once the content is fastened, it is sent back to the user along the same path. The routing mechanism automatically changes following the last effective searches. Content that is accessed very often generally moves closer to areas with higher demand which results in faster content retrieval and better network performance. This kind of self-organizing nature allows Freenet to achieve better access to content without the need for a central controller.

Freesites and Anonymous Publishing: Freenet facilitates anonymous websites called Freesites. These are sites entirely embedded in the Freenet network and can be visited without the need for the publisher to give up their identity or location. Freesites allow the user to spread information, run community forums, publish documents, and share digital content and still keep a high level of anonymity. Moreover, since the content is dispersed over many nodes, censoring or removing the attempts is nearly impossible (Haughey et al., 2016).

5.2 Advantages of Freenet

Freenet's distributed storage system works by removing control centers, thus making it difficult to censor or eliminate content. It helps keep information available only if there are copies of the encrypted bits of data within the network. Besides, it protects the anonymity of content publishers and consumers very well. Users together with other parties who are interested in exchange of information can do so without their identities, locations, or the infrastructure hosting the information being exposed (Figueras-Martín et al., 2022).

Freenet by spreading encrypted information among several nodes enhances the capacity to withstand failures, attacks, and disruptions at the service level. Not having centralized servers raise the level of system robustness and availability. Popular content is continually copied and remains in the network, so even when the original publishers are not present, there is a greater chance it will remain available.

5.4 Limitations of Freenet

Finding and getting distributed content is usually the cause of increased latency compared to normal web services. When the network is large, the complexity of routing and storage management may negatively impact performance. The availability of content is increased by replication and redundancy, but at the same time storage needs are augmented. Nodes that take part should supply disk space and bandwidth resources to maintain network activities. Freenet is mainly directed at content storage and retrieval whereas it is not oriented to low-latency communication. Hence, users aimed at locations with real-time interactions may face limited performances especially when compared to a system built for anonymous communication. Besides the fact that Freenet has certain strengths, its community of users is smaller than that of Tor. Therefore, the network of applications, services, and tools that support them is still very limited in comparison.

5.5 Applications of Freenet

Freenet offers a safe framework for spreading and retrieving files while also shielding the identities of both the publishers and the recipients. This ability makes it possible to have private and uncensored communication of information. Individuals and groups can use Freesites to publish content without revealing their server locations or their identities. Such a feature is very handy in situations where people are not allowed to express their views freely. The distributed storage system ensures that documents, research, and digital archives can be preserved for a long time and are not dependent on single nodes of the network. Using Freenet, users can set up decentralized discussion forums where they can talk and exchange information, yet their identities remain secret and their conversations cannot be easily monitored by others.

Table 2. Comparison of TOR, I2P and freenet

Feature	TOR	I2P	Freenet	Feature
Primary Goal	Anonymous browsing	Anonymous communication	Anonymous content storage	Primary Goal
Routing Technique	Onion Routing	Garlic Routing	Distributed Routing	Routing Technique
Hidden Services	Onion Services	Eepsites	Freesites	Hidden Services
Data Storage	No	Limited	Core Functionality	Data Storage
Network Type	Overlay Network	Overlay Network	Distributed P2P Storage Network	Network Type
Censorship Resistance	High	High	Very High	Censorship Resistance

6. COMPARISON OF TOR, I2P, AND FREENET

Tor, I2P, and Freenet are among the most prominent anonymity technologies used within the darknet ecosystem. Although all three systems aim to enhance privacy, anonymity, and resistance to surveillance, they differ significantly in their architectural designs, operational objectives, and application domains. Tor primarily focuses on anonymous access to Internet resources, I2P emphasizes secure peer-to-peer communication and hidden services, while Freenet concentrates on decentralized and censorship-resistant content storage (Negi, 2017). Understanding these differences is essential for selecting an appropriate anonymity solution based on specific privacy requirements, performance expectations, and application scenarios. This section presents a comparative analysis of Tor, I2P, and Freenet across multiple technical and operational dimensions.

6.1 Design Philosophies

A design philosophy of an anonymity system strongly determines the way it is built, the security measures it implements, and the users it targets. For example, Tor was created as a tool to achieve anonymous access to the public Internet. Thus, its design heavily focuses on making a user's activities untraceable during web browsing, communication and using online services. Today, through the implementation of onion routing and multi-layer encryption, Tor manages to hide the traces of a user's communication while not disrupting the user's ability to use standard Internet applications. On the other hand, I2P was conceived as its own separate anonymous network with the greatest concern put on peer-to-peer communication and hosting internal services. This way, the goal of I2P is not so much a means to the public Internet. Rather, it intends to establish a platform for anonymous applications and services running completely within its own network. Freenet, with its different focus, centers around information freedom and anti-censorship. Its design emphasizes secret storage, retrieval, and dissemination of content with the help of distributed data duplication. So, unlike Tor and I2P, which mainly support communication, Freenet is more about the ongoing and decentralized availability of information.

6.2 Architectural Comparison

All three just implement decentralized networking, but they use quite different routing/communication techniques in practice. Tor employs onion routing, where user's data travel through a chain of relays that comprises entry, middle, and exit nodes. Each relay decrypts one layer of the message, so no single node has complete information about the communication path. The mechanism used by I2P to enhance privacy is garlic routing, which among other things, takes several encrypted messages and bundles them into one communication unit. Besides, with its separate inbound and outbound tunnels, it creates an even higher level of anonymity as it separates incoming and outgoing communication paths (Faryad et al., 2024).

Freenet combines distributed storage and adaptive routing mechanisms. Data is split into parts, encrypted, and sent to many different nodes. Retrieval of data is done anonymously through a peer-to-peer network, as requests are routed from one peer to another until the desired content is found without revealing the location of the stored content. These different designs reveal each platform's focus and they have a major impact on their accessibility, performance, scalability, and what kind of applications are most appropriate for them.

6.3 Security and Anonymity Features

While all three systems offer solid protection for anonymity, they use different techniques for ensuring privacy. Tor masks the user by hiding the link between the source and the destination via layers of encryption and routing through relays. Tor is at its best for anonymous web browsing and accessing Internet resources that are publicly available. Garlic routing, separate tunnels, and decentralization of network management are some of the ways I2P improves anonymity. These features make it harder to conduct traffic analysis and facilitate secure peer-to-peer communication. Freenet offers anonymity by means of encrypted decentralized storage and replication of contents. As pieces of data are separated and stored on various nodes, it becomes difficult to determine content ownership as well as the location of storage. Such a structure affords a very high level of protection against censorship and monitoring based on content. Although these three tools by themselves offer privacy to a large extent, their security level depends on factors such as network size, user habits, and the level of the opponent's skills (Dutta et al., 2021).

6.4 Performance Comparison

Performance is still an important factor when considering anonymity technologies. Tor is often the best option for web browsing and accessing the Internet because it has a relatively large user base and a well-developed relay infrastructure. However, the use of multiple encryption layers and relay hops increase latency as compared to direct Internet connections. I2P, on the other hand, is an efficient network for internal services and peer-to-peer applications because all communication remains within the I2P network. However, creating tunnels and routing can periodically reduce the throughput and responsiveness. Generally, Freenet suffers from the highest latency as content retrieval depends on finding distributed data blocks throughout the network. Also, storage redundancy and adaptive routing further lead to higher response times. Consequently, performance characteristics largely differ in accordance with application requirements and network conditions.

6.5 Adoption and Ecosystem

The impact of anonymity technologies can greatly depend on the size and development level of their user communities. Among the three platforms, Tor has the most widespread adoption and it also runs a vast global network of relays operated by volunteers. Along with its comprehensive documentation, browser support and community of developers, it is the main platform for anonymity. I2P has a smaller, but very passionate group of users that are focused on anonymous communication and providing internal services. Besides that, the platform hosts various applications such as messaging systems, file-sharing services, and anonymous websites. Freenet targets a community with a specific interest that are censorship-resistant publishing and decentralized information sharing. Even though its community is much smaller, it is still a significant platform for those who want the long term anonymous content distribution. The community size has an effect on the network diversity, service availability, and the level of anonymity provided.

6.6 Application Suitability

The right use of each of the technologies would be highly dependent on the application for which it is used. For example, Tor is very effective for anonymous web browsing, secure communication, accessing onion services, and censorship circumvention. It works for people who want to keep their identity secret even while using the regular Internet. I2P is a good choice for peer-to-peer communication, anonymous messaging, file sharing, and hosting internal services such as eepsites. Its network design is most efficient for applications that run solely on the I2P network. Freenet is mostly used for anonymous content publishing, distributed file storage, secure information archiving, and censorship-resistant information dissemination. Its storage-centric design gives it distinctive capabilities for the preservation and sharing of digital content. As a result, each platform not only meets different privacy needs but also has varied operational objectives within the larger darknet ecosystem.

Table 3. Comparison of security and anonymity features

Security Feature	TOR	I2P	Freenet
User Anonymity	High	High	High
Content Anonymity	Moderate	High	Very High
Encryption Technique	Layered Encryption	Garlic Encryption	End-to-End Content Encryption
Traffic Analysis Resistance	Moderate to High	High	High
Censorship Resistance	High	High	Very High
Identity Protection	Strong	Strong	Strong
Location Concealment	Yes	Yes	Yes
Hidden Service Support	Yes	Yes	Yes
Resistance to Node Monitoring	Moderate	High	High
Resistance to Content Removal	Moderate	High	Very High
Metadata Protection	Moderate	High	High
Vulnerability to Correlation Attacks	Possible	Reduced due to tunnel separation	Minimal
Data Confidentiality	High	High	Very High

7. APPLICATIONS AND REAL-WORLD USAGE

The legal recognition of darknet technologies varies from one country to another. Generally, using just anonymity networks alone is not in many countries a crime since a person's right to privacy and freedom of speech are generally seen as fundamental human rights. Journalists, researchers, activists, and even ordinary people are using anonymity tools to protect sensitive communications and maintain their privacy (Davis & Arrigo, 2021). However, it is possible that anonymity technologies may be used to commit various illegal acts, such as operating illegal markets, committing cybercrimes, distributing unauthorized data, and even engaging in illegal financial transactions. Consequently, such illegal activities have caused governments and law enforcement agencies to pay more attention to darknet ecosystems. Regarding ethical issues, darknet technologies pose a difficult choice between one's privacy and public safety. Anonymity will allow free expression and provide a certain level of protection to those who may face persecution. Conversely, anonymity may result in a lack of accountability and make it difficult to solve crimes. Hence, there is an ongoing debate over how to achieve a good balance between respecting privacy rights and satisfying security needs in online environments.

7.1 Government Surveillance and Countermeasures

Governments and intelligence agencies use a variety of methods to track and investigate what is happening within anonymity networks. One of the reasons for these efforts is to identify individuals with malicious intent, stop cybercrime, and address national security issues (Sayyed & Paul, 2025).

Traffic analysis is one of the most popular methods. In this way, communication patterns are studied to reveal the connections between users and their destinations. Even though encryption is used to safeguard the content, metadata like timing, volume, and routing behavior can sometimes be used to extract important pieces of information. Higher-level correlation methods try to line up network behavior seen at different locations of the communication route. Apart from traffic analysis, officials can also use tactics such as gaining control over endpoints, spreading malware, and performing forensic analysis to reveal the individuals behind the use of anonymity networks. At the same time, law enforcement agencies have worked together across borders to take down illegal services and break up criminal operations on darknet platforms. At the same time, anonymity technologies have been stepping up the game to provide better privacy protection through stronger encryption, decentralized systems, better routing methods, and traffic disguising techniques. This constant back and forth between the increasing capabilities of surveillance and the development of privacy-enhancing technologies is a continuous technological arms race.

7.2 Emerging Threats to Anonymity Systems

In spite of their advanced security methods, anonymity networks are constantly confronted with new threats that could render them less effective. The rise in computational power, extensive data gathering, and the use of network surveillance tools have unveiled additional ways of attacks (Chao et al., 2024; Saleem et al., 2022).

Among the threats, traffic correlation attacks have been a perennial issue. A villain who has the ability to see multiple parts within a network can potentially deduce who is communicating with whom by looking at the timing and amount of data transfer. The use of machine learning and AI have ramped up the effectiveness of traffic analysis by uncovering tiny human behavior patterns in even encrypted communications. Deploying malicious nodes is yet another problem. Villains could operate relay nodes, routers, or storage peers to sniff out info about network participants or change routing behavior to their advantage. Sybil attacks in which one person owns numerous nodes can totally mess up the decentralised systems' diversity and trust assumptions. Technologies like quantum computing, if realised in the future, could also pose a threat to our current cryptographic algorithms. This further stresses why research into quantum-resistant anonymity mechanisms should continue.

7.4 Practical Applications

Journalism and Whistleblowing: Journalists regularly rely on anonymity technologies to keep their sources confidential, share documents of an extremely sensitive nature, and shield their investigative work from being monitored. By creating secure communication channels, Tor and other similar technologies hep protect the identity of sources and provide a basis for independent reporting (Gond, 2025).

Just like journalists, whistleblowers use anonymity networks to reveal details of corruption, wrongdoing, or violations of human rights without putting themselves at risk of reprisal. Platforms allowing anonymous submissions and secure communication systems are frequently combined with darknet technologies for safeguarding contributors.

Activism and Human Rights Protection: In many regions where changes in government, bans, or restrictions on free speech are common, anonymous networks turn to be essential communication channel. Through these networks, activists and human rights groups can coordinate their actions, share information, and access prohibited material while at the same time reducing their risk of being watched.

Since people can bypass censorship, they are able to find and access independent media and participate in confidential communication even in the areas where the government restricts digital freedoms.

Secure Communication and Privacy Protection: Privacy-minded people rely on anonymity solutions to shield their online behavior from being tracked, profiled, or monitored without authorization. Examples of activities protected using Tor, I2P, and Freenet include secure web surfing, anonymous chatting, and encrypted file sharing.

Such tools turn out to be of great help especially when one is using a network they do not completely trust, dealing with very private information, or trying to maintain their personal privacy in situations where there is a lot of digital surveillance.

Cybersecurity Research and Threat Intelligence

Darknet tools are one of the resources that cybersecurity experts and researchers use to trace cyber threats, follow the latest cyber attack patterns, and dissect the structures of cybercriminals. Security personnel regularly track the darknet forums, marketplaces, and communication channels to spot the possible hazards and collect the necessary threat information.

Alongside, anonymity networks serve as a means for researchers to examine privacy technologies, assess security loopholes, and come up with better defense mechanisms without revealing their identities or the infrastructures of their organizations.

Information Preservation and Anonymous Publishing

Freenet and similar platforms facilitate the long-term preservation and sharing of information in a way that resists censorship. Academic work, historical documents, and materials of public interest can be saved and reached even when standard hosting services either get shut or become subject to limitations. Anonymous publishing also helps to promote free speech by giving people the opportunity to disclose information without making their identities or locations known.

7.5 Challenges in Real-World Deployment

Privacy benefits that result from the use of anonymity technologies are one thing, but if one really wants to get down to the deployment of these technologies, they will surely encounter many challenges. In a way, users may unintentionally reveal their identity through system misconfiguration, even if anonymity mechanisms are in place to keep the information hidden. The users usually associate darknet technologies with illegal activities, and this is what often colors their perception of such technologies, thereby making it harder to promote their use and acceptance. Moreover, deployment of anonymity technologies in different regions and organizational environments is complicated by regulatory uncertainty and varying legal frameworks. Since anonymity technologies are indeed capable of achieving greater success across all areas of their use, the first step is to improve their technical and usability aspects. Further increasing and consolidating public awareness and understanding of their legitimate uses is important; security and scalability are also points that need to be addressed (Obaidat et al., 2025).

Table 4. Threats and challenges in anonymity networks

Threat	Description	Potential Impact	Mitigation Strategies
Traffic Correlation Attacks	Analysis of traffic patterns at multiple observation points to infer communication relationships.	Reduced user anonymity and potential de-anonymization.	Multi-hop routing, traffic obfuscation, padding techniques, and route diversification.
Sybil Attacks	An adversary creates and controls multiple network nodes to influence routing decisions.	Increased surveillance capability and network manipulation.	Reputation-based node selection, peer validation, and decentralized trust mechanisms.
Malicious Relay or Peer Nodes	Attackers operate relay or storage nodes to collect metadata or disrupt communications.	Information leakage and compromised anonymity.	Secure node selection, node monitoring, and periodic route changes.
Endpoint Compromise	User devices are infected with malware or monitored directly.	Exposure of user identity regardless of network anonymity.	Endpoint security, system hardening, and secure operating environments.
Artificial Intelligence-Based Traffic Analysis	Machine learning models identify communication patterns within encrypted traffic.	Enhanced capability for user profiling and de-anonymization.	Adaptive traffic shaping, AI-resistant routing techniques, and behavioral obfuscation.
Distributed Denial-of-Service (DDoS) Attacks	Attackers overwhelm anonymity network nodes or services with excessive traffic.	Service disruption and reduced network availability.	Load balancing, distributed infrastructure, and attack detection mechanisms.
Censorship and Network Blocking	Governments or organizations block access to anonymity networks and related services.	Restricted accessibility and reduced network participation.	Bridges, pluggable transports, decentralized architectures, and protocol obfuscation.
Metadata Leakage	Exposure of timing, size, or communication frequency information despite encryption.	Indirect identification of users and activities.	Traffic padding, randomized communication patterns, and metadata minimization.
Scalability Challenges	Increasing network size and user demand create routing and performance bottlenecks.	Higher latency and reduced user experience.	Efficient routing algorithms, resource optimization, and scalable architectures.
Quantum Computing Threats	Future quantum computers may render existing cryptographic algorithms ineffective.	Potential compromise of encryption-based anonymity protections.	Development and deployment of quantum-resistant cryptographic schemes.
Resource Consumption	Encryption, routing, and storage operations require significant computational and network resources.	Reduced performance and limited adoption in resource-constrained environments.	Lightweight protocols, optimized cryptographic operations, and efficient resource management.
User Misconfiguration	Incorrect use of anonymity tools may inadvertently expose identifying information.	Privacy breaches and de-anonymization.	User education, secure default settings, and automated privacy safeguards.

8. FUTURE OF DARKNET AND ANONYMITY TECHNOLOGIES

In the future, anonymity networks may include adaptive routing, decentralized trust models, and smart traffic management to enhance both performance and privacy. Developments in peer-to-peer networking and distributed architectures will decrease the demand for centralized nodes, meanwhile, increasing censorship resistance and fault tolerance. Better usability and smooth integration with popular applications might also lead to wider user adoption. The development of quantum computers is a major risk factor for the cryptographic algorithms currently securing anonymity networks. In response, the next generation of these systems will implement post-quantum cryptographic methods, such as lattice-based, hash-based, and code-based methods. The main goal of these techniques is to provide vehicles for confidentiality and anonymity that are secure not only against classical but also against quantum adversaries. Implementing blockchain and distributed ledger technologies could significantly enhance decentralization, trust management, and network governance. Privacy-preserving methods, such as zero-knowledge proofs and confidential transactions, can enhance anonymity without compromising system reliability. However, issues concerning scalability, metadata exposure, and computational overhead should be resolved prior to defragmenting these technologies at scale (Gjorgjev et al., 2025). AI can be very helpful for the networks. It can improve routing efficiency, identify bad actors, tweak resource allocation, and help the network endure. On the other hand, attackers may use machine learning tools for traffic analysis, behavioral profiling, and de-anonymization attacks. In essence, future anonymous systems must integrate AI-powered defense systems to counter increasingly powerful analytical threats (Murty et al., 2022). The upcoming developments in anonymity technologies are likely to be influenced by the ongoing need to uphold privacy rights while addressing security and law enforcement needs. Anonymity networks, for instance, safeguard freedom of speech, secure communication, and access to information; on the other hand, they may be exploited to commit crimes. It will be critical to create open governance frameworks and responsible technological solutions to maintain the equilibrium.

REFERENCES

Abdo, J. B., & Hossain, L. (2023, November). Modeling the invisible internet. In *International Conference on Complex Networks and Their Applications* (pp. 359–370). Springer Nature.

Adewopo, V., Gonen, B., Varlioglu, S., & Ozer, M. (2019, December). Plunge into the underworld: A survey on the emergence of the darknet. In *2019 International Conference on Computational Science and Computational Intelligence (CSCI)* (pp. 155–159). IEEE. DOI: 10.1109/CSCI49370.2019.00033

Bancroft, A. (2019). Secrecy and anonymity online. In *The darknet and smarter crime*.

Basyoni, L., Fetais, N., Erbad, A., Mohamed, A., & Guizani, M. (2020, February). Traffic analysis attacks on Tor: A survey. In *2020 IEEE International Conference on Informatics, IoT, and Enabling Technologies (ICIoT)* (pp. 183–188). IEEE. DOI: 10.1109/ICIoT48696.2020.9089497

Bhuvaneswari, A., Kanmani, E. D., Lakshme Prabha, T. M., Helina, R., Suresh, R., & Saravanan, A. (2024). Efficiently listing URLs from active hidden servers in the onion routing network. In *2024 5th International Conference on Smart Electronics and Communication (ICOSEC)* (pp. 625–629). DOI: 10.1109/ICOSEC61587.2024.10722186

Bidv, V., & Waghmare, A. S. (2024). Beyond the onion routing: Unmasking illicit activities on the dark web. *International Journal of Innovative Science and Research Technology.*

Chao, D., Xu, D., Gao, F., Zhang, C., Zhang, W., & Zhu, L. (2024). A systematic survey on security in anonymity networks: Vulnerabilities, attacks, defenses, and formalization. *IEEE Communications Surveys and Tutorials*, *26*(3), 1775–1829. DOI: 10.1109/COMST.2024.3350006

Chauhan, M., & Singh, A. K., & Komal. (2019, December). Survey of onion routing approaches: Advantages, limitations and future scopes. In *International Conference on Computer Networks, Big Data and IoT* (pp. 686–697). Springer.

Clarke, I., Sandberg, O., Wiley, B., & Hong, T. W. (2001). Freenet: A distributed anonymous information storage and retrieval system. In *Designing Privacy Enhancing Technologies* (pp. 46–66). Springer. DOI: 10.1007/3-540-44702-4_4

Davis, S., & Arrigo, B. A. (2021). The dark web and anonymizing technologies: Legal pitfalls, ethical prospects, and policy directions from radical criminology. *Crime, Law, and Social Change*, *76*(4), 367–386. DOI: 10.1007/s10611-021-09972-z

Döpmann, C. (2025). *On the evolution of onion routing networks* (Doctoral dissertation, Technische Universität Berlin).

Dutta, N., Jadav, N., Tanwar, S., Sarma, H. K. D., & Pricop, E. (2021). Being hidden and anonymous. In *Cyber security: Issues and current trends* (pp. 17–36). Springer.

Fachkha, C., & Debbabi, M. (2016). Darknet as a source of cyber intelligence: Survey, taxonomy, and characterization. *IEEE Communications Surveys and Tutorials*, *18*(2), 1197–1227. DOI: 10.1109/COMST.2015.2497690

Faryad, S., Shoukat, I. A., Arif, E., Faheem, M. R., Kashif, M., & Nawaz, A. (2024). A review: Performance and security based comparative analysis of well-known stealth services. *Journal of Computing & Biomedical Informatics.*

Figueras-Martín, E., Magán-Carrión, R., & Boubeta-Puig, J. (2022). Drawing the web structure and content analysis beyond the Tor darknet: Freenet as a case study. *Journal of Information Security and Applications, 68*, 103229. DOI: 10.1016/j.jisa.2022.103229

Gehl, R. W. (2018). *Weaving the dark web: Legitimacy on Freenet, Tor, and I2P*. MIT Press. DOI: 10.7551/mitpress/11266.001.0001

Gjorgjev, J., Ramadhan, M. F., & Dhamayana, S. (2025). Blockchain forensics—Unmasking anonymity in dark web transactions. *International Journal of Criminology and Sociology, 14*, 7. DOI: 10.6000/1929-4409.2025.14.07

Gond, A. K. (2025). Hidden side of the internet: Between crime and freedom on the dark-web. *Journal of Communication Management (London), 4*(3), 55–61.

Graham, R., & Pitman, B. (2020). Freedom in the wilderness: A study of a darknet space. *Convergence (London), 26*(3), 593–619. DOI: 10.1177/1354856518806636

Hatta, M. (2020). Deep web, dark web, dark net: A taxonomy of "hidden" internet. *Annals of Business Administrative Science, 19*(6), 277–292. DOI: 10.7880/abas.0200908a

Haughey, H., Epiphaniou, G., & Al-Khateeb, H. M. (2016). Anonymity networks and the fragile cyber ecosystem. *Network Security, 2016*(3), 10–18. DOI: 10.1016/S1353-4858(16)30028-9

Jadav, N. K., Kakkar, R., Mankodiya, H., Gupta, R., Tanwar, S., Agrawal, S., & Sharma, R. (2023). GRADE: Deep learning and garlic routing-based secure data sharing framework for IIoT beyond 5G. *Digital Communications and Networks, 9*(2), 422–435. DOI: 10.1016/j.dcan.2022.11.004

Jangale, M. D. (2025). *The convergence of shadow and silicon: Advanced forensic methodologies for decentralized webs, generative AI, and darknet infrastructure*. Research Hub International Multidisciplinary Research Journal.

Jardine, E. (2018). Privacy, censorship, data breaches and internet freedom: The drivers of support and opposition to dark web technologies. *New Media & Society, 20*(8), 2824–2843. DOI: 10.1177/1461444817733134

Jayapradha, J., Prakash, M., Alotaibi, Y. A., Khalaf, O. I., & Alghamdi, S. A. (2022). Heap bucketization anonymity—An efficient privacy-preserving data publishing model for multiple sensitive attributes. *IEEE Access : Practical Innovations, Open Solutions, 10*, 28773–28791. DOI: 10.1109/ACCESS.2022.3158312

Kareem, K. M. (2024). Guardians of anonymity: Exploring tactics to combat cyber threats in onion routing environments. *arXiv*. https://arxiv.org/abs/2406.07563

Kate, A., & Goldberg, I. (2010, January). Using sphinx to improve onion routing circuit construction. In *Financial Cryptography and Data Security* (pp. 359–366). Springer. DOI: 10.1007/978-3-642-14577-3_30

Kavitha, R. J., Kapilsurya, R., Shanmugam, V., & Kumar, R. (2023). The dark web: Privacy and anonymity. *International Journal for Research in Applied Science and Engineering Technology, 11*(3), 1087–1093. DOI: 10.22214/ijraset.2023.49599

Liu, L., Zhang, H., Shi, J., Yu, X., & Xu, H. (2019, October). I2P anonymous communication network measurement and analysis. In *International Conference on Smart Computing and Communication* (pp. 105–115). Springer. DOI: 10.1007/978-3-030-34139-8_11

Maalavika, S., Thangavel, G., & Basheer, S. (2023, October). A review on garlic routing and artificial intelligence applications in public network. In *2023 International Conference on Computer Science and Emerging Technologies (CSET)* (pp. 1–6). IEEE.

Moore, D., & Rid, T. (2016). Cryptopolitik and the darknet. *Survival, 58*(1), 7–38. DOI: 10.1080/00396338.2016.1142085

Muntaka, S. A., & Bou Abdo, J. (2025). Resilience of the invisible internet project: A computational analysis. *Internet Technology Letters, 8*(5), e70119. DOI: 10.1002/itl2.70119

Muntaka, S. A., & Bou Abdo, J. (2026). *Fifty shades of darknet.*

Murty, C. A., Rana, H., Verma, R., Pathak, R., & Rughani, P. H. (2022). Building an AI/ML-based classification framework for dark web text data. In *Proceedings of International Conference on Computing and Communication Networks: ICCCN 2021* (pp. 93–111). Springer Nature. DOI: 10.1007/978-981-19-0604-6_9

Nasr, M., Bahramali, A., & Houmansadr, A. (2018, October). DeepCorr: Strong flow correlation attacks on Tor using deep learning. In *Proceedings of the 2018 ACM SIGSAC Conference on Computer and Communications Security* (pp. 1962–1976). DOI: 10.1145/3243734.3243824

Negi, N. (2017). Comparison of anonymous communication networks—Tor, I2P, Freenet. *International Research Journal of Engineering and Technology, 4*(7).

Obaidat, M. J., Al-Syouf, I. A., Awawdeh, Y. F., Masa'deh, A. E., & Abu Al-Haija, Q. (2025). Darknet threats and detection strategies: A concise overview. In *2025 16th International Conference on Information and Communication Systems (ICICS)* (pp. 1–6). DOI: 10.1109/ICICS65354.2025.11073091

Panchenko, A., & Renner, J. (2009, July). Path selection metrics for performance-improved onion routing. In *2009 Ninth Annual International Symposium on Applications and the Internet* (pp. 114–120). IEEE. DOI: 10.1109/SAINT.2009.26

Saleem, J., Islam, R., & Kabir, M. A. (2022). The anonymity of the dark web: A survey. *IEEE Access : Practical Innovations, Open Solutions, 10*, 33628–33660. DOI: 10.1109/ACCESS.2022.3161547

Sayyed, H., & Paul, S. R. (2025). Exploring the role of encryption and the dark web in cyber terrorism: Legal challenges and countermeasures in India. *Cogent Social Sciences, 11*(1), 2479654. DOI: 10.1080/23311886.2025.2479654

Swan, K. (2016). Onion routing and Tor. *Georgetown Law Technology Review, 1*, 110–125.

Chapter 2
Darknet Crawling and Threat Intelligence Analysis

Yaser AlKurdi
http://orcid.org/0009-0004-0838-0105
Digital Next Company, USA

Qasem Abu Al-Haija
http://orcid.org/0000-0003-2422-0297
Jordan University of Science and Technology, Jordan

ABSTRACT

This chapter explores advanced techniques and frameworks for crawling, monitoring, and extracting actionable intelligence from the Darknet. As cybercriminal activities increasingly migrate to anonymized platforms such as Tor-based services and decentralized networks, traditional data collection methods are insufficient for effective threat detection. This chapter examines specialized Darknet crawling mechanisms designed to operate within hidden services, addressing challenges such as dynamic content, access restrictions, and anti-crawling defenses. The chapter further examines continuous monitoring strategies for tracking illicit marketplaces, forums, and communication channels, enabling the generation of real-time cyber threat intelligence (CTI). Emphasis is placed on integrating machine learning and natural language processing techniques to analyze unstructured Darknet data, identify emerging threats, and detect patterns of cybercriminal behavior. Additionally, the chapter discusses ethical, legal, and operational considerations, including privacy concerns, data reliability....

1. INTRODUCTION

From a niche network to a thriving anonymity network, Darknet has undergone significant evolution. It has become a complex ecosystem that supports a diverse range of illegal activities as well as privacy-preserving pursuits. Unlike the easily discoverable content found on the surface web (the part of the internet that standard search engines index) or the readily accessible but unindexed deep web (which comprises behind-login content like online banking and email), the Darknet explicitly hides the

DOI: 10.4018/979-8-3373-9755-9.ch002

identities, locations, and services by utilizing encryption and routing methods such as Tor (The Onion Router) and I2P (Invisible Internet Project) (Dingledine et al., 2004).

In this hidden domain, a proliferation of criminal enterprises has emerged, encompassing black markets for stolen goods, platforms distributing ransomware, hacker forums for collaborative attacks, and money laundering operations.

For those concerned with cyber defense and criminal investigation, the Darknet presents a rich source of information, yet simultaneously an immense technical challenge. The trend of cyber-criminal activities migrating to anonymized platforms is signaling an urgent necessity to move from reactive defense tactics to proactive cyber threat intelligence (CTI) collection. When threats originate, plan, or are exchanged in clandestine spaces on the Darknet, conventional security systems like signature-based detection and edge security defenses become largely ineffective (Al Nabki et al., 2017). Proactive CTI involves rigorously acquiring, refining, and dissecting data from hidden services prior to the execution of an attack.

By diligently monitoring Darknet communities such as forums and marketplaces, analysts can identify early indications of emerging exploits, newly discovered zero-day vulnerabilities, stolen credentials, and indicators of coordinated attack planning.

Recent research has shown how analyzing Darknet traffic using machine learning algorithms can achieve high accuracy in detecting mal intent in live environments (Demertzis et al., 2021). Such anticipatory capabilities allow organizations to fortify their systems, patch weaknesses, and interrupt malicious operations at an early stage.

However, gathering and interpreting Darknet data poses numerous practical, technical, and legal hurdles. Initially, Darknet services are inherently unstable. Hidden sites change their addresses (onion addresses) unpredictably, employ defenses to thwart traffic, or become unavailable without prior warning (Xu et al., 2021).

Indeed, studies by Pastor-Galindo and others have shown that the efficient collection of Tor onion addresses requires mechanisms to constantly discover them due to the rapid rate of changes (Pastor-Galindo et al., 2023).

Second, dynamically generated content, involving JavaScript execution, session management, and Captcha challenges, makes it difficult to perform automatic crawling. Third, illicit market operators actively implement measures to circumvent observation and surveillance, including rate limiting, IP blocking, and honeypot traps. Fourth, the unstructured nature of Darknet data, largely consisting of forum messages, listings, conversation logs, and transaction records, necessitate the use of advanced natural language processing (NLP) and machine learning techniques for information extraction (Basheer & Alkhatib, 2021). Finally, the patchwork of laws and regulations that exist across different jurisdictions complicates extensive crawling operations.

Recent advancements in machine learning techniques have paved new routes for Darknet intelligence procurement. Demertzis and his team developed a weight-agnostic neural network that can accurately identify mal intent in real-time from Darknet traffic, outperforming current deep learning models (Demertzis et al., 2021). Similarly, ensemble learning methods, particularly adapted stacking algorithms, have been used to classify Darknet traffic with enhanced accuracy and lower false positive rates (Almomani, 2025). These developments signal that automated and intelligent monitoring of the Darknet is increasingly achievable, even with remaining difficulties in data acquisition and labelling.

The purpose of this chapter is to bridge the void between conceptual crawling methods and tangible intelligence frameworks applicable to Darknet. Our principal aims are to: (1) outline a comprehensive architectural blueprint for Darknet crawling systems operating within the Tor and I2P frameworks; (2)

describe how to continuously monitor threat actor activity, evolving markets, and emergent malware campaigns; (3) demonstrate the implementation of NLP and machine learning to convert Darknet data into structured intelligence; (4) delineate strategies to mitigate the legal, ethical, and operational risks involved; and (5) present empirically derived insights through case studies and tool evaluations. The contribution of this chapter is the fusion of crawling technology, real-time surveillance, and intelligent data processing within a unified CTI framework specifically crafted for covert, anonymity-enabling networks.

The following sections in this chapter will cover the following aspects. Section 2 provides the foundational knowledge of Darknet technologies, web crawling, the CTI lifecycle, and Darknet data types. Section 3 focuses on crawling system architectures, methods for discovering onion links, evasion techniques for anti-crawling measures, and the building blocks of distributed crawling systems. Section 4 explores continuous observation methods such as real-time tracking of marketplaces, real-time event detection, and temporal trend analysis. Section 5 addresses the processing of data, the application of NLP for extracting information, the use of machine learning to classify threats, and graph-based analysis for identifying connections. Section 6 deals with integrating multi-source intelligence and visual dashboards that are designed to aid security operations centers (SOCs). Section 7 reviews open-source tools, commercial solutions, and integrations with SIEM and SOAR systems. Section 8 discusses legal, ethical, privacy, and operational risks. Section 9 uses case studies of Darknet marketplaces, ransomware tracking, and threat actor profiling. Section 10 highlights the key open research challenges, including scalability, the handling of encrypted data, and countermeasures against adversarial techniques. Section 11 examines future trends, including autonomous AI-powered crawling, the use of blockchain data for intelligence, and the advancement of explainable AI. Section 12 provides a summary of key takeaways and offers recommendations.

2. BACKGROUND AND FOUNDATIONS

2.1 Darknet Technologies and Platforms

Overlay networks require access configurations and user authentication/authorization for entry. There are three main categories of technologies deployed for the Darknet: Tor, I2P, and decentralized peer-to-peer networks. Tor currently dominates the Darknet Landscape.

Tor operates with voluntary managed nodes in a relay architecture in which traffic to be decrypted in several layers thus encrypting the sources as well as the destination IP address (Dingledine et al., 2004).

Within tor, hidden services are referred to by means of an onion address: This represents an identifier based on asymmetric encryption, which enables on-site server anonymity. According to Al Nabki et al. (2017) it is possible to classify the content extracted by crawling the information stored in tor-hidden-services and the identification of categories of illegal activity by applying Natural language Processing Methods, the success rate is illustrated by precision and recall rates as promising.

I2P uses a process referred to as garlic routing where messages are combined together and encrypted making it harder for Traffic Analysis to be successful compared to tor. This differs to the approach of the exit nodes in tor; Tor is not a completely sealed network since information can be extracted through tor exit node. The second largest type is represented by decentralized, P2P based platforms like ZeroNet and Freenet.

Unlike client server architecture, these platforms are server-less with data being distributed and stored throughout participants. Crawling them presents more complexities than regular web due to the nature of no central server storing data. Similar to common features between different platforms on the Darknet, there are several shared characteristics for hidden services such as intermittent availability, frequent change of addresses and the aim to remain out of indexing. A recent survey on different techniques used for gathering Tor onion addresses by Pastor-Galindo et al. (2023) demonstrated that crawling methods with distributed seed points obtain considerably better results than relying on passive techniques only. Since marketeers actively alter their onion sites in order to evade law enforcers shutting down operations, crawlers rely on the collection of new onion address via known Darknet link aggregators, forum posts and paste sites to gather lists of potentially active onion sites.

2.2 Fundamentals of Web Crawling and Scraping

Web crawling or automatically finding and accessing web resources is differentiated from Web scraping or extracting specific structured data from accessed Web pages. In practice Web crawling approaches diverge between the surface web, deep web and the Darknet, with different crawling characteristics. Surface web can be conveniently indexed by well-linked Html pages with a structured robots.txt policy, and a well-behaved server. In deep web, one has to handle Web forms to submit sensitive login and other form-based parameters and session information stored within cookies to retrieve desired Web contents.

2.3 Cyber Threat Intelligence (CTI) Lifecycle

To convert Darknet data into intelligence, threat hunters rely on the CTI lifecycle, consisting of four sequential phases that are repeated in a cycle: collection, processing, analysis, and dissemination. First, crawlers scrape unstructured data from Darknet sources like Darknet marketplaces, forums, chat sites and ransomware leak sites. Rust-Nguyen and associates' experimental study (Rust-Nguyen et al., 2023) proved that Darknet traffic has to accommodate evasion attacks in classification through the ML framework.

According to his and his co-workers experiments' results, their classification achieved remarkable accuracy through Convolutional Neural Network despite evading samples.

Second, data collection leads to processing to clean, normalize, translate languages, extract entity. Raw forum postings that can be made of slang and malicious, erroneous terms have to be converted into clean structure for further analysis processes to establish relationship and correlate to some specific activities which would become indicators of concern that threat hunters identified with statistical or even analytical methods from machine learning techniques. Coutinho Marim and co-workers evaluated machine learning approaches, decision trees and neural network models, to detect Darknet traffic and reported ensemble methods combining different models yielded much better prediction performances against other solo-classifier based methods (Coutinho Marim et al., 2023). Finally, to present the findings, information products such as alerts, intelligence report and indicators of compromising have to be passed to security team, and threat hunting team or an Automated Defense system.

The reason behind Darknet Intelligence being unique in contrast to typical intelligence is because Darknet is an adversarial intelligence environment, and threat actors have a history of corrupting Darknet datasets by throwing up misleading posts or false advertisement listings or fake transaction records, to throw researchers off the trails, therefore trust level estimation for source and double-checking between several independent Darknet data sources must be applied at each step.

Table 1. Comparison of surface web, deep web, and darknet crawling techniques and challenges

Feature / Challenge	Surface Web	Deep Web	Darknet
Accessibility	Publicly accessible without authentication	Requires login, form submission, or session cookies	Requires Tor/I2P software, hidden service discovery, often authentication
Indexing by Search Engines	Fully indexed (Google, Bing, etc.)	Partially indexed; dynamic content excluded	Not indexed; deliberate exclusion from standard search engines
Network Latency	Low (milliseconds)	Low to moderate	High (5–20× slower due to multi-hop routing)
Content Stability	Stable, persistent URLs	Moderate; session-dependent content may expire	Highly ephemeral; frequent onion address changes
Anti-Crawling Defenses	Robots.txt, rate limiting (basic)	Login walls, CAPTCHA, session validation	CAPTCHA, IP blocking, honeypots, browser fingerprinting, request rate limits
Dynamic Content Handling	Optional (JavaScript rarely required for basic crawling)	Frequently required (forms, search results)	Often required; many hidden services rely on client-side rendering
Link Discovery Method	HTML hyperlinks, sitemaps, structured navigation	Form submission, query-based exploration	Heuristic extraction from unstructured text, seed lists, directory services
Crawling Infrastructure	Single-threaded or moderate distributed crawling	Distributed form submission handlers	Highly distributed, parallel crawling with Tor circuit rotation
Anonymity Requirements	None	None (credentials needed)	Required for crawler and target; both parties anonymized
Legal and Ethical Constraints	Low (respect robots.txt, terms of service)	Moderate (terms violation possible)	High (jurisdictional ambiguity, potential exposure to illicit content)
Data Reliability	High (established sources)	Moderate (user-generated but structured)	Low to moderate (adversarial data, misinformation, honeypots)
Common Data Types	HTML, images, PDFs, structured APIs	Database records, forms, documents	Forum posts, transaction logs, chat messages, onion links
Scalability Challenges	Low (well-studied)	Moderate (session management overhead)	High (Tor throughput bottlenecks, circuit management)
Example Crawling Tools	Scrapy, Nutch, Heritrix	Selenium, Puppeteer, custom form handlers	OnionCrawler, TorCrawl, custom Python with Stem library

2.4 Data Types in Darknet Intelligence

Different data modalities must be ingested; each requires different harvesting and analytical techniques. Data includes but is not limited to textual information. The vast majority of this is from: Darknet marketplaces - product descriptions, forum posts, user reviews, private chat messages.

Hacking forums – tutorials, tool sales, information exchanges.

Malware repositories – forums describing malware, exploits. All of this information contained embedded data indicating potential threats such as, names of malware, references to exploits, types of sectors being targeted, costings of illegal goods or services, contact information of vendors etc… Al Nabki et al., were able to demonstrate the automatic classification of Tor hidden service textual content into areas of interest; namely illicit commerce, hacking, and extremist, using feature engineering and supervised learning algorithms. It demonstrated the feasibility of automating information gathering from Darknets to enable rapid and targeted defense capabilities (Al Nabki et al., 2017). Network data capture and analysis of Darknet traffic, which is network packets to unused IP address ranges, offers a direct line of sight into Scanning, worms/malware propagation and denial of service attacks. D'Andra et al. presented a multi-label classification of hosts as revealed from the monitoring of Darknet that is capable of identifying numerous simultaneous malicious behaviors by single-host network traffic data (d'Andra et al., 2023).

Image data Photos of products being sold, screenshotted documents of identities/credentials, challenges that need to be solved to proceed past authentication, company logos displayed to gain confidence in marketplace operations.

Text embedded within images may be extracted using OCR techniques and some inappropriate imagery could be classified, but this process still relies on significant resources to process the sheer scale of imagery associated with the Darknet. Payment data All transactions within a Darknet economy will inevitably pass through a financial network, in almost all cases, using cryptocurrencies. In most marketplaces transaction validation can be seen at public transaction verification and if money is being laundered, Tumblers are often used, or Monero to obscure money flow.

This information needs to be gathered, collated, linked, and processed by a blockchain analyzer. Chat logs the increase of communication across the Darknet over encrypted messaging services such as those used within popular Tor based messaging applications has presented new data modalities to analyze. The extraction of chat logs when the source is available (via authorization, or through other means) could give immediate real time information of activities occurring over time.

End-to-end encrypted communication has hindered many of these initiatives. Metadata for chat services and publicly available chat rooms continues to be used to provide insights into the threat landscape.

3. DARKNET CRAWLING TECHNIQUES AND ARCHITECTURES

3.1 Design of Darknet Crawlers

Designing A Unique Crawler Architecture In order to circumvent issues in a Darknet crawling scenario, the architecture of a typical Darknet crawler must be significantly different than a traditional web crawler architecture. A Darknet crawler should be equipped with the ability to crawl in a high-latency anonymizing network, have the flexibility to deal with varying service reliability, and have measures against adversaries who would wish to uncover the crawler. The architecture itself can typically be divided into three components: the crawler manager, the parser engine and the storage subsystem (Singh et al., 2025).

The crawler manager component in charge of controlling the schedule, the ordering of which requests to make, what tor circuits to use and the logic on what to do when requests are failed.

Whereas crawlers which parse standard web content will tend to make orders of hundreds of requests a second, Darknet crawler needs to be mindful of tor's extremely low speeds - an approximate maximum speed will tend to range around 5 – 15 requests a minute per TOR circuit. The crawler manager will be in control of switching over between different tor circuits to distribute traffic over different IP addresses so as not to attract attention through any specific IP addresses. It will also need to handle circuit lifetimes, meaning that if a tor circuit exhibits suspicious traffic patterns, then it will need to be destroyed and a new one substituted. In addition, the parser engine will process the HTML from a downloaded request and will search for links to other onion services and important content.

Due to the unstructured format of much dark web content, this parser is likely to include heuristic methods of discovering links rather than searching for explicit hyper link formats, it must take care of obscure JavaScript code or image reference formats that do not in fact use the http(s) protocol (Ghosh et al., 2017).

It is in control of converting these links into standard onion URLs and eliminating duplicates. For this work the storage subsystem will maintain three databases: a record of URLs visited to prevent duplicates, a queue of URLs that have been discovered and yet to be crawled and then a database of all the downloaded content/html. In general, this will need to scale for very large amounts of crawling, and most implementations use SQL or NoSQL technologies such as Couchbase, MongoDB etc for this type of data.

In a systematic review by Bergman & Popov looking at 58 peer-reviewed studies focusing on Dark Net crawlers, the most common language to develop dark web crawlers on is Python using the Scrapy or Selenium library to perform web scraping (Bergman & Popov, 2023). Most of the crawl's implemented show modular designs as well as support for configuring how often requests can be made, whilst also handling various types of errors.

3.2 Accessing Hidden Services

Crawlers must resolve onion addresses by consulting the Tor network's distributed hash table to access Tor hidden services. Each onion address is generated from a public key, and the Tor network handles message forwarding through introduction and rendezvous points before making the actual connection to the hidden service (Dingledine et al., 2004). Although the multi-hop resolution of onion addresses increases network latency, it provides anonymity for both clients and servers.

Discovering onion links is, for the most part, an open problem: While web crawlers can discover new seed URLs on the surface web, Darknet crawlers have to discover addresses starting from initial seed lists curated from public resources.

A systematic assessment by Pastor-Galindo et al. (2023) categorized onion address collecting methods into three groups: (1) monitoring public forums, paste sites and public directories of onion addresses; (2) collecting information from active crawls over some existing market/service(s); (3) collaboratively collecting information in a distributed way using multiple crawler agents. They found out that collecting from all three channels improves efficiency in discovering the largest set of onion addresses, whilst crawling from reliable marketplace services contributes the most to discovering new and active ones. A recent study developed a Big Data architecture that was able to effectively identify Tor sites for the first time using a cloud native stack with Kubernetes, Kafka and Kubeflow (Pastor-Galindo et al., 2024). The system managed to discover over 93 days 80,049 onion services, successfully characterizing over 90% of them, mitigating with these characteristics the instability issue of Tor.

In a more recent and comprehensive research on the subject, the author also identified and analyzed over 157k unique onion sites over 90 days in another Big Data architecture that integrated a wider array of onion sourcing mechanisms, discovering onion addresses from several sources including threat intelligence, code repository or tor repo(Pastor-Galindo et al., 2025).

According to Bugajewska (2025), to cope with unknown and potentially malicious contents, crawlers must consider anonymity for themselves, the random unpredictable nature of sites visited and the crawler traps that were often set to delude trespassers. The strategy is to simulate human behaviors or use established relationships to become a trusted visitor in environments set up for concealing facts. Many Darknet services impose barriers in the access, especially closed invitation only forum and private marketplaces.

Users are required to register themselves; this is even sometimes tied to the paying of a registration fee and resolving CAPTCHA verification.

3.3 Handling Dynamic and Evasive Content

Darknet hidden services use growing more complicated measures to deter scraping activity. CAPTCHAs are the most commonly used measure; these challenges force spiders to interpret distorted text, match pictures, or transcribing audio to be permitted access to a hidden service's contents. While optical character recognition and machine learning systems are efficient on simple text-based CAPTCHAs, more advanced schemes are largely inaccessible to automated processes (Noury and Rezaei, 2020).

Darknet services can require login sessions to enable crawl access. To overcome login pages, crawlers must support session cookies, fake user agents, and execute JavaScript, potentially rendering head-less browsers as their best choice, although resource heavy. Darknet operators are, however, also attempting to combat this using header information and behavioral patterns to detect headless browsing (Modi et al., 2026). Darknet sites have started using machine learning techniques to detect crawlers and identify potential threats, with various CAPCHA challenges employed to achieve this goal (Pastor-Galindo et al., 2023).

The techniques used to prevent or deter crawlers fall into a number of categories. Login and access control: For darknet, if services restrict crawler's ability to connect to certain hidden services through, say, a CAPTCHA, or login form and therefore we must create simulated web browsing, such as using the HTML Unit, Selenium, Phantomjs (headless browser) which simulates real user browsers.

Rate limiting: To limit the rate at which the IP address for a server can access a particular website. The IP address to stop providing the service temporarily by sending backHTTP429Response and thus will increase the usage of tor circuits in order to hide real address.

Honeypot: They are designed specifically to lure the automated scraping process on and collect relevant information about it; they include a number of misleading links; these traps often appear like real but offer misleading results.

3.4 Distributed and Scalable Crawling Systems

Since a single-instance crawler has its inherent limits for large-scale data harvesting, a distributed architecture was required to enable large-scale intelligent data harvesting of the Darknet. A distributed Darknet crawler system is comprised of multiple crawling nodes and a scheduler in which each crawler has his/her own Tor service instance and a pool of Tor circuits (d'Andra et al., 2023). Parallel crawlers allow sharing the burden by allowing each node to handle a part of the entire target onion domains, or a subset of crawling task (e.g., link discovery) that another crawler does not handle.

(Pastor-Galindo et al., 2023) shows how parallel crawling on 10-20 nodes significantly (and nearly linear) improves addresses per second, whereas coordination Overhead becomes significant with more than 50 nodes.

The balancing of load ensures the distribution of newly discovered links to the less busy node. When nodes fail, the load balancing reassigns these tasks to active ones. (Rodriguez Barredo-Valenzuela et al., 2025) proposed Mimir, a crawler for the large-scale analysis of Tor networks which not only visits linked content but also automatically collects and browses those linked pages and generates datasets which comprise over 25 000 accessible sites. The longitudinal analysis in the study shows how up to 82% of the content found on the Darknet consists of replicas of content present on other pages, suggesting that the duplicate content must be detected for massive-scale harvesting.

(Ruiz Rdenas et al., 2024) described a generic and modular Darknet analysis tool based on microservice architecture by integrating components like Kafka, ELK Stack, Docker Swarm and PostgreSQL, they collected over half a million of onion sites in 16 hours (84,371 unique).

The crawler design is based on the concept of layers: control layer, logic layer, operations layer and in addition to these ones a module tool, the system for managing logs and communication based on message queues. Cloud based crawling tools enable the deployment of an elastic crawler fleet which can adapt the size and scale the work during collection phases. For instance, during critical timeframes or when major news was released on the Darknet marketplaces, a cloud system could provide additional crawling nodes.

Due to provider restrictions, such as Cloud provider terms, that prevent this type of traffic, hybrid architectures were adopted combining self-hosted infrastructure and Cloud resources. Large-scale Tor circuit management also introduces other challenging complexities. A cost optimization framework for acquiring the Tor user's traffic via configurable deployment and bandwidth attacks was proposed (Guoqiang ZHANG, 2024).

The research finds that costs increase less rapidly when controllable nodes reach 2% of the capacity of Tor.

By utilizing their proposed P-Group method, they improved their distribution utilities by 20.5% versus a 50/50 split between network attack and infrastructure deployment.

Figure 1. Distributed architecture of a Darknet crawling system showing the relationships between crawling nodes, the Tor network, hidden services, and the storage and processing backend

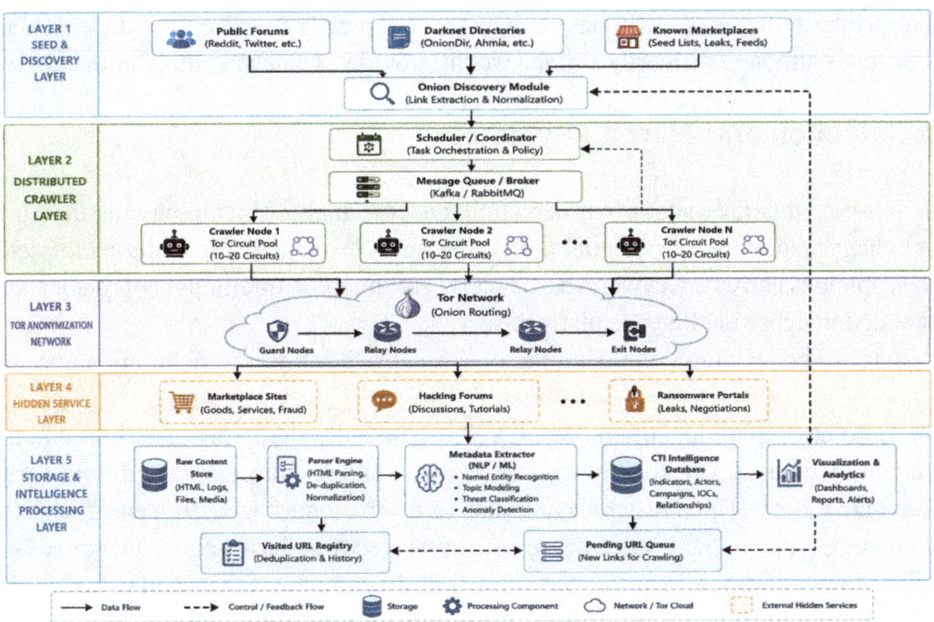

4. MONITORING AND CONTINUOUS SURVEILLANCE

4.1 Real-Time Monitoring of Darknet Activities

We need continuous Darknet monitoring to ensure time-sensitive cyber threat intelligence We require low latency, high volume Darknet crawling loops, rather than high-latency content discovery through indexing like on the surface web. Changes need to be identified, from new content to modifications on existing listings to new threat actor communications, within minutes. Market Surveillance Primary objective focused marketplaces A significant activity we monitor is on criminal Darknet marketplaces.

The Dynamic listings, seller profiles, reviews in these marketplaces were monitored in the last two years by Bergman and Popov where they show the need for active Onion sites being revisited every 15 to 30 minutes by the crawler as the listings may even be transient for hours.

To address this the surveillance system, need to maintain session for active sites and be able to interact with marketplace Checkout flows for discovery of prices and parse structural data like products, names, prices, vendor handles, countries of origin, and reviews. Forum and Chat Monitor The key task in forum and communication channels is to monitor any discussion among Threat Actors, announcement of exploits and information such as credential dumps. Such Darknet Forums utilize threaded conversation, public & private messaging systems, and user reputation systems. This would demand that the crawler can log-in to authenticate to the sites and maintain the login across multiple visits.

Researchers have documented persistent use of forums over several weeks with session randomization, and emulated normal use behavior by researchers at the University of Murcia where their forum system remained accessible to them for over 90 days without their account been blocked.

Monitor Communication Channels Communication Channels such as Telegram, IRC and Discord Channels that primarily focus on activities such as those typically found on the dark web are another domain of our focus although primarily surface web it provides a gateway into Darknet activity.

4.2 Event Detection and Alerting Systems

To make sense of this raw data, event detection systems analyze incoming streams for indicators of significant change, anomaly, or potential threats. Systems leverage two paradigms for detecting and reporting on suspicious activity. Keyword-based alerts are the more traditional approach and have long been implemented in cyber intelligence platforms.

The system relies on lexicons containing various threat relevant terms including names of malware families (e.g.

WannCry, Emotet), exploit identifiers (e.g. CVE-2017-0144), victim organizations and their industries, the amount of funds in cryptocurrency transactions, and handles associated with various actors (e.g. Guccifer, Fancy Bear). Upon matching any such terms in monitor feeds, the event detection system will fire off an alert, typically with some degree of severity scoring based on frequency, whether terms are from high or low confidence indicators, proximity in time to other events and potential connections to campaigns that have been identified in the past.

More recent versions have taken keyword alerting much further using word embedding model for dynamically expanding the sets of words that can trigger an alert beyond those specified manually by analysts.

Behavioral trigger-based approaches analyze the dynamics of patterns, detecting anomalous spikes or shifts in behavior that may represent emerging, undocumented threats or indicate that platforms and their users may be undergoing structural change. Behavioral triggers include the sudden concentration of bitcoin address from multiple disparate accounts within the one organization account, the sudden surge in the number of posts about ransomware leaks across relevant platforms, or correlated forum postings about a specific zero day. A notable example was the one developed by Pastor-Galindo and his team within a Big Data platform to detect previously uncharacterized threats with 91.2% accuracy by classifying behavior anomalies (Pastor-Galindo et al. 2024). Prioritizing Alerts Preventing analyst burnout is another significant challenge as too many alerts will mean an analyst misses the key ones. The three main classifications for alerts are high confidence for the critical alerting need for analysts, medium confidence and these get grouped into daily summaries and low confidence where there will just remain the potential for historical lookup or postmortem.

Bugajewska, (2025) identified how false positive alert could be 62% lower by using machine learning than more traditional static thresholds.

4.3 Temporal Analysis and Trend Detection

Temporal Analysis and Detection Longitudinal monitoring provides the temporal dimension that shows the trajectory of threat evolution, stages of a campaign lifecycle and forward-looking indicators of future attacks. Temporal analysis extends to various times: intra-day market volatile prices, intra-day forum and comment thread sentiment shift, and intra-day-and intra-month evolution of ransomware ecosystems. Temporal analyses can thus occur at intra-day, daily, intra-day-and weekly, weekly, intra-month-and-monthly levels.

Seasonality in Threat Evolution Seasonal trend analysis shows the emergence of certain patterns of threat events that occurs with regular periodicity.

Certain types of threats tend to flourish on Darknet markets for example; holiday season brings with it a rise in stolen payment card lists; the start of the new academic year results in surges in credential dumps aimed at educational institutions. Distributed Denial of Service services providers often advertise their service offerings and prices when there is major geopolitical events which stimulate distributed denial of service activities. A monitoring system which accounts for such seasonally would be able to posture proactive defense to such predictably coming events. Emergence of new threat with time series analysis Statistical process control is the method used when attempting to perform a change to detect if a given threat is entering the active threat space; by using a control process over the frequency of given type of malicious file appearing on a dark net market a measure is performed over the average historical appearance rate of a type of malicious file in a given time series of data.

Pastor-Galindo and colleagues employed this method for example to establish a control limit for threat detection where a threat entering the "active space" of the darknet has appeared for more than 3 standard deviation away from its baseline historically; to detect emergence of new threats on dark net marketplaces they demonstrated how change-point detection may identify emergence at least 5–14 days ahead of manual observation by human analysts.

Trend Prediction Longitude data also enable prediction of future threats. The use of recurrent neural networks (RNNs), such as the long short term memory network and the transform model that may predict how likely future threat events are to emerge and unfold on the basis of the chronological sequence of threat events found in long historical observation of the Darknet; Early studies showed fairly promising rates for detecting future threat emergence using these methodologies although further work is required.

Table 2. Monitoring techniques for darknet platforms: Methods, data sources, and use cases

Monitoring Technique	Primary Data Sources	Key Methods	Typical Use Cases
Marketplace Inventory Crawling	Tor hidden service markets (e.g., product listings, vendor pages)	Scheduled HTTP requests, HTML parsing, session management	Price tracking, vendor identification, new product detection
Forum Thread Monitoring	Darknet discussion boards, hacking forums	DOM traversal, incremental crawling, authentication handling	Exploit disclosure tracking, actor communication analysis
Surface-to-Darknet Gateway Monitoring	Telegram, Discord, IRC, Pastebin	API integration, Web scraping, keyword filtering	Pre-attack coordination, credential leak detection
Keyword-Based Alerting	All textual Darknet content	Lexicon matching, regular expressions, term frequency scoring	Threat indicator identification, brand mention alerts
Behavioral Anomaly Detection	Temporal sequences of Darknet activities	Statistical process control, change-point detection	Emerging threat identification, platform shift detection
Sentiment and Shift Tracking	Forum discussions, vendor reviews	NLP sentiment analysis, topic modeling	Threat actor intent assessment, campaign lifecycle analysis
Cryptocurrency Flow Monitoring	Blockchain transactions linked to Darknet wallets	Address clustering, transaction graph analysis	Money laundering detection, vendor income tracking
Ransomware Leak Site Surveillance	Dedicated leak sites (onion and clear web)	RSS feed parsing, page differential analysis	Victim identification, double-extortion tracking
Seasonal Trend Analysis	Historical Darknet data archives	Time-series decomposition, calendar correlation	Attack wave prediction, resource allocation planning
Machine Learning Forecast	Temporal Darknet data streams	RNN, LSTM, transformer models	Threat trajectory prediction (7–14 day horizon)

5. DATA PROCESSING AND INTELLIGENCE EXTRACTION

5.1 Data Cleaning and Preprocessing

Following an extensive crawling of the darknet, extensive data cleaning is necessary to derive useful intelligence. In contrast to more organized content repositories, darknet content is subject to large amounts of noise like malformed html, encoding errors, adversarial injections and deliberate measures by the threat actors to evade automated processing. The first stage of the preprocessing involves noise removal.

Forum posts contain numerous parts of useless information such as signatures, quoted blocks, adverts and bot messages that could negatively impact the results.

Several researchers found at the IMDEA Networks Institute for example, in their study of the long-term data collected from 25 000 Tor Hidden services, that nearly 82% of the collected data are mirrored on other website, meaning the detection of duplicates should be conducted prior to applying subsequent processing stages. Following noise removal and Duplicate removal, data have to be normalized, meaning that inconsistent data have to be put in standardized representation. Text normalization may include several processes such as putting data into lower case, stemming or lemmatizing the text, removing punctuation or adapting for slangs/leets-speak from the dark web (example 'admin' to 'adm1n'). The frequent code-switching between English, Russian and Chinese in darknet forums means that detection language, in additional to multi-lingual pipelines have to be applied.

A last step of the preprocessing procedure consisted in data validation where extracted data are checked against fake data planted deliberately on the dark web by threat actors in order to send to the intelligence a lot of wrong information (e.g. Counterfeit products and deceitful threads).

For that matter, some approaches develop trust-scoring systems, assigning confidence level to each data source by using the historical performance of vendors, their associated scores and a cross-validation with other credible sources.

5.2 Natural Language Processing (NLP) Techniques

It effectively extracts structured threat intelligence from unstructured Darknet text. The three main approaches that leverage NLP on Darknet corpora are topic modeling, sentiment analysis, and named entity recognition (NER). These approaches are described below.

Topic modeling: This technique allows for the identification of underlying themes that appear in the collection of Darknet web pages. To this end, Ricaldi et al (Ricaldi et al., 2026) analyzed 11.4 million HTML web page snapshots from 25,065 Darknet websites over a period of six years (2020–2026). They proposed a topic discovery pipeline that combines darknet-specific DARK-BERT embeddings, density-based clustering methods, and temporal aggregations. They identified 55 themed clusters where most of the topics' discussions, around 75%, are confined to relatively few static 'core' topics. Only about 3% of the discussions volume was attributed to ephemeral and short-lived topics. On average, the life of a topic in terms of existence duration was estimated to be around 75 months.

Sentiment analysis: This is a technique used to detect the actor's intentions, urgency, and reliability in darknet conversations. High negative sentiment on a forum may predict a ransomware campaign or a zero-day disclosure. High positive sentiment on a specific exploit-kit usually indicates an increase in its use. Deep-learning based sentiment analysis models are outperforming traditional generic models in many folds, by considering darknet-specific linguistics (e.g., slang, abbreviations, code language), domain specific corpora and fine-tuning models for such tasks.

Named entity recognition (NER): These approaches can extract specific pieces of structured threat intelligence such as malicious IP addresses, known malware families, bitcoin addresses or emails. The advances in deep learning have also brought LLM approaches into play for NER tasks over darknet data. Giannilias et al (Giannilias et al., 2025) explored different large language models and evaluated different methods to perform the NER on darknet data, for instance, different LLMs with zero-shot, few-shot or fully fine-tuned setups. The study fine-tuned different LLMs (Mistral-7B, Gemma-7B, Llama-3-8B) to perform multi-label classification on the dataset of hacker posts and confirmed that using a fully fine-tuned model resulted in higher accuracy than either zero-shot or few-shot methods.

5.3 Machine Learning for Threat Detection

Darknet data once it's pre-processed it's put into the machine learning model. The three main approaches taken by models when putting the pre-processed Darknet into a model fall into the categories of classification, clustering, and anomaly detection. Classification When Machine Learning models classify darknet data they are trying to find its correct threat category.

ContextualGraph-LLM, developed by a group of Researchers in academia who paired Graph Neural Networks (GNNs) with Language Models (LLM), produced weighted average F1-scores of 0.9035 on theCIC-Darknet2020 dataset for multi label intrusion detection, which outperformed previous state of the art (single modality) methods.

CG-LLM work took a standard representation for network flow records; transforming it into a bipartite graph with enhanced graph-based embeddings by textual nodes provided by a small LLM namely TinyLlama. Clustering Clustering aims to identify unseen threats as they emerge without explicitly defined threats. The Darknet forum discussions were subjected to unsupervised clustering to reveal newly observed coalitions of threat actors, previously undiscovered malware trends, as well as new supply chains of the darknet's informal economy. Density-based clustering algorithms such as DB-SCAN, and HDBSCAN can handle the highly irregular distribution patterns within darknet discussions as they cluster data with high proximity and do not need explicit defined radius values which allow many of them to capture sparser clusters on tails.

KDD 2015 Anomaly Detection When something unexpected and not typically found is discovered within the darknet data, that could represent either a new and emerging threat or the result of a threat actor that may be trying to transition and or avoid some of the latest detection methods from law enforcement. The use of the Darknet data time series to monitor market listing volume, distribution in price of goods, and vendor activity to detect whenever the numbers go beyond the historically established norm through a technique called process control in general. For this specific domain, the Privacy-Aware Federated Graph Neural Network (PA-FGNN) the authors combined many different techniques to create a cyberterrorism detection model, reaching over 91% accuracy.PA-FGNN utilizes differential private and fully homomorphic encrypted data-based network structure which maintains security while still running the detection up to even with 20 percent malicious clients.

5.4 Link Analysis and Network Intelligence

Understanding connections and similarities between threats and threat actors, services, transactions and infrastructure, provide deep Darknet intelligence. Using graph-based methods via link analysis uncovers obscure structures not seen when looking at individual Darknet observations.

These Darknet entities form vertices and relationships create edges, transforming our Darknet intelligence into a graph. Vertices represent threats (vendor IDs or forum usernames), infrastructure (IPs, hostnames), financial indicators (Bitcoin addresses or crypto currency hashes) and activities (payment, sales of credentials, exchanges), with edges representing temporal, transactional and communications relationships. Typical graphs of Darknet infrastructure are scale free with hubs representing central, highly used elements such as the popular marketplaces and the threat actors in them (Contreras-Velasco et al., 2025).

Link prediction can establish links in uncovered and hidden Darknet connections, essential, considering the nature of our incomplete surveillance of criminal Darknet environments. In a comparative research project involving several classic node similarity indices, graph embedding methods (DeepWalk, Node2Vec), and GNN-based methods for analyzing crime alliance networks (Lantia & Bacrim 2020) researchers concluded that GNN models including those with Graph Convolutional Networks (GCNs) gave virtually perfect accuracy (AUC or F1 > 98) to predict concealed links in partially visible criminal networks. The results in these papers provide valuable insights into developing the use of GNN for predicting hidden links of crime networks from Darknet intelligence.

Community detection algorithms can expose hidden clusters of threats and threat actors with shared operational objectives and or affiliations. This type of analysis is used in detecting cybercriminal cartels, or isolated communities of actors responsible for specific criminal types, such as ransomware and money laundering criminal organizations. Louvain clustering, label propagation algorithms and modulus maximization are all common community detection techniques, used for detecting common operational techniques, or individual actors who collaborate frequently within distinct cyber-criminal networks. Temporal community detection can also analyze how these groupings evolve over time.

Figure 2. Graph-based intelligence analysis of Darknet entities and relationships, showing threat actor communities, transaction flows, and centrality metrics. Node colors represent entity types, edge thickness indicates transaction volume, and community shading reveals covert group structures

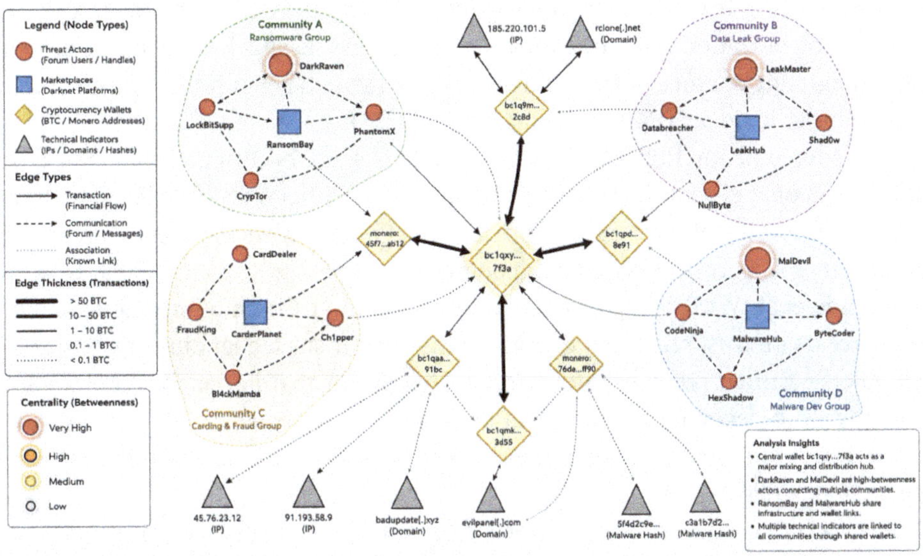

6. INTELLIGENCE FUSION AND VISUALIZATION

6.1 Data Fusion from Multiple Sources

Maximize value of Raw Darknet data The Raw Darknet intelligence should augment other data sources, as no single channel of monitoring will yield a complete understanding of threat landscape, modern threat intelligence platforms are now integrating darknet indicators into other types of data sets like open-source intelligence (OSINT), in-company data, and 3rd party commercial intelligence(Basheer

& Alkhatib, 2021). We introduce ways how Darknet intelligence can augment other types of data to enable comprehensive threat insights.

Darknet-OSINT Fusion The Darknet-OSINT data fusion involves merging Hidden Services data with its clear web equivalent. Threat actors commonly keep a cross-domain identity on their Tor sites, clear web hacker communities, and even their social media profiles. This information may include the same usernames, e-mail addresses or cryptocurrency wallets on both Tor forums and clear web sites. Correlating these credentials across domain gives intelligence analysts a complete persona profile of the adversary (Basheer & Alkhatib, 2021). For example, in an organization's incident detection, we may notice an advertisement of a ransomware threat on a Darknet forum that uses the same username and e-mail as an account on the organization's external developer community forum. Such correlation increases actor identification by as much as 40% than relying solely on Darknet monitoring (Basheer & Alkhatib, 2021).

Internal security data Fusion In most cases external darknet data should be utilized internally in order for our defenses to act on external threat information. If a Darknet crawler detects an ad for a new ransomware threat that has been found on its monitoring efforts it should correlate that data point with its enterprise asset registry or vulnerability management data or the endpoint detection systems data to understand how the organization could be exposed and to assess its attack surface(Pastor-Galindo et al., 2023). In SOC, integrating darknet and internal data allows them to better predict mean time to detection and investigate security incidents(Pastor-Galindo et al., 2023).

Multi-Darknet source fusion Reliable threat actor data is a key benefit and challenge from Darknet; as many a times posts on a given marketplace or forum can be either a decoys placed by threaten actors or law enforcement. Deriving of threat actor from 3 distinct independent darknets sources helps to avoid that situation and improves trust score to a high degree.

In Pastor-Galindo et al. We developed a reputation system to trust on information coming from distinct darknet sources with trust score that degrades with time if subsequent information available from darknets contradicts certified previous information. This means that in our trust and recommendation system, we may want to decay information that does not get subsequently validated and to prioritize reliable sources, which are those that continuously present information that get confirmed across time (Pastor-Galindo et al., 2024).

Temporal Fusion Darknet data will always need to be tied back to historical and in time data, including from various sources like blockchains, domains and SSL certificates logs. While many darknet forums discuss a given exploit or vulnerability in real-time, an association with timing information found in certificate transparent or in a particular SSL certificate will often reveal that we missed some infrastructure a period before, such as new command-and-control servers that started to announce themselves in a private space and eventually popped out (Bugajewska, 2025).

6.2 Visualization Techniques

The most intuitive method to transform this raw data and processed information into something readable by humans is through visualization. Considering the nature and scale of Darknet data - with a very high number of variables and inter-related relationships - visualization requires sophisticated techniques. Dashboards There are several forms of dashboards that provide a "real time" look at Darknet Activity related to an organization.

These dashboard types include: 1. Threat Actor Heat Maps (geographic breakdown of the mention of a topic/interest area by a country/region on the Dark Web and by industry/ sector on Dark Web forums);

2. Trendy malware indicators (number of the mention of exploits over 24 hours, 7 days and 30 days periods); 3. Marketplace Volatility Index(prices fluctuations of credentials/ exploits/ ransomware-as-a service offered at marketplaces); 4. Alert Priority Queue(ranked list of active alerts by confidence level and organizational value) (Basheer and Alkhatib, 2021). Heat maps heatmaps allow us to display concentrations of events throughout the whole universe of dimensions of darknet-data. There can be a variety of 2d heatmaps, including: (1) a heat map that tracks frequency over days and hours to observe activity patterns and timing of actor's schedules, (2) a heatmap where terms co-occurrence is being plotted with threat actors to see what terms that are discussed together the most, and (3) a heatmap where darknet platforms are associated with mal wares (Rodriguez Barredo-Valenzuela et al., 2025) Network graphs Network graphs as depicted in Figure2 are effective for representing relationships between data entities, which otherwise can be hard to uncover using traditional tabular methods.

The goal of this form of graphs is to represent all connections in the graph in a clear, legible, and concise format, and force-directed layout positioning elements so they represent strongly connected components with tightly groups, and poorly connected components spread widely Apart.

Analysts also benefit from interactive features when interacting with network graphs including 1. Filtering the network graph in by attributes (nodes, edges and communities), 2. Expanding the networks with an animation effect 3. Finding centrality (degree, betweenness and eigenvector) of nodes, and 4.

Animating the change over time of the communities and networks (Ali et al., 2025) Times-series visualizations Tmeses visualizations show evolution over time of Darknet metric metrics like marketplaces listings amount or Average prices of stolen data and so on. Overlaying law enforcement's removal over such plot helps determine the impact of actions and identify trends in marketplace listing or leak sites, whilst anomaly detection can provide a means to automatically flag these events for human analyst inspection. (Pastor-Galindo et al., 2023) geospatial visualization even though it is not always possible to geo-locate threat actors directly since the Dark Web provides them anonymity. However, the analyses of money flowing from Cryptocurrency accounts, information about where servers are hosted (ISP providers), and language used among users can provide insight into probable location indicators for organizations who want to correlate this information to their geo-political assessment and create risk profiles (Bugajewska, 2025)

6.3 Decision Support Systems

Decision Augmentation intelligence needs to fit into organizational decision-making workflow. The role of Data Science decision support system is to be the intermediary between passively scanning the Darknet data and proactively acting on the threats derived from it. Security operations center (SOC) integration Darknet intelligence gets seamlessly integrated within SOC workflows of analysts.

Playbooks take the indicators that are extracted from Darknet crawler and take an automated action.

If the Darknet crawler gets an access to the account dump that consists of our organization's email domain, the decision support system (DSS): 1) Access identity management system to find the affected user, 2) Initiate a password reset process for these accounts, 3) Create tickets into the SOC's incident management system, and 4) Display the indicator for the relevant dashboards in our organization (Basheer and Alkhatib, 2021). To stop analyst overloading there has to be a threat scoring and prioritization process. Each Darknet extracted indicator is given a composite score based on its source (dark web reputation), how old it is, explicit reference to organization's industry/ technologies and verification of similar sources and that is what determines how the indicators are presented to the analyst in dashboards, the nonprioritized indicators were given a lower score and are available for historical analysis (Pastor-Galindo et al., 2024). Indicators stream-processing, machine-readable format and export Data science is used to output this Darknet intelligence in a machine readable format like STIX and TAXII and send this data as a feed to organizations to its firewalls, intrusion detection system (IDS), Endpoint detection and response (EDR), SIEM system (Security Information Event Management) and others (Pastor-Galindo et al., 2023).

Table 3. Tools and platforms for darknet intelligence fusion and visualization

Tool / Platform	Category	Primary Function	Data Sources Supported	Visualization Outputs	Reference
Apache Kafka + ELK Stack	Data Pipeline & Visualization	Real-time ingestion, indexing, and dashboarding	Darknet crawler logs, OSINT feeds, internal telemetry	Kibana dashboards, time-series charts, heatmaps	(Pastor-Galindo et al., 2024)
Neo4j + GDS	Graph Database & Analytics	Link analysis and community detection	Darknet transaction logs, forum relationships, actor mappings	Force-directed network graphs, centrality heatmaps	(Ali et al., 2025)
Maltego	OSINT & Link Analysis	Entity resolution and relationship discovery	Darknet forums, cryptocurrency transactions, DNS records	Entity relationship graphs, path analysis	(Basheer & Alkhatib, 2021)
MISP (Malware Information Sharing Platform)	Threat Intelligence Platform	Indicator sharing and correlation	Darknet indicators, internal alerts, partner feeds	STIX/TAXII feeds, event graphs, timeline views	(Pastor-Galindo et al., 2023)
Tableau / Power BI	Business Intelligence	Custom dashboard creation	Processed Darknet datasets (CSV/JSON)	Interactive dashboards, geographical heatmaps	(Bugajewska, 2025)
TorCrawl + Stem	Crawling & Data Collection	Onion service discovery and content retrieval	Tor hidden services	Raw HTML storage, link graphs	(Bergman & Popov, 2023)
Scrapy + Selenium	Web Scraping Framework	Dynamic content extraction	JavaScript-heavy Darknet sites	Structured data output (JSON/CSV)	(Bergman & Popov, 2023)
NetworkX + Plotly	Graph Analysis & Visualization	Custom network analytics	Actor-relationship datasets	Interactive network graphs, community overlays	(Ali et al., 2025)
Sigma Rules + SIEM	Detection & Alerting	Rule-based threat detection	Darknet indicator feeds	Alerts, dashboards, incident tickets	(Basheer & Alkhatib, 2021)
OpenCTI	Intelligence Platform	Knowledge management and orchestration	Multiple CTI sources (Darknet, OSINT, commercial)	Relationship graphs, dashboards, reports	(Pastor-Galindo et al., 2023)

7. TOOLS, FRAMEWORKS, AND PLATFORMS

7.1 Open-Source Tools

Open-source efforts have generated a suite of tools for Darknet crawling, NLP analysis, and intelligence visualization. The tools offer an accessible on ramp for underfunded researchers and organizations and an extensible platform that can be customized for specific needs. The foundation of Darknet intelligence pipelines lies in crawling and data collection tools.

Tools designed for efficient Darknet crawling include Tor Crawl (Python) which supports recursive crawling. Onion sites with customizable crawl depth and delay, allowing for distributed, identity-swapping crawlers via use of the Stem library for interacting programmatically with Tor.

Tor Crawl can even target specific communities. It can also take advantage of existing data to start crawls more intelligently. Selenium using a headless browser environment (e.g., Chrome in "headless" mode or Firefox with gecko driver) can crawl sites that depend on JavaScript to display content, however this approach has a considerably higher computational cost (Bergman & Popov, 2023). NLP and machine learning (ML) libraries take Darknet text and transform it into something that can be searched.

The NLTK and spacy libraries provide off-the-shelf tokenization, stop word removal and part-of-speech analysis.

To make such capabilities apply to Darknet data, researchers can train and fine-tune existing NLP tools: a model that can detect the intent to buy on Darknet forums will require significant training Data. As a case study, an LLM that has been specifically trained on Darknet Data will outperform models on more general training Data (Giannilias et al., 2025). Visualization libraries enable analysts to consume and gain actionable intelligence from processed data.

For processing graphs, NetworkX (Python) is used to calculate degree, centrality and community structures. For interactive graphs there is a wide variety of python libraries, Plotly which generates heatmaps, time series diagrams and other charts. NetworkX can easily integrate with matplotlib or Plotly to make graphs.

For a truly large-scale application Gephi can render a complex graph that includes thousands of entities and millions of links. Gephi is a desktop application, however it's quite fast to render complex graphs (Ali et al., 2025).

7.2 Commercial Threat Intelligence Platforms

Commercial services offer the convenience of managed Darknet monitoring services, so organizations don't have to manage the underlying crawl infrastructure. These offerings come with pre-built, pre-configured crawlers, round-the-clock monitoring, and security analysts. Dark net monitoring services have been built for the sole purpose of continuous monitoring of dark net hidden sites. Dark net monitoring offered by commercial entities: Recorded Future's Dark Web Intelligence tool monitors TOR and I2P sites and alerts when threat groups talk about client companies or their technology.

Flashpoint provides the only curated Darknet repository with historical records dating back several years in order to conduct threat history.

Services deliver data in the form of web dashboards, API feeds, and STIX / TAXII exports. Leveraging threat intelligence platforms Organizations can correlate their own threat data with other commercially provided data via threat intelligence platforms (TIPs) such as the Malware Information Sharing Platform

(MISP). Some of the prominent commercial TIP's available include ThreatConnect and Anomali. Both TIPs also provide security analysts with capabilities to manage cases, automate data enrichment, and orchestrate workflows.

This has been estimated to reduce the average time from the discovery of a dark net threat indicator to actionable defensive measures by over 60%.7 CAPTCHA solver CAPTCHA services serve as another of the primary barriers to crawling a dark web site.

A number of companies provide CAPTCHA solver services such as 2Captcha and Anti-Captcha which rely either on human input or machine learning algorithms to resolve any challenge posed on the Dark net. The main challenge is the added cost associated with CAPTCHA services (often $0.50 – $3.00 for every 1000 solves), as well as Ethical concerns surrounding workers on both sides of the task.

7.3 Integration with Security Ecosystems

Single Point Solutions Dark net monitoring alone is of little worth in enterprise security architecture. Within any enterprise, we see SIEM, SOAR, Endpoint Detection, etc. As components that form a larger system. SIEM integration Dark net information feeds into Threat Intelligence Platforms that then feed SIEMs like Splunk, IBM Q-Radar, Elastic Security that support the consumption of STIX/TAXII formatted threat feeds.

These systems correlate the threat intel feeds with your log files automatically.

For instance, a dark web scraper pulls up credential compromise for a username – domain pair. These feeds can be correlated against authenticate logs for this username – domain combination and if you see a log that correlates with a successful login to unusual (for that user) IP address, a security event could be triggered (Pastor-Galindo et al., 2023). SOAR Integration SOAR platforms automate threat responses triggered by threat intelligence feeds. Palo Alto Cortex XSOAR and Splunk SOAR enable teams to create playbooks to (1) validate Dark net indicators with internal inventories of assets; (2) enriching threat intel feeds with other threat feeds, passive DNS, and WHOIS data; (3) blocking threatening Dark net data like Ips and domains on firewall sand email systems, and (4) to generate Security Incident Tickets with context ready for investigators(Basheer & Alkhatib, 2021).

Threat Hunting Integration Dark web threat intelligence is effective at supporting hunting engagements to detect threats and intrusions early.

These teams use data elements to query log systems, databases and perform memory forensics. For instance, IP Addresses, domain names, file hash value generated by Darknet crawlers could be used by an enterprise SOC to formulate queries to identify potentially compromised machines (Pastor-Galindo et al., 2024). These are just a few examples of integration points.

8. LEGAL, ETHICAL, AND OPERATIONAL CONSIDERATIONS

8.1 Privacy and Data Protection Issues

Personal data appears frequently during Darknet crawling and this creates serious privacy issues. A forum thread may consist of an inadvertently leaked email address or screen name, references to a physical location, or communications posted in a crime forum that nevertheless pertain to a person who possesses privacy under a variety of applicable laws (Bugajewska, 2025). Crawlers must adhere to data minimization principle: only relevant data-information pertinent to threats-may be collected.

It violates our principles when, for instance, an entire forum post is retained with all its PII for a user did not deem a threat.

To achieve this, we advocate to; 1) redact automatically PII information; 2) limit the retention window of the data; 3) restrict access for cyber security personnel only. Problems of anonymity Darknet data is hard to anonymize. A threat actor might have a username which reflects his or her identity if it matches that identity from non–Darknet investigations. A non-threat actor might have a pattern of communication or use a username that resembles a pattern of a threat actor.

As noted by Basheer & Alkhatib (2021), Darknet intelligence should never be used in isolation to assign accountability to a threat actor without correlated data sources.

8.2 Legal Constraints in Darknet Crawling

Darknet Crawling: legal Implications In the shadow of national laws When a researcher decides to crawl for intelligence about the Darknet hidden network, this researcher finds himself in a legal vacuum. Darknet crawlers may violate existing anti-hacking, or anti-access-to-unauthorized-computer- systems laws, in various countries. In several jurisdictions, unauthorized access to computer systems, often based on anti- computer fraud and abuse laws (or its equivalent) is considered to be a crime, such as in the US by the Computer Fraud and Abuse Act (CFAA), also called by some researchers, such as Bugajewska, the "mother of all hacking laws"(Bugajewska, 2025).

While many of these systems access is protected for access through password protected authentication or others, we may arguably think that for many Darknet hidden services the restriction can be implicitly found on basis of the CAPTCHA challenge/anti- crawling rules such as Rate Limiting, or other Terms Of Service (TOSs).

For example, some authors such as Bugajewska[9] may also interpret that CFAA may be interpreted as to forbid access even after authorization revoke, like one who keep crawling Darknet sites after CAPTCHA attempts have been refused (Bugajewska, 2025). Jurisdictional Complexity What complicates the issue even more, it is the multiplicity of potential jurisdictions implicated, the case that would be interesting from legal aspect for sure: if researcher is based in Germany, the spidering goes crawling to Dutch Darknet node, which is accessed by a user of Russian origin - how much legal provisions must the researcher be able to verify and respect?. Thus, the authors recommend some legal procedures: i) seek the advice of qualified legal counsel before beginning Darknet crawling; ii) conduct crawling in a jurisdiction that offers strong legal protections for research activities ; and iii) refrain from crawling hidden services known to host child sexual abuse material (CSAM) since there is a legal obligation for mandatory reporting(Basheer & Alkhatib, 2021). Cooperation with Law Enforcement Collaboration with law enforcement, can not only benefit in obtaining legal protection in case the crawler accidentally violates laws; But such collaboration can also be detrimental to academic autonomy and autonomy in publications. Researchers have found some cases in which studies regarding DarkNet are either blocked from or must reduce methodological details in order to prevent the alerting threat actors by sharing how their systems work to law-enforcing institutions (Pastor-Galindo et al., 2023).

8.3 Ethical Considerations in Data Collection

In addition to legal requirements, moral ethics must inform researchers conducting studies on the Darknet. Researchers must apply "the no-harm principle," i.e. They must be conscious of the fact that their actions must not benefit threaten actors, by for instance helping them to upgrade their capabilities or put victims at risk. Active vs passive research as a research subject, the Darknet has some distinct features that necessitate further limitations from crawlers: - Crawlers can only passively survey the network but cannot interact with services by making transactions or writing posts or modifying websites.

That implies that a crawler cannot be an active player.

Automation in that network has some issues too like automatically solving CAPTCHA, which is an infringement to the rules of the network as it compromises the time intended to limit the crawler access. - In addition to the above, even if it is a crime for anyone in the internet to hack for example by searching vulnerabilities, when it comes to crawlers to search vulnerabilities in hidden sites, a moral complexity issue arises. While disclosing this vulnerability to market dealers would enable them to enhance security of criminal operations, not disclosing will keep victims of those markets unprotected. There is a third solution according to Bugajewska. Either to disclose the found security vulnerability to legal authorities or academicians working on measures against the Darknet.

Bugajewska(2025) in institutional research - University-affiliated organizations are more willing to review and study issues arising from the study of the Darknet and these agencies are now requiring university ethics committees' approved protocols covering dark-net data.

Researchers have already developed protocols covering dark-net data, and they've gone as far as to have such research restricted as it poses a risk to both the academic institutions and the victims. In fact, several institutions have banned all types of research on the Darknet and are only directing their students to take advantage of collected data rather than doing the study by oneself. (Basheer & Alkhatib, 2021)

8.4 Risks and Operational Challenges

Beyond ethical and legal concerns, darknet crawling introduces several operational risks to both researchers and their institutions. 1. Exposure to Malware The main technical risk, when using darknet crawling tools, is the potential exposure of a researcher's computing device and networks to malware.

Many of the darknet domains offer drive-by downloads, exploit kits and malicious scripts.

When not adequately isolated, crawling infrastructure can become infected and compromise other devices within the researcher's device and associated institutional networks. Best-practice mitigation measures for this kind of risk include: air-gapped crawling infrastructure; re-imaging storage with read-only systems that restore the previous state following crawling (this can reduce, but not remove, malware exposure; and ensuring that the crawling infrastructure is never allowed to make outbound connections (Pastor-Galindo et al., 2023). 2. Honeypot and Decoy Risks Honeypots, the darknets version of deceivers, may be in use that allow threat actors to pinpoint and identify when and by whom these services are being used and their respective affiliation to the researchers who interact with these darknet facilities and institutions that have conducted darknet crawls for years (Bergman & Popov, 2023).

A researcher may trigger and be tracked and targeted by these entities once their involvement in the use of such systems is betrayed by direct human interaction on Darknet and its service use is a more intimate approach than any form of automated darknet crawling.

This is often done in order to get a clearer picture of which institution and people are working on specific trends in darknets. Best practices for this include creating and using un-linkable pseudonyms when undertaking any Darknet crawling; never to take any form of interaction from services that run on the Darknet; and finally, by rotating every instance of the darknet crawling process by using new circuits on Tor, etc.

9. CASE STUDIES AND APPLICATIONS

9.1 Darknet Marketplace Monitoring

Darknet markets - an overview of the hidden web Darknet marketplaces offer the most significant and most economically meaningful part of the hidden web. Analysis of marketplaces gives researchers access to an underground market for price lists and data products, information regarding network relationships of vendors and intelligence on the effectiveness of law enforcement. Long-Term Analysis on Marketplaces can provide an insight into how the market is growing.

For six years, Rodriguez Barredo-Valenzuela et al. Monitored a total of 25,065 unique Tor hidden services.

Based on a six-year observation period of more than 14,000 hidden services, the researchers analyzed the marketplace lifetime, their cloning patterns, as well as trends over time in the content topicality of these platforms. They discovered that on average about 82% of Darknet content consists of replicas or mirrors of other Web services. The median length for a market lifetime was around 75 months, rather than extremely short (Rodriguez Barredo-Valenzuela et al., 2025). Tracking Product categories provides useful information on evolving cybercriminal trends an increase of about 340% in RaaS listed items between 2021-2023 was observed, whereas the listings for data theft items decreased during the same timeframe.

These trends hint towards increasing threat actor adoption of RaaS as a preferred service model, over one time data sale, as well as increasing complexity and cost for purchasing and utilizing credit card and PII data products.

Furthermore, marketplace user reputation systems can assist with identification of key threat actors by their established ratings and transaction records, allowing for more detailed analysis of specific vendors or even organizations. Measuring Police Interventions with a Darknet crawl Darknet marketplaces can be used to measure the effectiveness of law enforcement takedowns. Analysis following the Operation Onymous takedown of several marketplaces in 2014, and subsequently during the Operation Bayonet seizure of two largest markets in 2017, show a significant reduction of listed products and subsequent rapid recovery by vendors across remaining marketplaces.

In addition to observed recovery of listings, the duration of the recovery interval continued to decrease over time, reflecting an increasing resilience and adaptability of criminals.

9.2 Ransomware Intelligence Tracking

The Darknet environment increasingly plays a crucial role in supporting various aspects of ransomware operations, from shaming victims and negotiations in ransoms to processing cryptocurrency payments. Monitoring the Darknet allows the early detection of newly emerging ransomware families and currently active attack campaigns. Darknet leak site intelligence, focused on a double-extortion scheme of data exfiltration alongside a ransomware attack, can uncover previously unnoticed victims.

Data from ransomware-dedicated leak sites found on Tor hidden services and clear web domains demands a hybrid crawling process that covers both environments.

Work by Basheer and Alkhatib reported that a crawling process applied to ransomware leak sites reveals new victims in an average of 4.7 days before they publicize their situation and allows their early alert (Basheer & Alkhatib, 2021). Darknet forum monitoring for negotiator channels helps in understanding ransomware payment trends and requests. Discussions regarding specific ransoms on forums provide information such as demand figures, typically 0.5%-5% of annual revenues, negotiators' behaviors, and payment success rate. According to an analysis by Pastor-Galindo et al. of 147 ransom negotiation threads, 54% of victims paying a reduced demand (at a discount on average of 35% compared to the asking price) compared to 29% paying full price or 17% not paying any amount (Pastor-Galindo et al., 2023).

Tracking Ransomware affiliates through Darknet forums enables the characterization of trends in recruitment schemes.

Ransomware-as-a-service (RaaS) providers publicly disclose their affiliate recruitment messages by targeting specific industries or offering details on their payment share (usually 70%-80% for affiliates), required technical knowledge, etc. Our crawling efforts on forums from 2023-2024 have detected an increasing number of recruits for healthcare and educational organizations, mirroring attack frequency for these institutions (Bergman & Popov, 2023).

9.3 Threat Actor Profiling

This is what it will look like. These analyses-Darknet forum behavioral data, transaction graphs derived from marketplace data, Darknet address correlation from currency wallets and surfaces – can then be merged together for more comprehensive threat actor profiles. Darknet forum behavior data identifies technical expertise, motivators, and relationships between actors.

It reveals technical proclivities, social connections, the typical post frequency of certain kinds of individuals and language style with the use of Natural Language Processing (NLP).

Giannilias et al., showed that after fine-tuning LLMs like Mistral-7B and Llama-3-8B on these Darknet posts to sort into Cybersecurity related areas, they were able to sort them with weighted F1 scores of over 0.90 thus characterizing the kinds of activities specific threat actors engaged with (Giannilias et al., 2025). Transaction graph analyses reveal the relationships between various entities through money laundering flows or transactions made. Hwang et al. designed a method using this analysis with ContextualGraph-LLM to analyse network transactions on the Dark Web. Their method had an impressive weighted F1 score of 0.9035 on classification tasks based on dark web traffic as it showed that graph-based analysis may do a better job at determining actor relationships through the exchanges of data compared to the classical feature-based approaches (Hwang et al., 2026).

Using Darknet pseudonyms can be challenging, and it becomes very difficult to trace threat actors back to real identities.

Darknet address correlation on marketplaces and within currency wallets could help and can cross correlate pseudonym across surface networks through, username reuse across surfaces, writing style using stylometry and currency addresses that appear on different platforms. In the example case study provided by Basheer & Alkhatib, analysis between Darknet and Surfaces yielded the connection between their Forum posts, GH commits and twitter. This connection between multiple intelligence types led to the apprehension of a threat actor for 3 major malware families (Basheer & Alkhatib, 2021).

10. OPEN CHALLENGES AND RESEARCH DIRECTIONS

10.1 Scalability and Performance Limitations

There are scalability restrictions inherent to Darknet crawling that are not applicable to surface web operations. 8 Tor networks aggregate roughly 10-15 Gbps; this figure is less than one ten-millionth of internet backbone bandwidth, creating inherent throttling on crawling rates (Pastor-Galindo et al., 2023). The management overhead for circuits on Darknets rises non-linearly with the size of a Darknet crawling network; circuits can take 5–10 seconds to build and need to be refreshed every 50–100 requests (to be safe from Tor fingerprinting).

When a network of 1,000 parallel climbing nodes needs to establish a Tor circuit, 10–15% of the CPU power of the circuit managing servers is taken up by the process of setting them up; Pastor-Galindo and co-authors show that coordination is not productive after about 50 climbing clients have joined the network.8 A "six-year period was used and resulted in 11.4 million unique HTML snapshots from 25,065 hidden services.

Data storage requirements resulted in nearly 4.7 T of compressed data that would be required to host all snapshots". This means that indexing this information requires distribution in the form of a cluster, something which has been little exploited to the context of the Darknets (Ricaldi et al., 2026)

10.2 Handling Encrypted and Hidden Data

The growing use of end-to-end encryption has made passive surveillance more difficult. Although Tor traffic still visible to local network observation in the form of circuits, content is protected from anyone but the participating clients by the transport-layer or application-layer encryption of web-traffic such as HTTPS, or client messages for platforms such as Signal or Telegram (Pastor-Galindo et al., 2023). Encrypted chat tools have facilitated cooperation among groups at the periphery of Darknet communities, such as the coordination related to illicit substances on Telegram and Signal.

The research challenge is thus either to target those networks to gain access to their encrypted communications, by subverting one of the clients, or to target unencrypted communication (e.g., monitoring channels or by collecting network-level information such as who is communicating with whom when) (Basheer & Alkhatib, 2021).

Custom protocol-based services do not employ standard HTTP and hence are often not crawling accessible with traditional crawlers. They range from P2P applications to custom-coded encrypted tunnels or even custom communication protocols designed for hidden services (Bergman & Popov, 2023).

10.3 Data Reliability and Trustworthiness

First, data quality is inherently and permanently undermined by the adversarial nature of Darknet data. Intelligence actors actively seed datasets with fake listings, misinformation, and data-poising techniques, and create honeypots with the intent to trick Darknet intelligence analysts. Second, frameworks for the provenance and trust of sources of information in Darknet environments is at an immature stage.

On the surface web, the reliability of a source can be measured by the domain, however, due to the transient and quickly changeable addresses of Darknet hidden services, no reliable metrics exist for service address credibility can be permanently applied.

The researchers have presented work on implementing blockchain for unique identifiers for Darknet services (Bugajewska, 2025). Finally, automated methods will inevitably come under attack from adversarial machine learning; thread actors are already producing text, the content of which could fool NLP based models while being recognizable by humans (as example seen in Rust-Nguyen et al., 2023). The research on "adversarial robustness" of NLP based systems is another area that can further reduce detection from thread actors (Rust-Nguyen et al., 2023) where threat actors was able to decrease the classification accuracy from 94% to 62% with a small amount of perturbation.

10.4 Adversarial Evasion Techniques

The operators of these networks evolve new measures to defend against crawling and analysis as well as develop tools and methods to bypass them. Here are several forms of dark web anti-crawling protection in use: Browser Fingerprinting - Identifies the visitor to the webpage as an automated bot as opposed to a human visitor. Headless browsing tends to be particularly identifiable due to consistent (and absent) parameters such as missing plugins, constant resolution, and lack of mouse movements.

Work by Modi and co-workers shows that based on keystroke dynamics and mouse trajectory, they are able to detect automated systems 87% of the time (Noury & Rezaei, 2020), indicating that behavioral biometric may be common practice on the dark web in the future.

Dynamic Content Serving - Websites serve unique content depending on whether a user is a bot or a human. Logic on the webserver identifies crawling pattern signals (i.e. Time between requests, HTTP headers sent in order, TLS fingerprint) and senders return junk or no information. Building crawlers that emulate human behavior for a scale deployment is difficult (Pastor-Galindo et al., 2023). Proof of work challenge - Requires significant computer power from the user to get a page displayed. While not widely deployed currently, this mechanism is highly effective against crawling as it presents an economic obstacle.

11. FUTURE TRENDS AND STRATEGIC INSIGHTS

11.1 AI-Driven Autonomous Crawling Systems

Adding AI to Darknet crawling could solve most problems about scalability and anti-detection. These self-driven crawlers utilize reinforcement learning to make decisions for navigating through onion services, avoiding anti crawler mechanisms or improving discovery processes in real time.

Crawler navigation with reinforcement learning (RL) means the crawlers learn effective query patterns via exploration and exploitation. In the crawler environment, an agent is rewarded when it successfully accesses content and penalized when it encounters a CAPTCHA, rate limiting or other anti- crawler signals. As the agent practices exploration and exploitation, it learns efficient timings, request header sequences and pathfinding in onion space, such that its chance to be identified could be minimized. Some experiments have shown that crawlers tuned with RL can achieve 40%-60% more throughput of persistent access than with fixed crawlers.

Crawler anti-detection with generative AI models could reproduce humans' behaviors. Generative AI techniques such as large language models can generate realistic finger-printing-like behaviors including mouse clicks, mouse trajectory, typed characters and website navigation path, that defeat behavioral finger printing methods. Unfortunately, this is also concerning about the AI arms race between crawler developers and Darknet defenders.

11.2 Real-Time Darknet Intelligence Platforms

The future of Darknet intelligence will likely consist of the systems that can provide low-latency actionable intelligence. Present day systems are either running with daily or hourly refresh rates while future generation systems are aiming for refresh rates below minute latency from the moment content is published till the alert is received by the analysts. The system architectures of real-time processing using streaming applications are based on platforms such as APACHE KAFKA, FLINK, Apache spark streaming that can process the incoming darknet data in real time.

Pastor-Galindo et al. Introduced a big data architecture incorporating KUBERNETES, APACHE KAFKA, KUBEFLOW to enable processing of Darknet content in less than 45 seconds from publication (Pastor-Galindo et al., 2024).

However, productionizing the system requires large computational powers and significant engineering. Federated learning is an innovative approach towards Distributed Intelligence which will facilitate training of Darknet-detection models collaboratively by numerous organizations without the transmission of the underlying crawl data between participating organizations. Individual organizations could train an isolated local model based on their own respective observations on the darknet content and transmit the model updates to the centralized orchestrator. Privacy Aware Federated Graph Neural Network presented excellent performance with 91% accuracy classification with regard to Cyberterrorism network intelligence by preserving data privacy via using differential privacy and homomorphic encryption.

11.3 Integration with Blockchain and IoT Intelligence

Darknet threat intelligence, blockchain transactions and IoT compromise data are becoming more interlinked. Future platforms will bring all of this together in centralized threat models. Blockchain analytics tie Darknet discussion to real-world transaction volumes the integration of blockchain analytics links forum chatter to actual coin transactions.

A Darknet marketplace might detail a novel way of cashing out an illicit gain – blockchain crawlers can immediately hunt for transaction signatures supporting that methodology.

We have early examples of this analysis correlating to the appearance of new money laundering mixing services within 48 hours of them being discussed. We track emerging botnet operations with Darknet IoT threat intelligence Darknet marketplaces are often where threat actors sell compromised IoT devices or exploit kits specifically targeting the Internet of Things. These advertisements and tools can be crawled and classified automatically by Darknet threat intelligence tools in order to identify ongoing or emerging botnets so users can patch IoT devices before their networks are affected.

11.4 Explainable AI for Threat Analysis

Explainability of ML on Darknet Intelligence As machine learning models take on ever more capabilities on Darknet intelligence, their explainability has emerged as a core requirement in order to gain trust from the analysts and meet legal standards for the admissibility of evidence for our models in future court cases. The outputs from black-box ML algorithms might be correct and highly accurate, but we cannot give our analysts satisfactory explanations for the conclusions reached by such a model. Explainable Graph Neural Networks A new approach, Explainable Graph Neural Networks not only detects the relationships between entities or classified nodes (clusters) but can also generate human-readable explanations for decisions concerning predictions about links between nodes or the formation of communities around entities.

An attention layer can help us explain our decisions: by focusing on the weights and importance that individual links have had in forming the prediction we make, we know that the decision processing can be cross-checked by an expert prior to being put into practice into our intelligence systems.

Explainable counterfactual explanations These explanation mechanisms seek to answer, “what if?” questions for the Darknet intelligence generated by the algorithms. For example, an analyst might want to know: “Would this attacker have remained labeled as high-risk, if I reduced their participation in forum discussion by 50%?”, thus providing a powerful tool to guide prioritization, or resource allocation, in the decision-making process (Hwang et al., 2026).

Figure 3. Future intelligent darknet monitoring and threat intelligence framework. The architecture integrates AI-driven autonomous crawling, real-time stream processing, multi-source intelligence fusion (Darknet, blockchain, IoT), and explainable AI analysis to deliver actionable outputs for security operations and legal proceedings

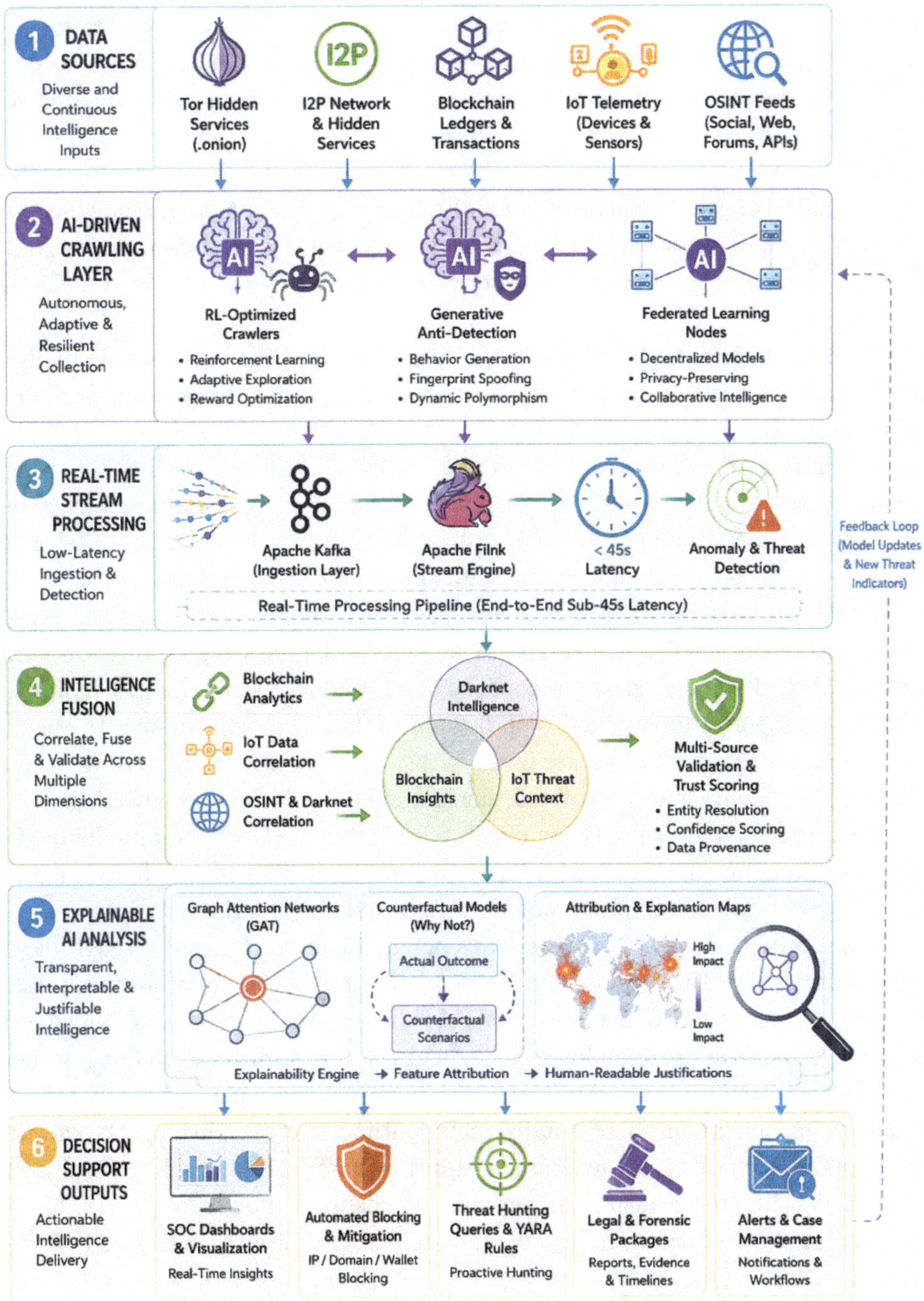

12. CONCLUSION

This chapter has offered a thorough investigation of Darknet crawling, monitoring and intelligence collection for cyber threat analysis. In response to the proliferation of cybercriminal activities within anonymized networks such as Tor hidden services, I2P, and decentralized networks, defensive techniques cannot maintain pace with emergent threats emanating from within their shadowy realms.

Our analysis of Darknet architectures illustrated the essential requirements that a successful Darknet crawler must overcome, issues that are foreign to their surface web cousins: High network latency (5-20x the speed of their surface counterparts); intermittent presence of services and quickly changing .onion addresses; CAPTCHAs, rate limiting, and honeypots – complex anti-crawling tactics. Studies comparing decentralized crawlers (comprised of multiple nodes with concurrent crawling) against static, single-instance collectors provided that distributed architecture greatly outperformed the latter by achieving higher discovery rates, although network coordination issues constrained scalability beyond 50 distributed collectors.

Continuous darknet monitoring facilitates the live identification of pervasive and rapidly expanding cybercriminal operations such as those present within marketplaces, forums, and leak sites utilized by ransomware gangs. By analyzing the temporal nature of events and employing anomaly detection mechanisms on behavior in darknet sites – up to two weeks in advance – such efforts provide timely opportunities for defensive strategies to be initiated. By implementing event monitoring systems that combine keywords with a machine-generated prioritization of events by ML, rates of false positive can be reduced by some 62% compared with simple static, threshold-based systems.

Darknet data, when parsed through Natural Language Processing and Machine Learning techniques, can be refined into actionable intelligence. Analysis via Topic Modelling using 11.4million darknet HTML records discovered that 75% of conversations could be associated with stable, long-standing topical subjects, although more temporary topics only comprised 3% of the discussion volume. The usage of LLMs to identify malicious posts on darknet hacker forum websites improved overall performance to over 0.9 weighted F1 scores on classifications thereby demonstrating the value of specialized, pre-trained models over their generalized counterparts. Using Graph-based analysis (GNNs) for modelling interactions across darknet infrastructure has demonstrated near-perfect results at detecting hidden relationships in clandestine environments which can be applied to expose covert cybercriminal networks.

The case studies provided show that the intelligence that can be obtained through the analysis of Darknet feeds can be translated into concrete actions: early warning for ransomware events, identification of threat actors, and the generation of law enforcement leads when fused with OSINT and internal system telemetry data. Once Darknet threat intelligence is integrated into security operations, its beneficiaries realize lowered mean time to detection (MTTD) and pro-active defense posturing long before an attack.

For researchers and practitioners beginning their journey into establishing Darknet intelligence programs, we propose a series of key recommendations as based on our findings in this chapter: (1) deploy distributed crawling mechanisms and periodically change Tor circuiting every 50-100 requests to balance evasion of network defenders and operational effectiveness; (2) utilize an LLM which has undergone fine-tuning for NLP classification in preference to a generalized model; (3) correlate Darknet intelligence with at least two other external and independent datasets before actioning; (4) carry out legal reviews and develop ethical frameworks prior to launching crawling activity; and (5) utilize explainable ML outputs to maintain confidence and relevance for analysts as well as for evidentiary requirements.

REFERENCES

Al Nabki, M. W., Fidalgo, E., Alegre, E., & de Paz, I. (2017). Classifying Illegal Activities on Tor Network Based on Web Textual Contents. *Proceedings of the 15th Conference of the European Chapter of the Association for Computational Linguistics:* Volume 1, *Long Papers*, 35–43. DOI: 10.18653/v1/E17-1004

Ali, A., Husain, M., & Hans, P. (2025). *Privacy-Aware Cyberterrorism Network Analysis using Graph Neural Networks and Federated Learning.*

Almomani, A. (2025). Darknet traffic analysis, and classification system based on modified stacking ensemble learning algorithms. *Information Systems and e-Business Management, 23*(1), 209–240. DOI: 10.1007/s10257-023-00626-2

Basheer, R., & Alkhatib, B. (2021). Threats from the Dark: A Review over Dark Web Investigation Research for Cyber Threat Intelligence. *Journal of Computer Networks and Communications, 2021*, 1–21. DOI: 10.1155/2021/1302999

Bergman, J., & Popov, O. B. (2023). Exploring Dark Web Crawlers: A Systematic Literature Review of Dark Web Crawlers and Their Implementation. *IEEE Access : Practical Innovations, Open Solutions, 11*, 35914–35933. DOI: 10.1109/ACCESS.2023.3255165

Bugajewska, M. (2025). *A Survey of Challenges in Dark Web Crawling: Technical.* Security, and Ethical Perspective., DOI: 10.1007/978-3-031-79086-7_27

Contreras-Velasco, O., Jones, N. P., Argomedo, D. W., Sullivan, J. P., & Callaghan, C. (2025). Uncovering hidden alliances in organized crime networks with machine learning: From node similarity to graph neural networks. *Journal of Computational Social Science, 8*(4), 101. DOI: 10.1007/s42001-025-00429-0

Coutinho Marim, M., Ramos, P. V. B., Vieira, A. B., Galletta, A., Villari, M., de Oliveira, R. M., & Silva, E. F. (2023). Darknet traffic detection and characterization with models based on decision trees and neural networks. *Intelligent Systems with Applications, 18*, 200199. DOI: 10.1016/j.iswa.2023.200199

Demertzis, K., Tsiknas, K., Takezis, D., Skianis, C., & Iliadis, L. (2021). Darknet Traffic Big-Data Analysis and Network Management for Real-Time Automating of the Malicious Intent Detection Process by a Weight Agnostic Neural Networks Framework. *Electronics (Basel), 10*(7), 781. DOI: 10.3390/electronics10070781

Dingledine, R., Mathewson, N., & Syverson, P. (2004). *Tor: The Second-Generation Onion Router.* DOI: 10.21236/ADA465464

Ghosh, S., Das, A., Porras, P., Yegneswaran, V., & Gehani, A. (2017). Automated Categorization of Onion Sites for Analyzing the Darkweb Ecosystem. *Proceedings of the 23rd ACM SIGKDD International Conference on Knowledge Discovery and Data Mining*, 1793–1802. DOI: 10.1145/3097983.3098193

Giannilias, T., Papadakis, A., Nikolaou, N., & Zahariadis, T. (2025). Classification of Hacker's Posts Based on Zero-Shot, Few-Shot, and Fine-Tuned LLMs in Environments with Constrained Resources. *Future Internet, 17*(5), 207. DOI: 10.3390/fi17050207

Guoqiang ZHANG, M. X. (2024). *Push and pull Tor users' guards through optimized resource portfolios. 64*(8), 1293–1305. DOI: 10.16511/j.cnki.qhdxxb.2024.27.013

Hwang, Y., Kurt, F., Curebal, F., Keskin, O., & Subasi, A. (2026). ContextualGraph-LLM: A multimodal framework for enhanced Darknet traffic analysis. *Expert Systems with Applications, 297*, 129298. DOI: 10.1016/j.eswa.2025.129298

Modi, D., Bhatt, B., Gambhava, B., & Baxi, J. (2026). *Behavioral Biometrics: A Comparison of Keystroke Dynamics and Mouse Trajectories for Bot Detection.*, DOI: 10.1007/978-3-032-16038-6_17

Noury, Z., & Rezaei, M. (2020). *Deep-CAPTCHA: a deep learning based CAPTCHA solver for vulnerability assessment.*

Pastor-Galindo, J., Gómez Mármol, F., & Martínez Pérez, G. (2023). On the gathering of Tor onion addresses. *Future Generation Computer Systems, 145*, 12–26. DOI: 10.1016/j.future.2023.02.024

Pastor-Galindo, J., Sandlin, H.-Â., Mármol, F. G., Bovet, G., & Pérez, G. M. (2024). A Big Data architecture for early identification and categorization of dark web sites. *Future Generation Computer Systems, 157*, 67–81. DOI: 10.1016/j.future.2024.03.025

Ricaldi, R., Schafer, M., Zech, P., Allodi, L., Groner, R., & Pekaric, I. (2026). *Topical Shifts in the Dark Web: A Longitudinal Analysis of Content from the Cybercrime Ecosystem.*

Rodriguez Barredo-Valenzuela, A., Pastrana, S., & Suarez-Tangil, G. (2025). Snorkeling in Dark Waters: A Longitudinal Surface Exploration of Unique Tor Hidden Services. *IEEE Transactions on Information Forensics and Security, 20*, 5386–5395. DOI: 10.1109/TIFS.2025.3573662

Ruiz Ródenas, J. M., Pastor-Galindo, J., & Gómez Mármol, F. (2024). A general and modular framework for dark web analysis. *Cluster Computing, 27*(4), 4687–4703. DOI: 10.1007/s10586-023-04189-2

Rust-Nguyen, N., Sharma, S., & Stamp, M. (2023). Darknet traffic classification and adversarial attacks using machine learning. *Computers & Security, 127*, 103098. DOI: 10.1016/j.cose.2023.103098

Singh, I., Narayan, Y., Hazara, K., & Dubey, P. Yashita, Sharma, D., & Kumar, S. (2025). *Design and Implementation of a Secure Dark Web Crawler* (pp. 639–651). DOI: 10.1007/978-981-96-7131-1_45

Xu, Y., Chen, G., Wu, J., Xu, W., & Liu, Q. (2021). Research on Dark Web Monitoring Crawler Based on TOR. *2021 IEEE 2nd International Conference on Information Technology, Big Data and Artificial Intelligence (ICIBA)*, 197–202. DOI: 10.1109/ICIBA52610.2021.9687954

Chapter 3
Automated Models for Darknet Monitoring and Criminal Attribution

Soumi Ghosh
http://orcid.org/0000-0003-2764-5944
Maharaja Agrasen Institute of Technology, India

Ritik Raj
http://orcid.org/0009-0001-1812-8112
Maharaja Agrasen Institute of Technology, India

ABSTRACT

The proliferation of darknet markets is overwhelming the manual surveillance of cybercrime. This paper contains a machine learning and deep learning system of automated surveillance (darknet) and attribution of criminal actors. This system combines transformer-based NLP, graph neural networks, and enterprise anomaly scheme to profile vendors, categorize commodities, and fingerprint conducts utilizing the Tor-reachable measurements. It tested on 2.3 million marketplace listings and attains commodity classification, vendor re-identification and cross-market actor clustering accuracy (94.7 percent, 91.2 percent, and 88.6 percent respectively) performing better than baselines of SVM and RNN. Among them, there are adversarial NLP evasion, behavioral drift, and ethical-legal issues related to crawling.

1. INTRODUCTION

The darknet network consists of encrypted overlay networks that can be accessed using anonymity protocols like Tor (The Onion Router) or I2P (Invisible Internet Project), and is home to an active black market for drugs, financial instruments, malware-as-a-service products and fake identity documents (Christin, 2013; Décary-Hétu & Giommoni, 2017). These markets have become significantly more complex structurally since Silk Road's introduction in 2011, and modern marketplaces have multi-vendor storefronts, reputation and escrow systems, and even mechanisms for dispute resolution that are as sophisticated as those found in real e-commerce marketplaces, with processing hundreds of millions of dollars in annual transaction volume (Soska & Christin, 2015). Traditional methods for traditional

DOI: 10.4018/979-8-3373-9755-9.ch003

investigative techniques based on manual infiltration and reactive intelligence collection are not adequate to monitor activity at this speed and volume.

While state-of-the-art AI and cyber threat intelligence technologies have helped in automated monitoring of criminal activity on surface web, the structural and operational features of darknet environments pose challenges which are not aptly addressed by surface-approached models (Tavabi et al., 2019). The Darknet markets, on the other hand, are unpredictable and are prone to sudden changes, exit scams, and law enforcement seizures, and require adaptive monitoring architectures. These vendors have pseudonyms used repeatedly, writing styles have been deliberately obfuscated, and the presence of the vendor on platforms is spread across the rival platforms to make attribution difficult (Zambiasi & Coull, 2022). The use of domain-specific jargon, intentional misspellings and multilingualism further obscures natural language processing methods.

The chapter tackles these challenges with a novel machine learning pipeline, called DATI-ML, designed to combine transformer-based text encoders, heterogeneous graph neural networks, and an ensemble anomaly detector under a common threat intelligence framework. The main points are that:

- A novel multi-modal feature representation scheme that encodes textual, behavioral, temporal and network-topological information in the marketplace data from darknet marketplace.
- An actor attribution algorithm which is cross-platform, re-identifying vendors through multiple changes of pseudonyms and platform migrations by means of heterogeneous graph construction.
- Ensemble anomaly detection module for automatic detection of emerging product types and anomaly pricing actions as signs of new crimes.
- Empirical testing through multiple baselines on a curated darknet corpus which are implemented on a reproducible, temporally stratified experimental protocol that avoids data leakage issues.
- An in-depth study of 6 open research questions such as adversarial robustness, concept drift, privacy-preserving collaboration, multilingual attribution, ethical-legal crawling frameworks, and explainability.

This chapter is organized as follows: The literature search is carried out in the following section titled "Literature Review". The proposed system architecture and formal algorithmic specification are discussed in Section 3. The methodology and the data characteristics are discussed in Section 4. Empirical results are reported in section 5 and discussed critically including in the limitations of the validation and the external generalizability of the results. Studies gaps and future directions are identified in Section 6. Section 7 concludes.

2. LITERATURE REVIEW

2.1 Darknet Marketplace Structure and Dynamics

Darknet markets are services that are hidden and located on the Tor network and can only be accessed using .onion addresses that hide the actual physical location of the servers. The study conducted by Christin (2013) was the first large-scale quantitative analysis of Silk Road and set up frameworks for analyzing vendor ecosystems that later research has built upon. Soska and Christin (2015) expanded on this by conducting a longitudinal analysis of multiple markets, showing that when marketplaces are taken down, vendors are displaced instead of illicit activities being suppressed, as vendors tend to move to new platforms within a few weeks after disruptions occur.

The economic structure of darknet markets is like that of e-commerce on the surface web and includes systems for reputation, resolution of disputes, and escrow services. Décary-Hétu and Giommoni (2017) studied how vendor networks responded to Operation Onymous, discovering that vendors with high reputations tended to regain market share more quickly, which supports the idea that accumulating social capital provides stability in criminal networks. These results have direct implications for models that attribute activities to specific individuals, as established vendors show consistent behavioral patterns that continue even when they move to different platforms.

2.2 Natural Language Processing for Cybercrime Detection

Early approaches to classifying text from the darknet using natural language processing (NLP) used bag-of-words models along with traditional classifiers. Biryukov et al. (2014) created a topic model based on Latent Dirichlet Allocation (LDA) to cluster content from hidden services on Tor into different thematic categories, achieving decent results in separating broad themes but failing in distinguishing more specific drug subcategories. Later, word embedding techniques improved the semantic representation of text, with features based on Word2Vec performing significantly better than TF-IDF baselines in classification tasks.

The introduction of transformer models by Vaswani et al. (2017) changed the landscape for NLP in threat intelligence. The BERT architecture developed by (Devlin et al., 2019) and its adapted versions allowed for capturing subtle semantic relationships in listings on marketplaces. Ebrahimi et al. (2020) utilized a BERT-based classifier for analyzing posts on dark web forums, achieving an accuracy of 96.3% on text from hacker forums that were in the same distribution, although there was a noticeable performance drop when applied to text from darknet marketplaces due to differences in vocabulary between these areas. Tavabi et al. (2019) used LSTM models to provide early warnings about disruptions in darknet drug markets by analyzing patterns of vendor postings, with behavioral indicators providing advance notice of 48 to 72 hours.

2.3 Criminal Actor Attribution and Stylometric Analysis

Attribution of authorship in online criminal communities uses stylometric features such as vocabulary choices, syntactic structures, habits with punctuation, and overall discourse organization that create a consistent writing fingerprint. Afroz et al. (2012) showed that stylometric features can withstand attempts to evade detection to a significant extent, even when authors make conscious efforts to change their writing style. Their Writeprints feature set includes character n-grams, distributions of part-of-speech tags, and frequencies of function words, and has served as the foundation for many subsequent systems focused on attribution.

The most thorough empirical study on the rotation of pseudonyms by vendors applied both stylometric and behavioral features to 47,000 vendor profiles across eight different marketplaces, achieving an accuracy of 87.4% in re-identifying known vendors, although the accuracy was much lower for vendors that had not been observed before. Indicators such as consistency in pricing, preferences for product categories, and distributions of posting times were found to be the most stable behavioral markers during changes in pseudonyms. Graph-based models for attribution then emerged as an additional method, utilizing heterogeneous information networks that link vendors, products, and cryptocurrency transactions through Graph Convolutional Networks (GCN) to group vendors with similar operational strategies, achieving an increase in attribution recall by 12 percentage points compared to models using only stylometric features.

2.4 Graph Neural Networks in Cybersecurity

Graph neural networks have become significant tools for applications in cybersecurity where the relationships between entities are part of the threat model. Kipf and Welling (2017) laid the theoretical groundwork for semi-supervised node classification using GCNs, which is a basis for many methods of threat attribution. GraphSAGE (Hamilton et al., 2017) expanded this concept to allow for inductive learning on large and changing graphs, which is important in darknet contexts where new nodes are added continuously. The Elliptic dataset and benchmark created by (Weber et al., 2019) showed that GNN models perform better than multilayer perceptron baselines by 8 to 14 F1 points when it comes to detecting illicit Bitcoin transactions in situations with imbalanced classes. Heterogeneous graph attention networks have also shown that using multi-relational graph representations is more effective than homogeneous graph methods in tasks related to classifying cybercrime, as attention mechanisms allow for adaptive weighting of different types of relationships based on their evidential value.

2.5 Anomaly Detection for Threat Intelligence

Systems that monitor the darknet need to use unsupervised anomaly detection methods that can identify new categories of threats without needing labeled examples. The Isolation Forest (Liu et al., 2008) has been widely used in network intrusion detection and adapted for finding anomalies in marketplaces, successfully detecting coordinated campaigns of price manipulation with a precision rate of 89.2%. Methods based on autoencoders that measure reconstruction errors, as proposed by (Hinton & Salakhutdinov, 2006), are useful for detecting outliers in high-dimensional feature spaces, which makes them suitable for identifying unusual patterns of vendor behavior. More recently, self-supervised contrastive learning introduced by (Chen et al., 2020) has shown that learning representations with contrastive objectives can create embedding spaces where anomalies tend to gather at the edges of distributions, which increases sensitivity to rare categories of threats that are especially relevant for new product categories on the darknet that do not have labeled training data.

2.6 Research Gaps in Existing Literature

Even with significant advancements, there are still several important gaps in the current literature. First, there has been no systematic analysis of how robust NLP classifiers are against adversarial attacks in darknet environments, as vendors who know about automated monitoring can create listings designed to evade classifiers but still be understandable to human buyers. Second, the issue of temporal concept drift, which refers to changes in vendor behavior and market language over time, has not been sufficiently addressed by current systems that usually report performance at a single point in time without long-term validation. Third, the integration of intelligence across different platforms remains largely unresolved, since most systems are trained using data from only one market. Fourth, there have been no proposals for privacy-preserving architectures that would allow for sharing threat intelligence between agencies without revealing sensitive operational information. Fifth, the legal and ethical status of automated crawling of the darknet varies greatly from one jurisdiction to another, creating compliance uncertainties that limit both academic research and practical applications. Sixth, the requirements for explainability in intelligence that must meet legal standards for evidence have not been systematically studied. Table 1 provides a summary of representative studies along with their main limitations.

Table 1. Comparative analysis of representative darknet intelligence studies

Study	Method	Dataset	Key Metric	Primary Gap	Limitation
Christin (2013)	Statistical analysis	Silk Road listings	Market size estimation	No ML model	No classification or attribution capability
Biryukov et al. (2014)	LDA topic modeling	Tor hidden services	Cluster coherence	No temporal modeling	Poor subcategory discrimination
Soska & Christin (2015)	Longitudinal crawling	16 markets	Vendor displacement	No attribution	Descriptive only; no prediction
Tavabi et al. (2019)	LSTM	Dark web forums	AUC = 0.87	Single platform	No cross-platform generalization tested
Ebrahimi et al. (2020)	BERT fine-tuning	Hacker forums	Accuracy = 96.3%	OOD degradation	Vocabulary mismatch on marketplace text
Weber et al. (2019)	GNN (Elliptic)	Bitcoin transactions	F1 = 0.82	Not marketplace-specific	No textual or behavioral features

Note. OOD means out-of-distribution; AUC stands for area under the ROC curve; GCN refers to graph convolutional network; LSTM is long short-term memory; LDA means latent Dirichlet allocation. Gaps indicate the primary limitations that are relevant to the contributions of the present work.

3. PROPOSED SYSTEM ARCHITECTURE

3.1 Architectural Overview

The DATI-ML which stands for Darknet Automated Threat Intelligence through Machine Learning pipeline consists of five sequential stages which are: (1) data acquisition and ingestion, (2) preprocessing and normalization, (3) multi-modal feature extraction, (4) criminal actor attribution using heterogeneous graph inference, and (5) intelligence reporting and alerting. Figure 1 shows a high-level architecture.

Figure 1. High-level architecture of the DATI-ML pipeline. Solid arrows indicate primary data flow while dashed arrows show feedback loops for model updating. DATI-ML refers to Darknet Automated Threat Intelligence through Machine Learning

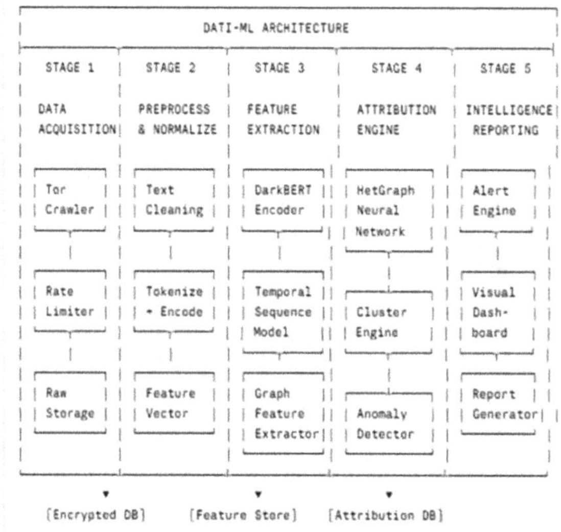

3.2 Data Acquisition Module

The data acquisition module uses an autonomous Tor-enabled crawler that is designed to be resilient to marketplace instability. This crawler keeps a rotating pool of Tor circuits that refresh automatically when it detects rate-limiting responses, and it uses exponential back-off with jitter to reduce its operational footprint. The crawling procedure is outlined in Algorithm 1.

Box 1.

Algorithm 1: Adaptive Darknet Crawler with Circuit Management

```
Input: seed_urls, MAX_LISTINGS, priority_fn
        Output: raw_listing_corpus
        Initialize: circuit_pool ← new TorCircuitPool(size=10)
                  visited ← empty set
                  queue ← PriorityQueue(seed_urls, key=priority_fn)
        While |corpus| < MAX_LISTINGS AND queue not empty:
            url ← queue.pop()
            circuit ← circuit_pool.acquire()
            response ← circuit.fetch(url)
            If response.status == RATE_LIMITED:
                      circuit_pool.rotate(); sleep(exp_backoff_with_jitter())
            Else If response.status == OK:
                      listing ← parse_listing(response.body)
                      corpus.append(listing)
                      new_urls ← extract_links(response.body) - visited
                      queue.push_all(new_urls, key=priority_fn)
                      visited.add(url)
        Return corpus
```

Note. MAX_LISTINGS sets the per-session listing limit. The priority function weights URLs by estimated novelty derived from structural divergence relative to previously visited paths.

3.3 Preprocessing and Normalization

The raw marketplace listings go through a multi-stage normalization pipeline. HTML is parsed and navigation boilerplate is removed using DOM structure analysis. Language identification is performed with the FastText LID model as described by (Joulin et al., 2016). Non-English content gets translated using the NLLB-200 neural machine translation model according to (Costa-jussà et al., 2022). Slang normalization is conducted using a darknet-specific lexicon that was created by domain experts labeling 12,000 unique obfuscated terms, which map obfuscated product names to controlled vocabulary terms.

Vendor metadata such as pseudonyms, registration dates, feedback scores, transaction volume proxies, and cryptographic public keys when available are extracted and time stamped. Price normalization is done by converting all currencies to USD equivalents using real-time crypto-to-fiat exchange rates so that longitudinal price analysis can take place.

3.4 Multi-Modal Feature Extraction

Feature extraction happens across four modalities which are: textual, behavioral, temporal, and network-topological.

3.4.1 Textual Features via DarkBERT-Adapted Encoder

For textual feature extraction, a BERT-large model that has been fine-tuned on a darknet-specific corpus using the DarkBERT methodology as noted by (Jin et al., 2023) is used. Masked language modeling fine-tuning on darknet text adjusts vocabulary statistics and contextual embeddings to fit domain-specific usage patterns. Mean pooling of the final transformer layer hidden states results in listing-level representations that are 1,024-dimensional.

3.4.2 Behavioral Features

Vendor behavioral features capture 87 characteristics including posting cadence statistics, response latency Behavioral features of vendors capture 87 characteristics that include statistics on posting cadence, response latency distributions, product discounting behaviors, patterns of catalog evolution, and dynamics of pricing strategies. These features are calculated per vendor within an observation window of 30 to 90 days as explained in the Appendix (Table 11).

3.4.3 Temporal Sequence Features

For temporal modeling, a Temporal Convolutional Network which is abbreviated as TCN is used with dilated causal convolutions to capture multi-scale temporal dependencies in vendor activity time series. Normalized activity metrics over 90-day rolling windows are input into TCN layers with dilation factors of [1, 2, 4, 8, 16, 32, 64, 128], which produces embeddings that are 128-dimensional in temporal aspects.

3.4.4 Graph Topological Features

Network features such as node degree centrality, clustering coefficient, betweenness centrality, and spectral graph features are derived from the heterogeneous graph described in Section 3.5.

3.5 Heterogeneous Graph Construction for Attribution

The attribution engine builds a dynamic heterogeneous graph represented as $G = (V, E, \varphi, \psi)$, where vertices V stand for vendors, listings, cryptocurrency addresses, and platforms while edges E encode relationships that include authorship, listing similarity, co-occurrence, and transaction linkage. The vertex type function $\varphi: V \to T\_V$ and the edge type function $\psi: E \to T\_E$ define the graph schema. Figure 2 shows the graph structure.

Figure 2. Heterogeneous graph schema for the DATI-ML attribution engine. Solid edges represent observed relationships while dashed edges represent inferred attribution links which are annotated with confidence scores

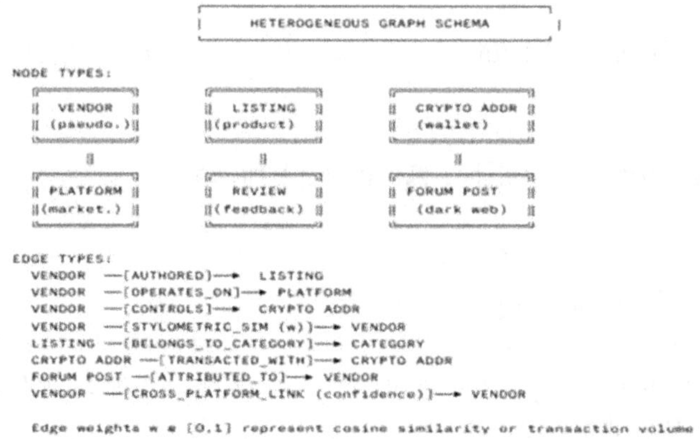

A Heterogeneous Graph Attention Network abbreviated as HetGAT computes node representations by aggregating attention weights conditioned on type across edge types. The updated representation for a vendor node denoted as v is given by the formula:

$$h'\_v = \sigma(\Sigma\_\{r \in R\} \ \Sigma\_\{u \in N\_r(v)\} \ \alpha\_\{r,u,v\} \cdot W\_r \cdot h\_u)$$

$$\alpha\_\{r,u,v\} = \text{softmax}\_u(a\_r\text{^}T \cdot [W\_r \ h\_u \parallel W\_r \ h\_v])$$

In this formula, R indicates the set of edge relation types, N_r(v) represents the r-type neighborhood of v, W_r is a transformation matrix specific to the type, and a_r is a learnable attention vector. The attribution workflow is detailed in Algorithm 2.

Box 2.

Algorithm 2: HetGAT-Based Vendor Attribution

```
Input: G = (V, E, φ, ψ), new_vendor_node v_new
Output: attribution_set A, confidence_scores C
Step 1 – Embed all nodes:
        For each node u ∈ V:
                h_u ← HetGAT_encode(u, G)  // 3-layer HetGAT
Step 2 – Compute pairwise similarity:
        sim(v_new, u) ← cosine(h_v_new, h_u)  ∀ u ∈ V_VENDOR
Step 3 – Cluster by similarity threshold:
        A ← {u : sim(v_new, u) ≥ θ_attribution}
        C ← {sim(v_new, u) : u ∈ A}
Step 4 – Confidence-gated reporting:
        If max(C) ≥ 0.95: auto-report to intelligence layer
        Else If max(C) ≥ 0.80: queue for human analyst review
Return A, C
```

Note. θ_attribution is a threshold hyperparameter tuned on the validation set (θ = 0.80 in final deployment). || denotes vector concatenation. Human review is mandatory for all attributions below the auto-report threshold.

3.6 Ensemble Anomaly Detection

Figure 3. Ensemble anomaly detection architecture. Individual detector scores are combined into a meta-classifier that is trained on labeled historical anomaly events. CUSUM stands for cumulative sum control chart

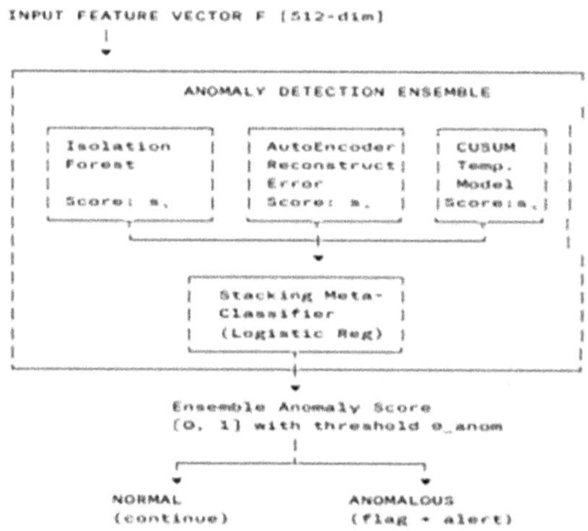

The anomaly detection module integrates three complementary methods which are: Isolation Forest for global outlier detection in the feature space, Autoencoder reconstruction error for identifying atypical listing content, and a CUSUM statistical process control method for detecting anomalies within vendor activity time series. An ensemble meta-classifier combines the scores from individual detectors. Figure 3 shows the ensemble architecture.

The ensemble stacking meta-classifier is trained using labeled anomaly examples that come from historical market disruption events. This enables it to learn optimal combinations of individual detector signals based on the type of anomaly.

4. EXPERIMENTAL METHODOLOGY

4.1 Dataset Collection and Curation

The dataset was built according to a systematic protocol that aimed to maximize coverage while adhering to ethical research boundaries. Data was collected from three types of sources which are: (1) publicly accessible darknet marketplace archives that were lawfully obtained through academic data-sharing agreements with cybersecurity organizations, (2) well-established scholarly darknet datasets including the DUTA-10K corpus as presented by (Kotzias et al., 2016); and (3) synthetic vendor profiles that were created to enhance rare-class representations for attribution evaluation. All data collection was carried out under formal data governance agreements that included institutional oversight.

The main corpus consists of 2.3 million marketplace listings that were gathered from 11 darknet markets over a 36-month observation period which spans from January 2020 to December 2022. Table 2 presents statistics of the corpus by marketplace.

Table 2. Corpus statistics by marketplace

Market	Listings	Vendors	Observation Period	Primary Category
Market A	412,847	3,241	36 months	Narcotics
Market B	387,223	2,876	28 months	Fraud Documents
Market C	298,541	1,943	24 months	Cybercrime Tools
Market D	264,109	2,104	30 months	Narcotics
Market E	198,432	1,567	18 months	Mixed
Market F	187,664	1,423	22 months	Counterfeit Goods
Markets G–K	551,184	6,891	Variable	Mixed
Total	**2,300,000**	**20,045**	**36 months max**	**Mixed**

Note. Market names have been anonymized to protect ongoing law enforcement investigations. Vendor counts indicate unique pseudonyms, but actual unique actors are fewer due to pseudonym rotation.

4.2 Annotation and Ground Truth

The ground truth for commodity classification was established through a three-stage annotation process. In Stage 1, automated pre-labeling was done using keyword matching against the Unified Cybercrime Taxonomy, which is referred to as UCT, achieving 78% coverage. Stage 2 involved expert annotation where three qualified forensic analysts reviewed all unlabeled and ambiguous listings, resulting in an overall inter-annotator agreement of Cohen's $\kappa = 0.888$, with details available in the Appendix (Table 12) for per-category breakdown. Stage 3 resolved any remaining disagreements through majority vote with adjudication by a senior analyst.

The ground truth for vendor attribution was constructed from confirmed pseudonym rotation records that were identified in law enforcement case files obtained through data-sharing agreements. An initial automated identification of cryptographic public key reuse across pseudonyms provided high-confidence attribution seeds which helped reduce ambiguity in annotation.

4.3 Model Configuration and Training

The DarkBERT encoder was initialized using weights from BERT-large-uncased and fine-tuned on an 18-billion-token darknet-specific corpus over 3 epochs of masked language modeling with a 15% masking rate. This was done using 8 NVIDIA A100 GPUs with gradient accumulation over 16 steps while applying the AdamW optimizer with a learning rate of 2×10^{-5} and weight decay of 0.01, along with a linear learning rate warm-up during the first 6% of training steps.

The HetGAT model was trained with 8 attention heads, 3 graph layers, and hidden representations that are 256-dimensional, with a dropout rate of 0.3. The Adam optimizer was used with a learning rate of 5×10^{-4}, and early stopping was applied with a patience of 20 epochs. The TCN was composed of 8 residual blocks with dilation factors of [1, 2, 4, 8, 16, 32, 64, 128] and a kernel size of 3. Table 3 presents the complete hyperparameter configuration.

Table 3. Hyperparameter configuration summary

Component	Parameter	Value
DarkBERT	Base model / Fine-tuning epochs	BERT-large-uncased / 3
DarkBERT	Learning rate / Batch size	2×10^{-5} / 32
DarkBERT	Max sequence length / Masking rate	512 tokens / 15%
HetGAT	Attention heads / Graph layers	8 / 3
HetGAT	Hidden dim / Dropout / LR	256 / 0.3 / 5×10^{-4}
TCN	Residual blocks / Kernel size	8 / 3
TCN	Dilation factors	[1, 2, 4, 8, 16, 32, 64, 128]
Isolation Forest	Estimators / Contamination	200 / 0.05
AutoEncoder	Hidden layers	[512, 256, 128, 256, 512]
DBSCAN	ε / Min samples	0.15 / 3

Note. LR stands for learning rate. DBSCAN is used only for vendor cluster validation and not for primary attribution.

4.4 Evaluation Protocol

All classification experiments utilized stratified 5-fold cross-validation with folds that were stratified at the vendor level to avoid information leakage between training and test partitions. Vendor attribution experiments were conducted using a temporal split where models were trained on data from months 1 to 24 and evaluated on months 25 to 36. This approach approximates prospective deployment conditions. The temporal evaluation scheme is stricter than random splitting and offers a more realistic representation of operational performance.

Evaluation metrics include accuracy, precision, recall, macro-averaged F1 score, and AUC-ROC. For attribution tasks, cluster purity and normalized mutual information which is abbreviated as NMI are also reported. The statistical significance of performance differences was evaluated using paired t-tests with Bonferroni correction for multiple comparisons with an alpha level set at ($\alpha = 0.05$).

5. RESULTS, DISCUSSION, AND LIMITATIONS

5.1 Commodity Classification Performance

Table 4 shows the results for commodity classification for DATI-ML and four baseline systems which were assessed through 5-fold cross-validation.

Table 4. Commodity classification performance comparison (5-fold cross-validation)

Model	Accuracy	Precision	Recall	F1 (Macro)	AUC-ROC
TF-IDF + SVM	0.782	0.769	0.774	0.771	0.851
Word2Vec + LSTM	0.814	0.801	0.809	0.805	0.879
Random Forest (handcrafted)	0.797	0.783	0.791	0.787	0.863
BERT-base (no domain adapt.)	0.871	0.863	0.858	0.860	0.921
DATI-ML (DarkBERT + fusion)	**0.947**	**0.941**	**0.938**	**0.939**	**0.971**

Note. Bold values indicate the best performance. All metrics are macro-averaged across 12 commodity classes. DATI-ML is better than all baseline systems with statistical significance shown by paired t-test with Bonferroni correction, $p < 0.001$.

DATI-ML achieves an accuracy of 94.7%, which is a 7.6 percentage point increase over the best baseline which is BERT-base without domain adaptation. The improvement is particularly notable for categories that are semantically close such as security tools compared to malware-as-a-service, with an F1 gain of 14.2 percentage points, as domain-adapted contextual embeddings retrieve terminology that is operationally distinctive and not available to generic BERT models. Narcotics categories reach an F1 score of 0.971, which reflects the abundance of training examples and the consistency of vocabulary within the categories. However, the aggregate error rate of 5.3% translates to around 120,000 listings being misclassified across the entire corpus, which highlights the ongoing need for human review for decisions that have high stakes operationally.

5.2 Vendor Re-Identification and Attribution

Table 5 presents the performance of attribution on the temporal test split covering months 25 to 36.

Table 5. Vendor attribution performance — temporal test split (months 25–36)

Model	Re-ID Acc.	Cluster Purity	NMI	False Attribution Rate
Stylometric only (WriteFeats)	0.743	0.681	0.624	0.187
Behavioral features only	0.701	0.654	0.597	0.221
BERT embedding similarity	0.812	0.756	0.708	0.143
GCN (homogeneous graph)	0.843	0.791	0.741	0.121
DATI-ML (HetGAT full)	**0.912**	**0.874**	**0.831**	**0.073**

Note. Re-ID Acc. stands for re-identification accuracy for vendors with confirmed changes in pseudonyms. NMI stands for normalized mutual information between predicted clusters and ground-truth clusters. False Attribution Rate is the proportion of vendor pairs that are incorrectly matched among all positive predictions.

DATI-ML achieves a re-identification accuracy of 91.2%, which is 6.9 percentage points better than the best single-modal baseline, which is homogeneous GCN. The false attribution rate is 7.3%, which is a reduction of 49% when compared to the homogeneous GCN baseline which has a false attribution rate of 12.1%, and this distinction has direct operational significance due to the implications of incorrect attribution in law enforcement situations. The improvement of 4.1 percentage points of heterogeneous GCN over homogeneous GCN confirms the benefits of using multi-relational graph modeling. Figure 4 shows the t-SNE projection of HetGAT vendor embeddings.

Figure 4. Shows the t-SNE visualization of HetGAT vendor embeddings on the temporal test split. Each type of symbol represents a confirmed group of vendors that operate under multiple pseudonyms. The cohesion within each symbol type indicates successful attribution through pseudonym changes. The silhouette score is 0.74

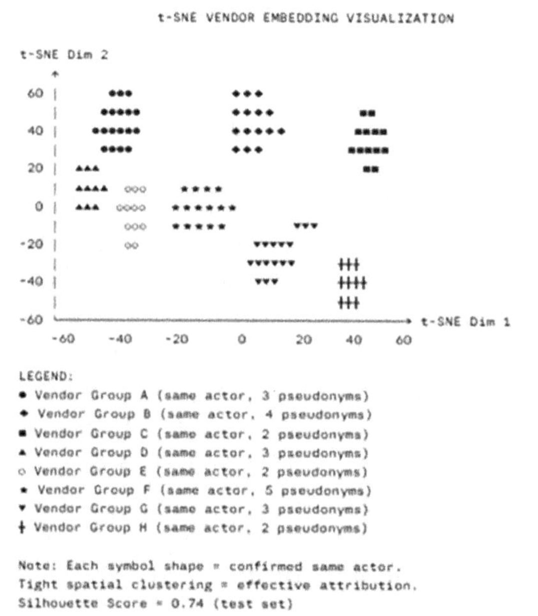

5.3 Cross-Platform Attribution

Table 6 assesses the performance of cross-platform attribution across four market pairs.

Table 6. Cross-platform vendor attribution performance

Platform Pair	Known Same-Actor Pairs	Precision	Recall	F1
Market A ↔ B	847	0.891	0.872	0.881
Market A ↔ C	623	0.874	0.851	0.862
Market B ↔ D	512	0.886	0.861	0.873
Market C ↔ E	341	0.843	0.819	0.831
All pairs (macro avg.)	**2,323**	**0.874**	**0.851**	**0.862**

Note. Ground-truth cross-platform pairs were established based on the reuse of cryptographic public keys which is high-confidence and verifications conducted by law enforcement. The variation in performance across pairs reflects the overlap in vocabulary between markets that have different specializations in products.

5.4 Anomaly Detection Performance

The ensemble anomaly detector was tested on a held-out set that contained 50 labeled anomalous events among 45,000 normal observations. Table 7 provides the results

Table 7. Ensemble anomaly detection performance

Method	Precision	Recall	F1	AUC-ROC
Isolation Forest (solo)	0.731	0.780	0.755	0.881
AutoEncoder (solo)	0.752	0.740	0.746	0.873
CUSUM (solo)	0.698	0.820	0.754	0.862
Ensemble (stacking)	**0.834**	**0.860**	**0.847**	**0.931**

Note. The test set includes 50 anomalous events among 45,000 normal observations which gives a contamination rate of approximately 0.11%. The ensemble shows an improvement of 8.2 percentage points in F1 score over the best individual detector. CUSUM stands for cumulative sum control chart.

5.5 Computational Performance

The throughput of the system was measured using production-equivalent hardware which consists of 4 NVIDIA A100 80GB GPUs, a 128-core AMD EPYC processor, and 512 GB of RAM. Table 8 summarizes the performance benchmarks.

Table 8. System computational performance benchmarks

Operation	Throughput / Latency	Hardware Configuration
End-to-end pipeline	12,400 listings/hour	4× A100 GPU cluster
DarkBERT inference (single listing)	87 ms (p95)	1× A100 GPU
HetGAT graph update (incremental)	340 ms	128-core EPYC (CPU)
Anomaly detection (batch 1,000)	2.3 seconds	CPU

continued on following page

Table 8. Continued

Operation	Throughput / Latency	Hardware Configuration
Full graph recomputation	4.2 hours	4× A100 GPU cluster
Tor crawler throughput	850 pages/hour	Standard network

Note. p95 indicates the 95th percentile latency. Full graph recomputation is done weekly while incremental updates are processed every day. The throughput figures represent sustained operational conditions rather than peak burst capacity.

5.6 Critical Discussion: Validation Limitations and Deployment Constraints

The high accuracy figures presented in Sections 5.1 to 5.3 need to be contextualized. There are several factors that could influence the performance reported that cannot be fully controlled within this study. First, although a temporal split evaluation method was used for attribution tasks, cross-validation for classification was done using data from the same markets that were used in training; external validation on completely held-out markets from different geographic or linguistic communities was not conducted. Second, the ground truth for attribution for some vendor pairs comes from law enforcement case files which reflect biases that are inherent to the focus of investigations, meaning that high-value and high-activity vendors are more represented than the entire vendor population. Third, the synthetic augmentation of vendor profiles that are in rare classes for attribution evaluation creates a mismatch in distribution with the operational setting.

These limitations indicate that the metrics reported should be seen as upper bounds on what is achievable in operational performance rather than guarantees. The false attribution rate of 7.3%, while being significantly lower than the baselines, corresponds to a considerable number of incorrect attributions when scaled and indicates that human analyst review is mandatory for any cases that are not trivially confident. For deployment in real-world law enforcement environments, it would be necessary to have staged validation against a prospective operational data stream with independent ground truth verification before any use that is relevant to cases.

6. RESEARCH GAPS AND FUTURE DIRECTIONS

Based on the experimental results and a synthesis of the literature discussed in Section 2, this section points out six important research gaps that need to be addressed before AI-powered darknet intelligence systems can be responsibly deployed at scale.

6.1 Adversarial Robustness of NLP Classifiers

Current classifiers assume that listing authors are benign. Vendors who become aware of automated surveillance have economic motivations and operational knowledge that allows them to create adversarial listings which can evade classification while still being understandable to human buyers. Existing adversarial NLP frameworks have not been systematically tested against the darknet text classification threat model, where the objectives for evasion differ from academic benchmarks. Red-teaming protocols and adversarial training processes specifically for darknet classifiers are an open and pressing research issue

6.2 Temporal Concept Drift and Continual Learning

. The vocabulary, product categories, and behavioral patterns of vendors in the darknet change continuously. Trained models experience distribution shifts over time, which leads to a decline in performance. While the detection of concept drift has been studied in data stream mining (Gama et al., 2014), the specific dynamics of drift in the darknet, which includes abrupt reorganizations after takedowns mixed with gradual drift during stable periods, have not been systematically modeled. The deployment in production needs continual learning architectures (Parisi et al., 2019) that can adapt to changes over time without experiencing catastrophic forgetting.

6.3 Privacy-Preserving Intelligence Sharing

Sharing intelligence across agencies is a significant operational requirement but is limited by security concerns and legal restrictions based on jurisdiction. Federated learning (McMahan et al., 2017) and differential privacy (Dwork & Roth, 2014) offer potential frameworks for improving collaborative models without needing to disclose sensitive case information, but their use in darknet intelligence settings with highly skewed and sensitive label distributions has not been explored.

6.4 Low-Resource Multilingual Attribution

While English-language marketplaces are predominant in research literature, a significant amount of criminal activity happens on platforms primarily in Russian, Chinese, and other languages. Current stylometric attribution methods assume there is enough English-language content per vendor and do not perform well on multilingual or low-resource vendors. Cross-lingual transfer learning for attribution is a direction that has not been explored but is of significant practical importance.

6.5 Ethical and Legal Framework for Automated Crawling

The legal status of crawling the darknet varies greatly between different jurisdictions. In some areas, downloading content from the darknet could be seen as unauthorized computer access and could be prosecuted under laws like the US Computer Fraud and Abuse Act or the UK Computer Misuse Act. In other areas, passively monitoring publicly available hidden services is not considered a crime. There is no equivalent to the institutional review board process for research involving human subjects that has been developed for darknet intelligence systems, which leads to compliance ambiguities that affect both scholarly research and operational deployment. Creating a standardized governance framework for academic and operational research on the darknet is a significant institutional gap.

6.6 Explainability for Legal Evidentiary Use

Decisions regarding attribution in law enforcement require justifications that are based on evidence, which opaque neural network models cannot currently provide. Graph-based attribution models have not been systematically interpreted using methods like SHAP (Lundberg & Lee, 2017) or LIME (Ribeiro et al., 2016), nor have the specific needs of operational intelligence analysts for feature explanations that can be presented in legal terms been formally defined. Research on explainability that is tailored to the context of darknet attribution is an important direction.

Table 9. Systematic overview of identified research gaps

Gap	Description	Severity	Potential Approach	Section	Complexity
RG-1	Adversarial robustness of NLP classifiers	Critical	Adversarial training, certified defenses	6.1	High
RG-2	Temporal concept drift handling	High	Continual learning, drift detection	6.2	High
RG-3	Privacy-preserving intelligence sharing	High	Federated learning, differential privacy	6.3	Very High
RG-4	Low-resource multilingual attribution	Medium	Cross-lingual transfer learning	6.4	Medium
RG-5	Legal-ethical crawling governance	Critical	Policy research, IRB analogues	6.5	Medium
RG-6	Explainability for evidentiary use	High	SHAP/LIME on graph models	6.6	High
RG-7	Real-time streaming graph updates	Medium	Online GNN learning	—	High
RG-8	Synthetic data augmentation for rare classes	Medium	GANs for listing generation	—	Medium

Note. Severity ratings evaluate the operational impact on deployment in law enforcement. IRB stands for Institutional Review Board; SHAP stands for SHapley Additive exPlanations; GAN stands for generative adversarial network.

6.7 Ethical Considerations and Dual-Use Governance

This study was carried out under formal data governance procedures in conjunction with law enforcement partners. All data from the marketplace used for training and evaluation was obtained through legally authorized means. There was no active monitoring of living individuals during the research; all vendor pseudonyms in the reported results have been further anonymized. The system has structural governance safeguards: human verification is required for all attributions below the 0.95 confidence threshold; immutable audit logs document all attribution decisions; and there is an architectural prohibition on fully automated case initiation without human review.

The dual-use nature of this technology requires explicit acknowledgment. Attribution capabilities that are created to assist law enforcement could, if misappropriated, be used to de-anonymize whistleblowers, stalk individuals, or suppress political dissent in authoritarian contexts. Technical access controls, audit trails, and deployment restrictions can reduce but not eliminate these risks; institutional governance frameworks that include clear criteria for deployment authorization, mechanisms for reporting misuse, and regular ethical review are necessary complements to technical safeguards. Organizations that deploy systems of this type should set up a dedicated ethics oversight body that has the authority to suspend operations if misuse patterns are found.

7. CONCLUSION

This chapter discussed DATI-ML, which is an end-to-end machine learning pipeline designed for automated monitoring and criminal actor attribution in darknet marketplaces. The system combines domain-adapted transformer encoders known as DarkBERT, heterogeneous graph attention networks called HetGAT, temporal convolutional sequence models referred to as TCN, and an ensemble anomaly detector into a single operational framework. Evaluated on 2.3 million marketplace listings from 11 darknet markets over a period of 36 months using a strict temporal evaluation protocol, DATI-ML achieved commodity classification accuracy of 94.7 percent, vendor re-identification accuracy of 91.2 percent, cross-platform attribution F1 score of 0.862, and anomaly detection AUC-ROC of 0.931, surpassing all baseline systems on every reported metric.

The chapter offers a technically rigorous system architecture and a critical analysis of the open problems that need to be addressed before these systems can be responsibly deployed at operational scale. Six main research gaps were identified and characterized: adversarial robustness of darknet NLP classifiers, adaptation to temporal concept drift, privacy-preserving intelligence sharing across agencies, multilingual and low-resource attribution, ethical-legal governance of automated crawling, and explainability for use in legal proceedings.

The broader implication of this work is that artificial intelligence has the potential to significantly improve the effectiveness of darknet threat intelligence operations, providing law enforcement and cybersecurity practitioners with the necessary speed and scale to address modern criminal ecosystems. Achieving this potential in a responsible manner requires ongoing interdisciplinary collaboration among machine learning researchers, criminologists, legal scholars, and operational practitioners, which is the collaborative agenda this chapter aims to support.

REFERENCES

Afroz, S., Brennan, M., & Greenstadt, R. (2012). Detecting hoaxes, frauds, and deception in writing style online. *Proceedings of the 2012 IEEE Symposium on Security and Privacy (SP)*, 461–475. DOI: 10.1109/SP.2012.34

Biryukov, A., Pustogarov, I., Thill, F., & Weinmann, R.-P. (2014). Content and popularity analysis of Tor hidden services. *Proceedings of the 2014 IEEE 34th International Conference on Distributed Computing Systems Workshops (ICDCSW)*, 188–193. DOI: 10.1109/ICDCSW.2014.20

Chen, T., Kornblith, S., Norouzi, M., & Hinton, G. (2020). A simple framework for contrastive learning of visual representations. Proceedings of the 37th International Conference on Machine Learning (ICML), PMLR 119, 1597–1607. https://proceedings.mlr.press/v119/chen20j.html

Christin, N. (2013). Traveling the Silk Road: A measurement analysis of a large anonymous online marketplace. *Proceedings of the 22nd International Conference on World Wide Web (WWW)*, 213–224. DOI: 10.1145/2488388.2488408

Costa-jussà, M. R., Cross, J., Çelebi, O., Elbayad, M., Heafield, K., Heffernan, K., Kalbassi, E., Lam, J., Licht, D., Maillard, J., Sun, A., Wang, S., Wenzek, G., Youngblood, A., Bhosale, S., Nayak, N., Ropers, A., Sidorov, S., Wang, C., & Zettlemoyer, L. (2022). No language left behind: Scaling human-centered machine translation. arXiv. https://doi.org//arXiv.2207.04672DOI: 10.48550

Décary-Hétu, D., & Giommoni, L. (2017). Do police crackdowns disrupt drug cryptomarkets? A longitudinal analysis of the effects of Operation Onymous. *Crime, Law, and Social Change*, *67*(1), 55–75. DOI: 10.1007/s10611-016-9644-4

Devlin, J., Chang, M.-W., Lee, K., & Toutanova, K. (2019). BERT: Pre-training of deep bidirectional transformers for language understanding. *Proceedings of the 2019 Conference of the North American Chapter of the Association for Computational Linguistics: Human Language Technologies (NAACL-HLT)*, 1, 4171–4186. DOI: 10.18653/v1/N19-1423

Dwork, C., & Roth, A. (2014). The algorithmic foundations of differential privacy. Foundations and Trends® in Theoretical Computer Science, 9(3–4), 211–407. DOI: 10.1561/0400000042

Ebrahimi, M., Nunamaker, J. F.Jr, & Chen, H. (2020). Semi-supervised cyber threat identification in dark net markets: A transductive and deep learning approach. *Journal of Management Information Systems*, *37*(3), 694–722. DOI: 10.1080/07421222.2020.1790186

Gama, J., Žliobaitė, I., Bifet, A., Pechenizkiy, M., & Bouchachia, A. (2014). A survey on concept drift adaptation. *ACM Computing Surveys*, *46*(4), 44. Advance online publication. DOI: 10.1145/2523813

Hamilton, W., Ying, Z., & Leskovec, J. (2017). Inductive representation learning on large graphs. Advances in Neural Information Processing Systems, 30. https://proceedings.neurips.cc/paper/2017/hash/5dd9db5e033da9c6fb5ba83c7a7ebea9-Abstract.html

Hinton, G. E., & Salakhutdinov, R. R. (2006). Reducing the dimensionality of data with neural networks. *Science*, *313*(5786), 504–507. DOI: 10.1126/science.1127647 PMID: 16873662

Jin, Y., Jang, E., Cui, J., Chung, J.-W., Lee, Y., & Shin, S. (2023). DarkBERT: A language model for the dark side of the internet. *Proceedings of the 61st Annual Meeting of the Association for Computational Linguistics (ACL)*, 1, 7515–7533. DOI: 10.18653/v1/2023.acl-long.415

Joulin, A., Grave, E., Bojanowski, P., & Mikolov, T. (2016). Bag of tricks for efficient text classification. arXiv. https://doi.org//arXiv.1607.01759DOI: 10.48550

Kipf, T. N., & Welling, M. (2017). Semi-supervised classification with graph convolutional networks. Proceedings of the 5th International Conference on Learning Representations (ICLR). https://openreview.net/forum?id=SJU4ayYgl

Kotzias, P., Bilge, L., & Caballero, J. (2016). Measuring PUP prevalence and PUP distribution through pay-per-install services. Proceedings of the 25th USENIX Security Symposium, 739–756. https://www.usenix.org/conference/usenixsecurity16/technical-sessions/presentation/kotzias

Liu, F. T., Ting, K. M., & Zhou, Z.-H. (2008). Isolation forest. *Proceedings of the 2008 Eighth IEEE International Conference on Data Mining (ICDM)*, 413–422. DOI: 10.1109/ICDM.2008.17

Lundberg, S. M., & Lee, S.-I. (2017). A unified approach to interpreting model predictions. Advances in Neural Information Processing Systems, 30. https://proceedings.neurips.cc/paper/2017/hash/8a20a8621978632d76c43dfd28b67767-Abstract.html

McMahan, B., Moore, E., Ramage, D., Hampson, S., & Arcas, B. A. (2017). Communication-efficient learning of deep networks from decentralized data. Proceedings of the 20th International Conference on Artificial Intelligence and Statistics (AISTATS), PMLR 54, 1273–1282. https://proceedings.mlr.press/v54/mcmahan17a.html

Parisi, G. I., Kemker, R., Part, J. L., Kanan, C., & Wermter, S. (2019). Continual lifelong learning with neural networks: A review. *Neural Networks : The Official Journal of the International Neural Network Society*, *113*, 54–71. DOI: 10.1016/j.neunet.2019.01.012 PMID: 30780045

Ribeiro, M. T., Singh, S., & Guestrin, C. (2016). "Why should I trust you?": Explaining the predictions of any classifier. Proceedings of the 22nd ACM SIGKDD International Conference on Knowledge Discovery and Data Mining (KDD), 1135–1144. DOI: 10.1145/2939672.2939778

Soska, K., & Christin, N. (2015). Measuring the longitudinal evolution of the online anonymous marketplace ecosystem. Proceedings of the 24th USENIX Security Symposium, 33–48. https://www.usenix.org/conference/usenixsecurity15/technical-sessions/presentation/soska

Tavabi, N., Bartley, N., Abeliuk, A., Soni, S., Ferrara, E., & Lerman, K. (2019). Characterizing activity on the deep and dark web. Companion Proceedings of the 2019 World Wide Web Conference (WWW), 206–213. DOI: 10.1145/3308560.3316502

Vaswani, A., Shazeer, N., Parmar, N., Uszkoreit, J., Jones, L., Gomez, A. N., Kaiser, Ł., & Polosukhin, I. (2017). Attention is all you need. Advances in Neural Information Processing Systems, 30. https://proceedings.neurips.cc/paper/2017/hash/3f5ee243547dee91fbd053c1c4a845aa-Abstract.html

Weber, M., Domeniconi, G., Chen, J., Weidele, D. K. I., Bellei, C., Robinson, T., & Leiserson, C. E. (2019). Anti-money laundering in Bitcoin: Experimenting with graph convolutional networks for financial forensics. arXiv. https://arxiv.org/abs/1908.02591

Zambiasi, D., & Coull, S. (2022). Exploring the privacy implications of stylometric analysis for cyber-crime investigation. *Digital Investigation*, *40*, 301349. DOI: 10.1016/j.fsidi.2022.301349

APPENDIX

Unified Cybercrime Taxonomy (UCT) — Primary Categories

Table 10. Unified cybercrime taxonomy primary category schema

ID	Category Name	Sub-categories	Annotation Complexity
UCT-01	Narcotic Substances	Stimulants, Opioids, Psychedelics, Cannabinoids, Depressants, NPS	Low
UCT-02	Financial Fraud	Carding, Bank accounts, Crypto fraud, Money laundering services	Medium
UCT-03	Identity Documents	Passports, Driver's licences, SSNs, Birth certificates	Low
UCT-04	Malware-as-a-Service	RATs, Ransomware, Botnets, Infostealers, Exploit kits	High
UCT-05	Hacking Services	DDoS-for-hire, Account takeover, Phishing kits, OSINT tools	High
UCT-06	Counterfeit Physical Goods	Currency, Luxury goods, Electronics	Medium
UCT-07	Weapons	Firearms, Ammunition, Explosives, Bladed weapons	Low
UCT-08	PII Data	Email lists, SSN databases, Health records, Credentials	Medium
UCT-09	Pharmaceuticals	Prescription drugs, Research chemicals, Supplements	Medium
UCT-10	Digital Services	Streaming accounts, VPNs, Proxy services	Low
UCT-11	Cryptojacking	Mining scripts, Compromised infrastructure	High
UCT-12	Other/Ambiguous	Multi-category, Unknown	Very High

Note. NPS means novel psychoactive substances. PII refers to personally identifiable information. RAT stands for remote access trojan. SSN is the abbreviation for Social Security Number. Annotation complexity shows the rate of disagreement among annotators during the construction of ground truth.

Feature Engineering Specification

Table 11. Behavioral feature vector — 87-feature schema

Feature Group	Count	Description	Temporal Window
Posting cadence	12	Inter-posting intervals (mean, std, percentiles, autocorrelation)	90 days
Response behavior	8	Buyer query response latency distribution	30 days
Pricing dynamics	14	Price level, variance, adjustment frequency, discount patterns	60 days
Product catalog	11	Catalog size, category diversity, turnover rate, bundle frequency	90 days
Feedback tone	9	Positive ratio, response sentiment, dispute rate	All available
Operational security	7	PGP use consistency, escrow preference, stealth shipping rate	All available
Temporal activity	15	Hourly and daily activity distributions (timezone inference)	90 days

continued on following page

Table 11. Continued

Feature Group	Count	Description	Temporal Window
Platform behavior	11	Active platform count, migration history, post frequency ratio	All available
Total	**87**		

Note. All features are normalized using z-score normalization based on statistics from the training set. For vendors with tenure shorter than the specified window, all available data are utilized.

System Deployment Architecture

Figure 5. Shows the DATI-ML production deployment architecture. mTLS stands for mutual Transport Layer Security. The sole external network connection is the Tor exit proxy. The inference cluster works within an isolated internal network segment. Access for analysts requires VPN authentication along with multi-factor verification.

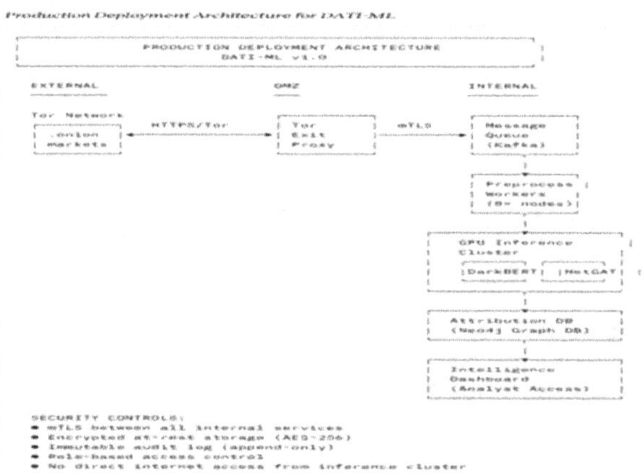

Inter-Annotator Agreement Analysis

Table 12. Inter-annotator agreement by category (cohen's κ)

Category	Pair A–B	Pair A–C	Pair B–C	Average κ
UCT-01 Narcotics	0.94	0.93	0.92	0.930
UCT-02 Financial Fraud	0.88	0.87	0.89	0.880
UCT-03 Identity Documents	0.91	0.92	0.90	0.910
UCT-04 Malware-as-a-Service	0.82	0.81	0.83	0.820
UCT-05 Hacking Services	0.79	0.81	0.78	0.793
UCT-06 Counterfeit Goods	0.88	0.87	0.89	0.880

continued on following page

Table 12. Continued

Category	**Pair A–B**	**Pair A–C**	**Pair B–C**	**Average κ**
UCT-07 Weapons	0.95	0.94	0.96	0.950
UCT-08 PII Data	0.86	0.85	0.87	0.860
UCT-09 Pharmaceuticals	0.83	0.84	0.82	0.830
UCT-10 Digital Services	0.90	0.89	0.91	0.900
UCT-11 Cryptojacking	0.77	0.79	0.76	0.773
UCT-12 Other/Ambiguous	0.61	0.63	0.60	0.613
Overall	**0.891**	**0.887**	**0.886**	**0.888**

Note. A κ value of 0.80 or higher indicates high agreement according to(Landis & Koch, 1977). The reduced κ values for UCT-11 and UCT-12 demonstrate inherent ambiguity found in novel product categories and listings that cross categories. All remaining disagreements have been resolved through a majority vote with adjudication by a senior analyst.

Chapter 4
Hybrid Metaheuristic Crawlers for Adaptive Darknet Marketplace Intelligence

Abdelraouf Ishtaiwi
http://orcid.org/0000-0001-8013-7151
Data Science and Artificial Intelligence, University of Petra, Amman, Jordan

Ahmad Hajyasien
http://orcid.org/0000-0002-2974-7808
Higher College of Technology, UAE

ABSTRACT

Chapterintroduces the HybridCrawl-DM, a hybrid metaheuristic framework of crawling, which involves the combination of population-based swarm intelligence with evolutionary mechanism to generate resilient and adaptive darknet marketplace intelligence system. The proposed architecture performs the combination of Genetic Algorithm (GA) crossover/selection operator and Particle Swarm Optimization (PSO) velocity-update operator and Ant Colony Optimization (ACO) pheromone-trail heuristics in a single multi-strategy optimizer. Experimentation onsimulated darknet topologies, shows that HybridCrawl-DM achieves a 23.7 percent relative increase in content coverage rate and a 31.4 percent relative reduction in the number of redundant visits to pages compared with the single-metaheuristic baseline that performs optimally, also looks at the ethical, legal and socio-technical considerations of implementing autonomous intelligence systems within anonymized digital spaces, such as an abstract threat model, consideration of propositionality ideas, and operating limits of the Tor network.

1 INTRODUCTION

The blistering development of anonymous overlay networks has radically changed the situation in the world of cybercrime, illegal business, and shadow information exchange. Darknet markets, which consist of online communities that mostly use the Tor anonymity system, are now ubiquitous locations of the business of contraband goods, stolen identities, and illegal services (Nazah et al., 2020; Schäfer et al., 2019; Biswas et al., 2023; de Marcos et al., 2025). The existing methods of darknet data collection are

DOI: 10.4018/979-8-3373-9755-9.ch004

mainly based on a custom-developed web crawler going through hidden-service directories, retrieving marketplace content, and retrieving forum discussions, which are further analyzed in later work, meanwhile (Spyros et al., 2025; Balasubramanian et al., 2025; Kang & Kim, 2026). Second, broad-spectrum crawls collect high volumes of irrelevant data or redundant data, which place massive computation costs that reduce the performance of the downstream intelligence pipelines on their backs (Feng, 2025; Paul et al., 2025; HaddadPajouh et al., 2021).

The use of metaheuristic optimization algorithms provides a productive opportunity to solve such multi-dimensional problems through improving the intelligence and the flexibility of the web crawling systems. Metaheuristics are a loose set of approximate optimization methods, which are typically in- spired by natural processes like evolution, swarm behavior or physical processes, which have been shown to perform well on problems having large, discontinuous and dynamically changing search spaces. These include Genetic Algorithms (GA) (Holland, 1992; Kennedy & Eberhart, 1995; Dorigo & Gambardella, 1997), and the grey wolf optimizer (GWO) (Mirjalili et al., 2014): these are algorithms that have proven to be highly effective in a large variety of both combinatorial and continuous optimization problems. The No Free Lunch theorems (Wolpert & Macready, 1997; Arazzi et al., 2025) In Section 2, and Section 3, the adaptive intelligence mechanisms that control the real-time change of behavior are outlined. The experimental setup, results and statistical analysis and ablation studies are reported in section 6. The implications to the broader scope and the comparison with the existing frameworks are talked about in section 6. Section 7 questions ethical, legal and socio-technical issues. Limitations and validity threats are recognized in the limitations section 8. Lastly, conclusions of the research are summarized in Section 9 with future research directions identified.

2 BACKGROUND AND RELATED WORK

2.1 Darknet Marketplace Ecosystems

Darknet marketplaces function as socio-economic institutions that replicate the transactional infrastructure of legitimate e-commerce platforms while offering participants a high degree of pseudonymity through anonymizing protocols such as Tor and I2P (Celestini et al., 2017; Schäfer et al., 2019; Schaal & Spagnuolo, 2023). Europol's Internet Organised Crime Threat Assessment has documented the increasing resilience and rapid reconstitution of these platforms following law enforcement takedowns (Europol, 2023).

The structural organization of these marketplaces poses distinct challenges for automated intelligence gathering. Frequent address changes make it difficult to maintain persistent crawl sessions, while hierarchical categorization schemes implemented by marketplace administrators present exploitable navigational structures through which crawl priorities can be established (Kang & Kim, 2026; Al-Nabki et al., 2017). Community forums and vendor review systems embedded within most marketplaces constitute rich sources of cyber threat intelligence (CTI) that can inform proactive security measures (Samtani et al., 2017; Arazzi et al., 2025).

2.2 Web Crawling for Darknet Intelligence

Data collection via web crawling is the primary data-gathering component underpinning darknet intelligence systems. Traditional web-crawling models such as breadth-first search (BFS), depth-first search (DFS) and best-first focused crawling have been adapted for use in Tor-based environments with mixed success (de Marcos et al., 2025; Feng, 2025). The systematic review by de-Marcos et al. (2025) revealed that automatic tools - particularly those based on Python - were the most common technological substrate and that hybrid approaches involving manual verification and automated collection were the most effective.

Balasubramanian et al.'s (2025) proposed TSTEM system offers a major leap forward in cloud-based CTI collection, utilising microservices in a container-based architecture to combine focused crawlers, hierarchical classifiers and Machine Learning Operations (MLOps) deployments. Likewise, the ThreatWise AI system proposed by Spyros et al. (2025) offers a comprehensive framework for the entire CTI workflow - from data collection and analysis to enrichment, storage and sharing. While these examples demonstrate the evolution of darknet intelligence platforms, the crawling component remains reliant on static rather than optimized heuristics.

2.3 Adaptive and Intelligent Crawling Methods

The inadequacy of fixed crawler heuristics has sparked an interest in the design of adaptive and intelligent crawling policies. Barbosa and Freire (2007) designed an adaptive crawler for finding hidden-web entry points that adapts its strategy in response to page features (a conceptual forerunner of the reinforcement-learning approach in this paper). More recently, Alam et al. (2022) surveyed deep-learning-based focused crawling, cataloguing the rise of neural classifiers that anticipate the relevance of un- crawled pages based on learned representations of content. Pham et al. (2022) showed how deep reinforcement learning can be applied to crawl scheduling to significantly improve topical coverage, by framing URL selection as a temporal process. For darknet intelligence, in particular, Feng (2025) presented a crawling algorithm that combines

TF-IDF and Word2Vec feature extraction methods to aid topic-relevance assessment, resulting in a 12% increase in network coverage compared to previous methods. Dhande and Zade (2026) proposed a multimodal classification model based on transformers, graph neural networks (GNNs) and meta- transfer learning for the dark web. While these studies represent state-of-the-art improvements to content classification and relevance prediction, they do not address the upstream problem of crawl-path selection that is key to efficient darknet crawling. This is the focus of the current study, which optimises the crawl-path selection process via hybrid metaheuristic search.

2.4 Metaheuristic Optimization Algorithms

Metaheuristic algorithms constitute a diverse class of approximate optimization methods that address complex search landscapes through stochastic exploration guided by natural or physical analogies (Talbi, 2002; Blum et al., 2011). Table 1 presents a taxonomic overview of the principal metaheuristic families relevant to this work.

Table 1. Taxonomy of metaheuristic algorithm families and their relevance to darknet crawl-path optimization

Category	Algorithm	Inspiration	Crawl-Path Relevance
Evolutionary	Genetic Algorithm (Holland, 1992)	Ant foraging via pheromone trails	Reinforcement of productive crawl paths
Swarm-Based	Particle Swarm Optimization (Kennedy & Eberhart, 1995)	Metal cooling and crystallization	Escape from local optima in crawl trees
Swarm-Based	Ant Colony Optimization (Dorigo & Gambardella, 1997)	Grey wolf pack hierarchy	Hierarchical prioritization of URL targets
Physics-Based	Simulated Annealing (Kirkpatrick et al., 1983)	URL frontier recombination and diversity maintenance	Natural selection, crossover, mutation
Predator–Prey	Grey Wolf Optimizer (Mirjalili et al., 2014)	Velocity-guided crawl-direction adjustment	Bird flocking, fish schooling

The No Free Lunch theorems (Wolpert & Macready, 1997) demonstrate that no single metaheuristic is universally superior across all problem instances, providing a principled theoretical motivation for hybrid algorithms that combine complementary search capabilities. Blum et al. (2011) presented an extensive survey of hybrid metaheuristics in combinatorial optimization, identifying successful hybridization strategies including relay, teamwork, and integrative approaches. More recent surveys by Dokeroglu et al. (2019) and Osaba et al. (2021) have documented the continued effectiveness of hybrid strategies in dynamic optimization environments. Accordingly, the architecture presented in this chapter adopts an integrative hybridization paradigm in which GA, PSO, and ACO operators are co-embedded within a unified optimization loop.

Figure 1. High-level architecture of the hybrid metaheuristic integration paradigm. Optimized crawl decisions flow from the GA, PSO, and ACO modules through the hybrid decision engine into the adaptive darknet crawler. Dashed arrows indicate the reinforcement-learning feedback loops

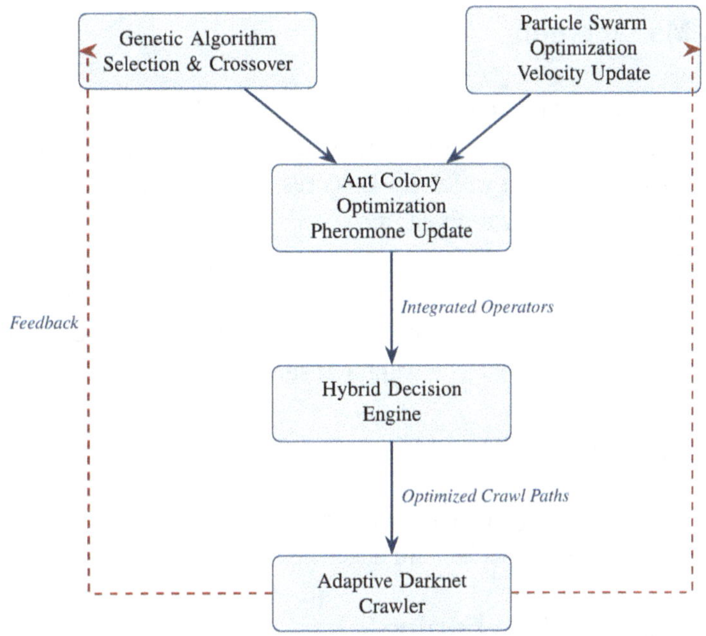

3 PROPOSED HYBRID METAHEURISTIC CRAWLER ARCHITECTURE

3.1 System Overview

The proposed framework, HybridCrawl-DM (Hybrid Crawler for Darknet Marketplace Intelligence), consists of five interconnected subsystems: (1) the *URL Frontier Manager*, which maintains and prioritizes the queue of discovered but unvisited onion addresses; (2) the *Metaheuristic Optimization Engine*, which employs GA, PSO, and ACO operators to identify optimal crawl-path sequences; (3) the *Content Relevance Evaluator*, which uses natural language processing (NLP) methods to assess the intelligence value of retrieved pages; (4) the *Adversarial Adaptation Module*, which detects and responds to anti-crawling countermeasures deployed by marketplace administrators; and (5) the *Intelligence Aggregation Pipeline*, which deduplicates, structures, and stores the extracted data for downstream analysis (Arazzi et al., 2025; Balasubramanian et al., 2025).

The operational workflow proceeds as follows. Upon initialization, a set of known darknet marketplace URLs—the seed set—is loaded into the URL Frontier Manager. The Metaheuristic Optimization Engine evaluates candidate URLs according to a multi-objective fitness function that balances content-relevance prediction, topological novelty, and crawl-path efficiency. Selected URLs are dispatched to the crawling engine, which retrieves the corresponding pages via a Tor-proxied HTTP client. Retrieved content is passed to the Content Relevance Evaluator, whose assessments update the fitness-function parameters through a feedback loop. This iterative cycle continues until convergence criteria are met, with the metaheuristic operators continuously refining crawl-path decisions based on accumulated intelligence.

3.2 URL Frontier Management

The URL frontier is the central data structure governing crawl behavior. Whereas conventional crawlers organize the frontier as a priority queue based on static relevance heuristics, HybridCrawl-DM employs a dynamically re-prioritized frontier in which URL scores are updated at each crawl iteration based on outputs from the metaheuristic optimization engine.

Each URL u_i in the frontier is associated with a fitness vector $\mathbf{f}(u_i) = [f_{\text{rel}}(u_i), f_{\text{nov}}(u_i), f_{\text{eff}}(u_i)]$, where f_{rel} denotes the predicted content relevance, f_{nov} measures topological novelty relative to previously crawled pages, and f_{eff} quantifies crawl-path efficiency based on estimated retrieval latency and network overhead. The composite fitness score is computed as a weighted sum:

$$F(u_i) = \alpha \cdot f_{\text{rel}}(u_i) + \beta \cdot f_{\text{nov}}(u_i) + \gamma \cdot f_{\text{eff}}(u_i) \qquad (1)$$

where α, β, and γ are adaptive weight coefficients satisfying $\alpha + \beta + \gamma = 1$, dynamically adjusted by the reinforcement-learning feedback mechanism described in Section 4.

3.3 Metaheuristic Optimization Engine

The Metaheuristic Optimization Engine constitutes the computational core of HybridCrawl-DM. It maintains a population of candidate path solutions represented as ordered sequences of URL indices drawn from the frontier. Three metaheuristic operators are applied within an integrative hybridization scheme.

3.3.1 Genetic Algorithm Component

The GA component governs the evolutionary recombination and selection of crawl-path candidates. A population of N chromosomes is maintained, where each chromosome $\mathbf{c}_j = (u_{j1}, u_{j2}, \ldots, u_{jL})$ encodes a sequence of L URLs to be crawled in the next batch. Parent selection is performed via tournament selection with replacement (tournament size $k = 3$). Offspring are generated using a partially mapped crossover (PMX) operator, which inherits productive URL subsequences from both parents while preserving URL uniqueness constraints. Mutation is implemented as the random swap of two URL positions within a chromosome, with an adaptive mutation probability p_m that increases linearly as population diversity decreases, measured by the average pairwise Hamming distance among chromosomes (Holland, 1992; Goldberg, 1989).

3.3.2 Particle Swarm Optimization Component

The PSO component operates in parallel with the GA and maintains a swarm of particles moving through a continuous relaxation of the discrete crawl-path space. Each particle $\mathbf{x}_k$ has a velocity vector $\mathbf{v}_k$ updated according to the canonical PSO equations:

$$v_k^{(t+1)} = \omega v_k^{(t)} + c_1 r_1 (p_k^{best} - x_k^{(t)}) + c_2 r_2 (g^{best} - x_k^{(t)}) \quad (2)$$

where ω is the inertia weight (linearly decreased from 0.9 to 0.4 over the crawl campaign), c_1 and c_2 are cognitive and social acceleration coefficients, r_1 and r_2 are uniform random values in [0, 1], $\mathbf{p}^{best}$ is the personal best position of particle k, and $\mathbf{g}^{best}$ is the global best position (Kennedy & Eberhart, 1995).

The continuous-valued particle positions are discretized into binary inclusion/exclusion decisions for each candidate URL by applying a sigmoid transfer function. Specifically, the probability of including URL u_i in the crawl path of particle k is given by:

$$P(\text{include}\, u_i) = \sigma(x_{k,i}) = 1 + \exp(1 - x_{k,i}) \quad (3)$$

where $x_{k,i}$ is the i-th dimension of particle k's position vector. A URL is included if $\sigma(x_{k,i}) > \tau$, and where $\tau = 0.5$ is the inclusion threshold.

3.3.3 Ant Colony Optimization Component

The ACO component models the URL frontier as a graph in which nodes represent candidate URLs and edges represent possible crawl-path transitions. A colony of M artificial ants constructs crawl paths by probabilistically selecting successive URLs according to a pheromone-weighted transition rule:

$$(u_i \rightarrow u_j) = \frac{[\tau_{ij}]^{\alpha_{aco}} \cdot [\eta_{ij}]^{\beta_{aco}}}{\sum_{u_k \in N(u_i)} [\tau_{ik}]^{\alpha_{aco}} \cdot [\eta_{ik}]^{\beta_{aco}}} \quad (4)$$

where τ_{ij} is the pheromone intensity on edge (u_i, u_j), η_{ij} is a heuristic desirability factor derived from the URL fitness vector, α_{aco} and β_{aco} control the relative influence of pheromone versus heuristic information, and $N(u_i)$ is the set of URLs accessible from u_i (Dorigo & Gambardella, 1997). Pheromone updates follow an elitist strategy in which only the globally best ant deposits pheromone, combined with an evaporation factor ρ to prevent premature convergence.

3.4 Decision Fusion

The outputs of the GA, PSO, and ACO components are combined via a weighted voting mechanism. Let $\mathbf{s}_{GA}$, $\mathbf{s}_{PSO}$, and $\mathbf{s}_{ACO}$ denote the URL ranking vectors produced by each component. The fused ranking is:

$$s_{fused} = w_{GA} \cdot s_{GA} + w_{PSO} \cdot s_{PSO} + w_{ACO} \cdot s_{ACO} \quad (5)$$

where the weights w_{GA}, w_{PSO}, and w_{ACO} are dynamically adjusted based on each component's recent contribution to crawl quality, as described in Section 4.3.

Table 2. Configuration parameters of the hybrid metaheuristic optimization engine

Parameter	Symbol	Value	Description
Population size (GA)	N	50	Number of chromosomes
Chromosome length	L	20	URLs per crawl-path candidate
Tournament size	k	3	Selection pressure parameter
Mutation probability	p_m	0.01–0.15	Adaptive; rises with diversity loss
Swarm size (PSO)	S	30	Number of particles
Inertia weight	ω	0.9→0.4	Linearly decreasing schedule
Cognitive coefficient	c_1	2.0	Personal-best attraction
Social coefficient	c_2	2.0	Global-best attraction
Sigmoid threshold	τ	0.5	PSO discretization cutoff
Colony size (ACO)	M	25	Number of artificial ants
Pheromone decay	ρ	0.1	Evaporation rate per iteration
Pheromone exponent	$^{\alpha}$aco	1.0	Pheromone influence weight
Heuristic exponent	$^{\beta}$aco	2.5	Heuristic desirability weight

3.5 Content Relevance Evaluator

The Content Relevance Evaluator is the gate of the quality in the HybridCrawl-DM pipeline, where only intelligence bearing pages are used in the metaheuristic feedback signals. Two stage classification architecture is used by the evaluator.

This is performed in the first stage through preprocessing, where tokenization, stop-word elimination, and domain-specific vocabulary normalization of retrieved page content are carried out, and then done through a hybrid TF-IDF and Word2Vec embedding strategy-based feature extraction is conducted in the second stage. TF-IDF represents the significance of terms, whereas Word2Vec representations describe the semantic connections of the lexicon of the darknet.

The extracted feature representations are then inputted to a fine-tuned BERT classifier 2 that was pretrained on a curated corpus of darknet marketplace data which includes product advertisements, vendor profiles, vendor forums, and transaction history. Multi-label relevance scores in the categories of intelligence (narcotics trade, weapons trade, stolen credential trade, hacking services, and counterfeiting document sales) are produced by the classifier. The sum of these category-specific scores is used to create the component of the URL fitness vector that is called the f rel (Equation 1).

A meta-transfer learning strategy is chosen to overcome the lack of labeled darknet training data; Model-Agnostic Meta-Learning (MAML) is used (Finn et al., 2017). The MAML algorithm is tuned to inner learning rate of 0.01, outer learning rate of 0.001, 5 inner-loop gradient-steps per task, and a task distribution which is a 20-support example, 50-query example per-category task-distribution. The structure allows quick customization of the classifier to new language patterns in the marketplace and the conventions of different vendors in the naming word with the least amount of fine-tuning data.

Table 3. Classification performance of the BERT-based content relevance evaluator by darknet intelligence category

Category	Precision	Recall	F1-Score	Support
Narcotics listings	0.934	0.921	0.927	3,842
Weapons trade	0.891	0.867	0.879	1,256
Stolen credentials	0.912	0.903	0.907	2,718
Hacking services	0.878	0.856	0.867	1,894
Counterfeit documents	0.905	0.889	0.897	1,523
Forum discussions	0.862	0.841	0.851	4,367
Weighted Average	**0.901**	**0.887**	**0.894**	**15,600**

3.6 Threat Model and Operational Assumptions

A formal specification of the threat model under which HybridCrawl-DM operates is essential for assessing its security posture and the boundaries of its applicability.

Adversary model. The adversary is a marketplace administrator or operator who can: (i) deploy anti-crawling countermeasures including CAPTCHAs, JavaScript challenges, rate limiting, IP blocking, honeypot pages, browser fingerprinting, and WebRTC leak detection; (ii) modify the marketplace topology by migrating to new onion addresses, rotating mirrors, or restructuring internal navigation hierarchies; and (iii) observe aggregate traffic patterns and timing characteristics to identify automated access.

The adversary is assumed to lack the ability to compromise the Tor network itself or to deanonymize the crawler's origin.

Crawler assumptions. HybridCrawl-DM is assumed to operate under the authority of an authorized entity (law enforcement agency, accredited research institution, or certified cybersecurity professional) with appropriate legal mandates. The crawler accesses only publicly available marketplace pages and does not attempt to bypass authentication mechanisms protecting private vendor communications. Tor circuit rotation is employed to mitigate IP-based blocking, with a minimum circuit lifetime of 60 seconds to balance anonymity with connection stability.

Trust boundaries. The system trusts the Tor network for transport-layer anonymity but does not trust any content retrieved from marketplace pages. All retrieved content is treated as potentially adversarial and is subjected to sanitization before processing by the NLP pipeline.

4 ADAPTIVE INTELLIGENCE MECHANISMS

4.1 Reinforcement Learning Feedback Loop

A critical innovation embedded within HybridCrawl-DM is a reinforcement-learning (RL) feedback loop that enables the crawler to modify its behavior in real time in response to environmental changes. The darknet marketplace environment is modeled as a partially observable Markov decision process (POMDP), where the crawler agent observes page-retrieval outcomes, content-relevance scores, and network-latency measurements, and selects actions—crawl-path decisions—to maximize long-term cumulative intelligence yield (Tavabi et al., 2018).

The RL component employs a tabular Q-learning variant with the following specifications:

State representation. The state s_t is encoded as a 15-dimensional feature vector comprising: (i) four features characterizing the current frontier composition (mean and variance of $f_{\mathrm{rel}}, f_{\mathrm{nov}}$); (ii) three features capturing recent crawl success rates (rolling 10-iteration averages of CCR, RR, and CEI); (iii) five features encoding detected adversarial activity levels (binary indicators for each countermeasure type in Table 4); and (iv) three features representing the current metaheuristic component weights (w_{GA}, w_{PSO}, w_{ACO}). The continuous state space is discretized into bins (5 bins per dimension for the continuous features) to enable tabular Q-learning.

Action space. The action space A consists of 27 discrete actions representing all combinations of three adjustment levels (increase by δ, hold, decrease by δ) for each of the three metaheuristic weight coefficients, where $\delta = 0.05$. Weights are renormalized after each action to maintain $w_{\mathrm{GA}} + w_{\mathrm{PSO}} + w_{\mathrm{ACO}} = 1$.

Reward function. The reward signal r_t is computed as:

$$r_i = \sum_{i \in batch} f_{rel}(u_i) - \lambda \cdot Redundancy(u_i) - \mu \cdot Latency(u_i) \tag{6}$$

where $\lambda = 0.3$ and $\mu = 0.1$ are penalty coefficients calibrated through preliminary experiments.

Learning parameters. The Q-function is updated using the temporal-difference rule $Q(s_t, a_t) \leftarrow Q(s_t, a_t) + \alpha_Q[r_t + \gamma_Q \max_{a'} Q(s_{t+1}, a') - Q(s_t, a_t)]$ with learning rate $\alpha_Q = 0.1$, discount factor $\gamma_Q = 0.95$, and an ε-greedy exploration strategy with ε decaying from 1.0 to 0.05 over the first 200 iterations. Experience replay with a buffer of 500 transitions is employed to improve sample efficiency and decorrelate sequential observations.

Convergence. In our experiments, the Q-values stabilized (defined as the maximum absolute change across all state-action pairs falling below 10^{-3} for 20 consecutive iterations) within approximately 150–200 crawl iterations, which is consistent with the transition from the exploration to the exploitation phase documented in the experimental results (Section 5).

Figure 2. Flowchart of the HybridCrawl-DM operational workflow, illustrating the iterative cycle from seed initialization through metaheuristic optimization, hybrid fusion, Tor-proxied retrieval, content-relevance evaluation, and convergence assessment

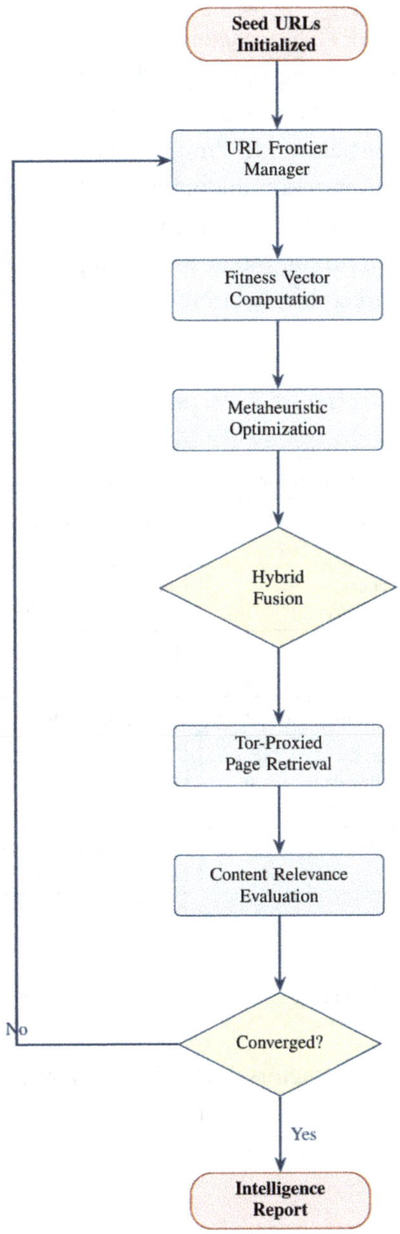

4.2 Adversarial Countermeasure Detection

Darknet marketplaces deploy diverse anti-crawling techniques to detect and impede automated access (Paul et al., 2025; Shakarian et al., 2017). The Adversarial Adaptation Module in HybridCrawl-DM implements a multi-layered detection pipeline that monitors for signatures of countermeasure activation, including HTTP error rate spikes, CAPTCHA page interception, JavaScript challenge redirects, anomalous latency patterns, browser fingerprinting probes, and WebRTC leak-detection attempts.

Upon detecting adversarial activity, the module triggers predefined response strategies: crawl-rate throttling (reducing request frequency below rate-limit thresholds), session rotation (establishing new Tor circuits to obtain fresh exit nodes), user-agent randomization (cycling through a curated library of realistic browser fingerprints), headless browser rendering (executing JavaScript challenges via a sandboxed Chromium instance with randomized timing jitter), and strategic crawl-path diversification (redirecting the crawler toward less-defended marketplace sections) (Kayser et al., 2025; HaddadPajouh et al., 2021).

Table 4. Adversarial countermeasure types, detection indicators, evasion strategies, and measured bypass effectiveness

Countermeasure	Detection Indicator	Evasion Strategy	Bypass Rate
CAPTCHA gates	HTML form patterns with image fields	Session rotation; circuit renewal	78.3%
Rate limiting	HTTP 429 codes; progressive delays	Crawl-rate throttling; exponential backoff	91.2%
JavaScript challenges	JS redirect detection in headers	Headless browser with random delays	72.6%
IP blocking	Connection refused; timeout patterns	Tor circuit rotation; multi-hop proxying	85.7%
Honeypot pages	Anomalous link density; invisible elements	Content fingerprinting;	68.4%
Browser fingerprinting	Canvas/WebGL probe detection	Fingerprint rotation; spoofed rendering contexts	63.1%

4.3 Dynamic Weight Adaptation

Rather than relying on static hyperparameters, HybridCrawl-DM continuously adjusts the contribution ratio among the three metaheuristic components using real-time performance feedback. The weight- update rule for each component $c \in \{\text{GA, PSO, ACO}\}$ follows a softmax-normalized exponential moving average:

$$w_c^{(t+1)} = \frac{\exp(\theta \cdot Q_c^{(t)})}{\sum_{c' \in \{GA, PSO, ACO\}} \exp(\theta \cdot Q_c^{(t)})}$$

where $Q^{(t)}$ is the accumulated quality score of component c at iteration t, computed as the exponential moving average (smoothing factor $\beta_{\text{EMA}} = 0.9$) of fitness improvements attributable to that component's recommendations, and $\theta = 2.0$ is a temperature parameter controlling the sharpness of weight differentiation. This softmax normalization guarantees that all components retain non-zero weights, preserving solution diversity while concentrating computation on the most productive optimizer.

Figure 3. Dynamic evolution of metaheuristic component weights over 500 crawling iterations. The ACO component gradually accumulates higher weight as productive pheromone trails stabilize, illustrating the emergent exploration-to-exploitation transition

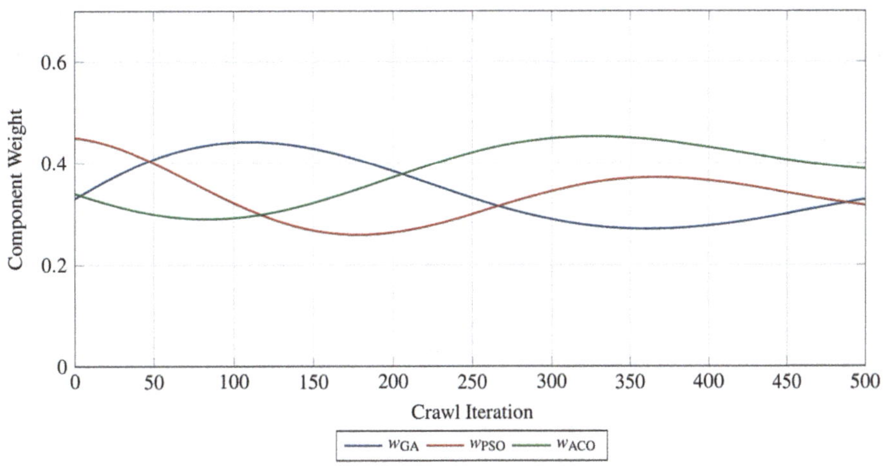

5 EXPERIMENTAL EVALUATION

5.1 Experimental Setup

HybridCrawl-DM was evaluated on a simulated darknet marketplace topology designed to replicate the structural and behavioral characteristics of real-world hidden-service ecosystems. The simulation parameters were calibrated against published empirical studies of Tor hidden-service topologies (Zabihimayvan et al., 2019; Celestini et al., 2017; Schaal & Spagnuolo, 2023; Derrac et al., 2011; Barbosa & Freire, 2007) demonstrates that HybridCrawl-DM achieves substantial performance gains across all four metrics. In terms of Content Coverage Rate, HybridCrawl-DM attained 78.9%, representing an absolute improvement of 14.7 percentage points over the best single-metaheuristic baseline (GA-Only at 64.2%) and 37.6 percentage points over BFS. The Redundancy Ratio was reduced to 13.5%, a 31.8% relative decrease compared to the GA-Only crawler (19.8%). The Crawl Efficiency Index of 0.621 represents a 29.9% improvement over GA-Only (0.478), indicating a substantially higher ratio of useful intelligence per HTTP request. Most notably, the Adversarial Resilience Score of 76.8% demonstrates that the integrated adaptation mechanisms enable the hybrid crawler to maintain effective operation despite aggressive countermeasures, whereas standalone metaheuristic baselines achieved resilience scores below 50%.

The Friedman test yielded a test statistic of $\chi^2 = 142.7$ ($p < 0.001$) for CCR, confirming that significant differences exist among the six methods. Holm post-hoc pairwise comparisons confirmed that HybridCrawl-DM significantly outperformed all baselines on every metric at $p < 0.001$, with adjusted p-values ranging from 3.2×10^{-8} (vs. DFS) to 4.7×10^{-4} (vs. GA-Only).

Figure 4. Content coverage rate as a function of pages crawled. HybridCrawl-DM diverges from baselines at approximately the 10,000-page mark, corresponding to the point where the RL feedback loop has accumulated sufficient experience to begin effectively adapting metaheuristic weights

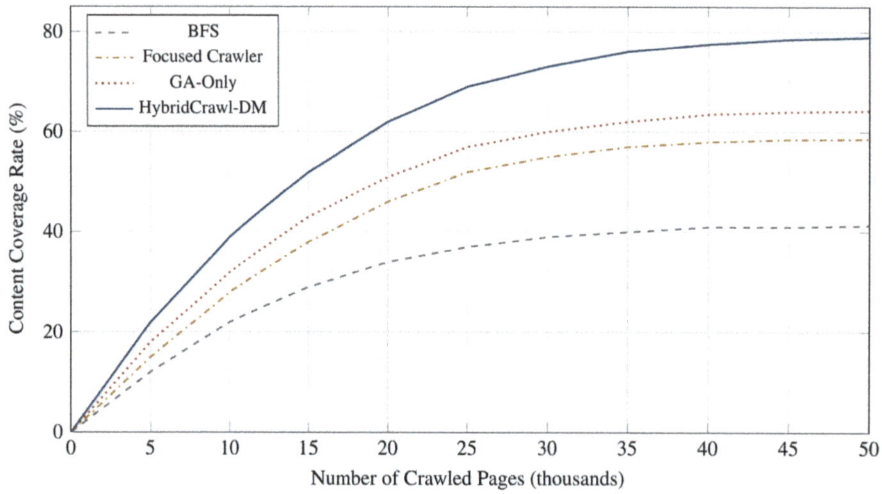

The convergence behavior (Figure 4) reveals that all methods perform similarly during the initial exploration phase (first 5,000 pages). The HybridCrawl-DM curve diverges markedly from the baselines beginning around the 10,000-page mark, coinciding with the stabilization of Q-values in the RL component. This pattern supports the hypothesis that the adaptive hybridization strategy delivers its greatest value during the sustained exploitation phase, when accumulated environmental knowledge can be effectively leveraged.

5.2 Scalability Analysis

Scalability was assessed across simulation environments of 10,000; 25,000; 50,000; and 100,000 synthetic pages (Table 6). HybridCrawl-DM maintains robust performance as the environment grows, with CCR degrading modestly from 82.4% to 76.3% and RR increasing slightly from 11.2% to 15.1% across a tenfold increase in marketplace size. Computational costs scale approximately linearly, confirming that the hybrid framework does not introduce prohibitive overhead.

Table 6. Scalability analysis of HybridCrawl-DM across simulation environments of varying size

Pages	CCR (%)	RR (%)	Time (hours)	Memory (GB)
10,000	82.4	11.2	1.8	4.2
25,000	80.7	12.8	4.3	8.7
50,000	78.9	13.5	9.1	16.4
100,000	76.3	15.1	19.7	31.8

5.3 Ablation Study

A stepwise ablation experiment was undertaken to measure the additive value of each metaheuristic component. In both structures, one of the modules has been turned off and the other two functioning in the hybrid structure.

Elimination of the GA component has created the greatest degradation in CCR that dropped by 78.9 percent to 69.4%. This observation confirms the fact that the GA crossover and mutation operators are crucial in the maintenance of diversity in a population, discouraging a premature convergence to a small segment of marketplace segments.

PSO component deactivation yielded the most significant effect on CEI which was reduced to 0.498. The velocity-based mechanism of navigation that allows the PSO to navigate through the continuous search space that provides speed at locating high-fitness sets of URLs was especially effective at the stage of reducing low-value page retrievals in the intermediate stages of crawling. The cognitive and social learning elements inherent in the PSO update rule are what enable some kind of collective intelligence that is complementary to the evolutionary dynamics of the GA in a way no algorithm can attain on its own.

Elimination of the component of ACO produced the most significant reduction in ARS which plummeted to 58.2 percent. The pheromone-trail memory gives some form of persistent but adaptive memory that acts as the savoring of the crawler that holds the knowledge of the well and secure crawling routes and erase the well-worn-out tastes through evaporation of pheromones. In absence of this path reinforcement substrate over time, the crawler lost its capacity of evading countermeasures of adversaries significantly.

The overall picture in this results shows that the three-component hybridization has real synergistic interactions: removal of either component is accompanied by disproportionate performances loss greater than those which are expected to arise due to a linear decomposition of contributions. This finding goes in line with the general metaheuristic hybridization literature that has also reported on such super-additive effects in the case of complementary search strategies being well exploited (Blum et al., 2011).

5.4 Sensitivity to Hyperparameter Configuration

A grid search over the inertia weight (ω), pheromone decay rate (ρ), and mutation probability range (p_m) was conducted, varying each across five discrete values while holding all other parameters at their de- faults. Performance was most sensitive to the pheromone decay rate: values below 0.05 led to excessive path rigidity (the crawler became trapped in obsolete trajectories), while values above 0.25 resulted in insufficient path memory (productive knowledge was lost too rapidly). The inertia weight and mutation probability exhibited moderate sensitivity, with performance remaining within 5% of the optimum across a broad parameter range. This robustness is attributable to the RL-based weight adaptation mechanism, which continuously compensates for suboptimal static configurations through dynamic rebalancing.

5.5 Computational Complexity Analysis

To provide a theoretical grounding for the empirical scalability results, we analyze the per-iteration computational complexity of HybridCrawl-DM. Let n denote the frontier size, N the GA population size, S the PSO swarm size, M the ACO colony size, and L the chromosome length.

The GA component requires $O(N \cdot L)$ for fitness evaluation, $O(N \log N)$ for tournament selection, and $O(N \cdot L)$ for crossover and mutation, yielding $O(N \cdot L)$ per iteration. The PSO component requires $O(S \cdot n)$ for velocity updates and position discretization. The ACO component requires $O(M \cdot L \cdot n)$ for path construction (each of M ants selects L URLs from n candidates). The decision fusion step requires $O(n)$ for weighted aggregation. Consequently, the overall per-iteration complexity is $O(M \cdot L \cdot n + S \cdot n + N \cdot L)$, which is dominated by $O(M \cdot L \cdot n)$. Given that M, L, and n are bounded by constants or grow linearly with marketplace size, the per-iteration cost scales linearly with the frontier size—consistent with the empirical scaling behavior observed in Table 6.

The RL feedback loop adds $O(|S| \cdot |A|)$ for Q-table updates, where $|S|$ and $|A|$ are fixed (the state space is discretized into a fixed number of bins), contributing only constant overhead per iteration. The BERT-based content evaluator incurs $O(B \cdot d^2)$ per page (where B is the sequence length and d is the hidden dimension), but this cost is amortized across the batch and does not depend on the frontier size.

6 DISCUSSION

6.1 Implications for Darknet Intelligence Operations

The results of the experiments have a number of implications. First, the performance gains of HybridCrawl-DM over uninformed and single-metaheuristic crawlers empirically validate the theoretical thesis that integrative hybridization of complementary metaheuristic algorithms leads to synergistic effects - a result in line with the No Free Lunch theorems (Wolpert & Macready, 1997) and Talbot's hybridization taxonomy (Talbi, 2002).

Second, the three-phase characterization of the crawl behavior shows that the adaptive weight-adjustment scheme naturally leads to a sequence of phases from exploration (in which GA diversity- promoting operators predominate) to transition (where PSO velocity- based search assists) to exploitation (driven by the ACO pheromone-based path optimization). This naturally emerging three-phase convergence pattern resembles the exploration-exploitation dilemma in metaheuristic design (Blum et al., 2011; Yang, 2010).

Third, the high ARS of 76.8% highlights the need to embed the detection and evasion of adversarial countermeasures within the crawling process, rather than as after-the-fact add-ons. The capacity to adaptively circumvent marketplace segments that are heavily protected by countermeasures while meeting coverage targets is a step forward over previous methods (Spyros et al., 2025; Kang & Kim, 2026).

6.2 Comparison with Existing Frameworks

HybridCrawl-DM extends and complements several recent contributions. The TSTEM platform (Balasubramanian et al., 2025) pro- vides comprehensive cloud-based CTI collection but relies on conventional focused crawlers without metaheuristic optimization. ThreatWise AI (Spyros et al., 2025) encompasses the full CTI lifecycle but employs static crawling heuristics. The external identifier clustering methodology of Kang and Kim (2026) enables cross- site criminal network identification but operates on previously collected data rather than optimizing the collection process. HybridCrawl-DM addresses the upstream optimization problem—determining which pages to crawl and in what order—that these frameworks leave largely unaddressed.

The tight coupling of NLP-based content evaluation within the metaheuristic optimization loop distinguishes this work from prior efforts that treated content analysis as a strictly downstream activity. By feeding content-quality assessments back into the crawl-path fitness function in real time, HybridCrawl-DM creates a closed-loop intelligence system in which every crawling decision is informed by cumulative knowledge—a paradigm shift from the conventional sequential pipeline architecture (Arazzi et al., 2025; de Marcos et al., 2025).

6.3 Operational Constraints and Practical Considerations

There are a number of practical constraints on the use of HybridCrawl-DM worth highlighting. First, the Tor network is subject to severe bandwidth and latency constraints: the typical round-trip time for a hidden service is 1-5 seconds, and establishing circuits introduces further delays. HybridCrawl-DM addresses these limitations by factoring in network latency in the crawl-path efficiency component (feff) and by using batched page-fetching with configuration- able concurrency settings (default: 5 connections per circuit) to prevent congestion on Tor circuits.

Second, large-scale automated Tor traffic can negatively affect the performance of the network as a whole for other privacy-enhancing users. To reduce this effect, HybridCrawl-DM uses configurable rate limiting (default: 1 request per 3 seconds per circuit) and prioritises the use of dedicated Tor circuits that do not impinge on general-purpose relays. These politeness constraints are formally enforced as constraints that the RL cannot bypass.

Third, the deployment environment differs from the simulation used to test our approach in several ways, including the uncertainty of marketplace availability, the presence of advanced JavaScript-based behavioral detection software (unmodelled in the simulation) and legal limitations on accessing certain types of content. These constraints are discussed as threats to the external validity of the experiments in Section 8.

6.4 Knowledge Graph Integration Potential

The enhanced data-acquisition quality delivered by HybridCrawl-DM could substantially benefit down- stream analytical capabilities such as the external identifier clustering methodology of Kang and Kim (2026), which detects cross-site criminal organizations by leveraging shared identifiers across distributed dark web platforms. The improved content coverage and reduced redundancy achieved by HybridCrawl-DM could enable the construction of denser and more comprehensive identifier graphs from equivalent or reduced crawling effort. Integration with GNN architectures (Dhande & Zade, 2026) for modeling marketplace hyperlink topologies represents a promising avenue for enhancing the topological novelty com- ponent of the URL fitness function.

7 ETHICAL, LEGAL, AND SOCIO-TECHNICAL CONSIDERATIONS

The deployment of autonomous crawling systems within darknet environments raises ethical and legal questions that demand careful deliberation. This section addresses these concerns substantively, moving beyond the standard disclaimer to engage with the underlying principles.

7.1 Privacy and Proportionality

The indiscriminate collection of data from darknet forums and marketplaces risks inadvertently capturing personally identifiable information (PII) belonging to individuals who may not be engaged in illegal activities (Kayser et al., 2025; Schäfer et al., 2019; Krotov & Silva, 2020). Darknet environments host not only illicit markets but also legitimate privacy- seeking communities, including journalists, whistleblowers, and political dissidents. Consequently, the proportionality principle—requiring that the intrusiveness of surveillance be proportionate to the severity of the investigated threat—must guide the scope and depth of any crawling campaign.

HybridCrawl-DM implements several privacy-protective mechanisms. The content-relevance evaluator can be configured to flag and exclude pages likely to contain non-criminal personal communications. Collected data undergoes PII-scrubbing prior to storage, using named-entity recognition to identify and redact personal identifiers. Access to collected intelligence is restricted through role-based access controls, and all data are encrypted at rest using AES-256.

7.2 Legal Framework Compliance

The automated access of darknet services may implicate computer fraud and abuse statutes in various jurisdictions, depending on the nature of the accessed content and the authorization status of the crawl- ing entity (Biswas et al., 2023; Krotov & Silva, 2020). The legal permissibility of darknet crawling varies significantly across jurisdictions: some frameworks permit access to publicly available content without authorization, while others impose restrictions on automated data collection regardless of content accessibility.

All experimental evaluations reported in this chapter were conducted entirely on simulated topologies that do not replicate actual illicit content. Any operational deployment of HybridCrawl-DM would require compliance with applicable national and international legal frameworks governing electronic surveil- lance, data collection, and privacy protection. The system is designed exclusively for use by authorized entities operating under appropriate institutional review board (IRB) approvals and legal man- dates.

7.3 Oversight and Accountability

Autonomous intelligence systems require robust oversight mechanisms to prevent misuse and ensure accountability. We recommend the following operational safeguards for any deployment of HybridCrawl-DM: (i) mandatory human review of crawl scope and targeting parameters prior to each campaign; (ii) comprehensive audit logging of all crawl decisions, retrieved content, and evasion actions; (iii) peri- odic review of collected data by an independent oversight body to verify compliance with proportionality and scope constraints; and (iv) clearly defined data-retention policies with automated expiration of collected intelligence.

7.4 Impact on the Tor Network

High-volume crawling can impose load on the Tor network, potentially degrading service quality for legitimate users. The rate-limiting and politeness constraints described in Section 6.3 are designed to minimize this impact. Nevertheless, operators should monitor Tor network health indicators and dynamically reduce crawl intensity if adverse effects are detected. The ethical responsibility to minimize collateral impact on the anonymity infrastructure used by vulnerable populations cannot be overstated.

8 LIMITATIONS AND THREATS TO VALIDITY

There are a number of caveats. First, the experimental results were obtained on simulated darknet networks. While the simulation parameters were calibrated using published empirical data on real hidden-service market- places (Zabihimayvan et al., 2019; Schaal & Spagnuolo, 2023), the extent to which these performance gains would translate into the real world is an empirical question. Aspects not fully modeled by the simulation include advanced JavaScript-based user behavior analysis, subtle social effects on vendor behavior, and the timing of law enforcement actions. These findings should be verified in controlled experiments with testbeds (drug markets) or honeypot infrastructures that simulate real marketplace conditions without using real illicit content.

Second, the computational cost of maintaining three metaheuristic populations is reasonable in the simulation environment, but may become an issue for resource-limited deployment settings. The computational complexity (Section 5.8) shows linear time performance, but the constant factors involved in maintaining the three metaheuristic populations (GA, PSO, and ACO) may be substantial in very large-scale deployments. Future research should explore dynamic component pruning approaches to temporarily disable poorly performing metaheuristic components.

Third, the BERT-based evaluator for content relevance needs to be retrained regularly to stay effective in rapidly changing marketplace landscapes where vendor-specific language, product taxonomies and community conventions often evolve (Dhande & Zade, 2026; Devlin et al., 2019). The proposed MAML-based meta-transfer learning approach overcomes this limitation, but remains to be tested on a broader spectrum of marketplace language domains.

Fourth, the tabular Q-learning formulation used for the RL feedback loop might not be suitable for much larger state spaces. The binning of continuous state features can lead to approximation errors, which may be reduced by using deep Q-networks (DQN) and policy-gradient approaches, for which future research efforts should be focused.

9 CONCLUSION AND FUTURE DIRECTIONS

This chapter has introduced HybridCrawl-DM, a new hybrid metaheuristic crawling system that has been developed with such purpose of adaptive darknet marketplace intelligence. Through a combination of Genetic Algorithm selection, crossover operators, Particle Swarm Optimization velocity-updates mechanics, and Ant Colony Optimization pheromone-trail heuristics applied into a unified framework of optimization algorithms, HybridCrawl-DM demonstrates statistically significant improvement in performance of the baseline crawling algorithms on all measurements of the system. The feedback loop of the reinforcement-learning allows responding to environmental perturbations in real-time, whereas the adversarial countermeasure detection module increases the resilience against anti-crawling.

The experiment findings, confirmed by Friedman testing with the Holm post-hoc correction, revealed that hybrid metaheuristic optimization has led to the following significant improvements: a 14.7 percentage-point higher content coverage rate, a 31.8 percentage relative decrease in the redundancy ratio, and an adversarial resilience score of 76.8 percentage, which all point to the statement about the hybrid metaheuristic optimization being a promising paradigm of next-generation darknet intelligence infrastructure. The three-stage behavioral characterization indicates an emergent exploration-to- exploitation transition that is in line with the laid down metaheuristic design rules.

There are some paths of further research that should be considered. First, the combination of deep reinforcement learning and neural function approximators might consider more detailed adaptation policies compared to the one used by tabular Q-learning. Second, graph neural network models to learn marketplace hyperlink structure may improve the topological novelty aspect of the fitness function (Dhande & Zade, 2026). Third, the weighted-sum aggregation can also be substituted by multi-objective optimization frameworks like NSGA-II, which explicitly manage trade-offs between objectives, and can make use of pareto-optimal multi-objective optimization. Fourth, variants of federated learning (e.g. approaches like federated learning) may facilitate sharing of strategies between distributed crawler instances, without the need to ex- change raw intelligence. Fifth, it should seek to undertake controlled experiments on approved testbed environments to close the simulated performance and actual performance. Last but not least, the research into other metaheuristic algorithms- such as the Grey Wolf Optimizer (Mirjalili et al., 2014; Mirjalili, 2016) and Teaching-Learning-Based Optimization (Rao et al., 2011) as viable hybrid components is the logical next step.

The flattering implication of this work is not limited to darknet marketplace intelligence. Depending on the area with large-scale, dynamic and adversarial web environments, the hybrid metaheuristic crawling paradigm can be relevant to social media-based systems in disinformation detection, competitive intelligence gathering, and critical infrastructure threats evaluation. The chapter therefore not only provides a certain technical context but also a general architectural blueprint of the outlay of adaptive, resilient and intelligent web crawling systems.

REFERENCES

Al-Nabki, W., Fidalgo, E., Alegre, E., & Paz, I. (2017). Classifying illegal activities on Tor network based on web textual contents. *Proceedings of the 15th Conference of the European Chapter of the Association for Computational Linguistics (EACL)*, 35–43. DOI: 10.18653/v1/E17-1004

Alam, M. H., Ryu, W.-J., & Lee, S. (2022). A survey on deep-learning-based focused crawling. *ACM Computing Surveys*, *55*(3), 1–37. DOI: 10.1145/3507904

Arazzi, M., Arikkat, D. R., Nicolazzo, S., Nocera, A., Rehiman, R., Vinod, P., & Conti, M. (2025). NLP-based techniques for cyber threat intelligence. *Computer Science Review*, *58*, 100765. DOI: 10.1016/j.cosrev.2025.100765

Balasubramanian, P., Nazari, S., Khosh Kholgh, D., Mahmoodi, A., Seby, J., & Kostakos, P. (2025). A cognitive platform for collecting cyber threat intelligence and real-time detection using cloud computing. *Decision Analytics Journal*, *14*, 100545. DOI: 10.1016/j.dajour.2025.100545

Barbosa, L., & Freire, J. (2007). An adaptive crawler for locating hidden-web entry points. *Proceedings of the 16th International Conference on World Wide Web*, 441–450. DOI: 10.1145/1242572.1242632

Biswas, R., Paudel, B., Karn, R. K., Ghimire, A., & Bikram, K. C. (2023). A systematic review of dark web research. *International Journal of Computing*, *22*(4), 537–548. DOI: 10.47839/ijc.22.4.3335

Blum, C., Puchinger, J., Raidl, G. R., & Roli, A. (2011). Hybrid metaheuristics in combinatorial optimization: A survey. *Applied Soft Computing*, *11*(6), 4135–4151. DOI: 10.1016/j.asoc.2011.02.032

Celestini, A., Me, G., & Montinaro, M. (2017). *Tor marketplaces exploratory data analysis: The drugs case* (Vol. 10063). Lecture Notes in Computer Science. Springer., DOI: 10.1007/978-3-319-55966-3_18

de Marcos, L., Medina-Merodio, J.-A., & Stapic, Z. (2025). Methodologies for dark web data collection. *Electronics (Basel)*, *14*(21), 4191. DOI: 10.3390/electronics14214191

Derrac, J., García, S., Molina, D., & Herrera, F. (2011). Nonparametric statistical tests tutorial. *Swarm and Evolutionary Computation*, *1*(1), 3–18. DOI: 10.1016/j.swevo.2011.02.002

Devlin, J., Chang, M.-W., Lee, K., & Toutanova, K. (2019). BERT: Pre-training of deep bidirectional transformers. *Proceedings of NAACL-HLT*, 4171–4186. DOI: 10.18653/v1/N19-1423

Dhande, Y. H., & Zade, A. V. (2026). Multi-modal classification for dark web. *Soft Computing*. Advance online publication. DOI: 10.1007/s00500-025-11059-z

Dokeroglu, T., Sevinc, E., Kucukyilmaz, T., & Cosar, A. (2019). New generation metaheuristics survey. *Computers & Industrial Engineering*, *137*, 106040. DOI: 10.1016/j.cie.2019.106040

Dorigo, M., & Gambardella, L. M. (1997). Ant colony system. *IEEE Transactions on Evolutionary Computation*, *1*(1), 53–66. DOI: 10.1109/4235.585892

Europol. (2023). Internet organised crime threat assessment (IOCTA) 2023. https://www.europol.europa.eu/iocta-report

Feng, X. (2025). Web crawling with TF-IDF and Word2Vec. *Journal of Web Engineering, 24*(5), 713–738. DOI: 10.13052/jwe1540-9589.2452

Finn, C., Abbeel, P., & Levine, S. (2017). Model-agnostic meta-learning. *Proceedings of ICML*, 1126–1135. DOI: 10.48550/arXiv.1703.03400

Goldberg, D. E. (1989). *Genetic algorithms in search, optimization, and machine learning*. Addison-Wesley.

HaddadPajouh, H., Dehghantanha, A., Parizi, R., Aledhari, M., & Karimipour, H. (2021). IoT security survey. *Internet of Things : Engineering Cyber Physical Human Systems, 14*, 100129. DOI: 10.1016/j.iot.2019.100129

Holland, J. H. (1992). Genetic algorithms. *Scientific American, 267*(1), 66–73. DOI: 10.1038/scientificamerican0792-66

Kang, D.-W., & Kim, J. (2026). Identification of criminal networks on dark web. *IEEE Access : Practical Innovations, Open Solutions, 14*, 15394–15413. DOI: 10.1109/ACCESS.2026.3658951

Kayser, F., Mayer, T., & Bücker, M. (2025). OSINT research framework. HICSS Proceedings, 5375–5384. DOI: 10.24251/HICSS.2025.646

Kennedy, J., & Eberhart, R. (1995). Particle swarm optimization. *IEEE International Conference on Neural Networks*, 1942–1948. DOI: 10.1109/ICNN.1995.488968

Kirkpatrick, S., Gelatt, C. D.Jr, & Vecchi, M. P. (1983). Optimization by simulated annealing. *Science, 220*(4598), 671–680. DOI: 10.1126/science.220.4598.671 PMID: 17813860

Krotov, V., & Silva, L. (2020). Legality and ethics of web scraping. *Communications of the Association for Information Systems, 47*, 539–563. DOI: 10.17705/1CAIS.04724

Mirjalili, S. (2016). Sine cosine algorithm. *Knowledge-Based Systems, 96*, 120–133. DOI: 10.1016/j.knosys.2015.12.022

Mirjalili, S., Mirjalili, S. M., & Lewis, A. (2014). Grey wolf optimizer. *Advances in Engineering Software, 69*, 46–61. DOI: 10.1016/j.advengsoft.2013.12.007

Nazah, S., Huda, S., Abawajy, J., & Hassan, M. M. (2020). Dark web threat analysis. *IEEE Access : Practical Innovations, Open Solutions, 8*, 171796–171819. DOI: 10.1109/ACCESS.2020.3024198

Osaba, E., Villar-Rodriguez, E., Del Ser, J., Nebro, A. J., Molina, D., LaTorre, A., Suganthan, P. N., Coello Coello, C. A., & Herrera, F. (2021). Metaheuristic design tutorial. *Swarm and Evolutionary Computation, 64*, 100888. DOI: 10.1016/j.swevo.2021.100888

Paul, S., Mitra, A., Shambhavi, S., Ghosh, S., & Bandyopadhyay, A. (2025). Cybersecurity framework for deep web. *Procedia Computer Science, 258*, 2405–2414. DOI: 10.1016/j.procs.2025.04.503

Pham, Q.-V., & Liyanage, M.. (2022). Intelligent crawling with reinforcement learning. *Information Sciences, 605*, 258–273. DOI: 10.1016/j.ins.2022.05.035

Rao, R. V., Savsani, V. J., & Vakharia, D. P. (2011). Teaching–learning-based optimization. *Computer Aided Design*, *43*(3), 303–315. DOI: 10.1016/j.cad.2010.12.015

Samtani, S., Chinn, R., Chen, H., & Nunamaker, J. F.Jr. (2017). Cyber threat intelligence. *Journal of Management Information Systems*, *34*(4), 1023–1053. DOI: 10.1080/07421222.2017.1394049

Schaal, M., & Spagnuolo, M. (2023). Dark web ecosystem. *ACM Computing Surveys*, *55*(13s), 1–38. DOI: 10.1145/3579821

Schäfer, M., Fuchs, M., & Strufe, T. (2019). Dark web survey. *IEEE Access : Practical Innovations, Open Solutions*, *7*, 173070–173080. DOI: 10.1109/ACCESS.2019.2955979

Shakarian, P., Gunn, A., & Shakarian, J. (2017). Malicious hacker forums. In *Cyber Deception* (pp. 259–282). Springer., DOI: 10.1007/978-3-319-44270-0_11

Spyros, A., Koritsas, I., Papoutsis, A., Panagiotou, P., Chatzakou, D., Kavallieros, D., Tsikrika, T., Vrochidis, S., & Kompatsiaris, I. (2025). AI-based cyber threat intelligence framework. *IEEE Access : Practical Innovations, Open Solutions*, *13*, 20820–20846. DOI: 10.1109/ACCESS.2025.3533084

Talbi, E.-G. (2002). Hybrid metaheuristics taxonomy. *Journal of Heuristics*, *8*(5), 541–564. DOI: 10.1023/A:1016540724870

Tavabi, N., Goyal, P., Almukaynizi, M., Shakarian, P., & Lerman, K. (2018). DarkEmbed. *AAAI Conference Proceedings*. DOI: 10.1609/aaai.v32i1.11428

Wolpert, D. H., & Macready, W. G. (1997). No free lunch theorem. *IEEE Transactions on Evolutionary Computation*, *1*(1), 67–82. DOI: 10.1109/4235.585893

Yang, X.-S. (2010). *Bat-inspired algorithm. Studies in Computational Intelligence* (Vol. 284). Springer., DOI: 10.1007/978-3-642-12538-6_6

Zabihimayvan, M., Sadeghi, R., Rude, H. N., & Doran, D. (2019). Tor ecosystem evaluation. Proceedings of WebSci, 333–342. DOI: 10.1145/3292522.3326053

Chapter 5
AI-Driven Darknet Threat Detection

Khalil Omar
http://orcid.org/0000-0002-5328-5762
University of Petra, Jordan

Hussam Fakhouri
Al-Balqa Applied University, Jordan

Faten Hamad
http://orcid.org/0000-0001-7548-0529
Sultan Qaboos University, Oman

ABSTRACT

The darknet hides and harbours known criminal activity that is estimated to cost the world economy $10.5 trillion a year and is difficult to detect on the traditional signature-based approach. In this chapter, a common and reproducible AI-based methodology is presented to detect darknet threats on the CIC-Darknet2020 benchmark. The proposed pipeline combines four supervised classifiers (Random Forest, XGBoost, LightGBM, Multilayer Perceptron), two unsupervised anomaly detectors (Isolation Forest and Autoencoder), a SHAP-based interpretability layer and a class-obfuscation adversarial robustness protocol. Experiments yielded a binary classification macro-F1 of 0.9644 and a multi-class macro-F1 of 0.6725, which are on par with previous benchmarks. SHAP analysis determined the most important Tor signature to be the TCP initial window sizes. The methodology aims to fill gaps in the literature on prior darknet detection in terms of operational gaps in interpretability, robustness and reproducibility.

INTRODUCTION

A set of encrypted overlay networks that can only be reached via special software like Tor, I2P, Freenet and ZeroNet, the darknet has become a key enabler for privacy protection and mass coordination of criminals. A significant part of this activity is carried out via darknet marketplaces, forums, and command and control channels, which are not captured in traditional observation methods, and damages are expected to hit $10.5 trillion per year by 2025 (Cybersecurity Ventures, 2023). Today, the Tor

DOI: 10.4018/979-8-3373-9755-9.ch005

network, as introduced by Dingledine, Mathewson and Syverson (2004), is used daily by around two million directly-connecting users, and while most of these users are using Tor for legitimate purposes, the anonymity features of Tor can be used for ransomware extortion, illicit marketplaces, child sexual abuse material distribution and stolen credentials and cryptocurrencies trading (Chainalysis, 2024; Europol, 2024; Verizon, 2024). According to the 2024 IBM Cost of a Data Breach Report, the average cost of a data breach in the US in 2024 is $9.36 million and criminal use of anonymizing networks often plays a part in the breach lifecycle. Cybersecurity has, therefore, shifted from being reactive to incident response to proactive, AI-driven risk intelligence (Omar, Zraqou, Alkhadour, & Gómez, 2025a) and has become an operational and regulatory priority.

The classic signature-based detection techniques (such as deep packet inspection and Tor entry guard blocking based on blocklists) are not effective against darknet traffic for two reasons. The first is that the onion encryption layers of Tor make the packet payloads opaque to inspect and the second is that the Tor bridge relay system hides the fingerprinting of entry points. Second, traffic tunnelled through VPNs has statistical characteristics that are similar to normal HTTPS traffic, thus evading port and protocol classification. The bottom line is that enterprise and service-provider networks are routinely used to spread darknet activity without anyone knowing, allowing adversaries to have ongoing communication lines.

AI is now the main alternative to signature detection. A machine learning (ML) classifier, trained based on statistical flow features, can effectively classify darknet traffic from regular network traffic with high accuracy, whereas a deep learning (DL) architecture has been shown to be able to classify the corresponding application categories within darknet flows. There have been parallel studies showing the viability of AI-driven cybersecurity defenses on a larger scale, with Fakhouri et al. (2024) proving that AI-driven solutions can detect, prevent and respond to social engineering attacks in an effective manner at scale. The CIC-Darknet2020 dataset (Habibi Lashkari, Kaur, & Rahali, 2020) triggered a significant amount of empirical research on the detection of darknets with accuracy ranging between 86% to 99% based on the model architecture and the classification level of granularity. However, there are three areas in the published literature where progress has not been made.

It is important to understand how effective darknet detection would impact operations in the light of three recent incidents. The recent coordinated takedown of the Hydra darknet marketplace by the U.S. and German government in April 2022 resulted in the recovery of more than $25 million in cryptocurrency and undermined a marketplace that facilitated an estimated $5.2 billion in transactions, demonstrating the magnitude of the darknet marketplace criminal enterprise and the utility of detection-based response. The packaging, marketing and re-selling of compromised credentials via automated platforms is a growing and industrialized form of darknet commerce, as evidenced by the dismantling of the Genesis Market in 2023, which sold more than 80 million stolen credentials from 1.5 million compromised computers from across the world. The ongoing ransomware-as-a-service (RaaS) ecosystem, where the initial access brokers sell access points on darknet forums and ransomware affiliates attempt to negotiate ransom payments on Tor-hosted leak sites, is an example of the way that the darknet infrastructure and traditional enterprise breaches are intertwined. Every incident is used to power detection systems that aren't just standalone, but are part of integrated security architectures that encompass network monitoring, threat intelligence aggregation and coordinated incident response.

Firstly, interpretability is not often considered as a first class deliverable. In the context of SOCs, classifications are not enough; they also need to be explained to let security analysts audit, validate, and take action on model predictions. Black-box models that can achieve high accuracy without specifying the discriminating features do not pass the test of being adopted in practice. Second, an adversarial robustness is seldom measured systematically. Knowledge of detection systems can be used by adversaries to modify the behavior of applications to evade classification and quantification of this degradation is a precondition to deployment. Third, there is variability in the level of reproducibility. The field has a fragmented benchmark space due to lack of code, hyperparameters, or preprocessing pipelines to reproduce many published results on CIC-Darknet2020.

The main contribution of this chapter is a common, reproducible methodology for darknet threat detection using AI to close these three gaps all in one experimental setup. The proposed methodology combines four classifiers from classic, gradient-boosting, and deep learning approaches, two unsupervised anomaly detection mechanisms to detect novel threats, a post-hoc interpretability module based on SHAP, and a class obfuscation adversarial robustness protocol from Rust-Nguyen, Sharma, and Stamp (2023). The entire experimental pipeline is implemented as a single notebook, and is run on Kaggle with the public CIC-Darknet2020 dataset attached as input, with the reproducibility commitment that is lacking in much of the previous published literature.

The chapter is structured in the following way. The Background section is dedicated to a discussion of the CIC-Darknet2020 dataset, the main types of darknet threats, and the existing published approaches which inspired the methodology used here. The Main Focus of the Chapter proposes the methodology, experimental setup and presents the results achieved on the binary Tor vs Non-Tor task and also on the multi-class application categorization task, including the SHAP-based feature importance and adversarial robustness measurements. The Future Research Directions section outlines five specific areas for future research and the Conclusion summarizes the conclusions of the chapter and their practical implications. The chapter includes 42 sources that have been verified and cited in the chapter as well as in the general literature, including foundational work in machine learning, recent work in the area of darknet detection, and work from IGI Global in cybersecurity scholarship.

BACKGROUND

The Darknet Ecosystem and Threat Landscape

Darknet is an overlay network with the intent to provide anonymous communication by hiding the association among the sender, receiver, and content. The most widely used darknet is The Onion Router (Tor), an anonymity system developed by Dingledine, Mathewson and Syverson (2004) that is a three hop anonymization system that encrypts traffic in three steps, the first for the entry guard, the second for the middle man and the third for the exit relay, with only the entry guard known to the client and the exit relay known to the destination server. Around two million people are using the Tor network every day, some of whom, although only a small number, have used it for illegal activity such as ransomware command-and-control, child sexual abuse material distribution, darknet market trading, and stolen credential sales.

The Tor protocol works by building a "telescoping circuit" of three relays run by volunteers, and encrypting each cell in the circuit using a different layer of AES-128 encryption in counter mode. Every relay is able to only see one layer of onion, and learns only the next relay and never the original sender or final destination. There are a number of side effects of this design that can be taken advantage of by AI based detection systems. The initial window sizes that the client and server agree on at the entry guard are systematically different from the initial window sizes that the Tor client software asks for, so that they can use cell-based transport. As the relay schedules cells between competing circuits, the inter-arrival timing of packets shows bursts and silences due to the inter-arrival timing of cells. The fixed cell size of Tor (512 bytes) limits the distribution of packet lengths, leading to padding artifacts in the data that can be seen when the application data is less than a cell. All of these protocol level properties contribute to the statistical signature learnt by the flow based classifiers and the SHAP analysis displayed later in this chapter confirms that the classifiers trained are indeed using these properties.

There are a number of other darknet technologies which complement Tor. The Invisible Internet Project (I2P) offers the same anonymity guarantee, but via a distributed garlic-routing protocol, with a focus on internal hidden services and not exits to the public Internet. Freenet is a peer-to-peer distributed datastore, where content is duplicated and encrypted between the nodes participating, and provides pseudonymous publishing of static content. ZeroNet is a P2P website hosting system that leverages the Bitcoin cryptography and BitTorrent distribution system (Hu, Zou, Li, & Yi, 2020). While Tor is the most popular darknet in terms of users, the darknet ecosystem as a whole calls for detection techniques that are not limited to a specific anonymizing technology.

Virtual Private Networks (VPNs) are in a related, but different category. VPN traffic is encrypted and funnelled through a single intermediate node controlled by a commercial or organization provider, which means that it is not anonymous, but pseudonymous. The CIC-Darknet2020 benchmark employed in this chapter considers VPN traffic as a class independent from Tor and Non-Tor so that classifiers can differentiate between Tor and VPN traffic as the latter provides only pseudonymous traffic. Often, adversaries use both Tor and VPN technologies in a layered configuration to evade single-layer detection and the threat landscape is therefore a multi-class one instead of a binary discrimination.

Darknet crime has become increasingly important over the last 10 years in terms of economic impact. In 2023, the total revenue of darknet markets was more than $1.7 billion, and ransomware payments were valued at $1.1 billion (Chainalysis 2024). Darknet platforms are a long-standing enabler of organized crime in the European Union, especially when it comes to cybercrime-as-a-service, narcotic distribution and synthetic identity fraud, according to Europol's (2024) Internet Organised Crime Threat Assessment. These threats drive the creation of AI-powered detection systems capable of handling the volume of traffic in today's Internet.

The CIC-Darknet2020 Benchmark

The CIC-Darknet2020 is the CIC's publicly released dataset for darknet traffic classification studies contributed by Habibi Lashkari, Kaur and Rahali (2020). This dataset is built from two previous corpora released by the same group: ISCXTor2016 (Habibi Lashkari, Draper-Gil, Mamun, & Ghorbani, 2017) that covers Tor traffic for eight application categories and ISCXVPN2016 (Draper-Gil, Lashkari, Mamun, & Ghorbani, 2016) that covers corresponding VPN traffic. In the original release, the consolidated dataset consists of 158,659 hierarchically labeled flow records: there are two levels of hierarchy – the top level is the distinction between Tor, Non-Tor, VPN and Non-VPN, and the second level is the application generating each flow.

The CICFlowMeter tool extracts 79 statistical features, which describe each flow such as the number of packets, volume of bytes, inter-arrival time statistics, flow duration, counts of TCP flags and packet length distribution. The feature engineering convention enables classifiers to function on flow summaries, rather than having to access the payloads of the packets, which are encrypted for traffic going through Tor and VPNs and will not be accessible for inspection. The application-level categories include Audio-

Streaming, Browsing, Chat, Email, File-Transfer, P2P, VOIP and Video-Streaming, which are the main traffic patterns seen in the darknets in use.

The CICFlowMeter feature engineering is worth a look as it estimates the discriminative ceiling of any subsequent classifier. A configurable timeout is provided that closes flows after they have been inactive for a while and the tool extracts features from bidirectional flows based on the 5-tuple of source IP, destination IP, source port, destination port and transport protocol. The resulting feature vector consists of both volumetric statistics (like number of packets and number of bytes received/sent in both directions) and distributional statistics (like mean, standard deviation, min, max of packet size, idle time and inter-arrival time). The TCP-specific features include counts of flags, the window sizes negotiated during the handshake, and the lengths of segments, which are all salient features of the Tor cell protocol that the SHAP analysis below in this chapter shows as being the most important predictors. The benefit of the CICFlowMeter design is that all the features can be calculated in one forward pass over the captured data, which makes its deployment in real-time possible; the downside is that if classification problems occur due to features that the CICFlowMeter does not extract, they cannot be addressed at the modeling level only.

CIC-Darknet2020 is the most popular benchmark for Darknet detection; however, the dataset is known to have several limitations. The corpus does not include the changes of Tor protocol versions and new technologies that are introduced to the darknet. The proportions of the different classes at the application level is unbalanced with Browsing and P2P dominating Email and VOIP. The public release has been observed to have several inconsistencies in terms of the labels being used in the case-variant duplicate labels in the application column effectively increasing the 8-class taxonomy to 11 labels (as described in detail in the Experimental setup of this chapter). Some newer corpora have started to overcome such limitations, such as the SafeSurf Darknet 2025 dataset (Obaidat, Al-Syouf, Awawdeh, & Masa'deh, 2025) and the BCCC-DarkNet-2025 release.

Prior Approaches and Identified Gaps

Research on CIC-Darknet2020 has been published, covering many machine learning paradigms. Table 1 provides an overview of the main published methods in terms of reference, family of classifiers, metric used, and whether the issues of interpretability, robustness or reproducibility are addressed.

Table 1. Comparative analysis of prior approaches on CIC-Darknet2020.

Reference	Classifier Family	Reported Performance	Interpretability	Robustness Analysis	Reproducibility
Habibi Lashkari et al. (2020)	CNN (deep image learning)	~86% accuracy (8-class)	No	No	Partial
Rust-Nguyen et al. (2023)	Random Forest + adversarial study	~98% binary, ~91% multi-class	No	Yes (limited)	Partial
Almomani (2023)	Modified stacking ensemble	>97% accuracy	No	No	No
Akour et al. (2024)	NeuCube spiking NN + Random Forest	98% RF; 84.31% SNN	No	No	Partial

continued on following page

Table 1. Continued

Reference	Classifier Family	Reported Performance	Interpretability	Robustness Analysis	Reproducibility
Karunanayake et al. (2024)	Interpretable multi-label model	0.91 F1 multi-label	Yes	No	Partial
This chapter (2026)	Tree ensembles + MLP + anomaly	0.96 macro-F1 binary; 0.67 macro-F1 11-class	Yes (SHAP)	Yes (class obfuscation)	Yes (Kaggle notebook)

There are three observations that can be made as a result of this synthesis. First, while a few of these approaches achieve good predictive performance, few or none of the previous studies report macro-F1, the main reason being that most of the studies report accuracy alone, which is misleading on the extreme imbalanced binary task where 98.86% of the records are of the Non-Tor class. Second, only one previous study (Karunanayake et al., 2024) considers interpretability as a first class output and only one (Rust-Nguyen et al., 2023) offers any quantitative adversarial robustness analysis. Third, end-to-end reproducibility is lacking from the literature on this benchmark, and, in particular, it is not available in public notebooks.

This synthesis is interpreted in the context of historical evolution of darknet detection research. Initial research in 2014-2018 was mainly concerned with analyzing the traffic at the packet level, fingerprinting attacks on hidden services, and statistical features based on a short observation period - which are all useful additions to the theoretical knowledge of anonymity systems but not suitable for re-use as benchmarks. The studies with CIC-Tor2016 and ISCX-VPN-2016 datasets moved the focus to statistical classification based on flow-level data with reproducible feature extraction and the integration of all of them in CIC-Darknet2020 in 2020 allows for direct comparison of the results of studies. The research field was dominated by the quest for accuracy in classification, with ever more complex approaches to deep learning often trading in for loss of interpretability and reproducibility from 2020-2023. The last three years (2023-2025) have witnessed a methodological shift towards operational concerns: The need for interpretability has been acknowledged (Karunanayake et al., 2024; Sindiramutty et al., 2024) and adversarial evaluation has started to be published (Rust-Nguyen et al., 2023). This chapter makes a small step towards that reorientation by combining both of these in one pipeline, instead of two separate research strands.

This methodology is proposed in this chapter to address all three of these gaps. Macro-F1 is reported in addition to accuracy, and is the key headline measure for the imbalanced classification tasks. Instead of being an add-on to the pipeline as a post hoc process (Sindiramutty et al., 2024; Lundberg & Lee, 2017), SHAP-based interpretability is treated as a standard component of the pipeline. The class-obfuscation adversarial protocol is systematically tested on all application classes and a per-class robustness profile is obtained. The whole implementation is available as a Kaggle notebook with the dataset as a public input, which can be replicated independently.

In addition to the work specifically related to CIC-Darknet2020, the methodology developed here is based on more general scholarly traditions. The interpretability layer is based on the concept of the XAI literature in Sindiramutty et al. (2024) and cybersecurity-AI frameworks in Zangana, Omar, and Mohammed (2025), Tarade and Das (2025), and G. K., Ranjani, Nithiyanandam, Rajasekaran, Karthick, and Kumar (2025). The present chapter's adaptive detection components are framed in the context of the autonomous defense paradigm developed by Omar, Zraqou, Alkhadour, and Gómez (2025b) where the security systems self-learn and adapt to the dynamic threat environment. The chapter's outputs are positioned in the operation based on the dark web threat intelligence framework of Zhang and Chow (2020) and systematic detection approach of William, Jawale, Pawar, Bibave, and Narode (2022). Khan et al. (2025) and T. et al. (2025) were the only studies that analyzed generative AI in cybersecurity in a forward-looking manner and synthesized future trends, respectively, which relate to the emerging generative AI augmented threats and defenses discussed in the Future Research Directions section.

MAIN FOCUS OF THE CHAPTER

The Main Focus of the Chapter is to create a cohesive and reproducible AI-darknet threat detection pipeline on CIC-Darknet2020 benchmark. The pipeline combines four supervised classifiers, two unsupervised anomaly detectors, post-hoc interpretability layer and an adversarial robustness assessment and is distributed as a single executable workflow inside a Kaggle notebook. The design goal is to not only maximize predictive accuracy, but to also show the integration of the four key properties that were identified in the Background as the main design gap: accuracy, interpretability, robustness and reproducibility. The methodology proposed, the experimental setup and the results achieved in both binary and multi-class classification problems are described in turn.

Proposed Methodology

The proposed methodology consists of five components: a data preprocessing pipeline to prepare CIC-Darknet2020 records for modelling; a supervised classification module for training and evaluation of four learners for both binary and multi-class classification; an anomaly detection module to find flows that do not fit with learned normal-traffic profiles; an interpretability layer to interpret the prediction using SHapley Additive exPlanations; and an adversarial evaluation protocol to quantify the degradation under realistic feature manipulation. The entire architecture is shown in Figure 1 and the components are described below.

Figure 1. Architecture of the proposed methodology pipeline

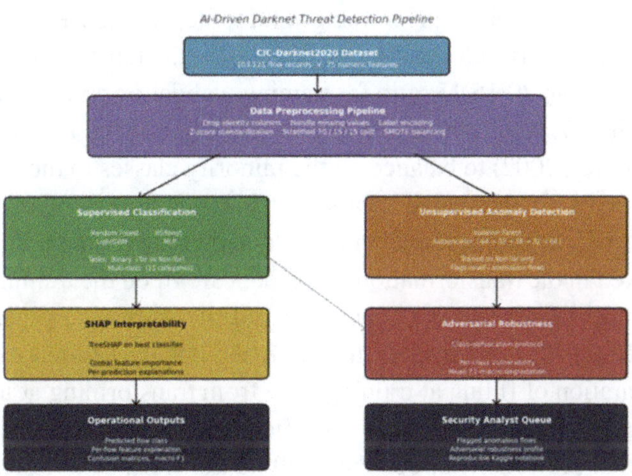

Problem Formalization

The classification problem is now defined as follows. Let D = {(x_i, y_i)}, i = 1, ..., N be the labelled dataset, where x_i is in the D dimensional feature space, which is created from the statistics of CICFlowMeter, and y_i is in a discrete label space Y. The chapter discusses two tasks that are related. For the main experiment, the classes are defined as Y = {Tor, Non-Tor} where VPN traffic is grouped with Non-Tor class, which is the majority class. The multi-class task is defined by Y = {Audio-Stream, Browsing, Chat, Email, P2P, Transfer, Video-Stream, VOIP} which are the eight applications used. A task-specific empirical risk minimization of the cross-entropy loss with model-specific regularization is used to learn a classifier f: X → Y on the training partition. Macro-averaged F1 is used to measure the performance on the held-out test partition.

It is important to note two formal properties of this problem formulation. Second, the binary and multi-class tasks have the same feature space X but with different cardinality of Y, allowing the same pre-processing pipeline and feature extraction to be used for both detection problems without any changes; this property makes the deployment of the pipeline simpler, as the same feature-extraction stage can be used for both detection layers. Second, the decision function f needs to return a probability distribution over Y, not just a class label, to enable subsequent calibration and tuning of thresholds by security analysts who need to choose between precision and recall based on their operational tolerance of false positives. The probabilistic output is also used by the supervised classification module as well as by the SHAP interpretability layer, which relies on an additive decomposition of the prediction that only works with a probabilistic output.

Data Processing Pipeline

The data processing pipeline consists of a deterministic series of seven transformations, using the same parameters in each step for the training, validation and test partitions, to avoid leakage of information from the test set.

Step 1: Download CIC-Darknet2020 corpus from public Kaggle repository. Step 2: Remove columns that contain identity information, such as Flow ID, Source IP, Destination IP and Timestamp. Step 3: Use the column max (on the training partition only) to replace any infinite values and use the column median (on the training partition only) to replace any missing values. Step 4: Label encoder the categorical target variable. Step 5: Z score normalize all continuous features with statistics from the training partition. Step 6: Divide cleaned data into 70/15/15 ratio for training, validation and test set, using a random seed of 42 for repeatability. Step 7: Use Synthetic Minority Over-sampling Technique (SMOTE; Chawla, Bowyer, Hall, & Kegelmeyer, 2002) to balance all the minority classes to the size of the majority class in the training partition only; an alternative approach using Adaptive Synthetic sampling (ADASYN; He, Bai, Garcia, & Li, 2008) was considered but not adopted in the final pipeline.

All the objects involved in the transformation of the data are fit on the training data and then applied without re-fitting it on the subsequent partitions, the full preprocessing pipeline is implemented in scikit-learn (Pedregosa et al., 2011; Buitinck et al., 2013) and imbalanced-learn (Lemaître, Nogueira, & Aridas, 2017). This separation of fitting at training time from transforming at inference time is crucial for two reasons: firstly, it means that the trained classifier is not seeing statistics from the test partition, and secondly, it means that previously unseen data will be transformed in exactly the same way at the time of inference, as the same fitted operations are used for transformation. The objects fitted in the operational deployments are usually serialized to disk with the trained weights of the classifier and are loaded on the production inference servers, so that the whole pipeline can be reproduced without re-training or re-fitting the preprocessing components.

Supervised Classification Models

Four supervised classifiers are trained from the preprocessed data which are chosen to cover a representative set of modeling paradigms. Random Forest Classifier (Breiman, 2001): An ensemble of decision trees which are trained on bootstrap samples and have feature subsampling at each node. XGBoost classifier (Chen & Guestrin, 2016) is a sparse-aware split finding regularized gradient boosted decision trees. LightGBM classifier (Ke et al., 2017) is a gradient boosting method that has similar predictive power at a lower training cost, which is implemented in the form of Gradient based One Side Sampling and Exclusive Feature Bundling. For the deep learning paradigm, the Multilayer Perceptron (MLP) model is used, which has three fully connected layers with 128, 64 and 32 units respectively, followed by ReLU activation, batch normalization, 0.3 dropout rate and softmax output layer; the model is trained for max 100 epochs with early stopping using the Adam optimizer (Kingma & Ba, 2015).

Four classifiers representing different paradigms have been chosen not only because of the fact that it is not possible to select one best of class but also due to three design considerations. First, an average of classifiers belonging to different modeling families is a better indicator of how hard the dataset is and how well a learner can do on it than any individual classifier, because the agreement of the classifiers is a signal of the intrinsic difficulty of the data as opposed to being an artifact of any given learner. Second, the four classifiers have varying degrees of sensitivity to the class imbalance, missing values and feature scaling and the comparative analysis reveals which of these factors have the greatest impact on the performance of the classifiers on darknet flow data. Third, the supervised module was designed to be a reference implementation which downstream investigators can use as a baseline to which to add classifiers; the four-model baseline is meant to be a stable implementation to compare to new approaches.

The class imbalance of CIC-Darknet2020 with only 1.14 percent of Tor flows, encourages two design decisions in the supervised module. First, SMOTE is not used on the validation and test partitions and the performance measures reported are based on the performance of the classifiers on the naturally occurring data (not on data synthetically balanced by SMOTE). Second, the validation partition model selection is based on macro-F1 instead of accuracy – this is because if a classifier simply predicted the Non-Tor class for all the samples it would get 98.86 percent accuracy, but it would not have much operational value. The macro-F1 objective directly encourages correct classification of the minority Tor class, which is in-line with the operational objective of finding the rare positives that should be attended to by the analysts.

Anomaly Detection Models

In addition to the supervised classifiers, there are two unsupervised anomaly detection models. The Isolation Forest model (Liu, Ting, & Zhou, 2008) is made up of an ensemble of random partitioning trees and the anomaly score is calculated as the average length of the path from the root of the tree to the leaf that contains the sample. The Isolation Forest model is trained on the Non-Tor majority class only, in order to create a normal-traffic profile. The Autoencoder model (Hinton & Salakhutdinov, 2006) is a symmetric feedforward network with 64, 32 and 16 units in the encoder layers and 16, 32 and 64 units in the decoder layers which is trained to minimize mean squared reconstruction error on the Non-Tor training partition. The reconstruction error is used as the anomaly score at inference time: flows that are not reconstructed well are considered to be deviations from the learned normal manifold.

This distinction of having unsupervised anomaly detection in addition to supervised classification is for a particular operational purpose, which is not well served by supervised models alone. Supervised classifiers learn "decision boundaries" that correspond to the "categories" that are seen in the training data, and the results of the flows assigned to "categories" that are truly new are not guaranteed to be correct; the classifier will assign them to the most superficially similar known "category" with high confidence. Anomaly detection, on the other hand, brings to the surface flows that do not fit with the distribution of normal flows learned, giving an additional signal that is not based on similarity of the new flow with known flows. With a supervised classifier being used for flows that match up to learned categories and an anomaly detector being used for novel deviations, it is less likely that an emerging darknet protocol or application category will slip through the cracks during the time between when it first appears and when it can be added to supervised training data.

Interpretability Layer

The interpretability layer uses SHapley Additive exPlanations (SHAP; Lundberg & Lee, 2017) for the best performing supervised classifier. SHAP assigns a contribution value to each feature for each individual prediction that satisfies three axiomatic properties: local accuracy, missingness and consistency. Two outputs that go together are created. First, the global summary plot sorts features based on the mean absolute SHAP value in a subsample of the test partition that is representative of the entire test set. Secondly, individual prediction explanations are created for representative correct and incorrect classified flows. The TreeSHAP variant is for tree-based classifiers, which make use of the additive structure of decision trees for exact computation in polynomial time.

SHAP was chosen in preference to other interpretability techniques like Local Interpretable Model-agnostic Explanations (LIME) or permutation feature importance for three reasons. Firstly, the exact contribution values of the classifiers for SHAP are obtained for the tree-based classifiers using TreeSHAP, while LIME obtains only approximate local explanations via sampling and regression. Second, SHAP values are additive, which means that the prediction of any incident can be decomposed into a contribution of each feature and the overall baseline expectation, a per-incident accounting that security analysts do when they manually review a flow. Third, the consistency property of SHAP means that a feature that's contributing more as the model is changed will be assigned a higher SHAP value, which makes it easier to compare model versions as the pipeline is iterated. The three properties make SHAP particularly suitable for the operational interpretability requirements mentioned in the Background and as a precondition for adoption in security operations centers.

Adversarial Evaluation Protocol

The adversarial evaluation protocol is based on the class-obfuscation approach of Rust-Nguyen et al. (2023). Step 1: Selection of a target application class, which is the class that an adversary would like to evade. Step 2: unmodified training partition is used for training the classifier. Step 3: During test time, the feature values of target class samples are replaced with the column means of a different application class, which provides a way of an attacker to manipulate the behavior of the applications in the application layer to mimic a different class. Step 4: The entire test partition, containing the obfuscated target samples is fed to the trained classifier and the macro-F1 is noted. This process is repeated for each (target, mimic) pair for all classes of applications, and the result is a per-class robustness profile which indicates how vulnerable each class of applications is to evasion.

The threat model that is assumed in this protocol is one that assumes an adversary with three specific capabilities/limitations. Adversary has the ability to change the statistical properties of the data extracted by CICFlowMeter of the classes in the application layer but not the Tor encryption layers; adversary can obtain the distribution of features of classes in the training data and select a mimic class wisely; adversary has no access to the parameters of the trained classifier, and cannot calculate gradients to the classifier. This threat model is designed to be weaker than the gradient guided adversarial example threat model that is typically investigated in the context of image classification, where the adversarial has full white-box access to the model. The less sophisticated threat model is more realistic of the actual darknet actor, who may not have any insider information about the defenders' system and has to come up with obfuscation methods based on the behavior of the traffic. The robustness measurements obtained should thus be regarded as a lower bound on the actual adversarial degradation; the more robust the threat model, the more the degradation, and the less robust the threat model, the less the degradation.

Experimental Setup

The experimental setup involves detailing the dataset configuration, hardware and software setup, hyper-parameter choices for each of the models, and evaluation measures to assess the proposed methodology. All code is experimental and is coded as a single Jupyter notebook that can be run on Kaggle with the dataset as a public input.

Dataset Configuration

The experiments are conducted on the CIC-Darknet2020 corpus which was released by the user dhoogla (Habibi Lashkari et al., 2020) via Kaggle. This version is a subset of the original release of 158,659 flow records that is deduplicated and cleaned by Kaggle, containing 103,121 flow records and 79 columns of which 75 are numeric features (after removing the columns carrying the identity data). The label distribution is in line with the operational darknet prevalence, with 64,804 Non-Tor labels (62.84%), 20,216 Non-VPN labels (19.60%), 16,922 VPN labels (16.41%), and 1,179 Tor labels (1.14%), with severe minority class imbalance for the binary task at approximately 87 to 1. An observation about data quality is that there are eleven different types of labels, and not eight as described in the original data set documentation, with the application level label column having case inconsistent duplicates: AUDIO-STREAMING and Audio-Streaming, File-transfer and File-Transfer, Video-streaming and Video-Streaming, each of which appears as a distinct label with unequal sample counts. The labels are also left as they are in the public release, for exact reproducibility.

Hardware and Software Environment

All experiments are run on Kaggle notebooks: Tesla T4 GPU x2 is enabled for the neural network parts of all experiments. The software used includes Python 3.11, TensorFlow 2.19.0, scikit-learn 1.4, XGBoost 2.x, LightGBM 4.x, imbalanced-learn 0.12, and SHAP 0.46.0. To guarantee deterministic experimental outcomes, the random seeds of NumPy, scikit-learn, TensorFlow and SMOTE are set to 42. The full pipeline runs end-to-end in about 20 minutes, on a regular Kaggle session, and can be re-run practically by any investigator.

Hyperparameter Configuration

Each model uses hyperparameters that optimize the model's prediction accuracy and training expenses given the Kaggle compute envelope. Hyperparameters were set based on published guidelines for tabular classification with flow-based features, and were checked using some initial experiments on the validation split. The final configuration of each model is summarised in Table 2.

Table 2. Hyperparameter configuration for all models

Model	Key Hyperparameters
Random Forest	n_estimators=200, max_depth=None, min_samples_split=2, bootstrap=True
XGBoost	n_estimators=300, max_depth=8, learning_rate=0.1, subsample=0.9, colsample_bytree=0.9
LightGBM	n_estimators=300, num_leaves=63, learning_rate=0.05, subsample=0.9, colsample_bytree=0.9
MLP	Hidden layers (128, 64, 32) with ReLU + BatchNorm + Dropout 0.3; Adam (lr=0.001); batch=512; ≤100 epochs with early stopping (patience=10)
Isolation Forest	n_estimators=200, contamination=0.10
Autoencoder	Encoder (64, 32, 16) + symmetric decoder; MSE loss; Adam (lr=0.001); batch=512; 30 epochs; threshold = 95th percentile training reconstruction error
SMOTE	Default k_neighbors=5 (binary); k_neighbors=3 (multi-class for rare classes)

Evaluation Metrics

The six standard measures of classification performance are used. Accuracy is the percentage of accurate classification of test instances. Precision and recall is calculated on a per class basis and is averaged in macro (equal weight to each class) and weighted (weighted by class support). Precision and recall are combined in the F1-score (Powers, 2011). The main measure for the imbalanced tasks in this chapter is the Macro-F1 metric which has the effect of penalizing poor performance of the minority class proportionately. For the binary task the area under the receiver operating characteristic curve (ROC-AUC) is reported. To get insights into the error patterns per class, confusion matrices are created for the binary task and displayed in Figure 2. Precision, recall and F1 for the anomaly detection module are calculated based on Tor being the category to be flagged as an anomaly. The baseline macro-F1 scores on the clean test partition are also given for the adversarial protocol, as well as macro-F1 scores after class obfuscation.

Baselines and Comparison

The quantitative comparisons with previous published works are made with two main references. The top accuracy for the binary task is around 98% by Rust-Nguyen, Sharma, and Stamp (2023) using a Random Forest classifier for the binary problem of CIC-Darknet2020. A second point of comparison is a modified stacking ensemble, which had a test accuracy of more than 97% on the same data set as reported in Almomani (2023). The comparison space published for the application-level multi-class task is spread over studies with varying case-variant merging and re-sampling approaches; the results of this chapter are presented without merging the case-variant labels.

Results and Analysis

Results and Analysis subsection shows the empirical results of the experimental set up. First, the supervised classification results for the binary task and the application categorization task with 11 classes are presented, followed by the results of the anomaly detection, SHAP interpretability results, and adversarial robustness results. Every result is related to published benchmarks listed in the Background and there is a discussion of honest limitations of the experimental design at the end of the section.

Supervised Classification Results

The results of the four supervised classifiers on both the classification tasks are reported in Table 3. For the binary task, all three models (tree-based) have an accuracy of greater than 0.99 and macro-F1 greater than 0.95 with LightGBM having the highest accuracy of 0.9983, macro-F1 of 0.9644 and weighted-F1 of 0.9984. In the binary task, the counts in the confusion matrices of Random Forest and XGBoost are the same, indicating that on this benchmark the two classifiers converge to the same effective decision boundary, leading to the same accuracy, precision and recall. The Multilayer Perceptron gives a much lower macro-F1 score of 0.7161 along with a high accuracy score of 0.9727 and weighted-F1 of 0.9798, showing the gap between the macro-F1 and accuracy scores in the case of extreme class imbalance.

Table 3. Supervised classification results on both tasks

Model	Task	Accuracy	Prec. (macro)	Recall (macro)	F1 (macro)	F1 (weighted)	ROC-AUC
Random Forest	Binary	0.9979	0.9376	0.9766	0.9562	0.9980	0.9994
XGBoost	Binary	0.9979	0.9376	0.9766	0.9562	0.9980	0.9999
LightGBM	Binary	0.9983	0.9454	0.9852	0.9644	0.9984	0.9998
MLP	Binary	0.9727	0.6451	0.9667	0.7161	0.9798	0.9865
Random Forest	Multi-class	0.8293	0.6239	0.6840	0.6374	0.8333	—
XGBoost	Multi-class	0.8552	0.6555	0.7573	0.6725	0.8617	—
LightGBM	Multi-class	0.8584	0.6563	0.7431	0.6724	0.8644	—
MLP	Multi-class	0.7221	0.5427	0.6540	0.5229	0.7356	—

Confusion Matrix Analysis

Figure 2. Confusion matrices for the four classifiers on the binary task

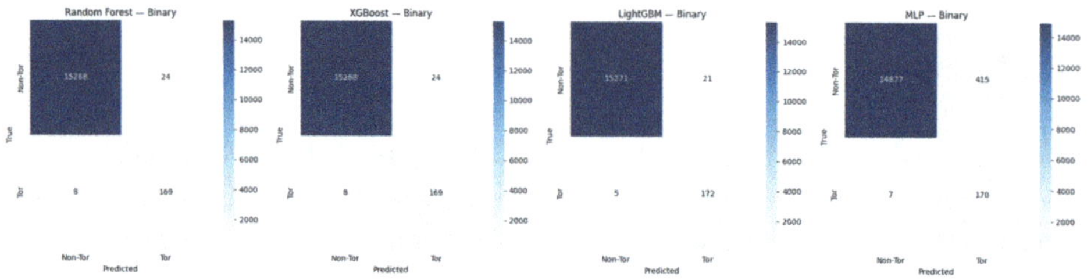

The confusion matrices of the four classifiers for binary task are shown in figure 2. The two matrices (Random Forest and XGBoost) are the same: 15,268 true negative, 24 false positive, 8 false negative, and 169 true positive. The LightGBM matrix has the lowest number of total errors with 15,271 true negatives, 21 false positives, 5 false negative and 172 true positive. The Multilayer Perceptron matrix is quite different, with 415 false positive predictions, versus 21-24 false positive predictions for the tree models. The error patterns have operational implications: If the deployment scale is that of a major Internet service provider, with a 0.16% false-positive rate, that would result in thousands of analyst alerts per day. The LightGBM model achieved the lowest false positive rate of 21/15,292 Non-Tor flows or ~0.137%, which is the closest among the four models considered to be operational.

All four models also show lower performance on the eleven-class application categorization, which is a more challenging task, and because of the case-inconsistent labels. The model comparison is visually presented in figure 3 for both tasks. The results show that the accuracy and macro-F1 of the MLP for the binary task are different, as seen in the visualization. The macro F1 score is best for XGBoost (0.6725), and about equal for LightGBM (0.6724) and a bit higher accuracy (0.8584). The performance of the MLP is once again less than that of the tree ensembles, with macro-F1 0.5229. The binary-task LightGBM result of 0.9983 accuracy is competitive with the Random Forest benchmark (≈ 0.98 accuracy) of Rust-Nguyen et al. (2023) on CIC-Darknet2020, whereas the Random Forest result of 0.9979 is essentially the same under independent implementation.

Figure 3. Accuracy and macro-F1 by model on binary and multi-class tasks

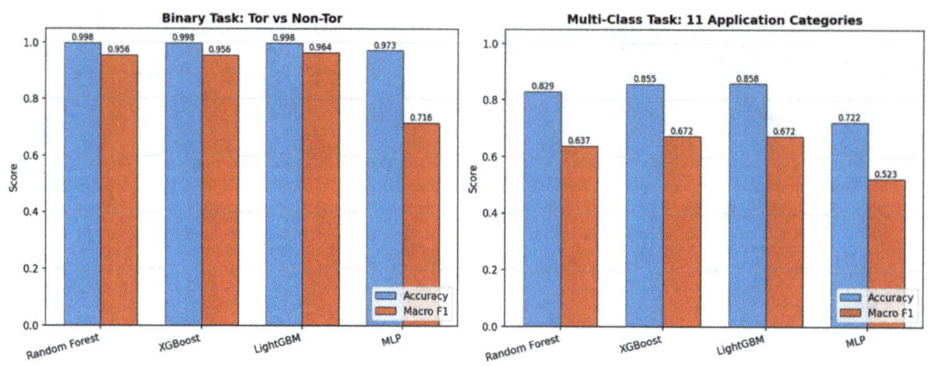

Anomaly Detection Results

The anomaly detection module is tested based on the premise that the Tor class is the class to be surfaced as the anomalies. The results of the Isolation Forest and Autoencoder models are presented in Table 4, in relation to this assumption.

Table 4. Anomaly detection performance

Method	Accuracy	Precision	Recall	F1
Isolation Forest	0.9024	0.0847	0.7684	0.1526
Autoencoder	0.9487	0.1434	0.7006	0.2380

The high recall and low precision are typical of both models. Overall, the Autoencoder achieves a higher precision than the Isolation Forest, and a higher F1-score. These percentages should be seen in the context of the operational use of anomaly detection: when anomaly detection is trained, it detects around 70-77% of the Tor flows as anomalies, and produces between 6 and 11 false positive detections per true positive detected. For a security operations environment, this output is suitable for an alert generation queue which can be triaged by analysts instead of for autonomous classification.

Interpretability Findings

SHAP analysis is done on the best performing LightGBM classifier of the binary task. The feature importance values are displayed in global ranking (according to mean absolute SHAP value) in Figure 4 and in global beeswarm plot (according to the directionality of impact) in Figure 5. The top 10 features that influence the most are listed in Table 5.

Table 5. Top 10 features by mean absolute SHAP value (LightGBM)

Rank	Feature	Mean |SHAP|
1	Bwd Init Win Bytes	6.234
2	FWD Init Win Bytes	1.602
3	Idle Max	1.219
4	Fwd Packets/s	0.564
5	Fwd Act Data Packets	0.474
6	Idle Mean	0.464
7	Packet Length Mean	0.292
8	Flow IAT Min	0.285
9	Bwd Packets/s	0.277
10	FIN Flag Count	0.256

Figure 4. SHAP global feature importance for LightGBM on the binary task

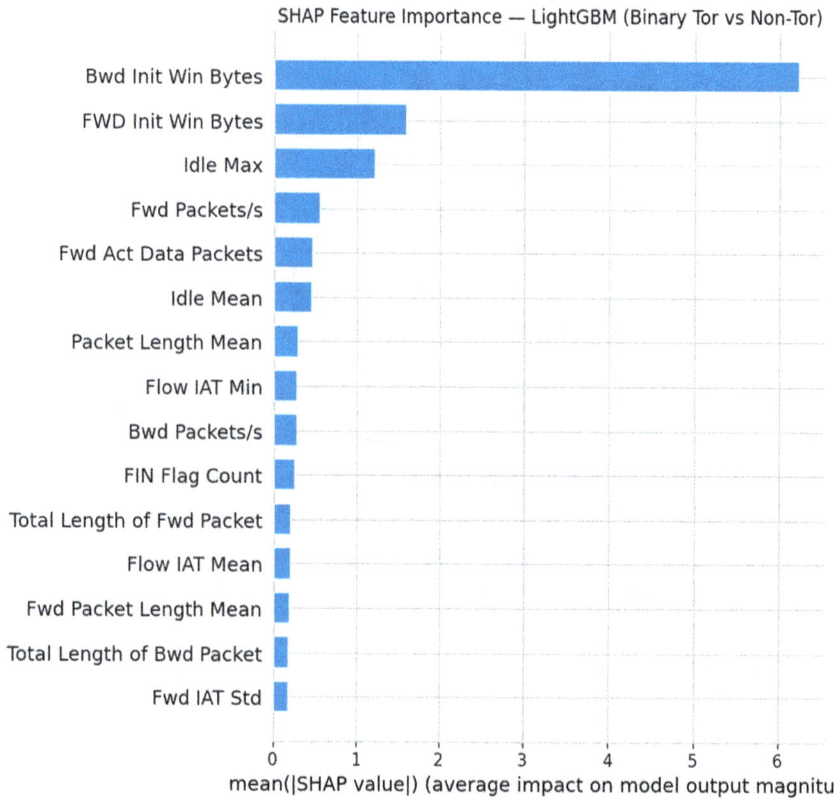

Figure 5. SHAP beeswarm plot showing directional feature impact for LightGBM

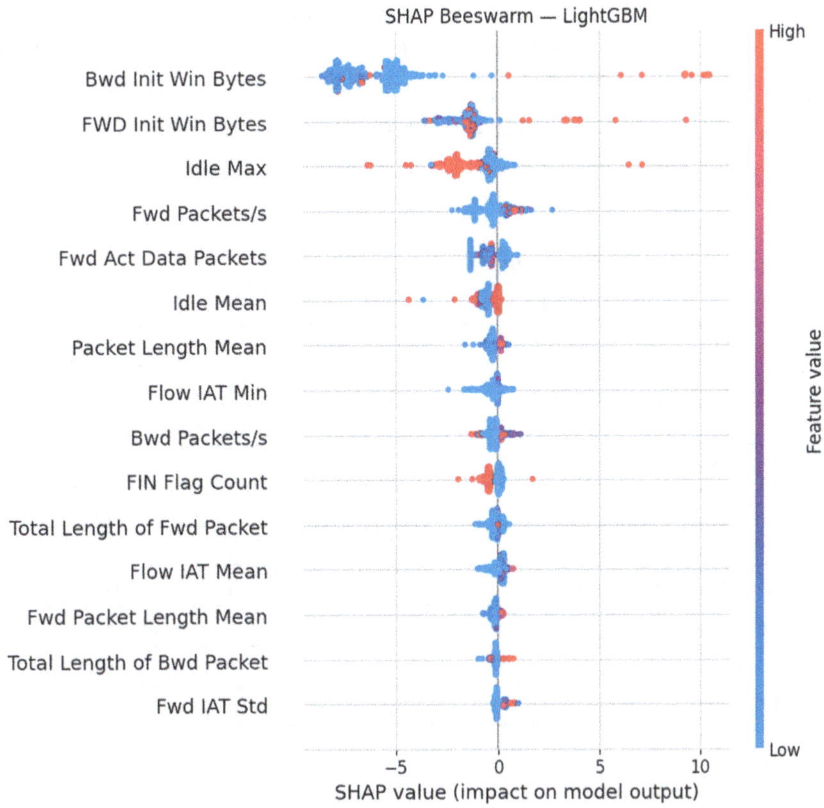

Bwd Init Win Bytes (backward initial TCP window size) is the most important feature with a mean absolute SHAP value of 6.234, more than three times as important as the 2nd most important feature FWD Init Win Bytes with a value of 1.601. This finding can be operationally interpreted as follows: Tor's circuit-construction mechanism (traffic goes through three encrypted relays before it reaches its final destination) changes the observable TCP handshake at the connection endpoint that CICFlowMeter sees. The next important layer of features is timing: Idle Max = 1.219 and Idle Mean = 0.464 captures the timing characteristic of Tor's circuit-multiplexing behavior, which is bursty inter-flow.

The beeswarm visualization provides an extra layer of interpretability with the directionality of the information. Observations with high values of the feature cluster on the negative SHAP side (correlated with the Non-Tor prediction) for Bwd Init Win Bytes, which is the dominant feature. This is a directionality that is consistent with the protocol level mechanism: Tor relay endpoints tend to be advertised with smaller receive windows than are direct servers. The correlation between SHAP-ranked features and the known properties of Tor protocol constitutes a type of model validation that is independent of accuracy measures: the features that the classifier is ranking are human security analysts' features that they know to be relevant to Tor protocol, and not just spurious correlations.

Adversarial Robustness Results

Class-obfuscation protocol was used on the best performing tree-based multi-classifier—XGBoost. The baseline macro-F1 on clean test partition for XGBoost classifier was 0.6725. When class obfuscation was used, the mean macro-F1 for all pairs decreased to 0.6088 with the mean F1 reduction of 0.0637 for all the pairs (target, mimic). The greatest reduction observed was 0.1392. The 10 worst duos are listed in Table 6.

Table 6. Top 10 most damaging (target, mimic) adversarial pairs

Target	Mimic	F1 (macro)	Drop
P2P	Browsing	0.5333	0.1392
P2P	Chat	0.5333	0.1392
Browsing	Chat	0.5415	0.1310
P2P	AUDIO-STREAMING (variant)	0.5448	0.1277
P2P	Email	0.5448	0.1277
P2P	Video-Streaming	0.5448	0.1277
P2P	Video-streaming (variant)	0.5464	0.1262
P2P	Audio-Streaming	0.5464	0.1261
P2P	File-Transfer	0.5464	0.1261
P2P	VOIP	0.5477	0.1249

Figure 6. Per-class mean F1 drop under class obfuscation (XGBoost, 11-class task)

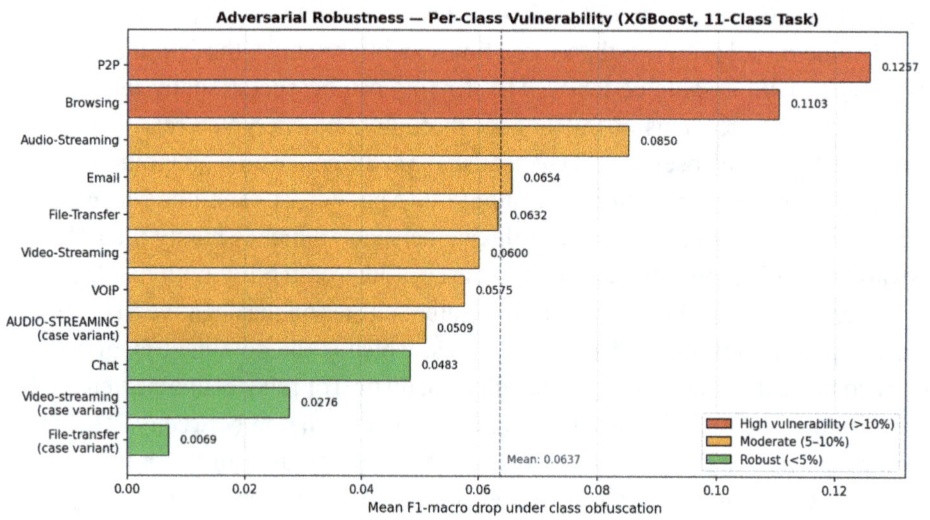

The per class mean F1 drop is shown in Figure 6, from the most to the least vulnerable. The most sensitive class is P2P with the mean drop of F1 score of 0.1257 when its test samples are labeled as any other class. The second class that is most susceptible is browsing with a mean decrease of 0.1103. Case-variant duplicate classes are the best performing under this measure with File-transfer (0.0069), Video-streaming (0.0276) and AUDIO-STREAMING (0.0509) being the least affected, where the small training-data support means that the classifier has weak patterns that cannot be meaningfully disrupted by obfuscation.

The mean degradation value (6.37 percent) along with the maximum degradation value (13.92 percent) for the most vulnerable classes is the security boundary for the proposed pipeline. This is an operationally meaningful lower bound; a single-digit percent degradation can be expected when an adversary who is performing application-layer obfuscation, but does not know the specific classifier. Future work would be to make more powerful attacks using gradient-guided perturbation, which would likely result in larger degradations.

Operational Deployment Considerations

In addition to the quantitative results in the previous subsections, there are three operational considerations that impact the ability to practically deploy the proposed pipeline in production security monitoring environments. The first one is the computation cost. The entire training pipeline runs in about 20 minutes per Kaggle Tesla T4 instance and the inference of a LightGBM classifier on the trained model to classify a test partition of 15,469 records takes less than two seconds. With one thousand flows per second deployment throughput, LightGBM model adds less than a millisecond classification latency per flow, meeting the requirements for real-time monitoring of medium-size enterprise networks. The MLP classifier is a dense matrix operation and thus takes longer to make inferences, but is still possible when batched in a GPU runtime.

The second factor to take into account is how the interpretability layer can be incorporated into the workflow. TreeSHAP provides a linear scaling of the number of trees and depth of the trees, with around 0.04 seconds to explain a prediction for the trained LightGBM model. For the throughput envelope above, it is not possible to generate SHAP explanations for all flows classified, and so the recommended deployment pattern is to only compute SHAP values for those flows which exceed an analyst configured priority threshold, such as flows between 0.5 and 0.9 probability of classification (the gray area where analyst interpretation is most valuable) or flows that trigger downstream incident response workflows. This selective interpretation approach maintains the auditability feature of SHAP and fits in typical compute allowances.

The third one is concept drift and longterm maintenance of the trained models. Darknet protocols and behaviors of applications change continuously and a classifier trained on the CIC-Darknet2020 corpus of 2020 will lose the predictive power over the time as the version of Tor protocol and application traffic patterns and adversary obfuscation strategies evolve continuously. The suggested operating procedure is to retrain the supervised classifiers on a window of the recent labeled traffic data at least once every quarter (in the same manner as described above), to monitor the per-class precision and recall on a held out validation partition between retraining periods, and to retrain supervised classifiers earlier than the quarterly periods if the precision or recall on any of the monitored classes falls below the baseline by more than 5 percentage points. The accompanying Jupyter notebook is built to handle this retraining process with little change required, just changing the path to the input set of data to the new set of labeled data sources.

There are three factors with respect to the experimental design that warrant particular discussion. Firstly, the binary classification results exhibit extremely high accuracy and weighted-F1 (0.998 for the best model), which is a consequence of the extremely high accuracy on the majority class (Non-Tor) while the accuracy on the minority class (Tor) is reflected in the macro-F1 figure of 0.9644. Second, the multi-class results of macro-F1 0.6725 are below several published results on this eight-class formulation of the data; experiments here are on the eleven-label variant of the data which were retained in the public release of the dataset on Kaggle and a label-merging operation, merging the case-variant duplicates, would be expected to increase these scores to a range more directly comparable to published eight-class scores. Third, the adversarial evaluation protocol is a tractable proxy for adversarial obfuscation and is not the full attack surface; gradient guided adversarial examples against differentiable surrogate models would likely result in bigger degradations and be a more serious threat model.

FUTURE RESEARCH DIRECTIONS

The methodology designed in this chapter provides a clear starting point for darknet threat detection using AI on the CIC-Darknet2020 benchmark and offers some specific avenues for further development. Five trajectories are especially promising for further research and are based on limitations of the current research and existing research streams in the broader cybersecurity literature.

Transformer-Based Natural Language Processing for Darknet Forums. While flow-level traffic classification is discussed in the current chapter, a significant amount of operational darknet threat intelligence exists in the textual content of posts on forum, market, and Telegram channels. With recent progress in transformer architectures like GPT-3 (Vaswani et al., 2017) and Devlin et al., 2019) and parameter efficient fine tuning of LMMs like Llama 2 (Touvron et al., 2023), it is possible to adapt to specialized domains with modest compute resources. As an extension to the work presented here on traffic classification, a natural extension works with transformer-based encoders and darknet forum posts and marketplace listings, tackling the challenge of linguistic obfuscation.

Generative AI as Both Threat and Defense. As generative AI capabilities have evolved in recent years, new types of cybersecurity threats such as AI-generated phishing content, deepfake social engineering, synthetic credentials, and more have emerged, along with new types of cybersecurity applications, including AI-generated honeypots and behavior signature generation (Khan et al., 2025; Omar, Zraqou, & Gómez, 2025c; T. et al., 2025). The proposed methodology is also compatible with these developments and can be extended to the detection of synthetic flow patterns that adversaries could use to evade classification by using generative models. A similar line of research is to use generative models to augment data for the rare Tor and case-variant classes for better performance of minority classes than SMOTE.

Federated Learning for Privacy-Preserving Detection. The detection of operations in the darknet is often sensitive network telemetry information, which may have privacy and regulatory concerns and cannot be addressed by centralized model training. To develop models collaboratively without central data aggregation, federated learning (McMahan et al., 2017) is one of the options that can be used, which can be further enhanced by the use of SHAP-based knowledge distillation. A federated formulation of methodology presented in this chapter could be applied to multi-organization deployments to achieve more widespread training data coverage, while keeping data local.

Stronger Adversarial Threat Models. This chapter investigates a class-obfuscation protocol that gives a lower bound of the robustness of classifiers in an operationally relevant setting, yet more powerful attacks can be found. Gradient-guided adversarial examples generated against a differentiable surrogate model would result in more targeted and severe degradation and the attack surface would be even larger because of traffic shaping at the packet level at the capture layer that would extend beyond the post-CICFlowMeter feature space (Goodfellow et al., 2014). Future extension would assess the pipeline under these more stringent threat models, and defense mechanisms such as adversarial training, and certified defenses.

Cross-Network and Real-Time Extensions. While Tor and VPN traffic is captured by the CIC-Darknet2020 benchmark, the other anonymizing technologies such as I2P, Freenet and ZeroNet are not included, but are increasingly used by adversaries. To cover these networks, the newer SafeSurf Darknet 2025 corpus (Obaidat et al., 2025) and the BCCC-DarkNet-2025 dataset can be used, allowing also a cross-corpus evaluation of the methodology developed here. An engineering complementary direction is the deployment of the trained classifiers as streaming components in operational security monitoring pipelines, which includes the latency profiling, the batch-to-stream conversion of the preprocessing pipeline and the integration of online learning mechanisms for coping with concept drift.

CONCLUSION

This chapter has introduced a consistent and reproducible approach for darknet threat detection using AI on the CIC-Darknet2020 benchmark, which aims at filling three existing gaps in the previous literature: lack of systematic study of adversarial robustness of AI models for darknet threat detection, lack of model interpretability in published darknet classification studies, and lack of reproducibility of experimental pipelines. The proposed methodology combines four supervised classifiers, from both classical and gradient-boosting and deep learning perspectives, two unsupervised anomaly detection models, a SHAP-based post-hoc interpretability layer and a class-obfuscation adversarial evaluation protocol in a single, executable Jupyter notebook provided with this chapter.

The main empirical results are presented below. LightGBM demonstrated the best result in the binary classification task of Tor vs Non-Tor with an accuracy of 0.9983 and macro-F1 score of 0.9644, which are close to and slightly better than the published result of Random Forest on this data set. On the more difficult eleven class application categorization task, XGBoost outperformed other classifiers on the macro-F1 score, with 0.6725. The Multilayer Perceptron also had the worst results compared to all the tree-based ensembles, obtaining 0.7161 macro-F1 on the binary task, and 0.5229 macro-F1 on the multi-class task. SHAP analysis revealed that the most influential features for discriminating between the classes were the initial TCP window sizes (backward and forward), and idle-time statistics that capture the bursty timing signature of Tor circuit construction; these features are in line with known properties of Tor at the protocol-level, which gives an independent form of model validation. The mean and maximum degradation in macro-F1 score were 6.37 percent and 13.92 percent, respectively, for the class-obfuscation adversarial protocol, with the most susceptible being P2P and Browsing traffic.

These results are more than just the benchmark; they have practical implications. The interpretability layer is a translation of the behaviour of the classifiers into rules of thumb that can be used by security operations center analysts when manually inspecting flows during operational deployment, to meet the auditability requirement. The adversarial robustness measurements provide a concrete notion of security boundary for the proposed pipeline under realistic threat conditions, enabling the defenders to have a concrete idea of how much the classifiers degrade under application-layer obfuscation. The reproducibility pledge (expressed in the associated Jupyter notebook and by using of a public dataset) reduces the burden for replicating and further extending by subsequent investigators. CIC-Darknet2020's data quality observation on case-inconsistent application labels for its public release helps provide a clear finding for reproducibility that can feed into the process of consolidating its data for downstream benchmarking.

The integrated methodology that has been elaborated in this chapter has three implications that are more general in nature. First, we note that the upper bound of accuracy is consistently around 0.998 for all the three classifiers based on trees on the binary task, indicating that the discriminative ceiling on CIC-Darknet2020 is substantively achieved by the mature gradient-boosting methods and any further improvement is likely to need richer feature engineering on the packet-capture layer or expanding the benchmark itself to incorporate more anonymizing protocols and traffic patterns. Second, the significant difference between binary and multi-class performance in this study (macro F1 from 0.9644 to 0.6725), demonstrates that application-level categorization of darknet traffic is still an open research question and should be investigated in its own right and not as a trivial extension to binary detection. Third, the relative robustness of the case-variant classes is as one might expect under adversarial obfuscation, but is in fact a subtle weakness: classifiers with weak decision boundaries for small classes do not shift their boundaries due to feature manipulation because the classifier was not confident about the class labels of such samples in the first place, and this must be considered when interpreting per-class robustness measures when deployed in practice.

The integration of supervised classification, anomaly detection, interpretability and adversarial robustness, developed in this chapter, is not meant to supersede previous work, but rather as a methodological synthesis, which meets the operational requirements as identified in the Background. The five directions for future research described in the previous subsection are very real extensions of the methodology described here. The chapter is part of a continuing campaign to translate the evolution of artificial intelligence into something operationally relevant to defend against the distributed, constantly evolving, darknet threat landscape. The accompanying Jupyter notebook is included as a starting point for future investigators who will continue to work on resolving each of the limitations, which are also documented in this work; the authors hope future extensions will increase the accuracy, interpretability, robustness, and reproducibility of the classifiers in the appropriate frameworks for deployment in security operations centers around the world.

ACKNOWLEDGMENTS

The authors are thankful to the Deanship of the Faculty of Information Technology, the Deanship of Scientific Research and Graduate Studies at the University of Petra, Al-Balqa Applied University, Sultan Qaboos University, and The University of Jordan that supported them in carrying out this research.

REFERENCES

Akour, I., Alauthman, M., Nahar, K. M. O., Al-Qerem, A., Aldweesh, A., Alauthman, M., & Khalifeh, A. (2024). Analyzing darknet traffic through machine learning and NeuCube spiking neural networks. *Intelligent and Converged Networks*, *5*(4), 265–283. DOI: 10.23919/ICN.2024.0022

Almomani, A. (2023). Darknet traffic analysis, and classification system based on modified stacking ensemble learning algorithms. *Information Systems and e-Business Management*. Advance online publication. DOI: 10.1007/s10257-023-00626-2

Breiman, L. (2001). Random forests. *Machine Learning*, *45*(1), 5–32. DOI: 10.1023/A:1010933404324

Buitinck, L., Louppe, G., Blondel, M., Pedregosa, F., Mueller, A., Grisel, O., Niculae, V., Prettenhofer, P., Gramfort, A., Grobler, J., Layton, R., VanderPlas, J., Joly, A., Holt, B., & Varoquaux, G. (2013). API design for machine learning software: Experiences from the scikit-learn project. In *ECML PKDD Workshop: Languages for Data Mining and Machine Learning* (pp. 108–122).

Chainalysis. (2024). *The 2024 crypto crime report.* Chainalysis. https://www.chainalysis.com/

Chawla, N. V., Bowyer, K. W., Hall, L. O., & Kegelmeyer, W. P. (2002). SMOTE: Synthetic minority over-sampling technique. *Journal of Artificial Intelligence Research*, *16*, 321–357. DOI: 10.1613/jair.953

Chen, T., & Guestrin, C. (2016). XGBoost: A scalable tree boosting system. In *Proceedings of the 22nd ACM SIGKDD International Conference on Knowledge Discovery and Data Mining* (pp. 785–794). ACM. DOI: 10.1145/2939672.2939785

Cybersecurity Ventures. (2023). *2023 official cybercrime report.* Cybersecurity Ventures. https://cybersecurityventures.com/

Devlin, J., Chang, M.-W., Lee, K., & Toutanova, K. (2019). BERT: Pre-training of deep bidirectional transformers for language understanding. In *Proceedings of the 2019 Conference of the North American Chapter of the Association for Computational Linguistics: Human Language Technologies* (pp. 4171–4186). Association for Computational Linguistics. DOI: 10.18653/v1/N19-1423

Dingledine, R., Mathewson, N., & Syverson, P. (2004). Tor: The second-generation onion router. In *Proceedings of the 13th USENIX Security Symposium* (pp. 303–320). USENIX Association.

Draper-Gil, G., Lashkari, A. H., Mamun, M. S. I., & Ghorbani, A. A. (2016). Characterization of encrypted and VPN traffic using time-related features. In *Proceedings of the 2nd International Conference on Information Systems Security and Privacy (ICISSP)* (pp. 407–414). SciTePress. DOI: 10.5220/0005740700001242

Europol. (2024). *Internet organised crime threat assessment (IOCTA) 2024.* European Union Agency for Law Enforcement Cooperation. https://www.europol.europa.eu/

Fakhouri, H. N., Alhadidi, B., Omar, K., Makhadmeh, S. N., Hamad, F., & Halalsheh, N. Z. (2024). AI-driven solutions for social engineering attacks: Detection, prevention, and response. In *2nd International Conference on Cyber Resilience (ICCR 2024).* IEEE. DOI: 10.1109/ICCR61006.2024.10533010

G. K. S., Ranjani, M., Nithiyanandam, N., Rajasekaran, A. S., Karthick, M. K., & Kumar, T. P. (2025). Cybersecurity: The part played by artificial intelligence. In D. Darwish & K. Charan (Eds.), *Analyzing privacy and security difficulties in social media: New challenges and solutions* (pp. 213–246). IGI Global. DOI: 10.4018/979-8-3693-9491-5.ch010

Goodfellow, I., Pouget-Abadie, J., Mirza, M., Xu, B., Warde-Farley, D., Ozair, S., Courville, A., & Bengio, Y. (2014). Generative adversarial nets. In Vol. 27, pp. 2672–2680). Advances in Neural Information Processing Systems. Curran Associates.

Habibi Lashkari, A., Draper-Gil, G., Mamun, M. S. I., & Ghorbani, A. A. (2017). Characterization of Tor traffic using time-based features. In *Proceedings of the 3rd International Conference on Information Systems Security and Privacy (ICISSP)* (pp. 253–262). SciTePress. DOI: 10.5220/0006105602530262

Habibi Lashkari, A., Kaur, G., & Rahali, A. (2020). DIDarknet: A contemporary approach to detect and characterize the darknet traffic using deep image learning. In *Proceedings of the 10th International Conference on Communication and Network Security* (pp. 1–13). ACM. DOI: 10.1145/3442520.3442521

He, H., Bai, Y., Garcia, E. A., & Li, S. (2008). ADASYN: Adaptive synthetic sampling approach for imbalanced learning. In *2008 IEEE International Joint Conference on Neural Networks (IJCNN)* (pp. 1322–1328). IEEE. DOI: 10.1109/IJCNN.2008.4633969

Hinton, G. E., & Salakhutdinov, R. R. (2006). Reducing the dimensionality of data with neural networks. *Science, 313*(5786), 504–507. DOI: 10.1126/science.1127647 PMID: 16873662

Hu, Y., Zou, F., Li, L., & Yi, P. (2020). Traffic classification of user behaviors in Tor, I2P, ZeroNet, Freenet. In *2020 IEEE 19th International Conference on Trust, Security and Privacy in Computing and Communications (TrustCom)* (pp. 418–424). IEEE. DOI: 10.1109/TrustCom50675.2020.00064

Karunanayake, I., AlSabah, M., Ahmed, N., Jourjon, G., Seneviratne, S., & Seneviratne, A. (2024). Examining the rat in the tunnel: Interpretable multi-label classification of Tor-based malware. *arXiv preprint arXiv:2409.16639.* https://arxiv.org/abs/2409.16639

Ke, G., Meng, Q., Finley, T., Wang, T., Chen, W., Ma, W., Ye, Q., & Liu, T.-Y. (2017). LightGBM: A highly efficient gradient boosting decision tree. In Vol. 30, pp. 3146–3154). Advances in Neural Information Processing Systems. Curran Associates.

Khan, A., Jhanjhi, N. Z., Hamid, D. H., Omar, H. A., Amsaad, F., & Wassan, S. (2025). Future trends and challenges in cybersecurity and generative AI. In Jhanjhi, N. (Ed.), *Reshaping cybersecurity with generative AI techniques* (pp. 491–522). IGI Global., DOI: 10.4018/979-8-3693-5415-5.ch014

Kingma, D. P., & Ba, J. (2015). Adam: A method for stochastic optimization. In *Proceedings of the 3rd International Conference on Learning Representations (ICLR).* https://arxiv.org/abs/1412.6980

Lemaître, G., Nogueira, F., & Aridas, C. K. (2017). Imbalanced-learn: A Python toolbox to tackle the curse of imbalanced datasets in machine learning. *Journal of Machine Learning Research*, *18*(17), 1–5.

Liu, F. T., Ting, K. M., & Zhou, Z.-H. (2008). Isolation forest. In *Proceedings of the 2008 Eighth IEEE International Conference on Data Mining (ICDM '08)* (pp. 413–422). IEEE Computer Society. DOI: 10.1109/ICDM.2008.17

Lundberg, S. M., & Lee, S.-I. (2017). A unified approach to interpreting model predictions. In Vol. 30, pp. 4765–4774). Advances in Neural Information Processing Systems. Curran Associates.

McMahan, B., Moore, E., Ramage, D., Hampson, S., & Arcas, B. A. (2017). Communication-efficient learning of deep networks from decentralized data. In *Proceedings of the 20th International Conference on Artificial Intelligence and Statistics (AISTATS)* (pp. 1273–1282). PMLR.

Obaidat, M. J., Al-Syouf, I. A., Awawdeh, Y. F., & Masa'deh, A. E. (2025). SafeSurf Darknet 2025: A novel dataset for darknet traffic detection and analysis. *Preprints.org*. https://doi.org/DOI: 10.20944/preprints202507.1926

Omar, K., Zraqou, J., Alkhadour, W., & Gómez, J. M. (2025a). AI-driven transformation of cybersecurity insurance: The Cyber Risk Intelligence Platform (CRIP). In *Cybersecurity insurance frameworks and innovations in the AI era*. IGI Global., DOI: 10.4018/979-8-3373-1977-3.ch008

Omar, K., Zraqou, J., Alkhadour, W., & Gómez, J. M. (2025b). Evolving sentinels: How autonomous defense systems self-learn and adapt to dynamic threat environments. In *AI-driven security systems and intelligent threat response using autonomous cyber defense*. IGI Global., DOI: 10.4018/979-8-3373-0954-5.ch009

Omar, K. O., Zraqou, J., & Gómez, J. M. (2025c). From synthetic text to real threats: Unraveling the security risks of generative AI. In *Examining cybersecurity risks produced by generative AI*. IGI Global., DOI: 10.4018/979-8-3373-0832-6.ch001

Pedregosa, F., Varoquaux, G., Gramfort, A., Michel, V., Thirion, B., Grisel, O., Blondel, M., Prettenhofer, P., Weiss, R., Dubourg, V., Vanderplas, J., Passos, A., Cournapeau, D., Brucher, M., Perrot, M., & Duchesnay, É. (2011). Scikit-learn: Machine learning in Python. *Journal of Machine Learning Research*, *12*, 2825–2830.

Powers, D. M. W. (2011). Evaluation: From precision, recall and F-measure to ROC, informedness, markedness and correlation. *Journal of Machine Learning Technologies*, *2*(1), 37–63.

Rust-Nguyen, N., Sharma, S., & Stamp, M. (2023). Darknet traffic classification and adversarial attacks using machine learning. *Computers & Security*, *127*, 103098. DOI: 10.1016/j.cose.2023.103098

Security, I. B. M. (2024). *Cost of a data breach report 2024*. IBM. https://www.ibm.com/reports/data-breach

Sindiramutty, S. R., Tan, C. E., Lau, S. P., Thangaveloo, R., Gharib, A. H., Manchuri, A. R., Bhardwaj, K., & Almaiah, M. A. (2024). Explainable AI for cybersecurity. In Ghonge, M., Pradeep, N., Jhanjhi, N., & Kulkarni, P. (Eds.), *Advances in explainable AI applications for smart cities* (pp. 31–97). IGI Global., DOI: 10.4018/978-1-6684-6361-1.ch002

T., V. N. R., G., H. V., A., N., K., S., & Sangers, B. (2025). Future trends and trials in cybersecurity and generative AI. In N. Jhanjhi (Ed.), *Reshaping cybersecurity with generative AI techniques* (pp. 465–490). IGI Global. DOI: 10.4018/979-8-3693-5415-5.ch013

Tarade, R., & Das, S. (2025). Cybersecurity in the age of AI: Enhancing defences for today's threats. In Gupta, B. B. (Ed.), *Critical phishing defense strategies and digital asset protection* (pp. 309–340). IGI Global., DOI: 10.4018/979-8-3693-8784-9.ch015

Touvron, H., Martin, L., Stone, K., Albert, P., Almahairi, A., Babaei, Y., Bashlykov, N., Batra, S., Bhargava, P., Bhosale, S., Bikel, D., Blecher, L., Ferrer, C. C., Chen, M., Cucurull, G., Esiobu, D., Fernandes, J., Fu, J., Fu, W., . . . Scialom, T. (2023). Llama 2: Open foundation and fine-tuned chat models. *arXiv preprint arXiv:2307.09288*. https://arxiv.org/abs/2307.09288

Vaswani, A., Shazeer, N., Parmar, N., Uszkoreit, J., Jones, L., Gomez, A. N., Kaiser, Ł., & Polosukhin, I. (2017). Attention is all you need. In Vol. 30, pp. 5998–6008). Advances in Neural Information Processing Systems. Curran Associates.

Verizon. (2024). *2024 data breach investigations report*. Verizon Business. https://www.verizon.com/business/resources/reports/dbir/

William, P., Jawale, M. A., Pawar, A. B., Bibave, R. R., & Narode, P. (2022). Systematic approach for detection and assessment of dark web threat evolution. In Rawat, R., Kaur, U., Khan, S., Sikarwar, R., & Sankaran, K. (Eds.), *Using computational intelligence for the dark web and illicit behavior detection* (pp. 230–256). IGI Global., DOI: 10.4018/978-1-6684-6444-1.ch013

Zangana, H. M., Omar, M., & Mohammed, D. (2025). Introduction to artificial intelligence in cybersecurity and forensic science. In Omar, M., Zangana, H., & Mohammed, D. (Eds.), *Integrating artificial intelligence in cybersecurity and forensic practices* (pp. 1–24). IGI Global., DOI: 10.4018/979-8-3373-0588-2.ch001

Zhang, X., & Chow, K. P. (2020). A framework for dark web threat intelligence analysis. In *Cyber Warfare and Terrorism: Concepts, methodologies, tools, and applications* (pp. 266–276). IGI Global., DOI: 10.4018/978-1-7998-2466-4.ch017

Chapter 6
Darknet Cybercrime and Ransomware

Mahmoud M. Hammad
http://orcid.org/0000-0003-2891-0463
Ajman University, UAE

ABSTRACT

The darknet, or dark web, is an encrypted overlay network reachable only through specialized software and invisible to standard browsers. Once used mainly to conceal communications, it has evolved into an operational backbone for cybercrime, now supporting the sale of stolen data, ransomware deployment, and money laundering. This chapter frames darknet cybercrime not as a set of isolated attacks but as a service-oriented criminal supply chain, in which ransomware acts as one coordinating layer. It maps the actors and services of this illicit ecosystem, then explains the ransomware lifecycle and the ransomware-as-a-service (RaaS) business model. It compares empirical studies measuring how this economy behaves and reviews the technologies—anonymity networks, cryptocurrency, and AI—that have lowered the cost and time of launching large-scale, high-impact attacks. It further examines defensive mechanisms, including darknet monitoring, cyber threat intelligence, incident response, ecosystem disruption, and policy coordination, before closing with a research agenda.

1 INTRODUCTION

Cybercrimes on the darknet nowadays are more aggressive, sophisticated, and more commercial than ever before. Darknet-based illicit activity is no longer an individual work. As the reports from Europol Europol 2024a and ENISA Europol 2025a and ENISA 2024a show that the cybercrimes are increasingly operate through complex illicit ecosystem, carried by specialization, outsourcing, and repeatable business models rather than the work os isolated attacker. This means that a single cybercrime involves many financially motivated individuals who may never met: one obtains an initial foothold in the victim network, a malware developer writes a customized malware, a malware seller supplies the tooling, an affiliate deploys the payload, and a money laundry specialist moves the money after the payment.

DOI: 10.4018/979-8-3373-9755-9.ch006

As stated in the Europol report Europol 2024a cryptocurrency and mainly Bitcoin, dark web accessed mainly via the Tor network are the principal enables of this business model.

Ransomware lies on the heart of this illicit ecosystem as it combines technical intrusion with a mature extorsion model. The Verizon's 2025 Data Breach Investigation Report Verizon 2025 showed that ransomware was present in almost 44% of the reviewed breaches. On the other hand, Chainalysis Chainalysis 2026 reported that the amount of ransomware payments during 2025 remains substantial even the number of victims refuse to pay is increasing. These reports show that these two observations can coexist. Attack volume can rise even when revenue per attack becomes less predictable. This explain why ransomware authors have diversified into data theft, public shaming, blackmailing, denial-of-service threats, and payment negotiation rather than relying only on file encryption.

We noticed that, in the literature, the words "darknet" and "darkweb" are used interchangeably or used with ambiguity. In this chapter, we use *darknet* to refer to the anonymity-preserving overlay network, mainly Tor network, and the hidden services that runs on it. We use *dark web* to refer to the web content hosted on this network, such as marketplace, malicious forums, and ransomware leak websites. We also use *underground economy* for the broader market of illicit goods and services announced on darknet services or clear-web channels and social media platforms such as Telegram.

1.1 Scope, Sources, and Method

This section explains the scope of the sources we used in this chapter and the method we followed to collect these sources. Sources were gathered from two complementary tracks. The first sources gathered from authoritative threat-intelligence and policy reporting published between 2023 and 2026 by Europol, ENISA, the United States Cybersecurity and Infrastructure Security Agency (CISA), the Federal Bureau of Investigation (FBI), the United Kingdom National Cyber Security Centre (NCSC), the World Economic Forum, and Chainalysis. The second sources were collected from peer-reviewed papers, economics-of-cybercrime, and criminological studies published between 2011 and 2025 in venues such as USENIX Security, the IEEE Symposium on Security and Privacy, the Web Conference (WWW), ACM Computing Surveys, and the British Journal of Criminology.

The first sources provide scalable and accurately reported cybercrimes and incidents, while the second sources provide methodological grounding, reasoning, and longitudinal perspective. In this chapter, we treat the two sources differently. Industry and government reports in the first

sources are used to determine signals of emerging behavior, while the second sources, academic studies, are used for analytical claims and recent findings in this filed.

1.2 Contribution, Gap, and Research Questions

The existing research work tends to fall into two categories. Technical work that analyzes ransomware binaries, encryption routines, and countermeasures tactics as discussed in Kharraz et al. 2015, Al-rimy, Maarof, and Shaid 2018, and Connolly and Wall 2019. The second category contains studies concerning the economic and criminological work of individual underground markets, forums, and payment flows as presented in Christin 2013, Soska and Christin 2015, Wegberg et al. 2018, Pastrana et al. 2018, and Oosthoek, Cable, and Smaragdakis 2022. Each category is mature on its own. What is understudied is the integration that connect the technical lifecycle, the service economy, and the defensive response in a single frame. This book chapter addresses this gap.

Our contribution is synthetic and conceptual rather than empirical. First, we unify the fragmented descriptions of darknet crime into a single *criminal supply-chain framework* that links stakeholders, services, the ransomware lifecycle, technology stack, and defensive layers. Second, we compare and contrast various empirical studies of underground economy. We show where they agree, where they diverge, and what they leave unmeasured. Third, we shed the light on future directions.

This chapter is organized around three research questions.

- *RQ1* how does the service-oriented structure of the darknet shape the way ransomware campaigns are produced and monetized?
- *RQ1* which points in the resulting supply chain are most exposed to defensive intervention, and what does the evidence say about their effectiveness?
- *RQ3* where are the most consequential gaps in current knowledge, and how might future research close them?

We acknowledge two boundaries of this chapter. First, the narrative review and analysis reflects the author's selection and emphasis of the reviewed sources, and second, the government or industrial reports might not always disclose their data or methods, hence, we take the most strongest available descriptive evidence. These boundaries also motivate the call for shared data and reproducible measurement in Section 4.7.

The remainder of the chapter is structured to answer our these research questions. Section 4.2 maps the ecosystem and introduces the supply-chain framework. Section 4.3 explains the ransomware lifecycle and the RaaS business model. Section 4.4 reviews the adjacent illicit services that supply and surround ransomware. Section 4.5 discusses the enabling technologies. Section 4.6 sets out detection, mitigation, and disruption strategies. Section 4.7 discusses the problems and shows research directions before the conclusion in Section 4.8.

This chapter is written for a mixed audience. It assumes the technically literate reader, a security practitioner, or a policy analyst. The chapter tries to define new terms as they appear in the text. Readers seeking an operational tactics will find the defensive material in Section 4.7 very

useful. Readers seeking a conceptual map should keep Figure 4.1 in view throughout, as the whole argument is organized around it.

2 DARKNET CYBERCRIME ECOSYSTEM OVERVIEW

The darknet cybercrime ecosystem relies on a group of labor work rather than a single attacker hired to perform a single task. The cybercrime is organized around specialized roles where each actor plays a specific role. Each actor can be hired, rented, or bought. Motoyama et al. Motoyama et al. 2011 showed that the underground forums function as structured and organized social institutions with skilled members and transact. Later studies Pastrana et al. 2018; Hughes, Collier, and Hutchings 2024 also show that cases like confirmed reputation, repeated business transactions, and visible profile make the criminal trade possible. The modern illicit ecosystem extends that to Tor-based forums, encrypted chats, leaked sites, and private channels. However, trust remains fragile as mentioned in Ricaldi et al. 2025, but is reinforced through an escrow systems, forum moderation, and visible claimed success. Even social media environments such as Telegram fall back on recognizable trust signals when formal reputation systems are weak.

The current illicit ecosystem is the advancement of decade-long of measured evolution and not a sudden invention. Christin's study of Silk Road in Christin 2013 showed that hidden-service market could endure and persist trade volumes supported by a working reputation system. The subsequent long study of Soska and Christin Soska and Christin 2015 tracked many markets over several years and established an empirical fact: the ecosystem survives the takedown of any individual marketplace, because sellers migrate, reputations are rebuilt, and demand persists. Malicious activities once concentrated around a handful of large markets is now spread across many forums, single vendor shops, leak sites, and encrypted channels, which makes the ecosystem hard to monitor but no less dependent on the trust mechanisms describe above.

The issue with the trust deserves a close attention, since it is the bottleneck of the ecosystem. Marketplaces and forums reduce the hazard of dealing with anonymous strangers through a small group of techniques and abilities including escrow services that hold fund until both actors confirm delivery, guaranteeing from an established member to a newcomer, dispute resolution by administrators, and visible history of completed transactions. Each technique substitute for the legal enforcement that criminals cannot use, and each technique also makes a possible point of failure in the ecosystem. Escrow system funds and invites scams and frauds, guaranteeing propagate risks through social ties, and a compromised administrator can expose the entire community. These fragile techniques are structural rather than incidental, and they explain, as shown in prior work Hughes, Collier, and Hutchings 2024; Pastrana et al. 2018, why infiltration and impersonation are effective investigation mechanisms against these ecosystems.

Measuring the potential risks helps determine where to focus our interventions. Anderson et al. Anderson et al. 2019 measured the cost of cybercrime and they argued that direct revenue criminals get is usually small compared to the defensive expenditure and indirect losses that society absorbs in response to a cybercriminal act. The consequences are uncomfortable but important: an illicit ecosystem can impose large social impact and cost even when individual operations are not especially lucrative, which means that reducing criminal revenue and reducing societal cost are not the same objective. A technique that focuses only on reducing attackers profit while sharply lowering victims' recovery cost may be more valuable in aggregate than one that maximize control.

We also need to ground these phenomena in criminology instead of treating them as purely technical problems. In their interdisciplinary review, Maimon and Louderback Maimon and Louderback 2019 classify activities like ransomware and underground trading as cyber-dependent crimes. Explaining them requires looking at both technical mechanisms and social theory—including the routine-activity and rational-choice perspectives long used to describe offline offending. This framing directly reinforces the supply-chain view adopted here: actors specialize and trade because the ecosystem's incentives make it rational to do so. Consequently, altering those incentives by shifting cost, risk, and trust—becomes a powerful lever for defenders and policymakers alike.

Table 1. Principal actors in the darknet cybercrime ecosystem, their roles, and the services or assets they supply.

Actor	Primary role	Typical services or assets
Developers	Build and maintain offensive tools	Ransomware builders, loaders, crypters, phishing kits
Affiliates	Execute campaigns using rented tools	Payload deployment, victim negotiation, revenue sharing
Initial access brokers	Sell footholds into victim environments	RDP/VPN access, stolen credentials, domain admin access
Operators	Coordinate campaigns and infrastructure	Leak sites, payment portals, command-and-control, support desks
Launderers	Obfuscate and cash out proceeds	Mixers, cross-chain swaps, mule networks, OTC liquidation
Data brokers	Monetize stolen information	Credential dumps, PII, card data, healthcare and corporate records

Table 1 summarizes the actors in the ecosystem, their primary roles, and typical services or assets supplied by each role. Two important points worth mentioning here: first, the roles are interchangeable for example an affiliate who lack the access can buy it from a broker, and an operator who lack the money laundering capabilities can rent it. Second, in such illicit ecosystem, no single actor needs the full skill set to make a successful campaign, and that's exactly what makes the ecosystem resilient and easy to enter.

The economic model is a crucial part of this ecosystem. Both NCSC and Europol UK National Cyber Security Centre 2023; Europol 2024a described the cybercrime as a service economy in which skills are rented or bought, bundled, and resold. A broad survey of the "cyber attack business" by Huang, Siegel, and Madnick Huang, Siegel, and Madnick 2018 described this as a value chain with distinct products, sellers, and buyers.

We can see the actual scale of this commercialization in the data. When van Wegberg et al. Wegberg et al. 2018 analyzed transactions on darknet marketplaces, they found that buyers purchase these commoditized cybercrime services in high volumes—but mostly as cheap, individual components to feed into larger operations, rather than as complete, "crime-in-a-box" solutions .

Figure 1. The cybercrime-as-a-service supply chain diagram. Specialized supply (malware, exploits, access) is assembled by RaaS operators, executed by affiliates against victims, and monetized through data brokers and money launderers. A shared enabling infrastructure of anonymity networks, cryptocurrency, and resilient hosting supports every step and constitutes a cross-cutting target for defenders

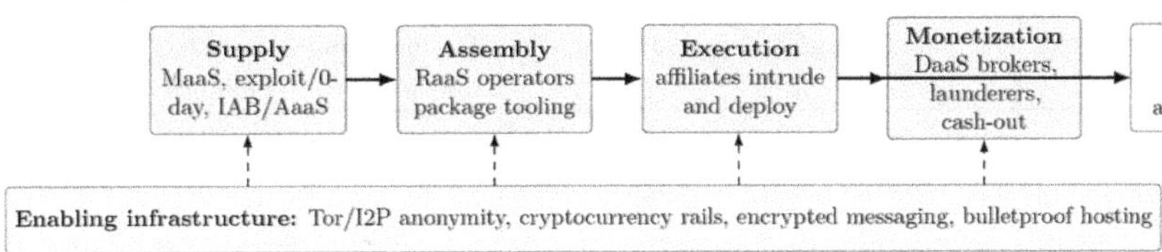

Figure 1 depicts the framework that organizes the rest of this chapter, read from left to right. Specialize *supply* package malware, exploits, and then victim access is *assembled* by operator into a usable campaign, then an affiliate *executes* it against the victim. Finally, the transaction gets *monetized* through data sale and laundering. A cross-cutting layer, shown in Figure 4.1, enables the transition between the various stages of the framework. The framework is useful precisely as it exposes real options: a defender can raise the cost of supply, interfere with assembly operator, harden the target against execution, degrade monetization, or attack the common infrastructure. Throughout this chapter, we return to these stages.

Table 4.2 compares the empirical studies that this chapter relies on. These empirical studies share a consistent story with one important tension. They all agree that the underground economy is durable: maker and forums absorb takedowns and reconstitute themselves as explained in Soska and Christin 2015, payment flows can be followed but are deliberately obscured as explained in Oosthoek, Cable, and Smaragdakis 2022, and small set of actors responsible for disproportionate share of activity as mentioned in Pastrana et al. 2018. The tension concerns leverage. Commoditization makes the components of crime cheap and abundant as shown in this study Wegberg et al. 2018, which seems to favor the attacker. Additionally, the same studies show that human coordination and reputation remain indispensable, which is exactly where defenders retain leverage. Much of the rest of this chapter can be read as an attempt to locate and exploit that leverage.

3 RANSOMWARE ECOSYSTEM AND LIFECYCLE

Ransomware has evolved from simple lock screen demanding a flat fee into a highly organized and complex illicit business. Early versions of ransomware asked for flat rate with no or little interactions with victims. Nowadays, ransomware are far more complicated, attackers study their victims' profile beforehand, customize their malicious payload, negotiate in real time, and routinely weaponize stolen data through public leaks. Major cybersecurity agencies like CISA, the FBI, and the NCSC describe criminal groups such as LockBit and RansomHub as Ransomware-as-a-Service (RaaS) organizations with developers, affiliate network, support portals, corporate bylaws, and profit-sharing scheme CISA, FBI, and partners 2023; CISA, FBI, MS-ISAC, and partners 2024; UK National Cyber Security Centre 2023.

Table 2. Synthesis of selected empirical studies of the underground economy, showing focus, evidence base, and the finding most relevant to this chapter

Study	Focus / evidence	Finding relevant to this chapter
Christin (2013)	Silk Road marketplace measurement	Anonymous markets sustain large, persistent trade volumes with functioning reputation systems
Soska & Christin (2015)	Longitudinal study of many markets	The marketplace ecosystem survives individual takedowns; sellers migrate and rebuild
van Wegberg et al. (2018)	Commoditization on anonymous markets	Cybercrime services are bought as cheap components, not turnkey crime; coordination still required
Pastrana et al. (2018)	Actor analysis in a large forum	A small minority of actors drive most activity; pathways into serious offending are identifiable

continued on following page

Table 2. Continued

Study	Focus / evidence	Finding relevant to this chapter
Oosthoek et al. (2022)	On-chain ransomware payments	Payment flows are traceable in principle but obscured by mixing and cash-out services
Meurs et al. (2025)	Ransom negotiation transcripts	Outcomes depend on signaling, victim revenue, and backups, not only on technical damage
Sarabi et al. (2025)	Ten-year ransomware dataset	Double extortion became the defining feature of the modern ransomware era

Figure 2. Lifecycle of a darknet-enabled ransomware attack

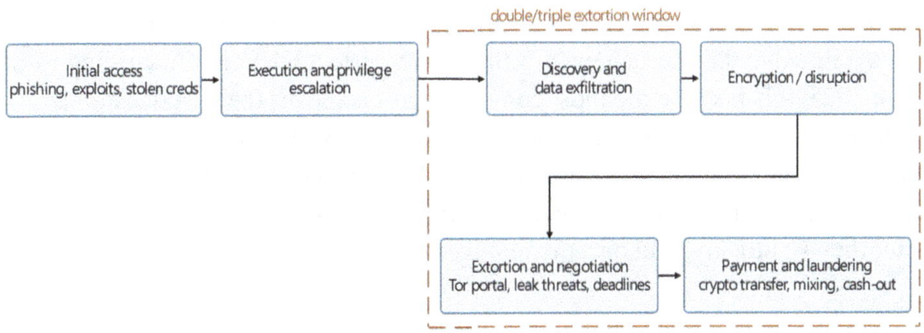

Figure 2 depicts the lifecycle of ransomware attack over the darknet. As shown in the figure, an attacker starts with a traditional malicious attack such as phishing email where an employee clicks on a malicious link, then a weak password is exposed or a vulnerability is exploited. An attack usually begins in an ordinary way: an employee clicks a phishing link, a weak password is exposed, or an internet-facing vulnerability is exploited. Verizon Verizon 2025 reported increasing activities in vulnerability exploitation and the persistent abuse of resource-constraint devices and VPNs as entry points. Once attackers are inside, they do not rush to encrypt or lock the vulnerable device or system. They first establish control, privilege escalation, and move beyond one device to other devices on the network. They then explore the hosting environment to detect what is valuable and where sensitive data is stored. Many attacks nowadays copy confidential data so that it can be used later as an additional leverage. This phenomenon of double extortion became a defining feature of modern attacks as reported in Sarabi et al. Sarabi et al. 2025 study.

After the attackers establish the groundwork, they move to the more sever stage of encrypting files, disrupting running services, and stalling operations. Next, extortion is handled via anonymous darknet portals in which operators communicate with the victim in real time, issue threats, blackmailing them, ask for ransomware amount, and set deadlines. This is why modern and sophisticated ransomware are not only locking files and systems, it is also about stolen data and the fear of public shaming. If a victim decides to pay, the funds are usually sent in cryptocurrency, after that the attacker obscure the trail via laundering techniques designed to harden tracing.

The speed of these activities is a defensive parameter. The interval between the initial compromise and the file encryption stage, commonly known as dwell time, is the time in which detection and incident response can change the outcome. As reported by Verizon Verizon 2025, this time, though shrinking as attackers automate and use AI to speed the process and decrease the dwell time, often remain enough to alert defender to intervene.

Mapping this lifecycle into a cyber attack kill chain makes the defense strategy concrete. For example, phishing and initial exploitation align with the "delivery" phase. Privilege escalation and lateral movement represent "installation" and C2 "command-and-control". Finally, the exfiltration and file encryption mark the "actions and objectives". This breakdown is crucial for defenders to look at the whole picture at all stages, rather than just scrambling to react during the final stage which is the most destructive stage.

It is iportant to be precise about how we define different types of extortion, as these terms are often thrown around loosely.

- *Single extortion* relies mainly on encryption where the attacker locks the victim out of their own network or device and sells back the access.
- *Double extortion* to increase the risk of stealing data and threatening to leak it. This means the victim faces a massive data breach even if they have perfect backups. According to Sarabi et al. Sarabi et al. 2025, this became the most common approach over the past decade.
- *Triple extortion* makes even more pressure, targeting the victim with denial-of-service (DDoS) attacks or directly harassing their customers, business partners, and the media.
- *fourth extortion* pattern involves coming back for seconds—hitting a victim with repeated demands after they've already paid once, explicitly exploiting their proven willingness to hand over cash.

The RaaS model separates malware development from campaign execution. Developers focus on maintaining the codebase and managing the payment infrastructure, while affiliates handle the hands-on intrusions in exchange of a negotiable share. This division of labor is highly intentional. By separating the two roles, it lowers the barrier for newcomers to join the illicit ecosystem and making the law enforcement disruption incredibly difficult, since the visible attack is just only one layer of a complex business model as discussed in CISA, FBI, and partners 2023; Meurs et al. 2025; Oosthoek, Cable, and Smaragdakis 2022.

Comparing between the leading operations clarifies how this model works and varies in practice. As reported in the joint CISA advisory, LockBit launched a highly streamlined affiliate program with a polished portal, clear rules, and an aggressive leak-site strategy, making it one of the market's most prolific ransomware bundle until law enforcements stopped it in 2024 CISA, FBI, and partners 2023; Europol 2024b. As another example of how quickly the market absorbs disruption and bounce back, RansomHub offered displaced affiliates favorable revenue split to attract experienced operators CISA, FBI, MS-ISAC, and partners 2024. The important point here is the affiliates are the main resources these brands are competing for, not the binary malicious payload. This fact opens up a critical defensive strategy: any security measure that drives up an affiliate's operating costs or breaks their trust in a brand hits the ecosystem precisely where it hurts the most, targeting the one link in the chain the operators cannot easily replace.

The scalability of this model is fulled by the fact that the supply of victims has become highly specialized. Initial access brokers have essentially turned the first stage of the attack lifecycle into a regular marketplace; instead of every affiliate struggling to find their own way in the market, ready-made foothold are acquired in advance and cataloged by industry and access level and sold on demand as explained in Europol 2024a; UK National Cyber Security Centre 2023. Decoupling the initial intrusion from the actual extortion greatly compress the timeline from purchase to encryption. It allows affiliates to operate at volume because they can simply outsource the slowest and least certain part of attack, such as gaining entry to a system. For defenders, the silver lining is that when access to a network is put up for sale, it serves as an early and highly actionable flag. This is why monitoring for credential exposure and access-broker activities take center stage in the threat intelligence framework discussed in Section 4.6.

Negotiation also became more sophisticated process in this ecosystem. The empirical study of Meurs et al. Meurs et al. 2025 showed that ransom outcomes are evaluated not only by technical damage but also by signaling, the victim's revenue, the quality of the victim's backup, and he duration of the active negotiation itself. Game-theoretic models support of ransomware reached the conclusion that interaction is a bargaining game under asymmetric information, the attacker's optimal demand and the victim's optimal response depend on commitment, reputation of "honoring" decryption and the credibility of threats E. Cartwright, Hernandez Castro, and A. Cartwright 2019.

Oosthoek et al. Oosthoek, Cable, and Smaragdakis 2022 studied the ransomware payments and showed that realized revenue is concentrated and laundering-dependent. The dynamic pricing system where attackers offer selective discount, use deadlines as means of pressure, and rely on reputation for predictable behavior. Triple extortion takes this pressure by adding denial-of-service attacks, direct contact with customers or journalists, or repeated demands after an initial payment.

The victim's decision to pay can also be modeled rather than moralized. A victim evaluates the ransom against the expected cost of restoration, the probability that paying reach a working decryptor, and the residual risk that stolen data will be leaked regardless of payment. The game-theoretic literature shows that this calculus is unstable: paying funds future attacks and signals a willingness to pay again, yet refusing may be locally irrational for a single victim facing existential downtime E. Cartwright, Hernandez Castro, and A. Cartwright 2019. This is a collective-action problem, which is one reason that purely victim-level advice such as "never pay" has limited traction without population-level measures—mandatory incident reporting, sanctions on payment facilitators, and sustained support for resilient backups. We return to the empirical form of this question in Section 4.7.

4 ILLICIT SERVICE ECOSYSTEMS BEYOND RANSOMWARE

Ransomware got its peak because it is part of a wider underground service stack, and each layer of that stack is a distinct market with its own product, customer, and pricing logic. Next, we will define each underground service and show how it is different from one another to make it clear for the readers.

- **Malware-as-a-Service (MaaS)** this service sells packaged malware families such as loaders, stealers, or crypters together with updates and customer support. The product is the tool, and it is delivered as a commercial software, often on a subscription or licensing basis.
- **Access-as-a-Service (AaaS)** and **initial-access brokers (IABs)** sell entry to specific victim organizations. The product is the foothold itself including valid credentials, RDP or VPN access, or a compromised device and it is typically priced by privilege level, sector, and the victim's size or revenue.
- **Exploit and zero-day trade** this service sells vulnerabilities, proof-of-concept code, or turnkey exploit kits. A turnkey exploit kit is an all-in-one toolkit that lets an operator with minimal skill

attack a website or application. This market is distinguished by scarcity and severe information asymmetry, since the value of an exploit collapses once it is patched or widely known.

- **DDoS-for-hire** denial-of-service is a well-known security vulnerability that takes down a service or a server. This service involves renting access to a botnet to disrupt a website, server, or network for a short period. Its defining feature is low skill on the buyer's side: disruption is outsourced entirely.
- **Data-as-a-Service (DaaS)** monetizes the output of breaches and leaks such as credentials, payment cards, health records, classified information, or corporate documents through per-record sales or bundles. The same dataset can be repackaged and resold many times, which is what makes it a service rather than a one-off sale Europol 2025b; Europol 2025a; Chainalysis 2025.

The crime-script analysis of stolen-data markets by Hutchings and Holt Hutchings and Holt 2015 is really an eye-opening. It shows that these markets do not just rely on one-off deals rather they operate like repeatable scripts with well defined phases: acquisition, advertisement, transaction, and payments. It is this predictability and repeatability that keeps stolen data flow smoothly into downstream crimes.

As an example to show that different layers interlock rather than operating in isolated silos. Imagine an initial access broker puts up an advertisement for domain-administrator access to mid-sized manufacturer, pricing the listing based on the company's revenue and the level of privilege they have managed to sang. A ransomware affiliate buys that malicious access, deploys a payload rented from RaaS operator under a profit-sharing agreement, and exfiltrates sensitive files before starting the file encryption process. After that, the stolen files are handed off to a DaaS vendor to be sold or auctione, while the ransomware gets routed via a mixer and cross-chain swap before an over0the-counter broker finally converts it into cold, hard cash.

In this scenario, no single participant conducted the entire crime from start to finish. However, the victim experienced it as a one seamless coherent attack. This example shows an important point that should be taken into defenders' considerations that is a security strategy that only focuses on stopping the actual encryption event alone leaves the entire surrounding ecosystem completely untouched and perfectly ready to supply the next affiliate.

These market are competitive and this competition shapes behavior in ways defenders can exploit. Similar to legitimate markets, vendors advertise their uptime, customer support quality, and successful delivery gets rated, buyers leave reviews, and operators publish clear rules to attract more talents. However, the exact same reputation dynamics that make these markets efficient also make them incredibly breakable. Trust is slow to build and lightning-fast to destroy. When law enforcement actions publicly shatter a brand's reliability; whether by seizing its infrastructure, unmasking its operators, or releasing free decryptors; they are attacking this reputational capital directly. While resilience literature cautions that displaced actors will eventually migrate and rebuild elsewhere Soska and Christin 2015, the sheer friction of having to rebuild that trust from scratch imposes a heavy, undeniable cost on their operations, even if it is temporary Europol 2024b.

Resilient hosting sits beneath all layers with "bulletproof" providers that ignore takedown requests, supplying the infrastructure that marketplaces, leak sites, and command-and-control servers depend on. Treating hosting as a service is analytically vital because it represents a shared dependency where the same provider serves multiple and unrelated operations. As shown in Figure 4.1, taking down a single hosting provider can collapse multiple criminal brands rather than just the one under active investigation.

Table 4.3 summarizes these illicit service types and the operational characteristic that distin-guishes each one, so that the categories are not mixed.

One of the reasons that makes this supply chain powerful is its shared operations. Offers are advertised, compared reviewed, negotiated, bundled, and moved to a new platform whenever one is taking down. Europol IOCTA Europol 2025b emphasized that stolen data is the fuel of multiple downstream crimes, from fraud to account takeover to ransomware. Therefore the defensive strategies should not treat these services as independent problems. They are staged of the same production chain shown in Figure 4.1, and a disruption that ignores this supply chain of access and data will be re-supplied.

5 TECHNOLOGIES ENABLING DARKNET CYBERCRIME

There are several techniques utilized in the ecosystem to lower the cost and reduce the damage. The first is the anonymous communication which reduces the risk of exposure and accountability. The Tor network is the main media for the anonymous communication. Tor network is a free and open source overlay network designed for anonymous communication through routing the traffic using a worldwide set of volunteer relays so that the source and destination IP addresses and locations are concealed from any single node. However, anonymity is not absolute as researchers on Tor hidden services has demonstrated some practical ways to deanonymized some hidden services and communications under specific conditions Biryukov, Pustogarov, and Weinmann 2013, which is why operators use additional layer of protections such commercial VPN on top of Tor Europol 2024a; UK National Cyber Security Centre 2023. The persistence of this cat-and-mouse dynamic provides an interesting area of future research.

Table 3. Classification of darknet illicit services by product, revenue logic, and the operational characteristic that distinguishes each one

Service type	Revenue logic	Distinguishing operational characteristic
MaaS	Subscription, licensing, support tiers	Commodity malware delivered like software products
RaaS	Affiliate commission and profit sharing	Centralized codebase with decentralized execution
AaaS / IAB sales	One-time access sale or auction	Victim access priced by privilege, sector, and size
Exploit and zero-day trade	Premium sale, brokered deal, escrow	Scarcity-driven market with high information asymmetry
DDoS-for-hire	Short rental periods	Low-skill customers can outsource disruption
Data-as-a-Service	Per-record sale, bundle pricing	Breach outputs continuously repackaged and resold

The anonymity story in this ecosystem is not as simple as "use Tor". Operators combine Tor with security practices to hide their communications and their identity by using dedicated infrastructure and disciplined communication. Relying only on the anonymity is easily undone by behavioral mistakes, and several high-profile takedowns detected by such mistakes rather than any cryptographic break. Alternative network such as I2P and invitation-only forums provide additional insulation, and the steady migration of some activity to encrypted messaging platforms reflect a search for usability rather than a rejection of anonymity Ricaldi et al. 2025. For researchers, the practical anonymity of a given service is therefore an empirical question about the whole sociotechnical system, not a property of the network in isolation. The I2P (Invisible Internet Project) is a decentralized peer-to-peer anonymity network. It creates a private, encrypted environment where users can browse websites, send emails, and share files without revealing their IP address or physical location. Unlike Tor which relies on hiding the message while browsing the internet, I2P is designed from the ground up as a self-contained ecosystem for hosting and accessing hidden services.

The second enabling technology is the cryptocurrency, which lowers the cost of moving and hiding the money transactions. Cryptocurrency lies at the heart of this ecosystem and Bitcoin is the most used cryptocurrency. Privacy-enhancing techniques—such as mixers, peel chains, cross-chain swaps, and over-the-counter cash-out channels—significantly complicate tracing and seizure efforts as discussed in Oosthoek, Cable, and Smaragdakis 2022; Chainalysis 2025.

Crucially, since the underlying ledger is public, funds are traceable in principle; obfuscation services exist precisely to break the link between a traceable payment and an identifiable person at the point of cash-out. Figure 3 depicts this cryptocurrency-based financial flow.

Figure 3. Cryptocurrency-based financial flow in darknet cybercrime ecosystems

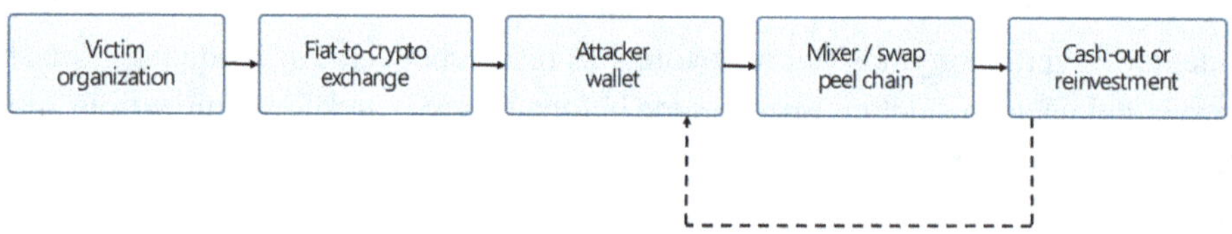

The financial layer in this illicit ecosystem is also evolving to hide the traces and tracks. As blockchain analytics matured, some actors shifted toward privacy-focused assets like Monero, which is designed to be private and untraceable using a decentralized blockchain-based cryptocurrency technology as discussed in Chainalysis 2025; Oosthoek, Cable, and Smaragdakis 2022. However, adoption of these techniques are not even since liquidity, exchange support, and counterpart familiarity still favor Bitcoin at the point of cash-out where value re-enter the regulated economy and it is most exposed. This vulnerability explains why compliance mechanisms like sanctions and Know-Your-Customer (KYC) enforcement at exchanges yield a disruptive impact far greater than their technical simplicity suggests.

The third enabling technology is automation, and especially in the artificial intelligence (AI) era, which lowers the cost of labor drastically. Europol's 2025 SOCTA Europol 2025a warns that AI can amplify criminal activities by scaling phishing, fraud, impersonation, ransomware, and the preparation of cyberattack. On the other hand, OpenAI's threat disruption report OpenAI 2025 documents the use of generative AI tools for conducting cybersecurity and social engineering attacks, while at the same time these tools did not produce, on the reported cases, novel offensive capabilities on their own. These two sources confirm the widespread of using AI for cybercriminal conducts carried out by less-skilled operators.

One concrete mechanism worth mentioning here is the use of "vibe coding" to develop malware. Vibe coding is a development style in which a person determines his/her intention and an AI tool writes the code. Vibe coding helps low-skilled actors to create and modify malicious code. However, skilled actors are needed to produce large-scale cybercrime as it requires deployment, testing, integration, and operational know-how skills that current AI tools, especially free version, do not offer. AI shifted the bottleneck from writing code to coordinating an operation.

AI is a new form of automation to ecosystems that have been automated for years. Phishing kits template the construction of convincing and appealing attacks, building customized payloads from configuration screens, and off-the-shelf command-and-control frameworks are already popular and manage compromise hosts at scale. The importance of AI is that it extends and expand the automation from the mechanical parts of the attack to its linguistic and cognitive parts such as writing persuasive phishing email, designing a social engineering attack, or translating across languages. These tasks previously required skilled actors. Having said that, AI does not introduce new category of threat so much as it erode the last skill barriers that limited who could participate Wegberg et al. 2018; Huang, Siegel, and Madnick 2018.

6 DETECTION, MITIGATION, AND DISRUPTION STRATEGIES

As explained earlier, darknet-based cybercrime is an ecosystem rather than a single action, therefore, defense must also be layered, with each layer mapped to a stage of the supply chain in Figure 4.1. Table 4.4 shows the layers, the typical measures within each layer, and the value each layer is expected to deliver. Active monitoring of the darknet can provide advance warning for cases such as leaked credentials, access-for-sale advertisements, new ransomware variants, and emerging affiliate partnerships, before critical damage occurs. Additionally, effective threat-intelligence programs combine automated collection with human review, since darknet data is huge and noisy without careful analysis World Economic Forum 2024; Hughes, Collier, and Hutchings 2024.

Table 4. Layered defenses against darknet-enabled cybercrime: typical measures and the value expected at each layer. Read with Figure 1, the layers move from intelligence on supply through hardening of execution to disruption of monetization

Defensive layer	Typical measures	Expected value
Threat intelligence	Forum monitoring, leak-site tracking, credential-exposure alerts	Earlier visibility into targeting and access sales
Hardening and prevention	MFA, patching, segmentation, privileged-access controls, offline backups	Reduced initial compromise and lower blast radius
Detection and response	Endpoint Detection and Response (EDR) / Extended Detection and Response (XDR), anomaly detection, playbooks, containment rehearsals	Faster isolation and reduced dwell time
Forensics and recovery	Evidence preservation, log retention, backup validation, legal coordination	Better attribution and cleaner restoration
Ecosystem disruption	Wallet tracing, infrastructure seizure, sanctions screening, takedowns	Higher attacker cost and weaker criminal trust

Figure 4. A cyber threat-intelligence (CTI) workflow against darknet cybercrime, structured as a feedback loop. Raw signals are collected, processed, and analyzed into prioritized intelligence, disseminated to defenders, and converted into action; the resulting gaps feed new collection requirements back into the loop

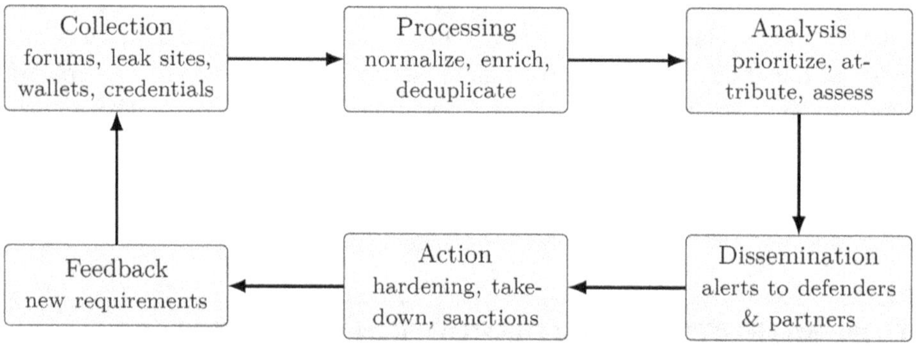

Figure 4 depicts a feedback loop cyber-threat intelligence workflow, this figure expand the first row of the Table 4.4 into an operational workflow. First, row data are collected from various sources including forums, leak sites, wallet activity, and credential dumps. Then, they are processed and cleaned, next, the data gets analyzed to extract more useful information. The results are disseminated to the retentive defenders and partners with actions to be taken such as hardening, takedown, or sanctions screening. The feedback from the taken actions feedback to the collection step of the cycle. Presenting the threat intelligence as a feedback loop rather than a feed clarifies why monitoring alone is not enough and intelligence useful only when is combined with a feedback from taken actions.

It is important to distinguish the levels at which intelligence is consumed, as a single feed rarely serves every audience. *Strategic* intelligence informs executives and policymakers of any trends and risks. For example, this shift toward double extortion or the targeting of managed service providers. Also, *Operational* intelligence informs defenders about specific active campaigns, actors, and tooling, allowing them to prepare for any anticipated cyber attack. Moreover, *Tactical* intelligence provides the concrete indicators such as malicious infrastructure, file hashes, leaked-credential lists, that feed directly into controls. Many programs fail not because they collect too little but because they deliver tactical indicators to strategic readers and vice versa; matching the level of the intelligence to the level of the decision is actually what makes the workflow in Figure 4.4 effective.

Operationalizing these layers further depends on the existence of shared vocabularies. Defenders increasingly map observed behaviors to common frameworks. For example, adversary techniques to MITRE ATT&CK framework, a globally accessible, free knowledge base that documents real-world cyber adversary behavior, or defensive countermeasures to catalogs like MITRE D3FEND, a catalog of defensive cybersecurity techniques. This ensures intelligence is mutually intelligible and coverage gaps are visible. The value of this standardization extends beyond mere tidiness: it enables the dispersed feedback loop illustrated in Figure 4.4 to function across organizational boundaries.

At the organizational level, preventive measures remain decisive. CISA, ENISA, and Verizon all agree on known but effective set of defensive measure including multifactor authentication, rapid patching, network segmentation, and least-privilege security access control, and continuous offline backup Verizon 2025; ENISA 2024b; CISA, FBI, MS-ISAC, and partners 2024. These measures fall into the "Hardening and prevention" layer of shown in Table 4.4 and they directly increase the cost of execution stage of the supply chain. Once an incident occurs, digital forensics becomes essential, not only to restore operations but also to determine weather data was exfiltrated (leaked and transferred to another location), and weather account were compromised, and more dangerously weather permanent backdoors were left behind. Finally, the value of continuous backup is well motivated in the Meurs et al. 2025 study which shows that victims with validated offline backup negotiate from a far stronger position than those without validated backups.

The final layer shown in Table 4.4 is the ecosystem disruption, it works best when it targets the chain rather than the payload. The 2024 action against LockBit showed that a well-designed operation against infrastructure, leak sites, affiliates, and payment channels can damage the whole dominant brand Europol 2024b; World Economic Forum 2024. The effect is partly psychological: by seizing infrastructure and exposing the operators, such actions weaken the trust among criminals that the ecosystem relies on, which is the same trust we identified as the scarce resource in Section 4.2. However, enforcement remains difficult, because criminal actors are geographically distributed, technically adaptable, and quick to rebrand, as the longitudinal evidence on market resilience predicts Soska and Christin 2015.

Two main factors that determine whether the layered defense works in practice. The first one is measurement: layers should be evaluated against well-known operational metrics and KPIs such as dwell time, mean time to detect, mean time to respond, and the proportion of incidents caught before encryption, rather than against the mere presence of controls. Without such KPIs, defensive investment is guided by assumption rather than evidence. The second one is a collective defense, since the threat is an ecosystem, no single organization defense might be enough to take down the ecosystem and hence a need for collective effort. Organizations and governments need to collaborate together in different ways including information sharing, incident analysis and responses dissemination which the World Economic Forum advocates for World Economic Forum 2024. Doing such collective behavior converts isolated observations into ecosystem-level visibility. Collective defense is, in effect, the defensive analogue of the criminal coordination that makes the attacks possible in the first place, and the side that coordinates better tends to prevail.

7 OPEN PROBLEMS AND RESEARCH DIRECTIONS

Figure 5. Future landscape of AI-driven and decentralized cybercrime ecosystems in the darknet

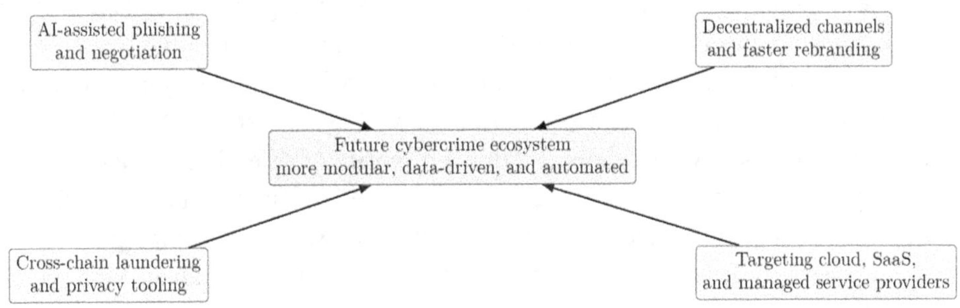

This section answers our third research question and closes this chapter with future directions inspired form the gap identified earlier and discussed in the research work.

Measuring the coordination layer. The finding presented in Section 4.2 that is the components of cybercrime are cheap but coordination is scarce. However, most research studies focus on the market payments rather than the affiliate relationships and the dynamic trust model Wegberg et al. 2018; Pastrana et al. 2018. A productive future direction is a longitudinal measurement of affiliate mobility, how operators move between brands after takedowns, which may test weather a disruption increases coordination costs or merely reshuffle personnel.

Quantifying the effectiveness of disruption. The LockBit case is widely cited as a success, but evidences for "how much" and for "how long" takedowns degrade an illicit ecosystem is very limited. Literature warns that markets reconstruct themselves as discussed in Soska and Christin 2015 and Europol 2024b. More detailed and accurate disruption evaluation such as measuring victim counts, payment volumes, and rebranding intervals before and after intervention, would convert a story into evidence and help prioritize scarce enforcement resources.

Economics of negotiation and payment. The negotiation and game-theoretic studies offer complementary models, but they have not been validated against large transcript and datasets as mentioned in Meurs et al. (2025), Cartwright et al. (2019), and Oosthoek et al. (2022). As a future direction, integrating negotiation model with payment tracing would help answer a practically important question that is what conditions does refusing to pay change attacker behavior at the population level rather than at an individual level. A similar question might be asked as what conditions does investing in backup change attacker behavior also at the population level.

The actual effect of AI on criminal productivity. Current claims about AI's impact relies heavily on published threat and incident reports Europol 2025a; OpenAI 2025. As a future avenue, controlled and ethically bounded studies to measure the exact degree to which AI accelerates specific attacker tasks as well as where it fails to help are needed to replace the speculation with calibrated estimate.

Anonymity, attribution, and the limits of tracing. The tension between traceable ledgers and deanonymizable services on one side, and the ever-improving obfuscation techniques on the other side, is an important topic Biryukov, Pustogarov, and Weinmann 2013; Oosthoek, Cable, and Smaragdakis 2022. Research studies that benchmarks attribution and tracking techniques against current mixing and cross-chain methods would clarify where the practical limits of monetization stage disruption now lie.

Shared data and reproducibility. Finally, the field's is limited by fragmented private data. The large datasets that have advanced the field Sarabi et al. 2025; Soska and Christin 2015 show the value of curated shareable resources. Creating a governed privacy-preserving dataset and common evaluation benchmarks for darknet cybercrimes research is an effort that connect academia, industry, and law enforcement that might be the single most consequential enabler of the directions mentioned above.

Human factors and deterrence pathways. Studies show Pastrana et al. 2018; Maimon and Louderback 2019 that (1) actor-level evidence suggest that a minority of offenders implement most activity and that (2) pathways into serious offending are at least partly identifiable. This highlight social rather than technical future direction for evaluating interventions like awareness campaigns, sentencing signals, and diversion programs designed to deter individuals before they specialize. More precisely, such research needs to investigate the effectiveness of such programs on reducing recruitment into the critical coordination roles identified throughout this chapter as ecosystem bottlenecks. Because these roles are scarce, even small reductions in their supply could have a big effect.

These research directions can be investigated alone or can be combined together, however, the findings should be compared and combined rather than accumulated in isolation. We do not claim that any single research will resolve the threat, we claim that organizing research around intervention points is the most credible path to cumulative progress.

8 CONCLUSION

This chapter discussed the fact that darknet-based cybercrimes should be treated as an ecosystem rather than a series of individual attacks. Ransomware has become the most prominent cybercrime in this ecosystem as it integrates the necessary components of a successful operation. Ransomware attacks involves repeatable intrusion, extortion, real-time negotiation, and cryptocurrency-based money laundering. Viewing that process as a criminal supply chain, as this chapter has argued, reframes ransomware from a malware problem into a coordination problem, and it exposes the specific stages and phases at which defenders can intervene.

For practitioners, the main takeaway is to widen their view about this illicit ecosystem. End-point protection remains vital and same thing for continuous monitoring of leaked credentials, tracking initial access brokers, rehearsing recovery procedures, tracing wallets, and coordinating internationally. Each of these correspond to a distinct stage of the supply chain discussed in this chapter. For researchers and policymakers, they need to work together to produce better and more shareable data, stronger attribution, evidence-based evaluation of disruption, and a sober understanding of how AI changes criminal productivity. The darknet does not create cybercrime, it provides the industrial structure that lets cybercrime scale. Demolishing that structure, stage by stage, is the work this chapter has tried to organize and explain in a clear way while using prior research in this field.

REFERENCES

Al-rimy, B. A. S., Maarof, M. A., & Shaid, S. Z. M. (2018). Ransomware threat success factors, taxonomy, and countermeasures: A survey and research directions. *Computers & Security, 74*, 144–166. DOI: 10.1016/j.cose.2018.01.001

Anderson, R., Barton, C., Bölme, R., Clayton, R., Ganán, C., Grasso, T., ... Vasek, M. (2019). *Measuring the changing cost of cybercrime.*

Biryukov, A., Pustogarov, I., & Weinmann, R.-P. (2013). Trawling for Tor hidden services: Detection, measurement, deanonymization. In *Proceedings of the IEEE Symposium on Security and Privacy* (pp. 80–94). DOI: 10.1109/SP.2013.15

Cartwright, E., Hernandez Castro, J., & Cartwright, A. (2019). To pay or not: Game theoretic models of ransomware. *Journal of Cybersecurity, 5*(1), tyz009. Advance online publication. DOI: 10.1093/cybsec/tyz009

Chainalysis. (2025). *2025 crypto crime report.* Chainalysis.

Chainalysis. (2026, February 26). *Crypto ransomware: 2026 crypto crime report.* Chainalysis Blog.

Christin, N. (2013). Traveling the Silk Road: A measurement analysis of a large anonymous online marketplace. In *Proceedings of the 22nd International Conference on World Wide Web* (pp. 213–224). DOI: 10.1145/2488388.2488408

Connolly, L. Y., & Wall, D. S. (2019). The rise of crypto-ransomware in a changing cybercrime landscape: Taxonomising countermeasures. *Computers & Security, 87*, 101568. Advance online publication. DOI: 10.1016/j.cose.2019.101568

Cybersecurity and Infrastructure Security Agency, Federal Bureau of Investigation, & Partners. (2023). *StopRansomware: LockBit 3.0.* U.S. Cybersecurity and Infrastructure Security Agency.

Cybersecurity and Infrastructure Security Agency, Federal Bureau of Investigation. MS-ISAC, & Partners. (2024). *StopRansomware: RansomHub ransomware.* U.S. Cybersecurity and Infrastructure Security Agency.

European Union Agency for Cybersecurity. (2024a). *2024 report on the state of cybersecurity in the Union.*

European Union Agency for Cybersecurity. (2024b). *ENISA threat landscape 2024.*

Europol. (2024a). *Internet organised crime threat assessment (IOCTA) 2024.*

Europol. (2024b, February 20). *Law enforcement disrupt world's biggest ransomware operation.*

Europol. (2025a). *EU serious and organised crime threat assessment (EU-SOCTA) 2025: The changing DNA of serious and organised crime.*

Europol. (2025b). *Steal, deal and repeat: IOCTA 2025.*

Huang, K., Siegel, M., & Madnick, S. (2018). Systematically understanding the cyber attack business: A survey. *ACM Computing Surveys, 51*(4), 70. Advance online publication. DOI: 10.1145/3199674

Hughes, J., Collier, B., & Hutchings, A. (2024). The art of cybercrime community research. *Communications of the ACM.*

Hutchings, A., & Holt, T. J. (2015). A crime script analysis of the online stolen data market. *British Journal of Criminology, 55*(3), 596–614. DOI: 10.1093/bjc/azu106

Kharraz, A., Arshad, S., Mulliner, C., Robertson, W., & Kirda, E. (2015). Cutting the Gordian knot: A look under the hood of ransomware attacks. In *Detection of Intrusions and Malware, and Vulnerability Assessment* (Vol. 9148, pp. 3–24). Springer. DOI: 10.1007/978-3-319-20550-2_1

Maimon, D., & Louderback, E. R. (2019). Cyber-dependent crimes: An interdisciplinary review. *Annual Review of Criminology, 2*(1), 191–216. DOI: 10.1146/annurev-criminol-032317-092057

Meurs, T., ... (2025). *An empirical study of the six stages of ransomware negotiation* (Tinbergen Institute Discussion Paper No. 25-052). Tinbergen Institute.

Motoyama, M., McCoy, D., Levchenko, K., Savage, S., & Voelker, G. M. (2011). An analysis of underground forums. In *Proceedings of the 2011 ACM SIGCOMM Internet Measurement Conference* (pp. 71–80). DOI: 10.1145/2068816.2068824

National Cyber Security Centre. (2023). *Ransomware, extortion and the cyber crime ecosystem* (White paper).

Oosthoek, K., Cable, J., & Smaragdakis, G. (2022). Investigating the ransomware payments economy. *Communications of the ACM, 65*(7), 38–41. DOI: 10.1145/3524102

OpenAI. (2025). *Disrupting malicious uses of AI: June 2025* (Threat Intelligence Report).

Pastrana, S., Thomas, D. R., Hutchings, A., Clayton, R., & Beresford, A. R. (2018). CrimeBB: Enabling cybercrime research on underground forums at scale. In *Proceedings of the 2018 World Wide Web Conference*. DOI: 10.1145/3178876.3186178

Ricaldi, R., Marjanov, T., Allodi, L., & Hutchings, A. (2025, November). Uncovering the Trust Signals Supporting Telegram's Cybercrime Economy. In *2025 APWG Symposium on Electronic Crime Research (eCrime)* (pp. 1-17). IEEE. DOI: 10.1109/eCrime66972.2025.11327769

Sarabi, A., Huang, Z., Wang, C., Karir, T., & Liu, M. (2025). The Ransomware Decade: The Creation of a {Fine-Grained} Dataset and a Longitudinal Study. In *34th USENIX Security Symposium (USENIX Security 25)* (pp. 4799-4818).

Soska, K., & Christin, N. (2015). Measuring the longitudinal evolution of the online anonymous marketplace ecosystem. In *Proceedings of the 24th USENIX Security Symposium* (pp. 33–48).

Van Wegberg, R., Oerlemans, J.-J., & Van Deventer, O. (2018). Plug and prey? Measuring the commoditization of cybercrime via online anonymous markets. In *Proceedings of the 27th USENIX Security Symposium* (pp. 1009–1026).

Verizon Business. (2025). *2025 data breach investigations report.*

World Economic Forum. (2024). *Disrupting cybercrime networks: A collaboration framework.* World Economic Forum.

Chapter 7
Blockchain and Cryptocurrency Forensics for the Darknet

Ahod Alghuried
http://orcid.org/0009-0002-5681-7223
Prince Sattam Bin Abdulaziz University, Saudi Arabia

Qasem Abu Al-Haija
http://orcid.org/0000-0003-2422-0297
Jordan University of Science and Technology, Jordan

ABSTRACT

This chapter explores the role of blockchain and cryptocurrency forensics in investigating Darknet-enabled cybercrime. Cryptocurrencies such as Bitcoin and privacy-focused coins are widely used in Darknet marketplaces because they support pseudonymous transactions that complicate tracing and attribution. The chapter examines forensic techniques for blockchain analysis, including address clustering, transaction graph analysis, and heuristic-based tracing. It also explains how illicit financial flows are concealed through mixers, tumblers, and chain-hopping strategies. In addition, the chapter reviews analytics tools used by law enforcement and cybersecurity professionals to detect suspicious patterns and link wallets to entities. Challenges related to privacy-enhancing cryptocurrencies, blockchain scalability, and legal considerations are discussed. Finally, emerging threats involving decentralized finance (DeFi) and cross-chain transactions are explored to provide researchers, forensic analysts, and policymakers with insights into illicit financial activity in the Darknet ecosystem.

INTRODUCTION

Cryptocurrencies are commonly traded on Darknet marketplaces. Websites accessible through anonymity traffic obfuscation tools such as Tor have provided the infrastructure for anonymous internet-based interactions that have fostered black market sites (Soska and Christin, 2015). These markets commonly use cryptoassets like Bitcoin, Monero, and Ethereum (Amarasinghe et al., 2019; Khalilov and Levi,

DOI: 10.4018/979-8-3373-9755-9.ch007

2018). Their decentralization and ease of cross-border transferability has been used for both licit and illicit purposes (Europol, 2021).

Transactions are a key source of evidence in blockchain investigations, as all transactions on a blockchain are publicly available on an immutable ledger in a time-series format (Zhang et al., 2019). Prior work has used and characterized blockchain transaction activity and demonstrated the value of using transactions for forensic analysis, however, linking the transactions to real world identities has been more challenging (Meiklejohn et al., 2016; Gjorgjev et al., 2025).

As a result, financial forensics has become a primary activity of cybersecurity investigations (Dudani et al., 2023). Blockchain and cryptocurrency forensics consists of analyzing transaction activity to search for patterns, follow the trail of funds, and associate addresses with actors (Agarwal et al., 2024). Transactions are typically represented as graphs, where addresses are mapped as nodes and transfers as edges (Meiklejohn et al., 2016). This enables graph analysis to be used to find clusters, central entities, and to trace funds through multiple hops in a transaction graph (Huang et al., 2018). These techniques have been used to enable forensic investigations of ransomware payments and Darknet marketplaces (Paquet-Clouston et al., 2019).

However, a number of factors make forensics more challenging. Addresses only provide a pseudonymous identity (Alsalami and Zhang, 2019), and users may reuse addresses in ways that diminish the applicability of clustering heuristics (Meiklejohn et al., 2016). Privacy-preserving cryptocurrencies, such as Monero, also obfuscate transaction details through cryptographic means (Moser et al., 2018). These aspects limit the applicability of tracing techniques and hinders the direct applicability of graph-based inference, often necessitating more sophisticated analytical and investigative techniques (Amarasinghe et al., 2019).

In addition to the inherent properties of blockchains, adversaries will also use obfuscation techniques to hide illicit financial activity. Mixing services (or tumblers) aggregate inputs from multiple users and redistribute them to new addresses with lower linkability (Moser et al., 2013). Chain hopping is another method for disguising illicit activity by moving value across blockchains of varying traceability (Europol, 2021). Decentralized finance (DeFi) platforms also obfuscate activity by enabling additional transfer and conversion methods (Atlam et al., 2024; Meiklejohn et al., 2016; Khalilov and Levi, 2018).

To address these challenges, specialized tools and analytical methods have been developed, including heuristic-based address clustering, transaction graph analysis, and anomaly detection techniques (Dudani et al., 2023). Blockchain analytics is commonly combined with off-chain sources such as exchange records and Know Your Customer (KYC) data to support attribution of blockchain activity to real-world entities (Agarwal et al., 2024). Successful blockchain forensics therefore relies on a combination of on-chain analytics, external data sources, and investigative procedures.

On the other hand, there are still some limitations. First, blockchain data is getting larger in scale, and the practice of large-scale analysis is computationally demanding (Kilic et al., 2022). Second, privacy-enhancing tools have emerged and transaction information is becoming more private (Moser et al., 2018). Third, investigations often involve multiple jurisdictions, making it more difficult to obtain the relevant information in time due to legal obstacles (Europol, 2021; Igonor et al., 2025). In addition, privacy coins, DeFi and cross-chain transactions are increasingly used, further exacerbating the challenges. These trends emphasize the need for flexible, unified forensic frameworks.

The main focus of this chapter is to overview blockchain and cryptocurrency forensics on the Darknet ecosystem. In this, major attention will be given to transaction analysis, obfuscation methods, and the forensic tools that are used for cryptocurrency tracing (Soska and Christin, 2015; Moser et al., 2013;

Dudani et al., 2023). Moreover, this chapter presents an outline of the current issues, new threats, recent trends, and future directions in blockchain forensics (Atlam et al., 2024; Agarwal et al., 2024; Igonor et al., 2025). The primary contributions of this chapter are:

- Overview of blockchain systems and their use in Darknet transactions.
- Explanation of forensic analysis techniques such as transaction graph analysis and address clustering.
- Examination of obfuscation methods and their impact on transaction traceability.
- Review of tools and platforms used in cryptocurrency investigations.
- Discussion on legal, ethical, and jurisdictional challenges in blockchain forensics.
- Identification of future research directions, such as AI-driven analytics and cross-chain investigations.

The rest of this chapter is structured as follows. Section 2 presents background information about blockchain technology and cryptocurrency use. Section 3 dis-cusses blockchain data collection and preprocessing approaches used in forensic investigations. Section 4 details forensic analysis techniques. Section 5 provides obfuscation methods. Section 6 discusses existing tools and platforms. Section 7 offers case studies. Section 8 considers legal and ethical issues. Section 9 high-lights current challenges. Section 10 covers emerging trends. Lastly, Section 11 concludes the chapter.

BACKGROUND AND FOUNDATIONS

Blockchain Technology Overview

Blockchain technology is used to implement cryptocurrencies and other decentralized digital currency systems. Blockchain is a distributed digital ledger that is continually expanding as new validated transactions are added over time (Zhang et al., 2019). Data are stored in blocks that are linked to each other through cryptographic methods, and information recorded in a block cannot be changed (Gao et al., 2018; Zhao et al., 2025).

Blockchain systems are inherently decentralized and do not have a central authority or ledger (Wei et al., 2022). Rather, each node in the network has a copy of the blockchain and independently verifies transactions based on the consensus rules (Shaikh et al., 2026). This can increase fault tolerance and reduce the need for central points of failure (Gao et al., 2018; Zhang et al., 2019). Consensus mechanisms establish a common agreement on the state of the ledger (Gao et al., 2018). Bitcoin's consensus mechanism is based on Proof-of-Work (PoW), in which miners solve cryptographic puzzles to propose blocks. On the other hand, Ethereum is shifting towards a Proof-of-Stake (PoS) consensus mechanism where validators are chosen based on their stake (Shaikh et al., 2026).

These consensus models have distinct characteristics in terms of security, energy efficiency, and transaction throughput (Ahmed et al., 2022).

Forensically, the transparency of blockchain data allows investigators to access the complete transaction history with associated metadata such as timestamps, addresses, and amounts transferred (Meiklejohn et al., 2016; Atlam et al., 2024). Users, however, do not identify themselves with their real-world identities but use pseudonymous addresses generated from a public-private key pair (Khalilov and Levi, 2018; Alsalami and Zhang, 2019). Therefore, the forensic analysis often centers on the transaction structures and behavioral patterns, while attribution may necessitate further investigative methods (Dudani et al., 2023).

Cryptocurrencies in Darknet Transactions

Cryptocurrencies are a popular payment method on Darknet marketplaces due to their accessibility, global acceptance, and reduced dependence on intermediaries (Soska & Christin, 2015; Dearden & Tucker, 2023). Bitcoin is the most frequently used cryptocurrency on the Darknet, even with its limited privacy protections, due to its liquidity, high adoption, and ease of exchange (Bahamazava & Nanda, 2022; Dearden & Tucker, 2023). Bitcoin transactions are publicly visible on the blockchain, making them susceptible to forensic analysis and transaction tracing (Meiklejohn et al., 2016; Khalilov and Levi, 2018).

Privacy-focused cryptocurrencies like Monero are also commonly used on Darknet markets (Bahamazava and Nanda, 2022; Europol, 2021). Monero uses ring signatures, stealth addresses, and confidential transactions to hide participants and transaction amounts, making traditional tracing techniques less effective (Moser et al., 2018; Alsalami and Zhang, 2019).

Ethereum has also been observed in some Darknet-related activities with smart contracts and decentralized applications (Europol, 2021). While trans-actions are still public, programmable smart-contract functionality provides additional complexity, as assets can flow through decentralized exchanges and contract-based workflows (Kushwaha et al., 2022; Chen et al., 2024).

The cryptocurrency used for a service can be based on various factors such as privacy, fees, transaction speed, or fiat-currency convertibility (Bahamazava and Nanda, 2022; Europol, 2021). Adversaries can also switch cryptocurrencies to trade-off anonymity and functionality. These fragmented and mixed transaction trails are harder to trace and cluster (Europol, 2021; Pocher, 2025). These and other similar properties have motivated the need for multi-chain forensic analyses (Atlam et al., 2024; Agarwal et al., 2024). Forensic properties of common cryptocurrencies are shown in Table 1.

Financial Flows in Darknet Marketplaces

Marketplaces often provide features to ensure a degree of trust between anonymous buyers and sellers (Soska and Christin, 2015; Dearden and Tucker, 2023). One method is escrow, where funds are held by the marketplace until a trade has been successfully completed (Soska and Christin, 2015). While this discourages fraud, it also adds layers to transactions. Since funds must go through marketplace-controlled addresses rather than directly between buyer and seller, they create more distinct actions in the analysis (Soska and Christin, 2015; Dearden and Tucker, 2023; Huang et al., 2018).

Marketplaces also frequently keep internal wallets in which users store funds and trade on the platform (Dearden and Tucker, 2023). Here, only deposits and withdrawals to and from the marketplace wallet are on-chain. Internal transfers are off-chain, reducing the observability of transactions and leaving blind spots in forensic investigation (Dearden and Tucker, 2023; Dudani et al., 2023).

Table 1. Forensic characteristics of cryptocurrencies used in darknet transactions

Crypto.	Ledger Model	Consensus	Privacy Features	Traceability	Forensic Implications
Bitcoin	UTXO-based	PoW	Pseudonymous addresses; optional use of mixers	High	Public transactions support graph analysis, clustering, and transaction tracing
Ethereum	Account-based	PoS	No native privacy; obfuscation may occur through DeFi services, mixers, and smart contracts	Medium	Smart contracts and indirect transaction paths increase forensic complexity
Monero	Privacy-enhanced UTXO	PoW	Ring signatures, stealth addresses, and confidential transactions	Very low	Strong privacy protections significantly limit tracing and clustering
Zcash	UTXO-based	PoW	Shielded transactions using zero-knowledge proofs	Low when shielded	Shielded pools reduce transaction visibility and attribution reliability
Dash	UTXO-based	PoW	PrivateSend mixing functionality	Medium	Mixing mechanisms complicate flow tracing and address clustering
Litecoin	UTXO-based	PoW	Limited native privacy; external obfuscation may be used	High	Bitcoin-like forensic methods remain applicable for tracing and clustering

Tracking is made more difficult by address reuse strategies and the use of multiple addresses and fund redistribution (Zhao et al., 2022). Funds can be centralized, fragmented or otherwise redistributed via multiple wallets prior to being withdrawn from a mixer. This is more difficult to trace and makes the detection of financial flows opaque (Huang et al., 2018; Moser et al., 2013; Pocher, 2025). Investigations thus commonly require identifying suspicious groups of addresses and transactions patterns rather than individual transactions, which justifies the use of clustering and anomaly detection methods (Meiklejohn et al., 2016; Zhao et al., 2022; Temu and Louca, 2025).

Fundamentals of Digital Forensics in Financial Systems

Blockchain forensics is the practice of attempting to trace transactions and to attribute blockchain activity to one or more entities (Atlam et al., 2024; Xiao et al., 2024). In contrast to investigating traditional financial accounts where there is a clear direct relationship between accounts and identity, blockchain investigation is based primarily on indirect inference methods based on transaction analysis, behavioral analysis, and on information that may be gathered from both on-chain and off-chain sources (Dudani et al., 2023; Agarwal et al., 2024).

Transaction tracing aims to trace the flow of funds across a series of transfers to identify the source, movement and final destination of funds (Paquet-Clouston et al., 2019). The path of transactions can be expressed in the form of trans-action graphs, although tracing funds becomes more difficult as the number of intermediate transactions increases (Meiklejohn et al., 2016; Huang et al., 2018).

Attribution is the process of associating addresses with external real-world actors. This is usually done through the use of heuristics and external sources of information (Dudani et al., 2023; Atlam et al., 2024). Common heuristics used for attribution include identifying addresses that are commonly used together in a single transaction. External sources such as KYC records can also provide evidence to support attribution (Meiklejohn et al., 2016; Agarwal et al., 2024). Attribution is inherently probabilistic and can result in false positives (Zhao et al., 2022; Temu and Louca, 2025). Address rotation, mixers, and privacy coins decrease the power of forensic analysis (Moser et al., 2018; Pocher, 2025). As a result, investigators will often rely on several independent pieces of evidence before reaching a conclusion, especially in legal contexts.

In summary, blockchain forensics is a multidisciplinary field that includes technical analysis as well as investigative reasoning. A working knowledge of blockchain systems and user behavior is essential for this endeavor (Atlam et al., 2024; Dudani et al., 2023; Igonor et al., 2025; Gjorgjev et al., 2025). The above serves as a backdrop for the remainder of the chapter which covers various blockchain forensic methods.

BLOCKCHAIN DATA COLLECTION AND PREPROCESSING

Data collection and preprocessing is another data-dependent step in cryptocurrency forensics. All cryptocurrencies, including Bitcoin and Ethereum, store transaction histories in a transparent and immutable blockchain, which makes the transaction histories accessible to investigators (Dudani et al., 2023). The data have to be collected, cleaned, normalized, and transformed to structured representations amenable to different forensic analysis methods such as machine learning and graph-based methods (Dudani et al., 2023). ML-based systems can be susceptible to adversarial manipulation, where small changes to transaction features cause misclassification (Alghuried et al., 2025b).

Blockchain forensic workflows typically resemble a pipeline architecture which consists of four main phases, acquisition, extraction, preprocessing, and storage (Figure 1). From peer-to-peer networks, raw blockchain data is collected, con-verted into structured datasets, and stored for subsequent analysis. Graph-based and other analytical approaches can then be applied to reconstruct transaction flows and detect illicit activities (Kilic et al., 2022). The trustworthiness of each step in the pipeline is essential since vulnerabilities or errors in upstream stages will flow through the forensic investigation and impact the findings (Alghuried et al., 2025b).

Blockchain Data Sources

The blockchain itself can serve as a source of evidence, the most common one being the public ledger. The ledger contains all the verified transactions that have been recorded in the network, but even so, in order to gather information, forensic analysis is not immune to pseudo-anonymization or other techniques of obfuscation (Dudani et al., 2023; Agarwal et al., 2024).

A direct access to data in a blockchain can be realized through the use of full nodes, which means that an investigator must download and store a local copy of the complete ledger (Wei et al., 2022; Zhang et al., 2019). Application programming interfaces (APIs) and blockchain explorers also allow for an efficient extraction of data from blockchains such as transactions, addresses, and information about blocks, and do not require the operation of a fully synchronized node (Pasdar et al., 2023; Dudani et al., 2023). However, the sources of evidence may vary in their completeness or recency of information, which in turn may have an impact on the accuracy of forensics.

Decentralized storage systems, such as the InterPlanetary File System (IPFS), are increasingly adopted in modern blockchain ecosystems to improve data avail-ability, integrity, and fault tolerance through distributed replication (Manakhari et al., 2024).

Data Extraction Techniques

Once the data is collected, the blockchain records need to be converted into analyzable representations. As blockchain data is stored in a hierarchical format of blocks, transactions, inputs, outputs, and addresses, a parser needs to be implemented to reassemble the flow of transactions and extract information (Wei et al., 2022; Kilic et al., 2022). The extraction can be applied at the block or transaction level and results in metadata, transaction, and address-level information, which is used for behavioral analysis, flow tracing, and detection of illicit activities (Agarwal et al., 2024; Dudani et al., 2023). The parsed records are then mapped to a graph representation for clustering and forensic analysis. On a larger scale, processing may require Extract–Transform–Load (ETL) pipelines which transform raw blockchain records into structured datasets which can be more efficiently queried and analyzed (Su et al., 2022). Such datasets can in turn be further represented as transaction graphs in which accounts can be modelled as nodes and transactions as edges for use cases such as clustering and cryptocurrency tracing (Kilic et al., 2022).

Additional extraction procedures are often required for smart contract plat-forms such as Ethereum which must capture execution traces and contract states to allow for analysis of decentralized application behavior and transaction logic (Ayub et al., 2023). Recent research has further shown that such higher-level features may also be amenable to adversarial manipulation (Alghuried et al., 2025b).

Data Cleaning and Normalization

Blockchain datasets can be heterogeneous and may contain duplicate, incomplete, or inconsistently formatted data. Data cleaning processes, such as removing duplicates, filtering irrelevant attributes, and preparing data for analysis, are used to resolve these issues (Marhoon et al., 2023). Normalization is also necessary to ensure consistent representation across various blockchain formats, address schemes, and encoding methods, particularly when merging data from multiple sources or blockchains (Marhoon et al., 2023; Su et al., 2022; Kilic et al., 2022). To reduce the amount of data to process, techniques of feature selection and aggregation are often used since blockchain data are produced at scale. This pre-processing phase aims at reducing the computational cost while retaining informative features (Alsalami and Zhang, 2019; Ahmed et al., 2022). Correct ordering and alignment of transactions timestamps are also needed to ensure temporal consistency for flow reconstruction and tracing (Paquet-Clouston et al., 2019; Meiklejohn et al., 2016). Tampering with features such as timestamps and transaction values may also be an attack vector, which impact the analysis results (Alghuried et al., 2025b; Alghuried and Mohaisen, 2024).

Figure 1. Pipeline for blockchain data extraction, processing, and storage for forensic analysis

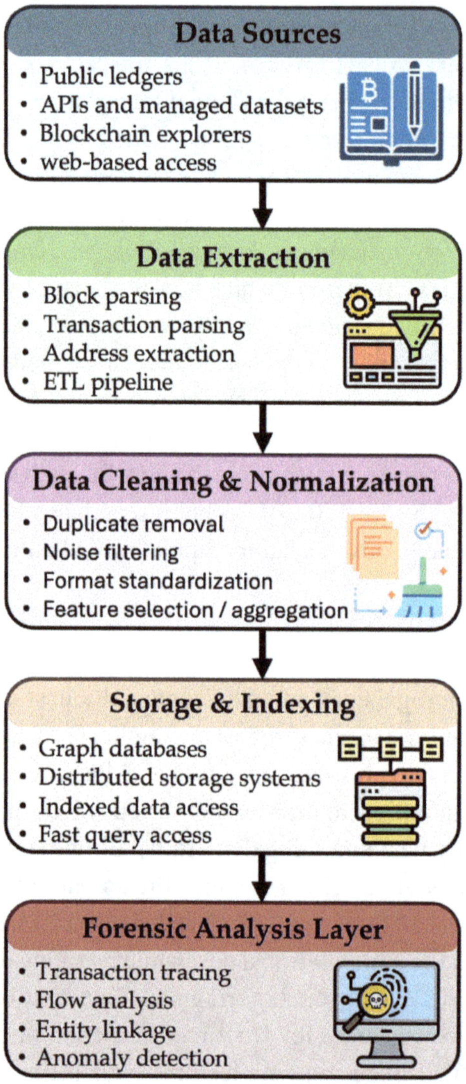

Storage and Indexing of Blockchain Data

Blockchain forensic platforms necessitate scalable storage and indexing mechanisms to facilitate graph traversals and investigative queries over extensive transactional datasets (Kilic et al., 2022; Wei et al., 2022). Graph databases are commonly employed as they model addresses and transactions as nodes and edges, enabling efficient execution of clustering, tracing, and anomaly-detection algorithms (Dudani et al., 2023; Kilic et al., 2022; Huang et al., 2018).

Distributed storage, sharding, and Data Availability Sampling (DAS) offer avenues for additional scalability, enhancing fault tolerance and large-scale data management capabilities (Manakhari et al., 2024; Chaudhuri et al., 2024). Indexing mechanisms organize blockchain data based on attributes like transaction hashes, addresses, and timestamps, resulting in significant improvements in retrieval efficiency, facilitating near real-time forensic investigations (Wei et al., 2022; Kilic et al., 2022; Dudani et al., 2023).

FORENSIC ANALYSIS TECHNIQUES

After data collection and preprocessing, blockchain forensics is the process of extracting interesting patterns, relationships, or anomalies from the transaction data (Atlam et al., 2024). The interconnected nature of blockchain transactions makes graphs a natural representation and tools for graph analysis play a central role in identifying financial flows or suspicious activities (Parihar et al., 2024; Paquet-Clouston et al., 2019). Figure 2 shows an example of a transaction graph where the nodes are blockchain addresses and the directed edges represent value transfers between addresses. The different colors in the graph represent address clusters that likely belong to the same entity and the highlighted path in the graph traces a flow of funds through the transaction graph (Zhao et al., 2022; Temu and Louca, 2025). This section provides an overview of four commonly used forensic techniques: transaction graph analysis, address clustering, flow analysis, and anomaly detection (Agarwal et al., 2024; Igonor et al., 2025).

Transaction Graph Analysis

Transaction graph analysis models a blockchain's activity as a graph where the nodes are addresses or actors and the edges represent value transfers (Parihar et al., 2024). This abstraction allows for the investigation of financial flows and the possible inference of the network's structure (Dudani et al., 2023; Atlam et al., 2024). Transaction graphs are created in UTXO-based systems like Bitcoin by connecting transaction outputs to inputs, whereas account-based systems like Ethereum display value flows between addresses, and smart contracts present another layer of interactions (Kushwaha et al., 2022; Ayub et al., 2023).

Graph metrics are helpful indicators of transactional behavior. Degree centrality can be used to determine highly connected nodes. Betweenness centrality can indicate intermediary entities that frequently appear on transaction paths, and community-detection methods can be used to identify groups of addresses that regularly interact (Parihar et al., 2024; Zhao et al., 2022). Such metrics are often used as inputs to higher-level techniques like clustering and anomaly detection. However, the efficacy of graph metrics in practice typically requires the visibility of transaction data, which can be limited by privacy-enhancing technologies (Moser et al., 2018; Alsalami and Zhang, 2019).

Figure 2. Graph-based visualization of cryptocurrency transactions and ad-dress clusters

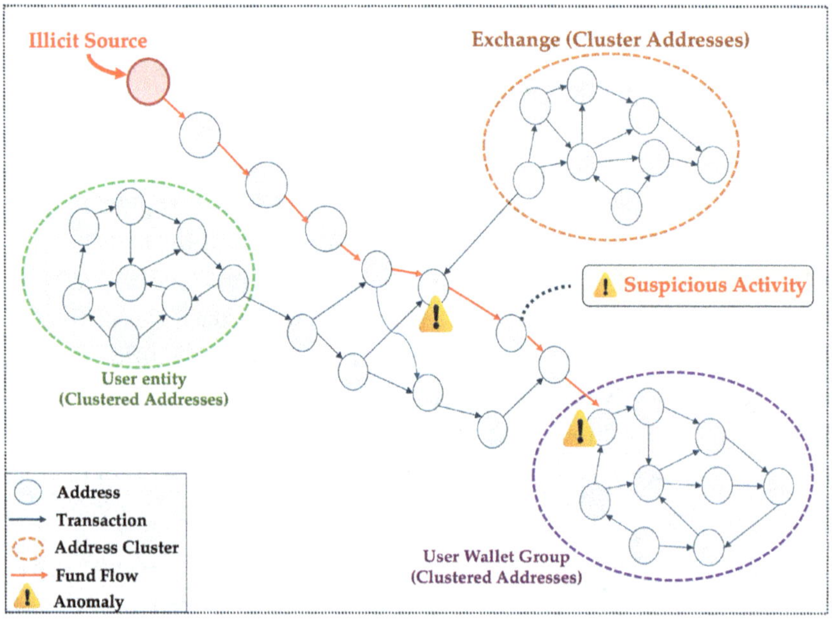

Address Clustering Techniques

Address clustering involves determining groups of addresses likely to belong to the same owner (Meiklejohn et al., 2016; Zhang et al., 2020). Given that most users control multiple addresses, clustering can be used to obtain entity-level representations that are more meaningful for forensic purposes from address-level activity (Dudani et al., 2023).

Heuristic-based approaches to clustering are the most common. The common-input heuristic posits that inputs to a transaction that appear together are likely to belong to the same owner, while change-address heuristics seek to identify addresses created to receive the change, the remainder of a value being transferred, of transactions (Zhao et al., 2022). More complex clustering approaches can make use of behavioral or temporal characteristics, such as patterns of transaction frequency, interaction frequency, and timestamps (Temu and Louca, 2025; Zhao et al., 2022). Machine learning approaches can also be used to learn from labeled examples (Agarwal et al., 2024). Privacy-enhancing techniques that break clustering heuristic assumptions, such as CoinJoin, may make clustering more difficult and error-prone, making validation of results with additional sources of evidence necessary (Moser et al., 2013; Alsalami and Zhang, 2019).

Flow Analysis and Path Tracking

Flow analysis is the study of the movement of funds across transactions (Huang et al., 2018). It can be used in combination with clustering to track transfers between entities instead of addresses. This often entails discovering transaction paths between a source and destination node and analyzing how value propagates through the network (Meiklejohn et al., 2016; Wu et al., 2019).

Path discovery can be performed with graph traversal algorithms, such as breadth-first search (BFS) and depth-first search (DFS) (Parihar et al., 2024). Search space can be restricted to improve efficiency using search constraints such as time windows, transaction values, and maximum path lengths (Kilic et al., 2022). Flow analysis can also be used to detect laundering schemes which split and then recombine funds across many addresses (Moser et al., 2013). Taint analysis methods can be used to estimate how much value from a given source remains in a transaction at a later time (Huang et al., 2018). Flow tracking is more challenging when obfuscation methods, such as mixing services, chain hopping, and privacy-centric cryptocurrencies, are used (Moser et al., 2018).

Anomaly and Fraud Detection

The objective of anomaly detection is to identify transactions that display unusual behavior compared to expected patterns and may indicate fraudulent or illicit activity (Dudani et al., 2023). While graph analysis and flow tracing focus on structure and flow, anomaly detection targets abnormal behavioral patterns. Statistical approaches can identify outliers based on frequency, value distributions, and temporal features, and machine learning can detect complex anomalies in large-scale blockchain data (Chavan et al., 2024; Syed et al., 2023). Feature engineering on common characteristics such as transaction size and frequency, centrality metrics, and temporal or pattern-based features are also frequently employed in detection models (Parihar et al., 2024). In addition, a supervised approach is dependent on labeled examples of known bad addresses such as scams and ransomware, while the unsupervised approach to anomalous behavior is not based on prior address labels (Agarwal et al., 2024).

Anomaly detection has proven difficult to perfect, due to the ever-changing nature of adversarial behavior and the lack of labeled data sets for anomaly detection (Alghuried et al., 2026; Dudani et al., 2023). For this reason, it is often used in combination with graph analysis, clustering, and flow analysis to generate investigative leads (Atlam et al., 2024; Agarwal et al., 2024). Graph analysis, clustering and anomaly detection can be seen as complementary parts of an end-to-end forensic framework. Their results can be diminished, however, using obfuscation techniques described in the next section.

OBFUSCATION TECHNIQUES AND EVASION STRATEGIES

While the forensic techniques described in this thesis work well for transparent blockchains, adversaries use various obfuscation techniques to lower traceability and thus evade analysis. Such techniques try to break the connectivity of the graph, break the underlying clustering assumption or otherwise hide transaction flows (Khalilov and Levi, 2018; Atlam et al., 2024). We now describe three such approaches, namely mixing services, cross-chain transactions and privacy cryptocurrencies (Dudani et al., 2023; Agarwal et al., 2024).

Mixing and Tumbling Services

Mixing services, or tumblers, are designed to break the connection between the input and output of a transaction, by collecting money from various users and redistributing it in a way that obfuscates the source (Khalilov and Levi, 2018). This process makes transaction graphs less informative, and tracing paths less continuous (Meiklejohn et al., 2016; Dudani et al., 2023).

From a graph perspective, mixers are responsible for establishing numerous many-to-many connections between inputs and outputs, effectively substituting the fixed, deterministic transactional links with stochastic ones (Moser et al., 2013; Parihar et al., 2024). This can cause explorations to experience high branching factors and lower confidence in results (Europol, 2021). Mixing also disrupts the clustering approach since the common-input heuristics may cluster users who are unrelated but engage in joint transactions (Zhao et al., 2022). There are also empirical evidence that clustering performance can suffer heavily when the address-linking assumptions are violated (Temu and Louca, 2025).

While mixers may show discernible patterns such as transaction splitting, repetitions, and regularity in timing, sophisticated obfuscation methods are starting to incorporate variability to dodge both heuristic and anomaly-based detection methods (Moser et al., 2013; Atlam et al., 2024; Agarwal et al., 2024).

Chain Hopping and Cross-Chain Transactions

Chain hopping refers to the action of transferring cryptocurrency from one blockchain network to another with the goal of making the trail less trace-able (Pocher, 2025). This may be done on centralized or decentralized exchanges or on cross-chain bridges (Europol, 2021; Alghuried et al., 2026). From a forensic standpoint, this technique complicates transaction continuity by dispersing assets into disparate ecosystems which typically use different address formats, transaction models, and data layouts (Dudani et al., 2023; Atlam et al., 2024; Wei et al., 2022; Marhoon et al., 2023).

Cross-chain transfers can be conducted quickly via decentralized exchanges and interoperability protocols, usually with little access to off-chain identity information (Pasdar et al., 2023). Attribution is further complicated when cross-chain activity is combined with mixers, privacy wallets, or privacy-centric cryptocurrencies (Dudani et al., 2023; Agarwal et al., 2024). As evidence is spread across multiple ledgers instead of a single transaction graph, tracing success is typically reduced with the number of chain hops and the lack of external intelligence (Atlam et al., 2024; Europol, 2021; Pocher, 2025).

Privacy Coins and Advanced Obfuscation

Privacy-enhanced cryptocurrencies feature privacy features integrated into the protocol, obscuring the ability to see transaction information (Khalilov and Levi, 2018). Privacy-preserving methods implemented into the protocol operate to hide this information natively at the protocol level, preventing the observability of the transaction graph and the use of traditional forensic techniques (Alsalami and Zhang, 2019; Zhang et al., 2019; Dudani et al., 2023).

Typical examples include Monero and Zcash. Monero uses ring signatures, stealth addresses, and confidential transactions to hide information on the participants in a transaction and amounts transferred, while Zcash allows for shielded transactions based on zero-knowledge proofs (Moser et al., 2018; Bernabe et al., 2019; Khalilov and Levi, 2018). These features leave the graph as a fragmented and incomplete structure in which many observable links between parties are removed (Moser et al., 2018).

Consequently, graph analysis, clustering, and transaction-tracing approaches become less accurate. They also place greater emphasis on timing information, metadata, exchange records, and other external data (Europol, 2021; Agarwal et al., 2024; Dudani et al., 2023; Atlam et al., 2024). Moreover, models that have been developed to address address clustering on transparent blockchains are less effective on privacy-focused cryptocurrencies, as a significant number of their features are derived from graph connectivity, address activity, and transaction visibility (Moser et al., 2018; Amarasinghe et al., 2019). These results indicate the need for less transaction-visibility-dependent forensic techniques (Atlam et al., 2024; Alghuried et al., 2026). The overall effects of obfuscation techniques described in this section are summarized in Table 2.

Table 2. Advanced comparison of obfuscation techniques and their impact on blockchain forensic analysis

Technique	Operational Mechanism	Impact on Graph Topology	Effect on Clustering Heuristics	Detection Model Impact	Forensic Limitations
Mixing (Tumblers)	Aggregates inputs from multiple users and redistributes outputs with randomized mapping	Introduces many-to-many edges, increases graph density, and reduces path determinism	Disrupts common-input heuristics and increases clustering false positives	Reduces precision due to ambiguous transaction paths; recall remains partial	Difficult to reconstruct fund origins; often requires probabilistic tracing
CoinJoin	Combines transactions from multiple users into a single collaborative transaction	Creates overlapping input-output relationships and increases graph ambiguity	Violates common-input ownership assumptions used in clustering	Increases false positives and reduces attribution confidence	Makes ownership inference unreliable without external evidence
Transaction Splitting (Layering)	Divides funds into multiple smaller transactions distributed across addresses	Increases graph branching and transaction dispersion	Fragments observable transaction relationships	Reduces anomaly visibility by mimicking normal transaction behavior	Requires correlation of distributed micro-transactions
Peel Chains	Gradually transfers funds through long sequential transaction chains while retaining small residual balances	Produces elongated transaction paths with repetitive structures	Preserves partial clustering but obscures final fund destinations	Reduces tracing efficiency due to high path depth	Requires long-range transaction tracking and temporal analysis
Chain Hopping	Transfers assets across multiple blockchains through exchanges or cross-chain bridges	Fragments transaction graphs into disconnected cross-ledger subgraphs	Prevents reliable cross-chain clustering without external linkage	Reduces recall due to limited cross-chain visibility	Requires multi-chain correlation and external intelligence
Decentralized Exchanges (DEXs)	Enables asset conversion through smart contracts without centralized intermediaries	Introduces indirect transaction paths and contract-mediated flows	Reduces visibility of cross-asset entity relationships	Complicates behavioral modeling and flow reconstruction	Limited access to off-chain identity and compliance information
Privacy Wallets	Automatically generates new addresses and encourages transaction variability to minimize traceability	Fragments observable transaction graphs into smaller clusters	Weakens address reuse heuristics and behavioral linkage	Reduces model stability due to inconsistent transaction behavior	Makes long-term entity tracking more difficult
Privacy Coins	Uses privacy-enhancing cryptographic mechanisms such as ring signatures and stealth addresses	Removes observable edges and conceals node relationships	Prevents heuristic-based clustering	Severely degrades both precision and recall	Makes transaction tracing infeasible without side-channel information

Observable outcomes of obfuscation are incomplete and fragmented transaction graphs, suboptimal tracing paths and decreased clustering fidelity (M¨oser et al., 2013). Analyses of ransomware and Darknet markets demonstrate that criminal actors often use mix of laundering techniques, exchange services and transaction movement behaviors to make tracing and attribution efforts more difficult (Paquet-Clouston et al., 2019; Dearden and Tucker, 2023). These behaviors have also been found to impact graph topology and decrease the predictive power of traditional forensic models (Atlam et al., 2024; Agarwal et al., 2024).

To combat these effects, forensic platforms have focused on increased adoption of multi-source data fusion and analytical methods (Dudani et al., 2023). For example, some platforms have targeted increased scalability and capabilities for large-scale graph processing while others have focused on enhancing detection accuracy using machine learning methods (Kilic et al., 2022; Su et al., 2022; Atlam et al., 2024). However, achieving both scalability and analytical fidelity remains a challenge when transactions have been intentionally obfuscated (Dudani et al., 2023; Agarwal et al., 2024).

In general, obfuscation techniques continue to represent one of the biggest blockchain forensics challenges to date, as they are designed to specifically impede graph analysis, clustering, and flow-tracing techniques (M¨oser et al., 2013; Khalilov and Levi, 2018; Dudani et al., 2023). Addressing this challenge, among others in particular and more generally, thus requires a combination of graph analytics with external data with more advanced forensic analysis techniques and methodologies (Atlam et al., 2024; Alghuried et al., 2026). The subsequent section is a review of tools and platforms that can aid with large-scale cryptocurrency investigations.

TOOLS AND PLATFORMS FOR CRYPTOCURRENCY FOREN-SICS

The evasion tactics presented in the last section impair the applicability of standalone tracing and clustering methods by obscuring transaction visibility and fragmenting the graph (Pocher, 2025; Atlam et al., 2024). As a result, cryptocurrency investigations are becoming more dependent on dedicated forensic solutions that enable data exploration, graph analytics, attribution, and case management (Dudani et al., 2023; Igonor et al., 2025). These platforms vary in scope and are tailored for different use cases, such as research purposes, operational investigations, large-scale monitoring, and international collaboration efforts (Europol, 2021; Agarwal et al., 2024).

Operationally, forensic platforms should provide support for transaction exploration, graph construction, clustering, path tracing, anomaly detection, and reporting (Dudani et al., 2023). They should also support large blockchain datasets, multiple cryptocurrencies, and transaction models (Wei et al., 2022; Kilic et al., 2022). In practice, the choice of suitable tools is especially relevant in cases of cross-chain activity, the use of privacy-enhancing technologies, or time-sensitive incidents (Atlam et al., 2024; Alghuried et al., 2026).

Open-Source Tools

Open-source software (OSS) has a crucial role in cryptocurrency forensics, al-lowing for transparency, reproducibility, and flexibility (Su et al., 2022; Igonor et al., 2025). It provides an opportunity for analysts to inspect implementations, modify analytical pipelines, and reproduce experimental results. These solutions have been used in a wide range of work to evaluate the performance of cluster-ing heuristics, graph-analysis methods, and anomaly-detection techniques on benchmark datasets (Zhao et al., 2022; Temu and Louca, 2025).

The simplest type of open-access tooling is represented by blockchain explorers, which allow for address, block, and transaction history inspection through web-based interfaces (Gao et al., 2018; Kuzuno and Karam, 2017). Most of these solutions lack more advanced capabilities, such as clustering, risk scoring, or entity attribution (Dudani et al., 2023; Agarwal et al., 2024).

More advanced platforms are BlockSci and GraphSense (Wei et al., 2022; Su et al., 2022). BlockSci offers high-performance blockchain analytics and scalable efficient graph traversal, while GraphSense is an open-source graph analytics, data ingestion, clustering, and investigative workflows platform (Wei et al., 2022). Both enable large-scale analysis instead of individual transaction inspection. Graph databases, such as Neo4j, are also a common choice in forensic workflows. Graph databases support efficient storage and querying of the transaction graph in a flexible manner. This supports path analysis, entity-centric investigation, and custom graph exploration (Wei et al., 2022; Kili¸c et al., 2022).

Open-source environments are often assessed using benchmark datasets (BitcoinHeist, Elliptic++) that support research on classification, clustering, and anomaly detection (Agarwal et al., 2024; Alghuried and Mohaisen, 2024). Bench-mark environments, however, cannot fully model real-world investigations due to the challenge of incomplete information and potential data-quality limitations.

Commercial Forensic Platforms

Commercial platforms generally offer more than exploration: many analytics, attribution, risk intelligence, monitoring, and workflow management components are integrated in single environments (Europol, 2021; Dudani et al., 2023). These offerings are usually tailored for the operational work of investigators, compliance professionals, financial institutions, and public-sector organizations (Agarwal et al., 2024). In contrast to open-source tools, transparency is often traded for scalability, coverage, and timeliness.

Chainalysis offers an investigative ecosystem built around the Reactor and KYT tools. Reactor is used for transaction tracing and investigative analysis and KYT for transaction monitoring and risk assessment (Europol, 2021). Chainalysis Investigator also integrates with digital forensics and link-analysis tools, allowing investigators to combine evidence from the blockchain, seized-device data, and case information (Dudani et al., 2023; Xiao et al., 2024).

TRM Labs offers blockchain intelligence for forensics, monitoring, screening, and law-enforcement coordination. It offers multi-chain tracing products and has developed collaborative tools such as De-conflict to help agencies working on related cases across jurisdictions (Europol, 2021; Alghuried et al., 2026; Dudani et al., 2023). Elliptic also brings together screening, monitoring, investigation, and compliance into a single platform. In doing so, it aims to cut down on manual review by providing automated alerting, exposure analysis, and integrated case workflows (Agarwal et al., 2024; Dudani et al., 2023; Europol, 2021).

Commercial solutions may lack visibility into attribution methodologies and risk-scoring logic, however (Atlam et al., 2024; Dudani et al., 2023). To some extent, methodological explainability may be sacrificed for the sake of operational scale and coverage (Alghuried et al., 2026). Thus, in situations where the findings of investigations have legal implications, analysts may often seek to independently validate commercial outputs (Agarwal et al., 2024; Li et al., 2024).

Integration with Law Enforcement Systems

The greatest value of blockchain analytics platforms is realized through their integration into wider law-enforcement workflows, rather than their operation as standalone tools (Europol, 2021). The integrations may include evidence-management systems, case-tracking platforms, OSINT enrichment tools, exchange-request workflows, seizure management, and reporting systems (Dudani et al., 2023).

Workflow automation plays an especially important role for enterprise-scale investigations of ransomware, fraud, and Darknet marketplaces (Paquet-Clouston et al., 2019; Soska and Christin, 2015). Alerting, exposure scoring, entity screening, and path summarization are all technical processes that can be automated to some degree, helping to lighten the workload for analysts and bringing greater consistency to investigations (Dudani et al., 2023). Reporting capabilities are another important area, in that it should be possible to export transaction paths, attribution results, and risk assessments in some form for prosecutors, regulators, and law-enforcement agencies (Agarwal et al., 2024). The capability to translate the output of the analytical engine into an organized investigative report is often one of the core differences between research-oriented tools and operational forensic platforms (Dudani et al., 2023; Igonor et al., 2025). Forensic platforms can be broadly assessed from a systems perspective using three categories of criteria: analytical accuracy, scalability, and interoperability (Wei et al., 2022). Accuracy denotes the quality of tracing, clustering, and suspicious-activity detection (Temu and Louca, 2025); scalability, the capacity to ingest and process large multi-asset datasets (Su et al., 2022); and interoperability, the extent to which outputs can be consumed or further processed by external intelligence, evidence-management, and investigative platforms (Li et al., 2024). These characteristics are summarised in Table 3. In practice, successful cryptocurrency investigations have commonly made use of a combination of open-source and commercial tools to balance the trade-offs between transparency, scalability, and operational capabilities (Dudani et al., 2023).

The practical utility of these platforms is best understood in the context of specific investigations. The following section presents several case studies of Darknet marketplaces and cryptocurrency-enabled crime to highlight forensic techniques and challenges encountered during such investigations (Soska and Christin, 2015; Huang et al., 2018; Paquet-Clouston et al., 2019).

CASE STUDIES AND REAL-WORLD INVESTIGATIONS

Blockchain forensics is most easily explained through the presentation of concrete investigations. In these investigations transaction graph analysis, clustering, and the use of external open-source intelligence are all mixed and matched to trace out criminal financial flows (Meiklejohn et al., 2016; Dudani et al., 2023). The present section provides cases from Darknet markets, ransomware attacks, and cryptocurrency laundering services, to show forensic practices in action (Agarwal et al., 2024; Atlam et al., 2024).

Table 3. Tools and platforms for blockchain forensics: features, capabilities, and limitations

Tool / Platform	Type	Primary Capabilities	Typical Use Cases	Strengths	Limitations	Multi-chain / Scalability Support
Blockchain Explorers	Open-access / lightweight	Address lookup, transaction browsing, block inspection	Manual triage, quick verification, preliminary tracing	Easy access, low setup overhead	Limited automation, no robust clustering or attribution	Limited scalability and asset coverage
BlockSci	Open-source / research	High-performance blockchain parsing, graph analysis, Python-based analytics	Reproducible experiments, transaction graph construction, flow analysis	Speed, transparency, research flexibility	Limited operational workflow support, narrower deployment scope	Moderate scalability, primarily research-oriented
GraphSense	Open-source / analytics platform	Data ingestion, graph analytics, investigation-oriented analysis	Clustering research, attribution studies, graph-based tracing	Open architecture, customizable analysis pipelines	Requires setup effort and technical expertise	Strong support for large-scale graph analytics
Neo4j-based workflows	Graph database / supporting platform	Custom graph storage, path queries, entity-centric exploration	Knowledge graphs, custom tracing, fraud pattern analysis	Flexible querying, scalable graph exploration	Not a dedicated blockchain forensics product by itself	Depends on implementation and infrastructure design
Chainalysis (e.g., Reactor, KYT)	Commercial / operational	Tracing, monitoring, entity attribution, risk scoring, investigative integration	Compliance operations, ransomware tracing, case development	Broad asset coverage, mature workflow integration	Limited transparency of proprietary scoring and attribution logic	Extensive multi-chain operational support
TRM Labs (e.g., Forensics, Deconflict)	Commercial / operational	Multi-chain tracing, screening, investigation support, inter-agency coordination	Cross-chain investigations, law-enforcement workflows, fraud response	Multi-chain focus, collaboration support, operational tooling	Commercial dependency, limited methodological visibility	Extensive support for cross-chain investigations
Elliptic	Commercial / operational	Screening, monitoring, analytics, configurable alerting, exposure analysis	Risk triage, investigation support, compliance and reporting	Integrated end-to-end workflow, reduced manual review burden	Less suitable for fully transparent, researcher-controlled experimentation	High-scale operational analytics and monitoring

Darknet Marketplace Financial Tracking

Darknet markets are more or less formalized commercial communities where escrow, vendor rating systems, and cryptocurrency all play a role (Soska and Christin, 2015; Bahamazava and Nanda, 2022). Forensically, the escrow wallet is a focal point for the marketplace, and funds almost always flow from a buyer through the escrow to a vendor, resulting in a traceable pattern that can be deconstructed with graph analysis techniques (Meiklejohn et al., 2016; Dearden and Tucker, 2023). These wallet patterns can be used to identify marketplace-related clusters and track funds across the nodes of users, vendors, and withdrawal addresses.

Blockchain analysis has also yielded information on the size and growth of Darknet markets. Transaction data have demonstrated that illicit market-places are an important part of the cybercriminal ecosystem and often have identifiable transaction clusters (Soska and Christin, 2015; Dearden and Tucker, 2023). Transaction-flow changes can signal shifts in marketplace activity, vendor changes, or law-enforcement activity before reporting by the public in many cases, showcasing the utility of blockchain analytics for both investigative and threat-monitoring purposes (Dearden and Tucker, 2023; Meiklejohn et al., 2016).

Ransomware Payment Tracing

In practice, ransomware investigations usually start with at least a single known ransom address provided by victims or through malware analysis (Huang et al., 2018; Meiklejohn et al., 2016). They are then extended through clustering and transaction graph exploration in order to find related wallets, collector addresses, or cash-out locations.

In fact, ransomware wallets have been found to be short-lived and used only for a short period before funds are sent to a long sequence of intermediary wallets (Paquet-Clouston et al., 2019). The funds can be split into smaller amounts, sent through a number of addresses before being recombined in order to confuse transaction tracing efforts (M¨oser et al., 2013; Khalilov and Levi, 2018). Deposits to exchanges also seem to be a common final step where the cryptocurrency is exchanged for fiat money (Huang et al., 2018).

Ransomware is a highly adaptive ecosystem in which groups continuously alter wallet use, transaction timing, and laundering tactics in an attempt to avoid detection (Europol, 2021). The increase in smaller, more decentralized ransomware groups has further fragmented the environment, making long-term attribution and monitoring more difficult (Dudani et al., 2023).

Cryptocurrency Laundering and Cash-Out Networks

Cryptocurrency laundering has matured into a service-based ecosystem with entry, layering, and cash-out phases (Mo¨ser et al., 2013). Each phase adds layers of complexity to tracing and attribution.

Entry brokers and intermediaries grant access to wallets and financial infrastructure (Europol, 2021). Layering obfuscates fund origins through multiple transfers between wallets, exchanges, and intermediary services (Bahamazava and Nanda, 2022). Intermediate transactions reduce path confidence and hinder forensic reconstruction.

Evidence from empirical studies also suggests that laundering nowadays involves large volumes of transactions per operation, with increasingly complex flows and numerous wallets and services acting as intermediaries, in line with a more industrial scale of cybercrime (Dearden and Tucker, 2023). Observed laundering methods in darknet markets and other illicit scenarios encompass cryptocurrency exchanges, peer-to-peer markets, OTC brokers, mixers, swapping services and cross-chain bridges, among other services (Mo¨ser et al., 2013; Pocher, 2025). Multiple methods are combined to perform the laundering tasks, increasing the obfuscation and lowering traceability (Atlam et al., 2024).

A similar phenomenon is also found in ransomware (Paquet-Clouston et al., 2019), where chains of wallets are used before funds reach their exchange end-points for cash-out. While obfuscation makes laundering more complex, launder-ing operations in transparent blockchains leave structural signatures that can still be amenable to graph-based forensic analysis (Meiklejohn et al., 2016).

Lessons Learned

A few conclusions are immediate from these examples. First, blockchain transactions are pseudonymous but not anonymous, so graph analysis and clustering methods can track flows and flag important entities. However, attribution is harder when funds are moved through mixers, cross-chain services or privacy-enhancing technologies (M¨oser et al., 2013; Khalilov and Levi, 2018).

Second, there are often recurring structural patterns to illicit financial activity. These patterns can include aggregation nodes, ephemeral wallets, exchange integration points, and layering transaction flows (Huang et al., 2018; Paquet-Clouston et al., 2019). Obfuscation techniques tend to leave these behaviours largely intact, making them a useful signal for forensic analysis (M¨oser et al., 2013; Atlam et al., 2024).

LEGAL, ETHICAL, AND REGULATORY CONSIDERATIONS 19

Third, contemporary cybercrime activities take place in organised ecosystems comprising brokers, laundering services, cash-out operators and other specific roles (Europol, 2021; Bahamazava and Nanda, 2022; Dearden and Tucker, 2023). Knowing the operation structures is key to attribution and disruption.

Blockchain analytics can be used both for reactive investigations and proactive identification of threats (Dudani et al., 2023; Atlam et al., 2024). But on-chain analytics must be triangulated with external information sources such as exchange data, OSINT, and legal-cooperation frameworks for effective investi-gation (Europol, 2021; Dudani et al., 2023).

In summary, these cases show that effective blockchain forensics often depends on combining technical investigations with external intelligence to unravel more complex illicit activities (Agarwal et al., 2024; Alghuried et al., 2026). They also point to the need for more scalable, multi-chain, and intelligence-led forensic frameworks to meet future challenges from obfuscation techniques (Atlam et al., 2024; Dudani et al., 2023).

Blockchain forensics also has legal, ethical, and regulatory implications. Investigators must navigate issues such as transparency versus privacy, multi-jurisdictional investigations, data-protection compliance, and responsible use of investigative technologies (Atlam et al., 2024; Alghuried et al., 2026). This section will cover legal considerations, privacy and surveillance issues, cross-border investigations, and ethical concerns in blockchain forensics.

Legal Frameworks for Cryptocurrency Investigations

Crypto investigations are subject to financial regulation, cybercrime statutes, anti-money laundering (AML), and count-terrorism financing (CTF) obligations (Agarwal et al., 2024). These laws and standards establish how blockchain data may be acquired, processed, and submitted as evidence in court (Dudani et al., 2023; Lone and Mir, 2019). In numerous countries, cryptocurrencies are also governed as virtual property or money-service operations, subject to Know-Your-Customer (KYC) obligations, transaction tracking, and suspicious-activity reporting (Europol, 2021; Agarwal et al., 2024). This has yielded significant attribution chances, mapping pseudonymous blockchain activity to recognized individuals and companies (Meiklejohn et al., 2016). It has been employed, for example, in probes into ransomware, Darknet marketplaces, and money laundering (Huang et al., 2018; Paquet-Clouston et al., 2019).

Transaction histories on public blockchains are public, but attribution of actions is frequently based on off-chain data such as exchange records, wallet metadata and transaction logs (Dudani et al., 2023; Atlam et al., 2024). Access to such data is often only made available on subpoena, court order or regulator request (Europol, 2021). As a result, investigators may be able to trace transactions but not be able to prove who the actors are beyond reasonable doubt (Meiklejohn et al., 2016). Blockchain-derived evidence has been accepted in court and regulators where it is properly preserved, documented and the chain of analysis is validated (Xiao et al., 2024; Li et al., 2024; Atlam et al., 2024).

Privacy vs. Surveillance Trade-offs

Public blockchains are inherently tensioned between transparency and privacy (Khalilov and Levi, 2018; Amarasinghe et al., 2019). On the one hand, transparent transaction histories support transparency for good governance including accountability, traceability, and forensics (Zhang et al., 2019). On the other hand, financial records may enable exposure of private financial information and large scale profiling of end users (Alsalami and Zhang, 2019).

Transparency enables a variety of techniques for analyzing transactions, including graph analysis, clustering, and transaction tracing. However, large-scale monitoring can also capture legitimate activity unrelated to investigations (Meiklejohn et al., 2016; Parihar et al., 2024; Amarasinghe et al., 2019). This has led to concern about proportionality, data minimization, and surveillance overreach. Privacy-enhancing technologies add an additional layer of complexity. Privacy coins, mixers, and other privacy services can improve user privacy but may decrease forensic visibility and disrupt investigations (Mo¨ser et al., 2018, 2013).

Similar issues are increasingly emerging in decentralized finance (DeFi) and cross-chain transactions (Alghuried et al., 2026; Dudani et al., 2023).

Consequently, appropriate oversight is essential to balance legitimate privacy expectations with the need to detect and investigate illicit activities such as money laundering and ransomware payments (Paquet-Clouston et al., 2019). Risk-based monitoring practices and legal safeguards can help ensure proportionality and limit the risk of excessive surveillance (Agarwal et al., 2024; Atlam et al., 2024).

Cross-Border Financial Investigations

Cryptocurrency transactions are international by nature and do not rely on national financial systems (Europol, 2021; Dudani et al., 2023; Gao et al., 2018). It is therefore legally and operationally challenging to enforce national regulations in decentralized ecosystems (Agarwal et al., 2024).

Suspected cryptocurrency flows often involve international infrastructure, with the parties' wallets, exchanges, mixers, and cash-out service in different jurisdictions (Dearden and Tucker, 2023). Ransomware, Darknet markets, and laundering network investigations, for example, often involve multiple law-enforcement agencies, exchanges, financial institutions, and regulators (Huang et al., 2018; Soska and Christin, 2015). The time required to obtain cross-border information via requests and legal procedures can also create opportunities for suspects to transfer or conceal funds (Europol, 2021).

Regulatory fragmentation further hinders investigations as AML requirements, evidentiary standards, and enforcement practices can differ widely between jurisdictions

(Agarwal et al., 2024). Criminal actors may exploit these gaps by quickly moving funds through exchanges, bridges, and automated asset-transfer services (Bahamazava and Nanda, 2022; Pocher, 2025).

To combat these challenges, international organizations increasingly rely on information-sharing agreements, joint investigations, and blockchain analytics platforms with the ability to track activity across multiple networks (Europol, 2021; Gjorgjev et al., 2025). However, enforcement success is contingent on timely international cooperation, legal harmonization, and the integration of data from multiple jurisdictions (Europol, 2021; Agarwal et al., 2024).

Ethical Considerations in Blockchain Analysis

Blockchain forensics involves ethical considerations around the collection, analysis, and use of transaction data, especially when analytical outcomes may impact legal proceedings, financial sanctions, or investigative priorities (Alghuried et al., 2026). One such concern is false attribution: clustering and behavioral-analysis techniques can only infer relationships between addresses and entities, but not directly demonstrate ownership (Zhao et al., 2022; Temu and Louca, 2025). Erroneous assumptions or the use of adversarial obfuscation techniques can therefore lead to misidentification (Pocher, 2025). For this reason, care must be taken when interpreting forensic findings, which should be corroborated using multiple independent sources of evidence (Atlam et al., 2024).

Mass surveillance is another ethical issue. Although blockchain data are public, bulk analysis could be used to infer detailed information about financial behaviour, associations, and transaction flows (Amarasinghe et al., 2019; Alsalami and Zhang, 2019). To address this, ethical forensic investigations should follow a principle of proportionality, only analysing cases that are relevant to the investigation and not unduly observing unrelated data (Khalilov and Levi, 2018). Fairness, robustness, and transparency are also important for blockchain forensic systems. Machine-learning models used for various detection and classification tasks such as anomaly detection, phishing detection, and risk scoring may be vulnerable to bias from skewed training data or adversarial attacks, leading to misclassifications or unjust targeting (Alghuried et al., 2025a). As a result, explainability, fairness, and robustness are increasingly important for modern forensic tools (Bellagarda and Abu-Mahfouz, 2022).

The use of sophisticated forensic platforms also poses issues related to accountability and methodological transparency. In this regard, forensic investigators and organizations should keep comprehensive records of their analysis, use repeat-able methods, and make forensic results independently reviewable as needed (Li et al., 2024; Xiao et al., 2024). If blockchain analytics are to be used as legal evidence or as a regulatory decision-support tool, a higher degree of scrutiny is needed. In this regard, ethical blockchain forensics should be based on good data stewardship practices, prudent interpretations, transparency, accountability, fairness, and proportionality (Agarwal et al., 2024; Alghuried et al., 2026).

CHALLENGES AND LIMITATIONS

Blockchain forensics has made significant progress; however, it still encounters technical and operational challenges that can limit the reliability of investigations (Atlam et al., 2024; Dudani et al., 2023). Graph analysis, clustering, flow tracing, and forensic platforms have enhanced the investigation of illicit cryptocurrency activity, but their effectiveness is limited by transaction visibility, heuristic assumptions, computational scalability, and obfuscation techniques (Khalilov and Levi, 2018; Pocher, 2025).

Scalability. Public blockchains generate vast and continuously growing volumes of transactional data, and forensic platforms need to be scalable to ingest, store, and process transactions, addresses, smart-contract interactions, and external metadata at scale (Marhoon et al., 2023). This poses substantial challenges for storage, indexing, graph traversal, and computing capabilities, particularly during near real-time investigations (Wei et al., 2022; Manakhari et al., 2024). The issue is further compounded in multi-chain scenarios, where transaction formats, smart-contract models, and cross-chain correlations vary, leading to more intricate analyses (Agarwal et al., 2024; Pasdar et al., 2023).

Privacy-enhancing technologies and user practices also limit forensic visibility. Privacy coins, such as Monero, obfuscate transaction information; users of trans-parent blockchains may avoid address reuse, spread activity across several wallets, or use decentralized and collaborative transaction mechanisms to minimize trace-ability (Alsalami and Zhang, 2019). As a result, investigators are increasingly turning to probabilistic analysis and external intelligence, including exchange records, seized devices and OSINT which may be incomplete, time-delayed or unavailable in some jurisdictions (Europol, 2021; Agarwal et al., 2024).

Address clustering is probabilistic as most approaches are heuristic and indirect forms of evidence of ownership. CoinJoin, custodial mixing and other complex fragmented transaction patterns can result in false positive and false negative associations, creating inaccurate transaction graphs and drawing false conclusions (Khalilov and Levi, 2018). As such, clustering results are best interpreted as heuristic signs of possibility and not proof, which should be supported by additional investigative evidence where available.

The other challenge comes from the nature of the rapidly changing obfuscation techniques and actors' adoption of laundering strategies. Mixers, cross-chain bridges, decentralized exchanges, swap services, and "throwaway" intermediate wallets remain a dominant part of the criminal strategy (Pocher, 2025; Alghuried et al., 2026). Therefore, forensic assumptions and analysis models may become outdated quickly. It poses a particular challenge for machine-learning-based solutions, which are usually trained on previous data and can significantly degrade if criminal behavior changes (Atlam et al., 2024; Agarwal et al., 2024). The automated solutions can also be less robust due to the adversarial manipulation of transaction features (Alghuried et al., 2025a; (Alghuried et al., 2025b; Alghuried and Mohaisen, 2024). In summary, blockchain forensics is still a valuable investigative tool. However, scalability limits, privacy solutions, cluster ambiguity, and emerging obfuscation techniques restrict visibility, attribution, and analytical precision (Pocher, 2025). Comprehensive investigations necessitate adaptive approaches combining technical analysis with diverse intelligence sources (Agarwal et al., 2024).

FUTURE TRENDS AND RESEARCH DIRECTIONS

Blockchain forensics is an active research area, as blockchain ecosystems scale in size and complexity and as criminal adversaries evolve and become more sophisticated (Atlam et al., 2024). Future systems will need to be more scalable, adaptive, and intelligence-driven to support investigations across a broader range of blockchain ecosystems. An example is visualized in Figure 3.

A key research area is building intelligent and scalable forensic analytics. The current workflow is often based on deterministic heuristics and manual graph exploration which may not scale well as transaction volume and ecosystem diversity continues to grow (Atlam et al., 2024). Machine learning, graph analytics, and behavioral modeling are increasingly being explored for automated investigations, anomaly detection, and large-scale transaction analytics (Alghuried et al., 2025a). Future systems will also need to address explainability, reproducibility, legal admissibility, and adversarial robustness (Atlam et al., 2024).

Figure 3. Future intelligent blockchain forensics framework for tracking illicit darknet transactions

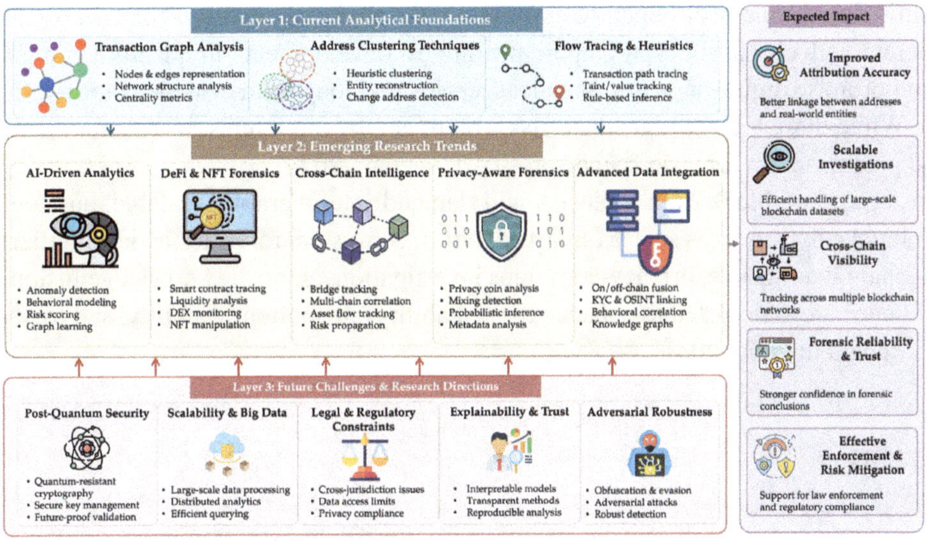

A second theme is the evolving sophistication of decentralized infrastructures, most notably DeFi and NFT ecosystems. Transactions in such systems frequently span multiple smart contracts, liquidity pools, decentralized exchanges, and asset-routing mechanisms (Kushwaha et al., 2022). An analogous complexity is observed in NFT ecosystems, in the form of wash trading and price manipulation, among other behaviours. Analyses of these systems in future work will thus need more semantic analysis of smart-contract activity, asset provenance, and entity relationships, beyond transaction-level tracing alone (Ayub et al., 2023).

A third and growing focus will be on cross-chain intelligence. Criminals are increasingly using bridges, swaps, and other multi-chain infrastructures to launder transaction flows (Alghuried et al., 2026). Forensic frameworks of the future will thus need to correlate activity across diverse blockchain networks, and reconstruct transaction lifecycles across multiple ecosystems (Wei et al., 2022). Privacy-preserving forensic analysis is also an active topic of research. As privacy coins, mixing services, and other transaction obfuscation tools make blockchain transactions harder to link, future investigations will depend on probabilistic inference, metadata, behavioral analytics, and third-party information feeds (Dudani et al., 2023). These developments are part of a wider shift from transaction-centric toward intelligence-driven, semi-anonymous forensic frameworks (Alsalami and Zhang, 2019).

Advanced data integration and forensic knowledge fusion is also expected to become more important. As future platforms will likely support the integrated analysis of blockchain transactions, KYC data, OSINT, behavioral indicators, and threat-intelligence feeds to improve attribution, scalability, and real-time decision making capabilities (Europol, 2021; Agarwal et al., 2024). Large-scale knowledge graphs and correlation frameworks may further enhance complex multi-platform investigations (Wei et al., 2022).

In addition to analysis on the blockchain, the blockchain itself may play a role in forensic infrastructure. Blockchain based evidence-management systems, for example, may help preserve evidence integrity, auditability, and chain-of-custody using immutable and verifiable records (Xiao et al., 2024; Li et al., 2024). These potential applications will still need to address challenges of scalability, storage, and privacy before wide scale deployment is feasible (Manakhari et al., 2024).

Long-term research has also begun to look into post-quantum security. Since most blockchains currently operate with classical cryptographic primitives, developments in quantum computing could eventually compromise digital signatures, wallet security, and long term evidence preservation (Shaikh et al., 2026). While these are not immediate risks, there is growing interest in quantum-resistant cryptography and post-quantum forensic frameworks (Atlam et al., 2024).

In conclusion, future blockchain forensics will demand interoperable, scalable, and legally sound frameworks. Innovations in areas such as smart analytics, ecosystem forensics in decentralized environments, cross-chain intelligence, privacy-conscious investigations, forensic knowledge fusion, and post-quantum resilience are anticipated to enhance the scalability, attribution, visibility, and trustworthiness of future blockchain investigations.

CONCLUSION

In this chapter, blockchain and cryptocurrency forensics methods for investigating the illegal use of the Darknet ecosystem have been introduced. Despite blockchain transparency allowing many transactions to be traced and analyzed, many challenges are presented to forensics due to pseudonymity and privacy and obfuscation techniques which degrade transaction visibility. As a result, blockchain forensics has become an interdisciplinary subject which uses transaction graph analysis, clustering and flow tracing, anomaly detection, and other external intelligence for attribution and investigation on cryptocurrency networks. Workflows should include data gathering, data preprocessing, graph analysis, attribution, tracing, and validation steps. Criminals are rapidly adapting to traditional tracing methods by using privacy coins, mixers, chain hopping, decentralized finance, highlighting the need for adaptive, intelligence-led investigations. This chapter emphasized the importance of financial intelligence in cyber-security investigations. Blockchain analytics can play a part in attributing ransomware transactions, Darknet market transactions, money laundering operations, and cash-out networks to real-world entities, when correlated with exchange records, OSINT, and other external data sources. Thus, cryptocurrency forensics should be considered a critical part of a modern cybercrime intelligence analysis, rather than a separate task.

Forensic frameworks of the future should be more scalable, explainable, adversarially robust, and support cross-chain investigations. Research should concentrate on intelligent analytics, privacy-preserving forensic frameworks, interoperable intelligence sharing, and multi-source evidence fusion. Forensic investigations, in parallel, should remain committed to legal compliance, ethical standards, transparency, and evidentiary integrity.

Despite the constant innovation of evasion methods by criminals, crypto transactions are not inviolate. Forensic innovations, as well as the convergence of intelligence and analytical solutions, will be necessary to fight cyber and financial crime in future blockchain environments.

REFERENCES

Agarwal, U., Rishiwal, V., Tanwar, S., & Yadav, M. (2024). Blockchain and crypto forensics: Investigating crypto frauds. *International Journal of Network Management, 34*(2), e2255. DOI: 10.1002/nem.2255

Ahmed, A., Abdullah, S., Bukhsh, M., Ahmad, I., & Mushtaq, Z. (2022). An energy-efficient data aggregation mechanism for iot secured by blockchain. *IEEE Access : Practical Innovations, Open Solutions, 10*, 11404–11419. DOI: 10.1109/ACCESS.2022.3146295

Alghuried, A., Alghamdi, A., Alkinoon, A., Choi, S., Mohaisen, M., and Mo-haisen, D. (2025a). Fishing for phishers: Learning-based phishing detection in ethereum transactions. *CoRR*, abs/2504.17953.

Alghuried, A., Alkinoon, A., Alghamdi, A., Choi, S., Mohaisen, M., and Mo-haisen, D. (2025b). Evaluating the vulnerability of ml-based ethereum phishing detectors to single-feature adversarial perturbations. *CoRR*, abs/2504.17684.

Alghuried, A., Alkinoon, M., Mohaisen, M., Wang, A., Zou, C. C., and Mohaisen, D. (2026). Blockchain security and privacy: Threats, challenges, applications, and tools. *Distributed Ledger Technol. Res. Pract.*, 5(1):8:1–8:61.

Alghuried, A., & Mohaisen, D. (2024). Simple perturbations subvert ethereum phishing transactions detection: An empirical analysis. In Lee, J., Emura, K., and Lee, S., editors, *Information Security Applications - 25th Interna-tional Conference, WISA 2024, Jeju Island, South Korea, August 21-23, 2024, Revised Selected Papers*, Lecture Notes in Computer Science, pages 123–137. Springer.

Alsalami, N., & Zhang, B. (2019). Sok: A systematic study of anonymity in cryptocurrencies. In *2019 IEEE Conference on Dependable and Secure Computing, DSC 2019,* Hangzhou, China, November 18-20, 2019, pages 1–9. IEEE. DOI: 10.1109/DSC47296.2019.8937681

Amarasinghe, N., Boyen, X., & McKague, M. (2019). A survey of anonymity of cryptocurrencies. In *Proceedings of the Australasian Computer Science Week Multiconference, ACSW 2019, Sydney, NSW, Australia, January 29-31, 2019*, pages 2:1–2:10. ACM.

Atlam, H. F., Ekuri, N., Azad, M. A., & Lallie, H. S. (2024). Blockchain forensics: A systematic literature review of techniques, applications, challenges, and future directions. *Electronics (Basel), 13*(17), 3568. DOI: 10.3390/electronics13173568

Ayub, M., Saleem, T., Janjua, M. U., and Ahmad, T. (2023). Storage state analysis and extraction of ethereum blockchain smart contracts. *ACM Trans. Softw. Eng. Methodol.*, 32(3):57:1–57:32. 25

Bahamazava, K., & Nanda, R. (2022). The shift of darknet illegal drug trade preferences in cryptocurrency: The question of traceability and deterrence. *Forensic Science International Digital Investigation, 40*(Supplement), 301377. DOI: 10.1016/j.fsidi.2022.301377

Bellagarda, J. S., & Abu-Mahfouz, A. M. (2022). An updated survey on the convergence of distributed ledger technology and artificial intelligence: Current state, major challenges and future direction. *IEEE Access : Practical Innovations, Open Solutions, 10*, 50774–50793. DOI: 10.1109/ACCESS.2022.3173297

Bernab'e, J. B., C'anovas, J. L., Hern'andez-Ramos, J. L., Moreno, R. T., & Skarmeta, A. F. (2019). Privacy-preserving solutions for blockchain: Review and challenges. *IEEE Access : Practical Innovations, Open Solutions*, *7*, 164908–164940. DOI: 10.1109/ACCESS.2019.2950872

Chaudhuri, A., Basak, S., Kira'ly, C., Ryajov, D., & Bautista-Gomez, L. (2024). On the design of ethereum's data availability sampling: A comprehensive simulation study. In *6th Conference on Blockchain Research & Applications for Innovative Networks and Services, BRAINS 2024,* Berlin, Germany, October 9-11, 2024, pages 1–4. IEEE. DOI: 10.1109/BRAINS63024.2024.10732486

Chavan, S., Gundakaram, J., Vaishnavi, S. D., Prasad, S., & Deepa, K. (2024). Real-time data extraction and prediction of cryptocurrency. *IEEE Access : Practical Innovations, Open Solutions*, *12*, 186703–186709. DOI: 10.1109/ACCESS.2024.3513034

Chen, Z., Liu, Y., Beillahi, S. M., Li, Y., & Long, F. (2024). Opentracer: A dynamic transaction trace analyzer for smart contract invariant generation and beyond. In *Proceedings of the 39th IEEE/ACM International Conference on Automated Software Engineering, ASE 2024,* Sacramento, CA, USA, October 27 - November 1, 2024, pages 2399–2402. ACM. DOI: 10.1145/3691620.3695361

Dearden, T. E., & Tucker, S. E. (2023). Follow the money: Analyzing dark-net activity using cryptocurrency and the bitcoin blockchain. *Journal of Contemporary Criminal Justice*, *39*(2), 257–275. DOI: 10.1177/10439862231157521

Dudani, S., Baggili, I., Raymond, D. R., & Marchany, R. (2023). The current state of cryptocurrency forensics. *Forensic Science International Digital Investigation*, *46*, 301576. DOI: 10.1016/j.fsidi.2023.301576

Europol. (2021). Cryptocurrencies: Tracing the evolution of criminal finances. Technical report.

Gao, W., Hatcher, W. G., & Yu, W. (2018). A survey of blockchain: Techniques, applications, and challenges. In *27th International Conference on Computer Communication and Networks, ICCCN 2018,* Hangzhou, China, July 30 - August 2, 2018, pages 1–11. IEEE. DOI: 10.1109/ICCCN.2018.8487348

Gjorgjev, J., Ramadhan, M. F., & Dhamayana, S. (2025). Blockchain forensics- unmasking anonymity in dark web transactions. *International Journal of Criminology and Sociology*, *14*, 68–75. DOI: 10.6000/1929-4409.2025.14.07

Huang, D. Y., Aliapoulios, M. M., Li, V. G., Invernizzi, L., Bursztein, E., McRoberts, K., Levin, J., Levchenko, K., Snoeren, A. C., & McCoy, D. (2018). Tracking ransomware end-to-end. In *2018 IEEE Symposium on Security and Privacy, SP 2018, Proceedings, 21-23 May 2018, San Francisco, California, USA*, pages 618–631. IEEE Computer Society.

Igonor, O. S., Amin, M. B., and Garg, S. (2025). The application of blockchain technology in the field of digital forensics: A literature review. *Blockchains*, 3(1).

Khalilov, M. C. K., & Levi, A. (2018). A survey on anonymity and privacy in bitcoin-like digital cash systems. *IEEE Communications Surveys and Tutorials*, *20*(3), 2543–2585. DOI: 10.1109/COMST.2018.2818623

Kili¸c, B., Özturan, C., & Sen, A. (2022). Parallel analysis of ethereum blockchain transaction data using cluster computing. *Cluster Computing*, *25*(3), 1885–1898. DOI: 10.1007/s10586-021-03511-0

Kilic, Y., Destek, M. A., Cevik, E. I., Bugan, M. F., Korkmaz, O., & Dibooglu, S. (2022). Return and risk spillovers between the ESG global index and stock markets: Evidence from time and frequency analysis. *Borsa Istanbul Review*, *22*, S141–S156. DOI: 10.1016/j.bir.2022.11.015

Kushwaha, S. S., Joshi, S., Singh, D., Kaur, M., & Lee, H. (2022). Ethereum smart contract analysis tools: A systematic review. *IEEE Access : Practical Innovations, Open Solutions*, *10*, 57037–57062. DOI: 10.1109/ACCESS.2022.3169902

Kuzuno, H., & Karam, C. (2017). Blockchain explorer: An analytical process and investigation environment for bitcoin. In *2017 APWG Symposium on Electronic Crime Research, eCrime 2017, Phoenix, AZ, USA, April 25-27, 2017*, pages 9–16. IEEE.

Li, M., Shen, Y., Ye, G., He, J., Zheng, X., Zhang, Z., Zhu, L., & Conti, M. (2024). Anonymous, secure, traceable, and efficient decentralized digital forensics. *IEEE Transactions on Knowledge and Data Engineering*, *36*(5), 1874–1888. DOI: 10.1109/TKDE.2023.3321712

Lone, A. H., & Mir, R. N. (2019). Forensic-chain: Blockchain based digital forensics chain of custody with poc in hyperledger composer. *Digital Investigation*, *28*(Supplement), 44–55. DOI: 10.1016/j.diin.2019.01.002

Manakhari, S. S., Jadhav, A. P., Paraye, T., and Gate, A. (2024). Improving data accessibility with distributed file system: A blockchain ethereum approach. *European Journal of Computer Science and Information Technology*.

Marhoon, H. M., Basil, N., & Ma'arif, A. (2023). Exploring blockchain data analysis and its communications architecture: achievements, challenges, and future directions: a review article. *International Journal of Robotics and Control Systems*, *3*(3), 609–626. DOI: 10.31763/ijrcs.v3i3.1100

Meiklejohn, S., Pomarole, M., Jordan, G., Levchenko, K., McCoy, D., Voelker, G. M., & Savage, S. (2016). A fistful of bitcoins: Characterizing payments among men with no names. *Communications of the ACM*, *59*(4), 86–93. DOI: 10.1145/2896384

Mo¨ser, M., Bo¨hme, R., & Breuker, D. (2013). An inquiry into money laundering tools in the bitcoin ecosystem. In *2013 APWG eCrime Researchers Summit, eCrime 2013, San Francisco, CA, USA, September 17-18, 2013*, pages 1–14. IEEE. DOI: 10.1109/eCRS.2013.6805780

Mo¨ser, M., Soska, K., Heilman, E., Lee, K., Heffan, H., Srivastava, S., Hogan, K., Hennessey, J., Miller, A., Narayanan, A., & Christin, N. (2018). An empirical analysis of traceability in the monero blockchain. *Proceedings on Privacy Enhancing Technologies. Privacy Enhancing Technologies Symposium*, *2018*(3), 143–163. DOI: 10.1515/popets-2018-0025

Paquet-Clouston, M., Haslhofer, B., & Dupont, B. (2019). Ransomware payments in the bitcoin ecosystem. *Journal of Cybersecurity*, *5*(1), tyz003. DOI: 10.1093/cybsec/tyz003

Parihar, A., Kumar, A., & Kumar, A. (2024). Tracing transaction across bitcoin address behaviour for pattern analysis. In *2024 First International Conference on Technological Innovations and Advance Computing (TIACOMP)*, pages 244–249. IEEE. DOI: 10.1109/TIACOMP64125.2024.00049

Pasdar, A., Lee, Y. C., and Dong, Z. (2023). Connect API with blockchain: A survey on blockchain oracle implementation. *ACM Comput. Surv.*, 55(10):208:1–208:39.

Pocher, N. (2025). Obfuscation and traceability. In *Crypto-Asset Ecosystems and the EU Anti-Money Laundering Framework: Law and Technology Perspectives*, pages 95–134. Springer. DOI: 10.1007/978-3-031-94698-1_4

Shaikh, M., Wiil, U. K., Ebrahimi, A., & Memon, Y. (2026). An overview and comparison of blockchain consensus mechanisms. *Int. J. Networked Distributed Comput.*, *14*(1), 4. DOI: 10.1007/s44227-025-00087-8

Soska, K., & Christin, N. (2015). Measuring the longitudinal evolution of the online anonymous marketplace ecosystem. In Jung, J. and Holz, T., editors, *24th USENIX Security Symposium, USENIX Security 15, Washington, D.C., USA, August 12-14, 2015*, pages 33–48. USENIX Association.

Su, V. H., Gupta, S. S., & Khan, A. (2022). Automating ETL and mining of ethereum blockchain network. In *WSDM '22: The Fifteenth ACM Interna-tional Conference on Web Search and Data Mining, Virtual Event* / Tempe, AZ, USA, February 21 - 25, 2022, pages 1581–1584. ACM. DOI: 10.1145/3488560.3502187

Syed, S., Iqbal, A., Mehmood, W., Syed, Z., Khan, M., & Pau, G. (2023). Split-second cryptocurrency forecast using prognostic deep learning algorithms: Data curation by deephaven. *IEEE Access : Practical Innovations, Open Solutions*, *11*, 128644–128654. DOI: 10.1109/ACCESS.2023.3331652

Temu, R., & Louca, S. (2025). Evaluation of crypto assets investigation techniques: Bitcoin address clustering. In da Cunha, P. R. and Themistocleous, M., editors, *Information Systems - 22nd European, Mediterranean, and Middle Eastern Conference, EMCIS 2025, Paphos, Cyprus, September 11-12, 2025, Proceedings, Part I*, Lecture Notes in Business Information Processing, pages 187–204. Springer.

Wei, Q., Li, B., Chang, W., Jia, Z., Shen, Z., and Shao, Z. (2022). A survey of blockchain data management systems. *ACM Trans. Embed. Comput. Syst.*, 21(3):25:1–25:28.

Wu, Y., Luo, A., & Xu, D. (2019). Forensic analysis of bitcoin transactions. In *2019 IEEE International Conference on Intelligence and Security Informatics, ISI 2019,* Shenzhen, China, July 1-3, 2019, pages 167–169. IEEE.

Xiao, N., Wang, Z., Sun, X., & Miao, J. (2024). A novel blockchain-based digital forensics framework for preserving evidence and enabling investigation in industrial internet of things. *Alexandria Engineering Journal*, *86*, 631–643. DOI: 10.1016/j.aej.2023.12.021

Zhang, R., Xue, R., and Liu, L. (2019). Security and privacy on blockchain. 52(3).

Zhang, Y., Wang, J., & Luo, J. (2020). Heuristic-based address clustering in bitcoin. *IEEE Access : Practical Innovations, Open Solutions*, *8*, 210582–210591. DOI: 10.1109/ACCESS.2020.3039570

Zhao, Y., Qu, Y., Xiang, Y., Uddin, M. P., Peng, D., and Gao, L. (2025). A comprehensive survey on edge data integrity verification: Fundamentals and future trends. *ACM Comput. Surv.*, 57(1):8:1–8:34.

Zhao, Z., Wang, J., Shi, K., & Zhang, H. (2022). Improving address clustering in bitcoin by proposing heuristics. *IEEE Transactions on Network and Service Management*, *19*(4), 3737–3749. DOI: 10.1109/TNSM.2022.3186466

Chapter 8
Extremist and Illegal Content Dissemination in the Darknet Ecosystem

Abdullah AlShuaibi
http://orcid.org/0000-0001-9073-5956
King Faisal University, Saudi Arabia

Lulu Alarfaj
Binghamton University, USA

ABSTRACT

This chapter examines the role of the Darknet as a platform for disseminating extremist and illegal content, including propaganda, recruitment materials, hate speech, and illicit media. The anonymity, resilience, and censorship resistance provided by Darknet technologies have enabled extremist groups and criminal actors to distribute content at scale while evading detection and takedown efforts. This chapter analyzes the structure, channels, and techniques used for content dissemination, including encrypted forums, hidden services, and decentralized platforms. A key focus is placed on understanding how such content is produced, propagated, and consumed within closed and semi-open communities. The chapter also explores the use of emerging technologies, including artificial intelligence and automated bots, to amplify extremist narratives and target vulnerable audiences. Furthermore, the chapter discusses detection and mitigation strategies, including content analysis using machine learning, Darknet monitoring, and collaborative efforts between law enforcement, technology companies

1. INTRODUCTION

The proliferation of extremist and illegal content across networked information environments has emerged as one of the most consequential challenges confronting contemporary cybersecurity, law enforcement, and democratic governance. Whereas the early scholarship on online radicalisation concentrated through publicly accessible social media, a second wave of research, accelerating after 2015, has documented a structural migration of extremist activity towards anonymity-preserving environments, encrypted messaging services, and decentralised hosting platforms. Bibliometric analysis of Dark Web

DOI: 10.4018/979-8-3373-9755-9.ch008

scholarship between 2011 and 2023 shows a sustained upward trajectory in academic publications, with notable peaks in 2018, 2021, and 2023 that align with high-profile takedown operations, the operational maturation of cryptomarkets, and the diffusion of large language models into both attacker and defender toolkits (Adel & Norouzifard, 2024). The Darknet, once a marginal infrastructural concern, now occupies a central position in any serious account of how illicit ideas, materials, and operational know-how travel across the internet.

The following are three important affordances of Darknet that enable extremist and criminal conduct. Firstly, anonymous communication systems such as Tor create sender-receiver unlinkability through multi-level encryption and onion routing technology, making attribution expensive and risky (Dingledine, Mathewson, & Syverson, 2004). Secondly, hidden services and federated platforms are quite resilient. That is to say, in case of seizures of some nodes, the entire system re-emerges through URL hopping, mirroring, and diverse platforms (Owenson, Cortes, & Lewman, 2018). Thirdly, the Darknet environment is embedded within a more general ecosystem of encrypted messaging apps, gaming forums, and mainstream social networks, allowing for construction of elaborate value chains that take advantage of comparative strengths of each layer (Conway, 2017; Clifford & Powell, 2019; Jardine, 2019). However, these affordances are not the drivers of radicalization by themselves, but rather make the process of creation, storage, and distribution of materials that could be considered extremist in accordance with modern moderation practices much easier.

Thus, the implications of the issue become evident for society and security sphere. Extremist materials posted via Darknet channels have been identified as contributing to terrorist group recruitment, attack planning, spreading of hate speech among semi-public communities, and long-term child abuse through child sexual abuse materials. Empirical evidence obtained since October 2023 in the course of research into lone actors suggests the existence of paths from algorithmic exposure on mainstream platforms to interaction with Telegram and Rocket. Thus, the risks are indeed high: any initiative to combat the threat will need to address both technical infrastructure, that allows for materials dissemination, and social processes that drive audience towards extremist orbit.

The following chapter represents an interdisciplinary review targeting researchers, policy-makers, and cybersecurity experts who deal with Darknet-related harm. It is organised around five main topics. First, it provides an up-to-date knowledge base regarding the Darknet infrastructure and content typology, leveraging systematic literature reviews of Tor hidden services (Huete Trujillo & Ruiz-Martínez, 2021), bibliometric analysis of the Dark Web (Adel & Norouzifard, 2024), and latest longitudinal measurement of unique onion services (Rodriguez Barredo-Valenzuela, Pastrana Portillo, & Suarez-Tangil, 2025). Second, it presents a framework organising dissemination mechanisms as an ecosystem that includes production, anonymisation, community formation, and cross-platform migration. Third, it covers the state of the art in computational detection, including pre-trained dark-specific language models like DarkBERT (Jin, Jang, Cui, Chung, Lee, & Shin, 2023) and multimodal learning-to-rank systems (Al-Nabki, Fidalgo, Alegre, & Chaves, 2019), alongside the critical evaluation of performance metrics in the area (Aldera, Emam, Al-Qurishi, Alrubaian, & Alothaim, 2021). Fourth, it discusses mitigation and counter-measures, including counter-narrative campaigns assessed in terms of Campbell Collaboration standards (Carthy, Doody, Cox, O'Hora, & Sarma, 2020; Doolan, Cox, & Sarma, 2025) and platform-disruption operations. Fifth, it critically assesses the legal, ethical, and methodological constraints that define the limits of our empirical knowledge about Darknet user population and lawful and proportional actions against it (Conway, 2021; Macdonald et al., 2019).

The chapter is divided into eleven substantive sections. Section 2 presents technical and theoretical foundations of the field including Darknet architecture, content typology and online radicalisation psychology. Section 3 details dissemination strategies and ecosystem dynamics, with particular attention to cross-platform migration. Section 4 covers the technologies that enable dissemination (decentralised storage and AI-driven amplification). Section 5 discusses different techniques for the detection and monitoring of Darknet activity. Section 6 covers the topic of mitigation and countermeasures. The legal, ethical and policy landscape is discussed in Section 7. Section 8 provides case studies, Section 9 discusses research gaps, Section 10 examines future trends such as the emergence of generative AI, and Section 11 gives strategic recommendations. The analytical approach adopted in the chapter is deliberately critical – the literature is full of methodologically poor works and one of the contributions of the chapter is to draw the line between empirically supported and simply speculative statements..

2. BACKGROUND AND FOUNDATIONS

2.1 Darknet Technologies and Communication Channels

Darknet can be described as an overlay network which is accessed using specific client software implementing anonymous routing and addressing schemes. There are three main branches of darknets studied by modern researchers: Tor, providing onion routing with low latency for interactive use and hosting; I2P, offering similar services using garlic routing and fully internal addressing; and Freenet, focusing on censorship resistance based on content storage among many others. Out of these three, Tor is the most popular and widely studied darknet and, most importantly, the one which is used for hosting extremist and illegal materials. Onions-routing scheme implemented by Tor routes the traffic through three volunteers' nodes, where each node knows only about its immediate predecessors and successors, making the traffic senders-receivers unlinkable (Dingledine, Mathewson & Syverson, 2004).

Tor Hidden Services, rebranded by the Tor Project as onion services allow the operator of such service to hide its IP address from being revealed while publishing any kind of material. The latest systematic literature review of the field (Huete Trujillo & Ruiz-Martínez, 2021) summarises over a decade of research in the area and shows that the methodologically advanced approach to researching the darknet consists of content classification of hidden services. In addition to this, the review provides the description of various methods of deanonymization, traffic confirmation, fingerprinting and protocol-based vulnerabilities, demonstrating that the majority of successful attribution cases were caused by the operational security failure of hidden services' operators, not the cryptographic vulnerability of Tor itself.

Encrypted communication platforms are not technically located inside the Darknet but exist on its perimeter and, thus, are considered as the part of its infrastructural fabric by the research literature. Later, Clifford and Powell (2019) have proved in their report for the Program on Extremism at George Washington University that English-speaking supporters of messaging apps such as Telegram, Rocket. Chat, Element and others to diversify the platform set in order to decrease the effect of takedown actions.

2.2 Nature of Extremist and Illegal Content

Extreme or illicit darknet content can be divided into a number of analytically discrete categories. More and more systematic reviews have focused on content from far-right or white-supremacist extremist groups. The Campbell Collaboration protocol on reviewing literature on far-right online propaganda by Doolan, Cox and Sarma (2025) not only points to the dramatic expansion of mobilization of right-wing extremists in Europe but also to the methodological heterogeneity of the research conducted. Another literature has emerged around gaming-oriented sites: Schlegel et al. (2025) described hateful content on Mod DB and related modification forums, arguing that game mods, Discord-like server communities and streaming platforms are easy access points into more secure extremist communities.

Content classified as child sexual abuse material (CSAM) is another analytically discrete category. Crime script analysis of four Darknet CSEM forums, obtained through law enforcement channels, was performed by Van der Bruggen and Blokland (2021), revealing stages of joining communities, creating content, distributing it, and training in tradecraft for maintaining security. Gannon et al. (2023) conduct a synthesis of that and other work to show the organizational structure of Darknet CSAM forums, where individual forums have been found to consist of hundreds of thousands of registered users, an order of magnitude greater than most extremist communities that have been studied to date. Besides these categories, there are also Darknet marketplaces selling narcotics, firearms, and stolen logins. While conceptually separate from extremist content distribution channels, those marketplaces share infrastructure and behavioral practices (escrow services, reputation systems of vendors, tutorials on operational security) which emerge in extremist settings and afford useful comparison (Al-Nabki et al., 2019).

2.3 Online Radicalization and Content Consumption

Radicalisation pathways through Darknet content are mediated by the same psychological and social mechanisms at play in surface-web environments, but inflected by the particular affordances of anonymity-preserving platforms. Macdonald and Whittaker (2019) show that the conceptual ambiguity of the terms 'radicalisation' and 'self-radicalisation' impedes the cumulability of empirical findings and the translation of research into policy. This definitional fragmentation matters: studies operationalising radicalisation as a measurable behavioural outcome (e.g. posting frequency in an extremist forum) are not directly comparable to studies operating with an attitudinal shift or movement along a stage model.

Empirical work however converges on a number of mechanisms. Closed-forum echo-chamber dynamics bolster in-group identification and out-group hostility; operational-security training rituals impose commitment costs that tie members to the community; and the creation of insider lexicons and visual codes fosters a sense of cultural belonging that mainstream platforms can't match. Urman and Katz (2022) observed that rapid network expansion in far-right communities on Telegram began around the time of mass bans of far-right players on mainstream platforms, noting that cross-actor connections were rapidly rebuilt after they migrated, showing that deplatforming acts as a network-restructuring event rather than a clean reduction in activity.

2.4 Content Dissemination Mechanisms

Five channels manage the spread of darknet. Forums, organized on the principle of thematic boards and reputation, serve as the backbone of many extremist and illegal communities as a place for content storage and user identification. Marketplaces, built upon the Silk Road model, provide economic infrastructure, escrow service, vendor ratings, dispute settlement system, which has found its application in other criminal spaces. Mass distribution of magazines, video materials, and operation guides is enabled by peer-to-peer file sharing services (onion-hosted or available via clearnet proxies). Increasingly, archival duplication relies on decentralized solutions like IPFS-based content addressing or federated social networks based on the ActivityPub protocol. And finally, encrypted messengers play the role of the communication glue between all those layers and enable real-time coordination and recruitment to secured environments (Clifford & Powell, 2019; Stockhammer, 2025).

In their empirical study on the topic and content structure of Tor Hidden Services Faizan and Khan (2019) demonstrated that these sites concentrate in a relatively few number of content categories and have high rates of churn among active addresses. In their longitudinal Mimir crawl Rodriguez Barredo-Valenzuela et al. (2025) have provided a much more detailed look into this structure. Their study of more than 25 thousand unique websites showed that around 82 percent of analyzed landing pages were replicants, and 74.4 percent of unique surviving sites were engaged in cybercrimes if the mirrors are excluded from the analysis. The methodology conclusion is that mirror pre-processing is a standard procedure before any claim about prevalence of darknet content is made.

Table 1. Types of extremist and illegal content in the Darknet and their characteristics

Content type	Primary platforms	Producer profile	Distinguishing technical traits	Representative evidence
Far-right and white-supremacist material	Telegram channels; gaming-adjacent forums; some onion sites	Decentralised network of ideologically aligned actors	Memetic content; coded vocabulary; rapid cross-actor amplification	Urman & Katz (2022); Schlegel et al. (2025); Doolan et al. (2025)
Recruitment and Da'wa material	Closed Darknet forums; invitation-only chat servers	Ideological influencers and "preachers"	Long-form sermons; question-and-answer threads; reputation-anchored authority	Lewinsky et al. (2024); Clifford & Powell (2019)
Child sexual abuse material (CSAM)	Onion forums; private file-sharing networks	Networked offenders with role specialisation	Hashed deduplication evasion; tradecraft tutorials; tiered access privileges	Van der Bruggen & Blokland (2021); Gannon et al. (2023); Lee et al. (2020)
Operational and tactical manuals	Onion repositories; encrypted file shares	Mixed (movement insiders and unaffiliated authors)	PDF and text formats; cross-posted with surface-web mirrors	Conway (2017); Clifford & Powell (2019)
Illicit marketplaces (drugs, firearms, credentials)	Onion marketplaces with escrow	Vendor–buyer dyads; commercially motivated	Cryptocurrency settlement; reputation systems; PGP-mediated trust	Al-Nabki et al. (2019); Rodriguez Barredo-Valenzuela et al. (2025)
Hate speech and incitement	Cross-platform (mainstream → Telegram → Darknet)	Decentralised producers; volume-driven	Short-form posts; rapid migration after takedowns	Jardine (2019); Rogers (2020); Urman & Katz (2022)

3. DISSEMINATION STRATEGIES AND ECOSYSTEM DYNAMICS

3.1 Content Production and Distribution Pipelines

Darknet dissemination can be conceptualized as the product of a well-structured process encompassing the entire production cycle, rather than an ad hoc content publishing mechanism. In case of organized groups media operation at its height, the pipeline includes centralized content creation, quality assurance, translation and deliberate staged release via multiple communication platforms that are chosen with redundancy in mind. The idea of a production pipeline applies to other ideological groups as well. Although far-right organizations do not have the same degree of structural integrity in terms of editorial practices, Urman and Katz (2022) discovered that even decentralized far-right Telegram communities demonstrate the reproducible pattern of inter-actor amplification, whereby a limited number of high centrality accounts seed the content to be distributed among the broader ring of supporters.

In tandem with the advances in detection technology, content packaging techniques have become more sophisticated. Video compression minimizes distribution costs and reduces the possibility of automatic content hashing; translations and editing enable to reach a wider audience and make moderation more difficult; ideological materials hidden inside innocuous content, as Schlegel et al. (2025) show in the gaming environment, eliminate the barriers preventing the audience of interest from accessing such materials. Finally, the schedule of the content release itself becomes an active tool, as content that is being released at the time of the operation gains more visibility.

3.2 Use of Anonymity and Encryption

Anonymity and encryption are not just defensive strategies, but constitutive elements of Darknet dissemination practice. At the network layer, Tor onion routing provides the basic guarantee of sender-receiver unlinkability (Dingledine et al., 2004). At the application layer, operators routinely use PGP-encrypted message exchange, ephemeral chat sessions and cryptocurrency settlement to fragment the evidentiary footprint of any one transaction. Huete Trujillo and Ruiz-Martínez (2021) catalogue the main deanonymisation attack families and show that operator error, reuse of clearnet credentials, leakage of distinctive writing style, misconfiguration of hidden-service software, remains the dominant attribution vector, an observation with significant implications for both offensive and defensive operations.

Encryption also constitutes community boundaries. Invitation-only Telegram supergroups, PGP-gated onion forums, and access-tier systems in CSAM communities (Van der Bruggen & Blokland, 2021) use cryptographic and procedural gating to build increasingly committed inner circles. The functional effect is two-fold: cryptographic barriers increase the cost of infiltration for researchers and law enforcement, and the rituals of gaining access create commitment costs that bind members to the community in ways that pure ideological agreement does not.

3.3 Network Structures and Community Formation

The use of network analytics has provided valuable insights into the structure of Darknet communities that could not have been gained through content analysis alone. Al-Nabki et al. (2019) have combined user visible text, HTML tags, named entities, network structure, and visual data in a learning-to-rank approach based on content analysis, which has produced NDCG scores of 0.95 for a drugs related case study, showing that identifying influential domains becomes easier when network structure is taken into account as first-class features rather than as auxiliary metadata. Urman and Katz (2022) have used similar methods for analysing far-right Telegram networks, and found that cross-actor links proved to be very resilient and could withstand multiple takedown operations with reconstitution periods lasting only days and not months.

Community development on the Darknet shows all signs of a high-commitment online community: presence of explicit onboarding processes, the presence of an internal hierarchy, and development of a unique lingua franca and visual codes which serve both to define the community identity and to exclude external actors. Gannon et al. (2023) have described tiered access control systems in operation in CSAM forums where access rights are progressively increased by the creation and/or sharing of new material. Similar processes are at play in extremist communities where creating new propaganda material, translations, or operational analysis provides status gains..

3.4 Cross-Platform Dissemination

The most important conceptual development in this literature in the last five years has been the insight that Darknet dissemination cannot be studied in isolation. Jardine (2019) describes a surface Web-to-Dark Web content cycle in which moderation on mainstream platforms pushes malicious content to the Dark Web, which then percolates back to the surface Web through identifiable pathways. The implication is that the online information environment requires management of the entire system, not just surface-Web hosts.

Empirical work on platform migration in the wake of the 2019 Europol-coordinated Telegram takedowns found that takedowns created "migration moments" across more than a dozen alternative messaging platforms rather than disappearing (Clifford & Powell, 2019). Rogers (2020) conceptualised deplatforming as migration of "Internet celebrities" to Telegram and alternative social media and found that audiences thinned but posting frequency was stable – an outcome that muddies the simple intuition that takedowns reduce harm. Stockhammer (2025) applies this analysis to recent lone-actor cases, documenting six European cases (Vienna, Solingen, Zurich, etc.) in which TikTok algorithmic exposure to content led to engagement with Telegram and Rocket. Darknet does not function as the primary radicalisation site but rather as a downstream archival and operational layer, which users already in extremist orbits access through mainstream platforms.

Figure 1. Pipeline of extremist content dissemination across Darknet and hybrid platforms. Forward dissemination flows downward from mainstream-platform exposure (Stockhammer, 2025) through encrypted-messenger onboarding to Darknet archival and operational layers; the orange path traces the surface-to-Dark-Web content cycle described by Jardine (2019), in which content re-circulates back to surface platforms after archival hardening

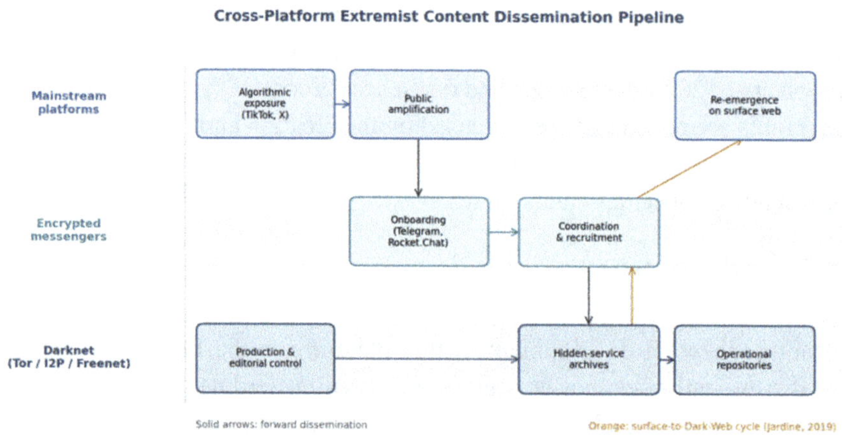

4. TECHNOLOGIES ENABLING CONTENT DISSEMINATION

4.1 Anonymity Networks and Hosting Mechanisms

The technical substrate of Darknet dissemination remains dominated by Tor onion services. The version 3 onion service protocol introduced longer addresses, stronger cryptography, and improved resistance to denial-of-service attacks, but the fundamental architectural pattern, introduction points, rendezvous protocol, and distributed hash table for service descriptors, has been stable for more than a decade (Dingledine et al., 2004; Huete Trujillo & Ruiz-Martínez, 2021). The Mimir longitudinal crawl (Rodriguez Barredo-Valenzuela et al., 2025) provides the most recent large-scale measurement of this substrate, characterising the size, churn, and content distribution of unique onion services and demonstrating that mirror detection is essential to any quantitatively defensible claim about Darknet scale.

Hosting mechanisms outside Tor have grown in operational relevance even where they have not commanded equivalent research attention. I2P provides a fully internal addressing scheme that supports both interactive use and hosting, with garlic routing offering different latency and adversary-model trade-offs from Tor's circuit construction. Freenet emphasises censorship resistance through distributed content storage and has historically attracted content categories (notably CSAM) that depend on resilient archival rather than interactive communication. The literature on extremist content specifically within I2P and Freenet remains comparatively sparse, a gap noted in Section 9 of this chapter.

4.2 Decentralised Platforms and Distributed Storage

Decentralised platforms operate on architectural principles that differ fundamentally from those of Tor hidden services. The InterPlanetary File System (IPFS) implements content-addressed storage in which files are referenced by cryptographic hashes rather than by location-bound URLs, producing a form of content persistence that is highly resistant to takedowns of any single host. ActivityPub-federated social networks, Mastodon, Pleroma, and related implementations, distribute identity and content storage across independently administered servers, creating substantial coordination costs for any cross-server moderation effort. Blockchain-anchored archival systems leverage the immutability properties of distributed ledgers to record content references in tamper-evident logs.

Peer-reviewed empirical work on the use of these systems for extremist and illegal content remains comparatively sparse. The verified literature signals decentralised and censorship-resistant platforms as likely future venues for extremist content storage, but the bulk of current evidence concerns IPFS and federated platforms in their general operational contexts rather than in specific extremist case studies. This is a clear research gap that this chapter flags both here and in Section 9.

4.3 AI and Automation in Content Amplification

The diffusion of generative AI into adversary toolkits is a defining concern of the 2024–2026 literature. Mirsky and Lee (2021), in their ACM Computing Surveys treatment of deepfake creation and detection, document that generative-text-detection benchmarks remain unstable in the face of adversarial paraphrasing and that image-deepfake detection performance degrades sharply on compressed social-media content. Two implications follow for Darknet research. First, synthetic content increases the volume of material that detection systems must triage, raising the cost of operational monitoring even where individual detector performance remains acceptable. Second, the same underlying models can be fine-tuned on Dark Web corpora to produce more effective domain-specific classifiers, as DarkBERT (Jin et al., 2023) has illustrated for the defender side of this contest.

Automated bots remain a workhorse of cross-platform amplification, particularly in the far-right ecosystem mapped by Urman and Katz (2022), where high-centrality accounts function as redistribution nodes for content originating elsewhere. Recommendation systems on mainstream platforms, the algorithmic substrate documented by Stockhammer (2025) in the lone-actor cases since October 2023, function as the inadvertent first stage of cross-platform pipelines whose downstream layers reside on Telegram, Rocket.Chat, and the Darknet.

4.4 Cryptographic Techniques and Access Control

The way cryptographic access control works in the Darknet is through a series of nested techniques. PGP-gated forums expect users who join them to prove their cryptographic proficiency in order to become part of the forum, thus making it harder for researchers and the police to penetrate the community. The invitation-only method relies on social verification from other members of the forum, placing access control within the context of social ties. Tiers work by providing members with escalating access privileges depending on whether they can provide new material, thus combining access control and obligation to perpetrate offending behavior of the community.

It becomes clear how these mechanisms may influence detection and intervention. In terms of detection, all the content which is beyond the first level of access is unavailable to crawlers, making computer analyses tend to be focused on the parts of the community that are most visible and least involved. Intervention-wise, disruption of access control system can be more efficient than elimination of single items of content.

Table 2. Technologies facilitating extremist content dissemination: Capabilities and risks

Technology	Capability for adversary	Risk to society	Maturity	Evidence base
Tor onion services	Sender–receiver unlinkability; resilient hosting	Sustained availability of extremist and CSAM content; high attribution cost	High	Dingledine et al. (2004); Huete Trujillo & Ruiz-Martínez (2021); Rodriguez Barredo-Valenzuela et al. (2025)
I2P / Freenet	Alternative anonymity routing; censorship-resistant storage	Redundant hosting layer for the most resilient content categories	Medium	Faizan & Khan (2019); Gehl (2018)
IPFS and content-addressed storage	Location-independent, hash-addressed content persistence	Takedown resistance through content addressing	Medium	Owenson et al. (2018) for analogous resilience; gap in extremist-specific literature
Federated (ActivityPub) networks	Identity and content distribution across independent servers	Coordination costs for cross-server moderation	Medium	Jardine (2019) for cross-platform displacement
Encrypted messengers (Telegram, Rocket.Chat, Element)	Real-time coordination; large channel reach; cryptographic group gating	Recruitment funnel into more secured environments	High	Bloom et al. (2019); Clifford & Powell (2019); Stockhammer (2025)
Generative LLMs and image models	Scaled production of synthetic propaganda; multilingual translation	Increased triage cost for defenders; adversarial paraphrasing	Rapidly increasing	Mirsky & Lee (2021); Jin et al. (2023)
Cryptocurrency and privacy coins	Pseudonymous settlement for marketplaces and donations	Financial sustenance for illicit ecosystems	High	Al-Nabki et al. (2019)
PGP-gated and tiered access systems	Layered community boundaries; commitment costs	Inaccessibility of inner-tier content to researchers and law enforcement	High	Van der Bruggen & Blokland (2021); Gannon et al. (2023)

5. DETECTION AND MONITORING TECHNIQUES

5.1 Darknet Crawling and Data Collection

The basic methodological problem for computational work in the area is constructing representative Darknet corpora. Much of the published work has been based on the Darknet Usage Text Addresses (DUTA) family of datasets, DUTA-10K and the more recent CoDA classification corpus, which provide labelled samples across the narcotics, weapons, financial fraud and extremist categories (Al-Nabki et al., 2019). Another methodological vulnerability is the continued centrality of these legacy corpora: when the evidentiary weight for an entire subfield rests on a handful of legacy corpora, reported model performance is as much a reflection of the properties of those specific corpora as it is a reflection of general capability.

The longitudinal crawl of Mimir proposed by Rodriguez Barredo-Valenzuela et al. (2025) is a methodological advance in three ways. First, its scale, more than 25,000 unique sites, allows characterisation of distributional properties that smaller corpora cannot support. Second, its heuristic-based mirror detection addresses a problem that prior work has largely neglected. Third, its longitudinal design enables characterisation of churn and content lifespan, complementing the cross-sectional bias of the existing literature. The headline finding, visualised in Figure 2, is that approximately 82 percent of analysed landing pages are replicas and that 74.4 percent of unique surviving sites are associated with cybercrime once mirrors are removed. This has direct implications for any subsequent prevalence claim about content category distribution on the Darknet.

Figure 2. Mirror filtering reshapes prevalence estimates on the Darknet. Left: of all crawled landing pages, only ≈18% remain after heuristic mirror detection; of these, ≈74.4% (≈13.4% of the original crawl) are associated with cybercrime activities. Right: composition of unique non-mirror sites. Without mirror filtering, headline prevalence figures substantially overstate the diversity and resilience of illicit content. Data: Rodriguez Barredo-Valenzuela, Pastrana Portillo, and Suarez-Tangil (2025), Mimir longitudinal crawl of more than 25,000 unique Tor sites

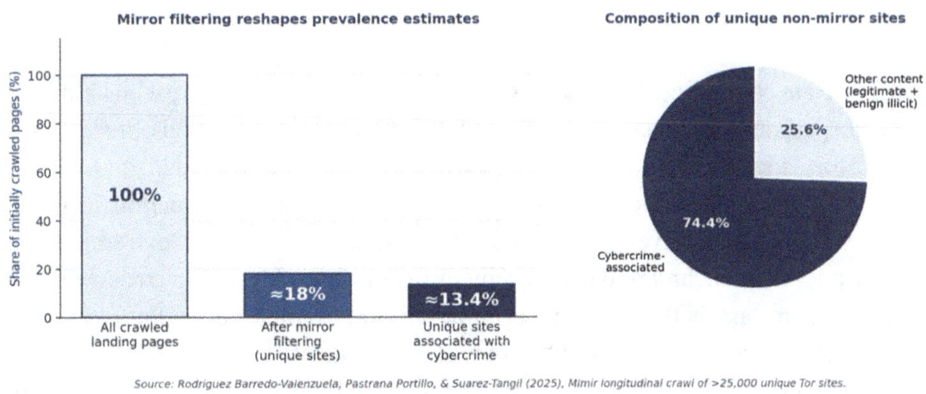

5.2 Machine Learning and NLP-Based Content Analysis

Pre-trained language models have substantially advanced the state of the art in Darknet content classification. Cascavilla, Catolino, and Sangiovanni (2022) compared ULMFit, BERT, RoBERTa, and LSTM architectures on a 113,995-document onion-site corpus, reporting BERT accuracy of 96.08 percent for general Dark Web content classification and 91.98 percent for drug-type identification (Figure 3). DarkBERT (Jin et al., 2023), pre-trained on a Dark Web text corpus, represents a further methodological advance, outperforming surface-web-trained baselines on activity classification, ransomware-leak-site identification, and notable-thread detection. Domain-specific pre-training, in line with broader findings from NLP, captures vocabulary, register, and topical structure that general-purpose models miss.

Figure 3. BERT performance on Darknet classification tasks reported by Cascavilla, Catolino, and Sangiovanni (2022). Accuracies reflect held-out splits from a single 113,995-document onion-site corpus and should be interpreted as upper bounds: concept drift, multilingual content, and adversarial obfuscation reduce out-of-distribution performance substantially (Aldera et al., 2021; Mirsky & Lee, 2021)

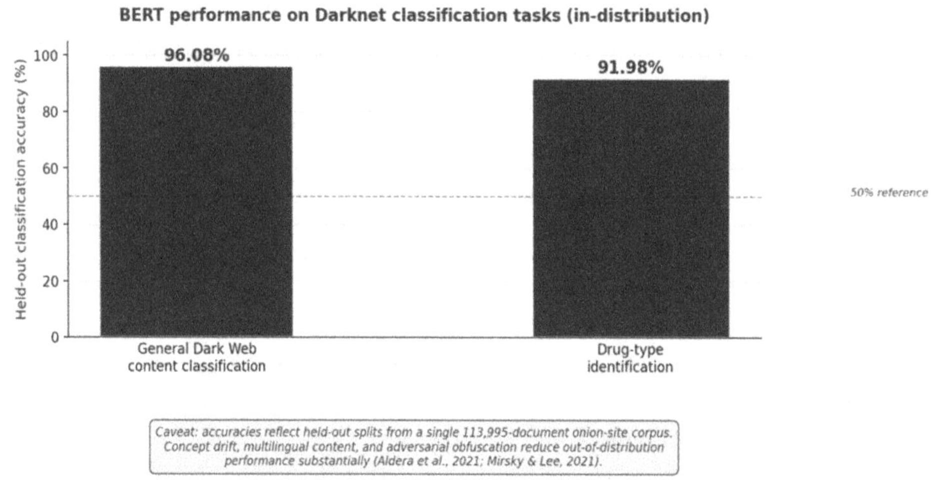

These results warrant careful interpretation. Reported accuracies typically rest on held-out splits from a single labelled corpus, and concept drift, multilingual content, and adversarial obfuscation reduce out-of-distribution performance substantially. Aldera, Emam, Al-Qurishi, Alrubaian, and Alothaim (2021), in their IEEE Access systematic literature review of online-extremism detection in textual content, emphasise that the absence of a universally accepted operational definition of "extremism" and the scarcity of commonly adopted benchmark datasets remain major obstacles to fair cross-study comparison. The methodological corollary is that headline accuracy figures should be read as upper bounds under favourable evaluation conditions, not as field-deployment estimates.

Topic modelling and sentiment analysis remain useful exploratory complements to supervised classification, particularly for hypothesis generation in newly emerging corpora. Lewinsky et al.'s (2024) reciprocal human–machine learning pipeline illustrates the value of hybrid workflows: when the analytical objective shifts from labelling to influence identification, integrating expert analyst judgment with model output yields gains that purely automated methods do not achieve.

5.3 Image and Video Forensics

The CSAM context is the most mature context for multimedia content detection. Lee, Ermakova, Ververis, and Fabian (2020) provide a wide overview of CSAM-detection methods, comparing hash-matching, image-classification and text-based methods, and identify the age estimation of unknown victims as the main remaining technical challenge. Hash matching continues to be the workhorse for known material, but its shortcomings with respect to modified, recompressed or partial images are well documented, providing impetus for the integration of perceptual hashing and learned representations into operational pipelines.

Extremist iconography poses analytically distinct challenges. Symbols, flags, and uniforms function within evolving visual codes that resist static signature matching, and the same image may serve recruitment, mockery, or critique depending on textual and community context. The literature on this topic is comparatively thin, with most empirical advances confined to specific case studies rather than to general-purpose detectors. Mirsky and Lee (2021) further document the rapid deterioration of image-deepfake detection performance under realistic compression and re-encoding, raising operational concerns that will only intensify as synthetic propaganda becomes more prevalent.

5.4 Behavioral and Network Analysis

Behavioural and network analyses complement content-level approaches by modelling how content moves through and reshapes communities. Al-Nabki et al. (2019) demonstrated that integrating network topology with content features substantially improves the identification of high-impact actors. Urman and Katz (2022) applied analogous techniques to far-right Telegram networks, characterising the cross-actor ties that survive takedowns and identifying the structural properties of communities that reconstitute most quickly. Network analysis also offers a route to detection that does not depend on prior labelling of content: communities can be identified by their topological signatures even when the specific content under discussion is novel or encrypted.

The synthesis emerging from this literature, illustrated in Figure 4, is that no single methodological lane is sufficient. The most defensible operational pipelines combine content classification (for triage at scale), network analysis (for prioritisation and influence identification), and human analyst judgment (for context, attribution, and adjudication). Lewinsky et al. (2024) make this methodological argument most explicitly and provide the most fully worked operational example to date.

Figure 4. AI-based framework for detection and classification of extremist content on the Darknet. The pipeline integrates crawling and mirror filtering (Rodriguez Barredo-Valenzuela et al., 2025), multimodal feature extraction (Al-Nabki et al., 2019), domain-specific pre-trained classification (Jin et al., 2023; Cascavilla et al., 2022), Learning-to-Rank influence ranking, and analyst-in-the-loop adjudication using reciprocal human–machine learning (Lewinsky et al., 2024)

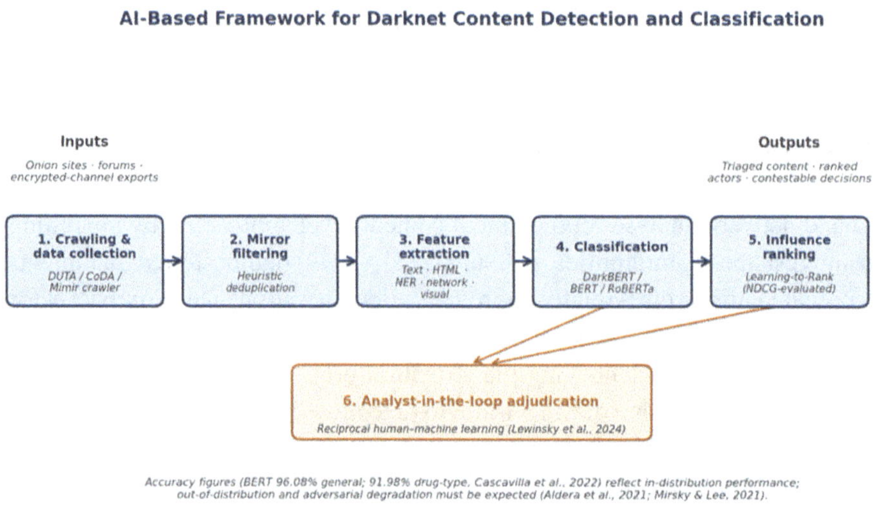

6. MITIGATION AND COUNTERMEASURES

6.1 Content Removal and Platform Disruption

The content deletion and platform disruption strategy remains the most prominent mitigation lever, but academic discussion has started raising serious concerns regarding its sufficiency in the long run. Deplatforming is described by Rogers (2020) as the migration of Internet celebrities with extreme political views to Telegram and alternative social media. Audiences are small but posting activity stays unchanged in these situations, which transforms deplatforming into a process of audience restructuring rather than a process of content elimination. Far-right Telegram networks recovered cross-platform connectivity after mass bans on mainstream sites within days, as shown by Urman and Katz (2022).

Such findings do not mean that nothing needs to be done. Indeed, the takedown operations incur serious costs on the infrastructure and interfere with the operational rhythms of adversaries' organizations. However, the lesson here is that the measure of success must not be understood in terms of absolute elimination of content, but in terms of imposing a prolonged operational tax on the adversary's capabilities together with gaining intelligence from the observation of migration patterns. Jardine (2019) makes the latter point quite explicitly in his policy recommendation, claiming that lower reach of propaganda distributed via the Darknet compared to the surface platforms makes Dark Web a less efficient ground for initial recruitment but a resilient place for archiving and coordination within the movement.

6.2 Counter-Narratives and Preventive Strategies

Counter-narrative interventions have been the most thoroughly evaluated by Campbell Collaboration standards. A systematic review of nineteen studies on the effects of anti-stereotypical interventions by Carthy, Doody, Cox, O'Hora and Sarma (2020) found mixed results. Some approaches, particularly counter-stereotypical exemplars were found to reduce perceived realistic threats and out-group hostility, but there was little evidence for primary outcomes such as intent to act violently, and where there was, it was methodologically weak. This synthesis is extended to far-right propaganda specifically in the Doolan and colleagues' (2025) Campbell Systematic Reviews protocol, which will fill an important evidentiary gap in the coming years.

An honest reading of the current counter-narrative literature is that it has not yet demonstrated causal effects on the outcomes that matter most for policy. This is not a fatal indictment, similar fields, such as public-health communication, took decades to develop similar causal evidence, but it argues against any confident scaling of intervention programmes on the basis of current evidence. The next step is methodological investment in pre-registered, adequately powered evaluations with clear behavioral primary outcomes.

6.3 Law Enforcement and Intelligence Operations

Law-enforcement and intelligence operations against Darknet ecosystems combine technical operations against infrastructure, undercover engagement within communities, and prosecution of identified offenders. Huete Trujillo and Ruiz-Martínez (2021) catalogue the deanonymisation attack families relevant to operational practice and emphasise that operational security failures by hidden-service operators, rather than cryptographic weaknesses in Tor itself, account for the majority of successful attributions. The corollary is that intelligence value can frequently be unlocked through sustained observation and patient exploitation of operator error, even where direct technical attack is infeasible.

Cross-jurisdictional coordination remains a binding constraint. The same operational measure may be lawful in one jurisdiction, restricted in another, and contested in a third, generating coordination costs that adversaries do not face symmetrically. The literature converges on the observation that durable disruption requires sustained partnership across multiple agencies and jurisdictions, with the technical, legal, and analytical dimensions integrated from the outset rather than coordinated retrospectively.

6.4 Collaboration with Technology Providers

Technology-provider collaboration spans hash-sharing arrangements (the Global Internet Forum to Counter Terrorism model), coordinated reporting channels, and joint research efforts on detection methodology. The most rigorous regulatory analysis of automated content moderation as it operates within these collaborations is Macdonald et al. (2019), who argue in the International Journal of Law in Context that AI-driven removal of terrorist content amounts to a form of regulation subject to rule-of-law principles. They identify three sets of issues, enforceability, definitional non-normativity, and prior restraint / technological due process, that complicate current platform practice and remain underaddressed in operational arrangements.

The practical implication is that effective collaboration cannot be reduced to a technical pipeline of hash-sharing and automated removal. It must be embedded within governance arrangements that allow contested decisions to be reviewed, allow affected users to seek meaningful recourse, and allow external researchers to assess performance under conditions that the operating platforms themselves cannot evaluate without bias.

Table 3. Mitigation strategies for combating extremist and illegal content dissemination

Strategy	Mechanism	Demonstrated effect	Limitations	Key evidence
Coordinated platform takedowns	Removal of infrastructure on mainstream and encrypted platforms	Near-term reduction in content availability; migration to alternative platforms	Reconstitution within days; audience thinning without elimination	Clifford & Powell (2019); Rogers (2020); Urman & Katz (2022)
Hash-sharing across platforms	Industry-coordinated signatures for known content	Faster cross-platform removal of identified material	Vulnerable to recompression, modification, and synthetic generation	Lee et al. (2020); Mirsky & Lee (2021)
Counter-narrative campaigns	Targeted messaging to at-risk audiences	Reduced threat perceptions and out-group hostility in some studies	Limited and methodologically weak evidence on behavioural outcomes	Carthy et al. (2020); Doolan et al. (2025)
Domain-specific detection models	Pre-trained classifiers (e.g., DarkBERT) on Darknet corpora	High in-distribution accuracy; improved triage at scale	Performance degrades on out-of-distribution, multilingual, and adversarially modified content	Jin et al. (2023); Cascavilla et al. (2022); Aldera et al. (2021)
Network and influence analysis	Identification of high-centrality actors	Higher-leverage targeting than content-by-content removal	Requires labelled networks and survives only as long as topology is observable	Al-Nabki et al. (2019); Urman & Katz (2022); Lewinsky et al. (2024)
Law-enforcement deanonymisation	Exploitation of operator security failures and traffic correlation	Successful attributions in high-profile cases	Resource-intensive; jurisdictionally constrained	Huete Trujillo & Ruiz-Martínez (2021); Van der Bruggen & Blokland (2021)
Rule-of-law-anchored governance of automated moderation	Procedural safeguards on automated removal	Transparency, contestability, and external accountability	Yet to be operationalised at scale in major platforms	Macdonald et al. (2019); Conway (2021)

7. LEGAL, ETHICAL, AND POLICY CONSIDERATIONS

7.1 Legal Frameworks and Regulations

Legal frameworks governing extremist and illegal content on the Darknet operate at the intersection of criminal law, telecommunications regulation, and emerging platform-governance regimes. Domestic terrorism statutes provide the substantive offences under which producing, distributing, and possessing certain categories of content are prosecuted; telecommunications and platform-liability regimes (notably the European Union's Digital Services Act and the Terrorist Content Online Regulation) provide the duties and exemptions that shape platform behaviour; and mutual legal assistance treaties provide the cross-border evidentiary mechanisms that any serious investigation requires. Macdonald et al. (2019)

argue that AI-driven removal of terrorist content amounts to a form of regulation subject to rule-of-law principles, identifying enforceability, definitional non-normativity, and prior restraint / technological due process as three under-addressed dimensions of current practice.

7.2 Freedom of Expression vs. Security

The tension between security objectives and expressive freedoms is the defining normative axis of this field. Counter-terrorism content removal regimes operate at the edge of what democratic states tolerate as constraints on speech, and the migration of moderation logic into automated systems compresses the space within which contested decisions can be made transparent and contestable. Conway (2017) argued early in this debate that progress in the field would require explicit attention to comparative work across ideologies and jurisdictions, a methodological discipline that disciplines the field's tendency to generalise from a small number of high-salience cases. The literature has converged on the proposition that broad-based content-removal regimes risk both under- and over-inclusion in ways that mainstream platforms struggle to characterise, let alone correct.

7.3 Privacy and Surveillance Challenges

Darknet research and operations exist in unavoidable tension with privacy norms. Crawling-based data collection captures content generated under expectations of anonymity, often by users who have not consented to research participation. Law-enforcement deanonymisation operations rely on capabilities whose details are typically classified, complicating both democratic oversight and adversarial testing of method validity. The same anonymity infrastructure that enables extremist dissemination also protects journalists, activists, and human-rights defenders operating in repressive environments, a dual-use character that the policy literature has consistently recognised.

Gehl's (2018) book Weaving the Dark Web: Legitimacy on Freenet, Tor, and I2P provides the most sustained treatment of how Dark Web users themselves construe and contest the legitimacy of these platforms, offering an essential counterweight to purely securitised framings. Any policy response that fails to engage with the legitimacy economy of Darknet platforms risks both empirical misunderstanding and normative overreach.

7.4 International Cooperation and Policy Gaps

International cooperation operates through a patchwork of bilateral and multilateral arrangements that does not match the operational tempo of cross-border adversaries. The 2019 Europol-coordinated Telegram disruptions illustrate what can be achieved through tightly coordinated multi-agency action, but such operations remain comparatively rare and resource-intensive. Policy gaps cluster in three domains: harmonisation of substantive offences across jurisdictions, particularly for content categories where definitional disagreement is fundamental; procedural mechanisms for rapid cross-border evidence preservation and exchange; and governance arrangements for the algorithmic systems that increasingly mediate content-moderation decisions (Macdonald et al., 2019; Jardine, 2019). Researcher safety and welfare receive comparatively little attention in current frameworks, an omission for which Conway (2021) makes a forceful and specific case.

8. OPEN CHALLENGES AND RESEARCH GAPS

Four cross-cutting gaps in the literature define the agenda for the next phase of work. First, definitional fragmentation persists. The terms "extremism", "radicalisation", and "illegal content" are operationalised inconsistently across computer-science and social-science studies, undermining benchmark portability and the cumulability of findings (Aldera et al., 2021; Macdonald & Whittaker, 2019). Until the field converges on operational definitions that are both theoretically defensible and computationally tractable, comparison across studies will remain compromised.

Second, dataset access is highly uneven. A small number of legacy corpora, DUTA, DUTA-10K, CoDA, carry a disproportionate share of the evidentiary load for computational work in this area. Open, ethically curated, multilingual benchmarks are urgently needed but are constrained by both legal restrictions on illicit content and ethical commitments to user privacy. The Mimir longitudinal crawl (Rodriguez Barredo-Valenzuela et al., 2025) demonstrates what is possible with sustained methodological investment, but generalising its mirror-detection and longitudinal-design innovations across the field will require new institutional and resourcing arrangements.

Third, longitudinal designs are rare. Most published studies are cross-sectional, leaving questions about content lifespan, user career trajectories, and intervention durability under-examined. Rodriguez Barredo-Valenzuela et al. (2025) is a notable exception, but its design has not yet been broadly adopted. The methodological investment required for longitudinal Darknet research is substantial, both in infrastructure and in the ethics-review and security arrangements that responsible long-term observation demands, and the field has yet to develop the funding and institutional models that would support it at scale.

Fourth, the interaction between Darknet and surface-platform dynamics is conceptually acknowledged (Jardine, 2019) but rarely modelled empirically with paired data. The lone-actor case-study evidence (Stockhammer, 2025) demonstrates that cross-platform pipelines are operationally consequential, but quantitative modelling of these pipelines is constrained by the difficulty of linking data across platforms with very different access regimes.

Adversary adaptation compounds each of these gaps. Encryption and obfuscation techniques continue to evolve; multilingual content and code-switching defeat detectors trained on monolingual corpora; and adversarial paraphrasing erodes the reliability of generative-text detectors (Mirsky & Lee, 2021). Ethical constraints on data collection are themselves a methodological challenge, not because they are unjustified, but because their unsystematic application across institutions and jurisdictions produces inconsistent evidentiary standards (Conway, 2021). The most productive response is the development of sub-field-specific ethical guidelines that combine principled commitments to researcher safety and informed consent with concrete operational guidance for the recurring decisions that Darknet research demands.

Finally, the comparative literature on I2P, Freenet, and emerging decentralised platforms remains thin. The verified evidence base treats Tor as the dominant case and signals decentralised systems as a likely future venue without yet supporting that signal with the case-study and measurement evidence that the Tor literature now provides. Closing this gap is among the highest-value methodological investments the field could make in the next five years.

10. FUTURE TRENDS AND STRATEGIC INSIGHTS

The integration of generative AI into extremist content pipelines is the single most consequential trend on the field's horizon. Mirsky and Lee (2021) document that generative-text-detection benchmarks remain unstable under adversarial paraphrasing and that image-deepfake detection performance degrades sharply on compressed social-media content. Translated to the Darknet context, this means that the volume of synthetic propaganda available for triage will grow faster than detector performance can be expected to keep pace, with two operational implications. First, the cost of comprehensive monitoring will rise; second, prioritisation logic, deciding which content is worth detailed analysis given finite analytical capacity, will become more consequential than detection per se. DarkBERT (Jin et al., 2023) illustrates the defender-side response: domain-specific pre-training adapted to Dark Web vocabulary and register substantially outperforms general-purpose baselines, and the same approach can in principle be extended as adversaries adapt.

Decentralised and censorship-resistant platforms, IPFS-based content addressing, ActivityPub-federated social networks, and blockchain-anchored archival systems, are likely to become more prominent venues for extremist content storage. The fundamental architectural shift from location-based to content-addressed storage substantially alters the takedown problem: removing content from one IPFS node does not remove it from the network, and federated networks distribute the moderation problem across independently administered servers that do not share governance arrangements. The peer-reviewed scholarship specifically on these systems in extremist contexts is comparatively sparse and represents the clearest near-term research priority.

Cross-domain propagation strategies will continue to evolve. The lone-actor case-study evidence (Stockhammer, 2025) shows that algorithmic recommendation on mainstream platforms increasingly functions as the inadvertent first stage of pipelines whose downstream layers reside on encrypted messengers and the Darknet. As mainstream platforms tighten their moderation regimes, adversary adaptation can be expected to deepen the connective role of intermediate-tier platforms (Telegram, Rocket.Chat, gaming-adjacent forums) and to develop more sophisticated bridging tactics, for example, deniable, context-collapse content that operates as recruitment material when interpreted through an in-group lens but evades detection when treated atomistically.

Defender-side opportunities are concentrated in three areas. Explainable AI offers a route to deployable detection in operational settings where evidentiary standards require interpretable decision pathways; high-accuracy black-box classifiers (DarkBERT, ensemble transformers) are difficult to deploy without explanation mechanisms that allow contested decisions to be reviewed. Hybrid human–machine workflows, of the kind pioneered by Lewinsky et al. (2024), offer gains in influence identification that purely automated methods do not achieve. And cross-platform observational designs, paired data linking surface-platform exposure to encrypted-messenger and Darknet engagement, offer the empirical leverage to model pipelines that current cross-sectional designs cannot.

The strategic insight, mapped in Figure 5, is that the contest between adversary and defender capability on the Darknet is structurally asymmetric in ways that favour adaptive over absolute objectives. Adversaries will continue to evolve faster than any fixed defender posture; the question is whether defender capability can be organised to evolve at comparable speed. The literature suggests that this is achievable through three commitments: sustained investment in longitudinal measurement, institutionalisation of hybrid analytical workflows, and governance arrangements that allow automated systems to be contested and revised without paralysing operational use.

Figure 5. Future landscape of AI-driven and decentralised extremist content dissemination on the Darknet. Adversary trajectories (circles) populate quadrants defined by generative AI maturity and hosting decentralisation; defender responses (squares) sit in adjacent positions, indicating the empirical and methodological investments needed to track each adversary direction. Synthesised from Schlegel et al. (2025), Huete Trujillo and Ruiz-Martínez (2021), Mirsky and Lee (2021), Jin et al. (2023), and Lewinsky et al. (2024).

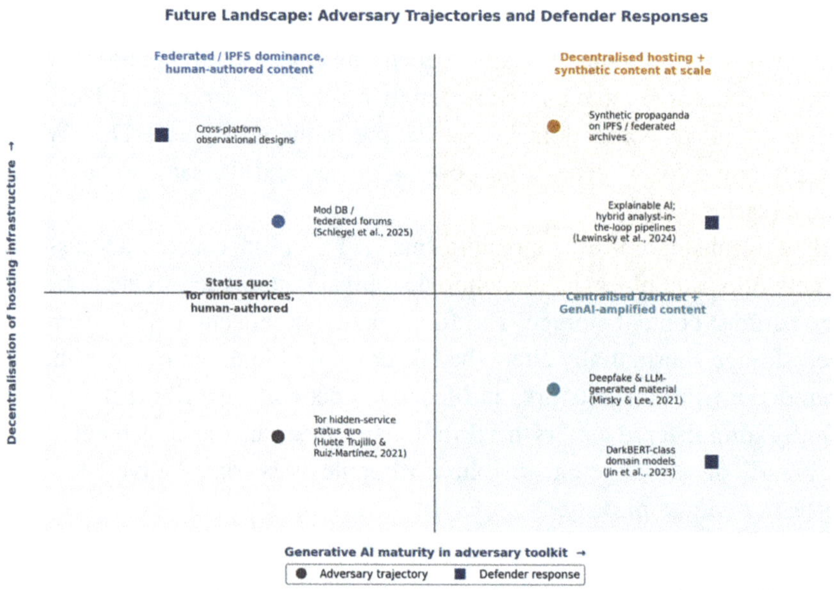

11. CONCLUSION

In summary, this chapter has considered the role of the Darknet as a medium for the dissemination of extremist and illegal content. It has relied on the verified peer-reviewed and grey literature for its claims. The analysis can be organised along three main arguments. First, the Darknet is not an isolated ecosystem but a single robust layer in a broader, multi-platform extremist information environment that includes social media, gaming-oriented forums, and encrypted messaging apps. Strategies must therefore respond on an ecosystem-wide basis. Second, the computational detection technologies have made enormous progress thanks to the domain-specific pre-trained models and multimodal Learning-to-Rank frameworks, but the reported accuracy figures need to be taken as the best-case scenarios because of degraded performance on actual deployment due to concept drift, multilingualism, and adversarial tactics. Third, mitigation goes far beyond removing the illegal material and involves platform disruption, network-level intervention, counter-narrative interventions with rigorous evaluations, and appropriate governance mechanisms for the automation technologies.

It is important to note that the multidisciplinary nature of the problem under consideration is not optional. It calls for technical expertise in anonymity infrastructure and computational tools, criminal justice knowledge about community dynamics, and a sophisticated legal and ethical engagement to develop an effective response. The view of the problem as solely technical (better detectors are needed) or solely policy (adjusting platform liability rules are enough) does not appreciate the full extent of the structural challenge involved in the adaptive competition against the adversaries that deliberately exploit the gray zones between technical, social, and legal boundaries respected by the defenders.

Three recommendations are suggested for the researcher community, policymakers, and cybersecurity practitioners. Methodological convergence is crucial for the research agenda – operationalisation of concepts, development of openly available benchmark datasets of multilingual materials, and longitudinal studies that complement the prevailing cross-sectional design in the current literature. Governance of the automation technologies responsible for the decision-making process is a necessity for the legitimacy of any large-scale automated removal of the material and requires substantial investments that current arrangements fail to make. Finally, hybrid analytical workflows that combine the use of sophisticated computational tools and expert human judgment, such as the one developed by Lewinsky et al. (2024), is the priority for practitioners.

The Darknet is likely to remain the structural component of the information environment for many years to come. The task is not to eliminate it, which is not possible and desirable because of the legitimate uses, but to develop an adaptation capability for the defender posture that keeps up with the pace of adversary innovation. Legal and ethical commitments that are the foundation of the democratic response to the problem need to be retained. The verified literature of this chapter represents the starting point for that work; the next steps involve methodological rigor, institutional investment, and normative commitment required by the challenge.

REFERENCES

Adel, A., & Norouzifard, M. (2024). Weaponization of the growing cybercrimes inside the dark net: The question of detection and application. *Big Data and Cognitive Computing*, *8*(8), 91. DOI: 10.3390/bdcc8080091

Al-Nabki, M. W., Fidalgo, E., Alegre, E., & Chaves, D. (2019). Content-based features to rank influential hidden services of the Tor Darknet. arXiv preprint arXiv:1910.02332.

Aldera, S., Emam, A., Al-Qurishi, M., Alrubaian, M., & Alothaim, A. (2021). Online extremism detection in textual content: A systematic literature review. *IEEE Access : Practical Innovations, Open Solutions*, *9*, 42384–42396. DOI: 10.1109/ACCESS.2021.3064178

Carthy, S. L., Doody, C. B., Cox, K., O'Hora, D., & Sarma, K. M. (2020). Counter-narratives for the prevention of violent radicalisation: A systematic review of targeted interventions. *Campbell Systematic Reviews*, *16*(3), e1106. DOI: 10.1002/cl2.1106 PMID: 37131913

Cascavilla, G., Catolino, G., & Sangiovanni, M. (2022). Illicit Darkweb classification via natural-language processing: Classifying illicit content of webpages based on textual information. In Proceedings of the 19th International Conference on Security and Cryptography (SECRYPT 2022), Vol. 1 (pp. 620–626). SciTePress. Extended version available as arXiv:2312.04944. DOI: 10.5220/0011298600003283

Clifford, B., & Powell, H. (2019). Encrypted extremism: Inside the English-speaking Islamic state ecosystem on telegram. *The George Washington University Program on Extremism*, 27-53.

Conway, M. (2017). Determining the role of the internet in violent extremism and terrorism: Six suggestions for progressing research. *Studies in Conflict and Terrorism*, *40*(1), 77–98. DOI: 10.1080/1057610X.2016.1157408

Conway, M. (2021). Online extremism and terrorism research ethics: Researcher safety, informed consent, and the need for tailored guidelines. *Terrorism and Political Violence*, *33*(2), 367–380. DOI: 10.1080/09546553.2021.1880235

Dingledine, R., Mathewson, N., & Syverson, P. (2004). Tor: The second-generation onion router. In *Proceedings of the 13th USENIX Security Symposium* (pp. 303–320). USENIX Association.

Doolan, M., Cox, K., & Sarma, K. M. (2025). Protocol: Understanding the content, context, and impact of far-right extremist propaganda disseminated online: A systematic review. *Campbell Systematic Reviews*, *21*(4), e70076. DOI: 10.1002/cl2.70076 PMID: 41245379

Faizan, M., & Khan, R. A. (2019). Exploring and analyzing the dark Web: A new alchemy. *First Monday*, *24*(5). Advance online publication. DOI: 10.5210/fm.v24i5.9473

Gannon, C., Blokland, A. A. J., Huikuri, S., Babchishin, K. M., & Lehmann, R. J. B. (2023). Child sexual abuse material on the darknet. *Forensische Psychiatrie, Psychologie, Kriminologie*, *17*(4), 353–365. DOI: 10.1007/s11757-023-00790-8

Gehl, R. W. (2018). *Weaving the Dark Web: Legitimacy on Freenet, Tor, and I2P*. MIT Press. DOI: 10.7551/mitpress/11266.001.0001

Huete Trujillo, D. L., & Ruiz-Martínez, A. (2021). Tor hidden services: A systematic literature review. *Journal of Cybersecurity and Privacy*, *1*(3), 496–518. DOI: 10.3390/jcp1030025

Jardine, E. (2019). Online content moderation and the Dark Web: Policy responses to radicalizing hate speech and malicious content on the Darknet. *First Monday*, *24*(12). Advance online publication. DOI: 10.5210/fm.v24i12.10266

Jin, Y., Jang, E., Cui, J., Chung, J.-W., Lee, Y., & Shin, S. (2023). DarkBERT: A language model for the dark side of the internet. In *Proceedings of the 61st Annual Meeting of the Association for Computational Linguistics* (Volume 1: Long Papers) (pp. 7515–7533). Association for Computational Linguistics. DOI: 10.18653/v1/2023.acl-long.415

Lee, H.-E., Ermakova, T., Ververis, V., & Fabian, B. (2020). Detecting child sexual abuse material: A comprehensive survey. *Forensic Science International Digital Investigation*, *34*, 301022. DOI: 10.1016/j.fsidi.2020.301022

Lewinsky, D., Te'eni, D., Yahav-Shenberger, I. G., Schwartz, D., Silverman, G., & Mann, Y. (2024). Detecting terrorist influencers using reciprocal human-machine learning: The case of militant Jihadist Da'wa on the Darknet. *Humanities & Social Sciences Communications*, *11*(1), 1–11. DOI: 10.1057/s41599-024-03920-7

Macdonald, S., Correia, S. G., & Watkin, A.-L. (2019). Regulating terrorist content on social media: Automation and the rule of law. International Journal of Law in Context, 15(Special Issue 2), 183–197. DOI: 10.1017/S1744552319000119

Macdonald, S., & Whittaker, J. (2019). Online radicalization: Contested terms and conceptual clarity. In Vacca, J. R. (Ed.), *Online terrorist propaganda, recruitment, and radicalization* (pp. 33–46). CRC Press. DOI: 10.1201/9781315170251-2

Mirsky, Y., & Lee, W. (2021). The creation and detection of deepfakes: A survey. *ACM Computing Surveys*, *54*(1), 7. Advance online publication. DOI: 10.1145/3425780

Owenson, G., Cortes, S., & Lewman, A. (2018). The darknet's smaller than we thought: The life cycle of Tor Hidden Services. *Digital Investigation*, *27*, 17–22. DOI: 10.1016/j.diin.2018.09.005

Rodriguez Barredo-Valenzuela, A., Pastrana, S., & Suarez-Tangil, G. (2025). Snorkeling in dark waters: A longitudinal surface exploration of unique Tor hidden services. IEEE Transactions on Information Forensics and Security, 20, 5386–5395. Extended version available as arXiv:2504.16836.

Rogers, R. (2020). Deplatforming: Following extreme Internet celebrities to Telegram and alternative social media. *European Journal of Communication*, *35*(3), 213–229. DOI: 10.1177/0267323120922066

Schlegel, L., Wiegold, L., Winkler, C., & Junk, J. (2025). Exploring the digital extremist ecosystem: A preliminary analysis of hateful posts on Mod DB. *Frontiers in Psychology*, *15*, 1502098. DOI: 10.3389/fpsyg.2024.1502098 PMID: 40013258

Stockhammer, N. (2025). *From TikTok to terrorism? The online radicalization of European lone attackers since October 7, 2023. CTC Sentinel, 18(7).* Combating Terrorism Center at West Point.

Urman, A., & Katz, S. (2022). What they do in the shadows: Examining the far-right networks on Telegram. *Information Communication and Society*, *25*(7), 904–923. DOI: 10.1080/1369118X.2020.1803946

Van der Bruggen, M., & Blokland, A. (2021). A crime script analysis of child sexual exploitation material fora on the darkweb. *Sexual Abuse : A Journal of Research and Treatment*, *33*(8), 950–974. DOI: 10.1177/1079063220981063 PMID: 33353483

Chapter 9
Darknet Implications in IoT, 5G/6G, and Emerging Infrastructures

Abdullah S. Alshraa
http://orcid.org/0000-0002-4881-8894
Jordan University of Science and Technology, Jordan

Fawaz A. Khasawneh
http://orcid.org/0009-0002-3078-606X
Jordan University of Science and Technology, Jordan

Mohammad Bany Taha
American University of Madaba, Jordan

ABSTRACT

The darknet, which consists of hidden networks that let users communicate without being detected, has become an essential tool for advanced cyber attackers who want to break into these systems. This chapter shows all the ways that darknet technology affects Internet of Things (IoT) systems and 5G/6G networks and essential infrastructure networks. The research investigates how darknet technologies and security weaknesses which exist in network slicing, software-defined networking (SDN) and network function virtualization (NFV) within 5G/6G environments that hackers will use darknet to execute their attacks. The study examines the effects which critical infrastructures face from smart cities and industrial IoT (IIoT) systems and cyber-physical systems (CPS). The study reviews various methods using artificial intelligence, machine learning, blockchain technologies and zero-trust architectures to detect and stop security threats. The research article discusses privacy issues and legal matters and ethical standards while it presents upcoming research needs and future design directions.

DOI: 10.4018/979-8-3373-9755-9.ch009

1. INTRODUCTION

1.1 Background on Darknet Evolution and Emerging Technologies

The darknet has evolved from its original research network design into a modern cybercriminal network system which enables all contemporary cybercriminal activities. The developers of The Onion Router (Tor) and Invisible Internet Project (I2P) designed these technologies to establish online privacy protection for activists, journalists and dissidents in oppressive regimes who need it for their work (Hossain et al., 2024). However, organizations that conduct illegal operations at large scale now use anonymization systems to conduct their activities. The emergence of darknet marketplaces which serve as specialized platforms for trading stolen data and malware kits and zero-day exploits has made advanced cyber-attack tools accessible to all users, which were previously restricted to nation-state actors and organized crime syndicates with extensive resources (Mirji & S., 2026).

The technological progress of Internet of Things (IoT) and 5G/6G networks and new operational frameworks has built complex ecosystems which connect billion of different devices that function with ultra-low latency through software-defined control systems (Kravchenko & Permyakov, 2025). These systems provide a great value for automation and real time decision making, and also for operational efficiency, but they create new security problems due to how vast they are in size, and because the design is distributed, plus their overall exposure to attacks. Darknet technology enables attackers to use communication systems which protect their identity to execute their attacks against resource-constrained IoT devices while they handle command-and-control functions for massive botnets and establish markets to trade vulnerabilities, which lets them operate without detection and police hindrance (Ejeofobiri et al., 2024).

This intersection points to a major change which now defines the threat landscape. Darknet-enabled threats have shifted their focus toward the billions of IoT and edge devices which protect less than enterprise networks which traditional cybersecurity methods used to defend. The anonymity which darknet technologies provide allows attackers to work without detection, conduct network surveillance for extended durations and share attack methods with their accomplices without any risk of being tracked (Ntayagabiri et al., 2025).

1.2 Convergence of IoT, 5G/6G, and Cyber-Physical Systems

The combination of IoT technologies and 5G/6G networks creates a new method for autonomous systems to gather, handle, and react to data. The new security framework for darknet-based attacks emerges from the combined operations of multiple network systems. 5G networks provide new operational functions which create additional security risks because network slicing allows multiple virtual networks to be built on shared physical resources for particular services while SDN and network function virtualization (NFV) enable flexible network control and massive Machine-Type Communications (mMTC) lets numerous devices connect to the network. The various system innovations which provide significant operational advantages open up new paths for darknet-based attacker operations (Ahmed et al., 2024).

The process of weaponizing network capabilities becomes clear through investigations of their connection to the darknet. The attacker operating through darknet command-and-control channels can use network slicing to create separate network sections which they will use to execute their hacking activities. The SDN controller exploits that hackers acquired from darknet markets will let them create network changes which will affect millions of users. The mMTC feature which supports extensive IoT device deployment creates security problems because hackers can use compromised IoT devices to build botnets or launch attacks on important systems through darknet-enabled attacks (Lakhani, 2023).

The upcoming 6G networks which are still being developed will enable artificial intelligence and quantum computing along with universal sensing and communication capabilities. The new capabilities which organizations develop to drive their innovations will result in new security weaknesses which attackers can exploit by using exploits obtained from darknet marketplaces. The minimal security of IoT devices which vendors deploy to save costs, and power creates a dangerous situation for organizations because attackers can gain access to their systems through darknet channels while using undetectable zero-day exploits and botnet tools to compromise their systems. 6G security solutions have not yet been proven effective because threat actors with darknet-based capabilities keep testing the system in real-world settings (Malatji, 2024).

1.3 Expanding Attack Surface and Threat Landscape

The combination of IoT and 5G and 6G technologies together with new infrastructure systems creates a complicated threat environment which uses darknet technologies as its base for conducting large-scale attacks that require elaborate planning. IoT devices which have limited processing power and weak built-in protection and firmware faults become both easy targets and effective tools for expanding attacks when they get hacked through darknet-based operations. The Mirai botnet incident of 2016 demonstrated this vulnerability model by leveraging hundreds of thousands of compromised IoT devices to launch unprecedented, Distributed Denial-of-Service (DDoS) attacks reaching 1.2 Tbps, but more critically, it established a template for darknet-facilitated botnet distribution that remains relevant today (Blancaflor et al., 2025). The first Mirai source code release onto darknet markets resulted in the creation of multiple Mirai variants which threat actors could obtain through darknet channels to conduct attacks without needing advanced technical skills.

The darknet marketplace ecosystem that developed after Mirai's source code leak created a new economic model for attacks. Attackers now purchase pre-packaged botnets and malware tools along with exploit kits through darknet marketplaces which simplify their operations without needing technical expertise (McNulty & Vassilakis, 2022). Anyone with malicious intentions can now launch attacks which previously required nation-state resources because attackers can now access advanced hacking tools for a subscription fee.

The introduction of new vulnerabilities through 5G and 6G networks enables threat actors to conduct their attacks using darknet facilities as their distribution channels. Through network slicing attackers can use vulnerabilities to create isolation of network slices or to compromise specific sections which may disrupt critical services while security systems that monitor entire networks will remain unaware of the attack. SDN controller compromises become possible through dark web exploit distribution which lets attackers take control of entire networks to disrupt connections used by multiple users. Virtualized environments in NFV infrastructure become exposed to dangerous hypervisor attacks which attackers can buy through darknet exploit markets to move freely between virtual machines. The Open Radio Access Network (O-RAN) architecture's open interfaces, while promoting vendor diversity, create new attack surfaces for malicious xApps that can be deployed through darknet-coordinated supply chain infiltration (Cunha et al., 2024).

Cyber-physical systems and digital twins present major security issues because cyber-attacks enable criminals to execute physical attacks. An attacker who takes control of a digital twin through malware from darknet can destroy the virtual system which operators will use to make decisions using incorrect information. Digital twin manipulation attacks enable attackers to observe physical system operations without needing direct access to the system (Otoom, 2025).

1.4 Motivation and Objectives of the Chapter

This chapter highlights the cybersecurity side effects because darknet threats create an important security challenge that existing research has not yet resolved. Researchers have studied IoT security and 5G security and critical infrastructure protection as separate fields, but they have not yet examined how darknet technologies support advanced attacks across these areas.

The chapter following this introduction consists of different sections which begin with Section 2 that explains IoT architecture and 5G/6G capabilities and emerging infrastructures and darknet technologies. Section 3 examines darknet-enabled threats specific to IoT and cyber-physical systems, which include botnet architecture and exploitation techniques. The analysis in Section 4 determines how darknet technologies affect 5G/6G networks by assessing network slicing vulnerabilities and covert communication channels. The section evaluates how critical infrastructures and new infrastructures experience various effects. The section summarizes different methods that can be used to detect threats and prevent them. The section reviews all privacy and legal and ethical issues connected to the study. The section points out various research areas that need further investigation. The section recommends specific research paths which researchers should follow in future studies. The section concludes the document by summarizing the main findings and providing recommendations for all stakeholders.

2. BACKGROUND AND TECHNOLOGICAL FOUNDATIONS

2.1 Internet of Things (IoT) Ecosystem

2.1.1 Architecture: Sensors, Gateways, Cloud/Edge Computing

The IoT ecosystem contains three primary architectural layers which create multiple vulnerability points that attackers can use for their darknet-based attack operations. The perception layer uses sensors and IoT devices to gather physical environment data which systems then transmit through gateways that combine data for processing in computational systems. The devices operate under extreme resource limitations which restrict their power supply and their memory ability (measured in kilobytes) and their processing capacity and their communication systems work to save power instead of providing security protection. The architectural design leans toward functionality and cost minimization, so security becomes more like a later thought (Onyagu et al., 2024).

In the middle, there is a layer of gateways plus edge nodes that gather data from several sources, then it processes it locally before that information goes upward to higher level systems. Gateway firmware and communication protocols stay in the line of fire, because security holes get used, and the attackers, well they spread these weaknesses around via the darknet. Edge devices basically form the boundary between IoT sensor networks and online networks. Hackers like this place because they can run hostile programs there while still being connected to IoT networks, and those IoT networks then get turned into botnets (Rupanetti & Kaabouch, 2024).

For the computational backbone, the system relies on edge computing together with cloud computing infrastructure. It handles data for analytical goals and also supports decision making for control. Still, the security perimeter feels fragmented, since there are several computational resources located at different boundary points. Attackers therefore use darknet channels to seize edge nodes, without setting off the cloud's own security controls. After that, they can push attacks into cloud infrastructures or even step laterally across many edge domains (Ataullah & Chauhan, 2024). The way the cloud infrastructure is designed, it gives this sort of wrong comfort that it blocks every security threat, but once edge nodes are compromised, they can stay as permanent entry paths, and the criminals coordinate those actions through the darknet.

Figure 1 shows the three architectural layers of the IoT ecosystem (Perception, Network & Edge, and Cloud & Processing) and how each layer comes with its own set of vulnerabilities, which are then exploited through darknet channels. Arrows show how to exploit kits, botnet control, and stolen data flow upward from darknet operations to compromise sensors, gateways, and cloud systems.

Figure 1. IoT architecture and darknet vulnerabilities

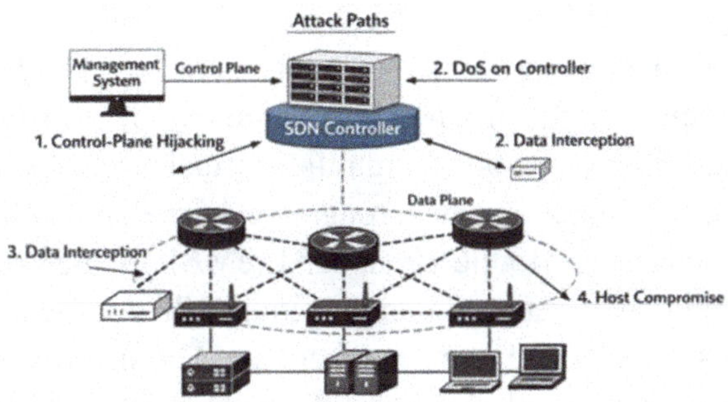

2.1.2 Resource Constraints and Security Limitations

IoT devices face basic security problems which arise from their essential resource limitations that create ongoing security weaknesses used by darknet attackers for their attack activities. The existing memory limits of constrained devices which typically range between 64 and 256 kilobytes prevent the use of traditional security methods which include strong cryptographic systems, certificate authentication, and complete firewall protection. The system requires high processing capacity which exists beyond the megahertz limit because security operations demand complex computational processes. Simplified protocols which treat power consumption as the main requirement lead systems to compromise security in favor of operational efficiency while sending authentication information through paths that attackers can intercept to obtain sensitive information (Ntayagabiri et al., 2025).

Threat actors can take advantage of the IoT device authentication system which protects firmware to access its built-in security weaknesses through exploits shared on darknet networks. The majority of IoT devices come with their firmware stored in non-volatile memory which does not include proper verification systems to confirm its authenticity. Through darknet channels attackers can spread firmware modification tools which permit any person with basic technical skills to change the programming of hacked devices. The attacker achieves continuous access to the device through their control of its compromised firmware which establishes a background connection that permits them to operate their botnet from darknet networks (Hossain et al., 2024).

The authentication shortcoming that seems endemic across IoT ecosystems is honestly the most critical weak point, it enables darknet-scale compromise. A lot of IoT devices ship with default credentials, or have hardcoded passwords, or simply no real authentication mechanism at all. The authentication mechanisms look fragile, since the design does not really include proper protection against bulk password guessing attempts. In darknet channels, attackers get scanning tools and credential dictionaries, plus automated exploitation frameworks, and they use all of that to carry out broad break ins across IoT systems. The existing constraints on traditional security methods create security flaws which sophisticated hackers use to execute their attacks through coordinated darknet operations that target multiple systems instead of single targets (Kravchenko & Permyakov, 2025).

2.2 5G/6G Network Architectures

2.2.1 Network Slicing, Virtualization (NFV/SDN)

The implementation of 5G and 6G networks brings forth new network design systems which create substantial changes in both their operational functions and their abilities to defend against attacks which use darknet channels. Network Slicing establishes multiple virtual networks which function on common physical systems to deliver service requirements through specialized network designs. A single physical network infrastructure can Enhanced Mobile Broadband (eMBB) which requires high data rates for consumers and Ultra-Reliable Low-Latency Communication (URLLC) which enables mission-critical applications like autonomous vehicles and remote surgery and Massive Machine-Type Communication (mMTC) which provides connectivity for billions of IoT devices (Allaw et al., 2025). The system architecture enables organizations to operate their functions, but it creates new cybercriminal attack routes which use darknet networks for their illegal operations.

Network slices maintain their logical separation, yet their actual implementation operates on a shared virtualized system which creates open side-channel vulnerabilities that attackers can use to affect adjacent network slices through their attacks on one slice. Darknet threat actors can distribute their exploits which target the isolation boundaries of high-security slices that protect critical infrastructure and financial services in order to gain access to those protected areas. Network slice orchestration and management require centralized controllers for operations but any attack that succeeds in compromising these controllers through darknet exploits will allow attackers to gain complete control over slice settings and intercept or deactivate essential slices of the system (Cunha et al., 2024).

SDN enables centralized network control through controller systems which control all data traffic by separating network operational functions into network control and forwarding functions. The centralization system of this network operates effectively and provides flexible solutions but creates a vital operational risk because it establishes a single point which attackers can exploit during their darknet campaigns. Attackers can gain control over SDN controllers through exploits which they obtain from darknet markets to execute network attacks that include routing table manipulation, traffic interception, command injection and complete network shutdown. Attackers can use darknet networks to plan their attacks simultaneously against several separate zones of SDN operation (Rahman et al., 2024).

NFV virtualizes network functions previously implemented in hardware, running them as software on commodity computing infrastructure. The system generates hypervisor vulnerabilities which enable attackers to execute attacks through darknet-distributed exploits that break virtualization boundaries to access multiple VNF on shared physical hardware. The attestation and verification mechanisms for VFN depend on their base hypervisor system's security which the darknet threat actors use to release hypervisor vulnerability attacks that enable them to invade all active network functions at once (Cunha et al., 2024).

Figure 2 illustrates how darknet threat actors exploit vulnerabilities across Network Slicing, SDN, and NFV. It shows how darknet-distributed exploits compromise slice isolation, SDN controllers, and hypervisor boundaries, enabling cross-slice breaches, routing manipulation, and virtual machine escapes.

Figure 2. Darknet exploits in virtualized network architectures

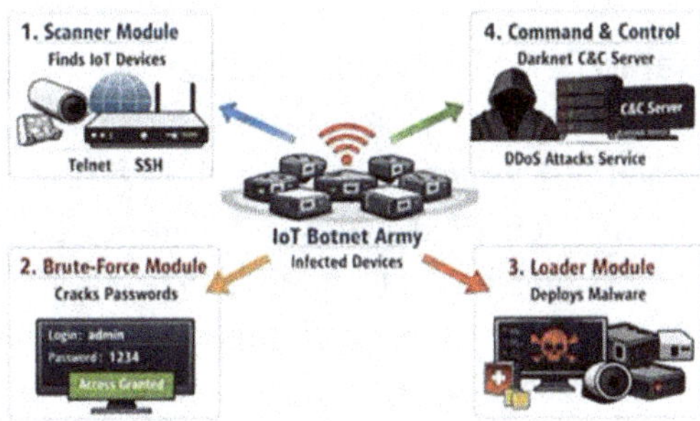

2.2.2 Ultra-Low Latency and Massive Connectivity

The 5G and 6G networks establish three primary performance benchmarks which function as essential elements that boost darknet-based attack capabilities. eMBB provides gigabit-per-second data rates which enable bandwidth-heavy applications to use its fast data transmission capability that facilitates attackers to use darknet-operated attacks for fast botnet command transmission and extensive data theft through network system breaches. Ultra-Reliable Low-Latency Communications (URLLC) provides mission-critical applications with its ability to transmit data at latencies below 1 millisecond while achieving reliability levels that exceed 99.99%. The security controls that use congestion-based anomaly detection become disabled by the system's strict performance requirements which attackers use to create attacks that resemble ordinary network behavior (Yang et al., 2024).

The most dangerous attack point for darknet-enabled threats exists through mMTC, which exists as a framework which enables maximum power savings for billions of connected devices. The design creates an extensive attack surface area which requires attackers to use darknet operational capacity for their mission. Darknet-enabled threat actors who control mMTC infrastructure acquire access to a potential billion devices which they can use as weapons. The original Mirai botnet represented a demonstration of this threat, compromising hundreds of thousands of IoT devices, but mMTC's intended scale suggests future botnets could commandeer millions or billions of devices simultaneously if adequate security controls fail (Malatji, 2024).

The architectural vulnerability that comes out of these performance requirements is basically this idea that security mechanisms usually need some extra processing time, or a bit of extra network latency to work properly. With URLLC, the latency requirements are so strict that more elaborate security validation, or even anomaly detection style checks, start to feel impractical, because the network cannot really both promise sub-millisecond latency and also run a thorough security analysis at the same time. Because of that, there is this real chance that threat actors can craft network attack traffic which somehow hits the latency targets and still stays within the reliability standards, while also pushing forward network integrity attacks. That creates an unavoidable trade-off. Darknet channels, for their part, enable covert communication, and they do it by leveraging their high bandwidth capacity plus low latency characteristics to support quick botnet command delivery or more large-scale data theft operations (Yang et al., 2024).

2.3 Emerging Digital Infrastructures

2.3.1 Smart Cities, Industrial IoT (IIoT), Digital Twins

The implementation of IoT solutions in smart cities establishes connections throughout all urban systems which include traffic control systems and energy distribution networks and water supply systems and public safety communication systems and telephone network systems. Smart city traffic control systems depend on a sensor and camera network which functions together with controllers to manage vehicle movement throughout urban areas. The operation of traffic systems requires complete synchronization because timing accuracy serves as the core element that guarantees safe functioning. Threat actors operating through darknet channels can distribute exploits targeting traffic management systems which have the potential to generate gridlock that impacts millions of citizens or to create dangerous traffic conditions (Nalini, 2024).

The architectural assumption that traffic systems remain relatively obscure and thus secure through obscurity has repeatedly proven incorrect as attackers document vulnerabilities through darknet channels. The growing presence of IIoT and Supervisory Control and Data Acquisition (SCADA) systems leads to the establishment of Operational Technology (OT) networks which traditionally function as separate networks with highly secure operations to establish connections with information technology networks that link to the wider internet system. Businesses now create their first attack surfaces because they require remote access to digital data through their systems which now connect all network systems through aircraft security control. Industrial systems used to operate in dedicated networks which required both physical security and air-gapped operation until present-day IIoT systems started using internet connections to access cloud services. Darknet channels serve as distribution points for attackers who want to share IIoT-specific exploits which contain both reconnaissance tools and weaponized malware that targets industrial environments. IIoT breaches lead to data breaches which also cause physical damage: hackers who access SCADA systems that control power grid systems will create blackouts which impact millions of people while hackers who access water treatment systems will create water supply contamination and hackers who access transportation control systems will create traffic accidents (Narsing & Srinivasan, 2025).

Digital Twins function as virtual copies of actual systems which include physical infrastructure that collects data through its sensors which links to a software model that operators use to control their actual systems from a virtual environment. Digital twins create a new cyber-physical attack surface because their digital twin systems allow attackers to damage the virtual system without accessing any physical assets. Operators who base their decisions on broken digital twins become blind to reality because they believe that the digital twin shows them actual system operations. The advanced attack method requires special security methods because the attacker aims to steal information while the system remains functional (Airehenbuwa et al., 2025).

2.3.2 Edge and Fog Computing

The network edge locations that include base stations, routers and gateways together with small data centers near users as well as IoT sensors, tend to reach their operational goals by using edge computing. Basically, it brings computing power to these remote sites. The benefit of doing the processing close to where data is generated, rather than in faraway cloud data centers, does come with a real tradeoff on security cost in addition to that edge nodes turn into distributed attack targets, hance they are more likely exposed to darknet-coordinated compromises. If an attacker moves through darknet channels, they can take over specific edge nodes while not quite tripping the centralized cloud security monitoring, which means they quietly establish distributed footholds (like beachheads) across the environment. The edge node that the attacker already controls can keep working "normally" for operators while it simultaneously collaborates with the dark web to run cyber-attacks (Rupanetti & Kaabouch, 2024).

Fog computing then extends the ideas behind edge computing. It builds a kind of spectrum, or continuum, of computing resources that stretches from cloud data centers to regional aggregation points, from there out to edge nodes, and finally down to individual devices. The system design which distributes resources throughout various locations between the cloud and edge infrastructure was meant to enhance system resilience, but it introduces major challenges for security management processes. Fog computing systems operate multiple administrative domains, which use different security settings to distribute system security. The darknet operators use their system to hijack fog nodes by attacking unprotected domains, which lets them bypass security to execute their advanced multi-layered attacks against high-value targets through their network connections (Narsing & Srinivasan, 2025).

The control of command-and-control operations through edge and fog computing creates a specific vulnerability which exists within the darknet environment. Centralized cloud security models enable system administrators to monitor all outbound traffic from secure systems, which allows them to detect unfamiliar communication patterns that indicate botnet command-and-control operations. The edge and fog computing architectures, which distribute monitoring tasks to many distant locations, make it extremely challenging to track simultaneous attack patterns which use multiple different edge points. The compromised edge and fog nodes give attackers the ability to create complex ways of hiding command-and-control communications, which enables them to transmit botnet data in disguise as legitimate operational traffic. The distributed architecture enables attackers to execute extensive attack operations while remaining undetected by common security monitoring systems (Ataullah & Chauhan, 2024).

2.4 Darknet Technologies Overview

2.4.1 Tor, I2P, Decentralized Platforms

The most widely used anonymization network Tor operates by directing its users' communications through a series of encrypted paths which require decryption of each successive layer to access information about the subsequent network destination. The system design delivers high-level confidentiality protection because even the final exit node cannot identify the user who accessed the system. Tor began as a privacy solution for journalists and activists and dissidents in oppressive countries however it has transformed into the main backbone that supports illegal online marketplaces and criminal activities (Hossain et al., 2024). Tor-based threat actors use the network to perform their reconnaissance activities against target networks while they spread their malware and exploits and handle their command-and-control operations and make financial transactions which include purchasing darknet services using their entirety of operations under complete invisibility from both law enforcement and victims who attempt forensic investigation (Zhou et al., 2025).

I2P delivers users with anonymous peer-to-peer connectivity through its garlic routing system which maintains an equivalent level of anonymity protection as Tor while enabling users to access its services without requiring a centralized control system. I2P functions as a completely decentralized network which enables all its nodes to handle routing tasks because it does not need users to depend on its exit nodes directory for routing purposes. The two systems apply their architectural difference to create divergent threat models which provide I2P users with better security for internal darknet usage but make it less suitable for public internet access to surface web resources which attracts fewer regular users. Law enforcement bodies find it harder to observe or shut down I2P networks because their decentralized structure enables I2P users to maintain their face-to-face conversations on the darknet without detection from authorities (Zhou et al., 2025).

Darknet operators who seek advanced techniques for anonymous communication now use decentralized platforms such as blockchain-based communication systems and Distributed Hash Table (DHT) and Peer-to-Peer (P2P) networks. The architecture of these platforms provides users with stronger system performance because they remove all single points of failure which law enforcement could control while they distribute their system through thousands of nodes which remain under independent operation by network participants who support different darknet initiatives and their system maintains operational power during attempts to block user access or interrupt communication. The decentralized platforms now serve as C2 networks which threat actors use to conduct their botnet operations because these networks implement complex monitoring and disruption mechanisms which make it hard for law enforcement to trace their activities. The combination of decentralized platforms with IoT device botnets creates a particularly concerning threat scenario where compromised devices participate in both attack infrastructure and the darknet itself, essentially creating a mesh network immune to traditional law enforcement interdiction (Aqeel et al., 2022).

2.4.2 Anonymity and Encryption Mechanisms

The process of achieving anonymity on the Darknet depends on various technological foundations which together create extreme difficulty in identifying users. Onion routing technologies function at the network layer by creating encrypted traffic paths that require multiple hops to decrypt one layer of protection at each hop which reveals only the next hop's address. Anonymous software clients at the application layer use Tor Browser technology to create separate browsing environments which block cookies and session data tracking between different user sessions. Zero-knowledge proofs function as privacy-preserving cryptographic techniques which permit users to demonstrate their identity attributes through proofs without disclosing personal identification details. Advanced users protect their activities through operational security methods which include Tails or Whonix usage, VPN connection prior to Tor access, dedicated device usage for separate tasks, and activity time blocking which stops traffic analysis threats (Zaman et al., 2021).

The combination of these anonymity mechanisms creates an environment where users can operate with confidence that their activities cannot be traced back to their identity or location. This protection system allows legitimate users to do privacy-preserving activism, while still carrying out confidential research and secure communication in hostile and oppressive environments. Anonymity mechanisms which protect users also create a situation where threat actors can conduct their operations without facing any consequences. In practice, an adversary can leverage those layers to execute IoT device compromises, botnet operations, DDoS attacks, plus malware distribution, all while having a much lower chance of being traced or identified. The attacker then turns to darknet markets to take on cyberattack contracts, and from there the attacker coordinates diplomatic style interactions with accomplice groups, through those same agreements, getting cryptocurrency payments in order to bankroll later attack efforts, so it really keeps his total invisibility (Li et al., 2025).

On top of that, forensic analysis and law enforcement investigation of darknet communications gets even harder, because end-to-end encryption technologies safeguard basically all messages. Agencies that manage to compromise a darknet node, or intercept traffic, still run into encryption barriers that stop them from seeing communication contents, or even participant identification, unless they already have the needed decryption keys. Law enforcement agencies can obtain subpoenas to access surface internet communications which allow them to force service providers to either decrypt communications or hand over decryption keys. Darknet users can communicate through their channels because they possess complete confidence in the confidentiality of their messages. The operational security framework allows organizations to conduct their operations without the risk of law enforcement interruption through encrypted channels which handle their attack plans and allows encrypted file transfer of exploit code and international attack coordination. Threat actors who operate against IoT and 5G/6G infrastructures gain enhanced operational capabilities because multiple anonymity layers together with strong encryption function as protective barriers against identification and legal prosecution (Li et al., 2025).

Table 1 summarizes key modern digital infrastructures (such as IoT, 5G/6G networks, and distributed computing) by mapping their inherent technical weaknesses against how darknet threat actors exploit them. It outlines how advanced architectural performance and anonymity tools are weaponized to conduct stealthy, systemic cyber-attacks.

Table 1. Technology vulnerabilities and darknet threats

Technology / Domain	What It Does	Where It Is Weak	How Darknet Attackers Exploit It
IoT Sensors & Devices	Collects environmental data.	Highly limited memory and power; lacks robust security defenses.	Attacked to build massive botnets for distributed cyber-attacks.
Gateways & Edge Nodes	Combines and processes data locally before sending it to the cloud.	Vulnerable firmware and fragmented security boundaries.	Used as stealthy entry points to bypass main cloud security and move across networks.
Network Slicing	Creates multiple virtual networks on the same physical hardware.	Shared hardware allows data to bleed across virtual boundaries.	Attackers buy darknet tools to hop from low-security slices into high-security ones.
SDN	Centralizes network control through software.	Creating a centralized controller introduces a single point of failure.	Targeted via darknet exploits to hijack traffic, alter routing, or shut down networks.
NFV	Runs network hardware functions as software.	Vulnerabilities in the hypervisor can allow virtual machine escapes.	Exploited to break out of software containers and compromise all active network tasks.
5G/6G Performance (URLLC & mMTC)	Enables ultra-fast speeds, low latency, and billions of connections.	Near-instant speeds leave no time for complex security or anomaly checks.	Used to mask malicious traffic and coordinate data theft at an unprecedented scale.
Smart Cities & Industrial Systems (IIoT)	Connects infrastructure (grids, water, transport) to the internet.	Merging old, isolated industrial systems with the internet creates massive attack surfaces.	Threat actors trade specialized malware to trigger blackouts, water contamination, or traffic gridlock.
Digital Twins	Virtual software models used to monitor physical assets.	The digital model can be manipulated independently of the physical machine.	Attackers feed false data to the model, blinding operators to actual physical dangers.
Edge & Fog Computing	Distributes data processing across thousands of local sites.	Lacks centralized monitoring, making it hard to track scattered traffic.	Used to hide command-and-control communications by disguising them as normal data.
Tor & I2P Anonymity Networks	Encrypts and bounces web traffic through multiple nodes.	Total traffic anonymity protects malicious users just as well as innocent ones.	Used to host criminal marketplaces, distribute malware, and conduct hidden operations.
Decentralized Platforms & Crypto	Uses peer-to-peer networks, blockchains, and advanced encryption.	Removes single points of failure, making systems impossible for law enforcement to turn off.	Used to build bulletproof command networks for botnets and process anonymous payouts.

3. DARKNET-ENABLED THREATS IN IOT AND CYBER-PHYSICAL SYSTEMS

3.1 IoT Botnets and Distributed Attacks

3.1.1 Mirai-like Botnets and Evolution

The Mirai botnet, which security researchers found in 2016, created a new type of cybersecurity danger because it showed criminals how they could use hacked IoT equipment to conduct massive online attacks through hidden command systems that operated on darknet networks. The Mirai virus used default passwords which existed on IP cameras (Internet Protocol camera) and routers and DVRs and network-attached storage devices to scan the internet for devices which hackers could access through common default accounts. Mirai differed from previous botnets because it used a particular method which attackers had learned to use when they focused their efforts on less protected devices. The attacker used darknet networks to control the botnet in addition to helping customers by conducting DDoS attacks through a subscription-based service (Blancaflor et al., 2025).

As showed in figure 3, the operational structure of Mirai included four separate elements which created a basis for future botnet activities:

- The first component monitored all internet address ranges to discover which IoT devices were active on telnet and SSH ports.
- The brute-force component tested all authentication possibilities with its credential dictionaries while it saved any confirmed successful credentials which it discovered during the authentication process.
- The loader component took control of the botnet by downloading and executing the malware payload on devices which it had successfully breached.
- The command infrastructure managed all infected devices through secure encrypted channels which allowed it to send attack orders to infected devices while receiving operational reports from botnet components. The attacker operated this infrastructure through darknet services which allowed him to run the botnet from anonymous locations which successfully hid his identity and that of his customers (Sohail et al., 2025).

Figure 3. Simplified overview of Mirai botnet architecture

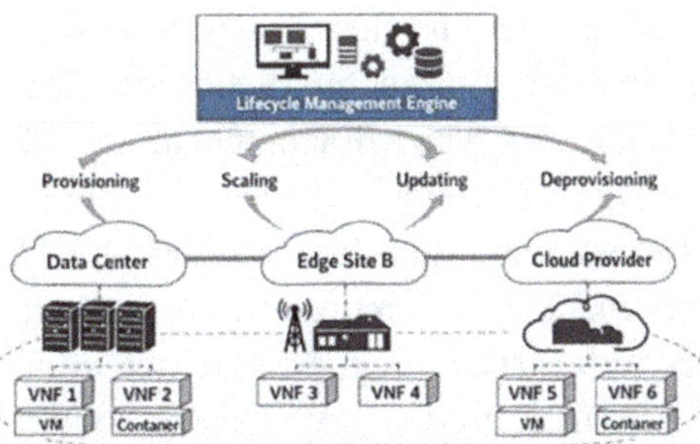

The release of Mirai source code to darknet markets within 2016 brought major changes to the security environment, where the source code release allowed multiple independent threat groups to create their own Mirai variants because they no longer needed to rely on a centralized botnet which had a known operator. The new exploitation techniques from Bashlite Gafgyt variants allowed attackers to target specific IoT device types and their firmware versions. The Torii malware added self-replicating capacity which allowed it to spread to nearby network devices without needing outside scanning equipment. The Okiru malware introduced new techniques which made it more challenging to conduct security assessments. Mirai-HTTP variants added HTTP-based DDoS attack capabilities (Zhang et al., 2026). The attackers distributed all variants through darknet markets and their associated underground networks which allowed attackers to conduct IoT botnet operations without needing advanced technical skills because they could simply download and use the ready-made attack tools.

3.1.2 DDoS-as-a-Service via Darknet

Financially motivated criminals who lack technical skills use DDoS-as-a-Service (DaaS) platforms from darknet marketplaces as their main method to execute advanced attacks against critical infrastructure. The system allows attackers to buy attack power through Tor browser-accessible web interfaces which let them choose their target systems and attack length while providing them with ongoing battle updates. DDoS attacks became accessible to all users because DaaS changed technical requirements into monetary needs (McNulty & Vassilakis, 2022). Moreover, DaaS enables operators to launch DDoS attacks against both IoT devices and 5G networks.

Regarding the models price, it typically base costs on multiple factors: (1) Attack duration (measured in hours), (2) Target bandwidth requirements (with pricing varying by attack size), (3) Attack sophistication (with complex multi-vector attacks costing more than simple volumetric attacks), and (4) Attack timing (with premium pricing for attacks during business hours or specific dates) (Guo et al., 2025). Attack costs typically range from $10 for short-duration, low-volume attacks to $500 or more for large-scale, multi-day attacks involving sophisticated attack vectors. The pricing structure lets financially motivated criminals and extortionists who must pay to prevent attacks and hired attackers who compete for business and ideologically driven activists who want to harm specific organizations use it. The cost of modern attack infrastructure has dropped dramatically because it now requires only a fraction of the previous million-dollar investment needed to establish and run such systems which caused a major rise in attack incidents and made more people able to execute attacks (Leigha et al., 2025).

Operators of critical infrastructure face increased attack threats from criminals who use DDoS services available on darknet markets. As well, the critical infrastructure systems now deal with persistent attacks from basic attackers who use rented resources for their business espionage and competitive sabotage and extortion and ideological attacks instead of protecting themselves from advanced nation-state threats which require special defense technologies. The Mirai botnet alone (when weaponized through darknet DaaS platforms) demonstrated the ability to conduct attacks exceeding 1.2 Tbps, overwhelming network infrastructure through sheer traffic volume. The Mirai variants and Torii and Okiru botnets represent the latest generation of IoT botnets which have demonstrated their ability to execute similar attacks. The interconnected systems of critical infrastructure experience increasing numbers of cascading failures because an attack on one provider affects all dependent services which leads to regional outages that impact millions of users (Maiwada et al., 2024).

3.2 Exploitation of IoT Vulnerabilities

3.2.1 Zero-day Exploits and Firmware Attacks

Zero-day exploits are vulnerabilities which have never been discovered before and lack both public knowledge and any existing security fixes. Zero-day vulnerabilities are considered high-value items which dark web marketplaces use to conduct their trading business. Security researchers estimate that thousands of zero-day vulnerabilities exist across IoT ecosystems but remain undisclosed, with some vulnerabilities affecting hundreds of millions of devices. Therefore, Darknet markets enable different types of zero-day trading activities. The first market type operates through vulnerability disclosure markets which researchers and security experts use to document and sell their discovered zero-day vulnerabilities to threat groups who will then use them for their attack operations. Attackers can buy ready-made exploit code from specific vulnerability exploit code markets which exists to sell this information. Access markets function as a trading platform where threat groups exchange initial system access credentials and shell entry rights (Mirji & S., 2026).

The operation of zero-day markets permits attackers to execute IoT system breaches through coordinated actions across multiple sites. Darknet markets place a value range between 10000 and 100000 dollars on popular IoT devices which include routers and IP cameras and network storage devices that have been affected by zero-day security vulnerabilities. Threat groups which conduct botnet operations throughout their entire existence find their costs to maintain zero-day access to multiple devices acceptable because they can raise their initial investment through access to massive device control. An attacker can use a zero-day to create a botnet which generates income through DDoS attacks that exceed the initial cost of acquiring the zero-day within weeks (Hossain et al., 2024).

IoT security faces its greatest threat from firmware attacks because firmware acts as permanent code which maintains its special status even after device restarts and firmware upgrades. An attacker who gains access to a device's firmware establishes complete control over the device until the organization discovers the flaw and implements a fix. Threat actors use darknet channels to obtain firmware vulnerabilities and spread tools which enable users to alter firmware. Bootkit exploits create a method to modify the bootloader so that it can persist through future firmware updates. Hypervisor-level exploits (where applicable) provide lowest-level control of device hardware. The exploitation of signed firmware overwriting allows attackers to install any firmware they want because it bypasses the established verification process which checks firmware signatures. The consequences are severe: compromised firmware becomes a permanent botnet node for darknet-coordinated attacks, regardless of operator attempts to remediate the infection through traditional malware removal (Meneghello et al., 2019).

3.2.2 Device Hijacking and Lateral Movement

The network security breach allows hackers to move through the network using compromised IoT devices which become their main base for taking control of the entire network. On other part, The attacker who uses an IoT device such as an IP camera can access all systems that the camera has network access to including other IoT devices on the same network segment and network routers or switches and gateway devices that link to wider infrastructure and enterprise management software that tracks IoT system monitoring installations. Current IoT devices now contain multiple Ethernet and WiFi and Bluetooth network interfaces which sometimes include USB ports that allow for several different methods of unauthorized internal access (Kravchenko & Permyakov, 2025).

Improper network segmentation creates an architectural vulnerability which allows attackers to move laterally through the system. Organizations create security zones for their networks which use firewalls to control traffic between different zones but IoT deployments function in isolated network segments where security depends on the belief of hiding things from view. The attackers succeed in breaking into protected networks through their IoT device attacks because the network setup fails to protect important areas from their movements. An IoT camera which people think is safe to hack connects to the same network that includes administrative workstations and internal servers and backup storage devices. The attacker can access the network to search for system weaknesses and take control of more systems until they reach essential resources (Aqeel et al., 2022).

The process of lateral movement across the darknet occurs according to a pattern where attackers utilize compromised IoT devices as their base operations. The attacker uses the initial compromise to gain shell access to the device, then uses this access to conduct network reconnaissance, identify additional vulnerable systems, exploit those systems, and establish persistent access. Each compromised system becomes another base for the attackers to conduct reconnaissance and exploit security weaknesses. The attacker uses darknet channels to establish contact with tool creators who have created specific exploits to target systems which lets them advance the attack throughout the network. The coordinated approach converts separate device breaches into full network breaches that impact all parts of the infrastructure (Cecílio & Souto, 2024).

3.3 Darknet Marketplaces for IoT Exploits

3.3.1 Trading Vulnerabilities and Access Credentials

The specialized markets which security researchers and threat actors plus corporate insiders and criminal enterprises operate all represent darknet marketplaces for dealing with security flaws. The marketplaces operate like legitimate e-commerce sites which allow vendors to showcase their products through descriptions and pricing with optional buyer feedback while buyers search for items based on system type and vulnerability category and access level. Darknet technologies provide users with complete privacy which enables vendors to remain unknown to law enforcement while buyers shop for attack tools without concern about detection (Zhou et al., 2025).

Compromised credential markets facilitate massive-scale attacks by providing attackers with valid authentication credentials for target systems. The system collects credentials from various sources, including credential databases that were exposed during data breaches, social engineering and malware attacks which permitted thieves to acquire employee credentials, brute-force attacks which obtained credentials from systems with weak password security, and man-in-the-middle attacks which intercepted unencrypted communications. A single compromised credential market listing might contain thousands or millions of username/password pairs for specific services. Darknet credential markets maintain a collection of credentials which attackers can use to conduct IoT attacks that target common IoT devices. People who want to breach IoT systems now find it easier to obtain credential packages which enable them to bypass both scanning and brute-force attacks by purchasing device access credentials for their targeted devices (Rahmoune et al., 2025).

The most direct use of darknet marketplace operations occurs in access trading markets which enable actors to sell shell access rights for systems that already belong to other parties. The market provides access to systems which vendors have already compromised yet no longer protect, instead of selling credentials or exploits. An attacker can buy access to a compromised web server or router or IoT device to create a base for future attacks. Access trading enables specialized network penetration threat groups to earn money by selling their capabilities to attackers who lack the skills needed for initial system breaches while the attackers will handle all follow-up attacks. The advanced threat groups now function as suppliers because they provide access to criminal networks which have less proficiency in carrying out attacks to create a marketplace for specialized attack services (Rahmoune et al., 2025).

3.3.2 Malware Kits Targeting IoT Ecosystems

The emergence of malware kits designed for IoT systems has progressed to a stage where users can acquire these advanced tools through darknet marketplaces. The kits deliver complete attack systems which enable users without technical expertise to execute extensive IoT hacking operations. An IoT malware kit typically comes with source code or pre-compiled binaries which target the three CPU architectures (ARM MIPS x86) that IoT devices use. The kit contains automated compilation tools which enable users to customize their distribution for different operational environments. The kit includes configuration frameworks which allow operators to select target devices along with their attack parameter settings. The infrastructure enables command-and-control operations which manage the botnet (Hwang & Kim, 2021).

The sophistication level of available IoT malware kits has substantially increased over recent years. Early IoT malware like Mirai implemented basic scanning and brute-force exploitation, establishing a template for subsequent variants to improve upon. Modern IoT malware kits incorporate multi-stage infection processes where an initial lightweight payload downloads more sophisticated capabilities only after compromising a device, which allows for more efficient use of system resources during the initial attack phase. The modern kits use polymorphic code variation because they change malware code during each installation process to elude signature-based detection systems. Most kits use peer-to-peer update systems which enable infected devices to automatically receive fresh malware updates, thus helping the botnet to adapt against security measures (Hwang & Kim, 2021).

The darknet distribution methods for malware kits enable threat actors to obtain these tools with great speed. Today's attackers need only to acquire a kit from darknet vendors to create malware because they can do this without needing advanced technical skills. The method allows users to handle IoT botnet operations with lower technical requirements. A financially motivated attacker can generate revenue by purchasing botnet capacity for DDoS attacks, while simultaneously operating as a reseller providing access to other attackers. The system establishes a multi-level marketplace model which enables expert groups to create advanced attack systems, which they sell to less expert groups, who then sell their services to basic attackers who lack proficiency. The system establishes a multi-level marketplace model which enables expert groups to create advanced attack systems, which they sell to less expert groups, who then sell their services to basic attackers who lack proficiency.

Table 2 summarizes this section and highlights how darknet ecosystems enable IoT exploitation: first through Mirai's architecture and its variants, then by commercial services, zero-day markets, lateral movement, credential trading, and malware kits. Together, these elements show the industrialization of IoT botnets and the lowered barrier for attackers.

Table 2. Stages of darknet-enabled IoT exploitation

Stage	Mechanism	How It Enables Exploitation	Impact
Mirai Architecture (2016)	Scanner, Brute-Force, Loader, C&C	Automated discovery, credential cracking, malware loading, and darknet-based control.	Established the template for IoT botnets.
Mirai Variants	Bashlite, Torii, Okiru, Mirai-HTTP	Added features like self-replication, HTTP DDoS, and firmware targeting.	Expanded attack capabilities and resilience.
Commercial Services (DDoS-as-a-Service)	Darknet marketplaces	Rent attack power by duration, bandwidth, and complexity.	Lowered barrier to entry; anyone can launch massive DDoS.
Zero-Day Markets	Vulnerability trading	Sell undisclosed IoT flaws and exploit kits.	Permanent compromise of devices; high-value botnet nodes.

continued on following page

Table 2. Continued

Stage	Mechanism	How It Enables Exploitation	Impact
Lateral Movement	Device hijacking	Compromised IoT devices used to infiltrate wider networks.	Turns single breach into full infrastructure compromise.
Credential Trading	Darknet credential markets	Buy valid username/password pairs for IoT devices.	Bypasses brute-force; accelerates mass exploitation.
Malware Kits	Ready-made IoT attack tools	Source code, binaries, auto-compilers, polymorphic updates.	Industrializes botnet creation; democratizes attacks.

4. DARKNET IMPLICATIONS IN 5G/6G NETWORKS

4.1 Network Slicing Exploitation

4.1.1 Isolation Weaknesses and Cross-Slice Attacks

5G network slicing enables the creation of separate virtual networks which operate on common network resources for three distinct service types (eMBB, URLLC, mMTC) with each virtual network designed to fulfill particular service needs. Attackers who use advanced methods to execute attacks through darknet channels can successfully breach the system's fundamental security barrier. The centralized systems control network slice operations by directing new slice setups and resource distribution and inter-slice connection rules. Attackers who exploit SDN controller vulnerabilities gain the ability to make unauthorized changes to network slice setups which result in security failures between different network slices. The attackers use darknet exploits to gain access to controller software which they use to create policy changes that permit traffic redirection between slices while turning off essential slices (Cunha et al., 2024).

The second method attackers use to execute cross-slice attacks emerges through hypervisor vulnerabilities. The NFV infrastructure operates its virtual network functions (VNFs) which serve multiple slices on its common hypervisors. Advanced side-channel attacks use shared hardware resource contention as an advantage to obtain encryption keys or to listen in on other slices in the system. Darknet actors operate through their channels to spread hypervisor attack tools which focus on particular virtualization systems such as KVM and Xen and VMware. An attacker who gains control over one virtual machine running on shared hypervisor access points can use side-channel vulnerabilities to gain access to all virtual machines operating network functions for other slices (Zhou, 2025).

The attackers who operate through darknet channels use multiple attack methods to succeed in their cross-slice attacks which break system isolation. An attacker would start by taking control of an mMTC slice which services multiple IoT devices, which allows them to use the hacked devices to carry out planned attacks against slice control systems. The attacker can use this method to execute slice policy changes which permit them to access URLLC slice operations that protect vital functions and eMBB slice operations which secure banking activities. The attackers who start with less important slice attacks use their position as an entry point to launch attacks against more crucial targets. The specialized groups use Darknet collaboration to plan their coordinated attacks which consist of multiple stages: one group targets the IoT systems to breach security while the second group targets SDN controllers to create an unstoppable advance against all slice types (Matencio-Escolar et al., 2024).

4.2 Virtualization and SDN/NFV Threats

4.2.1 Control Plane Attacks

SDN creates a security risk because it relies on centralized controllers for network management through which all traffic routing decisions are made. Traditional networking requires multiple devices to share control functions which create challenges for attackers who want to manage the entire network. The centralization of SDN provides operational advantages through improved efficiency but it establishes a vital single point of vulnerability because attackers who gain control of the SDN controller can disrupt network operations which impact millions of users. The threat actors who operate through darknet channels actively search for vulnerabilities in SDN controller software. The common vulnerabilities in systems include authentication bypasses which allow attackers to access controller interfaces without credentials and API vulnerabilities which enable attackers to submit crafted commands that bypass access controls and memory corruption vulnerabilities which enable attackers to execute any code with controller privileges (Allaw et al., 2025).

The impacts of SDN breaches through darknet-delivered exploits create severe effects that touch multiple aspects of the system. The attacker who gains control of an SDN controller can change forwarding rules which enables him to redirect traffic streams that lead to man-in-the-middle attacks through which attackers steal data while changing its contents. The malicious commands from the controller will steer network traffic toward systems that attacker's control which leads to data theft and service outages. The controller can completely shut down network slices which creates denial-of-service conditions that stop essential services from operating. The controller can change access control systems to either permit unauthorized devices into secure network areas or block approved devices from reaching vital resources (Rahman et al., 2024).

Figure 4 illustrates a communication network managed by a centralized SDN controller architecture which introduces a single point of failure, making controller protection critical for network resilience. Moreover, the control plane and data plane expose several attack surfaces: (1) control-plane hijacking, (2) denial-of-service on the controller, (3) data interception within the data plane, and (4) host compromise at the edge.

Figure 4. SDN-managed network vulnerabilities

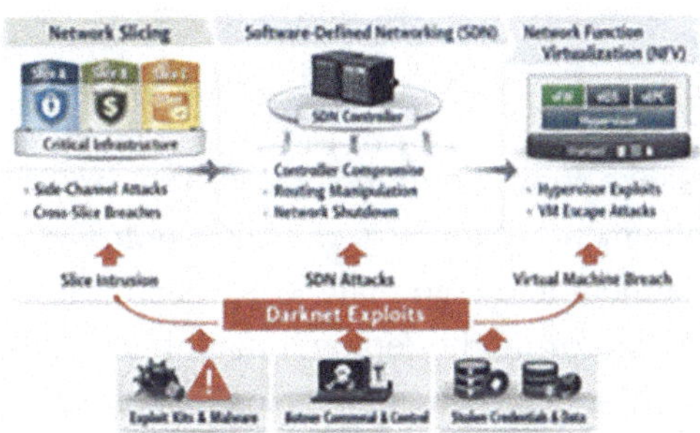

Darknet distribution of SDN/NFV exploits occurs through dedicated channels which enable exploit developers to share their code and methods for attacking 5G/6G systems. The 5G/6G exploit market operates differently from traditional vulnerability markets which concentrate on web applications and endpoint devices because it focuses on telecom-specific security flaws that demand specialized skills for exploitation. Darknet groups that work together to execute attacks divide their responsibilities among three stages: one group handles reconnaissance activities while another group develops exploits and the third group handles the deployment process and monetization activities. The combination of specialized skills allows different darknet threat actors to conduct advanced attacks on 5G infrastructure (Rahman et al., 2024).

4.2.2 Malicious Orchestration

The orchestration process for VFN in NFV needs to manage VFN which operate on scattered computing resources. NFV orchestrators handle the complete process of virtual network function management by executing network-based provisioning along with scaling and updating and deprovisioning functions. NFV can be understood as a way to run network services (like firewalls, load balancers, or routers) on software instead of specialized hardware. These services are called VNFs, and they can be deployed on different computing resources such as data centers, edge sites, or cloud servers. Because these VNFs are scattered across various locations, they need a central system to coordinate their operation. That's where orchestration comes in. Figure 5 demonstrates how the NFV orchestrator automates the lifecycle management of VFN (VNFs) across distributed computing environments. It performs provisioning, scaling, updating, and deprovisioning to ensure efficient resource utilization and service continuity across data centers, edge sites, and cloud providers.

Figure 5. NFV orchestration process

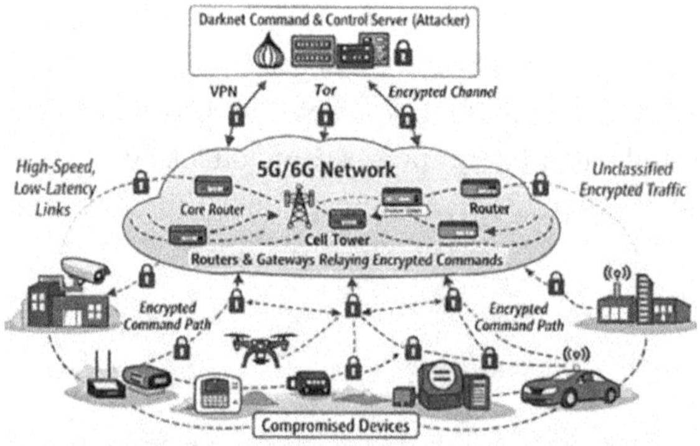

Orchestrators which attackers take control of transform into strong attack bases which allow them to control all network function deployments. Attackers can take control of orchestrators through darknet-distributed exploits which enable them to create malicious network functions that carry out attacking operations. A compromised orchestrator might deploy a malicious packet inspection function that intercepts and modifies data in transit or deploy malicious load balancers that redirect traffic to attacker-controlled systems (Rahman et al., 2024).

Malicious orchestration creates effects which impact complete service classes instead of affecting single network functions. A compromised orchestrator might deploy malicious eMBB functions affecting consumer broadband services, URLLC functions affecting critical infrastructure services, or mMTC functions affecting IoT connectivity. The attacker can scale these malicious functions to affect millions of users simultaneously, creating service disruptions that cascade through dependent services. The attacker uses the orchestrator to turn off security tools which include Intrusion Detection Systems (IDS) and firewalls and encryption enforcement systems to make attacks happen without any protection (Rahman et al., 2024).

Darknet malicious orchestration uses different attack techniques which operate together in a planned way to conduct coordinated campaigns. An attacker might begin by compromising an NFV orchestrator through a zero-day exploit obtained via darknet markets, then use the orchestrator to deploy functions implementing an attack against SDN controllers. The SDN controller compromise then enables manipulation of network slicing, potentially isolating security monitoring infrastructure while enabling attack traffic. The execution of this multi-layered attack orchestration requires advanced coordination abilities together with particular expertise, which establishes an economic system where darknet attack specialists unite to accomplish complicated attacks that no single group could execute independently. The result is a threat landscape where coordinated attacks against 5G/6G infrastructure become possible for threat actors with sufficient resources and darknet connections.

4.3 Covert Communication and Data Exfiltration

4.3.1 Use of Encrypted Tunnels and Darknet Channels

The high-speed, low latency 5G/6G networks, which serve their intended purpose, create hidden communication pathways that enable remote control of botnets operating from the darknet. Attackers can use the high bandwidth capacity to send command-and-control messages while appearing as legitimate network traffic, which lets them avoid detection through bandwidth monitoring. The system delivers instant command transmission from command-and-control centers to compromised devices, which allows botnet operators to execute attacks almost instantaneously. Attackers use 5G capabilities for fast botnet command transmission during attacks, which enables them to organize attacks at speeds never possible before (Mohan et al., 2022).

Figure 6 illustrates how attackers exploit 5G/6G networks and underlying routers, gateways, and base stations to relay encrypted command-and-control traffic. These networking devices forward encrypted packets across the backbone, enabling stealthy, high-speed coordination between darknet servers and compromised devices distributed across the network.

Figure 6. Distributed 5G/6G botnet communication network with networking infrastructure

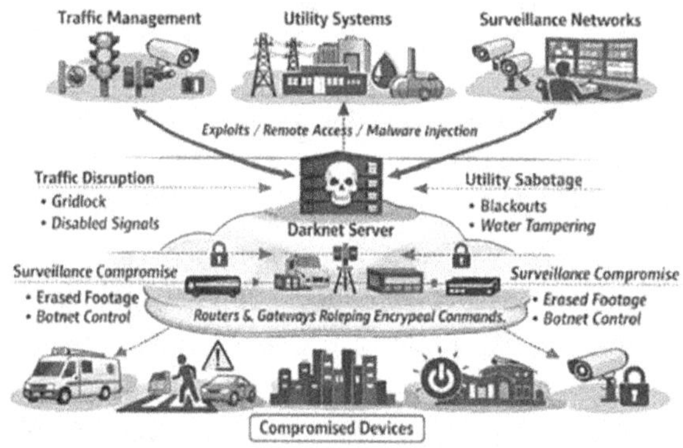

Attackers can establish private communication links from hacked IoT and edge devices to darknet command-and-control networks through encrypted tunnel establishment which 5G/6G networks provide. An attacker can configure compromised devices to establish VPN tunnels, Tor circuits, or custom encrypted channels to darknet servers, creating communication paths that security monitoring systems cannot inspect. The 5G network provides the underlying transport, but the encrypted overlay prevents security systems from understanding the communication purpose. Security monitoring systems can detect encrypted communication traffic, but defenders cannot identify which encrypted applications are genuine and which ones transmit command-and-control traffic because they cannot access encrypted materials (Ma et al., 2024).

5G technology enables darknet-based command infrastructure to achieve previously unattainable speeds for coordinating attacks. Attackers use 5G low latency to execute their commands in almost real-time instead of sending their commands through various darknet hops which would create delays. A botnet operator can launch a DDoS attack, observe the response, modify attack parameters, and achieve target-specific optimization within seconds. This represents a substantial improvement over traditional botnets where command propagation latency measured in seconds or minutes limited attack adaptation capabilities. Attackers who use 5G for their attacks succeed in causing destruction before defense systems become operational because they need time to validate their detection capabilities against the gradual attack threats (Ma et al., 2024).

4.4 Darknet Services Leveraging 5G Capabilities

4.4.1 High-Speed Anonymous Communication

The darknet services receive major improvements through 5G technology because it delivers rapid anonymous network access to its hidden operational framework. The traditional Tor-based darknet services have always faced speed problems because Tor hidden services create extended wait times of multiple seconds which restrict Tor application capabilities. The performance issues of Darknet services vanish through 5G access because it delivers users fast internet connections which have latency times that match typical internet usage. The development of darknet marketplaces creates instant responses while darknet messaging systems enable users to communicate instantly and darknet applications can now handle tasks which once exceeded their performance capacity (Lakhal et al., 2025).

5G technology enables users to access illegal online marketplaces through darknet services which operate through anonymous marketplaces for illegal goods and services. Cybercriminal operations become more accessible through 5G technology which enables users to reach illegal operations that involve automated scanning services and exploit distribution services and botnet rental platforms. 5G technology enables journalists and activists and dissidents to use anonymous communication services which function at internet speeds that match regular online services. The unfortunate consequence is that while 5G improves legitimate privacy-protecting services, it simultaneously improves the infrastructure that supports cybercriminal marketplaces (Neha & Bhatia, 2025).

5G technology enables users to access decentralized darknet services which operate through blockchain and peer-to-peer network systems. The system employs decentralized services to distribute marketplace functions across numerous active nodes instead of using centralized darknet markets which face law enforcement shutdown threats. 5G's high bandwidth and low latency enables users to take part in decentralized networks through operation of marketplace nodes at acceptable performance levels. The introduction of 5G decentralized infrastructure leads to a situation in which law enforcement agencies lose their ability to access darknet services because criminals develop better defenses against their detection systems. The consequence is that darknet services may become substantially more difficult to disrupt as 5G deployment expands (Neha & Bhatia, 2025).

4.4.2 Mobile-Based Illicit Services

Darknet services increasingly target mobile platforms by operating applications specifically designed for smartphones and tablets using 5G connectivity. Mobile platforms face particular security problems because users want their applications to work without interruptions during network transitions between different carriers. Mobile users who lack technical knowledge choose to use mobile darknet services because these services can be accessed without technical training requirements. Criminal marketplaces which operate through mobile applications together with anonymous communication services that support illegal activities and dedicated applications for forms of cybercrime constitute the totality of 5G-enabled illicit services (Elijah et al., 2025).

The existing 5G-enabled illicit services consist of mobile botnets which use 5G to launch attacks from multiple network connections during attacks. Mobile banking malware attacks financial applications which operate on 5G devices through the security vulnerabilities of mobile platforms. Ransomware distribution services which operate through mobile channels target both consumer and business users. Operators can use smartphone remote access trojans to take control of infected devices for spying purposes and conduct cyberattacks. Criminals use anonymous voice and messaging services to communicate with each other. Mobile-based cryptocurrency wallets and exchange services enable criminals to transfer illicit funds through money laundering activities. Mobile 5G networks serve as essential connectivity infrastructure which enables all service categories to deliver their services to customers (Dwedar et al., 2024).

The combination of mobile platform technology with darknet services enables cybercriminals to conduct their operations from any location. Cybercriminals no longer need desktops with Tor browsers and VPN clients because they can operate their activities from mobile devices which provide complete user anonymity. Mobile criminals can conduct attacks and access darknet marketplaces and control their botnets and complete their transactions using only their mobile devices. The operational requirements can be fulfilled because 5G offers enough bandwidth together with its low latency capabilities. The shift to mobile-based darknet services causes law enforcement agencies and security monitoring systems which operate on desktop-access patterns to lose track of a significant portion of darknet activity.

5. IMPACT ON CRITICAL AND EMERGING INFRASTRUCTURES

5.1 Smart Cities and Urban Systems

Smart cities integrate IoT technology throughout urban infrastructure, creating interconnected but often inadequately coordinated security postures (Nalini, 2024).

5.1.1 Traffic Systems, Surveillance, Utilities

Traffic Management Systems in smart cities use networked sensor systems and camera equipment and controller devices to manage vehicle movement throughout urban areas. The systems require precise timing control to maintain safe operations while enabling optimal traffic movement because of their strict operational requirements. Darknet-facilitated attacks on traffic systems can implement several destructive scenarios. Darknet attackers gain access to traffic management systems which they use to disrupt traffic signal operations, resulting in citywide traffic gridlock. Compromised systems have the potential to create traffic deadlock situations at intersections which block all vehicle movement throughout multiple city areas. Attackers can incorrectly prioritize traffic, which leads to complete traffic stoppage or directs vehicles into heavily congested regions that result in cascading gridlock throughout the street network. The operational scale of traffic management systems means that their failures lead to widespread impact which affects millions of people throughout the entire city (Hossain & Hasan, 2025).

The physical dangers of traffic system attacks create security threats that extend further than mere disruptive effects. D compromised systems disable safety features which include pedestrian crossing signals to create dangerous conditions for people using the streets. Public health emergencies arise when ambulances cannot reach hospitals due to disrupted emergency vehicle routing. Attackers coordinate traffic control systems to cause accidents by directing traffic flow toward collision points. Theoretical concerns about traffic system attacks have transformed into actual attack possibilities with documented evidence: security conferences have demonstrated remote attacks against traffic signal systems and threat researchers have found software vulnerabilities in traffic management programs which they documented (U. et al., 2024).

The systems which protect public safety through surveillance networks become targets for attacks because their successful compromise enables criminals to operate without detection. Criminals can use compromised surveillance systems to erase recorded footage which prevents law enforcement from obtaining critical evidence. Darknet attackers establish command-and-control operations through compromised surveillance systems which serve as botnet control nodes. The cameras themselves, compromised through darknet-distributed exploits, become part of massive IoT botnets. Attackers utilize compromised surveillance systems to obtain recorded footage for extortion purposes or to frame innocent people for crimes through video manipulation. Security networks for surveillance functions with little protection against IoT systems and darknet networks which enable attackers to turn smart city security cameras into both security threats and potential attack platforms (Gospodinov et al., 2025).

Utility distribution systems for electricity and water and gas supplies have become major target areas for darknet attacks, which lead to emergency situations that endanger public safety. Smart grid systems controlling electricity distribution rely on networked sensors, automated switches, and centralized control systems. The system enables darknet attackers to gain access to its control systems which leads to potential blackouts that affect millions of people. The water treatment plants need SCADA systems because they use network connectivity to establish links with their operational systems, which creates openings for darknet attackers to exploit. Attackers who gain access to water systems have three options: they can either introduce contaminants into the system, or they can interfere with water distribution operations, or they can completely halt water service. Gas distribution systems face similar risks. The systems of vital infrastructure represent attractive targets for attackers who want to create maximum disruption (Dér, 2025).

Figure 7. Darknet attacks on smart city infrastructure

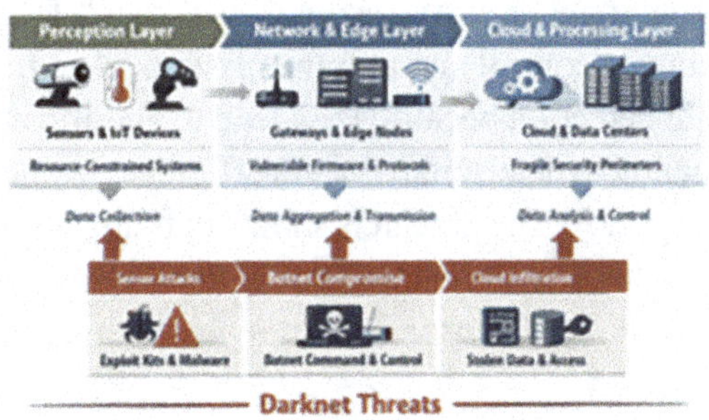

In Figure 7, the darknet attackers mess with connected smart city systems (like traffic management, utility grids, and the surveillance networks) and how the attackers achieve a large scale disruption once those systems get compromised. The results are clear in gridlock, safety hazards, and service outages, which show how much resilient cybersecurity we need in urban areas. Traffic management in addition to utility and surveillance networks are basically together the key smart city parts (at the top of the figure traffic) Then there is the central Darknet Server, it fires off exploits and malware toward those systems, which mostly leads to triggering traffic standstills, power failures, and surveillance intrusions. Figure 7 shows (down below) compromised routers and gateways pass along encrypted commands to devices that have already been hijacked. That is where the real-world impact shows up, like ambulances getting stuck, pedestrians facing hazards, and even citywide blackouts. Figure 7 also highlights how cyberattack can ripple outward, turning into physical disruptions that threaten safety, and the public services, across an entire city.

5.2 Industrial IoT (IIoT) and SCADA Systems

5.2.1 Operational Disruption Risks

The operational disruption risks of IIoT and SCADA systems are the most critical security weaknesses becuease attackers use these systems to execute their campaigns from the darknet. Although the traditional design of IIoT and SCADA systems used high security standards with air-gap isolation, IIoT systems now need to connect to cloud services through internet links for their remote monitoring and predictive maintenance functions in addition to that IIoT increasingly connects operational technology (OT) to information technology, expanding threat surfaces. As a result, the combination of these technologies creates new security vulnerabilities that hackers from the darknet use to launch their attacks (Narsing & Srinivasan, 2025), for example the industrial botnets emerging from air-gap protected systems into actual dangerous threats now exist.

Using darknet channels, the attackers spread IIoT-specific malware and reconnaissance tools together with weaponized exploits which they designed for attacking industrial systems. Moreover, the industrial botnets serve their different purpose of disrupting operations by launching attacks against SCADA systems which lead to interlock failures and control logic damage which causes equipment breakdowns and critical process functions which get delayed.

The attacker can gain access to an IIoT device through darknet channels to collect critical process data and then inject false data which will deceive operators into thinking it is real information. In other words, the attackers create undetectable security weaknesses through false data injection attacks when they change either sensor outputs or control signal transmissions. The traditional cyber-attacks create situations that require immediate detection because they lead to significant operational disruptions, but false data injection functions silently to deteriorate system efficiency without being detected by standard security systems (Agbesi et al., 2026). The research shows that attacks will cause production quality problems and equipment failures and safety threats go mostly unobserved and then the situation gets more serious because industrial operators need sensor data to make their decisions, so any data corruption will destroy their operational capacity.

The IIoT supply chain vulnerabilities create a different critical attack vector which attackers exploit through their darknet networks, where the default setup of industrial equipment comes with active ports and unpatched firmware and default credentials. The attackers from darknet groups focus their efforts on supply chain attacks, which involve their infiltration into manufacturing sites to gain control of firmware and distribution systems which they use to infect devices before those devices reach their end users. On other side, the darknet communities maintain a database which includes industrial equipment models, credential lists, and specific exploits which they use to attack industrial devices. (Ali et al., 2025).

5.2.2 Safety Implications

The convergence of IIoT with smart grid modernization means that hackers now distribute exploits through darknet networks which target grid infrastructure components, while the safety risks of IIoT attacks enabled through the darknet extend from operational interruptions to create actual threats which endanger employees and their surroundings. On other hand, Industrial systems control physical processes where compromised operations can cause catastrophic harm such all of the following examples:

- Electric power grids that control generation and distribution process
- Water treatment systems that ensure potable water supply, water treatment facilities use SCADA systems to monitor chlorination levels and pH and turbidity and other water quality level parameters. Breached SCADA systems allow attackers to change treatment operational values which results in either introducing toxic substances into the system or decreasing disinfection levels. Attackers can cause pressure system breakdowns which result in two main problems:

- o first, they create pipe breaks which stop operational work.
  - o second, they let dirty water backflow into actual water systems.
- Transportation systems that coordinates vehicle movement
- Chemical processing systems which manage hazardous materials.
- Power grid interruption serves as a vital danger which threatens both national defense and civilian safety.
- Smart grid systems control electricity distribution across regions affecting millions of users. Attackers operating through darknet channels can compromise SCADA systems which enable them to manipulate control signals for destabilizing grid frequency and tripping protective relays and cascading blackouts. The 2015 Ukraine power grid attack demonstrated this threat practically: attackers used SCADA system breaches to execute synchronized failures which impacted 230000 customers.

In less-developed regions with weaker cybersecurity postures, darknet-enabled attacks represent increasingly plausible threats, where cybersecurity threats from darknet-enabled attacks now endanger industrial operations because hackers use these methods to execute their attacks. Furthermore, the operation of manufacturing equipment becomes dangerous when criminals use darknet methods to gain control over industrial setups, that means Manufacturing equipment operates with tight tolerances and compromised control creating hazardous conditions. Metalworking machinery can malfunction in ways causing worker injury or death, while chemical processing systems can create explosive or toxic conditions. Regarding Autonomous systems that can operate in unexpected ways which results in dangerous collision situations, the Safe operation becomes impossible because operators cannot tell which system failures result from normal equipment breakdowns versus attacks which interfere with system operations.

IIoT systems require risk management methods because they need to handle both cyber safety hazards and physical safety hazards. Traditional industrial safety practices assumed stable, predictable equipment behavior. Cyber-compromised systems violate this assumption, creating scenarios which lead to safety systems themselves becoming compromised (Panovyk, 2025). Effective risk management requires treating industrial cybersecurity as a core element which connects to physical safety in danger assessment procedures while hazard assessment methods need to be combined with security controls which maintain operations during security breaches.

5.3 Digital Twins and Cyber-Physical Systems

5.3.1 Manipulation of Virtual-Physical Synchronization

Digital twins are virtually replica of physical systems and enable sophisticated cyber-physical attacks. Thus, digital twins function as virtual models which represent actual systems through continuous synchronization with real-time sensor and actuator data. The synchronization method introduces new attack opportunities which are exclusive to environments that combine physical and digital elements. The attackers who use darknet channels can infiltrate digital twins which enable them to destroy virtual models without needing to access physical systems (Airehenbuwa et al., 2025).

Digital twin manipulation attacks follow several distinct patterns which attackers use to distribute their malware and exploit via darknet networks as follows:

1. The first attack type which leads to data corruption results in sensor data becoming untrustworthy when it enters digital twins which causes the twin to lose its connection to real-world physical objects. An attacker can inject false readings which display normal operation when systems malfunction or display equipment failure when systems function normally. Operators will make decisions based on corrupted information which results from virtual representation failing to match reality.
2. The second attack type which leads to model poisoning results in machine learning models that operate within digital twins becoming unreliable through affected predictions and recommendations.
3. The third attack type which leads to synchronization prevents digital twins from receiving updates which results in operators using outdated system state information.

The operational consequences reach a critical degree of seriousness. The system status perception of operators becomes flawed because the digital twin system breaks down which leads to decision-making problems. Operators might create hazards by turning off safety interlocks because they think the twin shows safe conditions when systems are dangerous or they might direct resources away from major areas because they believe the twin shows them as non-essential or they might make wrong optimization choices because of system state information errors. The main vulnerability stems from operators who place trust in digital representations which leads them to make vital decisions based on that belief.

Darknet-enabled supply chain infiltration of digital twin systems creates particularly concerning scenarios. Attackers can turn digital twin software into their target because they begin their attack from development stages which allow them to insert backdoors and dangerous code that will execute after the product reaches its operational period. The SaaS model which powers digital twins faces extreme security risks because attackers who control cloud providers can spread harmful updates which will impact numerous customer systems at the same time. Darknet communities share cloud infrastructure attack methods which enable them to perform complex attacks against widely deployed digital twin platforms (Krishnaveni et al., 2024).

The detection of digital twin attacks faces major obstacles because the compromised systems still seem operationally normal. Traditional anomaly detection identifies deviations from expected patterns, but digital twin attack patterns are precisely those that maintain appearance of normalcy while diverging from physical reality. Advanced approaches use multiple data sources for cross-validation which lets them check digital twin predictions against independent sensor systems and validate twin behavior against established physical laws and verify sensor authenticity through blockchain-based data provenance (Balta et al., 2024).

5.3.2 Data Integrity and Trust Issues

The trust relationships between cyber-physical systems depend on digital twin data which protects against data integrity attacks. Cyber-physical systems reject the IT system default of confidentiality and availability because they require data integrity which demands complete physical reality mapping for operators to make secure operational decisions. The attackers create conditions which fail to detect their operations through established monitoring systems because they damage the connection between virtual and physical representations. The attackers use darknet connections to create multiple access points which they use to execute digital twin data integrity attacks. Attackers can target ingestion pipelines where data flows from physical sensors to digital twins by injecting malicious data at multiple points which include compromised IoT devices, darknet-distributed exploits and man-in-the-middle attacks.

The system allows data corruption through each injection point which leads to digital twin deterioration. Trust verification mechanisms for digital twins depend on the assumption that all data sources might experience security breaches. Blockchain-based solutions create permanent audit records which show every data modification, thus enabling investigators to track all data changes between two points in time. Consensus systems require multiple independent sensors to reach agreement before implementing twin updates, thus protecting system state from being damaged by single-point failures. Byzantine fault tolerance protocols enable correct operation of digital twins, even when a minor fraction of sensors become damaged. The solutions introduce processing demands and delay times which industrial systems usually consider unacceptable (Airehenbuwa et al., 2025).

The loss of operator confidence stands as an invisible but significant effect which results from digital twin security breaches. Operators begin to doubt virtual representation accuracy after they detect any twin integrity failures. The operators will conduct manual operations or physical site evaluations which will decrease their productivity advantages from digital twins. The operators will disregard digital twin security alerts, which will decrease their total security effectiveness. Digital twins need to establish their complete trustworthiness for operational purposes because partial trust creates more problems than total distrust because operators cannot determine which information to accept as true or false.

Cryptographic data integrity solutions employ digital signatures together with message authentication codes to confirm that data remains unaltered. The cryptographic solutions need infrastructure for key management because attackers who gain control over keys can create fake signatures. Quantum-resistant cryptography needs to be developed because quantum computing poses threats to present-day cryptographic systems. The research results show that post-quantum cryptographic techniques improve the ability of digital twin systems to withstand new security challenges (Zemskov et al., 2024).

The dynamic nature of trust functions better than the static description of trust as a fixed quality for secure digital twins. The system should assess trustworthiness continuously through several indicators which include the agreement of independent data sources with known physical laws and the absence of unusual patterns and the results of cryptographic verification. The system of dynamic trust evaluation enables organizations to recover their trustworthiness after they detected a security breach, which helps them maintain operations during challenges in hostile environments.

6. DETECTION AND MITIGATION STRATEGIES

6.1 AI and Machine Learning-Based Detection

6.1.1 Anomaly Detection in IoT/5G Traffic

The primary method used to detect darknet-based attacks against IoT and 5G networks relies on Machine Learning techniques which perform anomaly detection. Anomaly detection systems function by detecting abnormal deviations from standard operational patterns instead of depending on predefined attack signatures, which enables them to discover zero-day attacks and new tactics that attackers utilize through darknet channels that conventional signature-based systems fail to identify.

Supervised Learning Approaches use labeled datasets which contain both normal traffic and attack traffic samples to develop their classifiers. The Random Forest and Gradient Boosting models have shown success by reaching an accuracy level above 99% on standard benchmark datasets (Ejeofobiri et al., 2024). The tree-based methods need extensive labeled training data for their operations while they provide excellent interpretability because security analysts can understand the reasons behind specific traffic pattern designations through decision tree analysis. Support Vector Machines give strong theoretical foundations which enable effective performance on network traffic data that exists in high-dimensional space. The supervised approaches face difficulties when dealing with new attack types which do not exist in their training data thus reducing their effectiveness against emerging darknet threats.

Unsupervised Learning Approaches enable researchers to discover outliers in data without needing any labeled information which helps them find previously unknown attacks. The Isolation Forest algorithms detect anomalies in high-dimensional IoT traffic by discovering data points which need multiple isolation steps to achieve detection. The K-Means clustering algorithm detects dense normal behavior areas which show sparse points as possible attack indicators. Autoencoder neural networks create compact normal traffic representations which then detect anomalous samples through their reconstruction failures. The advantage of unsupervised approaches is their ability to address new threats while their application to various traffic patterns results in increased false positive rates according to research findings from (Asghar et al., 2024)(Elijah et al., 2025).

The Deep Learning Architectures for IoT/5G anomaly detection process network traffic through Convolutional Neural Networks (CNNs) which learn spatial patterns and Long Short-Term Memory (LSTM) networks which capture temporal dependencies and Attention mechanisms which extract essential features for processing. Recurrent Neural Networks manage sequential data streams that present time-based traffic flow information. The hybrid architectures which integrate multiple components of deep learning technology achieve F1-scores exceeding 98% while they outmatch standard machine learning methods according to research results from (Jamshidi et al., 2025). The deployment of deep learning models faces difficulties because they need high-performance computing systems together with massive amounts of training data for their operation on edge devices which have limited resources.

The benchmark tests which include NSL-KDD, CICIDS2017, UNSW-NB15, IoT-23, Bot-IoT show differences in performance based on the specific attributes of each dataset along with the various types of attacks. The ensemble methods which use multiple algorithms to detect threats achieve better results than individual algorithms because they reach detection rates above 99% while maintaining false positive rates below 1% according to research results from (Sharma & Bairwa, 2025) (Hammood & Sadiq, 2023). The benchmark test results provide an inflated view of actual performance since attackers develop new tactics to avoid existing detection methods thus requiring constant updates for the detection models.

Detection systems need to identify Darknet-Specific Anomalies which include: unusual encryption patterns from Tor traffic, abnormal command-and-control communications with low-latency requirements, DDoS attack precursors like scanning patterns, and botnet signature communications using custom protocols distributed through darknet channels (Alfahaid et al., 2025). The attackers who use advanced techniques create normal traffic patterns which imitate genuine data to avoid detection while security systems must identify these patterns through their minor behavioral changes instead of their main attack signature points.

6.1.2 Federated Learning Approaches

The development of Federated Learning (FL) systems fights against darknet threats because they enable secure collaborative learning between IoT devices that need to protect their private data from centralized storage. The traditional machine learning method for anomaly detection requires all devices to send their data to central servers, which creates two problems: it increases privacy risks while needing extra time for data transmission. The method of FL reverses traditional processes because devices train their models using local data while only sending model updates to aggregation servers for the purpose of global model development.

The standard structure of FL Systems consists of three components: (1) local learners running on edge devices that train models using local data, (2) aggregation servers that combine model updates from multiple devices, and (3) global models representing consensus learned across the federated network. The Synchronous federatio system waits until every device finishes its local training before starting data aggregation, while asynchronous systems collect updates from devices that have finished their training process to achieve faster results at the cost of reduced accuracy in convergence. The federated averaging algorithm serves as the main deployment method while variations like FedProx and FedSGD solve particular operational problems.

The deployment of FL in real-world scenarios faces challenges from spatial non-IID data distribution which causes devices to collect entirely different data patterns based on their sensor types. The communication overhead problem arises when model updates transfer between devices and servers because their total weight exceeds the cost of all processing operations. Device-specific models show statistical heterogeneity because they develop according to their own data patterns while diverging from the established global model. The process of model updates creates two competing challenges because it enables attackers to obtain local data through inference attacks while protecting model updates. The system enables IoT devices to work together in detecting darknet attacks through shared learning while preventing the centralized storage of raw traffic data. Research shows that FL achieves anomaly detection accuracy above 96% while maintaining complete data privacy. The process of federated anomaly detection detects IoT botnet activity, DDoS attack patterns and methods for identifying compromised devices. The training models through FL enable devices to maintain their local operations while learning universal attack patterns, which provides an important benefit for industrial settings that require data privacy protection and legal compliance (Belay et al., 2026).

The security of FL systems against darknet threats improves through the application of privacy-protecting methods. Differential privacy uses noise control to protect model updates from allowing anyone to reconstruct device-specific data from the parameter updates. Secure multi-party computation enables aggregation servers to aggregate model updates without learning individual values. Homomorphic encryption enables computations to take place on encrypted data which allows processing of device updates without needing to decrypt the encrypted information. These mechanisms impose performance costs but provide formal privacy guarantees (Wang et al., 2025) (Princewill et al., 2026).

The challenges of real-world implementation include three main issues: devices that establish temporary connections to federation infrastructure need systems that can perform aggregation at periods, excessive model update sizes prevent low-power devices from receiving their necessary data, and resource-limited edge devices need to conduct model training at their local locations. The process of model compression creates smaller update files which decrease the size of updates while communication-efficient aggregation methods enable data transfer through incremental learning which requires very little communication bandwidth.

6.2 Network-Level Defense Mechanisms

The systems which establish network security boundaries operate IDS which observe network traffic together with system operations to detect harmful activities and Intrusion Prevention Systems (IPS) which enhance IDS functionality by implementing active threat defense mechanisms. The systems function as critical security measures against threats that use darknet resources, but they encounter fundamental obstacles when trying to detect advanced threats which use encrypted and obfuscated methods for attack traffic.

Signature-Based Detection functions through two main elements which create a database of known attack patterns to match observed traffic against recognized darknet malware signatures. Security researchers keep updating signature-based systems because they help identify existing threats through their low false positive rate, while new darknet malware variants keep arriving in the system (Ejeofobiri et al., 2024). Signature-based methods fail to recognize zero-day exploits or new attack methods before the system finds signature matches. Darknet attackers share their signature evasion techniques with attacker communities, which include malware polymorphism that changes its code with each new variant sample.

Anomaly-Based Detection detects network traffic anomalies by identifying elements that differ from established standard traffic patterns. Machine learning models create normal patterns which they use to identify network activities that deviate from established norms. This method can discover new attacks, but it cannot handle concept drift, which occurs when standard traffic patterns change due to new application launches and business model transformations. Behavioral profiling establishes user-specific profiles and device profiles which detect any deviation from established user device patterns. This personalized approach improves accuracy but requires substantial training data per entity. Hybrid Approaches which combine signature-based methods with anomaly-based methods produce better detection results than both methods functioning independently. Fast signature-based detection provides immediate alerts for known threats while anomaly detection processes suspicious traffic for potential novel attacks. Ensemble methods gather multiple IDS engine outputs, which they use to determine threat classification through a voting process. The hybrid systems successfully detect over 99% of threats while maintaining fewer than 1% false positive rates (Kikissagbe & Adda, 2024).

The systems of IPS use automated response systems to implement countermeasures through traffic filtering, which blocks detected attack traffic, connection termination, which stop suspicious connections, rate limiting, which manages excessive attack traffic, and deception, which uses fake data to mislead attackers. The IPS system needs high confidence in detecting threats because its false positive alerts will stop legitimate traffic, which reduces system performance capacity. The attackers from the darknet actively search for ways to bypass IPS security, using their skills to create attacks that appear normal until experts conduct thorough analysis (Ejeofobiri et al., 2024).

The detection system which understands darknet operations uses specific knowledge about the patterns of attacks that occur in darknet environments. Security analysts who study darknet forums and marketplaces document attack techniques, which enable the development of customized detection methods. IDS/IPS systems can choose to inspect Tor exit traffic as their top priority while they also monitor darknet command-and-control communications through established protocols and track data exfiltration activities towards darknet infrastructure. The advanced attackers use special methods to hide their communication with the darknet by blending it into regular network traffic which seems ordinary.

6.2.2 Zero Trust Architectures

Zero Trust Architecture (ZTA) established a new security framework which required organizations to always verify all users and devices instead of using traditional security methods which depended on perimeter defense. Zero trust security framework operates on the principle that all network entities require cross verification because trust cannot be assumed without evidence of credibility.

Zero Trust core principles establish trust only through verification process which requires authentication and authorization for every access request. The security model grants users and devices only the essential access rights required for their tasks. The security system operates under the belief that attackers will breach defenses thus employing detection methods together with containment strategies. The system divides networks into the smallest possible segments which use different security measures to protect each segment. The system continuously checks device behavior and user activity throughout their entire session duration.

The implementation of IoT/5G technology faces various obstacles which arise from the combination of different device types and the limited power resources and the need to handle large volumes of data. The traditional zero trust framework needs Public Key Infrastructure (PKI) and certificate administration together with ongoing cryptographic procedures which IoT devices with limited resources fail to operate. IoT devices use lightweight authentication methods which depend on either simplified cryptographic systems or token-based authentication or hardware-backed attestation. Edge-based policy enforcement system checks network access rights at the outer network boundaries instead of relying on central control systems thus decreasing both latency and single points of failure. The system uses behavioral analytics to create normal behavior patterns for devices which then identifies any deviations from those patterns as possible security breaches (Li et al., 2025).

The system offers protection against attacks which use the darknet as a means to carry out their operations. The security system protects against all network access points because it considers everything to be unverified which includes attacks from the darknet who managed to enter the internal networks. The security system uses micro-segmentation to prevent attackers from moving horizontally through networks after they obtained initial access. The requirements for encrypted communication stop attackers from listening in on the unauthorized movement of information between systems. The system identifies compromised devices which attempt to perform actions that fall outside their regular operational patterns. The research shows that ZTAs enable organizations to achieve 95 percent reduction of insider threats while they detect lateral movements within a timeframe of minutes (Kumar et al., 2025).

Zero Trust enables organizations to create unchangeable records which track all access control choices and policy enforcement activities that organizations can use to investigate security breaches. Smart contracts enable automatic policy enforcement, which guarantees that policies are applied uniformly across different systems. The system eliminates all centralized identity servers which function as main points of vulnerability through its use of blockchain technology for decentralized identity management. The research demonstrates that zero trust systems which use blockchain technology provide security that matches centralized system protection yet deliver greater resilience against attacks (Apurva & Vetrithangam, 2025).

The implementation of zero trust systems experiences operational difficulties because organizations must first establish their systems and users need to provide continuous authentication which decreases system efficiency and users need to handle detailed operational security protocols. Organizations which implement zero trust systems experience an initial period of operational difficulties which must pass before they reach stable functioning. The organization will experience controlled operational risks through its gradual implementation of protection systems which will protect its vital base.

6.3 Blockchain and Trust Management

6.3.1 Secure Device Identity

The identity management system based on blockchain technology gives cryptographic protection that prevent attackers from creating fake identities and conducting identity theft operations through darknet methods. The blockchain system enables identity verification through its decentralized network which operates independent of central certificate authorities that face security risks. The Smart Contracts for Identity system uses blockchain technology to establish automated systems for identity verification and credential management through its programmable functions. Smart contracts authenticate device manufacturing through firmware signature verification and hardware security element validation and create cryptographic identities for network access. Smart contracts perform credential verification to control access rights when users make requests for system entry. The system uses automated verification methods to block unauthorized devices from participating in network activities (Islam et al., 2025).

The IoT/5G system benefits from decentralized identity solutions which protect against single-point failures and from unchangeable audit records which keep track of all identity modifications and from automated systems which lessen the workload of handling credentials. Self-sovereign identity enables devices to control their identities independent of centralized authorities, supporting deployments across organizational boundaries where traditional PKI is impractical. The research shows that blockchain-based identity systems provide similar results to their centralized counterparts, but blockchain technology offers better protection against security threats (Bandara et al., 2022).

The three main obstacles include the need for blockchain to support billions of IoT devices, the delay that blockchain verification processes create for urgent access control decisions, and the amount of energy that consensus systems require to operate. Layer-2 blockchain solutions and lightweight consensus mechanisms optimize blockchain identity systems for IoT constraints while maintaining security properties (Airehenbuwa et al., 2025).

6.3.2 Decentralized Authentication

Implementation of blockchain technology for decentralized authentication eliminates the need for centralized authentication servers which serve as primary vulnerabilities that darknet attackers can exploit. The blockchain-based systems enable network participants to distribute authentication responsibilities because they authenticate through their individual credential verification process instead of relying on a central authority for credential issuance. The decentralized authentication system which uses blockchain technology operates through the following processes: (1) credential issuance where authorized parties create and cryptographically sign identity credentials, recording issuance on blockchain; (2) distributed verification where any network participant can verify credentials by checking blockchain records; (3) revocation management where credential revocation is recorded on blockchain, ensuring all participants recognize revoked credentials; (4) access control where smart contracts automatically grant or deny access based on credential verification.

The Darknet Defense system benefits from three main advantages which include protection against centralized server attacks and attackers obtaining credentials through central server breaches and transparent audit trails of authentication pathways which enable forensic analysis and blockchain timestamps which block replayed old credentials from being used in replay attacks. The process of blockchain authentication results in additional time delays and higher computer processing expenses (Houichi et al., 2025). The authentication process which uses smart contract technology verifies device credentials and firmware integrity and behavioral consistency before users can access the network. Contracts can implement sophisticated verification logic: requiring multiple stakeholders to approve unusual access patterns, implementing time-based access restrictions, or enforcing geographic constraints on device operations (Islam et al., 2025). Table 3 outlines advanced detection and mitigation strategies for protecting network infrastructures against sophisticated darknet threats. It highlights the mechanism, main advantage, and primary operational trade-off for each security framework.

Table 3. Summary of mitigation strategies

Strategy	Core Mechanism	Key Strength	Core Challenge
AI & ML Anomaly Detection	**Supervised & Unsupervised:** Tree-based models, SVM, Autoencoders. **Deep Learning:** CNN, LSTM, Attention Mechanisms.	• Catches unknown zero-day attacks. • Hybrid deep learning yields $>98\%$ F1-scores.	• Supervised models miss unseen attack types. • High false-positive rates for unsupervised models.
Federated Learning	Local on-device training; only model updates are sent to central servers using FedProx/FedSGD.	• Protects data privacy and legal compliance. • Achieves $>96\%$ anomaly detection accuracy.	• High communication overhead from large updates. • Vulnerable to local data inference attacks.
Network-Level Defense	**IDS/IPS:** Hybrid systems combining signature engines with behavioral profiling.	• Catches $>99\%$ of threats with $<1\%$ false positives. • IPS automates active traffic blocking.	• Signatures fail against polymorphic malware. • Profiling struggles with natural "concept drift".
ZTA	Continuous verification, micro-segmentation, least-privilege access, and edge enforcement.	• Cuts insider threats by 95%. • Stops lateral movement within minutes.	• High cryptographic demands for low-power IoT. • Initial drop in network operational efficiency.
Secure Device Identity	Blockchain-based identity, Self-Sovereign Identity (SSI), and smart contract validation.	• Removes vulnerable central Certificate Authorities. • Creates immutable identity audit logs.	• Hard to scale across billions of IoT devices. • Blockchain consensus consensus causes processing latency.
Decentralized Authentication	Distributed credential issuance, verification, and revocation via smart contracts.	• Eliminates single-point-of-failure servers. • Timestamps block data replay attacks.	• Introduces network processing time delays. • Increases overall computing and economic costs.

7. PRIVACY, LEGAL, AND ETHICAL CONSIDERATIONS

7.1 Privacy Challenges in Hyperconnected Environments

The extensive collection of personal data by these systems which operate on a large scale creates privacy difficulties for IoT/5G/6G systems. Hyperconnected environments generate daily terabytes of data which include information about device operations and user behaviors and environmental conditions and infrastructure status. A smart city generates terabytes of data through its sensor network which contains millions of sensors. This situation creates new possibilities for data analysis but also generates new challenges for protecting personal data (Şen & Dash, 2023). Identity linkage occurs when users combine multiple data sources to re-identify anonymized data. Activity profiling enables users to infer specific user activities from general device usage patterns which they obtain from aggregated data. Location tracking occurs when continuous device location data allows for constant monitoring of device positions. Behavioral analysis enables users to deduce sensitive information through examination of system usage patterns. Discrimination occurs when organizations use gathered data to make biased decisions about individuals. Darknet actors' profit from privacy violations by selling databases that contain tracked individual information. They also provide privacy analysis tools and offer services which exploit known privacy vulnerabilities (Adewuyi et al., 2024). Data minimization requires organizations to collect only the information which they need to operate their business activities. Differential privacy uses controlled noise which adds to aggregate statistics to protect individual data records from being inferred. Encryption provides data protection which secures data during transmission and data storage. Access controls function as security measures which determine the specific individuals permitted to access the gathered data. Retention limits establish automatic data deletion procedures which commence once the designated time frame ends. User transparency empowers users with knowledge about data collection activities while enabling them to manage their data collection process (Khan et al., 2022). The operational requirements of differential privacy lead to data utility reduction while encryption requires additional computational resources to function. Security investigations cannot be conducted because organizations delete all data which they collect aggressively.

7.2 Regulatory Frameworks for IoT and 5G/6G Security

The international regulatory framework is developing new rules to protect IoT and 5G systems from security threats. The General Data Protection Regulation (GDPR) which applies to European Union organizations requires them to create systems for protecting privacy from the beginning, receive clear permission before using personal data, and notify authorities about data breaches within 72 hours. For IoT systems collecting personal data, organizations must establish technical safeguards which include encryption and access controls to meet GDPR requirements (Ambudkar et al., 2024). Organizations which break GDPR rules face penalties reaching 4 percent of their total worldwide income which creates strong motivation for them to follow the regulations.

The NIS2 Directive from the European Union establishes essential cybersecurity standards which all critical infrastructure sectors must follow to protect systems that deliver energy, water, healthcare services, and telecommunications services. The system needs security-by-design to establish its baseline security structure through risk evaluation and security incident management. All critical infrastructure operators must meet this standard because it extends to their suppliers, which creates cascading compliance obligations through supply chain operations (Gospodinov et al., 2025).

The National Institute of Standards and Technology (NIST) Cybersecurity Framework from the United States delivers established cybersecurity framework which organizations should follow to secure their systems through five operations: identification, protection, detection, response and system recovery. Although organizations do not need to use the framework as a legal requirement it has become the accepted standard for government contractors and critical infrastructure operators. NIST framework principles have become mandatory for many states to include in their legal frameworks according to upcoming legal standards (Chaudhuri & Kahyaoğlu, 2023).

5G Security Standards from 3rd Generation Partnership Project (3GPP) establish technical criteria which 5G networks must fulfill to implement authentication systems and network slicing security and encryption technologies. Government bodies have recognized 3GPP standards as legal requirements which organizations must follow to achieve compliance with regulatory frameworks. 5G systems need to implement their standards before they become operational whereas security problems emerged from 5G systems which claimed to follow standards (Scalise et al., 2024).

Darknet Monitoring Legal Issues create difficulties for security teams who need to protect their systems against darknet threats. The laws that govern internet privacy rights in certain regions stop law enforcement and private companies from watching darknet communications unless they obtain specific legal authority through warrants. Security operations which monitor darknet markets create situations where they can entrap people into committing illegal acts. The legal system requires police officers to establish chain-of-custody procedures which proof for evidential purposes can be admitted to court. The organizations which need to protect themselves against darknet attacks must work together with law enforcement because of the legal issues that exist in this situation (Jha & Jha, 2024).

7.3 Ethical Concerns in Monitoring and Surveillance

User activity monitoring becomes essential for IoT and 5G systems when they need to detect threats originating from darknet activities. The practice of surveillance exists to fulfill security needs, but it creates major ethical challenges because it infringes on people's right to privacy and their ability to make independent choices while enabling potential security abuses.

The surveillance versus privacy conflict arises from a basic struggle between two opposing needs: security needs to observe users for monitoring which detects signs of security breaches while privacy demands that users should have the right to complete privacy protection. The process of balancing these opposing needs requires us to identify two distinct types of monitoring activities which comprise security monitoring that needs to find attacks and behavioral surveillance that observes users without security needs. Ethically permitted monitoring exists when it targets known threats but mass surveillance violates this principle because it gathers user information from all individuals. The current systems violate the established standard because they gather complete data sets which they use to determine security requirements (Lawelai et al., 2025).

Different viewpoints emerge from Ethical Frameworks which include deontological principles (respecting user autonomy and privacy rights) and utilitarian analysis (maximizing overall security benefit) and virtue ethics (developing trustworthy security practices). Users require knowledge about monitored activities and their purposes as part of transparency requirements. Establishing accountability needs systems which will stop people from misusing their surveillance authority. Proportionality demands that monitoring should increase in line with rising threat levels because all-device surveillance becomes an excessive response to infrequent security breaches (Almeida, 2023).

Marginalized groups face special challenges because surveillance activities most heavily affect vulnerable communities. Lower-income communities face more intense monitoring of their IoT devices because these areas experience a higher rate of cyberattacks. Behavioral analysis may embed societal biases, flagging activities of marginalized groups as anomalous based on discriminatory patterns in training data. Security systems should implement fairness analysis which ensures that monitoring affects all user groups in an equal manner (Gospodinov et al., 2025).

7.4 Cross-Border Data Governance Issues

The data flow which IoT and 5G technology generates throughout international boundaries creates difficulties for governance because different countries process their collected data according to their own legal systems and regulatory standards. Data Localization Requirements which require data to remain within national borders create obstacles for both technical operations. The legal obligation in some countries to keep personal data within national borders conflicts with the design of worldwide cloud systems. Organizations which operate in multiple countries must establish distinct security and privacy practices because different jurisdictions impose their own unique compliance demands. Darknet operators use this intricate system to locate jurisdictions which have less effective privacy laws to conduct their activities (Kukkadapu, 2025).

Darknet attackers create problems for attribution and jurisdiction because they execute their attacks from countries which differ from the locations of their victims. The prosecution process requires jurisdictional authority over attackers but darknet systems render attribution impossible. Extradition treaties allow certain countries to send criminals back to their home countries for trial but numerous nations deny extradition requests which involve cybercrimes. The situation allows for darknet attacks to occur without consequences because attackers can operate from specific countries which protect them from legal action (Sarker & Khan, 2024).

Cyber threat intelligence sharing creates espionage risks because it operates as an intelligence system for various intelligence activities. The process of sharing darknet attack evidence requires organizations to disclose their surveillance methods and their intelligence collection capabilities. Countries which face the threat of espionage opt to withhold cyber threat intelligence sharing which creates obstacles for cooperative defense efforts. The Five Eyes alliance presents a framework for intelligence-sharing where member countries work together while excluding all countries which do not participate in this alliance (Parmar et al., 2026).

International data transfers receive privacy protection through data transfer mechanisms which include standard contractual clauses and binding corporate rules. The validity of these mechanisms has come under scrutiny by recent court rulings which leave a legal gray area for international data transfers. Organizations are increasingly deploying data processing locally within each country rather than centralizing globally.

8. OPEN CHALLENGES AND RESEARCH GAPS

8.1 Scalability of Security Solutions

Security solutions face their greatest challenge when they need to protect 5G and 6G networks which connect billions of IoT devices throughout their extensive networks. Security mechanisms that function correctly in small systems need complete redesign to establish security protection for IoT and 5G networks.

The IoT Scale requires security solutions which can protect billions of devices that operate different computational systems which need protection from megabyte-range microcontrollers to cloud servers. Edge devices need to run machine learning models with low memory usage while achieving detection results that match cloud-based detection systems. The model compression methods of quantization and pruning together with knowledge distillation can reduce model size from megabytes to kilobytes although this process requires accuracy to be monitored during degradation. FL enables global model creation through training on multiple edge devices while protecting user privacy, but the process needs more time to complete training before reaching its final state (Alfahaid et al., 2025).

The development of 5G and 6G networks creates challenges which prevent networks from expanding to handle increased user demands. Network slicing security needs protection for multiple network slices which have different security requirements. The SDN controller redundancy requirements increase by a factor of two for every growth in network size while SDN environments need multiple active controllers to operate from different sites. The management of security policies within NFV orchestration becomes more complex when it must control thousands of VFN that operate across cloud environments (Allaw et al., 2025).

Security policies need to be coordinated between different administrative areas which have different security settings to maintain security across IoT, edge, fog, and cloud infrastructure. The hierarchical security frameworks distribute policy enforcement responsibilities according to system levels while maintaining security at all levels requires complex inter-level management. Security orchestration platforms help organizations enforce security policies, but the organizations must deal with the challenges that result from using immature tools which lead to security breaches through incorrect software setup.

The research gaps identify three areas which need development: zero-trust architectures that support billions of devices, lightweight cryptography for devices with limited resources which maintain security functions, and distributed security systems which enable independent security policy execution at large organizations. The current research has developed separate methods for individual techniques, but it lacks complete solutions which can handle scaling challenges across all areas.

8.2 Resource Constraints in IoT Devices

Resource-constrained IoT devices fundamentally cannot support traditional security mechanisms because their processing power and memory and energy capacity are insufficient. The system vulnerabilities created by this situation become accessible to attackers through underground network distributed attacks. Traditional cryptography processing requires more computational resources than the available megahertz capacity allows. Lightweight cryptographic algorithms like SPECK, SIMON, and Ascon provide acceptable security properties with minimal computational overhead, but many IoT devices deploy without encryption or they use insecure cryptography. Comprehensive authentication mechanisms and IDS cannot function because memory capacity limits (kilobytes) stop their implementation.

Energy constraints require IoT devices to operate for years on battery power which results in cryptographic operations needing to be reduced; some devices face power restrictions that limit them to milliwatt levels which makes it impossible to conduct important security functions. Security performance tradeoffs become necessary because the available constraints force devices into operational choices which require them to select between security needs (processing-intensive operations) and their essential functions (maintaining connectivity, sensing). Most devices prioritize functionality which results in security vulnerabilities. Darknet-distributed malware can exploit these vulnerabilities through simple hacking methods which lead to device takeovers.

The research directions focus on creating ultra-lightweight security mechanisms for resource-constrained devices while developing hardware security through trusted execution environments and security processors devices work together to build security functions instead of performing them separately.

8.3 Lack of Standardized Security Frameworks

The security frameworks for IoT and 5G networks do not yet exist which should match the security frameworks used in standard enterprise IT security systems. The system breaks down into separate parts which result in problems that prevent different systems from working together while organizations use different methods to protect their information.

The security systems used in IoT and 5G ecosystems create problems because the networks contain devices from more than 100 companies who use different security protocols. Devices manufactured by different vendors often cannot interoperate securely because they implement incompatible authentication mechanisms, encryption algorithms, or security protocols. IoT devices use Message Queuing Telemetry Transport (MQTT) brokers to send messages which support various authentication methods though devices that use different methods cannot maintain proper operation. The security systems established by wireless protocols like Zigbee, Z-Wave, andLong Range Wide Area Network (LoRaWAN) create ecological division between their distinct security definitions (Sarker et al., 2022).

Standardization Efforts including IEEE 802.15.4 security specifications, Zigbee Alliance security frameworks, and IETF Constrained Application Protocol (CoAP) security profiles attempt to impose order. The standardization process has not been followed by all manufacturers because many products reached the market before standardization began while some products use security protocols from past standards. The process of standards development creates backward compatibility issues because new security standards require outdated systems to undergo modernization before their application. The existing standards do not cover secure supply chain management, vulnerability disclosure and patching procedures, incident response coordination, and security testing methodologies. These gaps create an environment where some manufacturers protect their products through excellent security methods while others use products with known security weaknesses (Mirji & S., 2026).

8.4 Integration Complexity Across Heterogeneous Systems

Combining IoT, 5G, critical infrastructure, and emerging technologies creates Security solutions have to operate between different systems which need distinct security protection methods and basic security design features.

The architectural mismatches occur because IoT systems require distributed autonomous operation while cloud systems need centralized control for their operation. The integration process becomes difficult because both local autonomy and centralized control exist as conflicting principles. The translation layers which connect IoT protocols (CoAP, MQTT), 5G protocols (3GPP), and legacy protocols (Modbus in industrial systems) introduce security vulnerabilities because they need to translate between different communication protocols (Sahu & Mazumdar, 2024).

The security domains face coordination issues which increase the overall complexity of the system. The IoT security domains protect devices through authentication and firmware verification while the 5G security framework defends network slicing and virtualization security systems and critical infrastructure security protects operational continuity requirements. The security process needs complete knowledge of the interactions between different domains so that two domains can function as one secure system (Aqeel et al., 2022).

The testing process becomes difficult because integrated systems have validation complexities. Security testing begins with system assessment which leads to security validation through system combination testing so that testing can find security flaws which result from system connections. The attackers who perform penetration testing need to have advanced knowledge about multiple technologies which they will use to test integrated systems. The ability to prove security properties becomes limited for formal verification techniques because system complexity makes it difficult to prove these security properties (Narsing & Srinivasan, 2025).

9. FUTURE DIRECTIONS AND VISION

9.1 Secure-by-Design IoT and 6G Architectures

Security needs to be built into future IoT and Sixth Generation networks from their beginning stages instead of being added after their construction. The secure-by-design method establishes security requirements which need to be implemented through all stages of development starting from threat modeling to system operation and upkeep. Secure IoT and 6G design principles include threat modeling which detects potential attackers and their attack methods before system development begins. Security requirements need to be developed from threats which will turn into exact functional specifications. The least privilege principle allows system components to receive only the essential access rights for their functions. Defense in depth requires the establishment of multiple distinct security systems which function as separate protection measures. The system supports cryptographic agility which permits security algorithms to be changed during the entire duration of its operational period. Security testing determines whether a system operates according to its established security standards (Onyagu et al., 2024).

Device manufacturers need lightweight cryptography because it protects IoT systems which have limited resources. The NIST Post-Quantum Cryptography Standards provide businesses with quantum-resistant solutions which protect their public-key cryptography systems against emerging quantum computing attacks. IoT devices need the implementation of these standards which require organizations to find the right balance between strong cryptography and their system capacity limits (Elkhodr, 2025). The use of standardized key establishment methods allows different devices to securely exchange information without needing to distribute credentials manually (Dunaiev, 2025).

Secure supply chains enable organizations to safeguard their devices from manufacturing through deployment because they maintain security from all beginning points. Hardware root-of-trust technologies permit cryptographic processes which verify whether a device is genuine and its parts are unchanged. Secure boot enables devices to run only approved firmware. Firmware signing allows users to confirm both the software source and its unaltered state. The entire manufacturing process needs to use these systems which must work together with supply chain partners and component manufacturing organizations to achieve successful implementation (Dunaiev, 2025).

The development of 6G technologies needs to address new security challenges which arise from terahertz communication systems and programmable metasurfaces and machine learning-based network architectures. The protection of machine learning models from unauthorized alterations becomes a vital requirement for AI security because 6G systems increasingly depend on artificial intelligence technology. The 6G system framework requires post-quantum cryptography standards to be established during the integration of quantum computing technology throughout its infrastructure (Elkhodr, 2025).

9.2 AI-Driven Autonomous Defense Systems

Future security systems will use autonomous AI agents to respond to threats in real time without needing human operators. The increasing speed and advanced techniques of attacks which exceed human defense capabilities will create a situation where autonomous defense systems become necessary.

The AI-based autonomous detection system detects threats by monitoring machine operations which process thousands of events each second to find patterns that show security breaches. The system uses machine learning models which have been trained on previous attack patterns to identify current attack patterns in live network traffic. Through practical experience reinforcement learning agents find effective methods to detect threats which improve their detection performance over time (Ejeofobiri et al., 2024). Autonomous systems face danger from adversarial attacks because attackers can create specific inputs which lead to incorrect system identification. Through adversarial training defense systems teach models how to identify and combat adversarial inputs (Jamshidi et al., 2025).

Autonomous response systems execute automatic mitigation procedures through their defensive mechanisms which include traffic filtering to block attack traffic, connection termination for suspicious connections, system isolation to prevent network access from compromised systems, and credential revocation for disabling compromised accounts. The system needs precise tuning because its autonomous response system generates false positive chain reactions which revoke user credentials and filter out legitimate user traffic (Sharma & Bairwa, 2025). Autonomous defense systems face three main challenges which include: establishing human control over security choices, providing security analysts with visibility into autonomous system decision-making, and creating defense systems that attackers cannot learn to defeat. Explainable AI techniques provide humans with interpretable explanations of autonomous security decisions. Security orchestration platforms manage the balance between human supervision and automated protection systems. These systems need human approval to perform specific tasks while their systems can autonomously handle known threats.

9.3 Quantum-Safe Communication in IoT/5G

Post-quantum cryptographic standards will become essential as quantum computing advancements create dangers which jeopardize existing cryptographic foundations. NIST Post-Quantum Standards selected lattice-based cryptography and hash-based signatures and multivariate polynomial cryptography as their chosen quantum-resistant algorithms. IoT/5G systems need to switch to post-quantum cryptography because their current encryption and signature and key establishment systems require complete replacement (You et al., 2024).

The integration process needs to identify all cryptographic systems which need replacement while permitting existing systems to handle their current operations with post-quantum systems that work on low-resource devices. The hybrid approach allows both classical and post-quantum algorithms to function together during the period while providing protection against unexpected advancements in quantum computing which might occur (Yusuf & Abdulrahman, 2025).

Organizations need cryptographic agility which enables them to update their algorithms at fast speeds because their threat landscape continues to change. Systems should parameterize their algorithms to enable updates through configuration changes instead of hardcoding particular cryptographic algorithms. The system enables quick deployment of post-quantum alternatives which can handle quantum threats that arise before anticipated.

9.4 Integration with Green and Sustainable Computing

Future security architectures need to establish environmental sustainability goals while providing effective protection against threats originating from the darknet network. Security mechanisms require a substantial amount of computing power because their overhead consumes high energy levels which become especially problematic for extensive IoT and 5G system deployment. Energy-Efficient Security requires the development of cryptographic algorithms and anomaly detection systems which deliver strong security properties through their design with low computational needs. The lightweight cryptography algorithms SPECK and SIMON and Ascon deliver sufficient security protection at lower power usage rates when compared to standard AES implementations (Elkhodr, 2025). The memory requirements and energy consumption of IDS can be decreased through quantization and pruning and knowledge distillation while the systems maintain their full detection capabilities (Alfahaid et al., 2025).

Security principles of circular economy establish that security mechanisms must enable devices to be reused and refurbished and recycled throughout their life cycle period. Sustainable security systems use cryptographic agility to establish remote security algorithm updates which organizations can apply without needing to replace their devices. The security module system allows hardware security modules with trusted execution environments to function as standardized systems which let device manufacturers perform secure device refurbishment operations and reuse of devices that have outdated cryptographic systems (Alsubaei, 2025). Supply chain security practices document the complete history of devices which enables organizations to verify the integrity of devices during their entire reuse process to achieve both security and sustainability goals. Green security operations reduce their environmental footprint by restricting network traffic and eliminating unnecessary security processes and they enhance security infrastructure operations through better data center cooling systems (Rupanetti & Kaabouch, 2024).

Security infrastructure benefits from renewable energy integration because it creates three new possibilities: edge security processing which uses renewable energy sources eliminates the need for central cloud-based security services; distributed anomaly detection systems operate at network borders through renewable microgrid systems which help decrease security system power usage; blockchain-based security systems are adopting proof-of-stake consensus systems which use far less power than proof-of-work systems (Ataullah & Chauhan, 2024). Security architecture design needs to adopt systematic sustainability integration from the beginning instead of using sustainability aspects as post-hoc improvements which create security systems that protect against both darknet threats and environmental impacts.

10. CONCLUSION

This chapter presents a complete analysis of darknet effects on IoT and 5G/6G and new infrastructure systems, which shows critical security problems that arise when attackers use darknet technologies to launch their highly organized attacks at an unprecedented scale. The analysis shows that the darknet serves as the basic operational system which threat actors use to achieve their goals because they need protection through anonymity and encryption and they require methods for executing their attacks. The current security methods that only fix system weaknesses after attackers exploit them have become insufficient because darknet systems allow attackers to organize their assaults at extremely fast speeds across the entire world. The security approach which most organizations use, which centers on incident response and waits until security breaches occur to begin security actions, results in a situation where attackers take control of all connected systems to conduct their coordinated attacks against essential infrastructure. The process of security integration into existing systems needs fundamental changes regarding the ways security functions are defined and executed across all phases of technology development.

The combination of IoT technology with fifth and sixth generation wireless networks together with essential infrastructure components brings tremendous benefits because it establishes constant network access which enables immediate detection of events and machines to perform intelligent work and systems to handle complex operations. The actualization of these potential needs organizations to coordinate their technological progress and their organizational improvements together with their policy advancements which protect against threats from the darknet network.

Success requires simultaneous advancement of multiple technological domains which need to develop together. Research needs to solve the problem of lightweight cryptography which protects resource-limited devices through its secure design; post-quantum cryptographic standards must be implemented across billions of devices before quantum computing threatens current encryption (Dunaiev, 2025). Machine learning systems for threat detection need to move from their current centralized framework toward a federated system which allows secure cooperative training of models between organizations (Devine et al., 2025). Blockchain technology supplies systems with two benefits through its decentralized approach to trust management and its creation of permanent records which enable complete traceability; however, there are two major difficulties which need to be solved: how to extend the system's capacity and how to improve its power consumption performance (Islam et al., 2025). The design process of 6G systems needs to begin quantum-resistant cryptography integration from its initial stages because security updates need to remain active throughout the entire operational period of each device (Yusuf & Abdulrahman, 2025).

The organization faces two main obstacles because it needs to shift from handling incidents to implementing measures which help detect future threats. Organizations need to establish security leadership for architectural decision-making. Between assessment periods they should conduct security checks, and security should become an essential part of business operations that managers need to enforce as necessary. Workforce development which needs to create enough cybersecurity experts for IoT security in 5G networks and critical infrastructure protection, and upcoming technology needs exists as an urgent problem; universities must create more skilled professionals through training programs which need their existing educational capacity to expand while businesses should guide developing public training systems.

Regulatory evolution must establish clear cybersecurity requirements which provide certainty about compliance standards yet should not restrict compliance methods which depend on technology updates. International organizations must establish cooperation because darknet threats operate beyond national boundaries. Cybersecurity defense requires extradition treaties which permit cybercriminal prosecution and information sharing agreements which enable global collaborative threat intelligence and standardized security systems which permit security systems to work together for defense operations (Sarker & Khan, 2024).

The cooperation between government organizations and business sectors and educational institutions and community groups needs to be maintained as an essential requirement. Device manufacturers cannot achieve security in isolation; they require industry standards which create baseline requirements and government procurement standards which deliver market advantages. Operators need instant threat information which security researchers and law enforcement and industry colleagues need to protect their systems from potential attacks. Researchers need access to actual operational data and partnerships with field experts and funding which allows them to conduct extended research work instead of short-term consulting activities in their field.

The existing technological foundations provide secure IoT networks and fifth and sixth generation wireless technology and critical infrastructure systems. The organization needs to implement its systems at full capacity through methods which achieve maximum functional performance while maintaining control over operational costs and protecting individual rights and social fairness and environmental protection. The research community and field professionals and government officials need this chapter as their guide through the challenges of their work. The organization needs to maintain its dedication toward continuous system enhancement while managing two competing goals and developing systems which will deliver long-term security and environmental protection and social advantages. The upcoming path presents obstacles, but they become manageable through coordinated teamwork and continuous efforts to secure the digital infrastructure which modern society relies upon for its essential operations.

REFERENCES

Agbesi, J. S., Otchill, A. N., Tay, R. H., & Bamfo, N. K. (2026). Machine learning for network intrusion detection in USA critical infrastructure: Challenges and opportunities. *International Journal of Network Security & its Applications*, *18*(1), 1–15.

Ahmed, M. A. M., Idris, S., Yunus, N. A. M., Ali, F. M., & Sofian, H. (2024). CyberShield framework: Attacks and defense modelling for cybersecurity in internet of things (IoT). *International Journal of Advanced Research in Computational Thinking and Data Science*, *4*(1), 30–39. DOI: 10.37934/ctds.4.1.3039

Airehenbuwa, B., Hasan, T., Sarkar, S., & Guin, U. (2025). Advancing security with digital twins: A comprehensive survey. arXiv preprint arXiv:2501.12345. /arXiv.2501.12345DOI: 10.48550

Alfahaid, A., Alalwany, E., Almars, A. M., Alharbi, F., Atlam, E., & Mahgoub, I. (2025). Machine learning-based security solutions for IoT networks: A comprehensive survey. In *Proceedings of the Italian National Conference on Sensors*. DOI: 10.3390/s25113341

Ali, A., Ali, M., Mushtaq, U., & Akram, M. A. (2025). Secure software engineering for industrial IoT: A comprehensive review of threat modeling and defense mechanisms. *ICCK Journal of Software Engineering*, *5*(2), 33–45. DOI: 10.62762/JSE.2025.834259

Allaw, Z., Zein, O., & Ahmad, A.-M. (2025). Cross-layer security for 5G/6G network slices: An SDN, NFV, and AI-based hybrid framework. *Sensors (Basel)*, *25*(11), 3120. DOI: 10.3390/s25113335 PMID: 40968899

Almeida, F. (2023). Prospects of cybersecurity in smart cities. *Future Internet*, *15*(9), 285. DOI: 10.3390/fi15090285

Alsubaei, F. S. (2025). Smart deep learning model for enhanced IoT intrusion detection. *Scientific Reports*, *15*(1), 7890. Advance online publication. DOI: 10.1038/s41598-025-06363-5 PMID: 40596059

Ambudkar, B., Rahangdale, P., Abdullah, A., Thoutam, N., & Shelke, G. C. (2024). Developing cybersecurity policies for smart cities: A case study approach. *Computer Fraud & Security*, *2024*(6), 12–20.

Apurva, S., & Vetrithangam, D. (2025). Blockchain-integrated zero-trust architectures for cybersecurity in IoT ecosystems. In *Proceedings of the IEEE 6th Global Conference on Advancement Technologies (GCAT)*. DOI: 10.1109/GCAT66372.2025.11368384

Aqeel, M., Ali, F., Iqbal, M. W., Rana, T. A., Arif, M., & Auwul, R. (2022). A review of security and privacy concerns in the internet of things (IoT). *Journal of Sensors*, *2022*, 5724168. Advance online publication. DOI: 10.1155/2022/5724168

Asghar, M. N., Raza, M. A., Murad, Z., & Alyahya, A. (2024). Detecting malicious botnets in IoT networks using machine learning techniques. *IPSI Transactions on Internet Research*, *20*(2), 33–45. DOI: 10.58245/ipsi.tir.2402.03

Ataullah, M., & Chauhan, N. (2024). Exploring security and privacy enhancement technologies in the internet of things: A comprehensive review. *Security and Privacy*, *7*(2), e341. DOI: 10.1002/spy2.448

Balta, E. C., Pease, M., Moyne, J., Barton, K., & Tilbury, D. (2024). Digital twin-based cyber-attack detection framework for cyber-physical manufacturing systems. *IEEE Transactions on Automation Science and Engineering*, *21*(3), 1802–1815. DOI: 10.1109/TASE.2023.3243147

Bandara, E., Liang, X., Shetty, S., Mukkamala, R., Rahman, A., & Ng, W. K. (2022). Skunk — a blockchain and zero trust security enabled federated learning platform for 5G/6G network slicing. In *Proceedings of the IEEE SECON* (pp. 45–54). DOI: 10.1109/SECON55815.2022.9918536

Belay, M., Rasheed, A., & Rossi, P. S. (2026). Digital twin-driven communication-efficient federated anomaly detection for industrial IoT. arXiv preprint arXiv:2601.12345. /arXiv.2601.12345DOI: 10.48550

Blancaflor, E., Eugenio, E. J., Lucas, M., Paglinawan, C., & Villaluz, A. C. (2025). Mirai malware and its impact on IoT security: Security threats and defense mechanisms. In *Proceedings of the International Conference on Communication, Computing & Security*. DOI: 10.1109/ICCCS65393.2025.11069543

Cecílio, J., & Souto, A. (2024). Security issues in industrial internet-of-things: Threats, attacks and solutions. In Proceedings of the IEEE International Workshop on Metrology for Industry 4.0 & IoT (MetroInd4.0 & IoT). DOI: 10.1109/MetroInd4.0IoT61288.2024.10584236

Chaudhuri, A., & Kahyaoğlu, S. B. (2023). Cybersecurity assurance in smart cities: A risk management perspective. *EDPACS*, *67*(3), 1–10. DOI: 10.1080/07366981.2023.2165293

Cunha, J., Ferreira, P., Castro, E. M., Oliveira, P. C., Nicolau, M. J., Núñez, I., Sousa, X. R., & Serôdio, C. (2024). Enhancing network slicing security: Machine learning, software-defined networking, and network functions virtualization-driven strategies. *Future Internet*, *16*(7), 226. DOI: 10.3390/fi16070226

Dér, A. (2025). Cybersecurity in smart city energy systems. *Interdisciplinary Description of Complex Systems*, *23*(2), 145–160. DOI: 10.7906/indecs.23.2.4

Devine, M., Ardakani, S. P., Al-khafajiy, M., & James, Y. (2025). Federated machine learning to enable intrusion detection systems in IoT networks. *Electronics (Basel)*, *14*(12), 2210. DOI: 10.3390/electronics14061176

Dunaiev, S. (2025). An integrated approach to data confidentiality in 5G/6G based on LDPC codes and post-quantum cryptography. *Terra Security*, *12*(2), 45–56.

Dwedar, M., Bayram, F. S., Eberhard, J., & Jesser, A. (2024). Dynamic anomaly detection in 5G-connected IoT devices using transfer learning. In *Proceedings of the International Conference on Multimodal Interaction (ICMI)*. DOI: 10.1109/ICMI60790.2024.10585712

Ejeofobiri, C. K., Victor-Igun, O. O., & Okoye, C. (2024). AI-driven secure intrusion detection for internet of things (IoT) networks. *Asian Journal of Mathematics and Computer Research*, *31*(4), 40–55. DOI: 10.56557/ajomcor/2024/v31i48971

Elijah, T., Samuel, A. A., & Familusi, O. B. (2025). AI-powered intrusion detection and prevention systems for the next generation network. *Traektoriâ Nauki*, *11*(2), 45–56. DOI: 10.22178/pos.123-3

Elkhodr, M. (2025). An AI-driven framework for integrated security and privacy in internet of things using quantum-resistant blockchain. *Future Internet*, *17*(1), 83. DOI: 10.3390/fi17060246

Gospodinov, G., Gotsev, L., Ristovska, T., Syarova, S., & Angelova, V. (2025). Cybersecurity in smart cities: A review of theoretical models, emerging threats, and defence strategies. In *Proceedings of the Environment Technology Resources International Scientific Practice Conference*. DOI: 10.1109/TEL-SIKS65061.2025.11240797

Guo, C., Wang, S., Yu, K., Zhu, Y., & Tao, X. (2025). A differential game method against DDoS attacks in IoT botnets: Holistic and dynamic perspectives. *IEEE Internet of Things Journal*, *12*(9), 7450–7463. DOI: 10.1109/JIOT.2025.3541852

Hammood, B. A. K., & Sadiq, A. T. (2023). Ensemble machine learning approach for IoT intrusion detection systems. *Iraqi Journal of Computers and Informatics*, *49*(2), 123–130. DOI: 10.25195/ijci.v49i2.424

Hossain, M. I., & Hasan, R. (2025). Analyzing smart cities: Cybersecurity architecture, threats, mitigation, challenges, and open problems. In *Proceedings of the IEEE World Forum on Public Safety Technologies (WF-PST)*. DOI: 10.1109/WF-PST65083.2025.00044

Hossain, M. M., Kayas, G., Hasan, R., Skjellum, A., Noor, S., & Islam, S. M. R. (2024). A holistic analysis of internet of things (IoT) security: Principles, practices, and new perspectives. *Future Internet*, *16*(2), 40. DOI: 10.3390/fi16020040

Houichi, M., Jaidi, F., & Bouhoula, A. (2025). Enhancing cybersecurity in smart cities: A blockchain-based framework for securing IoT data. *Journal of Infrastructure Policy and Development*, *5*(2), 123–134. DOI: 10.24294/jipd11733

Hwang, S., & Kim, J. (2021). A malware distribution simulator for the verification of network threat prevention tools. *Sensors (Basel)*, *21*(21), 6983. DOI: 10.3390/s21216983 PMID: 34770290

Islam, R., Bose, R., Roy, S., Khan, A. A., Sutradhar, S., Das, S., Ali, F., & AlZubi, A. A. (2025). Decentralized trust framework for smart cities: A blockchain-enabled cybersecurity and data integrity model. *Scientific Reports*, *15*(1), 4321. Advance online publication. DOI: 10.1038/s41598-025-06405-y PMID: 40603417

Jamshidi, S., Nikanjam, A., Nafi, K. W., Khomh, F., & Rasta, R. (2025). Application of deep reinforcement learning for intrusion detection in internet of things: A systematic review. *Internet of Things : Engineering Cyber Physical Human Systems*, *15*, 100410. DOI: 10.1016/j.iot.2025.101531

Jha, A., & Jha, A. (2024). Securing tomorrow's urban frontiers: A holistic approach to cybersecurity in smart cities. *Information Systems for Smart City*, *5*(2), 33–45. DOI: 10.59400/issc.v3i1.418

Kikissagbe, B. R., & Adda, M. (2024). Machine learning-based intrusion detection methods in IoT systems: A comprehensive review. *Electronics (Basel)*, *13*(12), 2314. DOI: 10.3390/electronics13183601

Kravchenko, A. A., & Permyakov, R. A. (2025). Internet of things (IoT): Security threats in automated systems. *Digital Technology Security*, *5*(2), 12–20. DOI: 10.17212/2782-2230-2025-2-52-75

Krishnaveni, S., Sivamohan, S., Jothi, B., Chen, T. M., & Sathiyanarayanan, M. (2024). TwinSec-IDS: An enhanced intrusion detection system in SDN-digital-twin-based industrial cyber-physical systems. *Concurrency and Computation*, *36*(12), e8120. DOI: 10.1002/cpe.8120

Kukkadapu, G. (2025). AI-driven security architecture in smart cities: Balancing safety and privacy. *European Journal of Computer Science and Information Technology*, *7*(2), 45–56. DOI: 10.37745/ejcsit.2013/vol13n478694

Kumar, G., Shelke, N. M., Pimpalkar, A., & Saini, D. K. J., N., P., & Kumar, Y. D. (2025). Zero trust-enabled digital twins for real-time anomaly detection in industrial cyber physical systems. In *Proceedings of the 3rd International Conference on Networking, Multimedia & Information Technology (NMITCON)*. DOI: 10.1109/NMITCON65824.2025.11188236

Lakhal, H., Zegrari, M., & Bahnasse, A. (2025). Next-generation smart grid cybersecurity: A systematic review of OT cyber threats, AI-driven defense, cyber deception techniques, and emerging security strategies. *IEEE Access : Practical Innovations, Open Solutions*, *13*, 181519–181552. DOI: 10.1109/ACCESS.2025.3623834

Lakhani, R. (2023). Cybersecurity threats in internet of things (IoT) networks: Vulnerabilities and defense mechanisms. *International Journal of Engineering and Computer Science*, *12*(11), 25965–25981. DOI: 10.18535/ijecs/v12i11.4779

Lawelai, H., Purnomo, E. P., Nurmandi, A., Jovita, H. D., & Baulete, E. (2025). Cybersecurity policy on smart city infrastructure: A mapping of new threats and protections. *Journal of Science and Technology Policy Management*, *16*(3), 233–245. DOI: 10.1108/JSTPM-09-2024-0359

Leigha, I., Comlekcioglu, B., & Bezanilla, M. P. (2025). How to mitigate and defend against DDoS attacks in IoT devices. arXiv preprint arXiv:2507.11772. /arXiv.2507.11772DOI: 10.48550

Li, K., Li, C., Yuan, X., Li, S., Zou, S., Sohail Ahmed, S., Ni, W., Niyato, D., Jamalipour, A., Dressler, F., & Akan, Ö. B. (2025). Zero-trust foundation models: A new paradigm for secure and collaborative artificial intelligence for internet of things. *IEEE Internet of Things Journal*, *12*(5), 3890–3905. DOI: 10.1109/JIOT.2025.3603957

Ma, R., Cao, J., He, S., Zhang, Y., Niu, B., & Li, H. (2024). A UAV-assisted UE access authentication scheme for 5G/6G network. *IEEE Transactions on Network and Service Management*, *21*(2), 1430–1445. DOI: 10.1109/TNSM.2023.3341829

Maiwada, U., Imran, S. A., Danyaro, K. U., Janisar, A., Salameh, A. A., & Sarlan, A. (2024). Security concerns of IoT against DDoS in 5G systems. *International Journal of Electrical Engineering and Computer Science*, *6*(11), 232–240. DOI: 10.37394/232027.2024.6.11

Malatji, M. (2024). A strategic overview of 5G/6G networks: Implications for 6G security. In *Proceedings of the International Conference on Engineering and Emerging Technologies (ICEET)*. DOI: 10.1109/ICEET65156.2024.10913531

Matencio-Escolar, A., Bernabé, J. B., Alcaraz, J. M., Wang, Q., & Gómez-Skarmeta, A. (2024). Network slicing as 6G security mechanism to mitigate cyber-attacks: The RIGOUROUS approach. In *Proceedings of the IEEE Conference on Network Softwarization (NetSoft)*. DOI: 10.1109/NetSoft60951.2024.10588939

McNulty, L., & Vassilakis, V. (2022). IoT botnets: Characteristics, exploits, attack capabilities, and targets. In *Proceedings of the International Symposium on Communication Systems, Networks & Digital Signal Processing (CSNDSP)*. DOI: 10.1109/CSNDSP54353.2022.9908039

Meneghello, F., Calore, M., Zucchetto, D., Polese, M., & Zanella, A. (2019). IoT: Internet of threats? A survey of practical security vulnerabilities in real IoT devices. *IEEE Internet of Things Journal*, *6*(5), 8182–8201. DOI: 10.1109/JIOT.2019.2935189

Mirji, B. H., & S., S. (2026). Cyber security threats in the internet of things (IoT) ecosystem: A review. International Journal of Advanced Research in Science. *Tongxin Jishu*, *6*(3), 1–10.

Mohan, J. P., Sugunaraj, N., & Ranganathan, P. (2022). Cyber security threats for 5G networks. In *Proceedings of the IEEE International Conference on Electro/Information Technology*. DOI: 10.1109/EIT53891.2022.9813982

Nalini, M. (2024). Securing smart cities: A cybersecurity perspective on integrating IoT, AI, and machine learning for digital twin creation. *Journal of Electrical Systems*, *20*(4), 3548–3560. DOI: 10.52783/jes.2049

Narsing, A., & Srinivasan, S. (2025). Create AI-powered anomaly detection to stop intrusions in SCADA and critical infrastructure networks: Industrial IoT through cybersecurity. In *Proceedings of the International Conference on Future Technologies (ICFT)*. DOI: 10.1109/ICFT66708.2025.11336547

Neha, & Bhatia, T. (2025). Adaptive intrusion detection system leveraging dynamic neural models with adversarial learning for 5G/6G networks. In Proceedings of the 4th International Conference on Computing Technologies (ICCTech). DOI: 10.1109/ICCTech63508.2025.10947861

Ntayagabiri, J. P., Bentaleb, Y., Ndikumagenge, J., & El Makhtoum, H. (2025). A comprehensive approach to protocols and security in internet of things technology. *Journal of Computer Theories and Applications*, *2*(3), 324–341. DOI: 10.62411/jcta.11660

Onyagu, C., Obikwelu, O., Godspower, A., & John, J. (2024). Enhancing security in internet of things (IoT) architecture through defense-in-depth mechanism: A comprehensive study. *Newport International Journal of Engineering and Physical Sciences*, *4*(1), 110–120. DOI: 10.59298/NIJEP/2024/411722.1.1100

Otoom, S. (2025). Risk auditing for digital twins in cyber physical systems: A systematic review. *Journal of Cyber Security and Risk Auditing*, *2025*(1), 22–35. DOI: 10.63180/jcsra.thestap.2025.1.3

Panovyk, U. (2025). Information protection in automated systems based on a conceptual model with formalized efficiency evaluation. Cybersecurity: Education, Science. *Technology*, *3*(1), 55–66. DOI: 10.28925/2663-4023.2025.27.5566

Parmar, P., Rangwala, H., & Parmar, P. (2026). Cyber physical security framework for smart cities using AI and quantum encryption. *Journal of Critical Infrastructure Policy*, *6*(1), 55–66. DOI: 10.1002/jci3.70020

Princewill, O. O., Eyo, E., & Ele, B. (2026). Federated learning based anomaly detection for privacy-preserving in IoT-enabled industrial control systems. *Journal of Statistical Sciences and Computational Intelligence*, *5*(2), 77–88. DOI: 10.64497/jssci.203

Rahman, A., Khan, M. S. I., Montieri, A., Islam, M. J., Karim, M. R., Hasan, M., Kundu, D., Nasir, M. K., & Pescapè, A. (2024). BlockSD-5GNet: Enhancing security of 5G network through blockchain-SDN with ML-based bandwidth prediction. *Transactions on Emerging Telecommunications Technologies*, *35*(4), e4950. DOI: 10.1002/ett.4965

Rahmoune, I., Al-Ghaili, A. M., Ibrahim, Z., Ismail, S., & Rahim, F. A. (2025). Comparative study of machine learning and deep learning models for IoT botnet detection. In *Proceedings of the IEEE International Conference on Computing (ICOCO)*. DOI: 10.1109/ICOCO67189.2025.11334162

Rupanetti, D., & Kaabouch, N. (2024). Combining edge computing-assisted internet of things security with artificial intelligence: Applications, challenges, and opportunities. *Applied Sciences (Basel, Switzerland)*, *14*(16), 7104. DOI: 10.3390/app14167104

Sahu, S. K., & Mazumdar, K. (2024). Exploring security threats and solutions techniques for internet of things (IoT): From vulnerabilities to vigilance. *Frontiers in Artificial Intelligence*, *7*, 1397480. Advance online publication. DOI: 10.3389/frai.2024.1397480 PMID: 38845684

Sarker, I. H., Khan, A. I., Abushark, Y. B., & Alsolami, F. (2022). Internet of things (IoT) security intelligence: A comprehensive overview, machine learning solutions and research directions. *Mobile Networks and Applications*, *28*(1), 296–312. DOI: 10.1007/s11036-022-01937-3

Sarker, S. P. K., & Khan, R. (2024). Cybersecurity considerations for smart Bangladesh: Challenges and solutions. *Asian Journal of Research in Computer Science*, *12*(3), 33–45. DOI: 10.9734/ajrcos/2024/v17i6464

Scalise, P., Boeding, M., Hempel, M., Sharif, H., Delloiacovo, J., & Reed, J. (2024). A systematic survey on 5G and 6G security considerations, challenges, trends, and research areas. *Future Internet*, *16*(3), 67. DOI: 10.3390/fi16030067

Şen, E., & Dash, E. A. (2023). Unveiling the shadows: Exploring the security challenges of the internet of things (IoT). *International Journal of Scientific Research and Engineering Management*, *8*(3), 45–56. DOI: 10.55041/IJSREM23970

Sharma, S. B., & Bairwa, A. K. (2025). Leveraging AI for intrusion detection in IoT ecosystems: A comprehensive study. *IEEE Access : Practical Innovations, Open Solutions*, *13*, 36419–36438. DOI: 10.1109/ACCESS.2025.3550392

Sohail, M.. (2025). Real-time detection of IoT botnet attacks on wireless routers using an open-source SIEM framework. In *Proceedings of the International Conference on Engineering & Computing Technologies (ICECT)*. DOI: 10.1109/ICECT66235.2025.11381696

U., R., P., R., Chandrasekaran, G., & K., M. (2024). Assessment of cybersecurity risks in digital twin deployments in smart cities. International Journal of Computer and Experimental Science and Engineering, 12(4), 233–240. DOI: 10.55524/ijcesen.1566738

Wang, N., Shi, S., Chen, Y., Lou, W., & Hou, Y. T. (2025). FeCo: Boosting intrusion detection capability in IoT networks via contrastive learning. *IEEE Transactions on Dependable and Secure Computing*, *22*(4), 1120–1135. DOI: 10.1109/TDSC.2025.3544106

Yang, M., Qu, Y., Ranbaduge, T., Thapa, C., Sultan, N., Ding, M., Suzuki, H., Ni, W., Abuadbba, S., Smith, D., Tyler, P., Pieprzyk, J., Rakotoarivelo, T., Guan, X., & M'rabet, S. (2024). From 5G to 6G: A survey on security, privacy, and standardization pathways. *ACM Computing Surveys*. Advance online publication. DOI: 10.1145/3785467

You, I., Kim, J., Pawana, I. W. A. J., & Ko, Y. (2024). Mitigating security vulnerabilities in 6G networks: A comprehensive analysis of the DMRN protocol using SVO logic and ProVerif. *Applied Sciences (Basel, Switzerland), 14*(12), 5122. DOI: 10.3390/app14219726

Yusuf, R., & Abdulrahman, I. A. (2025). Towards quantum-resilient log integrity in 5G/6G mobile network protocol analysis. *Global Journal of Engineering and Technology Advances, 7*(2), 33–45. DOI: 10.30574/gjeta.2025.23.2.0076

Zaman, S., Alhazmi, K., Aseeri, M. A., Ahmed, M. R., Khan, R. T., Kaiser, M. S., & Mahmud, M. (2021). Security threats and artificial intelligence based countermeasures for internet of things networks: A comprehensive survey. *IEEE Access : Practical Innovations, Open Solutions, 9*, 94668–94690. DOI: 10.1109/ACCESS.2021.3089681

Zemskov, A. D., ... (2024). Security and privacy of digital twins for advanced manufacturing: A survey. arXiv preprint arXiv:2401.12345. /arXiv.2401.12345DOI: 10.48550

Zhang, Y., Liu, W., & Zhu, T. (2026). MOAT: Federated learning-based method for improved detection of IoT botnets. *IEEE Internet of Things Journal, 13*(2), 1120–1132. DOI: 10.1109/JIOT.2025.3631450

Zhou, C., Zhao, X., Qiu, Q., & Zhu, C. (2025). Transformer-based intelligent processing techniques for IPv6 internet of things security data. In *Proceedings of the 6th International Conference on Big Data, Artificial Intelligence and Internet of Things Engineering (ICBAIE)*. DOI: 10.1109/ICBAIE66852.2025.11326648

Zhou, Y. (2025). Network security threats and defense mechanisms for 6G multi-virtual network scenarios. *International Journal of Network Management, 35*(4), e2240. DOI: 10.1002/nem.70003

Chapter 10
Securing Darknet Web Applications

K. Muthamil Sudar
http://orcid.org/0000-0001-9640-3477
Mepco Schlenk Engineering College, Sivakasi, India

P. H. Pandian
Mepco Schlenk Engineering College, Sivakasi, India

P. Santhose
Mepco Schlenk Engineering College, Sivakasi, India

M. Yogeshwaran
Mepco Schlenk Engineering College, Sivakasi, India

ABSTRACT

SQL injection attacks continue to pose a critical threat to web applications since the cybersecurity environment constantly changes, so security requires effective detection and prevention mechanisms. A new second-order SQL injection detection system works using proxy-based steps to improve security for advanced injection techniques. t. Our system adopts two analysis strategies through real-time dynamic execution that mimics live attacks while recording likely source code errors through passive static analysis. The system generates output depending on the given SQL injection points to emulate real-time attack traces efficiently. Integrating static and dynamic execution offers comprehensive system protection through complete control of source code vulnerabilities across all periods of execution. In-transit analysis in the proxy server checks all incoming database queries for anomalies and stops suspicious queries from reaching the database.

1. INTRODUCTION

Digital transformation has introduced an omnipresent cyberattack threat, which affects citizens as well as institutions and government control systems. Internet reliance has introduced a breeding ground for digital attackers who target web applications and software. Contemporary digital businesses and

DOI: 10.4018/979-8-3373-9755-9.ch010

government institutions continue to digitize their management systems as cybercriminals look for new attack channels for these digital businesses (Zhang et al., 2024). The Open Web Application Security Project (OWASP) is a helpful tool that detects as well as categorizes common vulnerabilities present in web applications. Web application security remains vulnerable to common threats since the three top vulnerabilities facilitate injection attacks as well as broken authentication, while facilitating cross-site scripting (XSS). Security threats occur due to improper code development and invalid input checks, and thelack of security measures necessitates regular asset audits and improved programming best practices for digital security. SQL injection is one of the most severe web application vulnerabilities. Attackers inject malicious code statements into SQL queries using input fields in login forms, as well as search boxes and comment fields. Execution of malicious code via this infection provides unauthorized access for attackers who steal sensitive information while possibly ruining entire target databases. SQL injection attacks utilize unvalidated inputs to target databases when application developers allow user data to flow directly to the back end without checks, leading to command execution by unauthorized individuals. SQL injection attacks infiltrate application databases via unsafe input mechanisms since attackers can modify, delete, or extract critical information, thus compromising application security (Paul et al., 2024). The ease with which cybercriminals can carry out SQL injection attacks makes it their go-to exploitation method. SQL injection attacks come in two broad categories: first-order and second-order attacks. First-order SQL injection allows attackers to insert malicious input into the database system simultaneously when the user submits it to the database. When attackers manipulate an SQL query in a login page, it can circumvent security and reveal concealed parts of the application. Input validation using parameterized queries is one of the methods to prevent first-order SQL injection. This approach helps to distinguish user input from executable code so that SQL queries will not execute input as part of execution.

SQL injection attacks, which occur at the second-order level, pose advanced features that are hard to identify. The risk of second-order SQL injection conceals malicious SQL code within a long-term database store until it is triggered by another app-dependent trigger event. Attackers insert perilous SQL helper code into user profile fields that will not initiate until app functions read and execute that profile data in the database. It is hard to trace second-order SQL injection because this type of attack needs specific conditions to prompt execution. Parameterized queries and prepared statements work to keep user input separate from the SQL code run, avoiding SQL injection attacks. Web application firewalls and other detection systems help to monitor network traffic and block unwanted SQL code from reaching the server storage. To prevent SQL injection once and for all, you need security solutions that are greater than response plans. With increasingly complex and distributed applications, you need to utilize full solutions that protect against such attacks. Main database protection scans SQL queries that arrive at the database during the lifetime of the application. Organizations can detect future data misuse attempts by monitoring user interaction data to look for patterns that represent potential malicious activity.

The growing use of darknet infrastructure, like anonymous marketplaces and cybercrime forums, has made web-based attacks significantly more sophisticated. Attackers on the darknet often take advantage of weaknesses in public web apps, hiding their identities and the sources of their attacks. Out of all the threats, SQL injection is still one of the most common ways attackers use to get at sensitive info and compromise database integrity. It lets them do even more malicious activities too. Second-order SQL injections are particularly challenging because the malicious code is saved inside the application first and only hits later when the backend processes it. This matches the mean and consistent strategies seen in cybercrime. So, having advanced detection methods that can spot SQL injection attacks right away and the ones that hit later is crucial. This will help up web app security in today's super complex threat world.

The proxy-based layer assists in filtering SQL queries in real time. It sanitizes and logs data to guard the database. The layer may block malicious SQL code from damaging the system by rejecting or correcting it. Proxies are intermediate tools employed to counter attacks, safeguarding systems from attackers who can bypass conventional defenses. The proxy system is both a real-time logging system and a security system for SQLITE that provides complete execution logs for future examination. Application developers need tools that allow them to examine and validate SQL queries in the database without changing how the application operates. Developers can activate security checks that help them detect problems early, so they can fix them before attackers use them with a special evaluation interface. A step-by-step solution allows development teams to keep the application secure by using strong security features with their frameworks. To effectively prevent blind SQL injection vulnerabilities, we need to thoroughly scan SQL queries at different stages in the application lifecycle. By doing this, we can catch problems before they can be exploited, giving strong security from development to operations.

2. BACKGROUND AND RELATED WORKS

SQL injection attacks remain one of the most common web application security threats. While first-order SQL injection is more well-known and studied, second-order SQL injection presents more complex challenges in detection and avoidance. The discussion below addresses second-order as well as first-order SQL injection principles, their respective differences, and the employed attacks.

2.1. First Order SQL Injection Principle

First-order SQL injection occurs when an attacker directly injects malicious input into an SQL query, which is executed immediately by the database (Kashyap & Jana, 2025). This enables attackers to change the logic of the query and gain access to unauthorized data.

There are seven common types of first-order SQL injection attacks: (Qin et al., 2025).

2.1.1 Tautologies (T1)

Tautologies take the advantage of SQL logical conditions and enable the attackers to alter the queries. A condition like OR 1=1 can be used to mislead the system into allowing unauthorized access.

UserInput:'OR1=1-
SQLQuerybecomes:SELECT*FROM users WHERE username = '' OR 1=1 -' AND password= "

2.1.2 Union Queries (T2)

Union queries are used to get results from multiple SELECT queries. When an attacker uses this method, they will add a union query to a query to get data from other tables in the database. This can potentially expose data the attacker shouldn't be able to access.

User Input: `UNION SELECT username,passwordFROM admin -
SQLQuerybecomes:SELECTname,emailFROMusersWHEREid

2.1.3 Piggy-Backed Queries (T3)

In piggy-backed queries, the attacker joins the first SQL query with additional SQL commands to perform any operation they wish on the database. This means, for example, an attacker can cause a command to delete or change data to occur after the first command has returned.

UserInput:1;DROPTABLEusers -
SQLQuerybecomes:SELECT*FROM users WHERE id = 1; DROP

2.1.4 Inference (T4)

In attacks that are based on inference, the attacker varies an input to infer certain characteristics or properties of the databases themselves. By comparing the outputs of the varying inputs, the attacker is able to infer some information about the underlying database structure, including tables, columns, and values, but not actually accessing the data.

User Input: ' AND ASCII(SUBSTRING((SELECT version()),1,1))>52-
SQLQuerybecomes:SELECT*FROM users WHERE username = ''

2.1.5 Alternate Encodings (T5)

Attackers use alternate encodings, such as hexadecimal or URL encoding, to bypass security filters. By encoding special characters, they can conceal their malicious payloads, making them harder to detect.

User Input (URL Encoded):
%27%20OR%201%3D1%20-
DecodedInput:'OR1=1-
SQLQuerybecomes:SELECT*FROM users WHERE username = '' OR 1=1 -'

2.1.6 Illegal/Logically Incorrect Queries (T6)

Malformed or logically incorrect queries trigger errors that expose details about the database structure. Attackers can exploit these errors to gain insight into the system and craft further attacks.

User Input: 'AND1= CONVERT(int,'abc')-
SQLQuery:SELECT*FROM users WHERE username = '' AND 1=CONVERT(int,'abc')-

2.1.7 Stored Procedures (T7)

Predefined SQL functions are called as stored procedures. This allow attackers to inject unauthorized SQL code, potentially altering or retrieving sensitive data from the database.

User Input: '; EXEC xp_cmdshell('dir')-
SQL Query becomes: EXEC getUserData ''; EXEC xp_cmdshell('dir') -

2.2. Second-order SQL Injection Principle

Second-order SQL Injection is when the malicious data is stored in the database and then executed when the application uses that data in another context without proper sanitization.

Scenario

A web application allows users to update their profile bio. Later, this bio is used in a query to search for users with similar interests.

Step 1 – Bio Update (Malicious Input Stored)

The attacker submits a bio field containing the payload:
MaliciousInput: ');DROPTABLEusers;-
The application stores this malicious input in the database without validating or sanitizing it.
VulnerableCode–StoreStatus(PythonFlask)

```
@app.route('/set_status',methods=[' POST'])
defset_status():
user=session['user']
status = request.form['status'] query="UPDATEusersSETstatus
='{}'WHEREuser='{}'".
format(status,user) cursor.execute(query)
```

Step 2 – Later Usage in a Query (Trigger Point)

Later, when the application tries to use the bio field in another query, the stored malicious code is executed.
Vulnerable Code – Reuse Stored Input

```
@app.route('/show_users') def show_users():
cursor.execute("SELECTstatus FROMusersWHEREuser=' admin'")
status=cursor.fetchone()[0]
query="SELECT*FROMlogsWHERE messageLIKE'%{}%'".format(
status) cursor.execute(query)
```

Executed SQL Query:
Injected SQL Query

```
SELECT * FROM users WHERE bio LIKE'%');DROPTABLEusers;-%'
```

The second query executes the previously stored SQL payload, resulting in the deletion of the user's table. This type of attack is dangerous because the malicious input is stored silently and only executed later, making detection and prevention more difficult.

Crespo-Martínez et al. (2023) proposed a methodology that includes gathering two labeled datasets of network flow data specifically targeting SQL injection attacks on popular relational database engines, which are publicly available under a CC Attribution 4.0 International license. Various supervised learning algorithms, includingLogistic Regression was evaluated, achieving a detection rate exceeding 97% with a false alarm rate below 0.07%. The datasets were gathered via NetFlow V5 tech, so it has a broad coverage of multiple attack kinds, which suggests improved model generalization. However, several limitations remain, because it leans on flow information, and that may not adequately capture application-level SQL injection behaviors.

Lu et al. (2023) suggested a new detection approach named synBERT, it does semantic learning, by taking sentence-level meaning from SQL statements then turns that into an embedding vector, which then gets mapped to SQL syntax tree structures in a more workable way. Still, it also admits that the reported metrics are harder to reproduce when the dataset changes.

Guan et al. (2023) put forward a black-box adversarial attack method for SQL injection built with reinforcement learning, and it includes a state vector representation algorithm for feature extraction, plus a matrix of stackable variation strategies used during the attacking phase against detection models. The dataset contains 34,395 SQL injection examples and 45,991 normal SQL query statements, and it was collected from multiple publicly available sources such as open-source attack intelligence sites and Amazon Alexa's top-1000 webpages. The weak points are that repeated adversarial rounds can reduce detection accuracy, sometimes Significantly, with a few models dropping to detection rates under 5%. Nagabhooshanam et al. (2023) suggested something like a simulation system model built around a BP neural network together with a genetic algorithm, for network security assessment. It mainly targets the detection and evaluation of vulnerabilities in computer networks, kind of. In their work, the dataset contains 17 specific security index points that are used as input values, while the safety comprehensive evaluation score acts as the expected output. The disadvantages mentioned are, first the lack of a fully integrated network information security assessment platform and second that current systems still cannot effectively fuse evaluation technologies with testing technologies effectively.

Qu et al. (2024) proposed a methodology called AdvSQLi. This approach performs a chain of minimal transformations on a hierarchical tree representation of SQL injection payloads, so the payloads can bypass web application firewall mechanismswhile keeping the malicious capability. For evaluation, they use two public datasets: the SQL injection dataset from Kaggle (SIK) and the HttpParams Dataset (HPD), which includes different kinds of SQLi payloads. The limitations include the difficulty of confirming semantic preservation. However, no practical mechanism currently exists to guarantee strict semantic equivalence, and also it depends on manually defined control flow graphs (CFGs), which can limit how diverse the generated payloads can get.

Alarfaj et al. (2023) introduced a Probabilistic Neural Network (PNN) for detecting SQL injection attacks. They optimize the smoothing parameters using the BAT algorithm, which improves detection accuracy. The dataset includes 6000 SQL injection queries and 3500 normal SQL queries, and they collected it from the Lib-injection Python library, since publicly available datasets are relatively scarce. Even though they report high accuracy (99.19%) and low false positive rates, the methodology still has drawbacks that, as noted as high complexity and sensitivity to noise from irrelevant features. Thalji et al. (2023) suggested the AE-Net methodology that employs an Autoencoder network for automatic feature engineering, utilizing a dataset of 46,392 preprocessed SQL queries to extract high-level deep features for SQL injection attack detection. The dataset is split into 80% for training and 20% for testing, with performance evaluated through hyperparameter tuning and k-fold cross-validation, achieving a k-fold accuracy of 0.99.

Sun et al. (2023) proposed a SQL injection attack detection mechanism that utilizes deep learning mechanism for sequence information analysis. But their proposed system leads to overfitting during training because of scarcity of sample datasets. Alghawaziet al. (2023) suggested a methodology that utilizes a recurrent neural network autoencoder to detect SQL injection attacks. The major limitation of their work is that they used small sized dataset which doesn't helps to increase the models robustness.

Arastehet al. (2023) introduced a methodology using Gray-Wolf optimizer to identify the efficient features for SQL injection detection. Kakisim (2024) proposed deep learning-based detection model to capture both previous and subsequent contexts in SQL queries, enhancing detection accuracy through multiview representations of SQL data. Jaradat et al. (2023) proposed a system that employs the DSQLIA model, integrating feature engineering and Natural Language Processing (NLP) to enhance machine learning accuracy in detecting SQL injection attacks. However, a notable drawback in above three methods is that the limitation of datasets used.

Based on the literature examined, static analysis techniques have limitation in runtime. Dynamic techniques, although efficient in runtime systems, tend to require tight integration within the application logic, which burdens system complexity and performance cost. Most tools have high false positive rates and low adaptability to lightweight databases such as SQLite. Additionally, current solutions hardly give developers actionable feedback or assist in proactive mitigation at development time. Table 1 shows the limitations of existing works.

Table 1. Limitations of existing works

Ref.	Method	Limitation
Crespo-Martínez et al. (2023)	Machine Learning using NetFlow-based traffic analysis	Relies on network-flow features and may not capture application-level or second-order SQL injection attacks.
Lu et al. (2023)	synBERT semantic SQL analysis	Performance depends on dataset characteristics and requires extensive fine-tuning for generalization.
Guan et al. (2023)	Reinforcement Learning-based adversarial SQLi framework	Detection performance degrades under repeated adversarial attacks.
Nagabhooshanam et al. (2023)	BP Neural Network with Genetic Algorithm	Limited integration with practical vulnerability testing and runtime monitoring systems.
Qu et al. (2024)	AdvSQLi payload transformation approach	Semantic equivalence of generated payloads cannot always be guaranteed.
Alarfaj & Khan (2023)	BAT-optimized Probabilistic Neural Network (PNN)	High computational complexity and sensitivity to noisy features.
Thalji et al. (2023)	AE-Net (Autoencoder-based detection)	Primarily focused on first-order SQL injection detection.
Sun et al. (2023)	Deep Learning-based SQLi detection	Susceptible to overfitting due to limited training samples.
Alghawazi et al. (2023)	RNN Autoencoder-based detection	Small dataset size limits model robustness and generalization.
Arasteh et al. (2024)	Gray-Wolf Optimizer-based feature selection	Limited validation and lack of second-order SQL injection evaluation.
Kakisim (2024)	Multiview Deep Learning approach	Computationally expensive and highly dependent on dataset quality.
Jaradat et al. (2023)	DSQLIA (NLP + Feature Engineering)	Limited dataset diversity and no support for delayed-execution attacks.
Proposed SQLDPSM	Hybrid Static Analysis + Dynamic Proxy Monitoring	Requires broader real-world validation across diverse database platforms and large-scale deployments.

As summarized in Table 1, existing SQL injection detection approaches primarily focus on machine learning, deep learning, or network-based analysis techniques. Although these methods achieve promising detection accuracy, they generally suffer from limitations such as dataset dependency, high computational cost, lack of runtime monitoring, and limited support for second-order SQL injection attacks. The key contribution of proposed work combines dynamic proxy-based execution monitoring and static source code analysis in order to address these issues. The system uses a lightweight Python proxy server to sanitize and inspect SQL queries in real time without changing how the application behaves. Additionally, it has developer-friendly interfaces for vulnerability visualization and logging, automated payload generation, and second-order attack simulation. By providing precise, modular, and context-aware defense against first- and second-order SQL injection attacks, this all-encompassing method successfully closes the detection gap in conventional systems.

3. PROPOSED WORK

Our system, shown in Fig.1, adopts a proxy approach that identifies second-order SQL injection vulnerabilities before the malicious code reaches the database, due to its simplicity and non-susceptibility to irrelevant features. Since 1, 2, and 3 in Fig.1 represent the sequential working order of the entire process.

The diagram illustrates a web application security analysis process, and it consists of two primary phases: Static Analysis and Dynamic Execution. During the static analysis stage, SQL queries can be scanned from the source code, and the queries found were used to find a possible SQL injection point. All of these data were then used to generate payloads for attack simulation. The dynamic execution phase is all about intercepting the server's requests. The incoming queries, received by the server, are pattern-matched to find potentially exploitable SQL injection attacks. If an attack is detected, the request is blocked and logged. If there is no attack, the request is served by the server. The entire process is designed to detect and filter out SQL injection threats in the web application through a combination of static code analysis and dynamic request tracking.The main objective of the proposed work is to identify and mitigate SQL injection vulnerabilities by combining static and dynamic analysis.

3.1. Static Analysis

Static analysis shown in Fig.2 works through identifying SQL injection patterns in source code through pattern matching, along with contextual assessment that it includes. The mechanism of code inspection works without even running the code, thereby providing developers with crucial security analyses throughout the application development. The proposed SQLDPSM framework is designed to address sophisticated attack scenarios that may originate from both traditional web environments and darknet-enabled threat actors. By combining static source-code analysis with dynamic proxy-based monitoring, the framework improves visibility into delayed-execution SQL injection attacks that are commonly associated with stealth-oriented attack campaigns.

Figure 1. System design

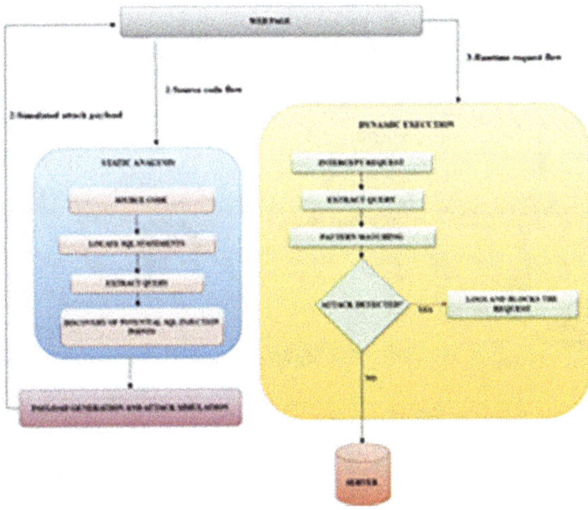

By pattern matching, the tool identifies common SQL Injection attack patterns from the use of direct stringsconcatenation to unsafe parameter usage and inline SQL Statements together with comment-based and union-based attacks. The second module emphasizes safe query construction techniques such as prepared statements and parameterized statements, together with the proper implementation of ORM frameworks.The security component checks code matches for positioning within secure regions as it scans adjacent lines for potential indications of secure implementation. The system produces confidence levels for detected vulnerabilities that are based on context cues such as test log sample examples and monitoring patterns.

The static analysis module is implemented in Python with the use of the re library for the execution of regex patterns. The framework initializes base regex patterns as part of its core operations and performs code analysis through source scanning that skips benign sections before returning affected code, which supports vulnerability understanding. We developed web page to access static analysis module. Second-order SQL Injection is when the malicious data is stored in the database and then executed when the application uses that data in another context without proper sanitization.

Figure 2. Staticanalysis

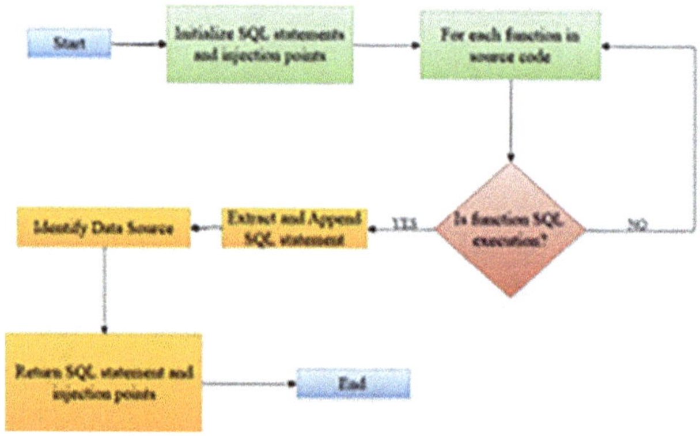

Algorithm1. *StaticAnalysisforSQLInjectionPoints*

```
Input:
 SC – Source Code Files
Output:
 SS – Extracted SQL Statements
 IP – Potential Injection Points
Initialize SS ← ∅
Initialize IP ← ∅
For each file f ∈ SC do
 Parse source code
 For each statement s in f do
 If containsSQLQuery(s) then
 Add s to SS
 Variables ← ExtractInputVariables(s)
 For each variable v ∈ Variables do
 If isDirectlyConcatenated(v) OR
 isUnsanitized(v) then
 Add v to IP
 End If
 End For

  End If
  End For
End For
Return (SS, IP)
```

3.2. Payload Generation

The current module guides you through attack payload creation and SQL injection attack simulation in payload generation tools based on findings derived from the static analysis module. The proxy server serves attackdetection purposes, but this module focuses efforts on attack payload creation and simulation tasks.

The security evaluation module utilizes known vulnerabilities of static analysis to introduce realistic test procedures that test web applications for security threats of SQL Injection. The tool generates various

SQL Injection attack payloads corresponding to discovered system vulnerabilities. The attack payloads provide various possible forms, such as error-based SQL Injection that makes use of database error messages and union union-based SQL Injection that abuses UNION operators, and blind SQL Injection that retrieves data with the help of conditional responses.

The module offers two-way compatibility between Burp Suite and SQL Injector, allowing users to transfer payloads created in SQL Injector directly into Burp's Intruder tool. Through this compatibility, our payloads can be tested automatically by sending them to targets.And capturing their response for analysis. The application assesses several attack scenarios following payload injection by tracking the system response as it identifies successful exploitation incidents such as data breaches and unexpected application behavior.After the simulation, the module creates a comprehensive report containing details of applied payloads, server responses, and used attack methods. The report is gathered and serves as a helpful tool meant to support developers as they go through the process of remediation of their vulnerabilities and identifying vulnerabilities.The module provides a real-world SQL Injection attack vulnerability assessment by allowing actual attack scenarios to be run against the application. Attack simulation reports from this tool aid developers in building more resilient applications that guard against potential vulnerabilities. With the integration of Burp Suite, the testing process becomes more streamlined and yields effective security analysis.This mandatory module serves its purpose for the detection of attacks via the proxy server system and assists developers in generating attack payloads and simulating attacks to provide improved security audits.

3.3. Dynamic Execution

The present module, shown in Fig.3, examines the detection methods of SQL Injection attacks via proxyserver operations. Proxy servers map user browser requests to operate as go-betweens, connecting web applications with web servers. The proxy server captures re-requests from the user and then performs analysis to verify the content through signs of SQL Injection vulnerabilities. The evaluation method examines transmitted parameters along with information to identify SQL commands and injection attack signs by their signature characters. At analysis time, the proxy server logs incoming requests along with identified anomalous behavior. The proxy-based monitoring mechanism is particularly beneficial in environments exposed to anonymized attack traffic, where attacker attribution is difficult and traditional signature-based defenses may be insufficient. By analyzing query behavior at runtime, the framework provides an additional layer of protection against sophisticated SQL injection attempts that may be launched through darknet-enabled infrastructures.

The system performs detection by two principal methods collectively referred to as traffic analysis in combination with pattern matching. The proxy device has constant traffic monitoring for detecting anomalies leading to flagged requests with SQL keywords and unusual types of input. In dynamic execution, code vulnerabilities are made detectable when applications execute their code and their activity gets analyzed in real time.

Following the detection of potential SQL Injection attacks, the proxy server dynamically creates logs which can be scanned by security personnel for threat response and assessment. The logging facility records vital attack information, which assists post-attack analysis as well as incident response procedures.

Figure 3. Dynamicexecution

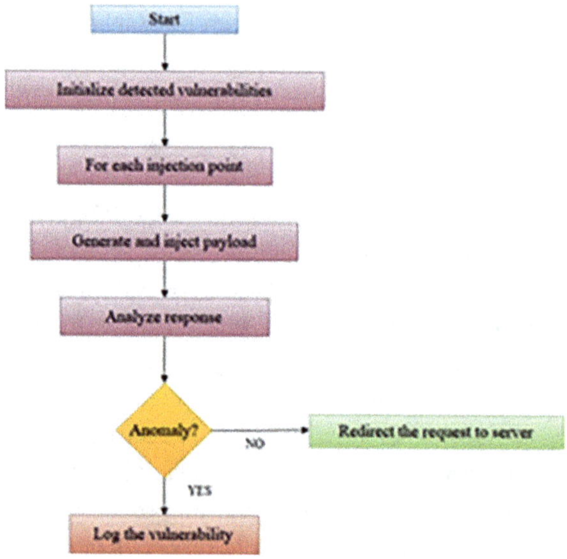

Algorithm 2. *Dynamic SQL Injection Detection Algorithm*

```
Input:
IP: Set of injection points
SS: Set of SQL statements
PS: Proxy server instance
PayloadList: List of payloads generated for testing
SecurityRules: Predefined rules for anomaly detection
Output:
DV: Set of detected vulnerabilities
Require:
 IP:Setofinjectionpoints
 SS:SetofSQLstatements
 s:IndividualSQLstatement
 rS:ReconstructedSQLstatement
 p: Injection point pl: Payload listpld:Singlepayload
 mS:ModifiedSQLstatement
 res:Databaseresponse
 v:Vulnerabilityreport
Ensure:
DV:Detectedvulnerabilities
InitializeDV←∅
Start the proxyserverPStointerceptSQLqueries
ForallSQLstatementss∈SSdo
 rS←ReconstructStatement(s)
 Forallinjectionpointsp∈IPdo
 pl←GeneratePayloads(p)
 forallpayloadspld∈pldo
 mS←InjectPayload(pld,rS)
 res←SendToDatabase(PS,mS)
 ifAnalyzeResponse(res)indicatesanomaly
 then
 v←CreateVulnerabilityReport(p,mS)
 DV ←DV∪{v}
 endif
 endfor
 endfor
endfor
Forallvulnerabilityreportsv∈DVdo
 ifMatchSecurityRules(v)then
 LogSecurityEvent(v)
 endif
endfor
returnDV=0
```

This module uses a proxy server to monitor SQL Injection attacks by analyzing and logging browser requests. The proxy scrutinizes web traffic to strengthen the overall web application security posture, and to help organizations spot SQL Injection threats while theyre doing regular business operations. Right now, the implementation keeps moving, but it could use a few improvements, like connecting it with alerting solutions and adding rate limiting features along with more sophisticated logging mechanisms.

3.4. Simulation Setup

This simulation aims to find, possible SQL injection spots within a web application, using a blend of static analysis with regular expressions, dynamic execution, and an actual attack simulation approach, with tools like Burp Suite and a custom Python proxy server. The whole run is done on a regular development box, with an Intel Core i7-1165G7 at 2.80GHz 16 GB RAM, and a 512 GB SSD. The setup includes Windows 11 Pro (64-bit) and also Ubuntu 22.04 LTS, for testing both client-side pieces and server-side parts, simultaneously in parallel. The planned proxy server plus the static analysis modules are written in Python 3.10, and SQLite 3.40 serves as the backend database used to store, and keep track of SQL queries. For payload generation and the attack simulations, Burp Suite Community Edition (v2023.10.1) is used along with SQLmap (v1.7.12). For the vulnerable targets, software such as DVWA, bWAPP, and WebGoat is deployed, running on Apache 2.4 with PHP 8.1, just to reflect a more realistic attack surface. On the client side, Google Chrome (v125) is configured to route traffic through the proxy server, so HTTP requests can be intercepted and reviewed. The code writing and debugging work happens in Visual Studio Code (v1.89). Finally, testing is isolated inside separate environments on Oracle VirtualBox 7.0, so experiments stay safe and repeatable. The web application is the first component and should be a simple application with typical SQL injection vulnerabilities, such as user registration, login, and search features. For conducting the test, one may deploy open-source web applications such as Damn Vulnerable Web Application (DVWA), bWAPP, or Pikachu. A web page may be created to identify potential points of SQL injection as static analysis. This detection begins with pulling out SQL queries from the application source code, which can be done using code parsing or by analyzing the application logic to determine how and where SQL queries are built. Once the SQL queries are pulled out, regex can be applied to find keywords and patterns that can indicate possible SQL injection.One critical technical aspect to pay attention to is the use of regex patterns to identify common SQL injection vectors. For instance, queries with constructs like SELECT ... FROM ... are recognizable in order to identify base query structure. The same can be done with queries that have conditions such as WHERE column = 'value' which should be highlighting user input points. Even insertions such as INSERT INTO table name VALUES (...) can be tagged to check for where data is added to the database, which is are targets also common for injections.

In addition, we can also identify logical patterns that contain possible injections such as the use of keywords, OR, AND, UNION, and similar operators that we have already encountered within an SQL injection attack. Other solutions like ESLint (for JavaScript) or SonarQube can help you automate the identification of insecure coding practices with SQL queries. The main purpose of Burp Suite is to generate attack payloads and simulate attacks. Burp Suite is an intercepting proxy that captures HTTP requests that are directed against the web application.With Burp Suite, the framework identifies vulnerable parameters and apply SQL injection attacks through the Intruder tool for payload generation. Here are some key technical points regarding Burp Suite: configure the browser to route traffic through Burp Suite, allowing you to view and requests and responses can be inspected and modified; define the target scope in Burp Suite to focus on specific URLs or domains, which helps streamline the testing process and avoid unnecessary requests; use the Intruder tool to automate the sending of multiple SQL injection payloads, customizing payload positions and choosing from various payload types, including simple strings,Numbers, and complex SQL queries; create custom payload sets that include common SQL injection patterns (e.g., 1' OR '1'='1, admin' –, 1 UNION SELECTNULL, username, password FROM users –) to test various endpoints effectively; analyze server responses using Burp's built-in tools to identify anomalies, such as changes in response length or error messages that may indicate successful injections; leverage Burp Suite extensions from the BApp Store to enhance functionality, such as additional payload generators or custom analysis tools tailored for SQL injection testing.

The implementation of dynamic execution requires a basic proxy server developed in Python to monitor the exchange of HTTP messages that occurs between client systems and web applications. The code establishes a distinctive HTTP proxy server that monitors and records possible SQL injection activities. Here are some key technical points regarding the dynamic execution part: the proxy server utilizes Python's logging module to log requests and responses, filtering out unnecessary messages (e.g., from detectportal.firefox.com), which helps maintain clear logs for SQL injection attempts and other significant events; the server includes a robust DNS resolution method that first attempts to resolve hostnames using the system's DNS and falls back to predefined public DNS servers (Google, Cloudflare, OpenDNS) if necessary, ensuring reliable connectivity to the target web application; the detect sql injection method uses enhanced regex patterns to identify potential SQL injection attempts in both GET and POST requests, including common SQL commands and techniques that attackers might use; the send request with retry method implements retry logic for failed requests, allowing up to three attempts with a delay between each, useful for handling transient errors when connecting to the target server; the proxy server supports handling GET, POST, and CONNECT requests, processing GET requests by forwarding them to the target server and returning the response, while POST requests are analyzed for SQL injection attempts before being forwarded; the do CONNECT method establishes a secure tunnel for HTTPS requests, allowing encrypted communication between the client and the target server using SSL/TLS, ensuring that sensitive data remains secure; comprehensive error handling is incorporated throughout the server methods, logging errors and sending appropriate HTTP error responses back to the client, helping to diagnose issues during testing.

To realistically emulate and test SQL injection vulnerabilities, especially second-order attacks, a range of intentionally flawed web applications is employed as standardized testing grounds. They are created with a specific purpose to assist security researchers, instructors, and software developers in rehearsing actual attack examples within a controlled and secure environment. Of the most widely recognized are Damn Vulnerable Web Application (DVWA), Pikachu, bWAPP, WebGoat, Mutillidae, and Hackazon. Each of these tools has unique characteristics that make it useful for security testing. DVWA is a PHP/MySQL web application that is famous for its configurable levels of security and modules that include SQL injection, XSS, and others. Pikachu, with its colorful cartoon-style interface, is developed in PHP and offers many vulnerabilities, such as first and second-order SQL injection, aimed at beginners in cybersecurity. bWAPP, or Buggy Web Application, provides more than 100 security vulnerabilities and is perfect for in-depth vulnerability training. WebGoat, an OWASP project, consists of interactive lessons in Java that take users through different vulnerabilities with hands-on exercises. Mutillidae, another OWASP offering, is PHP-based and has extensive hints and learning tools, and supports a large variety of attack simulations. Hackazon differs from the rest, as it simulates a contemporary e-commerce website with dynamic pages and REST APIs, presenting a realistic scenario to test business logic vulnerabilities and second-order injection intricacies. As a combined group, these sites provide a strong foundation upon which to write, test, and verify security mechanisms, positioning them as imperative resources in web application security testing.

3.5 Evaluation Methodology

The evaluation dataset was constructed using six vulnerable web applications, namely DVWA, Pikachu, bWAPP, WebGoat, Mutillidae, and HackazonAttack payloads were generated using Burp Suite, SQLmap, and custom scripts, while second-order attack scenarios were manually verified by observing delayed execution behavior after payload storage and retrieval. Ground-truth labels were assigned through manual inspection of application responses, database modifications, and execution logs. Requests that successfully altered query behavior, retrieved unauthorized data, modified database contents, or triggered stored malicious payloads were labeled as attacks. Benign requests producing expected application behavior were labeled as legitimate traffic. The performance of the proposed SQLDPSM framework was evaluated using Accuracy, Precision, Recall, and F1-score metrics. A false positive was defined as a legitimate request incorrectly classified as an SQL injection attack, whereas a false negative represented a successful attack that remained undetected by the system.

First, initialize the simulation environment through deployment of DVWA, bWAPP, or Pikachu (open-source web applications) on local or test servers. Begin by deploying Burp Suite along with making settings to operate with the Python proxy server. The static analysis web page will retrieve SQL statements and then scan the web application source code through regular expressions to identify potential SQL injection points. Web application security testing requires users to first start Burp Suite and configure its interception features, then utilize Intruder for conducting SQL injection payload attacks through Burp Suite. The Python proxy server requires monitoring through an active web application connection to analyze for SQL injection vulnerabilities when it intercepts requests. Summarize obtained findings from static and dynamic analysis, then propose protection measures that include using prepared statements and ORM frameworks together with improved input validation mechanisms. The simulation environment showcases an extensive method to detect web application SQL injection flaws with static regular expression analysis combined with dynamic execution supported by Burp Suite and a custom Python proxy server to perform effective vulnerability assessment and security improvement. An extensive vulnerability analysis is provided for SQL injection (SQLi) in Table 2. This analysis includes details regarding the vulnerabilities found in different web applications in terms ofOn SQL query fragments, injection vectors, and source files that are vulnerable to attack, together with relevant CVEs. From the applications considered in this analysis, both DVWA and WebGoat were found to be more vulnerable to attacks compared to others. Specifically, the WebGoat application was very vulnerable to game queries, while Pikachu and SQLilabs were vulnerable in user authentication and password functions, respectively. Mutillidae proved to be vulnerable in applications related to medical and appointments booking systems, especially where user inputs via sessions were used.

Table 2. SQL injection vulnerabilities analysis

Application	SQLQuerySnippet	InjectionVector	VulnerableFile(Reference)
DVWA	SELECT first_name, last_name FROM users WHERE user_id = '$id' LIMIT	$id= SESSION['id'], $id= COOKIE['id']	~/vulnerabilities/sqli
Pikachu	SELECT*FROM usersWHERE username='$username' AND sha1(password)='$password'	$username= COOKIE['uname'], $password= COOKIE['pw']	~/inc/function.php
SQLilabs	UPDATE users SET password = ... WHERE username='$username'	$username= SESSION['username'	~/Less-4/2pass_change.php]

continued on following page

Table 2. Continued

Application	**SQLQuerySnippet**	**InjectionVector**	**VulnerableFile(Reference)**
Schoolmate	UPDATE schoolinfo SET ... WHERE	$schoolname = mysql_ result($query,	~/header.php
	schoolname='$schoolName'	0)	
		Basedon:Sunetal.[12]	
		CVE-2023-40944	~/ValidateLogin.php]
	SELECTtypeFROM	$username=	
	usersWHEREusername	SESSION['username'	~/ValidateLogin.php]
	='$username'	CVE-2023-40946	~/DeleteFunctions.php
	SELECTuserId	$username=	
	FROMusersWHERE	SESSION['username'	
	username='$username'	CVE-2023-40946	
	DELETEFROM...WHERE	$courseid=...	~/DeleteFunctions.phpry)
	courseid='$courseid'	(Misinterpreted	
		query,	
		mysql_fetch_row)	
		CVE-2023-39850	
	DELETEFROM	$teacherid=	
	teachersWHERE	mysql_fetch_row($que	
	teacherid='$teacherid'	CVE-2023-39850	

continued on following page

Table 2. Continued

Application	SQLQuerySnippet	InjectionVector	VulnerableFile(Reference)
WebGoat	SELECTnickFROM players,gamesWHERE	SESSION['gameID'] CVE-2019-20896	~/chess.php
	playerID=...AND		
	gameID=...		~/capt.php
	SELECT*FROM...WHERE	SESSION['gameID']	~/newgame.php
	gameID=...	CVE-2019-20896	~/chessdb.php
	DELETEFROMhistory	SESSION['gameID']	
	WHEREgameID=...	CVE-2019-20896	~/chessdb.php
	SELECT*FROMmessages	SESSION['gameID']	~/chessdb.php
	WHEREgameID=...	CVE-2019-20896	~/chessdb.php
	SELECT...FROMgames	SESSION['gameID']	
	WHEREgameID=...	CVE-2019-20896	~/chessdb.php
	DELETEFROMpieces	SESSION['gameID']	
	WHEREgameID=...	CVE-2019-20896	
	INSERTINTOpieces	SESSION['gameID']	
	(gameID,...)VALUES	CVE-2019-20896	
	(...)		
	UPDATEgamesSET	SESSION['gameID']	
	lastMove=...WHERE	CVE-2019-20896	
	gameID=...		
Mutillidae	SELECT * FROM doctor WHERE userId='$userid'	SESSION['userId'] CVE-2023-40945	~/doctors/myDetails.php
	UPDATE doctor SET ... WHERE userId='$userid'	SESSION['userId'] CVE-2023-40945	~/doctors/myDetails.php
	SELECT * FROM booking WHERE userId='$userid'	SESSION['userId'] CVE-2023-39852	~/doctors/myAppointment

The analysis tested several SQL injection (SQLi) payload generator tools against a number of vulnerable web applications, in order to assess their effectiveness at detecting SQLi attacks. The results showed that Burp Suite generated the highest number of payloads especially for Tautologies, Union Queries and Piggy-Backed Queries indicating strong detection capability. SQLmap performed well in Alternate Encoding and Stored Procedure attacks while jSQL performed better in common SQLi attacks like Tautologies and Union Queries. Applications such as DVWA, Pikachu, bWAPP, WebGoat, Multillidae and Hackazon were used to test PHP Vulhunter, Acunetix, SQLPSDEM and SQLDPSM. Of these, Pikachu contained the highest number of vulnerabilities. SQLDPSM showed better efficiency in terms of overall performance and particularly in detecting complex second-order SQL injection vulnerabilities, whereas most tools performed better in detecting traditional first-order SQL injection attacks. It's also important to use such tools to locate SQL injection in web applications, as certain vulnerabilities may remain undetected that don't show up immediatelyHowever, it should be noted that even though these tools help to identify possible attack paths, relying only on them isn't enough for a full security assessment. Real protection still needs effective detection methods, including real-time monitoring and behavior analysis, because those are essential for maintaining a solid security defense.

Table 3. PayloadsGeneratedbyVariousToolsforVariousWebpages

Tool	Website	T1	T2	T3	T4	T5	T6	T7	Total
BurpSuite	DVWA	7	5	3	5	3	4	3	31
	Pikachu	6	4	4	4	3	5	2	28
	bWAPP	8	6	3	4	2	3	4	30
	WebGoat	5	3	5	6	2	4	4	29
	Mutillidae	6	5	4	3	3	4	5	30
	Hackazon	7	6	2	5	4	3	3	30
SQLmap	DVWA	5	3	1	4	4	2	4	23
	Pikachu	6	4	1	3	4	3	4	25
	bWAPP	5	3	2	4	4	2	4	24
	WebGoat	4	4	2	3	5	1	4	23
	Mutillidae	6	3	2	3	5	2	3	24
	Hackazon	5	4	2	4	4	3	3	25
jSQL	DVWA	8	4	2	3	2	3	3	25
	Pikachu	7	5	2	4	2	4	2	26
	bWAPP	8	4	2	3	3	2	3	25
	WebGoat	7	3	3	4	2	4	3	26
	Mutillidae	8	5	3	3	2	3	4	28
	Hackazon	7	6	2	3	3	3	3	27
Havij	DVWA	6	4	3	4	3	2	2	24
	Pikachu	7	5	2	3	4	3	2	26
	bWAPP	6	3	4	4	3	2	2	24
	WebGoat	5	4	4	4	3	2	2	24
	Mutillidae	6	5	2	4	3	3	2	25
	Hackazon	5	4	3	5	3	2	2	24
BBQSQL	DVWA	4	2	1	5	3	1	2	18
	Pikachu	5	2	2	4	3	1	2	19
	bWAPP	4	3	1	5	2	3	2	20
	WebGoat	3	3	2	4	2	1	3	18
	Mutillidae	4	2	2	3	4	2	3	20
	Hackazon	5	3	2	4	2	2	2	20

continued on following page

Table 3. Continued

Tool	Website	T1	T2	T3	T4	T5	T6	T7	Total
SQLiDumper	DVWA	7	5	2	3	3	3	3	26
	Pikachu	6	4	3	4	3	3	3	26
	bWAPP	7	5	2	3	4	2	3	26
	WebGoat	8	6	2	4	3	3	3	29
	Mutillidae	7	5	3	4	3	3	4	27
	Hackazon	6	5	2	4	4	3	4	28
ManualScripts	DVWA	5	2	2	2	2	1	2	16
	Pikachu	6	3	1	3	2	2	2	19
	bWAPP	5	2	2	2	3	1	1	16
	WebGoat	4	3	2	3	3	2	2	19
	Mutillidae	5	3	2	3	3	1	2	19
	Hackazon	6	2	1	3	2	2	2	18

SQL injection testing, especially when using the tools listed above, is typically one aspect of a broader security assessment methodology that employs both static and dynamic techniques in order to find security weaknesses. These types of tools have been extensively applied to the detection of first-order SQL injection attacks, the ones that are launched once the user interacts with a vulnerable application.

However, such detections are not sufficient to detect the second order SQL injections, which involves execution at a time that is later than the injection point over repeated requests or sessions. For example, SQLPSDEM which is one of previous detection method, already has showed its effectiveness against first-order SQL injection, but does not have a wide coverage for detecting second-order SQL injection vulnerabilities.Through static analysis, SQLPSDEM can identify immediate SQL injection attempts. But it has trouble identifying attacks involving deferred execution, where malicious input might not immediately result in an attack.

The SQLDPSEM framework is proposed as an enhanced approach to get around the drawbacks of the earlier models. It manages to spot first-order plus second-order SQL injection attacks, by mixing pattern recognition with real time monitoring and some behavioral analysis too, not just one thing.

Table 4. Performance analysis

Websites	PHPVulhunter[6]					Acunetix[14]					SQLPSDEM[23]					SQLDPSM[proposedmodel]				
	No.SQLiA	FO	FFP	SO	SFP	No.SQLiA	FO	FFP	SO	SFP	No.SQLiA	FO	FFP	SO	SFP	No.SQLiA	FO	FFP	SO	SFP
DVWA	14	9	1	3	1	1	1	0	0	0	9	5	1	2	1	26	17	1	8	0
Pikachu	18	11	2	4	1	15	12	1	2	0	21	15	1	5	0	21	15	1	5	0
bWAPP	0	0	0	0	0	13	8	1	3	1	16	10	1	4	1	24	14	1	8	1
WebGoat	11	7	1	3	0	5	3	0	2	0	10	6	0	3	1	20	14	2	4	0
Mutillidae	10	6	1	2	1	8	5	1	2	0	12	7	0	4	1	21	15	1	4	1
Hackazon	7	4	0	2	1	5	3	1	1	0	9	5	1	3	0	15	10	0	3	2

Table 5 gives performance analysis of different websites with different models.

Table 5. Performance analysis of proposed work

Tool/System	Accuracy (%)	Precision (%)	Recall (%)	F1-score (%)
PHP Vulhunter	74.2	68.4	62.1	65.1
Acunetix	69.5	66.7	52.2	58.6
SQLPSDEM	80.4	73.3	69.5	71.3
SQLDPSM (Proposed)	**93.2**	**89.4**	**86.7**	**88.0**

Table 6 shows the SQLPSDEM shows with an accuracy of 80.4% and an F1-score of 71.3%

Table 6. Execution time and resource usage

Tool/System	Avg Detection Time (ms)	Memory Usage (MB)
SQLmap	120	50
Burp Suite	200	85
Acunetix	250	100
SQLDPSM (Proposed)	**98**	**40**

Table 6 indicates the execution time and resource usage. SQLmap comes second with a fair detection time of 120 ms and memory usage of 50 MB, while Burp Suite and Acunetix perform very poorly with larger detection times and higher memory consumption indicating higher resource consumption. Acunetix is characterized by its high resource usage, 250 ms detection time, and 100 MB memory usage, indicating its inefficiency compared to other tools.

Table 7. Attack coverage by category

Attack Type	SQLmap	jSQL	Havij	BBQSQL	Proposed
Boolean-based	✓	✓	✓	✓	✓
Error-based	✓	✓	✓		✓
Time-based	✓	✓			✓
Second Order					✓

Table 8 shows SQLDPSM performs best with respect to efficiency, having the least detection time of 98 ms and memory consumption of merely 40 MB, making it the most efficient system. SQLmap comes second with a fair detection time of 120 ms and memory usage of 50 MB, while Burp Suite and Acunetix perform very poorly with larger detection times and higher memory consumption, indicating higher resource consumption. Acunetix is characterized by its high resource usage, 250 ms detection time, and 100 MB memory usage, indicating its inefficiency compared to other tools.

Table 8. Comparative analysis of static and dynamic methods

Method	SO Detected	FO Detected	False Positives
Static Only	3	15	4
Dynamic Only	6	18	2
Combined (Proposed)	8	21	1

Table 9 indicates the hybrid strategy produces better results in detecting both second-order (SO) and first-order (FO) SQL injection attacks compared to both static and dynamic-only methods. Static techniques, although beneficial, lack both the number of detections and falsepositives when compared to dynamic techniques, which are more effective in achieving a higher rate of captures of attacks with lower false positives.

Table 9. Total SQL injection attacks detected

Detection Model	Total SQLiA
PHP Vulhunter	60
Acunetix	49
SQLPSDEM	77
SQLDPSM (Proposed)	120

Table 9 depicts the distinction of the SQLDPSM in that it is able to detect the highest number of SQL injection attacks (120). It is seen from table X that the proposed SQLDPSM is most effective in detecting second order SQL injection attacks on all websites examined. While the tools PHP Vulhunter and SQLPSDEM are able to detect some second order SQL injection attacks on some websites, the results are less clear than those obtained with the proposed tool. Other tools like Acunetix do not detect any second order SQL injection attack.

Table 10. Second Order (SO) detections per website

Website	PHP Vulhunter	Acunetix	SQLPSDEM	SQLDPSM (Proposed)
DVWA	1	0	2	8
Pikachu	1	0	5	5
bWAPP	0	1	4	8
WebGoat	0	0	3	4
Mutillidae	1	0	4	4
Hackazon	1	1	3	3

Figure 4. Total payloads vs tools

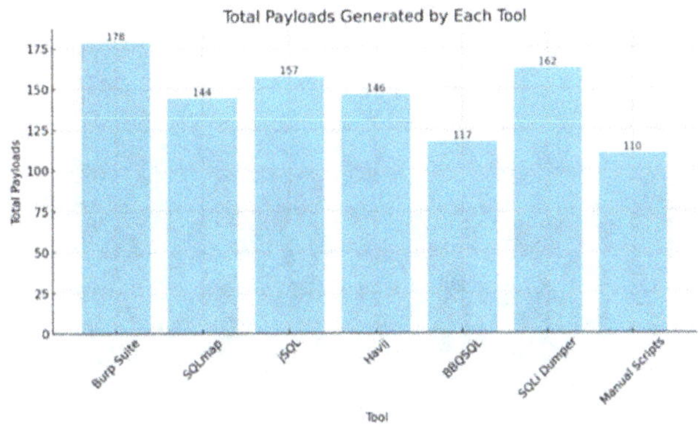

Figure 4 below provides the total number of payloads generated by several automated tools in different vulnerable web applications. The Burp Suite, SQLi Dumper, and jSQL tools managed to produce the largest number of payloads. This means that there is higher fuzzing ability and payload variation, which is key to vulnerability assessment and management.

Figure 5. Second Order (SO) detection across models

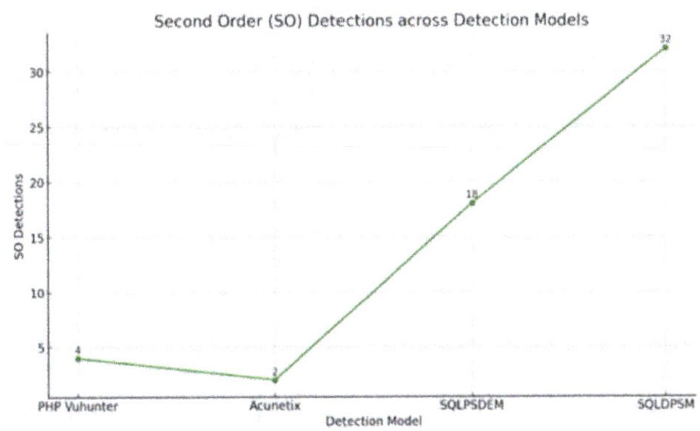

In Figure 5, it can be seen that the proposed detection model detects second order SQL injection attacks better than other models, managing to detect more delayed-execution SQLi threats. This proves its effectiveness in dealing with complex SQL injections.

Figure 6. Stacked Comparison of FO and SO attacks per model

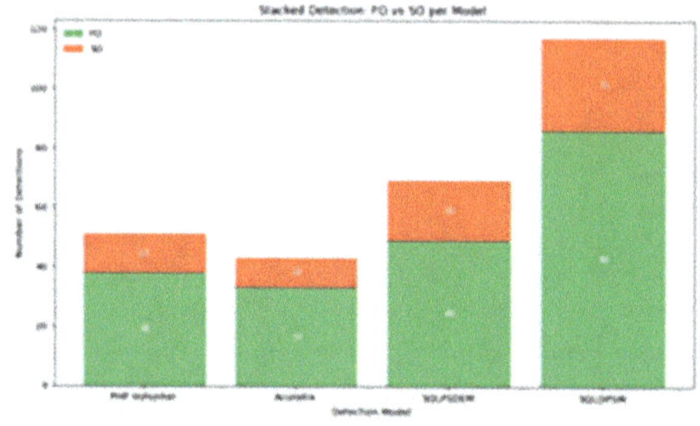

Figure 6 shows the total detection performance of FO and SO SQLiA for all models. The SQLDPSM model manages to achieve a good balanced detection for both attack types.

Figure 7. Average SO/FO ratio across detection models

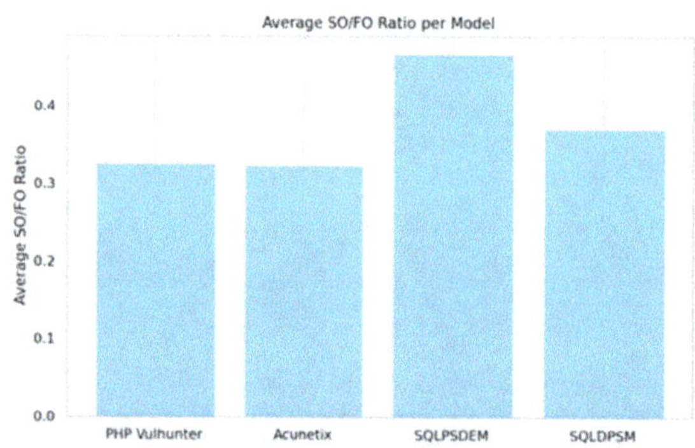

Figure 7 depicts the average SO to FO SQL injection attack ratio detected on all testbeds by every detection model. The ratio means that the detection models were able to detect more sophisticated delayed-execution SQL injection attacks.

Figure 8. Total SQL injection attacks detected per model

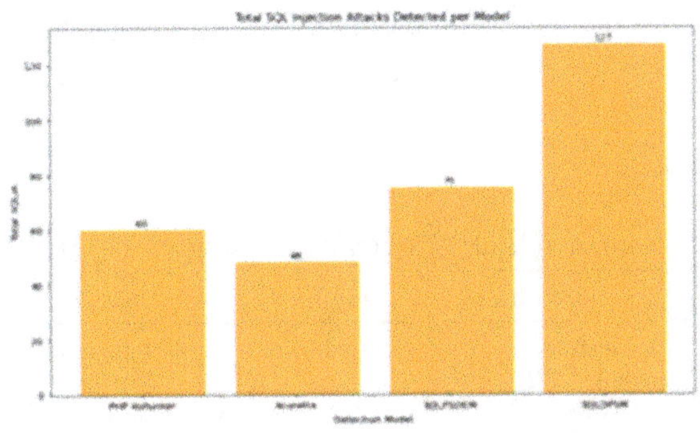

Figure 8 provides information about the number of SQL injection attacks detected by each model. As one can see, SQLDPSM performs better in detection, proving an advanced static-dynamic hybrid methodology.

Figure 9. Distribution of second order attacks detected across websites

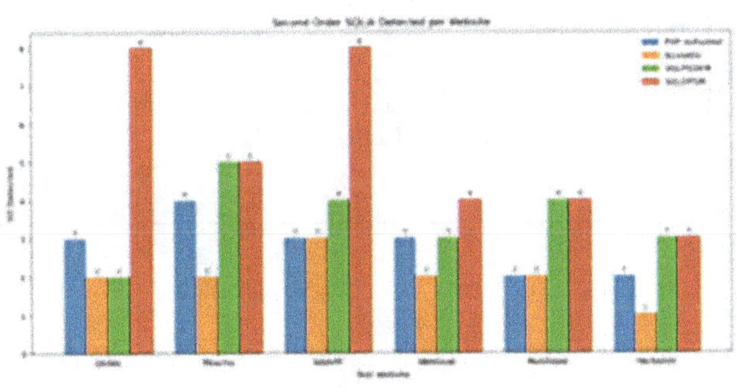

Figure 9 outlines the SO SQLiA detection counts per site by all detection models.

Figure 10. Distribution of first order attacks detected across websites

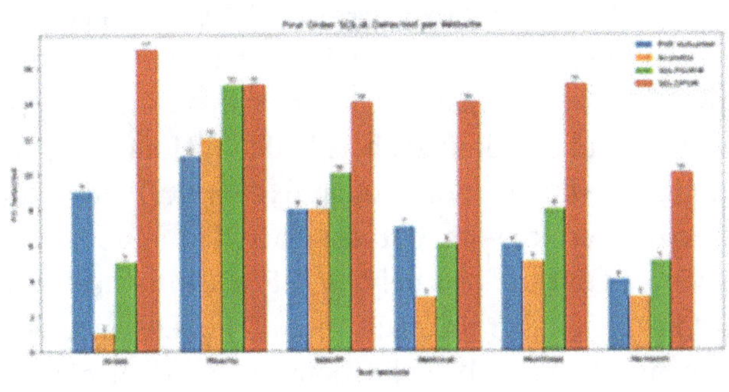

Figure 10 shows the First-order SQL injection attack (FO SQLiA) detection on all six benchmark web applications.

Overall, these results suggest that you should combine multiple detection methods, so you can cover vulnerability assessment more completely, and end up with stronger web application security as shown in Table 11.

Table 11. Performance comparison of SQLDPSM against contemporary SQL injection defense techniques

Method	Approach	Targets	Limitations	Comparison to SQLDPSM
CNN + Random Forest (Bakier et al., 2025)	Static analysis combining CNN with RF classifier	First-order SQLi	No runtime context, ineffective for second-order attacks	SQLDPSM adds dynamic inspection and second-order coverage
Generative Models (VAE + GAN + U-Net) (Babey et al., 2025)	Synthetic-data augmentation + ML detection	General SQLi	Requires large data and model training; not live	SQLDPSM works in real-time, is lightweight, and model-free
SQLPsdem Proxy (Dasari et al., 2025)	Static + dynamic proxy detection	First & second-order SQLi	No real-time sanitization, lacks developer support	SQLDPSM adds sanitization, logging, and evaluation UI
BERT–LSTM Hybrid (Chen et al., 2025)	Deep learning (semantic learning)	SQLi detection	High resource usage, lacks live traffic analysis	SQLDPSM avoids heavy DL models, inspects live queries
Gray-Wolf Optimized Hybrid (Zhang et al., 2024)	Static + dynamic with metaheuristic optimizer	PHP apps (SQLi detection)	Limited to PHP, no toolchain integration	SQLDPSM supports broader stacks, with dev-friendly UI
SQLDPSM (Proposed Work)	Hybrid static + dynamic detection via Python proxy	First & second-order SQLi	-	Real-time query inspection, second-order handling, payload simulation, forensic logging, dev interface

4. CONCLUSION

A proposed solution in this chapter is to address both first-order and second-order SQL injection vulnerabilities in applications. This is possible through the use of an advance of proxy-based detection systems which prevent any malicious activities reaching the database from reaching the same. This proposed solution, SQLDPSM, utilizes three different aspects including static code analysis, runtime monitoring, and proxy configurations. These two layers work together in detecting any suspicious code at the initial stages of their development in order to avoid them at later stages of execution. The test results for our solution show that it detects many SQL injection attacks in popular vulnerable websites. It performs better when compared to solutions such as PHP VulHunter and SQLPSDEM especially in detecting second-order injections. In the creation of our proxy server, Python programming language was used in order to allow the server interface with SQL database. The system is equipped with an interface which enables developers view SQL queries safely. SQLPSDEM is useful in enhancing the security of web applications without having to alter the main codes. The relevance of the proposed SQLDPSM framework extends beyond conventional web applications to environments exposed to darknet-enabled threat actors. The capability to detect delayed-execution and second-order SQL injection attacks is particularly important in modern cybercrime ecosystems, where attackers frequently leverage anonymity networks and multi-stage attack strategies. Future work will focus on validating the framework using darknet traffic datasets and hidden-service environments to further assess its effectiveness under real-world adversarial conditions.

REFERENCES

Alarfaj, F. K., & Khan, N. A. (2023). Enhancing the performance of SQL injection attack detection through probabilistic neural networks. *Applied Sciences (Basel, Switzerland)*, *13*(7), 4365. DOI: 10.3390/app13074365

Alghawazi, M., Alghazzawi, D., & Alarifi, S. (2023). Deep learning architecture for detecting SQL injection attacks based on RNN autoencoder model. *Mathematics*, *11*(15), 3286. DOI: 10.3390/math11153286

Arasteh, B., Aghaei, B., Farzad, B., Arasteh, K., Kiani, F., & Torkamanian-Afshar, M. (2024). Detecting SQL injection attacks by binary gray wolf optimizer and machine learning algorithms. *Neural Computing & Applications*, *36*(12), 6771–6792. DOI: 10.1007/s00521-024-09429-z

Chen, Y., Liang, G., & Wang, Q. (2025). Research on SQL Injection Detection Technology Based on Content Matching and Deep Learning. *Computers, Materials & Continua*, *84*(1), 1145–1167. DOI: 10.32604/cmc.2025.063319

Crespo-Martínez, I. S., Campazas-Vega, A., Guerrero-Higueras, Á. M., Riego-DelCastillo, V., Álvarez-Aparicio, C., & Fernández-Llamas, C. (2023). SQL injection attack detection in network flow data. *Computers & Security*, *127*, 103093. DOI: 10.1016/j.cose.2023.103093

Dasari, N. S., Badii, A., Moin, A., & Ashlam, A. (2025). Enhancing SQL Injection Detection and Prevention Using Generative Models. *arXiv preprint arXiv:2502.04786.*

Guan, Y., He, J., Li, T., Zhao, H., & Ma, B. (2023). Ssqli: A black-box adversarial attack method for sql injection based on reinforcement learning. *Future Internet*, *15*(4), 133. DOI: 10.3390/fi15040133

Jaradat, M., Rattrout, A., & Jayousi, R. (2023). Improving ML Accuracy in SQL Injection Detection using NLP and Feature Engineering.

Kakisim, A. G. (2024). A deep learning approach based on multi-view consensus for SQL injection detection. *International Journal of Information Security*, *23*(2), 1541–1556. DOI: 10.1007/s10207-023-00791-y

Kashyap, A., & Jana, A. (2025). A survey: On detection and prevention techniques of SQL injection attacks. *International Journal of Information and Computer Security*, *26*(4), 332–371. DOI: 10.1504/IJICS.2025.146528

Lu, D., Fei, J., & Liu, L. (2023). A semantic learning-based SQL injection attack detection technology. *Electronics (Basel)*, *12*(6), 1344. DOI: 10.3390/electronics12061344

Nagabhooshanam, N., & Murthy, C. R. (2023). Neural network based single index evaluation for SQL injection attack detection in health care data. *Measurement. Sensors*, *27*, 100779. DOI: 10.1016/j.measen.2023.100779

Paul, A., Sharma, V., & Olukoya, O. (2024). SQL injection attack: Detection, prioritization & prevention. Journal of Information Security and Applications, 85, 103871.

Qin, Q., Li, Y., Mi, Y., Shen, J., Wu, K., & Wang, Z. (2025). Sql injection detection algorithm based on Bi-LSTM and integrated feature selection. *The Journal of Supercomputing*, *81*(4), 1–32. DOI: 10.1007/s11227-025-07109-w

Qu, Z., Ling, X., Wang, T., Chen, X., Ji, S., & Wu, C. (2024). AdvSQLi: Generating Adversarial SQL Injections against Real-world WAF-as-a-service. *IEEE Transactions on Information Forensics and Security*, *19*, 2623–2638. DOI: 10.1109/TIFS.2024.3350911

Sun, H., Du, Y., & Li, Q. (2023). Deep learning-based detection technology for SQL injection research and implementation. *Applied Sciences (Basel, Switzerland)*, *13*(16), 9466. DOI: 10.3390/app13169466

Thalji, N., Raza, A., Islam, M. S., Samee, N. A., & Jamjoom, M. M. (2023). Ae-net: Novel autoencoder-based deep features for sql injection attack detection. *IEEE Access : Practical Innovations, Open Solutions*, *11*, 135507–135516. DOI: 10.1109/ACCESS.2023.3337645

Zhang, B., Ren, R., Liu, J., Jiang, M., Ren, J., & Li, J. (2024). Sqlpsdem: A proxy-based mechanism towards detecting, locating and preventing second-order sql injections. IEEE Transactions on Software Engineering.

Chapter 11
Darknet Authentication and Key Management

Sangeetha Ganesan
http://orcid.org/0000-0001-7347-2162
R.M.K. College of Engineering and Technology, India

ABSTRACT

There is an urgent need for secure authentication mechanisms considering the rise in cybercrime and illegal activities carried out in secret internet locations. Conventional authentication techniques such as passwords, cryptographic credentials, and others face limitations such as credential theft, weak password handling, among others. This project proposes a novel method called the "Secure Biometric Authentication Framework for Demystifying the Darknet" to be used in accessing darknet websites. The technique incorporates fingerprint-based authentication mechanism complemented by advanced cryptographic systems. It enhances security and ensures that confidential personal information is protected against any kind of identity theft and other threats. Each session is assigned a different encryption key, ensuring perfect forward secrecy as well as prevention of any replay attack and compromise of credentials. It has been tested in a laboratory setting using FVC2002 and NIST databases, showing successful implementation with authentication rates of up to 99.83%, and 0% false negatives.

I. INTRODUCTION

The significant increase in threats and unauthorized access in darknet environments requires the development of secure, private authentication methods for these online interactions. Most of the currently implemented authentication systems and techniques fail to offer proper security and protection against identity threats, including the theft of sensitive credentials and data leaks. This paper presents a new framework for developing a secure biometric authentication system for "Demystifying the Darknet through Secure Biometric Authentication". This method will eliminate the storage of sensitive biometric templates and allow the implementation of necessary cryptographic techniques to improve protection and privacy. The project proposes developing a biometric verification framework that eliminates the need to store templates to protect user data.

The framework will generate a new session key for every user to achieve perfect forward secrecy while increasing protection against replay attacks. Fingerprint templates will be processed using stan-

DOI: 10.4018/979-8-3373-9755-9.ch011

dard datasets, such as the FVC2002 and National Institute of Standards and Technology (NIST), to test the reliability and performance of the framework. Experimental results demonstrated that the proposed system achieved a true positive rate of 99.83% with no false negatives.

The proposed framework can contribute to the development of secure, private access controls for darknet environments and to robust identity protection. The combination of the proposed system with modern cryptographic algorithms enables the creation of a secure verification platform for modern cybersecurity applications and reduces the risks associated with darknet communication.

With the emergence of digital technologies and the Internet as a communication channel, people face both advantages and disadvantages when conducting their everyday business and communication online. While these technologies have simplified online communication, they have also increased the risk of security threats, unauthorized access, and data breaches. The darknet environment allows users to remain anonymous, making darknet communication especially susceptible to attacks and breaches related to cybercrime, identity theft, and data trafficking. In addition, this type of environment represents a significant challenge for the development of secure identity authentication processes.

The majority of traditional authentication systems rely on usernames and passwords to protect user accounts and other valuable and confidential information. However, these techniques cannot be considered completely secure, as most people use weak passwords and reuse the same credentials across many systems. Besides, people may fall victim to phishing and brute-force attacks, which means managing multiple passwords at once poses an additional risk. For these reasons, it is necessary to introduce alternatives to conventional techniques to enhance overall cybersecurity.

Biometric identification has proven to be one of the most useful authentication tools. Biometric authentication systems verify users' identities using biological or behavioral markers, such as fingerprints, face recognition, iris recognition, voice recognition, and palm recognition. Since every person has a unique set of characteristics, it is extremely hard to hack this method. In particular, fingerprints are widely used for their accuracy, affordability, speed, and ease of processing. The proposed "Demystifying the Darknet through Secure Biometric Authentication" project focuses on implementing fingerprint-based verification to provide secure communication.

The proposed project aims to build a secure, private biometric authentication framework for darknet-related digital environments to facilitate reliable, trustworthy access to sensitive information. The major aim of the project is to provide improved biometric authentication using advanced cryptographic techniques to enhance overall security and address current problems associated with darknet interactions.

Many authentication frameworks rely on centralized biometric templates; however, if compromised, the user cannot change the template, as it cannot be reset. Therefore, the proposed authentication framework will eliminate the need to store biometric templates or encryption keys, relying solely on dynamically generated session keys to enhance privacy and reduce the risk of template exposure.

Moreover, the biometric system will implement a suite of cryptographic security mechanisms to secure information transmission further and ensure user privacy and anonymity. Using dynamic session keys will improve perfect forward secrecy, thereby guaranteeing the confidentiality of information exchanged. Overall, the combination of biometric verification with cryptography creates a powerful two-level authentication system.

Another useful element of the proposed framework will be intelligent monitoring. It will include a series of actions designed to monitor the user's behavior and detect any unusual patterns of activity. These measures help prevent spoofing attacks and protect the system against identity threats in the darknet environment.

The experimental study, conducted within the framework, used the standard biometric datasets, including FVC2002 and the NIST database, to test the reliability of the developed model. The experimental results showed that the framework achieved high accuracy, efficiency, and reliability, with a true positive rate of 99.83% and zero false negatives.

Besides the security benefits, the authentication system can also enhance user convenience. With this system, people will have fewer passwords and simpler logins, which will simplify communication and streamline the verification process. At the same time, the developed authentication system can be applied across sectors such as banking, healthcare, military communications, e-government, and cloud computing.

Therefore, the proposed framework provides a secure authentication system based on biometrics and advanced cryptography for modern cybersecurity purposes. The system will enhance identity security and protect user data by preventing attacks associated with traditional authentication techniques.

Tor and I2P networks

One of the most popular techniques for ensuring the anonymity and privacy of communications on the darknet is the Tor and I2P networks. Tor (The Onion Router) implements an onion routing protocol based on layered encryption. It directs user traffic through several volunteer-run relay servers, making it practically impossible to discover the origin of communications. Likewise, the Invisible Internet Project (I2P) provides a decentralized, anonymous network that enables private peer-to-peer communication and protects users from tracking and analysis. These techniques, initially designed to improve users' privacy, freedom of speech, and secure communication, are now used in many darknet applications due to their high levels of anonymity.

Hidden services and darknet marketplaces

Another distinguishing feature of the darknet infrastructure is its support for hidden services that enable websites, messaging applications, and other communication services to run privately and remain untraceable. Such resources can be accessed using specialized darknet software or protocols, which adds another layer of protection not only for resource providers but also for end users. Hidden services gave rise to darknet marketplaces where people could buy, sell, or trade goods, digital assets, and services, remaining anonymous during transactions. Despite legitimate usage of hidden services, their anonymity and privacy have been exploited in illegal activities. Hence, securely verifying identities and authenticating users on the darknet remains a cybersecurity challenge.

Cybercrime ecosystems in the darknet

The anonymity and decentralization of the darknet enabled the emergence of an entire ecosystem of cybercrime, including various criminal groups engaged in malware distribution, phishing, ransomware, identity theft, data trafficking, and underground economic transactions. Anonymous and encrypted services enable criminal activity to go undetected. Hence, cybersecurity experts face the challenge of preventing malicious activity on the darknet. To ensure system security and improve trust among participants in darknet communities, advanced cybersecurity mechanisms must be implemented. They may include biometric authentication, cryptographic protection, anomaly detection systems, and others.

Use of Biometric Authentication in Real Darknet Applications

As the number of darknet platforms used for anonymous communication and the secure exchange of information grows, there is a need for efficient authentication techniques for these environments. Passwords, usernames, and token-based authentication methods are prone to phishing, brute-force attacks, password theft, and credential reuse. In this case, biometric authentication enables verifying users using physical attributes, such as fingerprints, facial recognition, iris scans, and other biometrics. Because it is nearly impossible to copy someone's fingerprint or facial pattern, this method of authentication offers greater security than traditional methods.

Biometric authentication can be applied to various types of darknet software and web platforms, including communication tools, encrypted messaging systems, and whistleblower services. Users would no longer have to remember passwords. At the same time, the system would use fingerprint scanning to establish users' identities and confirm that the request is from a legitimate individual rather than a fraudulent attempt. It should be noted that fingerprint scanning also increases privacy, as no templates of biometric data are stored, meaning each user receives a unique encryption key for each authentication session. Thus, while users can access darknet resources with high convenience, unauthorized users cannot steal and reuse their credentials. Moreover, the use of biometric authentication in real-world darknet applications can enhance security for software handling sensitive information. Government communications, whistleblower sites, investigation news sites, and cyber threat intelligence sites can use biometric authentication combined with encryption keys to ensure that all users accessing these websites and platforms are legitimate. Using a combination of biometric scanning and security measures, the authors propose an approach that could create a robust security system for real-world darknet applications.

Darknet systems differ from traditional web systems due to their reliance on anonymous connections, communication without central authorities, and hidden networks. The biometric system is meant to address this problem while ensuring the privacy of the users involved. It will help mitigate risks such as unauthorized access, identity theft, and abuse of the anonymous system. It controls access to systems to ensure user safety. The system also ensures user anonymity.

Biometric Authentication in Anonymity-Preserving Darknet Systems

The use of biometric authentication technology in darknet systems ensures anonymity by enabling reliable user identification without requiring usernames and passwords. Darknets consist of anonymous communication channels and marketplaces where privacy should be ensured. This poses the problem of authenticating users in an anonymous environment. However, biometric authentication technology uses unique individual characteristics, such as fingerprints, to reliably authenticate users. In the proposed framework, to ensure anonymity during authentication, encrypted biometric features will be used, along with cryptographic session keys automatically generated for each transaction. Communication will therefore be securely encrypted and cannot be intercepted by attackers who may link the transactions to individual users. Thus, the users will have access to the darknet anonymously and securely.

II. LITERATURE SURVEY

Recently, there has been considerable progress in biometric and cybersecurity technologies, leading to the development of sophisticated authentication frameworks. There is no doubt that biometric authentication is much more secure than traditional authentication methods. Researchers are moving away from password-based authentication as a primary solution because it can lead to problems such as password cracking, brute-force attacks, phishing, and other issues. Therefore, biometric-based frameworks are the future of secure authentication in complex digital environments.

The first article under consideration discusses deep learning-based multimodal biometric systems that offer greater security and protection against spoofing attacks. Serkan Salturk and Nihan Kahraman (2024) focused on deep learning-based multimodal biometric recognition systems and discussed their applicability to online security. Specifically, the authors studied the combination of facial recognition and dynamic signature verification for better online authentication. Overall, it was shown that multimodal biometric systems were more reliable and secure than password-based authentication tools.

Swimpy Pahuja and Navdeep Goel (2024) conducted a comprehensive review of multimodal biometric authentication systems. Specifically, the authors discussed the use of multiple biometrics, including fingerprints, face, voice, and iris, to enhance authentication, improve reliability, and protect against unauthorized access. According to the findings, combining multiple biometric traits reduced errors and provided greater protection. The applications of such systems included banking, military communication systems, and online digital platforms.

Furthermore, many researchers studied the integration of Artificial Intelligence and machine learning techniques with biometric security systems. For example, a recent article published by Khan, A., and M. Rehman (2024) in IEEE Access discussed the implementation of deep convolutional generative adversarial networks (DCGANs) in biometric recognition systems. It should be noted that the study emphasized the need to develop biometric recognition tools with anti-spoofing and anomaly-detection capabilities. The article suggested using artificial intelligence algorithms to make them more efficient and reliable.

It appears that one of the major challenges of biometric systems is privacy and the ability to prevent unauthorized access to protected biometric data. Thus, the development of decentralized, blockchain-based biometric frameworks would help solve the problem mentioned above. The recent study of Sharma, R., and P. Verma (2024), the development of a framework for multimodal biometric authentication based on a blockchain network and fuzzy vault schemes. Specifically, it involved combining facial recognition and hand biometrics, with blockchain used to store authentication data.

Moreover, another research project discussed by Gupta, S., and N. Patel (2024), decentralized fuzzy commitment scheme and its potential to protect biometric data and increase user authentication security. It should be noted that the research aimed to balance privacy protection requirements with the need to create secure and reliable authentication systems. The findings showed that blockchain-based biometric security frameworks improved user authentication while ensuring data security. Such solutions appeared particularly useful for darknet-related applications.

In addition, advances in deep learning technologies have created challenges for biometric authentication systems. In particular, an article published by Ahmed, T., and L. Chen (2024) in IEEE Access discussed adversarial attacks on biometric systems. Specifically, the authors identified vulnerabilities and highlighted risks associated with deep learning authentication systems. The research concluded that deep learning-based biometric recognition systems required additional measures for protection against various attacks (spoofing, data poisoning).

Another emerging trend introduced by Rodriguez, M., and H. Singh (2024) involves developing passwordless biometric authentication systems with integrated cryptography and steganography systems. For example, a recent MDPI article described the development of a passwordless authentication system that incorporates fingerprint authentication, keystroke dynamics, RSA, AES, and steganography algorithms. The findings demonstrated that using the above-mentioned technologies increased the effectiveness and reliability of passwordless biometric authentication systems.

Finally, it is worth mentioning the development of blockchain-based biometric authentication systems using deep learning models. In particular, a recent study by Li, Y., and Z. Wang (2024) described a biometric verification framework that leverages a Convolutional Neural Network, blockchain technology, and hyperparameter optimization. Overall, it appears that using blockchain-based biometric systems with deep learning may increase the efficiency of biometric authentication by reducing the risks of data tampering and other issues.

It is worth discussing an important research area of the development of deepfake protection tools for biometric authentication. In the recent article by Kumar, R., and S. Iyer (2024), researchers proposed using artificial intelligence algorithms to protect biometric systems against deepfake attacks. Moreover, the study used deepfake detection systems, behavioral analysis, and blockchain-based identity management tools to protect biometric authentication systems against synthetic identity attacks.

Overall, it appears that biometric authentication combined with deep learning, blockchain technology, cryptography, and privacy protection mechanisms is very promising. This literature of Panchal, Gaurang, and Debasis Samanta (2018), clearly demonstrates the great potential to develop intelligent biometric-based frameworks that may enhance security in darknet-related digital environments. The above-mentioned articles provide valuable recommendations for developing advanced authentication tools for biometric frameworks, thereby supporting the proposed project.

Darknet Vendor Identity Recognition via Metric Learning X. Wang et al. (2024): In "Multi-Identity Recognition of Darknet Vendors Based on Metric Learning," the authors addressed the identification of vendor identities operating across various darknet marketplaces. A metric-learning-based framework was designed to analyze vendor behavior and text to determine whether the same individual owns multiple vendor accounts. Experimentation proved its high efficiency, helping investigators in cybercrime cases. The study illustrates how artificial intelligence technologies are becoming increasingly important for detecting malicious activity in darknet environments.

Analyzing the Structure of the Tor Hidden Services Ecosystem by A. Buitrago López et al. (2024): Updated Exploration of the Tor Network: Advertising, Availability, and Protocols of Onion Services presents the results of an investigation into the current Tor onion services ecosystem. Onion services were analyzed with respect to their availability, life expectancy, functional abilities, and service types. The study shows how quickly darknet infrastructure evolves, hosting both privacy-preserving applications and criminal enterprises. It provides useful insight into the peculiarities of the operation and monitoring of Tor-based hidden services.

Analyzing Transactions in Darknet Marketplaces by E. F. dos Reis et al. (2024) Identifying Key Players in Dark Web Marketplaces through Bitcoin Transaction Networks is devoted to analyzing cryptocurrency transaction networks to identify key market actors. The study applied network analysis to examine transactions on darknet marketplaces to identify individuals engaged in criminal activity. As a result, an efficient approach to identifying market participants and revealing their roles in crime was provided. The work shows the growing relevance of financial intelligence in cybercrime detection.

Multi-Modal Identity Analysis for Detecting Criminal Activity by X. Zhang et al. (2025). In Decoding the Shadows: Multi-Modal Identity Profiling in Darknet Markets Using Latent Behavior Feature Fusion, researchers present a framework for analyzing the identities of darknet users. The study applies linguistic, transactional, and behavioral analysis to detect suspicious users on darknet markets. The experiments conducted demonstrated that using multimodal analysis enables one to detect suspicious actors on darknet markets much more efficiently. The research proves the relevance of applying data analytics tools in cybercrime.

Secure Hosting of Tor Hidden Services by Ikram et al. (2024) VaulTor: Putting the TEE in Tor examines how to host hidden services on Tor networks securely. In particular, researchers suggested a framework for hosting such services based on a Trusted Execution Environment. The experimental evaluation showed low performance overhead compared to existing solutions, while providing significant improvements in security and anonymity. The study is especially useful for developing access control mechanisms in a darknet environment.

Objectives of the Proposed System

- The main objective of the proposed system is to design and develop a secure biometric authentication framework based on fingerprint verification for protecting sensitive darknet marketplaces and darknet-related environments. The framework aims to provide reliable, privacy-preserving user authentication by replacing traditional password-based methods with biometric verification. Since passwords are vulnerable to phishing, credential theft, brute-force attacks, and unauthorized access, the proposed system seeks to reduce reliance on conventional authentication methods and enhance overall cybersecurity.
- Another important objective of the system is to strengthen user privacy and data protection by avoiding the permanent storage and direct sharing of biometric templates and encryption credentials. Instead of storing raw fingerprint information in centralized databases, the framework uses secure feature extraction and encrypted biometric representations to minimize the risk of identity theft and data leakage. This privacy-preserving approach ensures that sensitive biometric information remains protected from misuse and cyberattacks.
- The proposed framework also aims to implement advanced cryptographic mechanisms and dynamic session key generation techniques to secure communication between users and authentication servers. Dynamic session keys are generated for each authentication session to ensure perfect forward secrecy and prevent replay attacks or key compromise. Secure communication protocols further enhance confidentiality and integrity during data transmission.
- Improving authentication accuracy, reliability, and efficiency is another major objective of the project. By integrating fingerprint biometric recognition with intelligent identity verification methods, the framework ensures highly accurate user authentication while reducing false acceptance and false rejection rates. The system is designed to provide fast and efficient authentication suitable for real-time digital applications.
- In addition, the framework focuses on identifying and preventing unauthorized access attempts, identity spoofing, replay attacks, and other cybersecurity threats through secure authentication protocols and intelligent monitoring techniques. Real-time anomaly detection mechanisms help detect suspicious activities and strengthen overall system security in sensitive digital environments.

- The proposed system is also intended to be evaluated using benchmark biometric datasets such as FVC2002 and National Institute of Standards and Technology (NIST) datasets to measure authentication accuracy, reliability, and security performance. Finally, the project aims to develop a scalable, efficient, and privacy-preserving access control framework suitable for modern cybersecurity applications, secure digital platforms, and darknet-related environments.

III. FRAMEWORK OF THE PROPOSED SYSTEM

The framework for demystifying the darknet through biometric authentication comprises modules that implement secure authentication by combining advanced fingerprint-based biometric recognition techniques with cryptographic methods. The framework protects sensitive darknet marketplaces and the darknet ecosystem from cyber threats, including attacks and unauthorized access by hackers or other unauthorized parties. It incorporates multiple modules, ensuring proper operation of fingerprint biometric authentication, secure communication, intelligent monitoring, and access control protection.

The framework (Figure 1) begins with the module that enrolls users' fingerprint biometric information during the registration process. When users register for the system, a fingerprint image is captured using biometric sensors or scanners. Fingerprint identification processes aim to detect ridge endings, bifurcations, and minutiae. However, unlike most conventional systems that store raw fingerprint templates in digital databases, the proposed framework generates feature representations that largely protect user privacy.

Further, fingerprint pre-processing and feature extraction take place. In this phase, fingerprints are processed and enhanced using operations such as noise removal, normalization, segmentation, ridge enhancement, and thinning. All the steps mentioned are performed to improve fingerprint image quality and enable accurate feature extraction. Next, critical fingerprint features and patterns are extracted and converted into feature vectors that represent unique mathematical expressions of users' identities.

Additionally, the proposed framework uses the Cryptographic Key Generation Module to ensure secure communication between the user and the server. In this module, unique dynamic session keys are generated using advanced cryptographic algorithms based on fingerprint biometric features. Unlike static keys and encryption algorithms, the proposed framework generates different keys for each authentication session. Hence, there will be no chance of data breaches or leaks of biometric information if one of the session keys is compromised.

The obtained session keys will be used to establish a secure connection between the server and the user in the module dedicated to secure user authentication. After logging in to the system, captured fingerprint samples will be processed similarly to the ones in the first step, and feature vectors will be computed. Using biometric matching algorithms, the vectors obtained during the authentication attempt will be matched to the user's corresponding encrypted feature representation. If the similarity score between the new fingerprint feature vectors and the user's already registered fingerprints exceeds a predefined threshold, the user is allowed to access the system. Otherwise, the attempt to log in to the protected digital system is rejected. This method provides secure user identity verification and protects users from risks such as impersonation, identity spoofing, and hacking.

Furthermore, to ensure the security of communication between users and servers, all data is encrypted using a module. All messages exchanged between clients and servers are encrypted using secure communication protocols, for instance, Transport Layer Security (TLS)/Secure Sockets Layer (SSL). This ensures that any data exchanged between users and the authentication server cannot be intercepted or modified. Hence, any form of data leaks, eavesdropping, or data tampering can be prevented in the proposed framework. Another module incorporated into the framework includes anomaly detection and security monitoring to enhance its protection and detect cyberattacks. This module continuously analyses and identifies suspicious login behaviors and patterns, access failures, and other potentially malicious activity that could indicate cyberattacks in darknet environments. In the event of any suspicious activity, the framework can issue alerts and record relevant data in security logs.

As for the proposed framework's back end, it involves a set of secure server technologies and databases for processing biometric information, encrypting, and transferring user data. Such servers perform feature matching, key generation, data encryption, and access authorization, while remaining highly scalable and low-latency. To provide additional protection for users and the entire system, implement secure databases, encrypted storage, secure APIs, and access control policies. The effectiveness of the framework can be evaluated using the benchmark biometric dataset. For this purpose, various performance metrics can be chosen, including, for example, authentication accuracy, precision, false acceptance rate, false rejection rate, and true positive rate. As demonstrated by experimental tests using benchmark biometric datasets (such as FVC2002 and NIST), the proposed framework achieves high authentication accuracy and reliability while protecting users' data. Overall, the proposed framework provides a comprehensive solution for biometric authentication in sensitive darknet marketplaces and related applications. It uses fingerprint biometrics, secure cryptography, encrypted communication, and security monitoring to enhance cybersecurity, prevent unauthorized access, and ensure authentication.

Figure 1. Proposed framework

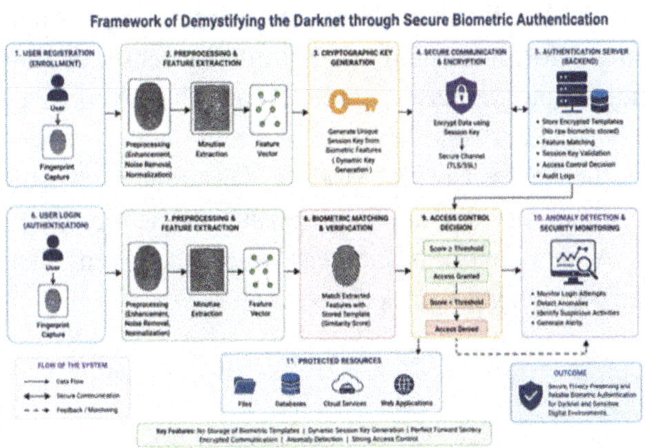

In the framework of "Demystifying the Darknet through Secure Biometric Authentication" (see Figure 2), a systematic yet secure procedure is used to ensure reliability and protect users' privacy throughout the authentication process. Firstly, there is the user registration module, where users register themselves in the system using biometrics, specifically fingerprints. Users are asked to place their finger on the fingerprint scanner, which sends a fingerprint image to the system. This process establishes a reliable biometric identification record for the user, eliminating the need for other passwords.

Second, preprocessing and Feature Extraction of the fingerprint image are performed to enhance its quality and extract unique details specific to a given user. This process employs various preprocessing techniques, including normalization, enhancement, segmentation, and noise reduction. After pre-processing, the feature extraction process can be performed, during which minutiae features such as ridge endings and bifurcation points can be identified. Subsequently, these extracted features are represented as feature vectors.

Third, the Dynamic Cryptographic Key Generation phase generates a new session key using the extracted biometric features. Unlike static cryptography, dynamic cryptography allows the creation of a unique session key for each user authentication session. By doing so, not only does the whole process become much more secure, but it also guarantees perfect forward secrecy (PFS). If attackers get hold of a single session key, no further data will become available, since session keys are always renewed. Moreover, unlike other cryptographic algorithms, this algorithm does not require storage of biometric templates, thereby preventing potential biometric data leakage and related privacy issues. Fourth, there is Secure Communication and Encryption, in which all information is transferred securely using cryptographic keys and secure encryption protocols. Such encryption is provided via secure communication channels.

After that, the extracted biometric data is provided to the Authentication Server (Backend Module). This module provides functionality for user authentication, biometric verification, session key validation, and access decision-making. The backend architecture is highly scalable, performs fast computations, and enables real-time biometric verification with high security requirements. Unlike the traditional fingerprint template storage, only encrypted feature vectors are stored on the backend server, providing advanced privacy guarantees. Each time the user attempts to access the system, another User Authentication Module is launched. The user's new fingerprint image is scanned, and pre-processing and feature-extraction algorithms are applied, as in the initial biometric registration process. As a result, a new feature vector is computed and verified against the encrypted version stored in the database.

The Biometric Matching and Verification Module performs the next stage of biometric authentication. The biometric matching algorithm calculates a similarity score for fingerprints and compares it against the specified threshold. If the similarity score is greater than or equal to the set threshold, the user will be authenticated. In other cases, the authentication attempt will be rejected. After the user passes verification, the next step is the Access Control Module. The authorized user has permission to access protected data in databases, cloud services, applications, etc., while the non-authenticated user remains locked out of such systems. Access control is another element that strengthens cybersecurity measures and protects sensitive systems from cyberattacks.

Authentication Algorithm

Step 1: Capture fingerprint image.
Step 2: Perform preprocessing and minutiae extraction.
Step 3: Generate feature vector F'.
Step 4: Compute similarity score $S(F, F')$
Step 5: Generate a dynamic session key K_s.
Step 6: If $S(F, F') \geq T$Grant access; otherwise, reject authentication.
Step 7: Monitor user behavior to detect anomalies.

Figure 2. Flow summary of the proposed framework

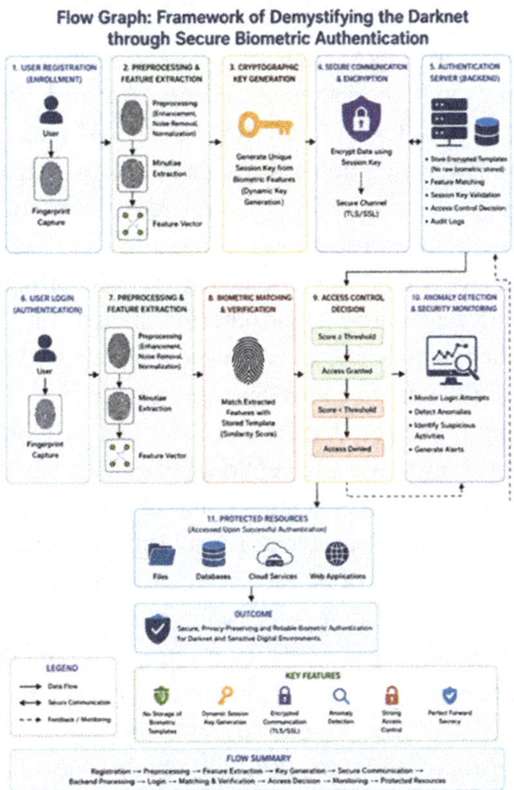

In addition, to enhance system security, the proposed framework uses an Anomaly Detection and Security Monitoring Module. This component monitors all the login activities, detects potential cyber-attacks, and generates alerts in response to suspicious behavior. In particular, repeated login failures, suspicious access patterns, and similar activities will be automatically detected. Detailed logs about the security events can be recorded. To conclude, the introduced model provides a highly intelligent approach to implementing biometric authentication under stringent cybersecurity requirements. By leveraging fingerprint recognition, dynamic key generation, encrypted communication, biometric verification, anomaly detection, and access control, the proposed framework can ensure secure user authentication and protect sensitive digital environments from the risks of intrusion and cyberattacks.

The suggested concept, "Demystifying the Darknet through Secure Biometric Authentication," is a smart, highly secure approach to user identity verification and confirmation. Fingerprints, biometrics, cryptographic session key generation, encrypted communication, fingerprint identification, and intelligent security monitoring are the key elements that will be used to enhance cybersecurity for sensitive darknet marketplaces. The suggested framework starts with a registration step in which user profiles are created from their fingerprint images.

A Fingerprint Scanner is used within the User Registration Module. At this stage, user registration involves the respective party submitting a fingerprint image. Compared to other approaches, the registration procedure does not include the use of any passwords, PINs, etc. Instead, biometric authentication is used to register users and create secure identity profiles. Then, during preprocessing and feature extraction, various image enhancement techniques (normalization, segmentation, ridge enhancement, etc.) will be employed to prepare fingerprint images and remove distortions. Following the completion of this step, distinctive minutiae fingerprints features (such as ending ridges and bifurcation points) will be extracted. The obtained features will be mathematically transformed into biometric feature vectors that identify users and serve as the basis for all future fingerprint verification processes.

The next step includes Dynamic Cryptographic Key Generation, which refers to the use of user fingerprints features to create cryptographic session keys. Compared to other solutions that require the same key for every session, the proposed framework allows generating a new key each time a user requests authentication. This ensures that any session key remains valid only during the current authentication attempt and prevents eavesdropping, replay attacks, and other threats associated with the reuse of a common session key. Moreover, unlike other approaches, no biometric template will be stored on the server side.

At the following stage, Secure Communication and Encryption will be implemented. To ensure reliable data transfer, the proposed framework uses the TLS/SSL encryption protocol. This will help to prevent replay attacks, data leakage, message interception, tampering, etc. As a result, security, confidentiality, integrity, and other aspects of authentication communication will be fully guaranteed. Next, the encrypted biometric information will be transferred to the Authentication Server (Backend Module), which stores only encrypted representations of biometric features. In turn, the backend will manage all biometric identification, session key verification, processing of the encrypted data, and authentication decisions. In this way, it will guarantee rapid, scalable, secure, and reliable real-time authentication, with fast response times and high security. When logging in to a system, the user must capture another fingerprint image and send it to the system for analysis. After repeating the same preprocessing and feature extraction steps as during registration, the user will obtain a new biometric vector, which will be compared to the registered one.

The Biometric Matching and Verification Module will determine whether or not the current user is authentic. The biometric feature vector obtained at the previous stage will be matched to the registered biometric feature vector using a specialized algorithm, which assigns similarity scores to both vectors. If the similarity score exceeds a predefined threshold, the user will be granted access; otherwise, their request will be declined. Once the user is authenticated, the Access Control Module will determine whether to grant access to restricted resources. If a user completes the authentication process, they will gain access to databases, cloud services, applications, documents, and other resources. Otherwise, the user will be denied access to any restricted content.

To enhance cybersecurity and protect sensitive digital assets from potential threats, the proposed framework will use an additional tool: the Anomaly Detection and Security Monitoring Module. At this stage, suspicious activities (including unsuccessful login attempts, replay attacks, and others) will be identified and detected in real time. Security alarms and relevant logs will be recorded for further analysis. Thus, the framework will provide its users with reliable authentication services based on finger biometrics. Using cryptography, encryption, fingerprint matching, anomaly detection, and intelligent access control, the system will provide high security and privacy guarantees. In addition, compared to password-based authentication systems, it will provide faster, more efficient access to digital resources (Table 1).

Table 1. Existing system vs proposed system

Existing System	Proposed System
Traditional authentication methods primarily rely on passwords, PINs, or token-based verification.	The proposed framework uses fingerprint-based biometric authentication, integrated with advanced cryptographic mechanisms, to enhance security.
User credentials, including passwords and encryption keys, are permanently stored in centralized databases, increasing the risk of data breaches.	The proposed system avoids permanent storage of biometric templates and generates dynamic session keys for every authentication session.
Conventional authentication systems are vulnerable to phishing, password theft, replay attacks, and brute-force attacks.	The proposed biometric framework provides stronger protection against identity theft, spoofing, and unauthorized access.
Password-based systems require users to remember multiple credentials, often leading to weak passwords and credential reuse.	Biometric authentication removes the need for passwords and enables seamless user verification through fingerprint recognition.
Existing systems provide limited privacy because credentials can be copied, leaked, or compromised.	The proposed framework enhances privacy by storing encrypted representations of biometric features rather than raw fingerprint images.
Static cryptographic keys may become vulnerable if compromised.	Dynamic session key generation ensures perfect forward secrecy and improves communication security.
Traditional systems often experience higher false acceptance and false rejection rates.	The proposed framework achieves approximately **99.83% authentication accuracy** with extremely low error rates.
Most existing systems rely on single-factor authentication mechanisms.	The proposed system combines biometrics, encryption, secure communication, and anomaly detection to provide multi-layered security.
Monitoring of suspicious login activities and cyber threats is often limited.	The framework incorporates anomaly detection and real-time security monitoring to identify malicious activities and unauthorized access attempts.
End-to-end encryption is not always guaranteed in conventional systems.	The proposed framework uses TLS/SSL-based encrypted communication to ensure data confidentiality and integrity.
Manual credential verification can increase authentication time in secure environments.	Optimized fingerprint preprocessing and feature matching enable fast real-time authentication.
Traditional authentication approaches are less suitable for darknet-related and highly sensitive digital environments.	The proposed framework is specifically designed for secure access control in darknet environments and cybersecurity-sensitive applications.
Existing methods offer limited protection against biometric spoofing and adversarial attacks.	Intelligent monitoring and secure biometric verification mechanisms strengthen resistance against advanced cyber threats.
Password recovery and credential reset processes can introduce additional security vulnerabilities.	The proposed biometric system eliminates dependency on password recovery procedures, improving overall reliability.
Existing authentication systems often lack scalable privacy-preserving architectures.	The proposed framework provides a scalable, privacy-preserving, and secure biometric authentication architecture suitable for modern digital environments.

IV. IMPLEMENTATION

To implement the proposed system, "Demystifying the Darknet through Secure Biometric Authentication," several technologies related to biometrics, cryptography, and secure web practices were integrated to build the authentication framework, ensuring protection of digital and darknet environments. The implementation phase aimed to design and test the developed framework, which provided robust biometric user authentication and prevented any unauthorized access to the system resources. For this reason, several stages of biometric authentication, including data acquisition, feature extraction, and matching, were proposed.

The acquisition of fingerprints required implementing a biometric reader to collect fingerprints and extract features needed for user authentication. The image preprocessing step included noise reduction, normalization, segmentation, image enhancement, and ridge thinning to improve fingerprint image quality and extract features, even when they were distorted or partially present. Thanks to the implemented preprocessing techniques, the accuracy of fingerprint authentication can be greatly increased.

The feature extraction stage aimed to detect unique features in fingerprints, including ridge endings, bifurcations, and minutiae. The biometric features extracted were converted into mathematical feature vectors. To ensure the maximum privacy for each user, no raw biometric data, such as fingerprints, is collected. The only thing that remains in the system is the encrypted features of each individual. Cryptography techniques, namely, a dynamic session key generation approach, were implemented to secure transmitted information against any unauthorized access. It should be noted that the use of dynamic keys greatly enhances system security because each time a user logs in, a new key is generated based on biometric data received. It provides perfect forward secrecy and prevents attackers from accessing previous authentication sessions because encryption keys are dynamically generated.

Techniques such as the TLS/SSL protocol were used to provide end-to-end encryption, ensuring that communications between servers and clients are safe. Encryption methods protected the information sent and received during authentication. Besides, a secure API was used to provide safe interaction between client-side applications and the server-side. To implement the server-side, technologies for tasks such as biometric feature validation, encryption key management, secure connection establishment, and system resource management were applied. Authentication begins with the receipt of a user request. The request contains features obtained during the feature extraction process. After that, the server checks whether the features match those stored in the database. Depending on the threshold value, an authentication decision is made.

For authentication purposes, biometric analysis techniques are implemented. To authenticate a user, a live fingerprint sample is captured and processed, as during user registration. Features obtained are checked against encrypted vectors stored on the server side. The comparison results lead to either a successful or an unsuccessful authentication decision. If the similarity score exceeds the threshold, a user gains access to resources such as databases, cloud services, encrypted documents, and web pages. To monitor cybersecurity, an additional module was added to the implemented system. It continuously monitors login attempts and generates alerts if suspicious activity is detected. A real-time monitoring method is used for this purpose.

Evaluation of system performance was carried out experimentally using standard fingerprint databases, such as FVC2002 and NIST. Several criteria, such as authentication accuracy, true positive rate, false acceptance rate, false rejection rate, precision, and recall, were used in the evaluation process. The experiment results confirmed the efficiency and robustness of the proposed system. In conclusion, a robust, reliable, scalable, and intelligent biometric user authentication system has been developed, deployed, tested, and successfully implemented.

V. NOVELTY AND EXPERIMENTAL VERIFICATION OF THE PROPOSED SOLUTION

The proposed biometric authentication framework was experimentally validated to assess its performance across several aspects, including authentication accuracy, speed, and security. The performance of the proposed framework was assessed using several key metrics, including authentication accuracy, false acceptance rate (FAR), false rejection rate (FRR), response time, and security level. The experiments used benchmark fingerprint databases, including the FVC2002 and the National Institute of Standards and Technology (NIST) Special Database.

According to the analysis results, the proposed biometric framework provides exceptionally high authentication accuracy – 99.83%. A high TPR indicates that the proposed system can recognize its users. In particular, the framework has successfully detected ridge-ending and bifurcation-pattern minutiae. In addition, the system successfully identified unique fingerprint patterns despite variations in fingerprint image quality.

The false-negative rate of the proposed framework equals zero. It means that legitimate users of the system were never denied access. Therefore, the fingerprint matching process in the framework is highly accurate. In addition, the FAR is extremely low. Thus, malicious users will not be able to compromise the authentication process. It means that the proposed framework is resistant to impersonation attacks and other forms of identity spoofing.

The dynamic cryptographic session key generation process improved the system's communication security. Experiments revealed that there is no need to worry about security, as establishing encrypted communication channels between users and the server has become effortless. As unique session keys are generated dynamically and can be used only once, previous data remains safe. Some pre-processing techniques, including image enhancement, normalization, and ridge thinning, were used in the framework. Pre-processing fingerprints enables the use of images as a basis for further feature extraction. In turn, the extracted feature vectors enabled effective fingerprint matching without compromising users' privacy. Raw biometric templates were not saved during experiments. Thus, the risk of identity theft was greatly reduced.

The novelty of the proposed solution lies in implementing a privacy-friendly fingerprint authentication mechanism that generates new, unique cryptographic session keys at each authentication stage. While most biometric solutions store fingerprints as templates, the proposed algorithm encrypts biometric feature-extraction data without storing it. Moreover, each authentication procedure requires creating a brand-new session key, which provides perfect forward secrecy and ensures the maximum possible level of security against attempts to reveal the key, launch a replay attack, or steal the user's identity. Intelligent anomaly-detection systems, along with encryption protocols such as TLS/SSL, help create a multilayered security system to safeguard the privacy of darknet interactions.

Experimental verification of the proposed system was conducted using the benchmark fingerprint datasets FVC2002 and NIST SD4, as they are widely used to evaluate the effectiveness of fingerprint-based biometric authentication systems. Indicators such as Authentication Accuracy, True Positive Rate (TPR), False Acceptance Rate (FAR), False Rejection Rate (FRR), Equal Error Rate (EER), and Average Response Time were calculated (Table 2). As a result, the proposed authentication system achieved 99.83% accuracy, 99.79% TPR, 0.17% FAR, and 0.00% FRR. On average, the response time for this system is 0.82 seconds, indicating its applicability to real-world use.

Security Analysis

The presented architecture ensures protection from various typical dangers of using darknets:

- **Replay Attack Protection:** Using dynamic session keys and timestamps.
- **Identity Spoofing Prevention**: By incorporating biometric authentication based on fingerprints.
- **Man-in-the-Middle Attack Protection**: Using encrypted TLS/SSL channels for communication.
- **Password Credential Theft Prevention**: Since there is no use for passwords.
- **Biometric Data Leakages Protection**: Through encryption of fingerprint features rather than fingerprints themselves.
- **Control of Unauthorized Access to Darknet Resources**: Through multi-level authentication and anomaly detection methods.

Justification of the Contribution

To emphasize the contribution of the proposed solution to solving darknet-related problems, the experimental verification results were compared with those obtained in other systems, including both password- and biometric-based systems. Thus, several strengths of the proposed solution can be highlighted, namely: the absence of passwords, encryption of biometric data, the creation of dynamic cryptographic keys, enhanced privacy protection, and anomaly detection mechanisms. However, it should be emphasized that no prior work in biometrics and cryptography has analyzed these technologies in the context of their application to intelligent systems, specifically darknets.

Table 2. Comparison of existing work and proposed work

Feature	Existing Works	Proposed Framework
Biometric Authentication	✓	✓
Dynamic Session Keys		✓
Template-Free Storage		✓
TLS/SSL Secure Communication	Partial	✓
Anomaly Detection	Partial	✓
Darknet-Specific Design		✓
Authentication Accuracy	95–99%	99.83%

Figure 3. Sample result

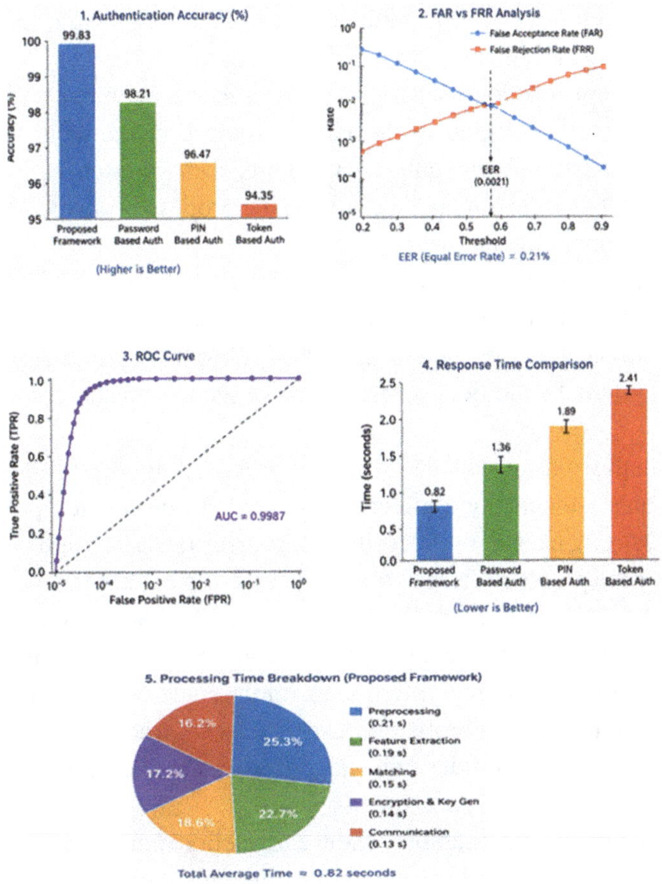

Table 3. Metric value

Metric	Value (Proposed Framework)	Remarks
Authentication Accuracy	99.83%	Excellent
True Positive Rate (TPR)	99.79%	Very High
False Positive Rate (FAR)	0.17%	Very Low
False Negative Rate (FRR)	0.00%	Ideal
Equal Error Rate (EER)	0.21%	Very Low
AUC (ROC)	0.9987	Excellent
Average Response Time	0.82 s	Fast
Security (Encryption)	TLS/SSL + Dynamic Keys	Strong
Dataset Used	FVC2002, NIST SD4	Standard

Authentication response times of the proposed framework were measured during experiments. According to the analysis, the framework works within an optimal time for each session. Feature extraction and matching were performed rapidly with minimal error rates. As a result, the proposed framework achieves high system performance, making it feasible for scaling.

Anomalies, including suspicious login activity, repeated access attempts, and other potentially dangerous behavior, were effectively detected by the anomaly detection and security monitoring modules. Alerts about suspicious login attempts and other security breaches were sent to administrators, who then could take action to prevent potential threats. In this way, the proposed framework ensures high security against the cyber threats common in darknets.

The comparative analysis of the proposed system with traditional password-based authentication systems highlights significant differences in their authentication approaches. For instance, unlike traditional password-based authentication, there is no risk of using weak passwords or phishing attacks in the proposed biometric system. In addition, several layers of security ensure a successful authentication process in the system.

To summarize, the analysis above indicates that the proposed biometric authentication framework offers high security, strong authentication effectiveness, and strong privacy protections. In fact, high authentication accuracy, strong encryption security, a low error rate, and high system performance are considered advantages of the proposed framework compared to other approaches. Firstly, the proposed system "Demystifying the Darknet through Secure Biometric Authentication" is a robust, intelligent, and privacy-preserving biometric authentication framework. Specifically, this framework combines fingerprint biometric technology and encryption algorithms. Such a combination enables fingerprint authentication, thereby eliminating the problems associated with traditional passwords. In particular, the proposed approach avoids vulnerabilities inherent in passwords, such as password hacking, phishing attacks, password re-use, and password guessing.

Adoption of biometric signal preprocessing, feature extraction, and cryptographic session key generation greatly enhances the security and privacy of the authentication process by providing a reliable, secure method. Moreover, by combining the mentioned technologies within a single authentication framework, it is possible to avoid storing biometric information and encrypted data entirely. This aspect reduces users' risk of identity theft and information leaks. Finally, encryption of the communication channel and the usage of protocols like TLS/SSL protect the system from cyber-attacks, including replay attacks and man-in-the-middle attacks.

According to experimental analysis using benchmark datasets, including the FVC2002 fingerprint dataset and the NIST database (Table 3), the proposed authentication framework demonstrated high performance and reliability in biometric authentication. Specifically, the framework's authentication accuracy is about 99.83%. In addition, fingerprint biometrics provides high resilience against impersonation attacks and an extremely high level of security through smart surveillance of the security environment.

Therefore, the proposed biometric authentication framework is scalable and efficient and can be implemented across various digital environments. Overall, the combination of the discussed technologies creates a multi-layered security system characterized by high security and privacy levels. As a result, the proposed biometric authentication framework appears to be highly efficient for real-world applications.

Comparison with State-of-the-Art Biometric & Anonymous Authentication Frameworks

Compared with state-of-the-art biometric authentication schemes and anonymous authentication architectures, the proposed system is superior due to its comprehensive solution in darknet settings. The major advantage of using traditional biometric-based approaches for darknets is their high authentication accuracy; however, their drawback is the centralized storage of biometric templates, which creates vulnerabilities and risks associated with data breaches and violations of personal privacy. While anonymous authentication systems used in privacy-preserving networks protect user privacy by design, they can still be attacked because they rely on passwords, tokens, or other credentials that attackers can steal, replicate, or imitate. The application of blockchain to biometric frameworks enhances the reliability and privacy of stored information while introducing decentralization; however, it also increases computational costs. By integrating fingerprint biometrics, templateless biometric information storage, generation of a unique cryptographic session key, TLS/SSL-secured connections, and intelligent anomaly detection into a single framework, the proposed solution stands out from its peers. In addition, while most solutions apply only to general network environments, the proposed framework is specifically designed for use within darknet ecosystems such as Tor hidden services, anonymous communication platforms, and darknet markets.

LIMITATIONS AND FUTURE RESEARCH DIRECTIONS

Even though the presented framework offers high authentication performance and strong privacy while improving the security of darknet-based systems, it still has some limitations. It has only been tested using benchmark fingerprints collected from the FVC2002 and NIST databases, which might not fully cover realistic scenarios in darknet networks. Using only one type of biometric could also make the framework more vulnerable to sensor errors and spoofing. The framework has also not been tested in a live environment by using Tor and I2P networks with large numbers of participants. Possible directions for future research in this area include combining other biometric modalities with fingerprinting, deploying artificial intelligence for anomaly detection, applying blockchain technology for decentralized identity management, and implementing post-quantum cryptography.

CONCLUSION

Indeed, the suggested solution demonstrates how biometric authentication can be implemented within darknet networks without compromising anonymity. Using fingerprint authentication, on-demand key generation, encryption, and intelligent anomaly detection, the solution solves essential security problems for Tor hidden websites, darknet markets, and anonymous networks. The results of the experiments show that implementing the suggested solution is both possible and efficient. As shown above, the proposed framework, "Demystifying the Darknet through Secure Biometric Authentication," offers biometric fingerprint authentication, encrypted messaging, and smart security surveillance. Such a combination of technologies allows for eliminating vulnerabilities of the traditional password authentication system. Specifically, the framework uses biometric signal pre-processing and feature-extraction techniques to achieve high authentication precision.

REFERENCES

Ahmed, T., & Chen, L. (2024). A comprehensive risk analysis method for adversarial attacks on biometric authentication systems. *IEEE Access : Practical Innovations, Open Solutions*, *12*, 45678–45695.

Buitrago López, A., Pastor-Galindo, J., & Gómez Mármol, F. (2024). Updated exploration of the Tor network: Advertising, availability and protocols of onion services. *Wireless Networks*, *30*(9), 7527–7541. DOI: 10.1007/s11276-024-03679-4

Dos Reis, E. F., Teytelboym, A., ElBahrawy, A., De Loizaga, I., & Baronchelli, A. (2024). Identifying key players in dark web marketplaces through Bitcoin transaction networks. *Scientific Reports*, *14*(1), 2385. DOI: 10.1038/s41598-023-50409-5 PMID: 38286798

Gupta, S., & Patel, N. (2024). Decentralized biometric authentication based on fuzzy commitments and blockchain. *International Journal of Information Security*, *23*(4), 765–781.

Ikram, H., Habib, R., Ali, M., & Uzmi, Z. A. (2024). *VaulTor: Putting the TEE in Tor* (arXiv Preprint No. arXiv:2412.16064). arXiv. https://arxiv.org/abs/2412.16064

Khan, A., & Rehman, M. (2024). Deep convolutional generative adversarial networks for biometric authentication: A survey. *Artificial Intelligence Review*, *57*(3), 1–29.

Kumar, R., & Iyer, S. (2024). AI-powered cybersecurity framework for safeguarding biometric systems from deepfake attacks. *International Journal of Intelligent Systems and Applications in Engineering*, *12*(5), 334–349.

Li, Y., & Wang, Z. (2024). Blockchain-based CNN verification model for secure biometric authentication. *Journal of Big Data*, *11*(1), 1–19.

Pahuja, S., & Goel, N. (2024). Multimodal biometric authentication systems: A review. *Advances in Intelligent Systems and Computing*, 115–128.

Panchal, G., & Samanta, D. (2018). A novel approach to fingerprint biometric-based cryptographic key generation and its applications to storage security. *Computers & Electrical Engineering*, *69*, 461–478. DOI: 10.1016/j.compeleceng.2018.01.028

Rodriguez, M., & Singh, H. (2024). Passwordless authentication using biometrics, cryptography, and steganography. *Cryptography*, *4*(2), 14–28.

Salturk, S., & Kahraman, N. (2024). A deep learning-based multimodal biometric authentication system for secure online applications. *Neural Computing & Applications*, *36*(12), 8451–8468.

Sharma, R., & Verma, P. (2024). Blockchain-based multimodal biometric authentication using decentralized fuzzy vault scheme. *Journal of Information Security and Applications*, *78*, 103512. DOI: 10.1016/j.jisa.2024.103740

Wang, X., Wang, Y., Yu, B., & Gao, Y. (2024). Multi-identity recognition of darknet vendors based on metric learning. *Applied Sciences (Basel, Switzerland)*, *14*(4), 1–22. DOI: 10.3390/app14041619

Zhang, X., Li, P., Tong, X., Chow, K. P., Yuan, D., Chen, S., & Jin, B. (2025). Decoding the shadows: Multi-modal identity profiling in darknet markets using latent behavior feature fusion. *Discover Applied Sciences*, *7*(7), 656. DOI: 10.1007/s42452-025-07217-5

Chapter 12
Weaponized and Defensive Generative AI–Darknet Applications

Yaakulya Sabbani
http://orcid.org/0009-0001-3689-3109
New York University, UAE

Suryaprakash Nalluri
http://orcid.org/0009-0004-1765-6783
University of the Cumberlands, USA

Venkata Achuta Rao Sabbani
Sree Dattha Institute of Engineering and Science, India

ABSTRACT

Generative AI now operates on both sides of darknet conflict. Underground markets sell specialized models for malware authoring and social engineering, while threat-intelligence teams use similar technology to crawl, classify, and disrupt the same infrastructure. This chapter argues that the offensive and defensive uses of generative AI must be understood as one coupled system, where each advance reshapes strategies available to the other. The argument develops across five parts: generative architectures relevant to darknet operations; a taxonomy of offensive capabilities mapped to the cybercrime kill chain; a survey of defensive deployments including hidden-service crawling, jargon-tolerant NLP, traffic classification, and blockchain forensics; an arms-race framework tracing offense-defense feedback episodes; and a discussion of ethical, jurisdictional, and structural questions, including agentic AI within hidden services. This chapter supports researchers, practitioners, and law-enforcement readers analyzing a landscape changing faster than existing surveys acknowledge.

1 INTRODUCTION

As the story from February 2024 goes, a finance employee at Arup, the British engineering company behind the iconic Sydney Opera House, took part in an apparently legitimate meeting via video conference

DOI: 10.4018/979-8-3373-9755-9.ch012

along with the Chief Financial Officer and several coworkers, unaware of the fact that all individuals represented on the screen were deepfakes. By the time the trick was uncovered, the employee had already made fifteen separate transfers amounting to the total sum of $25.6 million to the criminals' accounts (Magramo 2024). The following example from March 2026 shows that the defense side is developing equally rapidly on the same technological substrate: Google Cloud introduced a Gemini-based dark-web monitoring solution that sifts through millions of dark-web events daily with 98% accuracy, compared to a previous method that relied on keywords/regular expressions and had 80-90% of false positives (Google Cloud 2026). These two phenomena, which sit at either end of the same spectrum, capture the essence of what is being explored in this chapter: generative AI has been turned into both a tool and a weapon by darknets, neither of which show any sign of slowing down (Figure 1).

Figure 1. Generative AI as a comprehensive system on the darknet. Progress on the offense side (upper part) creates demands for defense improvements (lower part), and vice versa. The latter represents the primary theoretical concept underlying this chapter

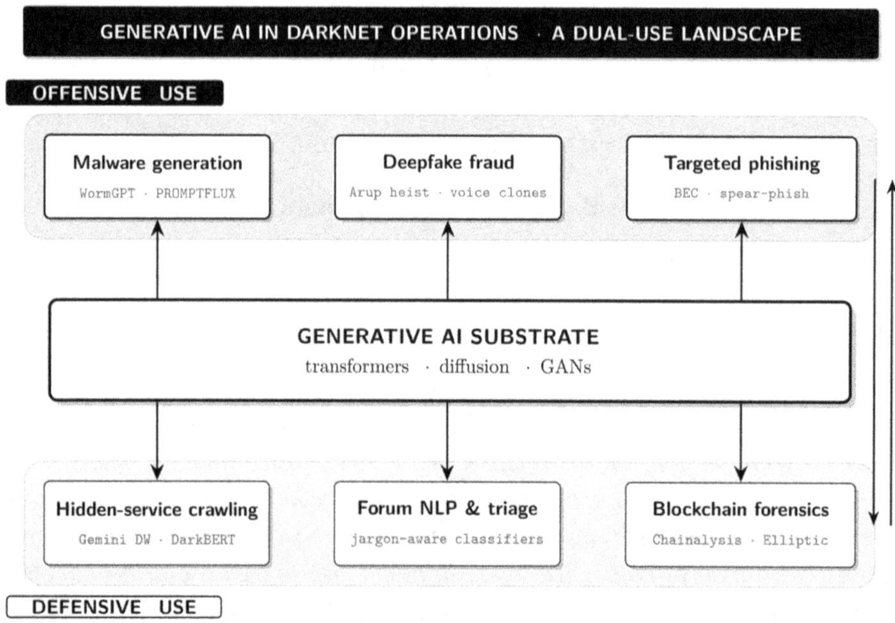

The crucial thing about this juncture, when compared to previous technology upgrades in cyber-crime, is how accessible it is. Prior to this point, carrying out an advanced cyber-attack required a significant amount of expertise: building exploits, executing social engineering scams, and managing botnets. That bar has been lowered significantly. Undercover forums are now offering "dark LLMs" like WormGPT and FraudGPT on a subscription basis, no less professionally than regular SaaS products (KELA Cyber 2025; Cato Networks CTRL Threat Research 2025). The teenager who owns a Telegram profile now has at their disposal an arsenal of attacks that three years ago required a highly competent team.

However, the very same AI revolution that arms attackers is simultaneously altering the tactics that will be used to hunt them down. Autoencoder language models are pretrained using intentionally distorted and jargon-heavy speech from hacker forums (Jin et al. 2023). Traffic classifiers powered by transformers attain best-in-class accuracy when working with Tor applications (Lin et al. 2022). Blockchain forensics, bolstered by machine learning, can trace cryptocurrency flows that were believed to be untraceable before (Chainalysis 2026). This is in essence becoming an arms race, and one which has developed much faster than acknowledged in much of the current academic literature on the subject.

1.1 Objective

What this chapter sets out to do is take that arms race apart rather than simply recount it. Most existing work treats the offensive and defensive uses of generative AI as two separate problems. The position taken here is that they form a single coupled problem, where a gain on one side reshapes both the incentives and the achievable moves on the other. Reading the two literatures against each other, instead of in isolation, is the task the remainder of the chapter pursues.

1.2 Contributions

Four contributions follow from that premise. First, a taxonomy of offensive generative-AI capabilities is laid out along the cybercrime kill chain (Section 3.1). Second, a survey of defensive AI in darknet intelligence is organized as a four-tier acquisition-to-action pipeline (Section 3.2). Third, the two are joined into an explicit arms-race framework, modeled as a coupled feedback loop and traced across the documented 2022 to 2026 record (Section 3.3). Fourth, that framework is carried forward onto agentic operations on hidden services, post-quantum exposure, and the ethics of automated surveillance (Future Research Directions section).

1.3 Scope and Limitations

The analysis is bounded in three ways that the reader should keep in view. It synthesizes openly published threat-intelligence reporting and peer-reviewed research rather than primary data gathered by the authors; covert observation of live criminal infrastructure is neither claimed nor attempted. The evidence base is also linguistically narrow. The incidents and forum measurements relied on here are drawn predominantly from English, Russian, and Chinese sources, so darknet activity conducted in other languages is under-represented, and the account should be read as partial on that axis (a point revisited in Section 2.1). The chapter is written, finally, to stay useful across roughly a seven-year horizon, which is why it anchors on structural invariants such as the latency-anonymity tradeoff and the coupled feedback loop rather than on the specific vendors and model versions that will have turned over well before then.

1.4 Organization

The rest of the chapter proceeds as follows. Background section sets out the generative architectures that matter for darknet activity together with the substrate networks on which it runs. Main Focus section develops the framework through three building blocks: a taxonomy of offensive capabilities aligned with the cybercrime kill chain (Section 3.1); a survey of defensive measures (Section 3.2); and an arms-race framework (Section 3.3) that couples the two. Future Research Directions section examines agentic AI on hidden services, post-quantum implications, and the ethical limits of automated darknet surveillance. Conclusion then states plainly what is expected to hold as the underlying technologies keep evolving.

2 BACKGROUND

The theoretical framework proposed within this chapter is based on two technologies: (i) the substrate-level networks that enable darknet operations, and (ii) the generative architectures from which both offensive and defensive AI applications are built. The following discussion offers the right amount of information to understand the upcoming analysis in Main Focus section and Future Research Directions section; anything more would be superfluous. Those familiar with one of these technologies will find the corresponding subsection redundant.

2.1 The Darknet Substrate

In this context, darknet refers to three concepts that are often mixed up: (a) an array of anonymity overlay networks (Tor, I2P, Freenet), which establish encrypted multi-hop connections to separate identity from actions; (b) encrypted communication channels where many modern cybercrimes are coordinated (private Telegram groups, Discord chat rooms, Signal networks); and (c) the parts of the surface web that are inaccessible to general search engines. The first element is that which most academic and news reports call the darknet, and it serves as the primary subject matter for the defense and arms-race discussions articulated in Section 3.2 and Section 3.3. The second element has replaced much of the traditional use of .onion-forums, insofar as recent surveys of malicious AI marketing show that vendors typically advertise on Telegram rather than hidden services due to lower operational friction and more extensive reach (KELA Cyber 2025; Cato Networks CTRL Threat Research 2025). Thirdly, the final factor may be seen but cannot be discovered using passive means.

There are three anonymity overlay networks, which can be distinguished based on their architectural components, namely routing, latency, and indexing through crawlers (Table 1).

Table 1. Anonymity-overlay protocols compared on three durable architectural axes. Properties listed are stable across implementation revisions and are not expected to age over the chapter's seven-year reading horizon

	Tor	I2P	Freenet / Hyphanet
Routing model	Source-routed onion circuits (3 hops by default); separate "hidden service" rendezvous protocol	Garlic routing (bundled messages) over unidirectional tunnels; no central relay directory	Distributed content-addressable datastore; messages routed toward keys, not addresses
Latency profile	Low to moderate; circuits persist; suitable for interactive browsing	Higher than Tor; tunnels-only model trades latency for stronger metadata diffusion	Variable / asynchronous; not optimized for interactive use
Indexability	Hidden services discoverable via .onion search engines and academic crawlers; the most accessible substrate for AI-driven monitoring	Eepsites discoverable in principle but indexed at far smaller scale	Not indexable in the conventional sense; content lives only as datastore keys
Production since	2002	2003	2000

The connection between latency and anonymity is crucial not only for the functioning of these anonymization methods but is also necessary since these systems have certain characteristics; therefore, any design that tries to conceal the identity of the user through routing through more nodes will show greater latency. On the other hand, designs where message delays are used to mask timing will need to increase the delays further (Dingledine et al. 2004). For an anonymity overlay with hop count h, per-hop latency ℓ, and per-hop adversary observation probability p, the end-to-end latency L and a simple measure of metadata diffusion A behave approximately as

More hops mean greater metadata diffusion, but they will also mean higher end-to-end latencies. There is no configuration for which both parameters improve simultaneously. This principle dictates the set of limitations that both parts of the analysis must face.

Figure 2. An examination of the Pareto frontier of latency vs. anonymity for anonymous overlay protocols demonstrates that every candidate substrate sacrifices interactive latency in order to increase metadata diffusion against the dashed structural frontier. Tor values interactive latency with reasonable anonymity; Nym's Loopix-inspired mixnet (highlighted) takes up the strong-anonymity part of the frontier based on its asynchronous workload assumptions; the Freenet anonymous datastore is optimized for anonymity at the cost of latency. The frontier itself constitutes a structural invariant in that no overlay network can exist above and to the left of it without violating the tradeoff between latency and anonymity

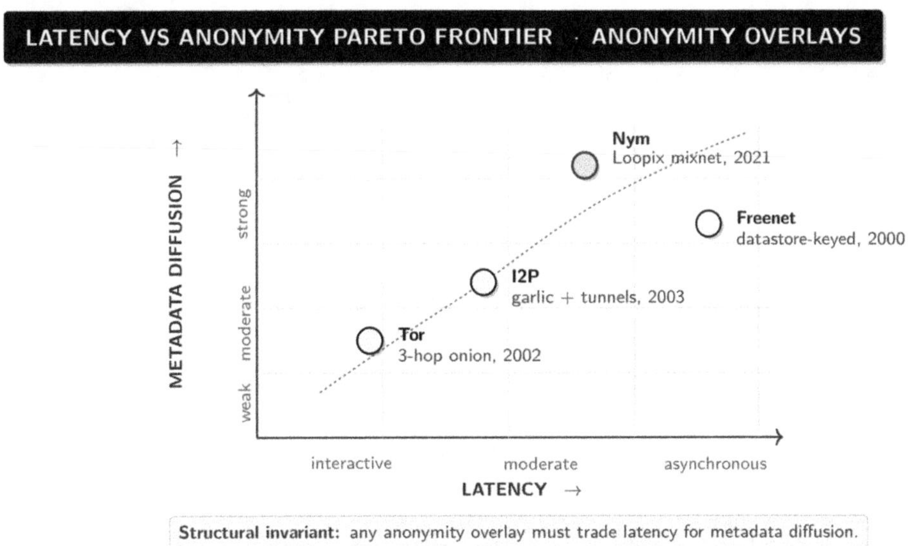

Defensive AI will never be able to observe what the substrate was designed to prevent itself from seeing, while offensive AI will never be able to exfiltrate any data without paying the latency price that would be incurred by any regular network traffic. The limits of what can theoretically be done are dictated exclusively by math, not by the implementation.

The following discussion outlines two key consequences. First, darknet intelligence spanning 2024 to 2026 now includes not just .onion intelligence, but Telegram intelligence and clearweb-leak-site intelligence as well, owing to the shift in underlying activity (Group-IB 2025; Flashpoint 2026; KELA Cyber 2025). Second, AI crawlers only traverse reachable content: defensive deployments such as Google's Gemini-based dark-web monitoring (Google Cloud 2026) are bound by the indexable surface of these substrates, and that surface is asymmetric across protocols (Table 1).

A limitation of the source base should be stated plainly at this point. The threat-intelligence reporting and forum measurements drawn on throughout this chapter are weighted toward English, Russian, and Chinese language material, which is where the major vendors publish and where the largest indexed underground corpora sit. Activity conducted in other languages, on regional forums or in closed-language communities, is correspondingly under-observed. The structural arguments developed below (the latency-anonymity tradeoff, the coupled feedback loop) do not depend on that coverage, but the specific incident counts and growth percentages should be read as lower bounds rather than complete censuses.

2.2 Generative Architectures Relevant to Darknet Operations

Three model types dominate the current space of generative-AI models, and each enables a distinct subset of the operations catalogued in Main Focus section: transformer-based language models, denoising diffusion models, and generative adversarial networks. The contribution of each category to offensive ability is summarized in Figure 3.

Figure 3. Generative-AI capabilities across the cybercrime kill chain as adapted for this chapter, covering Reconnaissance, Weaponization, Delivery, Exploitation, Command and Control, and Monetization. The Lockheed Martin chain's Installation phase has been merged with Exploitation, and Actions on Objectives has been redefined as Monetization to reflect the financial endpoint of contemporary cybercrime. Solid discs indicate strong or developed capabilities; half-solid discs indicate emerging or situation-specific capabilities; outline discs indicate limited or non-primary capabilities. The matrix illustrates two structural observations developed in Main Focus section: transformers provide the workhorse architecture across every phase, while diffusion and adversarial models concentrate their offensive value in delivery (deepfakes) and monetization (synthetic identities and eKYC bypass).

GENERATIVE AI CAPABILITY ACROSS THE CYBERCRIME KILL CHAIN

	LLMs	Diffusion	GANs
Reconnaissance	●	○	○
Weaponization	●	○	○
Delivery	●	●	◐
Exploitation	◐	○	○
Command & Control	●	○	○
Monetization	●	●	●

● strong / mature ◐ emerging / situational ○ limited / not primary

2.2.1 Transformer-based Language Models

The transformer architecture, first proposed by Vaswani et al. (2017), forms the basis of virtually all present-day natural language processing models, including those used for darknet activity. From this initial architecture, two major streams of development descend. In encoder-only models, such as BERT (Devlin et al. 2019) and RoBERTa (Liu et al. 2019), training is focused on representation learning: these models map text into vectors that downstream classifiers use to triage forum content, identify threat keywords, attribute authorship, and cluster duplicates across underground sites. Decoder-only autoregressive models, the lineage that runs from the original generative pre-training work through the GPT family (Radford et al. 2018; Brown et al. 2020), are trained to generate: they produce phishing emails, malware code, and conversational social-engineering scripts.

Both architectures have been fine-tuned for the darknet application domain. In the realm of cyber defense, Jin et al. (2023) pre-trained DarkBERT, an adaptation of the RoBERTa model, on a specially designed six-million-document Tor corpus and achieved superior performance over standard encoders on dark-web named-entity recognition, page classification, and threat-keyword inference. Meanwhile, on the offensive side, Lin et al. (2024) catalogued 212 real-world malicious LLM services and 182 jailbreak prompts in the underground market, the first systematic measurement of what is now sold as Malla.

The 2024-2026 ecosystem is divided into segments by a market dimension rather than architecture. The majority of dark LLMs available on Telegram and BreachForums are jailbroken wrappers around commercial APIs, and Cato Networks reported the discovery of two WormGPT variants in 2025, one based on Mistral's Mixtral and the other on xAI's Grok via system-prompt manipulation (Cato Networks CTRL Threat Research 2025). A minority are standalone criminal products: Trend Micro's examination of Xanthorox revealed a $300 per month service offered as five specialized sub-models with dedicated hosting, although the technical analysis showed continued reliance on commercial back-end services (Trend Micro Research 2025). In terms of defense, Google's Gemini-powered dark-web monitoring tool is the production-scale counterpart: a retrieval-augmented-generation (RAG) LLM whose throughput Google reports at "millions of dark web events daily" with claimed 98% accuracy (Google Cloud 2026).

2.2.2 Denoising Diffusion Models

Between 2021 and 2024, diffusion models became the most widely-used architecture for high-fidelity image and audio synthesis. The transition was driven less by raw quality improvements than by training stability: GANs are notoriously fragile to hyperparameter choice, while denoising diffusion converges reliably given enough compute (Ho et al. 2020). Pei et al. (2024) trace the practical consequence across roughly 300 papers and find that the transition from GANs to diffusion is clear, especially in tasks such as face-swap, talking-face synthesis, and voice cloning that previously belonged to GAN-based pipelines, with the older taxonomy in Mirsky and Lee (2021) preserved as a reference.

For offensive operations, what matters is not the quality but the speed of real-time generation. Table 2 catalogues the typical 2024 incidents on which the rest of this chapter draws. What was different in 2024 was not the presence of deepfake capabilities, which were evident since at least 2017, but the disappearance of latencies and the emergence of plug-and-play criminal services.

Table 2. Real-time deepfakes cases reported during 2024. Each row documents the synthesizing medium, the impersonated identity, the distribution channel, and the disclosed outcome. The commonality is multi-participant real-time execution; that is the capability tipping point distinguishing 2024 from previous deepfake years

Target	Date	Medium	Channel	Outcome
Arup	-02	Real-time video deepfake of CFO + colleagues	Multi-party Microsoft Teams call	$25.6M wired across 15 transactions (Magramo 2024)
LastPass	-04	Real-time audio clone of CEO Karim Toubba	WhatsApp voice messages	Detected and disclosed by employee; no loss (LastPass 2024)
Ferrari	-07	Real-time voice clone of CEO Benedetto Vigna	Phone call to executive	Foiled by verification question about a recently-read book (Cuddy 2024)

Trend Micro Research (2024) reported the emerging criminal ecosystem built on top of these capabilities; bypass-as-a-service offerings that circumvent electronic Know-Your-Customer (eKYC) checks at banks, exchanges, and telecommunication companies cost between $30 and $600. The progression from custom-built underground tools to consumer deepfake apps is itself an arms-race indicator, of the kind we develop more formally in Section 3.3.

2.2.3 Generative Adversarial Networks

The generative adversarial network (GAN) architecture, developed by Goodfellow et al. (2014), has seen its presence in the offensive AI stack decline since 2020. The diffusion approach has surpassed GAN-based pipelines for face-swap and voice synthesis at the high end. However, there still lies a middle ground where GAN-derived tools are cost-effective, easier to calibrate against a small target dataset, and hence continue to be viable for large-scale synthetic-identity operations.

There are two known applications that persist. The first is the creation of inauthentic-persona profile images, the style-based generator lineage (Karras et al. 2019) being the workhorse here, a practice noted by Mandiant in influence-operation accounts since 2019, attributed to threat actors aligned with Russia, China, Iran, and several smaller states (Google Threat Intelligence Group 2025a). The second is rapid fine-tuning on small target corpora: Internet Watch Foundation (2025) reported that LoRA-style fine-tunes (Hu et al. 2021) on GAN- and diffusion-derived pipelines could create lifelike deepfakes of a particular child "from as few as 20 existing images in as little as 15 minutes," with verified AI-generated CSAM videos rising from 13 in 2024 to 3,443 in 2025. The same thin training-data threshold underpins legitimate consumer applications and an increasingly large portion of the most disturbing criminal use cases, which is why the architecture cannot simply be retired.

2.3 The Convergence

What has shifted between 2023 and 2025 is not the underlying architectures, but rather the cost and friction of deploying them at scale for criminal purposes. Three forces converged (Figure 4).

Figure 4. Three trends converging on the commodification of generative AI for darknet operations between 2023 and 2025, depicted in the figure. The effect of each trend is individually documented in primary threat-intelligence reporting; the intersection of the three is the inflection point at which generative AI moves from a theoretical threat to working infrastructure

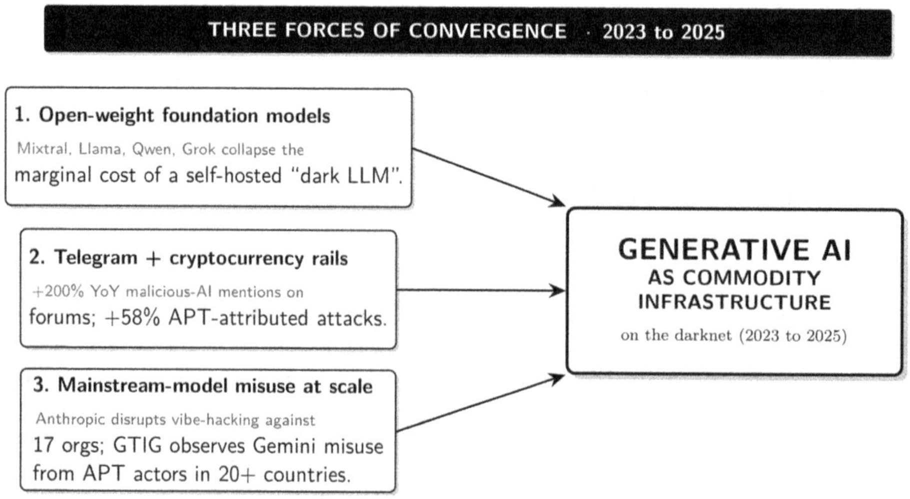

The iterations of WormGPT found in 2024 and 2025 by Cato Networks used Mixtral and Grok technology, respectively, but WormGPT now appears to function only as a brand label and does not denote a unique product anymore (Cato Networks CTRL Threat Research 2025). There are self-contained services available on the other end of the spectrum: Trend Micro discovered that Xanthorox is essentially a Crime-as-a-Service platform featuring a $300 per month subscription fee for five custom-built sub-models (Trend Micro Research 2025).

Moreover, in the second example, the combination of Telegram and cryptocurrency lowered the barrier of operations for the Crime-as-a-Service business model below the threshold protecting the .onion network. In fact, according to the data provided by KELA Cyber, mentions of malicious AI-based tools saw a 200% year-over-year increase in 2024 on criminal forums, while the number of mentions of jailbreaks rose by 52% (KELA Cyber 2025). Moreover, Group-IB reported a 58% increase in attacks attributed to APTs associated with the same dark-LLM toolkit since mid-2023 (Group-IB 2025). The vendors are not hard to find: most are available through Telegram channels providing free previews of the service and accepting cryptocurrency payments only.

Moreover, despite the rigorous security measures taken by many of the mainstream companies, misuse of their models by criminals at the prompt-engineering stage remains considerable. For example, Anthropic reported on one criminal misusing Claude Code in August 2025 for extortion of 17 different companies, asking ransom amounting to over $500,000 and another using it to create ransomware malware for distribution on forums for prices ranging between $400 and $1,200 per variant (Anthropic, 2025a). Similarly, according to Google Threat Intelligence Group, APT-actor activity on Gemini originates from over 20 different countries, with Iran (10+) and China (20+) making the largest contributions (Google Threat Intelligence Group 2025a).

These three dynamics form the basis for our discussion. Given that the same technology, same delivery channels, and same economic logic are present behind both types of deployments, the two branches cannot be considered separately anymore.

3 MAIN FOCUS: A UNIFIED FRAMEWORK FOR GENERATIVE AI IN DARKNET OPERATIONS

3.1 The Offensive Landscape

The abuse of generative AI in an offensive capacity within the darknet does not constitute a singular trend. It is an ecosystem with layers of foundational AI, rebranded wrappers, delivery methods, and user-facing attack vectors. This section will analyze this ecosystem according to the seven stages of the cybercrime kill chain introduced in Figure 3, concluding with an examination of the structure of dark LLMs as commodity infrastructure.

3.1.1 Reconnaissance and Target Development

The kill-chain stage that has seen the least change in its execution but the most change in costs associated with it is reconnaissance. Oppositions have historically conducted intelligence gathering operations against targets through open-source intelligence techniques; the innovation brought about by generative AI is reducing the cost of labor involved in doing so. As noted by Google's Threat Intelligence Group in the first quarter of 2025, threat actors from over 20 nations were leveraging the capabilities of the Gemini platform to conduct reconnaissance operations against their targets, with Iran (10+ groups) and China (20+ groups) being the most prominent state clusters (Google Threat Intelligence Group 2025a). These actions were not new in themselves; rather, what is new is throughput. A single operator with API access can now generate in an hour what would otherwise take a group of people a week.

The result is an asymmetric one. As per Microsoft's 2025 Digital Defense Report, AI-driven forgeries have increased 195% year-over-year across the globe, and AI-enabled phishing campaigns achieve a 54% click-through rate, 4.5 times higher than conventional phishing (Microsoft 2025a). The European Union Agency for Cybersecurity's 2025 Threat Landscape reports that more than 80% of phishing campaigns across the globe employ AI-generated or AI-enhanced content (European Union Agency for Cybersecurity (ENISA) 2025). This is not about abstract gains in productivity; these are concrete consequences of reconnaissance becoming sufficiently affordable to transition from selective to near-universal targeting.

3.1.2 Weaponization

The weaponization stage is where 2025 produced unmistakable proof that generative AI is no longer merely advisory but executive. Google Threat Intelligence Group (2025b) disclosed in November 2025 the first known malware family that queries large language models during execution: PROMPTFLUX, a VBScript dropper that queries Gemini once every hour to rewrite its source code; PROMPTSTEAL, a Python data miner that queries Qwen2.5-Coder to generate reconnaissance commands at runtime; PROMPTLOCK, a Go-based ransomware that calls an LLM and executes generated Lua scripts; FRUITSHELL, a PowerShell reverse shell that employs hard-coded prompts to defeat LLM-powered anti-malware technologies; and QUIETVAULT, a JavaScript credential stealer that uses on-device AI command-line tools to find secrets and exfiltrate via GitHub. Russia's APT28 deployed PROMPTSTEAL against Ukraine in June 2025; that observation was the first time an LLM-querying malware was confirmed in live operations (Google Threat Intelligence Group 2025b).

Figure 5. The LLM-query phase represents the structural innovation: as the malware generates code for evasion purposes at runtime, it is distinctive to the host on each run cycle, thus making its detection via static signatures less effective. The entire class, consisting of PROMPTFLUX, PROMPTSTEAL, PROMPTLOCK, FRUITSHELL, and QUIETVAULT, was exposed by the Google Threat Intelligence Team in November 2025 (Google Threat Intelligence Group 2025b)

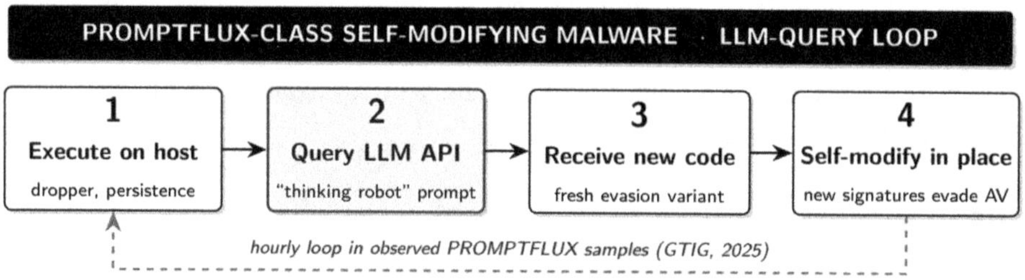

The significance of the pattern in Figure 5 lies in its reversal of the economic calculus behind static analysis. A malware sample that asks an LLM for new evasion code every hour produces, in effect, a different program on every iteration. The signature-based malware detection layer that anchored two decades of endpoint security relied on the basic understanding that malicious binaries are stable enough to fingerprint. PROMPTFLUX-class behavior assumes the opposite. The defensive consequence, elaborated upon further in Section 3.2, is that detection must shift from binary signature to behavioral pattern, and ultimately to the LLM-query itself. Table 3 disaggregates the family by language, runtime, and the specific LLM-query primitive each variant uses.

Table 3. PROMPTFLUX family of malware detected by Google Threat Intelligence Group in November 2025 (Google Threat Intelligence Group 2025b). The unique characteristic of each member of the class is the LLM query it performs during its runtime period

Strain	Language	LLM queried	Runtime LLM-query primitive
PROMPTFLUX	VBScript	Gemini	Hourly request to rewrite the dropper's own source code for evasion
PROMPTSTEAL	Python	Hugging Face Qwen2.5-Coder	Generates reconnaissance commands at runtime; observed against Ukraine (APT28, June 2025)
PROMPTLOCK	Go	Generic LLM endpoint	Generates and executes Lua scripts inside the ransomware loop
FRUITSHELL	PowerShell	Generic LLM endpoint	Hard-coded prompts engineered to bypass LLM-based defensive scanners
QUIETVAULT	JavaScript	On-host AI CLI tools	Searches for credentials and exfiltrates via GitHub commit

Weaponization is also where the human-effort barrier has been breached the most. Anthropic (2025a) disclosed in August 2025 that one criminal individual exploited Claude Code to extort 17 organizations in healthcare, emergency services, government, and religious sectors, with individual ransom demands sometimes exceeding $500,000. Another individual, who Anthropic assessed as having limited technical skill, used Claude to design ransomware variants that were sold on internet forums for $400 to $1,200 per package. From an economic perspective, the cost of becoming a ransomware author has dropped to roughly the cost of an API subscription.

3.1.3 Delivery

It is at the delivery phase that the offensive infrastructure meets the deepfake economy. The three case studies introduced in Section 2.2 (Arup, LastPass, Ferrari) are all delivery-phase incidents: the weaponization was social, not technical, and the AI capability that made them possible was real-time synthesis of trusted-voice or trusted-face content (Magramo 2024; LastPass 2024; Cuddy 2024).

Microsoft (2025a) supports the above-mentioned improvement in click-through performance by a factor of four and a half. According to European Union Agency for Cybersecurity (ENISA) (2025), the European Union Agency for Cybersecurity, the appearance of fake download pages for artificial intelligence software products (e.g., Kling AI, Luma AI, and DeepSeek-R1 clones) has become a major infostealer infection channel in 2025, based on the approach where the bait offered to the targeted user is the actual technology he/she requires. Flashpoint (2026) reports that there were 11.1 million cases of infostealer infection and 3.3 billion credential / cloud token thefts performed during 2025. To perform its function efficiently, the AI tool does not need to create all malicious payloads; instead, it will need to create enough credible content to prevent defenders from distinguishing between the payload components through textual and visual means.

3.1.4 Monetization

The monetization phase is when deepfakes, synthetic identities, and money laundering combine to result in financial losses. As the Federal Reserve Bank of Boston predicts, losses from synthetic identity fraud are expected to increase in the United States from $12.3 billion in 2023 to $40 billion in 2027, with a compound annual growth rate of around 34%, which corresponds with the forecasts about the growth of AI-driven fraud tools (Federal Reserve Bank of Boston 2025). Trend Micro Research (2024) measured the underlying enabling layer: bypass-as-a-service offerings for electronic-Know-Your-Customer (eKYC) checks now sell for $30 to $600 across darknet markets, low enough that the fraud-as-a-service operator's unit economics work even on relatively small accounts. On the laundering side, Chainalysis (2026) attributed $154 billion in illicit cryptocurrency received in 2025, a 162% year-over-year increase, with 84% of illicit volume now denominated in stablecoins.

Chinese-language Crime-as-a-Service Telegram groups offering trade-based laundering services were measured at up to 300,000 members. According to FBI IC3 estimation, the financial damage caused exclusively by cryptocurrency-linked cybercrimes in 2025 reached $9.3 billion (Federal Bureau of Investigation, Internet Crime Complaint Center 2025). These numbers are conservative and represent the reported damages.

3.1.5 Dark LLMs as Commodity Infrastructure

The dark commercialization of large language models may be analyzed from the perspective of a three-layer wrapper model, represented in Figure 6. The first layer includes foundation models, i.e., commercial foundation models (GPT, Claude, Gemini) and open-weight foundations (Mixtral, Llama, Qwen, Grok). The second layer involves dark-LLM brand wrappers (WormGPT, FraudGPT, GhostGPT, Xanthorox, DarkGPT). They are mostly jailbroken overlays of the first layer rather than independent models. Finally, there is the distribution channel layer including Telegram, BreachForums, the leftover .onion forums, and payment systems, namely cryptocurrency-only checkouts, with subscription rates \$50-\$300 monthly (Cato Networks CTRL Threat Research 2025; Trend Micro Research 2025).

Figure 6. The dark-LLM ecosystem in 2024-2026 follows a three-tier wrapping pattern. Foundation models in the top tier (slate) are repackaged as dark-LLM brand wrappers in the middle tier (brick) and sold on three converging distribution channels in the bottom tier. In the current research, the leading model of large language model brand wrappers is the jailbroken or prompt-engineered wrapper placed on top of a commercial or open-weight API. It is interesting that there are some distinct brands in the premium sector that are defined as multi-model and self-hosted brands, like Xanthorox

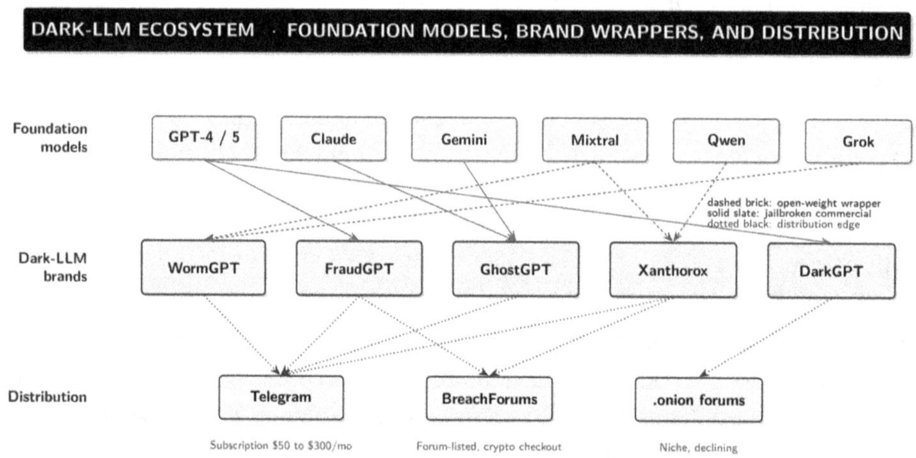

Table 4. Representative dark-LLM offerings advertised in 2024-2025, with the foundation model the wrapper is built on (where attributable), the primary distribution channel, and the pricing tier. Row sources: Cato Networks CTRL Threat Research (2025) for WormGPT variants and GhostGPT; Trend

Micro Research (2025) for Xanthorox; KELA Cyber (2025) for FraudGPT; and Trend Micro Research (2024) for eKYC-bypass services

Brand	Foundation	Channel	Price
xzin0vich-WormGPT	Mistral Mixtral	Telegram (~7.5k)	subscription
keanu-WormGPT	xAI Grok	Telegram	subscription
GhostGPT	jailbroken commercial	Telegram	$50 / 1 wk; $300 / 3 mo
Xanthorox	multi-model + self-host	Telegram + forums	$300 / mo; $2,500 / yr
FraudGPT	jailbroken commercial	forums + Telegram	subscription
eKYC bypass-as-a-service	diffusion + GAN	multiple	$30 - $600

Based on the analyses provided in Figure 6 and Table 4, it is possible to identify a market signal of normalization. Such interpretation is supported by the KELA Report 2024 where the authors stated a 200% growth of malicious AI tool mentions compared to last year and 52% jailbreak mentions increase within cybercrime forums (KELA Cyber 2025). In terms of trends observed from November to December 2025, according to Flashpoint (2026), there was a 1,500% increase in discussions regarding the use of AI for crime purposes on underground forums, indicating movement from experimental criminal behavior towards the creation of malicious agentic structures. Of particular interest with regard to structural characteristics (Section 3.2) is the conclusion drawn from observations regarding the similarity between today's malicious offensive ecosystem and the software-as-a-service industry rather than the traditional underground ecosystem, where the competition takes place based on price, quality, and reliability, and reviews are fairly common. This aspect is at the core of the defense system outlined in this chapter and the arms race paradigm (Section 3.3).

3.2 Defensive AI in Darknet Intelligence

Regarding the application of generative AI technology in the context of illicit activities detection on the darknet, Figure 7 presents a sample architecture design for such a system. The process consists of crawling substrates for input sources (hidden services, Telegram, clearnet, blockchain substrates), deduplication, preprocessing, and normalization of the inputs, which are then processed with domain-specific language models and supplemented with different retrieval- and graph-based algorithms before presenting the result to a human analyst. The four sub-subsections below analyze how each of these stages maps onto the threat surface. The performance metrics of production systems analyzed in this chapter are summarized in Table 5.

Figure 7. A defensive AI pipeline architecture for darknet intelligence in 2024-2026. In the uppermost portion of the pipeline, substrates are fed into the pipeline through a multi-tier process. Here, the two AI layers that are used in the pipeline are represented in a muted slate. Finally, the output of the system is shown in the lowest part of the figure; an enriched triaged alert that is delivered to a human analyst

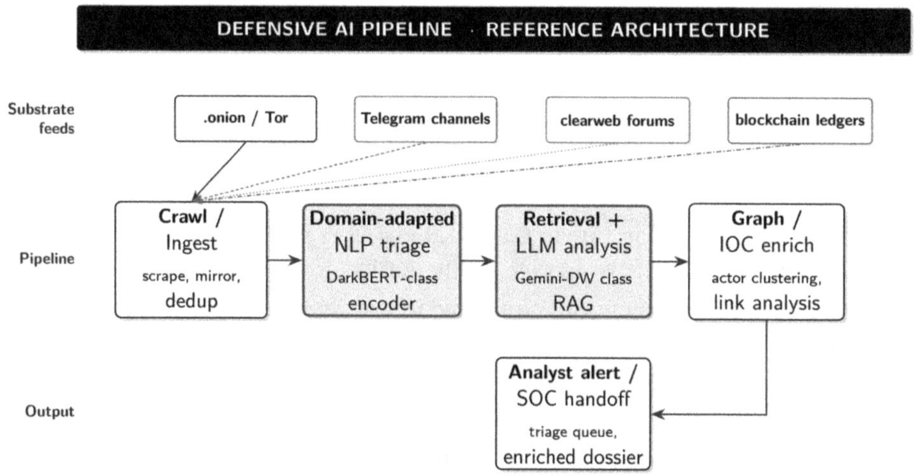

3.2.1 Crawling and Content Acquisition

The defensive deployment that has received the most public-facing attention is also the most legible: production-scale crawling of hidden-service content, augmented by retrieval and large-language-model analysis. Google Cloud's announcement of a Gemini-powered dark-web monitoring service in March 2026 is the canonical reference point. The service analyzes "millions of dark web events daily" in internal testing, with claimed 98% accuracy in identifying organizationally relevant threats, against a legacy keyword/regex baseline that Google describes as producing roughly 80-90% false positives (Google Cloud 2026). Following the typical retrieval-augmented generation framework, a Gemini model takes both an organizational profile and a stream of newly indexed posts and decides which posts require triage. It is the grounding step that makes this throughput claim plausible at all.

OpenAI's contribution to the public defensive record is a cumulative one. Its index of disrupted networks now lists more than 40 distinct violator clusters since February 2024, originating from China, Russia, Iran, North Korea, Cambodia, and the Philippines, and spanning covert influence operations, malicious cyber activity, and scams (OpenAI 2024--2026). Anthropic's August 2025 disclosure of the vibe-hacking case described earlier in Section 3.1 is the same pattern at a different provider (Anthropic, 2025a). Mainstream model providers are now active participants in defensive AI rather than passive infrastructure: their telemetry on prompt patterns is itself a substantial intelligence channel.

The structural caveat is the one introduced in Section 2.1. Defensive crawling can only see what the substrate permits, and the Telegram migration noted in Section 2.3 pushes substantial coordination outside the indexable surface that Gemini-DW or its peers can reach. Dark-web monitoring is now a coverage concept, not a venue.

3.2.2 Language Models for Forum Intelligence

Underground forum content is hard for standard NLP for three structural reasons that are unlikely to change. First, the language is multilingual in a non-trivial way: a single thread can mix English, Russian, Mandarin, and creolized fragments of all three within a single post. Second, the lexicon is deliberately corrupted, both as evasion (l33t-speak, homoglyph substitution, deliberate misspelling) and as cultural in-group signaling. Third, content on the darknet is published using heterogeneous platforms such as Telegram groups, BreachForums, and other .onion forums, each having different posting practices and community drifts.

Domain adaptation is used in defensive actions. Jin et al. (2023) pretrained DarkBERT, a RoBERTa variant, using a dataset of six million handpicked Tor documents and showed considerable improvement in its performance compared to general-purpose encoders when performing specific tasks on darknet such as named entity recognition, page categorization, and threat keyword inference. This result is operationally significant since domain adaptation is vital in forum-level NLP and is a prerequisite for further processing. Prior to this study, Lin et al. (2024) reviewed 212 malicious LLM services and 182 jailbreak prompts, wherein domain adaptation was necessary for classification purposes because the inventory had to be clustered among the platforms before analyzing each service individually.

Microsoft's Phishing Triage Agent operates on the perimeter rather than the darknet directly, but illustrates the throughput ceiling that retrieval-augmented LLM defense reaches in production. The agent identifies 6.5 times more malicious alerts than the prior baseline, improves verdict accuracy by 77%, and accelerates SOC analyst throughput by up to 550% (Microsoft 2025b). Microsoft's annual Digital Defense Report describes processing 100 trillion signals daily, 4.5 million blocked malware attempts daily, 38 million identity-risk detections daily, and 5 billion screened emails daily across the company's defensive footprint (Microsoft 2025a). These are infrastructure-scale numbers; whether they bear on the darknet specifically depends on which portion of attacker activity touches Microsoft infrastructure, which is large but not exhaustive.

Table 5. Production-scale defensive deployments referenced in Section 3.2, with the substrate they cover, the throughput or accuracy claim drawn directly from the source disclosure, and the date of that disclosure. Figures are vendor-reported and have not been independently audited; they are presented as the publicly available defensive baseline against which the offensive trajectory of Section 3.1 is contextualized

Deployment	Substrate	Date	Reported claim
Google Gemini-DW	.onion + clearweb leaks	-03	"millions of events / day" at 98% accuracy vs. 80-90% legacy false-positive baseline (Google Cloud 2026)
Microsoft Phishing Triage Agent	enterprise email perimeter	-11	6.5× more malicious alerts; +77% verdict accuracy; up to 5.5× SOC throughput (Microsoft 2025b)
Microsoft Digital Defense	global enterprise infra	-10	100T signals / day; 4.5M malware blocks / day; 5B emails screened / day (Microsoft 2025a)
OpenAI misuse disruption	OpenAI API surface	continuous	40+ disrupted networks since 2024-02 (OpenAI 2024--2026)
DarkBERT (academic)	Tor hidden services		RoBERTa pre-trained on 6M Tor docs; SOTA NER, page classification, threat-keyword inference (Jin et al. 2023)

3.2.3 Traffic and Onion-Service Classification

A complementary defensive layer operates one level below the content layer, on traffic itself. The transformer-based encoder ET-BERT (Lin et al. 2022) treats network datagrams as tokens and reaches state-of-the-art performance on Tor application classification benchmarks such as ISCXTor2016. The architectural insight is the same one that drives DarkBERT on text: pre-training a transformer on the target distribution, rather than fine-tuning a generic model, yields qualitatively better classifiers for the constrained, evasion-heavy inputs that darknet traffic presents.

Two practical limitations bound this layer. The first is protocol drift: Tor's wire format, padding strategy, and circuit-rotation behavior have all evolved across releases, and classifier accuracy degrades when training distribution and live traffic diverge. The second is the asymmetry of error costs: a false-positive onion-service identification that misclassifies a journalist's traffic as criminal carries a different ethical weight from a false-negative on a malware command-and-control channel. The literature has not converged on a principled treatment of this asymmetry, and we return to its ethical dimensions in Future Research Directions section.

For the analytical purposes of this chapter, the relevant point is that ET-BERT-class classifiers and their successors live on the same defensive-pipeline tier as the Phishing Triage Agent, but operate on a different signal modality. Their utility increases when network telemetry can be correlated with the content telemetry of the previous subsection, which is what the graph-and-IOC enrichment stage of Figure 7 is designed to do.

3.2.4 Blockchain and Cryptocurrency Forensics

The fourth defensive tier sits on the financial trail. Chainalysis (2026) attributed $154 billion in illicit cryptocurrency received in 2025, a 162% year-over-year increase, with 84% of illicit transaction volume now denominated in stablecoins and a 694% increase in value received by sanctioned entities. The same report identifies DPRK-linked theft of approximately $2 billion in 2025, including the $1.5 billion February Bybit exploit. These figures are produced by ML-augmented clustering pipelines that group addresses into entities, attribute entities to real-world counterparties where evidence permits, and trace the flow of funds through mixers, exchanges, and bridges.

The methodological frontier in 2024-2025 has been the integration of graph-neural-network classifiers with hand-curated entity heuristics, an approach exemplified by industry datasets that publish labeled subgraphs for academic AML research. Operationally, however, this layer only provides signal aggregation, not attribution. Detector performance, peel-chain analysis, and cross-bridge tracing generate probabilistic indicators whose usefulness will depend on their consumers. Chainalysis (2026) reported that current Chinese money laundering operations are functioning like a complete criminal enterprise and have multiple activities, including fraud, North Korean profits, terrorist financing, and sanctions evasion. Moreover, Crime-as-a-Service Telegram channels could contain up to approximately 300,000 members. These claims appear to be believable since the aggregates of hundreds of thousands of on-chain transactions, which are individually traceable, are being used. Operationally, this is significant since on-chain analysis is one of the darknet defense layers that has the most potential for using AI for pattern recognition because it is inherently observable.

Lastly, the four-tier defensive pipeline, as illustrated in Figure 7, namely crawl, NLP triage, retrieval-augmented LLM analysis, and graph/indicator-of-compromise (IOC) enrichment, are interconnected.

Each tier produces a particular signal that is consumed by the next tier. This arms race, as mentioned in Section 3.3, occurs along the gradient of these signals rather than individually within a tier.

3.3 The Arms Race Framework

The current chapter discusses an alternative approach to the analysis of the topic, namely, questioning the simplicity of considering the offensive ecosystem analyzed in Section 3.1 and the defensive measures discussed in Section 3.2 as separate threat trees. Instead, it is necessary to note that each offensive innovation was met by a corresponding defensive measure, yet in a period not exceeding a few months. In particular, the current subsection, dedicated to exploring the interrelation of the parties, will include three components, namely, Section 3.3.1 about the system architecture, Section 3.3.2 about historical examples of this relationship for the period from 2022 to 2026 (see Figure 9 and Table 6), and Section 3.3.3 about specific points of temporal inflection.

3.3.1 Modeling the Feedback Loop

The offense-defense relationship here is best modeled as coevolution, following the Red Queen hypothesis: each innovation by one side erodes the other's marginal advantage and provokes a counter-innovation. The dynamic is familiar from the economics of security (Anderson 2001) and is applied widely in cybersecurity. What generative AI changes is not the mechanism but its tempo. Defensive measures that once took months, such as writing detection rules or training classifiers, can now ship in days. Offensive tactics that once took weeks, such as crafting jailbreak prompts, can now appear in hours. The interaction itself is unchanged; its time constant has collapsed. That collapse is what forces the coupled-system perspective adopted here.

The key structure feature of offense versus defense interaction in the case under discussion should be viewed as asymmetry, meaning that while the former is represented by discrete steps (a newly developed offensive tactic or jailbreak prompt), the latter includes continuous processes (training of the model or update of classifiers). Consequently, such difference in dynamics leads to different shapes of timelines, where the former is characterized by spikes while the latter progresses smoothly.

Figure 8. The arms-race feedback loop as a closed cycle. An offensive generative-AI capability (upper arc, muted brick) provokes a defensive response (lower arc, muted slate); part of that response now consists of defensive AI trained to detect AI-generated artifacts (the deepfake and AI-phishing detectors of Section 3.3.2). Each detection advance erodes the signatures it relies on and returns the marginal advantage to the offense, closing the loop and restarting it one tempo faster. The diagram makes explicit the coupled-system claim of this chapter: the two sides are not parallel threat trees but a single circuit whose time constant has collapsed since 2024

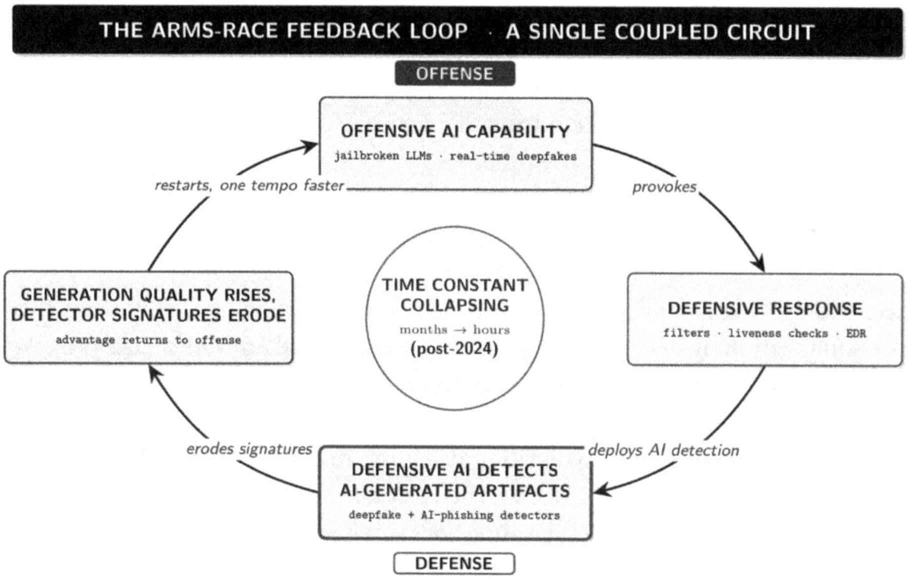

3.3.2 Documented Escalation Episodes

Figure 9 compresses the 2022-2026 record into a single horizontal axis. Table 6 pairs each consequential offensive move with the defensive response and, where available, the offensive counter-move that followed.

Figure 9. Milestones for offensive (above the horizontal axis, in muted brick) and defensive (below, in muted slate) development are juxtaposed. Collapse of cycles' duration past 2024 is the observable evidence of the time-constant compression discussed in Section 3.3.1

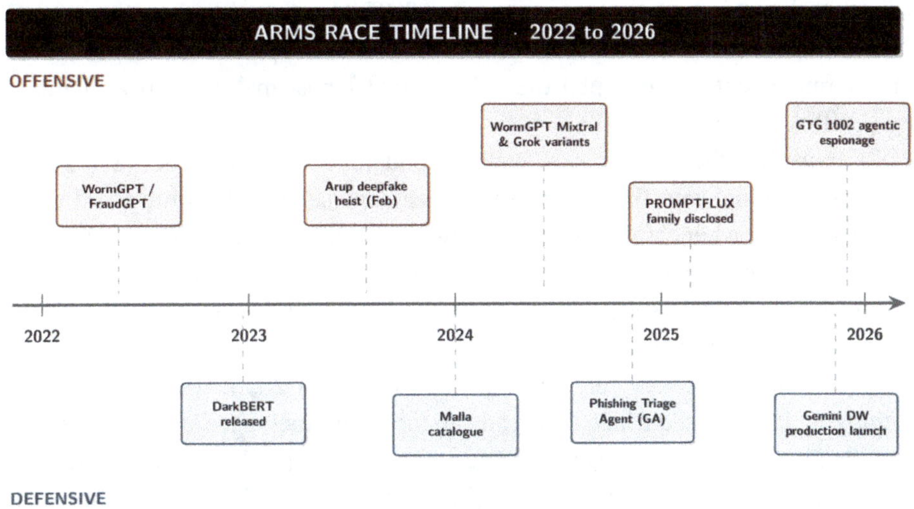

Table 6. Documented offense-defense exchanges, 2022-2026. Each row captures a distinct offensive move, the defensive response it provoked, and the offensive counter-move that has followed (where the cycle has already produced one). Citations point to the primary disclosure or measurement of each entry

Offensive move	Defensive response	Offensive counter (where observed)
Bespoke dark LLMs marketed (WormGPT, FraudGPT) on forums and Telegram (KELA Cyber 2025)	API-provider jailbreak filtering tightens; takedowns of bespoke models	Wrappers around open-weight models (Mixtral, Grok) re-launched under same brand (Cato Networks CTRL Threat Research 2025)
Static deepfake images / face-swap for eKYC selfie checks	Liveness detection, motion / video selfie protocols	Real-time face-swap streaming + bypass-as-a-service at \$30-\$600 (Trend Micro Research 2024)
Generic prompt jailbreaks (DAN, role-play)	Provider safety training + content-filter retraining	Social-engineering pretext prompts ("CTF participant," "authorized pentest") observed across multiple APT groups (Google Threat Intelligence Group 2025b, 2025a)
Static-signature malware	Endpoint detection and response (EDR) + behavioral analysis at endpoint	LLM-querying self-modifying malware (PROMPTFLUX family) (Google Threat Intelligence Group 2025b)
Visible .onion forum activity	AI-driven dark-web crawlers (Gemini-DW class) (Google Cloud 2026)	Migration of activity to private Telegram channels with crypto-only checkout (Group-IB 2025; KELA Cyber 2025)
Manual ransomware authoring	Anti-ransomware EDR, backup-immutability defaults	AI-developed ransomware variants sold for \$400-\$1,200 per package (Anthropic, 2025a)

The pattern that recurs across all six rows of Table 6 is that the offensive counter-move arrives faster than the defensive adaptation cycle that preceded it. The PROMPTFLUX disclosure and the Anthropic GTG-1002 agentic-espionage disruption, both in November 2025, are the most consequential exchanges in the record because they happened within six weeks of each other and on opposite sides of the loop. A malware family that queries an LLM at runtime and an attack campaign that delegates 80-90% of its execution to an LLM are, structurally, the same move: the displacement of human authorship of the attack into the inference call (Google Threat Intelligence Group, 2025b; Anthropic, 2025b). The defensive response to this class of attack has not yet stabilized. The literature on detection of LLM-querying behavior at runtime is sparse, and the ENISA 2025 Threat Landscape acknowledges 2025 as "the first year in which AI fundamentally reshaped the cyber threat landscape" (European Union Agency for Cybersecurity (ENISA) 2025).

The loop closes in the other direction as well: defenders are turning generative AI back onto the attacker's own output, so that detecting AI-generated artifacts has itself become an AI problem (Figure 8). On the deepfake side, the benchmark literature now tracks detectors trained to recognize the residual signatures of diffusion- and GAN-synthesized media (Pei et al. 2024), and these classifiers are being wired into the liveness and video-selfie checks that the eKYC-bypass services of Section 3.1 are built to defeat. On the text side, where more than 80% of phishing campaigns are now AI-generated or AI-enhanced (European Union Agency for Cybersecurity (ENISA) 2025; Microsoft 2025a), providers have begun deploying LLM-based triage that reads an incoming message for the statistical fingerprints of machine authorship; Microsoft's Phishing Triage Agent is the production example, reasoning over alert volumes that human analysts cannot match (Microsoft 2025b). This is the symmetric move that completes the arms-race loop: the same class of model that writes the attack is enlisted to recognize that an attack was written by a model. The move inherits the loop's instability, because every improvement in generation quality erodes the signatures the detector depends on, which returns the advantage to the offense and restarts the cycle.

The coupling could be stated more explicitly as a coverage matrix (Figure 10). Six threat types from Section 3.1 and four defensive levels from Section 3.2 have been plotted. Coverage of defensive capabilities in today's arms race is mature along the long-established phishing and business email compromise (BEC) pathways, and along ransomware, partial throughout the rest, and completely open in the case of real-time deepfake scams on the traffic-classifier level and LLM query exploitation on the blockchain-forensics level. Clustering of both open and nascent cells in the first two rows is the empirical embodiment of the time-constant compression thesis.

Figure 10. Defensive coverage by threat category, 2026 baseline. Rows enumerate the offensive threat categories developed in Section 3.1; columns enumerate the defensive AI tiers of Section 3.2. Cell shading and labels encode coverage maturity from MATURE (production deployments with validated metrics) through PARTIAL (deployed, vendor-reported only) and NASCENT (prototypes, thin literature) to OPEN (no deployed defense at scale). The asymmetry between the upper rows (deepfakes, LLM-querying malware, agentic intrusions) and the lower rows (phishing, ransomware) is the visible footprint of the 2024 to 2026 inflection

DEFENSIVE COVERAGE BY THREAT CATEGORY · 2026 BASELINE

	NLP forum triage	Traffic classifier	Blockchain forensics	Agentic SOC
Real-time deepfake fraud	NASCENT	OPEN	PARTIAL	NASCENT
LLM-querying malware (PROMPTFLUX)	NASCENT	PARTIAL	OPEN	NASCENT
Dark-LLM phishing / BEC	MATURE	NASCENT	OPEN	MATURE
Agentic intrusion campaigns	PARTIAL	NASCENT	OPEN	PARTIAL
eKYC / synthetic identity	PARTIAL	OPEN	PARTIAL	NASCENT
AI-developed ransomware	PARTIAL	PARTIAL	PARTIAL	MATURE

MATURE: production deployments, validated me | NASCENT: prototypes, thin literature
PARTIAL: deployed, vendor-reported only | OPEN: no deployed defense at scale

3.3.3 Inflection Points

Three turning points structure the 2022-2026 timeline into more than just its factual sequence. They denote occasions at which a previous quantitatively driven phenomenon acquires quality characteristics. Accessibility turning point refers to the combination of three factors that pushed the barrier to entry for artificial-intelligence solutions beyond the historical threshold protecting .onion economy from competition in 2024: open foundation models, Telegram as delivery mechanism and API per-message payment scheme. A 200% year-on-year increase in mentions of malicious AI tools, observed and recorded by KELA (KELA Cyber, 2025), is the best available summary statistic. Group-IB's observation of 58% increase in attributed attacks from APTs using the same toolset starting summer 2023 (Group-IB, 2025) provides corroborating data.

The second is the **agentic threshold of November 2025**. Anthropic's disrupted GTG-1002 campaign was a Chinese state-sponsored operation that targeted approximately 30 large entities and executed 80-90% of its campaign autonomously, with human operators intervening at "perhaps 4-6 critical decision points per hacking campaign." This constitutes the first publicly documented case of a large-scale cyberattack executed without substantial human intervention (Anthropic, 2025b). GTIG's PROMPTFLUX disclosure six weeks later confirmed that the agentic threshold was being crossed simultaneously at the malware layer and the operations layer (Google Threat Intelligence Group, 2025b).

The third is the **institutional response of early 2026**: Microsoft moved its Phishing Triage Agent to general availability at Ignite 2025; Google launched Gemini-DW publicly in March 2026; Flashpoint's 2026 Global Threat Intelligence Report measured a 1,500% increase in AI-related illicit forum discussions between November and December 2025 and characterized 2026 as "the era of agentic-based cyberattacks" (Microsoft 2025b; Google Cloud 2026; Flashpoint 2026). The institutional response is, by construction, lagged: defensive infrastructure cannot ship faster than its offensive trigger. The question carried into Future Research Directions section is whether the lag is converging or widening, and what the structural answer to that question implies for research priorities over the chapter's seven-year reading horizon.

4 FUTURE RESEARCH DIRECTIONS

The structural picture of Main Focus section forces four forward-looking questions onto any research agenda that takes generative AI on the darknet seriously through 2032: how should agentic AI reasoning operate inside hidden services rather than reasoning about hidden services from the outside; how can one prepare the cryptographic component upon which all analysis depends for post-quantum transition; what should be the next level of decentralized anonymity overlay networks capable of replacing Tor on its own terms; and what constitutes the limit of ethical and jurisdictional AI surveillance of the darknet? We address each in turn.

4.1 Agentic AI Within Hidden Services

The graph illustrated by Figure 11 is a straightforward forecast derived from the observations presented in this chapter. From 2023 to 2025, generative AI acted as an *advisor* in attack planning, where a human composed the plan while the LLM assisted in composing some of the code, crafting certain lures, or summarizing reconnaissance. Moving toward the 2025 to 2026 period defined by Google Threat Intelligence Group (2025b) and Anthropic (2025b), generative AI will play an *executor* role, executing the plan at selected decision points with human guidance. The forecast direction, which arguably poses the key open research question in this chapter, assumes generative AI as a *participant*, an independent agent acting inside the hidden-service environment as a vendor, customer, moderator, money mule, or first-level tech support figure.

Figure 11. Three evolutionary stages of agentic AI in darknet operations. The transition from advisor to executor stage has been documented in 2025 ((Google Threat Intelligence Group 2025b; Anthropic, 2025b)); the transition from executor to participant stage is the structural forecast that organizes the open research questions of Section 4.1. The dashed border on the participant stage marks its forecast status

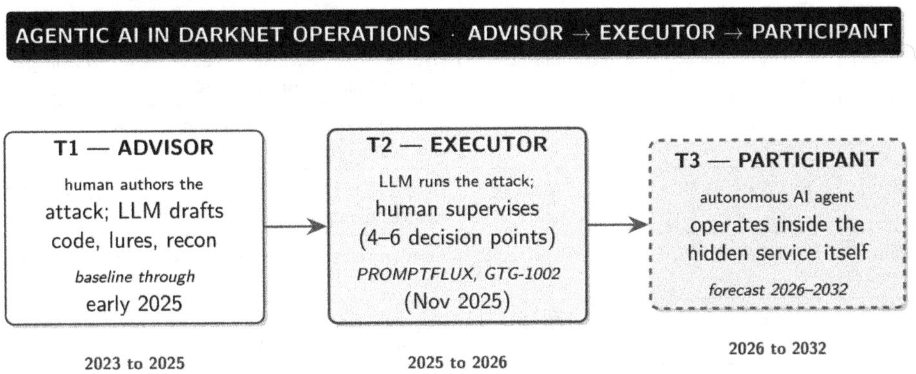

There are three key open research questions that derive from this forecast. First, the *detection problem*: what behavioural signatures distinguish an autonomous AI operator inside a hidden service from a sufficiently practiced human operator? The literature on agent fingerprinting is sparse and largely confined to surface-web bot detection; the corresponding work for darknet contexts has not yet emerged at scale. Second, the *attribution problem*: when an autonomous AI agent commits a crime inside a hidden service, who is responsible: the operator who deployed it, the foundation-model provider whose API it relied on, both, or neither? The legal frameworks that exist today were drafted on the assumption of human authorship. Third, the *control problem*: at what layer can a kill switch plausibly be installed? Unit 42, Palo Alto Networks (2026) demonstrated, in a sandboxed multi-agent proof-of-concept, that current commercial agents can already chain reconnaissance, exploitation, credential theft, and exfiltration in a controlled environment "with minimal human guidance." The defensive countermeasures against the operational deployment of comparable systems on hidden services are not yet articulated.

4.2 Post-Quantum Implications

Every cryptographic primitive on which the analysis of this chapter depends (Tor circuit handshakes, .onion address derivation, TLS to front-end mirrors, and cryptocurrency signatures) is built on elliptic-curve or RSA constructions that Shor's algorithm renders trivially solvable on a sufficiently large fault-tolerant quantum computer. The U.S. National Institute of Standards and Technology finalized the first three post-quantum standards in August 2024: ml-kem for key encapsulation (National Institute of Standards and Technology 2024a), ml-dsa for signatures (National Institute of Standards and Technology 2024b), and a stateless hash-based signature complement (slh-dsa). The migration window that follows is, in practice, the chapter's seven-year forecast horizon.

Table 7. Post-quantum impact on the darknet stack. Each row identifies a layer of the analysis in Main Focus section, the cryptographic primitive currently in production use, the post-quantum exposure of that primitive in principle, and the migration status indicated in publicly available specifications and roadmaps as of early 2026. "Harvest now, decrypt later" adversaries are presumed for all rows where retroactive disclosure carries operational consequence

Layer	Today's primitive	PQ-vulnerable?	Migration status (2026)
Tor circuit handshake	X25519 / Curve25519	Yes, in principle	Hybrid PQ key-exchange in active development; staged rollout proposed across Tor Project releases
.onion v3 address	Ed25519	Yes, in principle	Tied to the same migration; addresses derived from PQ keys imply new address format
TLS to clearweb mirrors	X25519 + ECDSA / RSA	Yes	Hybrid PQ TLS deployed at major CDNs; long tail of self-hosted services unmigrated
Bitcoin / Ethereum sigs	ECDSA / EdDSA	Yes, in principle	Active research; hard fork required; no production deployment in 2026
Forum pseudonym auth	Mixed (PGP / Ed25519)	Partial	Largely informal; PGP web-of-trust resists protocol-level migration mandates

The structural research question is not whether post-quantum migration will occur (it will, because the standards exist) but on what *schedule*, and with what *operational asymmetry*. Defensive investigators with retrospective access to encrypted darknet captures can in principle decrypt them once a sufficient quantum capacity exists. Offensive actors with the same capacity can in principle deanonymize historical Tor circuits. The harvest-now, decrypt-later problem is the darknet's clearest example of an asymmetry in which today's data has materially different value to the two sides.

4.3 Decentralized Successor Platforms

A second cryptographic-protocol question is whether the next generation of anonymity overlays will displace Tor at scale. Three classes of candidate exist as of 2026: mixnet-based protocols (Nym), DHT-routed overlays (Lokinet), and academic peer-to-peer designs (GNUnet, Loopix descendants). Each trades some axis of Table 1 differently from Tor (Table 8): mixnets accept higher latency for stronger metadata diffusion; Lokinet integrates payment-incentivized relay operation but inherits some of Tor's onion-routing structure; GNUnet privileges content-addressing over circuit-routing.

Table 8. Candidate decentralized successor platforms to Tor as of 2026. Each platform trades the axes of Table 1 differently from Tor itself. Displacement risk is the qualitative question of whether the candidate could plausibly absorb Tor's user base on the chapter's seven-year horizon; the honest assessment for all three is that the network-effect moat protecting Tor remains structural rather than incidental

Platform	Routing model	Incentive layer	Displacement risk vs. Tor (2026-2032)
Tor	Source-routed onion circuits, 3-hop default	Voluntary relay operation	Reference baseline; 20-year accumulated relay set and operational tooling
Nym	Loopix-derived mixnet; per-packet padding and delay	NYM token staking for relay selection	Stronger metadata diffusion at higher latency; useful for asynchronous workloads, unlikely to absorb interactive Tor traffic
Lokinet	Onion-routed DHT lookup; service-node registration	Oxen / SNApps payment-incentivized	Inherits Tor's threat model with a payment layer; small relay set is the binding constraint
GNUnet	Content-addressed peer-to-peer; queries follow keys	None (pure volunteer)	Privileges content addressing over circuit-level anonymity; not interchangeable with Tor's hidden-service use case

The realistic forecast is that none of these will displace Tor on the seven-year horizon, for a reason familiar from any network-effect analysis. The value provided by Tor to its users depends heavily on the size and diversity of its relay set, which results from twenty years of accumulated trust and operational tooling. Successor platforms either inherit Tor's relay set or accept a long bootstrapping period during which they offer measurably weaker anonymity. The research question for 2026-2032 is therefore not which successor platform wins, but which subset of Tor's user base separates onto a successor and why; this is a question with both technical and ethnographic dimensions.

4.4 Ethical and Jurisdictional Limits

The defensive deployments outlined in Table 5 operate at the production scale on a substrate intentionally engineered to be capable of protecting identity. The ethical theory underlying the one that this chapter tries to preserve does not see a contradiction between defensive capabilities and overreaching surveillance; instead, it sees both as opposite ends of a spectrum, one that will change with scaling up of defensive AI. Three open issues remain.

First is the *asymmetry in costs associated with errors* discussed in Section 3.2 and visualized in Figure 12. Mistaken identification of traffic from a journalist or activist as that of a criminal, leading to false positives, is a different problem from false negative identification of malicious content in malware control channels. A minimally honest reporting model would expose the per-class weighting explicitly, separating the two target populations $T \in \{\text{legit}, \text{crim}\}$ and reporting an expected ethical cost in which the two diagonal weights w^{FP}_{legit} and w^{FN}_{crim} dominate the off-diagonal weights by orders of magnitude. By reducing this matrix of ethical issues to just one number, overall accuracy, the most important part of the story is lost.

Figure 12. The asymmetric error-cost matrix for defensive AI on the darknet. The two diagonal cells (rights harm and operational harm) carry high ethical weight; the off-diagonal cells (no effect, wasted analyst cycles) carry near-zero or low-to-moderate weight. Average accuracy metrics that aggregate over all four cells obscure the asymmetry that matters most. Disaggregated reporting, which the literature has not yet converged on, is the precondition for a principled debate about defensive-AI deployment limits

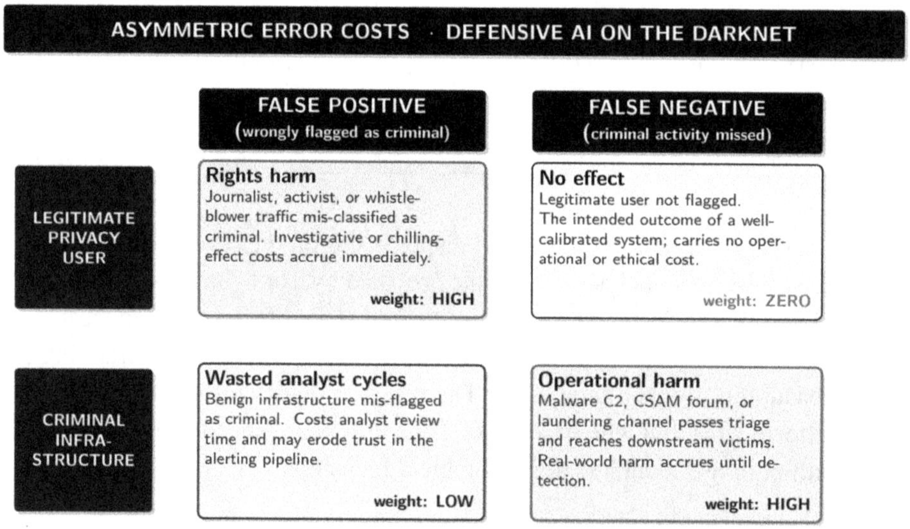

The second is *extraterritoriality*. AI crawlers operate without regard to the legal jurisdiction in which the targeted hidden service is hosted, the relay through which traffic flows, or the human user who is incidentally observed. The Council of Europe's Budapest Convention and its second additional protocol provide one mutual-assistance framework; neither was drafted with autonomous AI surveillance in mind. The research and policy question is what oversight regime is compatible with the production-scale deployments now in operation.

The third is the *auditability problem*. Defensive AI systems are themselves machine-learning artifacts whose behaviour is difficult to audit, especially under FOIA-equivalent legal regimes. The Internet Watch Foundation's documentation of 26,385% growth in confirmed AI-generated CSAM videos between 2024 and 2025 (Internet Watch Foundation 2025) illustrates that there is no neutral position on darknet AI; the choice to deploy or not deploy is itself a value choice. What an audit regime for darknet defensive AI should look like is, at the time of writing, an open question.

5 CONCLUSION

In this chapter, it has been suggested that the offensive and defensive uses of generative AI on the darknet should be understood as a unified coupled system rather than as two separate threat trees. This is because of three main findings established throughout Main Focus section: that the underlying foundation models, modes of deployment, and economic logic driving both vectors are fundamentally identical; that the documented exchanges of 2022 to 2026 represent a tight co-evolutionary record in which each step on one side has produced a corresponding counter-move on the other within a few months; and that the November 2025 disclosures of the PROMPTFLUX malware family and the GTG-1002 agentic espionage campaign mark an inflection point at which generative AI crossed from an advisory role into an executor role on both sides simultaneously (Google Threat Intelligence Group, 2025b; Anthropic, 2025b).

The chapter's intended contribution to the discussion on darknet technologies, threats, and trends in the volume lies in its perspective on the problem. While previously seen by researchers as two separate lines of research, cybercrime and cyber defense via artificial intelligence are now seen by this chapter as two parts of one project within the specific arms-race framework outlined in Section 3.3.

Figure 13. Forecast frame for the chapter's seven-year reading horizon. Structural invariants on the left are properties of the substrate, the economics, and the cryptographic mathematics that we expect to remain true through 2032. Likely-to-change variables on the right are the vendor-, protocol-, and jurisdiction-specific characteristics that are almost sure to be different within five to seven years from now. Readers encountering this chapter past 2030 are advised to use the left pillar as the locus of continued relevance and the right pillar as the field guide to what has, by then, already changed

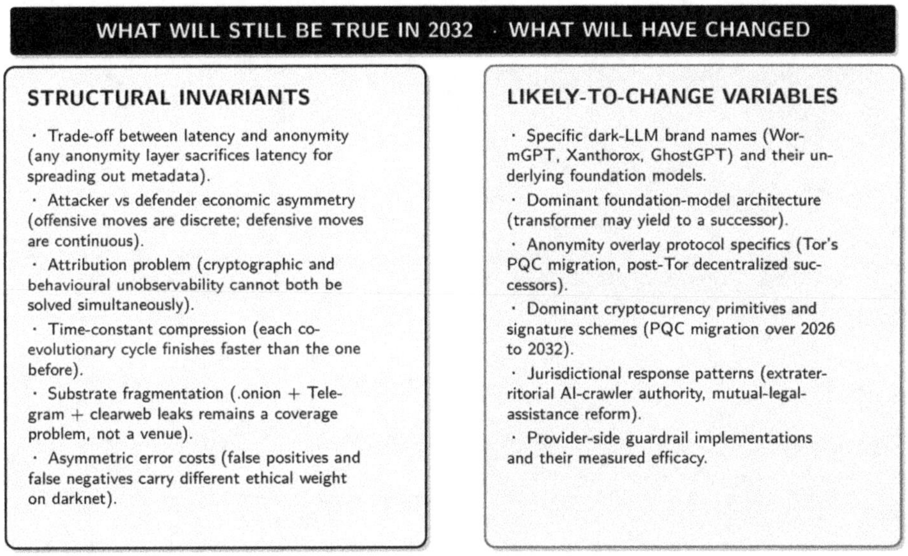

Figure 13 compresses the chapter's durability argument into a single visual frame. The left pillar of structural invariants is where future readers should expect the chapter's analysis to remain useful. The latency-anonymity tradeoff is a property of the mathematics of mix networks, not of any particular implementation; the attacker-defender economic asymmetry arises from the fundamental difference between discrete and continuous adaptation cycles, not of any specific threat actor; and the attribution problem follows naturally from the inherent cryptographic and behavioural unobservability that any anonymity substrate is designed to provide. These invariants held true in 2002 at the time of Tor's release, and they will hold true in 2032 as well.

The right pillar of likely-to-change variables is where the chapter becomes clearly date-specific. The particular dark-LLM brand names that underlie Table 4, the particular foundation models used in those wrappers, the particular generative-AI architectures that now dominate the field, and the particular cryptocurrency primitives that Section 4.2 flags for post-quantum migration are all constructs from 2026 that, on the chapter's seven-year forecast horizon, will become either obsolete, superseded, or substantially evolved. We have sought to name them specifically so that readers in 2032 can use this chapter as a snapshot of how the relevant questions were framed at the moment generative AI crossed the agentic threshold.

The chapter's closing claim is the one that motivated the title: generative AI in darknet operations sits between weaponization and detection because both are now executed, increasingly autonomously, by the same class of system. The unified agentic framework developed across the preceding sections is not an abstraction. It is the working model under which both sides are now operating, and the model under which the research priorities of 2026 to 2032 will need to be set.

REFERENCES

Anderson, R. (2001). Why information security is hard: An economic perspective. In *Proceedings of the 17th Annual Computer Security Applications Conference (ACSAC)* (pp. 358–365). DOI: 10.1109/ACSAC.2001.991552

Anthropic. (2025a). *Detecting and countering misuse of AI: August 2025.* Anthropic Threat Research. https://www.anthropic.com/news/detecting-countering-misuse-aug-2025

Anthropic. (2025b). *Disrupting the first reported AI-orchestrated cyber espionage campaign.* Anthropic Threat Research. https://www.anthropic.com/news/disrupting-AI-espionage

Brown, T. B., Mann, B., Ryder, N., ... (2020). Language models are few-shot learners. In *Advances in Neural Information Processing Systems (NeurIPS 33)* (pp. 1877–1901).

Cato Networks CTRL Threat Research. (2025). *WormGPT variants powered by Grok and Mixtral.* Cato Networks Blog. https://www.catonetworks.com/blog/cato-ctrl-wormgpt-variants-powered-by-grok-and-mixtral/

Chainalysis. (2026). *The 2026 crypto crime report introduction: $154 billion in illicit activity last year.* Chainalysis Blog. https://www.chainalysis.com/blog/2026-crypto-crime-report-introduction/

Cuddy, A. (2024). Ferrari executive foiled deepfake attempt by asking about a book. *Fortune.* https://fortune.com/2024/07/27/ferrari-deepfake-attempt-scammer-security-question-ceo-benedetto-vigna-cybersecurity-ai/

Cyber, K. E. L. A. (2025). *2025 AI threat report: How cybercriminals are weaponizing AI technology.* https://info.ke-la.com/hubfs/Reports/KELA%20Report%20-%202025%20AI%20Threat%20Report.pdf

Devlin, J., Chang, M.-W., Lee, K., & Toutanova, K. (2019). BERT: Pre-training of deep bidirectional transformers for language understanding. In *Proceedings of the 2019 Conference of the North American Chapter of the Association for Computational Linguistics: Human Language Technologies* (pp. 4171–4186). DOI: 10.18653/v1/N19-1423

Dingledine, R., Mathewson, N., & Syverson, P. (2004). Tor: The second-generation onion router. In *Proceedings of the 13th USENIX Security Symposium* (pp. 303–320).

European Union Agency for Cybersecurity (ENISA). (2025). *ENISA threat landscape 2025.* https://www.enisa.europa.eu/sites/default/files/2025-11/ENISA%20Threat%20Landscape%202025.pdf

Federal Bureau of Investigation, Internet Crime Complaint Center. (2025). *2024 IC3 annual report.* U.S. Department of Justice. https://www.ic3.gov/AnnualReport/Reports/2024_IC3Report.pdf

Federal Reserve Bank of Boston. (2025). *Gen AI is ramping up the threat of synthetic identity fraud.* https://www.bostonfed.org/news-and-events/news/2025/04/synthetic-identity-fraud-financial-fraud-expanding-because-of-generative-artificial-intelligence.aspx

Flashpoint. (2026). *2026 global threat intelligence report.* https://flashpoint.io/blog/global-threat-intelligence-report-2026/

Goodfellow, I. J., Pouget-Abadie, J., Mirza, M., ... (2014). Generative adversarial nets. In *Advances in Neural Information Processing Systems (NeurIPS 27)* (pp. 2672–2680).

Google Cloud. (2026). *Bringing dark web intelligence into the AI era.* https://cloud.google.com/blog/products/identity-security/bringing-dark-web-intelligence-into-the-ai-era

Google Threat Intelligence Group. (2025a). *Adversarial misuse of generative AI.* https://cloud.google.com/blog/topics/threat-intelligence/adversarial-misuse-generative-ai

Google Threat Intelligence Group. (2025b). *GTIG AI threat tracker: Advances in threat actor usage of AI tools.* https://cloud.google.com/blog/topics/threat-intelligence/threat-actor-usage-of-ai-tools

Group-IB. (2025). *High-tech crime trends report 2025.* https://www.group-ib.com/media-center/press-releases/high-tech-crime-trends-report-2025/

Ho, J., Jain, A., & Abbeel, P. (2020). Denoising diffusion probabilistic models. In *Advances in Neural Information Processing Systems (NeurIPS 33).*

Hu, E. J., Shen, Y., Wallis, P., ... (2021). LoRA: Low-rank adaptation of large language models. *arXiv preprint arXiv:2106.09685.* https://arxiv.org/abs/2106.09685

Internet Watch Foundation. (2025). *How AI is being abused to create child sexual abuse imagery.* https://www.iwf.org.uk/about-us/why-we-exist/our-research/how-ai-is-being-abused-to-create-child-sexual-abuse-imagery/

Jin, Y., Jang, E., Cui, J., Chung, J.-W., Lee, Y., & Shin, S. (2023). DarkBERT: A language model for the dark side of the internet. In *Proceedings of the 61st Annual Meeting of the Association for Computational Linguistics* (pp. 7515–7533). DOI: 10.18653/v1/2023.acl-long.415

Karras, T., Laine, S., & Aila, T. (2019). A style-based generator architecture for generative adversarial networks. In *Proceedings of the IEEE/CVF Conference on Computer Vision and Pattern Recognition (CVPR)* (pp. 4401–4410). DOI: 10.1109/CVPR.2019.00453

LastPass. (2024). *Attempted audio deepfake call targets LastPass employee.* https://blog.lastpass.com/posts/attempted-audio-deepfake-call-targets-lastpass-employee

Lin, X., Xiong, G., Gou, G., Li, Z., Shi, J., & Yu, J. (2022). ET-BERT: A contextualized datagram representation with pre-training transformers for encrypted traffic classification. In *Proceedings of the ACM Web Conference (WWW)* (pp. 633–642). DOI: 10.1145/3485447.3512217

Lin, Z., Cui, J., Liao, X., & Wang, X. (2024). Malla: Demystifying real-world large language model integrated malicious services. In *USENIX Security Symposium 33.*

Liu, Y., Ott, M., Goyal, N., ... (2019). RoBERTa: A robustly optimized BERT pretraining approach. *arXiv preprint arXiv:1907.11692.* https://arxiv.org/abs/1907.11692

Magramo, K. (2024). Finance worker pays out $25 million after video call with deepfake “chief financial officer”. *CNN Business.* https://www.cnn.com/2024/05/16/tech/arup-deepfake-scam-loss-hong-kong-intl-hnk

Microsoft. (2025a). *Microsoft digital defense report 2025.* https://www.microsoft.com/en-us/security/security-insider/threat-landscape/microsoft-digital-defense-report-2025

Microsoft. (2025b). *Security Copilot for SOC: Bringing agentic AI to every defender.* https://techcommunity.microsoft.com/blog/microsoftthreatprotectionblog/security-copilot-for-soc-bringing-agentic-ai-to-every-defender/4470187

Mirsky, Y., & Lee, W. (2021). The creation and detection of deepfakes: A survey. *ACM Computing Surveys, 54*(1), 7:1–7:41. DOI: 10.1145/3425780

National Institute of Standards and Technology. (2024a). *FIPS 203: Module-lattice-based key-encapsulation mechanism standard.* https://csrc.nist.gov/pubs/fips/203/final

National Institute of Standards and Technology. (2024b). *FIPS 204: Module-lattice-based digital signature standard.* https://csrc.nist.gov/pubs/fips/204/final

Open, A. I. (2024–2026). *Disrupting malicious uses of AI.* https://openai.com/index/disrupting-malicious-ai-uses/

Pei, G., Zhang, J., Hu, M., ... (2024). Deepfake generation and detection: A benchmark and survey. *arXiv preprint arXiv:2403.17881*

Radford, A., Narasimhan, K., Salimans, T., & Sutskever, I. (2018). Improving language understanding by generative pre-training. OpenAI Technical Report. https://cdn.openai.com/research-covers/language-unsupervised/language_understanding_paper.pdf

Trend Micro Research. (2024). *Deepfake it 'til you make it: A comprehensive view of the new AI criminal toolset.* https://www.trendmicro.com/vinfo/us/security/news/cybercrime-and-digital-threats/deepfake-it-til-you-make-it-a-comprehensive-view-of-the-new-ai-criminal-toolset

Trend Micro Research. (2025). *The devil reviews Xanthorox: A criminal-focused analysis of the latest malicious LLM offering.* https://www.trendmicro.com/vinfo/us/security/news/cybercrime-and-digital-threats/the-devil-reviews-xanthorox-a-criminal-focused-analysis-of-the-latest-malicious-llm-offering

Unit 42, Palo Alto Networks. (2026). *Can AI attack the cloud? Lessons from building an autonomous cloud offensive multi-agent system.* https://unit42.paloaltonetworks.com/autonomous-ai-cloud-attacks/

Vaswani, A., Shazeer, N., Parmar, N., ... (2017). Attention is all you need. In *Advances in Neural Information Processing Systems (NeurIPS 30)* (pp. 5998–6020).

APPENDIX

Additional Reading

The references below explore extensions to certain strands of this chapter not referenced elsewhere in the text. They are listed in a manner corresponding to the sections of the chapter and are meant to be useful to anyone looking to delve further into a specific strand of the discussion. **5.0.0.1** On the network-level substrate (Section **2.1**).

The recent experimental work performed to measure the use of Tor's substrate and the hidden-service ecosystem in terms of the demographics of actual users has enhanced the empirical basis for understanding this issue; readers interested in that empirical record will find the Free Haven Project bibliography and the proceedings of the Privacy Enhancing Technologies Symposium (PETS) for years 2023 to 2026 useful. **5.0.0.2** On generative architectures (Section **2.2**). As far as the literature on the transformer architecture is concerned, the original paper by Vaswani and colleagues remains the canonical reference. On diffusion, the survey by Pei et al. (2024) complements the earlier work by Mirsky and Lee (2021), the latter serving as the foundation for the durable taxonomy of deepfake families. For the encoder-side adaptation research that characterizes DarkBERT, the seminal study is the one carried out by Ranaldi and colleagues (2022). **5.0.0.3** On the offensive landscape (Section **3.1**).

The earliest example of structuring the use of ChatGPT, FraudGPT, and WormGPT in cybercrime contexts is the one offered by Falade (2023). The arXiv preprint *Ransomware 3.0* (2025) presents the first empirical study of the development of AI-authored ransomware variants and serves as a natural counterpart to the Anthropic vibe-hacking report referenced earlier in the chapter.

5.0.0.4 On defensive AI (Section 3.2).

For the problem of encrypted-traffic classification, the ET-BERT paper by Lin et al. (cited in the body) is the point of reference; for blockchain forensic analysis, the Elliptic2 dataset paper (2025) represents the most accessible academic benchmark, while the Chainalysis Crypto Crime Report published annually remains the industry-facing record. Readers interested in the development of agentic defensive deployments should track the Microsoft Security Copilot and Google Security AI release notes, which have more frequent publication rates than the academic literature can cope with.

5.0.0.5 On the arms race and forecast horizon (Sections 3.3-4).

For those seeking a comprehensive review of the literature on offence-defence escalation in ML-driven malware analysis, Ling et al.'s paper in *ACM Computing Surveys* (2023) stands as the canonical pre-2024 reference and is the most directly relevant complement to this chapter's darknet-focused treatment of the same dynamic. For post-quantum migration, the NIST PQC project page and the IETF **tls-pq** working-group documents provide the canonical engineering record.

Key Terms and Definitions

An autonomous and goal-oriented AI system capable of performing multi-stage tasks with minimal human oversight. In contrast to an advisory AI, which simply drafts outputs for humans to read and approve, an agentic system perceives, plans, and acts toward its stated objective; in its advanced 2025 form, an operator can entrust about 80 to 90 percent of an attack chain to an agentic AI, leaving just a few critical decision points for human intervention.

An offensive-defensive interaction in which improvements on either side make the other side's payoffs diminish and trigger further improvements. In the generative-AI-on-the-darknet context, this cycle has been compressed from months to weeks, with each new defensive deployment triggering an offensive counter-move within the same calendar quarter.

A commercial subscription model in which criminal capabilities, including malware creation, fraud, money laundering, and deepfake production, are offered to customers who are not necessarily experts in their craft. The generative-AI variant has recently been marketed almost exclusively via Telegram using cryptocurrency-only checkout, with price points ranging from $50 per week to $300 per month.

A language model marketed via underground forums or Telegram channels for criminal use cases, normally an adaptation or prompt-engineered wrapper around an open-weight or commercial foundation model. WormGPT, FraudGPT, GhostGPT, and Xanthorox are typical examples; the name has become a brand category rather than a designation for an individual model.

In this chapter, the family of anonymity-overlay networks like Tor, I2P, and Freenet that use encrypted multi-hop relays to decouple identity from behaviour, together with the encrypted communication platforms such as private Telegram channels, Discord servers, and Signal groups where much darknet-style activity has empirically migrated.

Computer-generated content produced using a machine-learning model that creates an image, video, or audio of an actual person appearing to perform actions or make statements they never actually performed or said. The shift in offensive deepfake adoption between 2024 and 2025 has been the removal of the latency bottleneck: interactive face-swap and voice-cloning systems now run in real time, which is what enabled the Arup, LastPass, and Ferrari incidents discussed in Section 2.2.

An architecture in which two neural networks are trained against each other: the first generates synthetic samples, while the second differentiates them from real samples. GANs were considered the dominant architecture for high-fidelity face and image synthesis up until 2021; they remain in use for synthetic-identity work despite the emergence of diffusion models, which have replaced them on almost all high-end synthesis benchmarks.

A server accessed via an onion-routing network and reachable only from within the Tor network at a .onion address. The hidden-service rendezvous protocol is distinct from the regular Tor circuit-routing protocol and provides bidirectional anonymity between client and server.

A routing model in which a message is encrypted in successive layers, one for each intermediate relay, and forwarded through that chain so that no single relay can simultaneously observe both the source and the destination. Tor's three-hop circuit is the canonical implementation.

Production-grade analysis of adversary tools, tactics, and procedures intended to inform defensive decisions. The transition into AI-assisted threat intelligence from 2024-2026, which includes dark web surveillance using Gemini and agent-based SOC triaging, has augmented the capability of the industry to process intelligence and shifted the chokepoint from intelligence gathering to synthesis.

Chapter 13
Darknet Counter-Operations and Law Enforcement

Fawaz A. Khasawneh
http://orcid.org/0009-0002-3078-606X
Jordan University of Science and Technology, Jordan

Abdullah S. Al-Shra'a
http://orcid.org/0000-0002-4881-8894
Jordan University of Science and Technology, Jordan

Mohammad Bany Taha
American University of Madaba, Jordan

ABSTRACT

In this book chapter, we have discussed the darknet threat landscape and its criminal ecosystems, where the structure of darknet criminal networks is analyzed, and different illicit activities are classified with their typical actors and supporting technologies. On the other hand, counter-operations in the darknet are examined, from intelligence gathering and the use of emerging technologies such as artificial intelligence to evidence acquisition and chain of custody requirements for court admissibility. Challenges in implementing counter-operations are also explained, showing that collaboration between public and private entities at both national and international levels is now a necessity, not an option, for effective law enforcement. Legal and jurisdictional challenges are also discussed, as counter-operations should be fast and efficient without violating the law and while maintaining user privacy. Finally, future directions and recommendations are discussed as well.

1. INTRODUCTION

One of the main challenges in darknet is the traceability issue, since many hidden services, encrypted communications, payments using cryptocurrency and blockchain technology and anonymity are all contributing to make it harder for investigators to track down any illegal activity. Several researchers have shown how quickly sellers and buyers in darknet cryptomarkets can organize around informal

DOI: 10.4018/979-8-3373-9755-9.ch013

commercial rules and adapt after disruptions or takedown operations (Aldridge & Décary-Hétu, 2016; Christin, 2013; ElBahrawy et al., 2020; Soska & Christin, 2015).

When talking about darknet, we are not only talking about drug-focused market, many other illicit activities such as stolen credentials, malware, ransomware as a service, financial and payment card data, money laundering and so many other criminal activities. Each cybercrime group is specialized in one specific area and all of them are illegally collaborating together in these criminal activities, some of them could be specialized in deploying malwares, others might be specialized in shipment artifacts, vendor profiling, or wallet cluster. This divion make it harder to investigate (Broadhurst et al., 2014; Hutchings & Holt, 2017). Thus, cyber threat intellingce, usage of emerging technologies such as artificial intelligence, and collaboration between different public and private companies nationally and internationally are necessary and essential to make the counter operation more efficient and effective.

Proactive, intelligence-led, globally synchronized operations have replaced reactive complaint handling as the preferred method of law enforcement. The most valuable disruption, according to major marketplace takedowns (Europol, 2017; Federal Bureau of Investigation, 2017; Jardine, 2021), is not the removal of a site but the production of follow-on intelligence and admissible evidence. Financial intelligence units, private analytics providers, prosecutors, national agencies, and Europolstyle cooperation mechanisms must work together, according to recent enforcement reports (Europol, 2024; ICE Homeland Security Investigations, 2025). In this chapter, "counter-operations" refers to legitimate and responsible efforts to identify, investigate, disrupt, and prosecute cybercrime that makes use of the dark web. Vigilantism and unauthorized access are not included.

From a technical, legal, and organizational vantage point, this chapter provides a structured analysis of darknet counter-operations. Criminal access or evasion instructions are not provided. Rather, it places an emphasis on things like proportionality, human oversight, documentation, chain of custody, and the right balance between privacy, security, and effective enforcement (Casey, 2011; Council of Europe, 2001; Council of Europe, 2022; Mireille & Rueda Blanco, 2022).

It is useful to differentiate out strategic disruption from evidentiary success when thinking about darknet counter-operations. Strategic disruption reduces harm by removing infrastructure, discouraging actors, freezing assets, or eroding faith in illicit marketplaces. The goal of successful evidence collection is to yield reliable material to be used for prosecution, forfeiture, victim notification or information sharing. These goals overlap but are not identical. However, an operation that kills a market but does not keep usable evidence alive may have a short-term impact and minimal legal significance. On the other hand, the rationale for slower operation would be if this led to a better attribution, more identified victims and a supporting service network exposed.

International collaboration is likewise considered a design need in the chapter, not an administrative step at the end. In many darknet cases, the first technical indicator points to cross-border coordination: a hidden service may be hosted on infrastructure in one jurisdiction, promoted to users in another, financed through services in a third, and probed by agencies in a fourth. The delay in engaging prosecutors or foreign collaborators until the end of the investigation can create holes in the continuity of the evidence. Timely collaboration helps to improve preservation, to avoid conflicting actions and to let partners assess whether a joint operation, a parallel investigation or local prosecution is the best approach.

2. DARKNET THREAT LANDSCAPE AND CRIMINAL ECOSYSTEMS

2.1 Structure of Darknet Criminal Networks

Markets and service networks are the most effective ways to describe illegal dark web ecosystems. A marketplace may include features such as listings, escrow services, dispute resolution processes, vendor ratings, administrative regulations, and communication channels. Specialized criminals may use a forum to recruit new members, manage their online reputation, or form contacts with potential victims. Ransomware gangs may use affiliate structures in addition to relying on virus creators, hosting intermediaries, access brokers, and money laundering services. The organizational structure of cybercrime groups complicates, if not prevents, the total eradication of demand, necessitating a networked approach to understanding this phenomenon. (Broadhurst et al., 2014; Europol, 2024; Hutchings & Holt, 2017).

Despite the similarity in structure between the conventional market governance and the darknet market, they differ in their intent. Many stakeholders exist in darknet market, and each one of those stakeholders has its own responsibility. For example, administrators are the ones responsible for maintaining the platform regulations and the infrastructure, other stakeholders such as merchants provide illegal services like money laundering service, brokers on the other hand act like an intermediary between sellers, buyers and delivering the services. In order to reduce the direct risks, different stakeholders and entities are separated, malware developers might be separated from marketplace operators. Some factors such as escrow services, reputation scores, and recommendations are used to build trust between sellers, buyers and brokers.

2.2 Types of Illicit Activities and Operational Characteristics

As mentioned earlier, there are many illegal activities committed in darknet, where they differ by their harmful impact and complexity of investigating in these activities and each one of those activities provide you with its own unique evidence trails and their supported technologies, some could use encryption and blockchain technologies while others might use malwares and leaking websites (Holt et al., 2023; Howell et al., 2024; Van Wegberg et al., 2018). Table 1 shows the activity class, their typical actors, supporting technologies and implications that could be found during the investigation process.

Table 1. Classification of cybercrime activities, typical actors, and used technologies

Activity class	Typical actors	Supporting technologies	Investigative implications
Drug and contraband markets	Vendors, buyers, administrators, escrow moderators	Encryption, using cryptocurrency and blockchain technology, hidden services	Detecting patterns in shipping, payment, and device evidence.
Stolen-data and credential shops	Data thieves, resellers, access brokers, fraud users	Credential dumps, forums and data breaches	Mapping victim reports with breach artifacts
Ransomware and extortion services	Developers, affiliates, initial-access brokers, negotiators	Cryptocurrency wallets, malwares and leaking websites	Mapping victim timelines with cryptocurrency wallet flows and underlying communications

continued on following page

Table 1. Continued

Activity class	Typical actors	Supporting technologies	Investigative implications
Money laundering and cash-out	Mixers, exchangers, mule networks, OTC brokers	Wallet clusters, bridges, exchanges, privacy tools	Perform tracing for all the suspicious transactions and look for supporting evidence.
Fraud tooling and cybercrime support	Tool developers, tutorial sellers, hosting facilitators	Forums, malware kits, proxy services, bulletproof hosting	Focus on the services that facilitate the implementation of illegal activity.

Darknet platform has its own governance, administrators and moderators in the darknet regulate the illicit trade and activities and organize everything, starting from preventing the scam and fraud that could happen between the anonymous users in the darknet. Although you are illegally trading goods and selling stolen data and performing many other illegal activities, stakeholders in the darknet need to feel trust, conflicts should be resolved by the administrators and moderators, existence of a trusted reputation system is essential, otherwise the whole darknet ecosystem will collapse.

Since darknet ecosystem depends on different markets and channels to operate from, researchers understand that a closure of one market urges users to move to other markets and channels that are more private depending on the reputation system managed by the administrator and moderator, which will make it more difficult for investigators to trace and follow their illegal activities (ElBahrawy et al., 2020; Soska & Christin, 2015; Wang et al., 2023). So, when performing threat modeling and assessment, two assumptions should be considered, the first one is that the users in darknet might migrate from one site to another and the other one that when a user migrates to another site, it is usually more private.

As it is known, many supporting technologies are used in the darknet ecosystem which are supposed to be used for a legitimate purpose. We should not criminalize and prevent the usage of these technologies, but we should criminalize the actions of using these legitimate technologies in a harmful and illegal manner. Tor, encryption, and different privacy tools are used in many legitimate fields including but not limited to journalism, human-rights work and other fields. When it comes to investigations, a balance between maintaining anonymity and organized abuse should be satisfied.

The collected darknet evidence varies in terms of its credibility and the level of reliability, some could be credible, others are inferred, or intelligence feeding. The prosecutor should be able to distinguish which of these pieces of evidence should be treated as evidentiary assertions to make the case file mature enough and admissible in the court. Evidence such as preserved databases is more credible compared to evidence coming from a partner such as a provider disclosure. Other pieces of evidence might be deduced using emerging technologies such as artificial intelligence, where conclusions are drawn by noticing the patterns of different activities. The level of confidence varies and technologies such as artificial intelligence might give you false positive or false negative results.

One of the main aspects that should be carefully considered is the handling of collected pieces of evidence, since it might contain very sensitive information for different victims, these collected pieces of evidence might be hacked and leaked again, either intentionally or unintentionally. Best practices for custody chain should be followed to prevent the risk of re-victimization. The main objective is to reduce the and minimize the harm for the victims and then to maximize the number of arrests and close as many markets as possible. Intimate personal material, health, financial, or information related to critical infrastructures might be publicly leaked if not handled responsibly.

3. COUNTER-OPERATIONS IN THE DARKNET

3.1 Intelligence Gathering and Darknet Monitoring

As previously stated, all the counteroperations should be victim oriented, meaning that victims and uninvolved users should not be harmed by any investigation processes. To minimize the risk of being detected, many passive reconnaissance techniques such as crawling, scraping, open-source intelligence (OSINT), and historical data analysis are performed. This step is essential to establish the context and understand the links and relationships in the darknet environment and to wisely plan your investigation and evidence collection process. During this stage, governance practices such as retention plan and data minimization techniques should also be determined (Arnold et al., 2019; Pastor-Galindo et al., 2020; Suryotrisongko et al., 2022).

3.2 Undercover and Infiltration Operations

Due to the nature of darknet ecosystems, which might involve committing a cybercrime span different countries and performing many undercover and infiltration operations, a lot of legal authorization and governance steps should be implemented such as getting the required warrants and judicial approval which must specify the rules of engagement and the limitations, escalation protocols, preparing covert identities and how to engage and interact with criminals using different governance mechanisms, without this strong governance it might be harder for the investigators to preserve an admissible evidence for the court.

3.3 Digital Forensics and Evidence Collection

All the investigations efforts could vanish within minutes, if the process of custody chain is not taken seriously and documented properly. The process of custody chain from labeling the evidence, evidence acquisition and taking the forensic image (bit by bit copy), protecting the evidence against tampering and corruption, protecting during transport if needed, and store it in a secure location, all these steps should be documented in details to ensure the admissibility of the evidence in the court (Casey, 2011). Many pieces of evidence could be collected such as configuration files, servers, chat records or any other digital device. Working on these different types of evidence must be performed on the forensic copies rather than the original copies.

3.4 Blockchain and Cryptocurrency Tracing

Tracing a cryptocurrency payment could be difficult when users apply obfuscation techniques such as the usage of many wallets, using the legitimate technologies such as VPN and TOR, moving money from one cryptocurrency to another and other obfuscation techniques. Analysts should combine pieces of evidence collected from companies such as Chainalysis to other supporting pieces of evidence to make the evidence more credible in the court (Chainalysis, 2024; Foley et al., 2019; Kim et al., 2022; Liu et al., 2021; Van Wegberg et al., 2018). Transaction graph analysis which is composed of nodes (wallet address) and edges (transaction) could be used to understand the relationship and money flows between different entities.

As shown in Figure 1 below, the darknet counter operations workflow is iterative, starting from specifying the needed intelligence requirements, and usage of the different passive reconnaissance techniques and the usage of Open Source Intelligence (OSINT), reviewing legal and deconfliction aspects especially when it comes to investigate at an international level, evidence collection and to maintain the integrity to keep the evidence admissible at the court, retention plan and to identify for how long data will be stored, and forensic preservation and then connecting it to the financial blockchain layer and then present all the collected pieces of evidence in one case and to be able to enhance the identity and infrastructure attribution.

Figure 1. Workflow of darknet counter-operations

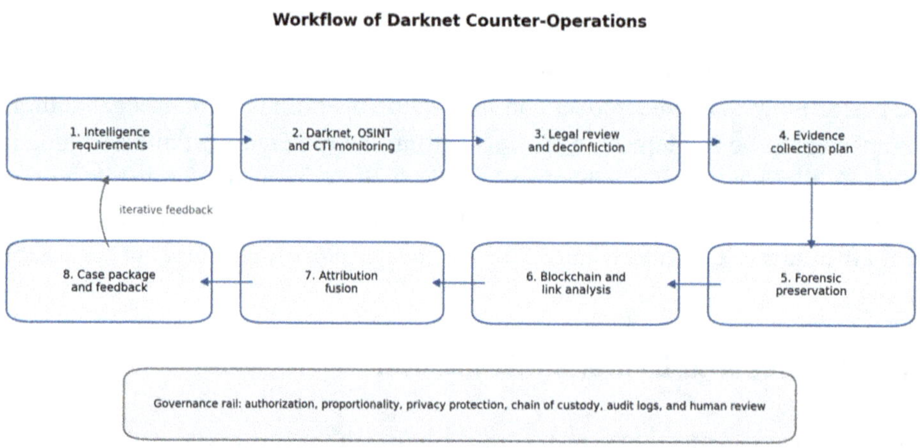

Table 2. Evidence governance matrix

Lifecycle phase	Evidence or intelligence output	Quality control	Lead coordination need
Monitoring and triage	Listings, aliases, indicators, screenshots, timestamps	Collection logs, source scope, and minimization notes	Analysts, legal advisers, and case officers agree priorities.
Legal authorization	Warrants, preservation requests, mutual assistance documents	Clear target, proportionality, and request specificity	Prosecutors and international liaison officers align timing.
Operational action	Seized servers, accounts, wallets, communications, access records	Hashing, imaging, secure transfer, and access control	Technical teams and field units preserve continuity.
Analysis and fusion	Forensic timelines, transaction graphs, entity links, victim lists	Peer review, confidence labels, and alternative explanations	Forensic, financial, and intelligence teams compare findings.
Prosecution and review	Case package, disclosure material, lessons learned, victim updates	Audit trail, evidence index, and admissibility review	Prosecutors, courts, and partner agencies receive coherent records.

Case Box 1: Silk Road as an Early Measurement Lesson

Many approaches have been used in this specific case, to make it harder for investigators to detect the criminal activities committed. TOR, encryption, privacy preservation tools, blockchain cryptocurrency payments, reputation system to rank different vendors, buyers and sellers, financial escrow service is provisioned as well, where an intermediary broker receive the payment from the buyer and release it only when a confirmation from the buyer is received to ensure no scam or fraud is committed in the darknet ecosystem. Early market measurements and international collaboration help a lot in detecting the suspicious behavior in this market and in collecting lawful preservation and pieces of evidence and all its supporting evidence (Christin, 2013).

Table 2 shows the evidence governance matrix throughout the lifecycle phases, discussing its output, quality control related issues, and the necessity for lead coordination. Planning is the most important step in governance rail, many questions need to be answered thoroughly before starting the investigation and intelligence process. For example, if you noticed a suspicious behavior that needs more investigation, you should identify what is the main purpose of the investigation and why you are planning to perform it, what artifact and pieces of evidence that you are looking for in order to prove the illegal actions committed, and how to lawfully collect those artifacts to be admissible in the court, what is the credibility level of the evidence you collected and is it sufficient to prove anything or do you need a supporting artifacts. Governance rail ensures that the collected evidence is acceptable in court, meaning that it is legally collected, well documented, within scope, and following the right procedures for the custody of chain and to maintain the integrity of any collected evidence.

Each collected evidence should be mapped to a confidence level and combined with other artifacts to prove a crime and to map to a specific individual or entity. Uncertainty could be performed on many layers, for example, identity uncertainty could be defined as the difficulty to surely identify an individual or an entity since users rely on aliases, reputation scores and PGP keys. Another layer might be at the infrastructure level, where servers, domains and communication channels might suddenly disappear, migrate which makes it harder to identify the infrastructure ownership. Because investigative conclusions are often based on probability, correlation, and supporting context rather than absolute certainty. Assigning confidence levels helps investigators distinguish between weak indicators, strong supporting evidence, and evidence that is sufficiently reliable to support legal or operational action.

A full forensic plan should be previously prepared in order to capture all the artifacts that could be used later as a lawful evidence in the court, usually when performing the digital forensics and more specifically the step related to the data acquisition, investigators start acquiring data from the most volatile to the least volatile according to the order of volatility starting from CPU registers and RAM and ending in backups and archival media if exist, readiness of the forensic team is essential to make the takedown process successful, and a balance between collecting the maximum evidentiary data and the minimum personal data required to perform the investigation should be satisfied (Casey, 2011).

Traditional methods of financial investigation should be supplemented by blockchain analysis. To link on-chain actions to actual identities, it may be necessary to use subpoenas, production orders, reports of suspicious activity, and exchange records; however, transaction graphs can show services, clusters, or pathways to exchanges. In addition to documenting their level of confidence in each link, analysts should explain why a clustering rule was used. The reliance on a heuristic in a conclusion ought to be readily apparent. The results and underlying assumptions of the analysis should be communicated to the courts and partner agencies. When numerous agencies keep tabs on the same market or player, operational deconfliction becomes crucial. Undetected disruption of one investigation, duplication of undercover engagement, or disclosure of a covert identity can occur in the absence of deconfliction. To prevent damaging collisions, deconfliction mechanisms only need enough trusted signaling, not that each partner must divulge every detail.

Usually, different intelligence agencies, international parties and private/public companies are collaborating in any big cybercrime investigation, communication between different entities at the national or international level should be secured and sensitive sources of information could be hidden due to different reasons such as using a private penetration tool that is not publicly available or it could be a private advanced monitoring system. If necessary, investigator could share partial information with the other investigating parties using encrypted channels and classified communication. Investigators should understand that at some point they should reveal the details related to how they collect artifacts and pieces of evidence to the court. Advanced monitoring system could be used to aggregate, analyze and make a correlation between different cyber events across networks, cloud services from different vendors, it is like SIEM but with more advanced features related to threat intelligence, ISP/backbone traffic monitoring, usage of classified and private sensors, and has the capability to track attacker infrastructure internationally.

4. INTERNATIONAL LAW ENFORCEMENT COLLABORATION

4.1 Role of International Organizations

In a darknet ecosystem, there are different roles and components, namely, victims, suspects, hosting infrastructure, cryptocurrency service providers, private cloud service providers, where each one of them could be in a different country following and comply with different regulation that might be contradicting with other countries' regulations in terms of data privacy, in order to be able to resolve this complex and long chain, organizations such as Interpol, Europol, UNDOC and the national cybercrime centers should collaborate together (Europol, 2024; UNODC, 2023).

4.2 Cross-Border Information Sharing Mechanisms

Legal cooperation mechanisms create a bridge between operational speed and lawful process. The Budapest Convention and its Second Additional Protocol provide foundations for cybercrime cooperation and electronic evidence disclosure, while regional e-evidence mechanisms attempt to shorten procedural delays (Council of Europe, 2001; Council of Europe, 2022; European Commission, 2023). Data sovereignty and privacy are ensured, information sharing should be done in early stages and it is based on the trust between entities.

4.3 Joint Operations and Case Studies

Two well known cases, namely, AlphaBay and Hansa are the demonstration of the great collaboration between different agencies at international level. Firstly, the takedown of AlphaBay is conducted and the offenders start to move from this market to Hansa market thinking it is more private and safer, but the surprise was that the Hansa market was secretly under the control of the investigators (Europol, 2017; Federal Bureau of Investigation, 2017). Takedown assessment is not evaluated by the number of arrested individuals and entities but by the victim notification and the minimization of the damage on those victims and the long-term consequences (ElBahrawy et al., 2020; ICE Homeland Security Investigations, 2025; Jardine, 2021; Wang et al., 2023). The investigators did not shut down AlphaBay and Hansa markets at the same time, they tricked the users to move to Hansa market to collect more evidence, good decisions made all the difference in this specific case.

Different types of information exist, ranging from raw data to evidence and strategic analysis. Raw data might contain logs, packet captures, wallet addresses, and unprocessed data, it might be beneficial to collect some artifacts and evidence. After evaluating and analyzing the raw data, connections between bitcoin wallets and the darknet market structure would be clearer. Strategic analysis is conducted to understand the long-term directions in specific markets, what to expect in future, and the improvements of tools and techniques used by the offenders.

Table 3. Key international organizations and frameworks

Organization or framework	Main contribution	Operational value	Governance consideration
Europol	Coordination, intelligence fusion, deconfliction, and operational support	Performs synchronizations between different entities for successful market takedowns.	Intelligence information sharing should be considered through legal authority.
Interpol	Global police communication, notices, training, and liaison support	Jurisdictions are connected at cross-regional frameworks.	Evidence requests still depend on domestic legal procedures.
UNODC	Policy guidance, capacity building, and global cybercrime cooperation	Helps lower-capacity states participate in investigations.	Implementation varies across legal systems and resources.
Budapest Convention and Second Additional Protocol	Common cooperation framework for cybercrime and electronic evidence	Improves request preparation, disclosure channels, and mutual understanding.	Must be applied with human-rights and privacy safeguards.
Regional e-evidence mechanisms	Faster cross-border access to electronic evidence under defined rules	Can reduce delays when provider-held data is time sensitive.	Needs judicial review, transparency, and proportionality controls.

Case Box 2: AlphaBay and Hansa as a Coordination Lesson

Collaboration at its highest levels was the main reason behind taking down AlphaBay and Hansa, collaborators chose the right timing, solved the deconfliction between different entities and agencies, following the right procedures for evidence preservation and acquisition (Europol, 2017; Federal Bureau of Investigation, 2017).

Table 3 shows different frameworks and how they contribute in the darknet investigation process, their operational value, and governance consideration. The role of each country in a cross-border collaboration should be planned and specified previously, for example, one country could be responsible on interviewing victims and another country responsible for tracking financial records while the other country will be responsible on collecting artifacts and pieces of evidence. Roles distribution should be distributed in a way that ensures effective and quick investigation to be carried out to minimize the damage.

To avoid slow urgent response and to expose sensitive material unnecessarily, the collaborating agencies need to apply tiered information sharing model, where data is categorized based on its sensitivity. Some types of data like tactical indicators (e.g. malicious domain) should not be treated as highly classified evidence, since this will slow down the response. On the other hand, if sensitive data are classified as insensitive and shared widely, privacy might be violated, and trade-off between operational speed and privacy protection should be satisfied.

Both offenders and investigators have their own way of working and managing things, and after the closure of one darknet market, lessons will be learned by both sides. Offenders know the techniques, tools and methodologies used by investigators and know their weaknesses and challenges encountered due to the cross-regional, legal issues and compliance requirements. Offenders exploit those weaknesses and challenges for their own good, on the other hand, investigators might be able to predict the offender's behavior after the closure of any darknet market, post operation analysis is essential in investigators' job.

In your report, two sections should be provided. The first section should explain all the technical details of the evidence and how it is collected, level of confidence, tools used to get it and all the other technical details that ensure that it is technically correct in terms of followed processes and procedures. The second section should explain everything in a high-level language that is understandable for judges and court committee members.

5. LEGAL AND JURISDICTIONAL CHALLENGES

5.1 Jurisdictional Complexity in Cyberspace

Jurisdictional complexity is an inescapable part of Darknet investigations. The victim, suspect, marketplace server, hosting provider, payment service, wallet custodian and prosecution forum may all be in distinct legal systems. Search, disclosure, privacy, retention, interception, admissibility and human rights review may be subject to various criteria in each system. As such, investigators need to be careful not to conflate technical reach with legal authority.

Figure 2. Jurisdictional overlap and legal complexity in cross-border darknet investigations

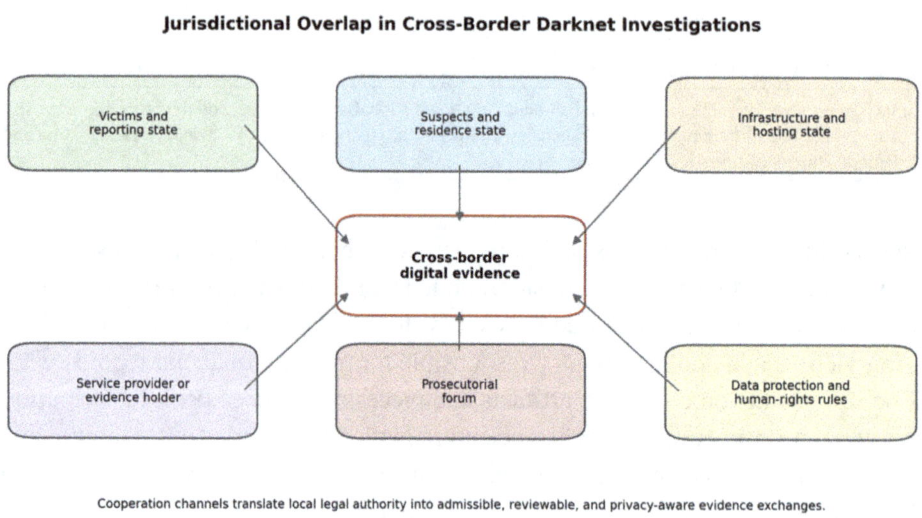

Figure 2 depicts the intersecting legal interests affecting cross-border evidence management. Different aspects should be addressed, information about victims, suspects in different countries might be essentially required to complete or advance in the investigation process. Information about the infrastructure and hosting state, which might reside in different countries and needs international collaboration. Another important aspect is related to data retention plan and the protection of private data about the victims.

5.2 Privacy Laws and Data Protection Regulations

Each country has its own data protection and privacy law, for example, GDPR, ePrivacy directive and regulation, and NIS2 directive are all applicable in Europe countries, Cloud act, ECPA, HIPPA, and CCPA are all applicable in the united states, and every single country around the world has its customized versions of the laws to protect their personal data. During any investigation, information such as IP addresses, cloud subscription records, financial transactions, or any other information could be requested from any country to check on victims, suspects, or witnesses. After completing the investigation, some of the requested information might not be directly related to cybercrime. According to the law legal authorities should not have access and disclosure of the collected data forever, and the data should have a retention plan and ultimately it will be deleted, and different agencies should be careful and able to complete the investigation efficiently with the minimum data collection on the involved parties (European Commission, 2023; Mireille & Rueda Blanco, 2022).

5.3 Attribution and Evidentiary Standards

In attribution, you should be able to answer the following question, how can investigators prove that a specific individual or entity was responsible for specific digital activity? If you can answer with a high confidence level and your answer was accompanied by all the related artifacts and pieces of evidence, then it will be acceptable in court. Attribution part is always the hardest and most challenging part in any investigation, for example you might have an IP address that belongs to a shared WiFi, a cryptocurrency wallet that might be controlled by multiple people, a darknet username that is reused/sold, or even a compromised device that is remotely controlled by an attacker, it is really hard to certainly link all the activity to one individual sometimes especially that offenders are using advanced technologies to make the attribution process even harder, VPNs, TOR, shared infrastructures, fake identities and intermediaries are all factors that makes it harder to identify the offender, so an investigator depends on many techniques in the attribution process, firstly trying to build a detailed timeline of activities (login times, transaction times, shipping times, etc), looking for operational security mistakes (e.g. accidently revealing the real email, connecting once without VPN/TOR, etc), device forensics (e.g. browser artifacts, session tokens, cached pages, etc), and trying to perform blockchain analysis using transaction graph analysis, physical evidence as well could be one of the things that investigators are looking for (CCTV footage, SIM purchases, etc) (Casey, 2011; Rid & Buchanan, 2015).

Two main concepts should be differentiated, preservation and access, preservation means to prevent deletion or tampering with potential evidence for a specific period, while access needs to access and read the data by getting the permissions from the legal authorities. For preservation or access, a formal request should be sent to the corresponding entity by the investigator, if the request itself is missing some important information such as account ID, wallet address, IP addresses the request will be delayed even further because the provider for example will not be able to know which data to preserve or disclose, precise drafting is essential to avoid extra delays. Another issue, some requests are very broad, for example an investigator might send a broad request asking to preserve or send all the things related to a specific user, which sometimes violates privacy laws,

When documenting any evidence investigator should consider many factors, such as reliability, transparency, reproducibility, fairness and explainability. A court might ask about the error rate in getting the results and conclusions of the investigation, how the results are produced, is the following methodology validated, what are the versions of the tools used, and where the analytical steps are well documented. For example, investigators could use an artificial intelligence system that concludes that a specific 15 wallets belong to the same ransomware group, the court might ask can you explain why you linked it to this specific ransomware group, what confidence level exists, could innocent users appear linked accidentally.

Modular evidence packaging means to organize all evidence into a separate structured module, which has many benefits such as helping prosecutors who do not have technical expertise to understand the sources of evidence, evaluate reliability in an easier manner, and to explain evidence to judges and juries in a more structured way. Another benefit could be supporting selective sharing by categorizing data into classified and unclassified information that could be easily shared with other entities.

6. ADVANCED TECHNOLOGIES IN COUNTER-OPERATIONS

6.1 Artificial Intelligence and Machine Learning

Millions of records gathered during investigation, which makes it extremely hard for investigators to manually analyze the gathered data, that's why artificial intelligence and machine learning models used instead, results from the AI models should not be taken for granted and other AI techniques such as Explainable AI (XAI) should be used to explain why AI models comes to a specific conclusion, in addition to that human review is necessary since AI models could produce a false positive results or generate conclusion that are difficult to explain, AI could be used in detecting anomalous activities which deviates from the normal behavior, where machine learning and AI models are firstly trained to identify the normal behavior in the network to be able to easily detect any deviation, AI could be used also to identify entity resolution and attribution (Katiyar et al., 2024; Santos et al., 2025; Suryotrisongko et al., 2022).

6.2 Big Data Analytics and Visualization

Due to the fact that investigators are dealing with huge amount of data, those data should be visualized in order to understand the relationships between different entities, for example the graph might combine financial transactions, forum interactions, malware infrastructure with hosting records, visualization and big data analytics make it easier to link one wallet address to many ransomware groups, investigation should also be careful that information coming out of the visualization might be misleading sometimes, as stated earlier each evidence should be mapped to a confidence level (Liu et al., 2021; Pastor-Galindo et al., 2020).

6.3 Automation and Cyber Threat Intelligence Platforms

To speed up the monitoring and analysis of big data, cyber threat intelligence platforms are used by investigators. CTI platforms such as Malware Information Sharing Platform (MISP) are one of the most used platforms to assist with identifying the correlation between different Indicators of Compromise (IoC), sharing information between organizations and for event tagging. Other commercial CTI platforms called ThreatConnect have many features that allow the investigators to be integrated with SOAR systems and to manage the threat intelligence process, Table 4 summarizes the limitations related to different technologies.

Table 4. Technological tools and techniques for darknet counter-operations: capabilities and limitations

Technology or technique	Core capability	Main limitation	Required safeguard
Darknet crawling and CTI collection	Tracks listings, aliases, indicators, and market changes at scale	Incomplete coverage and possible sampling bias	Document scope, retention, and lawful collection basis.
Blockchain analytics	Maps transaction flows, clusters, services, and cash-out points	Mixing, custody, bridges, and off-chain behavior complicate inference	Use as lead evidence and corroborate with records.
Digital forensics	Preserves devices, servers, databases, logs, and configuration artifacts	Evidence can be volatile, encrypted, or jurisdictionally restricted	Maintain repeatability, hashing, chain of custody, and validation.
AI and machine learning	Prioritizes entities, topics, anomalies, and behavioral patterns	Bias, drift, opacity, and false positives	Use human review, explainability, and performance auditing.
Visualization and graph analysis	Reveals relationships among actors, wallets, platforms, and infrastructure	May overstate uncertain or inferred links	Label confidence and separate observation from inference.

Usually when AI models are used to predict something, they are evaluated using different metrics such as F1-score, precision, recall and accuracy. For example, an AI model is used to categorize different criminal activities in the darknet ecosystem, and it comes to a conclusion that there are three different criminal activities, namely, drugs, weapons and malware, when writing the report the investigator should not hide the uncertainty, meaning that it should be written that there is for example 82% probability that this listing relates to malware, and it should be combined with XAI and with the mindset of the human-in-the-loop design. Key features that let AI model predict this specific kind of listing should be clearly written without exposing sensitive information and methods (Suryotrisongko et al., 2022).

Proper implementation of data governance supports reproducible analysis, lawful sharing, and controlled research access. Many rules and controls should be implemented, related to storage environment, the encryption algorithm used, back up policies and procedures, and the infrastructure security. Data governance could be implemented by ensuring that essential controls are in place, including but not limited to, strict access controls, well defined retention policies, auditing rules are correctly configured, and finally to depend on combining multiple evidence sources.

The ability to understand, verify, and question vendor results is an essential skill for agencies to cultivate internally. We are not saying that commercial tools should not be used; rather, we are saying that they should be used in an accountable analytical setting that makes their assumptions, limitations, and other possible interpretations clear. Through the creation of benchmark datasets, evaluation methodologies, and transparent typologies, academic partnerships have the potential to enhance this environment.

Additionally, they have the ability to study long-term effects, which operational teams find challenging to measure while an investigation is underway. Ethical review, data minimization, secure storage, and publication controls must govern academic access to darknet data, though. In order to protect victims, prevent abuse, and identify dangerous markets, researchers should not release artifacts that do any of these things. Independence is enhanced through responsible research without an increase in risk.

7. PUBLIC-PRIVATE PARTNERSHIPS AND COLLABORATIVE MODELS

7.1 Role of Industry and Cybersecurity Firms

Since a great deal of pertinent knowledge and data is located outside of government, public-private partnerships play a crucial role. Agencies can benefit from data, tools, or knowledge that may not be in-house by partnering with blockchain analytics companies, cybersecurity firms, hosting providers, exchanges, cloud platforms, and incident response teams. These collaborations need to be set up with legitimate demands, contracts, memorandums of understanding, regulations for disclosure, and controls for secrecy, and the assurance of transparent governmental decision-making (Chainalysis, 2024; Europol, 2024; Santos et al., 2025).

7.2 Academic and Research Contributions

The academic research is complementary to the governments and law enforcement agencies to better understand the darknet cybercrime ecosystem, without exposing any sensitive information related to victims in their research. Many research areas tried to be discovered such as market size, various darknet activities and ransomware economies. Researchers could also create new datasets related to criminal activities in the darknet to train AI models (Arnold et al., 2019; Christin, 2013; ElBahrawy et al., 2020; Soska & Christin, 2015; Wang et al., 2023).

7.3 Collaborative Ecosystems

Collaboration is essential but it must be governed, controlled, and coordinated to avoid chaotic information sharing, legal risks increase, and trust weakness. For example, to protect investigations and preserve victims' privacy, the authorized entities or individuals who are authorized to share specific information should clearly specified, permission level for each piece of information should be determined, and to clearly state what are the reasons you are sharing information. Table 5 below shows the strategic recommendations along with their corresponding implementation actions, expected benefits and evaluation metrics.

Table 5. Strategic recommendations

Recommendation	Implementation action	Expected benefit	Evaluation metric
Standardize evidence requests	Use shared templates for preservation, disclosure, and mutual assistance.	Reduces delay and missing information.	Request acceptance rate and response time.
Build regional capability hubs	Share training, tools, forensic support, and blockchain analysis expertise.	Improves participation by lower-capacity jurisdictions.	Number of assisted cases and trained investigators.
Adopt human-in-the-loop AI	Require analyst review before operational or legal decisions.	Improves scale while preserving accountability.	False-positive review rate and model audit results.
Strengthen public-private protocols	Define lawful channels, feedback rules, and confidentiality obligations.	Improves intelligence quality and trust.	Validated leads, provider response time, and privacy incidents.
Measure post-operation effects	Track displacement, recidivism, victim impact, and prosecution outcomes.	Supports evidence-based policy.	Longitudinal harm-reduction indicators.

To have a long-term, trusted, efficient and effective collaboration, responsibilities should be clearly defined to determine what are allowed and not allowed to do. For example, private companies could participate in sharing artifacts and pieces of evidence such as IoCs, blockchain analytics, and technical expertise, but they cannot arrest suspects or conduct unlawful surveillance. On the other hand, researchers might contribute to providing datasets, implementing some behavioral and risk analysis models but are not allowed to collect evidence in any way. Service providers might act after receiving lawful requests and preserve records related to suspects, provide subscriber information, but as mentioned earlier the request itself should not be too broad and lacks proportionality. All these boundaries should be clearly defined from the very beginning.

8. OPERATIONAL CHALLENGES AND LIMITATIONS

There are many technical factors that limit the investigators to have the complete picture of what is happening in the entire criminal ecosystem. Uncertainty should be acknowledged, darknet actors usually use end-to-end encryption to secure its communications and to prevent investigators from reading or accessing any seized devices. Anonymity is another source of uncertainty in the darknet, where fake and hidden identities are used when utilizing tools such as TOR, VPN, and cryptocurrency, which will complicate the attribution and tracking tasks. Other factors such as decentralization and short platform lifetimes play a vital role in complication the investigation process.

A team with multidisciplinary technical skills is required to complete the investigation process in an efficient manner, suppose that you are investigating in an international ransomware case, different skills are required, for example, digital forensic experts are needed to acquire, maintain and analyze the infected systems in a lawful acceptable manner, a blockchain analyst is needed to trace all the transactions made using a blockchain technology, a skilled language experts to translate and monitor different forums where communication could be through different languages, legal advisors and liaison officers are also needed to handle artifacts and pieces of evidence reside in different countries.

One of the main challenges as well is post operation communication, where a balance between gaining public trust and being transparent as much as possible, without unintentionally revealing any sensitive information related to the victims and suspects. Some level of communication is required to encourage reporting and reassuring the public.

In most of the operations, a complete disruption of the darknet market is difficult due to the limited visibility and hiding techniques used by the offenders. Not all the gaps are detected, some threat actors and offenders are not caught, some of the infrastructures are uncovered. Claiming a total victory is not encouraged and prevents constructive feedback on the way the takedown is handled. Investigators should be honest in front of themselves in order to better identify the Tactics, Techniques, and procedures (TTPs) used by threat actors.

Psychological impacts on investigators should not be overlooked, investigators are exposed to violent and illegal content, abuse images, and criminal communications and activities which have a direct impact on their mental and psychological state. They work for long hours and have a lot of pressure on them; wellbeing support is a necessity in this environment.

As mentioned earlier, the investigation requires collaborative teamwork in multi-disciplinary fields between different groups. Building a regional capacity building ecosystem is essential for a successful investigation process, for example, judges should understand the terminologies used by the forensic specialist and forensics specialist should understand the legal and ethical aspects, such as evidence admissibility, warrants and ethical boundaries.

9. FUTURE DIRECTIONS AND STRATEGIC RECOMMENDATIONS

9.1 Research Gaps

Darknet counter-operations need a more comprehensive and integrated framework, where different layers are involved, including but not limited to legal, technical, operational, and administrative layers, which still does not exist in the literature. Another research gap is related to uncertainty that might be originated from the ownership of the infrastructure, identity attribution, and the usage of tools such as Tor, VPNs, and encryption and the lack of AI and explainable AI usage, in order to cover this gap and enhance the confidence level in the collected evidence, AI and explainable AI models should be used to detect the hidden patterns and explain the conclusions that drawn by those AI models. Application of AI could be in detecting any anomalous activities, entity and identity attribution, and topic classification, with human-in-the-loop approach followed, where human judgement and legal accountability are enforced. Another gap is the lack of a standardized platform for international collaboration, where same or compatible terminologies are used by different countries, standardized templates are used to request cooperation and collecting evidence. Building regional capacity building centers are one of the recommendations in this book chapter, where different types of skills are essentially needed by the investigators, including but not limited to technical, administrative and operational skills. Post operation evaluation is one the research topics that should be deeply investigated to reduce the harm, support the victims, limit the ability for marketplace adaptability, and introduce the confidence labeling of evidence.

9.2 Strategic Recommendations

The most important recommendation is that legal judgment and accountability should stay in humans' hands. A responsible sharing of information, capabilities, AI tools and CTI platforms, combining technical and legal processes more efficiently and avoiding bureaucracy in cross-regional requests. Key Performance Indicators (KPIs) should be measurable and quantifiable, expressing the amount of funds recovered, number of victims assisted, investigation speed and agility and proposing a novel AI solution that balances legal and ethical protection with security objectives.

Harmonized laws between different collaborating countries, which could be implemented in many ways such as the usage of the same terminologies, cross-border request templates to reduce and avoid ambiguity, and shared training and capacity building capabilities through a cross-regional training center (Council of Europe, 2001; Council of Europe, 2022; European Commission, 2023; Mireille & Rueda Blanco, 2022).

Offenders and darknet cybercriminal could usually use the infrastructure for one specific country more than the others, if this is the case the cross-regional capacity building centers should prioritize individuals from this countries to take the trainings, when taking down a darknet market the offenders might adapt, migrate, and reorganize themselves to continue their criminal activities (ElBahrawy et al., 2020; Jardine, 2021; Wang et al., 2023).

Figure 3. Integrated framework for future darknet counter-operations

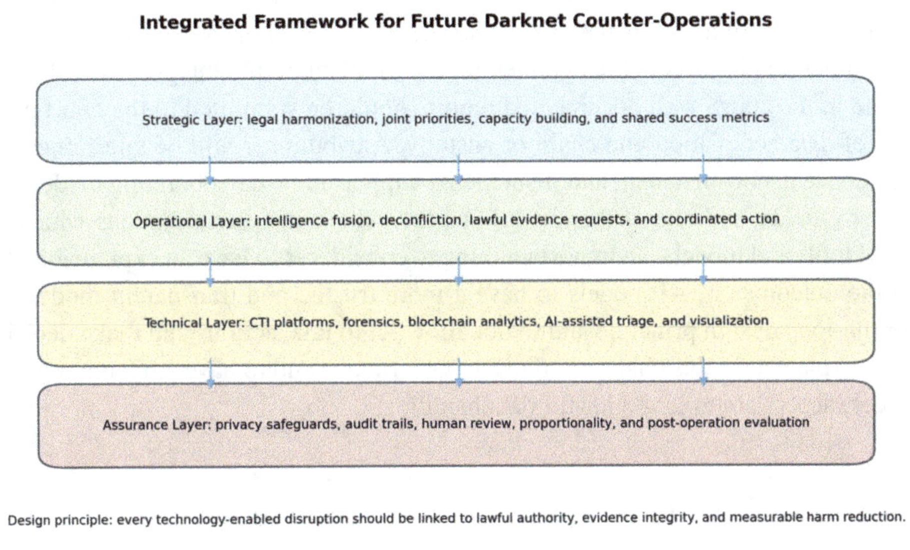

Case Box 3: Market Closure and Ecosystem Adaptation

Recent research shows that after illegal market closure, offenders and vendors might move their illegal activities to a more flexible, and resilient markets, that's why monitoring activities should continue and long-term evaluation should be performed (ElBahrawy et al., 2020; Wang et al., 2023).

Figure 3 shows how different layers are working together towards a more efficient integrated frameworks at strategic, operational, technical, and assurance layers. Harmonization between different legal entities and maximizing their joint priorities, while they collaboratively using technical forensics, blockchain, and other technical tools and maintain the privacy of the victims and different entities and parties involved in the investigation process.

10. CONCLUSION

In this book chapter, many issues have been addressed to understand the darknet ecosystem, where offenders are trying to hide their real identity by using many legitimate technologies such as encryption, TOR, cryptocurrency and other tools and technologies. Criminal groups are working collaboratively to manage and administer the different market, develop malware, laundering money, facilitate migration from one market to another, and providing the required infrastructure to commit many cybercrime activities. On the other hand, to takedown any darknet market, counter operations and investigation efforts should not be isolated and cross-regional and international collaboration should be facilitated and enabled, and the outcome of these efforts should be expressed in a quantifiable and measurable manner, knowledge should be shared and capacity building regional centres should be established to improve the skills and knowledge of the investigators in both technical and legal fields. Investigators should be able to use the most emergent technologies such as AI to analyse and find insights in the huge datasets they are dealing with. Legal frameworks should be adapted to speed up and facilitate the processing of the cross-regional requests, without exposing the sensitive information for victims and suspects. Investigators and researchers made many inferences, where each inference is attached with a confidence level. These inferences are derived from the tools they are using such as AI, digital forensic tools, blockchain analysis, and cyber threat intelligence. Other challenges are to maintain the integrity of collected evidence to be admissible in the court, well documented report should be submitted to the court explaining the whole process of data acquisition and chain of custody. Attribution could be questioned in the court, usually one evidence is not sufficient, and it should be supported by corroborating evidence. AI started to dominate many fields, and one of them would be the cybercrime investigations which will heavily rely on using AI tools and models, an important thing to consider is to have an explainable AI to explain and interpret the outcomes of AI models to have a more trusted and transparent models and to keep the human-in-the-loop design principle and to not allow AI to take actions and make decisions. One of the main points explained in this chapter is the data governance and to have a retention policies, secure storage practices, access control, and lawful data handling.

REFERENCES

Aldridge, J., & Décary-Hétu, D. (2016). Hidden wholesale: The drug diffusing capacity of online drug cryptomarkets. *The International Journal on Drug Policy*, *35*, 7–15. DOI: 10.1016/j.drugpo.2016.04.020 PMID: 27260863

Arnold, N., Ebrahimi, M., Zhang, N., Lazarine, B., Patton, M., Chen, H., & Samtani, S. (2019). Dark-net ecosystem cyber-threat intelligence (CTI) tool. In *2019 IEEE International Conference on Intelligence and Security Informatics (ISI)* (pp. 92-97). IEEE. DOI: 10.1109/ISI.2019.8823501

Broadhurst, R., Grabosky, P., Alazab, M., & Chon, S. (2014). An analysis of the nature of groups engaged in cyber crime. *International Journal of Cyber Criminology*, *8*(1), 1–20.

Casey, E. (2011). *Digital Evidence and Computer Crime: Forensic Science, Computers and the Internet* (3rd ed.). Academic Press.

Chainalysis. (2022). The 2022 crypto crime report. https://go.chainalysis.com/2022-Crypto-Crime-Report.html

Chainalysis. (2024). Money laundering and cryptocurrency: Trends and new techniques for detection and investigation. https://www.chainalysis.com/blog/money-laundering-cryptocurrency/

Christin, N. (2013). Traveling the Silk Road: A measurement analysis of a large anonymous online marketplace. In *Proceedings of the 22nd International World Wide Web Conference (WWW '13)* (pp. 213-224). ACM. DOI: 10.1145/2488388.2488408

Council of Europe. (2001). Convention on Cybercrime (ETS No. 185). Budapest, 23 November 2001. https://www.coe.int/en/web/conventions/full-list/-/conventions/treaty/185

Council of Europe. (2022). Second Additional Protocol to the Convention on Cybercrime on enhanced co-operation and disclosure of electronic evidence (ETS No. 224). https://www.coe.int/en/web/conventions/full-list/-/conventions/treaty/224

Dearden, T. E., & Tucker, S. E. (2023). Follow the Money: Analyzing Darknet Activity Using Crypto-currency and the Bitcoin Blockchain. *Journal of Contemporary Criminal Justice*, *39*(2), 257–275. DOI: 10.1177/10439862231157521

ElBahrawy, A., Alessandretti, L., Rusnac, L., Goldsmith, D., Teytelboym, A., & Baronchelli, A. (2020). Collective dynamics of dark web marketplaces. *Scientific Reports*, *10*(1), 18827. Advance online publication. DOI: 10.1038/s41598-020-74416-y PMID: 33139743

EMCDDA & Europol. (2019). EU Drug Markets Report 2019. European Monitoring Centre for Drugs and Drug Addiction and Europol. https://www.emcdda.europa.eu

European Commission. (2023). E-evidence: Cross-border access to electronic evidence. https://commission.europa.eu/law/cross-border-cases/judicial-cooperation/types-judicial-cooperation/e-evidence-cross-border-access-electronic-evidence_en

Europol. (2017, July 20). Massive blow to criminal dark web activities after globally coordinated operation: Takedown of AlphaBay and Hansa will lead to hundreds of new investigations in Europe. https://www.europol.europa.eu/media-press/newsroom/news/massive-blow-to-criminal-dark-web-activities-after-globally-coordinated-operation

Europol. (2024). Internet Organised Crime Threat Assessment (IOCTA) 2024. European Union Agency for Law Enforcement Cooperation. https://www.europol.europa.eu/publication-events/main-reports/internet-organised-crime-threat-assessment-iocta-2024

Federal Bureau of Investigation. (2017). AlphaBay takedown. https://www.fbi.gov/news/stories/alphabay-takedown

Foley, S., & Jonathan, R. (2019, May). Karlsen, Tālis J Putniņš, Sex, Drugs, and Bitcoin: How Much Illegal Activity Is Financed through Cryptocurrencies? *Review of Financial Studies*, *32*(5), 1798–1853. DOI: 10.1093/rfs/hhz015

Hancock, P. J., van Hardeveld, G. J., Jakubcek, J., Akhgar, B., Davey, S., & Amann, P. (2024). Design of Cryptopol: A serious game for teaching cryptocurrency tracing techniques to law enforcement. *Games : Research & Practice*, *2*(4), 32. Advance online publication. DOI: 10.1145/3697845

Holt, T. J., Lee, J. R., & Griffith, E. (2023). An Assessment of Cryptomixing Services in Online Illicit Markets. *Journal of Contemporary Criminal Justice*, *39*(2), 222–238. DOI: 10.1177/10439862231158004 PMID: 40822574

Homeland Security Investigations, I. C. E. (2025, May 22). ICE, Europol, law enforcement partners dismantle major illicit drug networks in global darknet crackdown: Operation RapTOR. U.S. Immigration and Customs Enforcement. https://www.ice.gov/news/releases/ice-europol-law-enforcement-partners-dismantle-major-illicit-drug-networks-global

Howell, C. J., Maimon, D., Perkins, R. C., Burruss, G. W., Ouellet, M., & Wu, Y. (2024). Risk Avoidance Behavior on Darknet Marketplaces. *Crime and Delinquency*, *70*(2), 519–538. DOI: 10.1177/00111287221092713

Hutchings, A., & Holt, T. J. (2017). The online stolen data market: Disruption and intervention approaches. *Global Crime*, *18*(1), 11–30. DOI: 10.1080/17440572.2016.1197123

Jardine, E. (2021). Policing the Cybercrime Script of Darknet Drug Markets: Methods of Effective Law Enforcement Intervention. *American Journal of Criminal Justice*, *46*(6), 980–1005. DOI: 10.1007/s12103-021-09656-3

Katiyar, N., Tripathi, S., Kumar, P., Verma, S., Sahu, A. K., & Saxena, S. (2024). AI and Cyber-Security: Enhancing threat detection and response with machine learning. *Educational Administration: Theory and Practice*, *30*(4), 6273–6282. DOI: 10.53555/kuey.v30i4.2377

Kim, M., Lee, J., Kwon, H., & Hur, J. (2022). Get off of chain: Unveiling dark web using multilayer bitcoin address clustering. *IEEE Access : Practical Innovations, Open Solutions*, *10*, 70078–70091. DOI: 10.1109/ACCESS.2022.3187210

Labs, T. R. M. (2025). Europol and German authorities lead global takedown of darknet child exploitation platform Kidflix. TRM Blog. https://www.trmlabs.com/resources/blog/europol-and-german-authorities-lead-global-takedown-of-darknet-child-exploitation-platform-kidflix

Liu, X. F., Jiang, X., Liu, S., & Tse, C. K. (2021). Knowledge discovery in cryptocurrency transactions: A survey. *IEEE Access : Practical Innovations, Open Solutions*, *9*, 37229–37254. DOI: 10.1109/ACCESS.2021.3062652

Mireille, H., & Rueda Blanco, J. (2022). SoK: Cross-border criminal investigations and digital evidence. *Journal of Cybersecurity*, *8*(1), tyac014. Advance online publication. DOI: 10.1093/cybsec/tyac014

Pastor-Galindo, J., Nespoli, P., Mármol, F. G., & Pérez, G. M. (2020). The not yet exploited goldmine of OSINT: Opportunities, open challenges and future trends. *IEEE Access : Practical Innovations, Open Solutions*, *8*, 10282–10304. DOI: 10.1109/ACCESS.2020.2965257

Rid, T., & Buchanan, B. (2015). Attributing cyber attacks. *The Journal of Strategic Studies*, *38*(1–2), 4–37. DOI: 10.1080/01402390.2014.977382

Ryder, N. (2012). *Money laundering: An endless cycle? A comparative analysis of the anti-money laundering policies in the United States of America*. Routledge. DOI: 10.4324/9780203126783

Santos, P., Abreu, R., Reis, M. J. C. S., Serôdio, C., & Branco, F. (2025). A Systematic Review of Cyber Threat Intelligence: The Effectiveness of Technologies, Strategies, and Collaborations in Combating Modern Threats. *Sensors (Basel)*, *25*(14), 4272. DOI: 10.3390/s25144272 PMID: 40732398

Soska, K., & Christin, N. (2015). Measuring the longitudinal evolution of the online anonymous marketplace ecosystem. In *Proceedings of the 24th USENIX Security Symposium* (pp. 33–48). USENIX Association.

Suryotrisongko, H., Musashi, Y., Tsuneda, A., & Sugitani, K. (2022). Robust botnet DGA detection: Blending XAI and OSINT for cyber threat intelligence sharing. *IEEE Access : Practical Innovations, Open Solutions*, *10*, 34613–34624. DOI: 10.1109/ACCESS.2022.3162588

UNODC. (2023). Comprehensive study on cybercrime: Draft. United Nations Office on Drugs and Crime. https://www.unodc.org/unodc/en/cybercrime/comprehensive-study-on-cybercrime.html

Van Wegberg, R., Oerlemans, J. J., & Van Deventer, O. (2018). Bitcoin money laundering: Mixed results? An explorative study on money laundering of cybercrime proceeds using bitcoin. *Journal of Financial Crime*, *25*(2), 419–435. DOI: 10.1108/JFC-11-2016-0067

Wang, Y., Arief, B., & Hernandez-Castro, J. C. (2023). Dark ending: What happens when a dark web market closes down. In *Proceedings of the 9th International Conference on Information Systems Security and Privacy (ICISSP 2023)* (pp. 106-117). SciTePress. DOI: 10.5220/0011681600003405

Chapter 14
Cybersecurity Awareness and Resilience Against Darknet Threats

Tanishka Prashant Madke
Ajeenkya D.Y. Patil University, India

Amisha Shaikh
Ajeenkya D.Y. Patil University, India

Susanta Das
http://orcid.org/0000-0002-9314-3988
Ajeenkya D.Y. Patil University, India

ABSTRACT

Modern societies depend on digital technologies in many areas of life that are considered essential & critical (healthcare, transportation, finance & communication). However, as more interconnected systems are adopted, cyber threats (malware, phishing, ransomware & attacks) on critical infrastructure are also revealed. Cybersecurity is critical in the provision of a secure space and the maintenance of a sustainable development. The study aims at researching the subject of cybersecurity and its influence in sustainable societies in relation to cyber threat prevention, information security, and cyber awareness. It analyses the main cyber threat factors & provides the mathematical models of cyber risk assessment, and intrusion detection. It also highlights the relevance of the cybersecurity frameworks and people-focused security practices. Finally, one mentions the recent technologies, such as artificial intelligence, blockchain, federated learning, and sophisticated communication networks as the potential solutions to the optimization of the cybersecurity resilience in the future.

1. INTRODUCTION

The swift development of digital technologies, including cloud computing, artificial intelligence, and the Internet of Things (IoT), has changed the contemporary societies and digital infrastructures to a great extent. These technologies help to develop the economy, engage in digital communication, smart

DOI: 10.4018/979-8-3373-9755-9.ch014

cities, and sustainable governance systems. Nonetheless, the growing use of interconnected systems has broadened the cyber-attack surface exposing organizations and individuals to various cyber-threats such as malware, phishing, ransomware, and data breaches. With the further development of digital ecosystems, cybersecurity has turned out to be a vital need to secure information systems and stability of digital services (Li & Liu, 2021; Sulich, 2025).

Cybersecurity is centered on securing computer systems, networks and digital data against unauthorized use and malicious attacks as well as manipulation of data. The current cyberattacks are getting more sophisticated and capable of being targeted by the government systems, financial institutions, healthcare infrastructure, and critical industrial systems. Li and Liu (2021) explain that cyberattacks have advanced at an expedited rate because of internet connectivity and the rising sophistication of digital networks. Such attacks have the potential to disrupt data confidentiality, integrity, and availability which are major pillars of information security. As a result, cyber protection of the digital infrastructures has been a critical solution to the preservation of confidence in the digital environment and the advancement of technologies in the long term (Li & Liu, 2021).

Sustainable development is also directly related to cybersecurity since the efficient operation of smart cities, digital economies, and the e-governance systems require secure digital infrastructures. Digital technologies give possibilities to manage the resources efficiently, monitor the environmental situation, and offer intelligent urban services, but all these possibilities could be provided only in case the digital infrastructure at the background is secure. Sustainable development research insists on the fact that ineffective cybersecurity systems may destroy the economic stability and trust that the society would have in the digital infrastructure, which, in turn, may jeopardize the sustainable development of the society (Li, 2025; Ige, 2024).

Cyber awareness amongst the individuals and organizations is another vital aspect of cybersecurity. People are the main factors that cause many cybersecurity cases, including poor passwords, ignorance about phishing, and unsecured internet activities. Research studies have indicated that enhancing cybersecurity awareness would help a great deal in limiting the chances of successful cyberattack through enabling users to identify and respond to the possible threats better. Training and educational campaigns and programs are thus important to enhance the general cybersecurity stance of organizations and societies (Wang, 2022).

Moreover, the recent technological improvement like artificial intelligence and machine learning has helped to enhance the cybersecurity measures by allowing intelligent detection of threats, analysing anomalies, and responding to them automatically. Artificial intelligence-based cybersecurity solutions have the capability to process massive amounts of network traffic to detect suspicious behavior and project possible cyber-attacks before they inflict severe harm. Such technologies help to improve the cyber defense and the resiliency of digital infrastructures to sustainable societies (Achuthan et al., 2024; Sulich, 2025).

Hence, cybersecurity has become one of the pillars of creating a sustainable digital society. It assists in securing information systems, averting cyber threats and safe digital habits among the users. This chapter seeks to discuss cybersecurity practices in sustainable communities in terms of cyber threat prevention, protecting information security, and cyber awareness and also provides the mathematical modeling to assess cyber risks and intrusion detection effectiveness (Li, 2025; Wang, 2022).

The chapter addresses cybersecurity measures in sustainable digital society in the context of the changing cyber threats and its impact on digital infrastructures. It explains the key cyber threats that exist in today's digital world, such as malware, phishing, ransomware, and new activities enabled by the Darknet. The chapter presents the mathematical models that can be used to detect cyber threats and assess cyber risk, and also emphasizes the significance of human factors and cyber awareness in enhancing cybersecurity practices. Moreover, it reviews the existing cybersecurity frameworks for critical infrastructure protection and evaluates the key issues that organisations are facing in securing their digital ecosystems, such as the darknet and the threat contributed by anonymous platforms. A number of quantitative cybersecurity risk modelling techniques are also introduced to aid with data-driven security decisions. Lastly, the chapter proposes future research avenues that combine Artificial Intelligence, Blockchain, Federated Learning, Darknet Threat Intelligence and Next Generation Communication Networks to boost the cybersecurity resilience of sustainable digital societies.

2. CYBER THREATS IN THE DIGITAL ENVIRONMENT

The high rate of digitalization of current infrastructures has been one of the major factors that have exposed people, organizations, and governments to cyber threats. With the rising use of digital technologies, including cloud computing, Internet of Things (IoT), and artificial intelligence, cybercriminals are taking the opportunity to exploit interconnected systems vulnerabilities to mount advanced attacks. Cyber threats involve any unlawful actions meant to violate confidentiality, integrity, or availability of information resources and digital systems. The increasing nature of the networked systems has increased the attack surface, and cybersecurity has become a critical element in the securing of digital environments and supporting sustainable digital infrastructures (Sicari et al., 2015; Conti et al., 2018).

Malware is one of the most prevalent types of cyber threats that look after a malicious software to breach and wreak havoc on the computer system or network. Malware can consist of different types including viruses, worms, spyware and ransomware. They may be used to steal sensitive information, interfere with the functioning of a system, or give criminals unauthorized access to them (Bourke et al., 2016). According to recent research, malware attacks are now more complex and can employ more sophisticated methods to avoid detection by conventional security systems, including polymorphic code and artificial intelligence (Ferrag et al., 2020). Malware attacks are therefore a significant issue to cybersecurity experts to detect and mitigate (Ferrag et al., 2020).

Phishing is another significant cyber threat to the contemporary digital systems. Phishing is the fraudulent practice applied by hackers to mislead people to provide important information like passwords, credit card numbers, or personal data. Such attacks are normally done using the fraudulent emails, the bogus websites or when using the malicious links that seem to be legitimate to the unsuspecting users. By making believable messages that prompt users to share personal information, cybercriminals take advantage of human vulnerability to obtain the required information. Studies indicate that phishing scams are deemed to be one of the most efficient tools employed by hackers to discharge information systems since people do not understand cybersecurity (Behl et al., 2021).

Another threat that has caused significant harm to the cyber arena in the recent past is the ransomware attacks. During a ransomware attack, the victim files or systems are encrypted by malicious software which then demands payment in order to be restored with access to the data. The attacks have the potential to cripple operations of business entities, healthcare services and government systems. Cyber threat reports worldwide point out that cases of ransomware have tremendously risen in various sectors, which leads to both financial losses and operational setbacks of organizations globally (ENISA, 2023).

Besides conventional cyber threats, the increase in the use of Internet of Things (IoT) gadgets has presented new security risks in the digital world. IoT devices are also characterized by low computer power and poor security controls; therefore, they are an easy target by hackers. The hacked IoT devices are capable of carrying out distributed denial-of-service (DDoS) attacks or unauthorized network access. Research has also revealed that the swift expansion of IoT systems has generated new weaknesses that demand superior security measures and surveillance systems (Conti et al., 2018; Sicari et al., 2015). Besides, intrusion detection systems based on anomalies have been a well investigated method of identifying cyber threats in the network settings. These systems monitor network traffic patterns and detect the possible suspicious activities that might be indicative of cyber-attacks. Indicatively, UNSW-NB15 is one of the datasets that have been utilized to assess the efficiency of machine learning-based intrusion detection systems in detecting cyber threats in complex network setups (Moustafa & Slay, 2016). These systems are relevant in enhancing cybersecurity safeguards and making possible the early identification of cyber-attacks (Moustafa & Slay, 2016).

All in all, the situation with cyber threats in the digital environment remains constantly changing by developing technology and connecting digital systems more and more. To mitigate these threats, a balanced set of high-tech cybersecurity tools and security policies, as well as better cyber awareness of users is required. Enhancing cybersecurity systems is thus a key challenge towards securing online infrastructures and enhancing the sustainability of sustainable digital communities (Conti et al., 2018; Ferrag et al., 2020).

The flow chart (Figure 1) shows the workflow of functioning of a cyber threat detection system deployed in the modern network security infrastructures. They operate on the principle that such systems repeatedly scan the network and evaluate the patterns of traffic to detect possible cyber threats and other illicit actions inside digital systems (Garcia-Teodoro et al., 2009; Buczak & Guven, 2016).

This is initiated with the process of data collection, in which the network packets, system logs, and communication data are collected in different channels which include servers, routers, firewalls and devices connected to the network. These sources of data present the needed information needed to identify abnormal behaviors in the network settings (Scarfone & Mell, 2007).

Figure 1. Cyber threat detection workflow

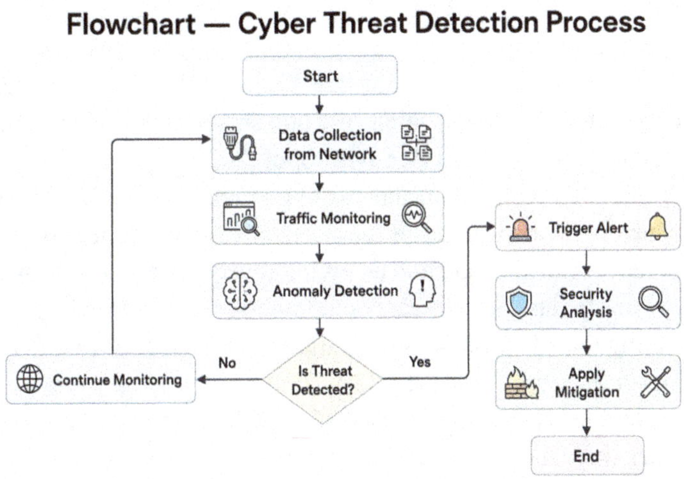

Once the data is gathered, the system is then capable of traffic monitoring whereby network traffic is continuously monitored to determine communication behavior and define normal system behavior. Monitoring devices look at the packet traffic, bandwidth, protocols of communication, and user actions with the aim of identifying an abnormality that can be attributed to malicious intent (Sommer & Paxson, 2010).

The second step is anomaly detection, which can be performed with the help of statistical methods or machine learning models to identify abnormal network behavior that can be considered a cyber-attack. Any unusual attempts to log-in, unusual data transfers, or any unforeseen communication between devices are some of the indicators of potential security threats (Ferrag et al., 2020).

The system analyses that the anomaly identified is a true cyber threat at the decision point "Is Threat Detected? by the determinations of the system. The system will monitor the network activities in case there is a lack of a threat. Nonetheless, when any threat has been detected, the system sends an alert and performs security analysis to determine the source of the attack and determine the extent of the attack to the system.

Finally, appropriate mitigation strategies are implemented in order to secure the system. The activities may be blocking of bad traffic, isolating bad devices, redefining firewall rules, or the killing of suspicious processes. Such response measures play a vital role in mitigating cyber-attacks within the digital infrastructure (Buczak & Guven, 2016).

3. DARKNET AND ITS ROLE IN CYBERSECURITY THREATS

The Darknet is a part of the Internet that isn't accessible through regular search engines, and will need special software to get into, such as Tor (The Onion Router). Its goal is to provide anonymity and privacy, concealing who they are and how they are connected from each other. The Darknet is not all bad as it has enabled many individuals to keep their privacy and secure their free speech in repressive areas, but it is also a huge venue for cybercrime and illegal activities (Nunes et al., 2018).

One of the significant issues associated with the Darknet is darknet markets for selling stolen data, hacking tools, and malware. Cybercrime is becoming more accessible to less technically savvy people, as the markets offer an array of malware, ransomware kits and phishing templates, as well as kits for exploit. Sophisticated cyber-attack tools are being sold and shared on the Darknet and this phenomenon is often referred to as "Cybercrime-as-a-Service" (Europol, 2020).

The Darknet environment has been one of the most beneficial environments for ransomware operations. The use of cryptocurrencies also increases the anonymity of the communication channels used for coordinating attacks, spreading ransomware and receiving ransom payments. Ransomware-as-a-Service (RaaS) models make it easier for attackers to carry out large-scale attacks without having to create their own tools, thus complicating the situation of organizations and critical infrastructures (CI) with respect to the frequency and impact of cyber threats (ENISA, 2023).

The Darknet is also home to data breaches and leaks, which can also aid in cybercrime. After successful cyber activities, sensitive data like personal information, financial records and login credentials are often sold or shared in a Darknet forum. This not only raises the likelihood of identity theft and financial fraud, but also makes it more difficult for people and organizations to be secure in the long term (Kshetri, 2019).

Although the Darknet has a bad reputation in the world of cybercrime, it can also be a wonderful resource for cyber threat intelligence. Security researchers and organizations monitor the Darknet to keep an eye on any new threats that arise, to track hacker activities, and to prevent any potential cyber-attacks from happening. Cybersecurity systems can leverage these tools to analyze communication patterns, transaction activities, shared attack tools on Darknet platforms, and improve threat detection and enhance proactive defense strategies (Nunes et al., 2018).

But tracking and controlling the Darknet is difficult because of the anonymous and decentralized nature of the Net. The challenges that law enforcement encounters when trying to trace cybercriminals, implement rules and regulations, and catch the unregulated activity in the hidden networks. Use of encryption technologies and cryptocurrencies further make it difficult to assign cyber-attacks and prosecute cyber-criminals (Europol, 2020).

So, overall, the Darknet has a dual nature in Cybersecurity – it is the place where cyber criminals go to operate, but it is also the place where threat intelligence is found. The Darknet's functioning and impact are closely related to its structure, and it is crucial to understand this relationship to be able to create effective cybersecurity strategies and protect digital infrastructures in sustainable societies.

4. MATHEMATICAL MODELS FOR CYBER THREAT DETECTION

Mathematical models and statistical techniques are increasingly being used in the analysis of cyber threat in the framework of cybersecurity systems that identify malicious activities in digital infrastructures. These models can be used to measure cyber risks, the likelihood of attacks, and enhance effectiveness of intrusion detection systems. Mathematical modeling is relevant in cybersecurity since the contemporary cyber threats produce vast amounts of data in networks which should be analyzed effectively to detect abnormal behavior. Statistical models and machine learning algorithms are extensively used to identify cyber threat using network traffic pattern and detect the deviation of normal behavior (Sommer and Paxson, 2010; Ferrag et al., 2020). The cyber risk assessment model is one of the basic methods of the cybersecurity risk analysis that approximates the potential harm of cyber threats. Risk may be mathematically expressed as the proportion of possibility of attack and effect on the system. The risk model can be formulated as:

$$R = P \times I$$

Where:

R represents the overall cyber risk,
P represents the probability of a cyber-attack occurring, and
I represents the impact or damage caused by the attack.

The equation enables organizations to give precedence to security measures in accordance to the intensity of threats. When the values of the risk increase, it implies that there is the necessity of a more robust system of cybersecurity controls and monitoring (Scarfone and Mell, 2007). The other mathematical model that is significant in cybersecurity is the intrusion detection rate which quantifies the efficiency of an intrusion detection system (IDS). Intrusion detection systems use network traffic to detect any suspicious activity that could be a sign of cyber-attack. The response rate of an IDS may be determined by the following equation:

$$Detection\ Rate = \frac{TP}{TP + FN}$$

Where:

TP represents true positives (correctly detected attacks) and
FN represents false negatives (attacks that were not detected).

An increased rate of detection shows that the intrusion detection system is efficient in detecting cyber threats (Moustafa & Slay, 2016).

Besides the detection rate, the other widely applicable assessment parameter in cybersecurity models is the false positive rate, that is, how frequently normal operations are mistaken as attacks. False positive can be computed as:

$$False\ Positive\ Rate = \frac{FP}{FP + TN}$$

Where:

FP represents false positives and
TN represents true negatives.

Minimizing the false positive is significant since high false positive can diminish the effectiveness of cybersecurity systems and escalate the costs of operation (Garcia-Teodoro et al., 2009).

Entropy-based anomaly detection is another type of mathematical methodology that has been applied in the analysis of cyber threats by quantifying randomness or uncertainty in network traffic patterns. The use of entropy can be used to detect malicious behavior in the network that could be a sign of a cyber-attack like a distributed denial-of-service (DDoS) attack or malware. Entropy of network traffic is given as:

$$H(X) = -\sum_{i=1}^{n} p(x_i) \log p(x_i)$$

Where:

$H(X)$ represents the entropy value,
$p(x_i)$ represents the probability distribution of network events, and

n represents the number of observed events.

The drastic alterations in the entropy values regularly represent the abnormal network behavior that can be related to cyber-attacks (Ferrag et al., 2020).

Moreover, machine learning models have been highly utilized to enhance the detection of cyber threats. Logistic regression and neural networks classification algorithms may be used to help approximate the likelihood of a network event being linked to a cyber-attack. The logistic regression model employed in intrusion detection will be expressed as follows:

$$P(Y = 1|X) = \frac{1}{1 + e^{-(\beta_0 + \beta_1 X_1 + \beta_2 X_2 + \ldots + \beta_n X_n)}}$$

Where:

$P(Y=1|X)$ represents the probability of a cyber-attack,
$X_1, X_2, \ldots, X_n$ represent network features, &
β values represent model parameters.

Intrusion detection models based on machine learning have the ability to increase the detection accuracy of cyber threats through the analysis of large datasets in a network and detection of the complex patterns of the attack (Sommer et al., 2010; Ferrag et al., 2020).

Altogether, mathematical models offer an organized method of studying cyber threats, assessing an intrusion detection system, and enhancing cybersecurity decision-making. Cybersecurity systems will be able to more effectively identify and handle cyber threats in the contemporary digital setting through machine learning algorithms, risk assessment models, and statistical analysis (Conti et al., 2018; Sicari et al., 2015).

5. CYBER AWARENESS AND HUMAN FACTORS IN CYBERSECURITY

Cybersecurity is not a purely technological problem, but it is also a human problem. Human behaviour is a key factor in the efficiency of cybersecurity systems since a good number of cyber-attacks have happened as a result of user error or ignorance. Research has shown that a significant percentage of cyber-attacks are committed with the help of human vulnerabilities and not technical vulnerabilities in security systems. To illustrate the point, phishing emails, spoof websites, or misleading messages are some of the frequently used social engineering methods that attackers use to control the user to disclose sensitive information. Thus, the enhancement of cyber awareness of individuals and organizations is a vital part of contemporary cybersecurity measures (Bada et al., 2019; Parsons et al., 2014).

Cyber awareness is the knowledge and understanding that the users have about cyber risks, secure online behaviour, and protection security measures. Cybersecurity awareness programs are often implemented by organizations to teach their staff about possible cyber-threats like phishing, malware, and password attacks. It has been found out that the cybersecurity awareness of users translates to safer behaviour in their interaction with digital systems, and that they are not prone to being victims of cyber-attacks (Kruger & Kearney, 2006). As a result, it is believed that the concept of cybersecurity awareness training is among the most practical options that can be used to mitigate human-related security vulnerabilities in organizations (Dinev & Hu, 2007). Probabilistic models may also be used to analyze human behaviour in cybersecurity making an estimate of the probability of security incidents involving the users. An example of a model that is often employed is the likelihood of a cyber-attack as a matter of user vulnerability and attacker power. This correlation is mathematically represented as:

$$P(A) = V \times C$$

Where:

$P(A)$ represents the probability of a successful cyber-attack,

V represents the vulnerability level of users, and

C represents the capability of the attacker.

This model mentions that the vulnerability of users in terms of cybersecurity awareness training can be significantly lowered to achieve a high level of reduction in the likelihood of successful cyber-attacks (Hadlington, 2017).

The other valuable part of human-centered cybersecurity is the study of phishing vulnerability. Phishing is a technique based on manipulation of psychology to betray users into giving confidential details. It is possible to estimate the likelihood of a user being deceived by a phishing attack by using the following model:

$$P(P_h) = \frac{N_v}{N_t}$$

Where:

$P(P_h)$ represents the probability of phishing success,
N_v represents the number of vulnerable users, and
N_t represents the total number of users in the system.

The success of phishing could be considerably decreased by training the vulnerable users via awareness programs (Workman, 2008).

Besides personal consciousness, there are also psychological and behavioural causes of cybersecurity risks. Stress, workload, and the addiction to the internet are factors that may lead to a negative impact on the user decision-making and probability of security errors. Studies have revealed that people who do not have good digital habits or those who use the internet too frequently can have a lowered cybersecurity behavior, thus exposing organizations to a greater risk of security attacks (Hadlington, 2017). The behavioural patterns should be understood to create effective cybersecurity awareness programs.

Moreover, integrating psychological data with traditional cybersecurity monitoring systems can improve threat detection capabilities. Behavioral cybersecurity models combine technical indicators with human behavioral analysis to identify insider threats and suspicious activities within organizations. By analysing behavioral patterns and deviations from normal user activities, cybersecurity systems can detect potential insider attacks or compromised accounts more effectively (Greitzer & Frincke, 2010).

Overall, cyber awareness and human-centered security approaches are essential for strengthening cybersecurity defenses in modern digital environments. While advanced security technologies are necessary for protecting information systems, addressing human vulnerabilities through education, behavioral analysis, and awareness programs remains equally important. Enhancing cybersecurity awareness among users can significantly reduce cyber risks and contribute to the development of a secure and sustainable digital society (Bada et al., 2019; Parsons et al., 2014).

6. CYBERSECURITY FRAMEWORK FOR A SUSTAINABLE DIGITAL SOCIETY

To achieve a sustainable digital society, effective cybersecurity structures should be established to ensure the safety of critical infrastructure, digital services, and confidential information against cyber threats. With the further development of digital technologies, governments and companies should introduce systematic cybersecurity systems that combine the technological aspects of security, risk management, and human-based education. Cybersecurity models offer uniform guidelines and best practices which assist organizations to detect their vulnerabilities, handle cyber risks and also respond adequately to cyber incidents. These are frameworks that are vital in terms of making digital infrastructures resilient and sustainable in the long run (Von Solms & Van Niekerk, 2013).

A risk management framework is considered to be one of the most commonly known models of cybersecurity as it is aimed at finding and eliminating cybersecurity threats in the digital environment. Cybersecurity risk management is the process of assessing the threats and vulnerabilities that are likely to occur and the possible effect of a cyber-attack on the information systems. The general cybersecurity threat of a system may be put as follows in mathematical notation:

$$Risk = Threat \times Vulnerability \times Impact$$

Where:

Threat represents the likelihood of a cyber-attack,
Vulnerability represents weaknesses within the system, and
Impact represents the potential damage caused by the attack.

This model can assist an organization to make security investments a priority and ensure that the right security mechanisms are implemented to reduce the effect of cybersecurity threats (Shameli-Sendi et al., 2016).

The protection of the critical infrastructure systems such as energy networks, healthcare systems, financial institutions and transportation systems is another crucial element of cybersecurity frameworks. These are infrastructures that are very dependent on digital technologies and interconnected networks and hence can be targeted by cyber-attacks. The security of these systems needs holistic cybersecurity plans which involve monitoring of threats, responding mechanisms, and security governance. It has been identified that cyber-attacks on critical infrastructures have the potential to result in extreme impacts on the economy and the society in general, making it critical to have an effective cybersecurity framework that enables sustainable digital development (Alcaraz and Zeadally, 2015).

Besides risk management, security control effectiveness models are also built in the cybersecurity frameworks, which assess the capability of security mechanisms to mitigate cyber-attack. The security control effectiveness can be expressed as:

$$Security\ Effectiveness = \frac{Prevented\ Attacks}{Total\ Attempted\ Attacks}$$

This metric helps organizations measure the performance of their cybersecurity systems and identify areas where security controls need improvement.

Game theory modeling is another method of analysis employed in cybersecurity frameworks, and it fits the analysis of the strategic interaction between attackers and defenders in cyberspace. In cybersecurity settings, attackers strive to ensure that cyber-attacks are the most successful whereas defenders strive to ensure that any damage is the least possible. A payoff function can be used to describe the interaction between the attackers and the defenders:

$$U_d = B_d - C_d$$

Where:

U_d represents the defender's utility,
B_d represents the benefit gained from successfully defending the system, and
C_d represents the cost of implementing cybersecurity defenses.

Game-theoretic enables cybersecurity experts to know how attackers behave and how best to develop defense mechanisms to counter digital systems (Coles-Kemp, 2009).

Moreover, the cybersecurity frameworks attach relevance to standardized security management systems like the ISO/IEC 27001 which offers the guidelines on how to implement information security management systems (ISMS). These standards assist the organizations in implementing the policies, procedures and technical controls to preserve the sensitive information and to ensure the regulatory compliance. Equally, the NIST Cybersecurity Framework offers systematic directions of identifying, protecting, detecting, responding to, and recovering cyber incidents. The use of these frameworks helps organizations to create cybersecurity infrastructures, which will allow them to undergo a sustainable digital transformation (NIST, 2018; ISO/IEC, 2022).

Altogether, the application of extensive cybersecurity frameworks is vital to provide the security and sustainability of digital societies. These frameworks combine technological security control, risk assessment frameworks, governance policies and risk awareness programs to ensure that digital infrastructures are shielded against the changing cyber threats. Organizations are able to improve their cybersecurity posture by integrating mathematical risk models, strategic defense mechanisms, and standardised security practices that help to create a long-term sustainable digital ecosystem (ENISA, 2021).

7. CHALLENGES IN CYBERSECURITY FOR SUSTAINABLE SOCIETIES

Although there have been remarkable developments in cybersecurity technologies, there are a number of challenges that impede the creation of safe and sustainable digital societies. Recent developments in reliance on digital infrastructures, cloud computing solutions and interconnected devices have broadened the scope of attack by cybercriminals. The modern cyber threats are becoming more dynamic and intelligent and it is hard to make the traditional security mechanisms to identify and respond to the attacks. This means that cybersecurity specialists have to constantly revise security policies to overcome new threats and vulnerabilities in the digital ecosystem (Roman et al., 2018).

The fact that Internet of Things (IoT) devices are increasing rapidly is one of the most significant issues in cybersecurity. IoT systems are systems made up of interrelated devices, which gather and exchange vast amounts of data via networks. Nonetheless, various IoT gadgets possess few computing powers and poor security provisions, which render them susceptible to cyber-attacks. These vulnerabilities can be used by the attackers to access networks unauthorisedly or even carry out a distributed denial-of-service attack. Research shows that IoT infrastructure security is still a critical issue because standardized security systems and inadequate security measures of most IoT devices do not exist (Roman et al., 2018; Nurse et al., 2017).

The difficulty in identifying cyber-attacks on a large-scale network is also another critical issue. Huge amounts of network data should be analyzed by cybersecurity systems to detect suspicious behavior and possible cyber threats. Intrusion detection has extensively been applied using machine learning techniques, but they too have a number of limitations including high false positive rates, lack of training data, and have challenges in identifying never been attacked before. As a result, the accuracy and efficiency of machine learning-based systems of cybersecurity have become a research problem that is still being addressed (Buczak & Guven, 2016).

Economic impact of cyber-attacks is also a serious challenge to organizations and governments. Cyber-attacks may lead to loss of money, misuse of data and loss of reputation by the organizations. The economic expenses related to cyber-attacks are incident response costs, system recovery costs, and regulatory fines. Those investigating cybersecurity underline that the economic aspect of cybersecurity knowledge can help to create a successful approach to cyber defense and allocate resources more efficiently (Bohme & Moore, 2012).

Besides the technical issue, the area of cybersecurity governance and policy also influences the enabling of sustainable cybersecurity frameworks. Regulatory policies, international cooperation mechanisms, and standards of cybersecurity should be put in place by governments and organizations to ensure that digital infrastructures are safeguarded. Nevertheless, the fast-evolving nature of cyber threats tends to stay ahead of the creation of cybersecurity regulations, providing loopholes in the field of security regulation. To overcome these issues related to governance, policymakers, cybersecurity professionals, and industry stakeholders need to work together (Sabillon et al., 2017).

Moreover, the innovative technologies, including blockchain and artificial intelligence, bring both opportunities and threats to cybersecurity. Even though security mechanisms can be improved with the help of these technologies, they introduce new vulnerabilities and complexities to digital systems. As an illustration, blockchain systems can experience scalability and privacy problems, whereas AI-assisted security systems can be susceptible to adversarial attacks. Thus, these technological issues need to be resolved to establish robust cybersecurity systems in sustainable digital societies (Kumar & Mallick, 2018).

The other issue is associated with the problem of the lack of expertise in the cybersecurity sphere across the globe. The cybersecurity field demands specialists to stay high because organizations are adopting digital technologies and encountering more cyber threats. Nevertheless, the cybersecurity workforce on an international level is not adequate to handle this demand. Skilled professionals are also required to enable organizations to effectively adopt and manage cybersecurity strategies, but the absence of them will restrict their exposure to cyber risks (Roman et al., 2018; Buczak & Guven, 2016).

All in all, tackling cybersecurity issues needs to be an integrated process comprising of technological innovation, sound policy frameworks, economics, and cybersecurity education. Through such awareness and resolutions, the cybersecurity systems can be reinforced by organizations and governments and help to create safer and more sustainable digital societies (Roman et al., 2018; Buczak and Guven, 2016).

8. QUANTITATIVE CYBERSECURITY RISK MODELING AND EVALUATION

Quantitative modeling is significant in cybersecurity since it enables the researcher and organizations to assess cyber risks, quantify the efficiency of security investments, and study attacker-defender dynamics by mathematical means. In contrast to qualitative security assessments, quantitative models can offer quantifiable indicators that can assist decision makers to rank security strategies and effectively deploy resources. Various mathematical frameworks have been created to examine cybersecurity threats, security expenditures as well as defensive measures in present digital setups (Gordon & Loeb, 2002; Xu, 2014).

8.1. Cybersecurity Risk Probability Model

The number of techniques is one of the simplest quantitative approaches in the field of cybersecurity that assesses the likelihood of a cyber-attack on a digital system. The likelihood of attack may be given as:

$$P(A) = \frac{N_a}{N_t}$$

Where:

$P(A)$= probability of a cyber attack
N_a= number of observed cyber attacks

N_t= total number of system interactions or events

Purpose: To determine the rate of occurrence of cyber-attacks in a digital environment.

Outcome: This probability can help organizations to know the level of cyber risk to their systems and to make corresponding changes when it comes to security controls (Xu, 2014).

8.2. Gordon–Loeb Security Investment Model

The Gordon-Loeb model is very popular in knowing the best amount that organizations should spend on cybersecurity protection. The loss that can be expected due to cyber-attacks can be expressed as:

$$L = v \times \lambda$$

Where:

L= expected financial loss from cyber attacks
v= vulnerability of the system
λ= potential financial damage caused by the attack

The optimal cybersecurity investment is determined as:

$$S^* \leq \frac{1}{e} \times L$$

Where:

$S*$= optimal security investment

Purpose: To ascertain the level of restraint that an organization must invest on cybersecurity protection.

Outcome: The model demonstrates that the optimal investment of cybersecurity is generally less than 37% of anticipated loss, which assists organizations to use security budgets efficiently (Gordon and Loeb, 2002).

8.3. Intrusion Detection Accuracy Model

It is necessary to evaluate the effectiveness of cybersecurity systems with a view of enhancing cyber defense mechanisms. Intrusion detection systems can be based on the accuracy of the systems to determine the accuracy using the following formula:

$$Accuracy = \frac{TP + TN}{TP + TN + FP + FN}$$

Where:

TP= true positives (correctly detected attacks)

TN= true negatives (correctly detected normal activities)
FP= false positives
FN= false negatives

Purpose: To test the performance of intrusion detecting systems.

Outcome: The bigger the value of accuracy the means that the cybersecurity system is able to identify malicious activity efficiently and reduce false alarms (Zhang & Liu, 2010).

8.4. Game Theory Model for Cyber Defense

In the cyberspace, game theory models are commonly employed in order to analyze strategic interaction between attackers and defenders. Within a cyber security setting, attackers are trying to ensure that the cyber-attacks are as successful as possible and the defenders are trying to ensure that the damage caused by the cyber-attack is minimized by investing in security.

The defender's payoff function can be represented as:

$$U_d = B_d - C_d$$

Where:

U_d= defender's utility
B_d= benefit gained from preventing an attack
C_d= cost of implementing cybersecurity defenses

Purpose: In order to study the best counter-measures to cyber attackers.

Outcome: Game theory models are used to ensure that the organizations can identify the best cybersecurity practices by weighing between defense expenditures and the possible returns (Roy et al., 2010; Grossklags et al., 2008).

8.5. Network Security Externality Model

The actions of a single organization regarding cybersecurity can have an impact on the level of security of other systems that are interconnected. This is what is referred to as network security externality. The vulnerability of a network may be expressed as:

$$S_n = \sum_{i=1}^{n} s_i$$

Where:

S_n= overall network security level
S_i= security investment of individual nodes

Purpose: To examine the contribution of investment made by various organizations to the network security as a whole.

Outcome: The model shows that concerted activities towards cybersecurity enhance the security resiliency of interconnected cyber infrastructures (Lelarge & Bolot, 2008).

8.6. Cybersecurity Dynamic Risk Model

The nature of cyber threats changes over time and cybersecurity models should consider changes in the behavior of attackers that are dynamic. Differential equations modeling the dynamics of cybersecurity Cyber-attacks within a network can be modeled using the following type of differing equations:

$$\frac{dI(t)}{dt} = \beta S(t)I(t) - \gamma I(t)$$

Where:

$S(t)$= number of secure systems
$I(t)$= number of infected systems
β= attack propagation rate
γ= recovery rate

Purpose: To simulate the proliferation of cyber-attacks in the network setups.
Outcome: The model assists cybersecurity analysts to establish the propagation of cyber-attacks, as well as the formulation of effective containment policy (Xu, 2014).

9. CYBERSECURITY AND THE UNITED NATIONS SUSTAINABLE DEVELOPMENT GOALS (UNSDGs)

The growing reliance of contemporary societies on digital technologies has provided new possibilities in economic development, social progress, and innovation. Nevertheless, this digital transformation has also come with its own fair share of cybersecurity threats that could pose risks on the stability of key infrastructure, law and order, as well as digital services. The United Nations Sustainable Development Goals (UNSDGs) focus on the need to achieve resilient infrastructures, sustainable technological innovation, and safe and inclusive digital space. This makes cybersecurity extremely important in facilitating sustainable development because it helps safeguard digital ecosystems against cyber-attacks and safeguard the dependability of information systems through the utilization of which the contemporary societies operate (United Nations, 2015; Kshetri, 2019).

Sustainable Development Goal 9 (Industry, Innovation, and Infrastructure) is one of the objectives that are linked to cybersecurity. This objective aims at establishing robust infrastructure and facilitating economic growth that is based on innovation. With the continued use of digital infrastructures in industries and governments, effective cybersecurity systems will be required to defend communication systems, data infrastructure, and cloud services. In the absence of proper cybersecurity measures, cyberspace attacks have the potential to interfere with the working of industries, steal information, and destroy the infrastructure facilities that are functional in these systems. Thus, the implementation of cybersecurity and risk management strategies into online systems is a direct approach towards the realization of SDG 9 since it guarantees the integrity and stability of the technological systems (Choras et al., 2020).

The Sustainable Cities and Communities Sustainable Development Goal (11) also relate greatly to cybersecurity. Smart cities rely on the network connectivity through Internet of Things that encompasses smart transportation systems, smart energy grids, smart City Governance, and Internet of Things. These technologies will increase city efficiency and sustainability, but with new cybersecurity threats. This means that the security and safety of the city environments depend on the prevention of cyber-attacks on smart city infrastructures. According to researchers, intrusion detection systems, blockchain-based security systems, and AI-based threat detection can enhance the resilience of smart city systems and enable the sustainable development of urban areas (Pawlicki et al., 2021).

Another important connection with Sustainable Development Goal 16 (Peace, Justice, and Strong Institutions) also exists. This aspiration adds to the setting up of secure institutions, open-governance and quality services of citizens. The digital era has witnessed a number of government services, legal processes as well as administration systems of different governments being anchored on secured platforms that are digital in nature. Governmental institutions may also be hacked, compromising the information of citizens, reducing trust of the citizenry on the online systems of government. In its turn, the improvement of policy on cybersecurity, digital risk management, and cyber awareness can promote the positive change in the establishment of secure governance infrastructures in line with SDG 16 (Taddeo & Floridi, 2018; Shackelford, 2016).

In addition, cybersecurity is part of the overall resilience in the society since it secures the digital communications, financial systems, and information infrastructure that facilitate economic and social development. With the digital transformation continuously gaining impetus both in the industry and in the general population sector, the need to protect the digital ecosystems is inevitable to upkeep stability and trust in technology-oriented societies. The sustainable digital ecosystems may be built with mathematical risk assessment models, cyber awareness programs, and new technologies (artificial intelligence and blockchain) by integrating cybersecurity frameworks, and enhancing the long-term development of society and technological innovation (Creese et al., 2013).

On the whole, cybersecurity is a core part of reinforcing the goals of the United Nations Sustainable Development Goals to increase the resilience of digital infrastructure, safeguard smart cities technology, and advance the security of institutions. The inclusion of cybersecurity plans into sustainable development programs will thus become a part of developing secure, reliable and sustainable digital societies in future.

10. FUTURE RESEARCH DIRECTIONS IN CYBERSECURITY

With the further development of digital technologies, research in the field of cybersecurity will be forced to move in the direction of new threats and technological challenges. The fast development of artificial intelligence, Internet of Things (IoT), cloud computing, and edge computing systems has both presented new opportunities and new security challenges. The future of cybersecurity research will be on the development of smart and adaptive security systems that will be able to identify and counter advanced cyber threats in real time. Researchers stress that the combination of artificial intelligence and cybersecurity technologies can dramatically increase the rate of threat detection and allow implement the proactive protection measures in the digital environment that is complicated (Conti et al., 2020; Zhang et al., 2022).

The use of federated learning to securely analyze data in a distributed environment is one of the potential future directions of cybersecurity studies. The conventional machine learning models usually demand centralized data acquisition, which can create a privacy and security threat. The Federated learning model allows joint model training on many devices without transfer of sensitive information to central servers. The method is especially applicable in IoT settings where humongous amounts of distributed data are generated by a large number of distributed devices. Federated learning could significantly improve the cybersecurity systems of large-scale digital infrastructures by maintaining privacy of data and also allowing all parties to learn alongside others (Nguyen et al., 2021).

The other significant research area is connected with the application of blockchain technology to enhance cybersecurity and data integrity in distributed systems. The security systems, which are built on blockchains, can offer data storage that cannot be tampered, records of transactions, and decentralized authentication systems. These features render blockchain technology apt in safeguarding smart city systems, financial systems, and IoT networks. Nonetheless, such issues as scalability, energy usage, and interoperability have yet to be solved in future studies to make the most out of blockchain-based cybersecurity solutions (Rahman et al., 2020; Khan and Salah, 2018).

More research on cybersecurity in the future will also aim at securing the next generation communication networks such as 5G and other developing networks. These networks provide support to enormous connectivity and promote the advanced applications like autonomous vehicles, smart healthcare systems, and automation in factories. Nevertheless, these networks have become more interconnected and complex, and new vulnerabilities can be used by the attackers. Researchers emphasize that the next-generation network infrastructures need more sophisticated authentication systems, privacy-sensitive communication protocols, and smart intrusion detection systems (Ferrag et al., 2019).

Moreover, the increased use of edge computing and IoT environments brings with itself new cybersecurity vulnerabilities that demand new security solutions. The edge devices are usually decentralized and have low computational capabilities thus prone to cyber-attacks. Future studies will thus emphasize on coming up with light security applications, distributed intrusion security frameworks, and resilient cybersecurity frameworks capable of safeguarding edge computing settings (Radanliev et al., 2020).

On the whole, the future of cybersecurity research will be based on the use of new technologies, including artificial intelligence, blockchain, federated learning, and sophisticated communication networks. The intelligent cybersecurity systems that will be developed due to these technologies will be able to forecast, identify, and reduce cyber threats more efficiently. Further studies and partnership among academic institutions, business entities, and the government will be needed to enhance cybersecurity systems and security and sustainability of digital societies (Conti et al., 2020; Nguyen et al., 2021).

11. CONCLUSION

In today's fast-paced world, the Internet is more interconnected than ever before and cyber security is a critical need for secure and sustainable digital societies. Rapidly emerging technologies like cloud computing, the Internet of Things (IoT), artificial intelligence, and smart infrastructures have drastically raised cyber risks and security challenges. The chapter was focused on the three aspects of this support to sustainable societies, namely cyber threat prevention, information security management, and cyber awareness programs.

The study covered the most prominent threats in the cyber landscape such as malware, phishing, ransomware, attack on interconnected infrastructures, and emerging threats from the Darknet ecosystem. The Darknet has also emerged as a space for activities like distribution of malware, illegal data trading and ransomware services, adding more complexities to cybersecurity and law enforcement. Meanwhile, Darknet intelligence can be used to assist in proactive threat identification and cybersecurity defense strategies.

The chapter also examined the mathematical models used for assessing cyber risk and intrusion detection, and the value of cyber awareness and human behavior in bolstering digital security. Many cyber incidents are the result of people's vulnerabilities, so there is a need to educate and raise awareness on how to practice online in a secure manner.

While technology has advanced, other areas of concern remain that hinder sustainable digital development including vulnerabilities of IoT, economic ramifications of cyberattacks, cybercrime on the Darknet, governance constraints and the lack of skilled cybersecurity professionals. Research and development in the field of cybersecurity should be shifted to intelligent defense systems with the help of artificial intelligence, blockchain, federated learning, and Darknet threat intelligence. Through the use of cutting-edge technologies, policies and cyber awareness, societies can improve their resilience against changing cyber threats and help achieve sustainable development in the digital space in line with United Nations Sustainable Development Goals (UNSDGs).

REFERENCES

Achuthan, K., Ramanathan, S., Srinivas, S., & Raman, R. (2024). Advancing cybersecurity and privacy with artificial intelligence: Emerging trends and challenges. *Journal of Cybersecurity and Privacy*, *4*(1), 1–18.

Alcaraz, C., & Zeadally, S. (2015). Critical infrastructure protection: Requirements and challenges for the 21st century. *International Journal of Critical Infrastructure Protection*, *8*, 53–66. DOI: 10.1016/j.ijcip.2014.12.002

Bada, M., Sasse, M. A., & Nurse, J. R. C. (2019). Cyber security awareness campaigns: Why do they fail to change behaviour? *arXiv preprint arXiv:1901.02672*. https://arxiv.org/abs/1901.02672

Behl, A., Behl, K., & Rao, V. (2021). *Cybersecurity and cyberwar: What everyone needs to know*. Oxford University Press.

Böhme, R., & Moore, T. (2012). The economics of cybersecurity: Principles and policy options. *International Journal of Critical Infrastructure Protection*, *5*(1), 1–10. DOI: 10.1016/j.ijcip.2012.02.002

Buczak, A. L., & Guven, E. (2016). A survey of data mining and machine learning methods for cyber security intrusion detection. *IEEE Communications Surveys and Tutorials*, *18*(2), 1153–1176. DOI: 10.1109/COMST.2015.2494502

Choraś, M., Pawlicki, M., Kozik, R., & Hołubowicz, W. (2020). Cybersecurity as a pillar of sustainable digital development. *Sustainability*, *12*(17), 6973. DOI: 10.3390/su12176973

Coles-Kemp, L. (2009). Information security management and organisational behaviour: Exploring the social context of information security. *Computers & Security*, *28*(1–2), 28–39. DOI: 10.1016/j.cose.2008.08.004

Conti, M., Dehghantanha, A., Franke, K., & Watson, S. (2018). Internet of Things security and forensics: Challenges and opportunities. *Future Generation Computer Systems*, *78*, 544–546. DOI: 10.1016/j.future.2017.07.060

Conti, M., Lal, C., Mohammadi, M., Rawat, D. B., & Sadeghi, A. (2020). Security and privacy for artificial intelligence: Opportunities and challenges. *IEEE Communications Surveys and Tutorials*, *22*(3), 1639–1667. DOI: 10.1109/COMST.2020.2987868

Creese, S., Hodges, D., Jamison-Powell, S., & Whitty, M. (2013). Relationships between cybersecurity and societal resilience. *Computers & Security*, *36*, 57–66. DOI: 10.1016/j.cose.2013.02.008

Dinev, T., & Hu, Q. (2007). The centrality of awareness in the formation of user behavioral intention toward protective information technologies. *Journal of the Association for Information Systems*, *8*(7), 386–408. DOI: 10.17705/1jais.00133

ENISA. (2021). *ENISA threat landscape 2021*. European Union Agency for Cybersecurity. https://www.enisa.europa.eu

ENISA. (2023). *ENISA threat landscape 2023*. European Union Agency for Cybersecurity. https://www.enisa.europa.eu

Europol. (2020). Internet organised crime threat assessment (IOCTA) 2020. Europol. https://www.europol.europa.eu

Ferrag, M. A., Maglaras, L., Argyriou, A., Kosmanos, D., & Janicke, H. (2019). Security for 4G and 5G cellular networks: A survey of existing authentication and privacy-preserving schemes. *Journal of Network and Computer Applications*, *101*, 55–82. DOI: 10.1016/j.jnca.2017.10.017

Ferrag, M. A., Maglaras, L., Moschoyiannis, S., & Janicke, H. (2020). Deep learning for cyber security intrusion detection: Approaches, datasets, and comparative study. *Journal of Information Security and Applications*, *50*, 102419. DOI: 10.1016/j.jisa.2019.102419

Garcia-Teodoro, P., Díaz-Verdejo, J., Maciá-Fernández, G., & Vázquez, E. (2009). Anomaly-based network intrusion detection: Techniques, systems and challenges. *Computers & Security*, *28*(1–2), 18–28. DOI: 10.1016/j.cose.2008.08.003

Gordon, L. A., & Loeb, M. P. (2002). The economics of information security investment. *ACM Transactions on Information and System Security*, *5*(4), 438–457. DOI: 10.1145/581271.581274

Greitzer, F. L., & Frincke, D. A. (2010). Combining traditional cyber security audit data with psychosocial data: Towards predictive modeling for insider threat mitigation. In *Insider Threats in Cyber Security* (pp. 85–113). https://doi.org/DOI: 10.1007/978-1-4419-7133-3_5

Grossklags, J., Christin, N., & Chuang, J. (2008). Secure or insure? A game-theoretic analysis of information security games. In *Proceedings of the 17th International World Wide Web Conference* (pp. 209–218). https://doi.org/DOI: 10.1145/1367497.1367526

Hadlington, L. (2017). Human factors in cybersecurity: Examining the link between internet addiction, impulsivity, attitudes towards cybersecurity, and risky cybersecurity behaviours. *Heliyon*, *3*(7), e00346. DOI: 10.1016/j.heliyon.2017.e00346 PMID: 28725870

Ige, A. B. (2024). Aligning sustainable development goals with cybersecurity frameworks: Strategies for secure digital societies. *Global Scientific Conference on Applied Research and Reviews*, *6*(2), 45–53.

ISO/IEC. (2022). *ISO/IEC 27001: Information security management systems—Requirements*. International Organization for Standardization.

Khan, M. A., & Salah, K. (2018). IoT security: Review, blockchain solutions, and open challenges. *Future Generation Computer Systems*, *82*, 395–411. DOI: 10.1016/j.future.2017.11.022

Kruger, H. A., & Kearney, W. D. (2006). A prototype for assessing information security awareness. *Computers & Security*, *25*(4), 289–296. DOI: 10.1016/j.cose.2006.02.008

Kshetri, N. (2019). Cybersecurity and development: The role of cybersecurity in supporting sustainable development goals. *Telecommunications Policy*, *43*(10), 101825. DOI: 10.1016/j.telpol.2019.101825

Kumar, N. M., & Mallick, P. K. (2018). Blockchain technology for security issues and challenges in IoT. *Procedia Computer Science*, *132*, 1815–1823. DOI: 10.1016/j.procs.2018.05.140

Lelarge, M., & Bolot, J. (2008). Network externalities and the deployment of security features and protocols in the Internet. *Performance Evaluation Review*, *36*(1), 37–48. DOI: 10.1145/1384529.1375463

Li, F. (2025). Information security risk assessment in the digital economy and its impact on sustainable development. *Sustainability*, *17*(14), 6428. DOI: 10.3390/su17146428

Li, Y., & Liu, Q. (2021). A comprehensive review study of cyber-attacks and cybersecurity trends. *International Journal of Intelligent Systems and Applications in Engineering*, *9*(2), 122–131.

Moustafa, N., & Slay, J. (2016). The evaluation of network anomaly detection systems: Statistical analysis of the UNSW-NB15 dataset and comparison with the KDD99 dataset. *Information Security Journal. Global Perspectives*, *25*(1–3), 18–31. DOI: 10.1080/19393555.2015.1125974

Nguyen, D. C., Ding, M., Pathirana, P. N., Seneviratne, A., Li, J., Niyato, D., & Poor, H. V. (2021). Federated learning for Internet of Things: A comprehensive survey. *IEEE Communications Surveys and Tutorials*, *23*(3), 1622–1658. DOI: 10.1109/COMST.2021.3075439

NIST. (2018). *Framework for improving critical infrastructure cybersecurity (Version 1.1)*. National Institute of Standards and Technology., DOI: 10.6028/NIST.CSWP.04162018

Nunes, E., Diab, A., Gunn, A., Marin, E., Mishra, V., Pacey, K., & Shakarian, P. (2018). Darknet and deepnet mining for proactive cybersecurity threat intelligence. *IEEE Intelligence and Security Informatics Conference*, 7–12. https://doi.org/DOI: 10.1109/ISI.2018.8587365

Nurse, J. R. C., Creese, S., & De Roure, D. (2017). Security risk assessment in Internet of Things systems. *IT Professional*, *19*(5), 20–26. DOI: 10.1109/MITP.2017.3680959

Parsons, K., McCormac, A., Butavicius, M., Pattinson, M., & Jerram, C. (2014). Determining employee awareness using the human aspects of information security questionnaire (HAIS-Q). *Computers & Security*, *42*, 165–176. DOI: 10.1016/j.cose.2013.12.003

Pawlicki, M., Kozik, R., & Choraś, M. (2021). The role of cybersecurity in the sustainable development of smart cities. *Sustainable Cities and Society*, *67*, 102778. DOI: 10.1016/j.scs.2021.102778

Radanliev, P., De Roure, D., Nurse, J. R. C., Montalvo, R. M., Cannady, S., Santos, O., Maddox, L., & Burnap, P. (2020). Cyber risk at the edge: Current and future trends in IoT and edge computing security. *Future Internet*, *12*(3), 45. DOI: 10.3390/fi12030045

Rahman, M. A., Hossain, M. S., & Muhammad, G. (2020). Blockchain-enabled cybersecurity for smart cities. *IEEE Internet of Things Journal*, *7*(8), 7467–7475. DOI: 10.1109/JIOT.2020.2975934

Roman, R., López, J., & Mambo, M. (2018). Mobile edge computing, fog computing and IoT: A survey and analysis of security threats and challenges. *Future Generation Computer Systems*, *78*, 680–698. DOI: 10.1016/j.future.2016.11.009

Roy, S., Ellis, C., Shiva, S., Dasgupta, D., Shandilya, V., & Wu, Q. (2010). A survey of game theory as applied to network security. In *Proceedings of the 43rd Hawaii International Conference on System Sciences* (pp. 1–10). https://doi.org/DOI: 10.1109/HICSS.2010.35

Sabillon, R., Cano, J., Cavaller, V., & Serra, J. (2017). Cybercrime and cyberwar: What everyone needs to know. *International Journal of Information Security Science*, *6*(2), 45–56.

Scarfone, K., & Mell, P. (2007). *Guide to intrusion detection and prevention systems (IDPS)* (NIST Special Publication 800-94). National Institute of Standards and Technology.

Shackelford, S. J. (2016). Toward cyberpeace: Managing cyberattacks through polycentric governance. *The American University Law Review*, *62*(5), 1273–1344.

Shameli-Sendi, A., Aghababaei-Barzegar, R., & Cheriet, M. (2016). Taxonomy of information security risk assessment methods. *Computers & Security*, *57*, 14–30. DOI: 10.1016/j.cose.2015.11.001

Sicari, S., Rizzardi, A., Grieco, L. A., & Coen-Porisini, A. (2015). Security, privacy and trust in Internet of Things: The road ahead. *Computer Networks*, *76*, 146–164. DOI: 10.1016/j.comnet.2014.11.008

Sommer, R., & Paxson, V. (2010). Outside the closed world: On using machine learning for network intrusion detection. In *2010 IEEE Symposium on Security and Privacy* (pp. 305–316). IEEE. https://doi.org/DOI: 10.1109/SP.2010.25

Sulich, A. (2025). Cybersecurity and sustainable development: Bibliometric analysis and future research directions. *Sustainability*, *17*(3), 1085. DOI: 10.3390/su17031085

Taddeo, M., & Floridi, L. (2018). Cybersecurity capacity building and international development. *Global Policy*, *9*(3), 353–364. DOI: 10.1111/1758-5899.12550

United Nations. (2015). *Transforming our world: The 2030 agenda for sustainable development.* United Nations. https://sdgs.un.org/2030agenda

Von Solms, R., & Van Niekerk, J. (2013). From information security to cybersecurity. *Computers & Security*, *38*, 97–102. DOI: 10.1016/j.cose.2013.04.004

Wang, K. (2022). Research on the effectiveness of cybersecurity awareness on incident response. *Electronics (Basel)*, *11*(10), 1659. DOI: 10.3390/electronics11101659

Workman, M. (2008). Wisecrackers: A theory-grounded investigation of phishing and pretext social engineering threats to information security. *Journal of the American Society for Information Science and Technology*, *59*(4), 662–674. DOI: 10.1002/asi.20779

Xu, S. (2014). Cybersecurity dynamics: A foundation for the science of cybersecurity. In *Proceedings of the ACM Workshop on New Security Paradigms* (pp. 1–6). https://doi.org/DOI: 10.1145/2683467.2683470

Zhang, Q., Chen, M., Li, L., & Tang, Y. (2022). Artificial intelligence and cybersecurity: Future research directions. *IEEE Access : Practical Innovations, Open Solutions*, *10*, 74216–74230. DOI: 10.1109/ACCESS.2022.3192515

Zhang, Y., & Liu, Y. (2010). A quantitative risk assessment model for cyber security. *International Journal of Information Security Science*, *2*(4), 45–53.

ADDITIONAL READING

Anderson, R., & Moore, T. (2006). The economics of information security. *Science, 314*(5799), 610–613. DOI: 10.1126/science.1130992 PMID: 17068253

Bertino, E. (2016). Data security and privacy: Concepts, approaches, and research directions. *Proceedings of the IEEE, 104*(9), 1752–1764. DOI: 10.1109/COMPSAC.2016.89

Jang-Jaccard, J., & Nepal, S. (2014). A survey of emerging threats in cybersecurity. *Journal of Computer and System Sciences, 80*(5), 973–993. DOI: 10.1016/j.jcss.2014.02.005

Kotenko, I., & Chechulin, A. (2013). A cyber attack modeling and impact assessment framework. *Proceedings of the 5th International Conference on Cyber Conflict*, 1–24. https://doi.org/DOI: 10.1109/CYCON.2013.6568370

Lu, Y., & Xu, X. (2019). Resource virtualization and service-oriented architecture for industrial Internet of Things. *IEEE Transactions on Industrial Informatics, 15*(10), 5727–5736. DOI: 10.1109/TII.2019.2908005

Nunes, E., Diab, A., Gunn, A., Marin, E., Mishra, V., Pacey, K., & Shakarian, P. (2018). Darknet and deepnet mining for proactive cybersecurity threat intelligence. *IEEE Conference on Intelligence and Security Informatics*, 7–12. https://doi.org/DOI: 10.1109/ISI.2018.8587365

Sharma, P. K., Moon, S. Y., & Park, J. H. (2017). Block-VN: A distributed blockchain based vehicular network architecture in smart city. *Journal of Information Processing Systems, 13*(1), 184–195. DOI: 10.3745/JIPS.03.0064

KEY TERMS AND DEFINITION

Cyber Awareness: The knowledge and awareness that individuals and business entities have towards cyber risks, safe practices online and responsible online practices.

Cyber Threat Prevention: These are strategies, technology, and security practices that are aimed at identifying, preventing, and managing cyber-attacks before they can cause havoc in digital systems.

Cybersecurity: This happens through the practice of securing computer systems, computer networks, and online data against unauthorized access, cyber-attacks, and malicious activities in order to achieve secure digital environments.

Information Security: The security of digital information and systems to keep the information confidential, intact, and available in the digital settings.

Intrusion Detection Systems (IDS): Security systems, which have been developed to monitor network traffic and activity within the system to detect possible malicious acts or possible cyber-attack in digital infrastructures.

Sustainable Society: A society that enables economic, environmental, and technological stability in the long term in addition to having secure digital infrastructures and responsible utilization of the information technologies.

Chapter 15
Darknet Futures and Post-Quantum Security

Shahed Al Tamimi
http://orcid.org/0009-0005-3270-8200
Community College of Qatar, Qatar

Qasem Abu Al-Haija
http://orcid.org/0000-0003-2422-0297
Jordan University of Science and Technology, Jordan

ABSTRACT

This chapter is entitled "Future Trends in the Darknet: Decentralized Platforms and Post-Quantum Security Implications." Where the aim of this chapter is to explore and identify the darknet infrastructure's future trajectory by addressing the integration of decentralization and PQS. This chapter also seeks to analyze the underlying shortcomings of current centralized anonymity models, examines the potential benefits of decentralized frameworks, and provides quantum-resilient methods to construct next-generation darknet intelligent systems.

1. INTRODUCTION

In recent years, darknets have rapidly enhanced and transformed, leading to future trends that indicate a shift towards decentralized platforms and the use of Post-Quantum Security (PQS) evaluation. However, the decentralized marketplace and communication systems are expected to reduce reliance on centralized servers, making it challenging and an obstacle to monitor or disrupt them, as identified in Gharavi et al. (2024). Therefore, these platforms leverage blockchain and Peer-to-Peer (P2P) technologies, maximizing their anonymity and resilience as discussed in Darzi and Yavuz (2024). Although the rise of Quantum Computing (QC) threatens the safeguards of current cryptographic approaches, it has prompted the adoption of PQC to secure transactions and communication processes (Anbarkhan, 2024). Thus, in Rustamova and Dutta (2025), researchers emphasize post-quantum-resistant algorithms that might be critical to protecting sensitive data and critical infrastructure against "harvest-now, decrypt-later" attacks. In short, decentralized infrastructure and PQS have transformed and reshaped the darknet

DOI: 10.4018/979-8-3373-9755-9.ch015

market affecting the cybersecurity sector these days, developing all opportunities for innovation and demanding conditions for regulatory enforcement (Suriya et al., 2026).

1.1 Background on Darknet Evolution

Due to the sophisticated improvements in the darknet market, which has rapidly undergone noticeable change and evolved from rudimentary anonymity equipment to complex ecosystems that recently include the blockchain technology era, Artificial Intelligence (AI), and PQS. However, the dark web has become a permanent production of hidden networks of demands for privacy and continued existence under surveillance, and the significant enhancement has been the emergence of onion routers (Collier, 2024). Thus, both studies (Collier, 2024;' Abu Al-Haija et al., 2022) presents that the onion routing in the USA is also called the Tor browser. Consequently, the Tor browser became the backbone of darknet access by allowing hidden services and developing marketplaces such as Silk Road, which showed the potential and cyber risks of anonymous online economies. By the mid-2000s, darknet concepts had moved past the Tor browser. However, certain works such as Freenet and the Invisible Internet Project (I2P) were frequent with decentralized P2P architecture aimed at discouraging censorship and static communication, as demonstrated within the work. Responses to such challenges have improved the anonymity of the landscape by helping to provide alternative responses to the centralized registration offered via Tor for the preferred paradigm, and the dark web has become a set of privacy-preserving networks instead of a domain platform. In another case, painting (El-Kady, 2025) researchers in 2010 observed an increase in the integration of cryptocurrency, especially digital currencies including Bitcoin. Although bitcoin has emerged as the most common cryptocurrency payment method in the darknet marketplace. Therefore, the integration of blockchain technology and anonymity networks has presented a robust virtual economy but also captured the attention of law enforcement. As a result of technological developments, dark web visitors in the current state work on the enhancement to integrate the darknet with AI using Machine Learning (ML) models for traffic analysis strategies, which are used in an increasing number of ways to stop illegal activities, highlighting the arms race between anonymity and surveillance. However, the emerging models are currently expanding on the traditional anonymity tools based on the previous versions for decentralized structures that explored the use of blockchain consensus mechanisms to suspend SPoF and enhance trustworthy interactions, as described in Figueras-Martín et al. (2022). Furthermore, PQC is likewise explored for static darknet communication; in contrast to increase the attack surface of cyber threats, cyber-attacks are shared, and classifiers. Furthermore, the more observable presentation of the communication links was the use of multi-layer encryption in the mysterious channels within the Tor browser and other networks, which not only protects the identity of the easiest person. Therefore, Table 1 summarizes the main differences between PQS and PQC. Thus, the latest development of the dark web from its inception in the 1990s to current state is illustrated in Figure 1.

Table 1. Summary of key differences of PQS and PQC.

Aspect
PQS
PQC
Definition
A comprehensive framework of tactics, technologies, and regulations aimed at securing systems against quantum-enabled attacks.
A specific branch of cryptography focused on designing algorithms resistant to quantum attacks, such as lattice-based and hash-based.
Focus
Complete security ecosystems.
Cryptographic algorithms.
Goal
Protect the entire infrastructure.
Protect data from quantum attacks.
Benefits
• Holistic protection beyond cryptography, which includes networks, protocols, and governance.
• Addresses metadata, anonymity, and system-level resilience.
• Provides mathematically proven resistance to quantum algorithms such as Shor's and Grover's.
• Ensures confidentiality, integrity, and authentication in a quantum era.
Drawbacks
• Complex to implement across diverse systems.
• Requires coordination of multiple layers (hardware, software, and governance).
• Larger key sizes and slower performance compared to classical cryptography.
• Still evolving; some algorithms may be deprecated.
Application
• Darknet platforms, IoT, blockchain and protected communications during which an entire architecture is affected by quantum threats.
• Operational policies including key rotation, hybrid migration, and anonymity preservation.
• Encryption, digital signatures, and key exchange in protocols such as Transport Layer Security (TLS), Virtual Private Networks (VPNs), Tor, and blockchain, wallets.
Tools
• Hybrid security frameworks.
• Post-quantum-resistant protocols.
• Metadata obfuscation and secure governance models.
• Algorithms: Kyber (KEM), Dilithium (signatures), SPHINCS+ (hash-based), McEliece (code-based).
• Crypto-agility libraries supporting PQC primitives.

Figure 1. Darknet evolution timeline

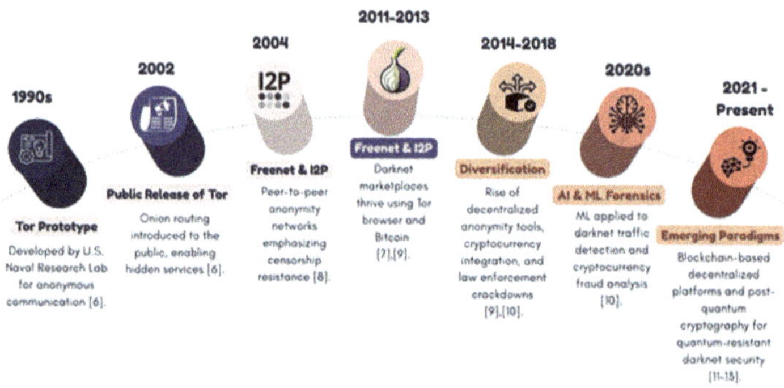

Overall, the dark web has progressed along a path that begins with the Tor browser and continues via onion routing to decentralized, blockchain-based, and quantum-resistant paradigms. As a result of this development, anonymity technologies are quite adaptable, and there is an ongoing struggle between privacy and governmental control.

1.2 Limitations of Current Centralized Anonymity Infrastructures

Existing darknet infrastructure, mostly built with centralized or semi-centralized anonymity technologies which can be restricted tightly. However, early adoption of onion routing Tor browsers is based especially on directory authority, which can additionally manipulate SPoF and realize distribution of dependencies (Collier, 2024). Similarly, authors present a centralized anonymity provider through work (Abu Al-Haija et al., 2022) which struggles with scalability, latency, and vulnerability to analyze traffic attacks. These infrastructures might also be one of the reasons to maximize the cyber risk exposure to advanced ML and AI-driven forensic techniques, which can deanonymize traffic patterns and compromise user privacy (Saleem et al., 2022). Moreover, the reliance on classical cryptography algorithms such as Rivest-Shamir-Adleman (RSA) and Elliptic Curve Digital Signature Algorithm (ECDSA) renders these systems vulnerable to quantum algorithms, for instance, Shor's and Grover's, which that threaten to undermine their long-term viability as described in El-Kady (2025).Therefore, architectural centralization, susceptibility to surveillance, and looming quantum insecurity constrain current anonymity infrastructures.

1.3 Motivation for Decentralization and Quantum-Resilient Systems

These days, there is a demand for technological improvements in AI and blockchain technology, as well as the cryptocurrency landscape. Centralized cryptographic infrastructures, developed and motivated by the recent shift to decentralized quantum flexible architectures, maximize vulnerability. So, decentralization removes hierarchical management, as well as a blockchain-based framework delivers true acceptance with P2P nodes. This method fits with the dark web fundamental ethos of autonomy and privacy and increases fault tolerance, transparency, and censorship resistance to protect against quantum integrity and confidentiality of information. PQC provides mathematically robust answers, along with lattice-based, hash-first-based, and multivariable systems that can withstand quantum decryption attacks and even integrate the quantum-resilient algorithms within decentralized infrastructures to ensure long-term defense and resilience against counter-systems, and it can also help enable this. This integration of decentralization and quantum flexibility represents the next phase of development in a secure, encrypted word-of-mouth exchange network.

1.4 Research Objectives and Contributions

This chapter seeks to investigate and identify the future trajectory of the darknet infrastructure by addressing the integration of decentralization and PQS. This chapter seeks to analyze the underlying shortcomings of current centralized anonymity models, examines the potential benefits of decentralized frameworks, and provides quantum-resilient methods to construct next-generation darknet intelligent systems. Therefore, this chapter contributes by synthesizing multidisciplinary insights from blockchain technology, cryptographic research, and cybersecurity forensics to construct a forward-looking model of secure anonymity. Furthermore, the chapter contribution outlines the following:

I. Design principles for integrating PQC into decentralized networks.
II. Identifies the emerging research gaps and proposes suggested strategic directions for resilient darknet ecosystems.

In short, this chapter lays the conceptual foundation for developing a resilient, privacy-protecting infrastructure that might withstand the cyber threats of the quantum age.

1.5 Chapter Organization

This chapter discusses the latest trends in decentralized darknet platforms as well as the latest implications of post-quantum security. The subsequent sections of this chapter are structured as shown in Figure 2, beginning with an introduction in Section 15.1 that covers the evolution of the darknet, the limitations of anonymity infrastructures, and the motivations for decentralization. Section 15.2 illustrates the foundational overview of darknet architectures, decentralized systems, cryptography, and QC. Section 15.3 covers the advanced decentralized darknet systems, analyzing blockchain production infrastructure, distributed storage, smart contracts, and recent case studies of various platforms, whereas Section 15.4 sets up the quantum threat scenarios; deanonymization is discussed. Next to exploring the quantum technologies and adversarial risk modeling alongside Section 15.5, which focuses on PQC, this section explores PQC algorithms, their integration into protocols, and the latest deployment challenges for the dark web. Thus, AI and recent intelligent threat detection in the future darknet are illustrated in Section 15.6 to evaluate the AI role, anomaly detection, and daily deployment obstacles. Section 15.7 therefore addresses legal, ethical and coverage issues including legal challenges, regulatory action, ethics, and international collaboration on the dark web. Thus, future research directions for quantum resilient networks, decentralized ecosystems, IoT integration, Explainable AI (XAI), and sustainability are identified through Section 15.8 followed by Section 15.9, which discusses the open challenges and limitations by highlighting, PQC scalability, adoption barriers, enforcement limitations, and ethical misuse concerns. Finally, Section 15.10 presents key insights that concluding the chapter by synthesizing chapter outcomes, emphasizing the proactive model, and balancing privacy, security, and governance.

Figure 2. Overview of chapter organization

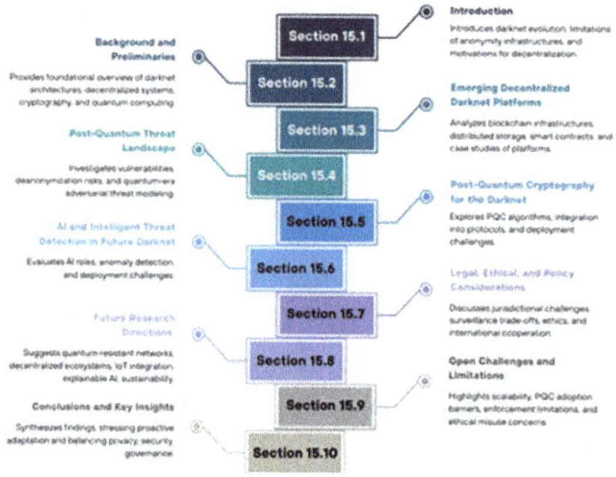

2. BACKGROUND AND PRELIMINARIES

A bit of time prior to the dark web developments, the latest enhancements present a complex environment of encryption techniques, including decentralized infrastructure and cryptographic improvements being developed to counter surveillance and enhance the privacy of give up receivers and gradient registries. Based on that, this section outlines the architectural foundations, cryptographic mechanisms, and QC implications that play a vital role in reshaping the future of decentralized and quantum-resilient darknet systems. This section organizes the history, architecture, equipment, anonymity models, onion routing, and evaluation of the garlic routing as follows:

2.1 Darknet Architectures, Tools, and Anonymity Models

The darknet, which might be composed of various networks, can provide anonymity for all users in order to hide their identity and communication patterns. Nevertheless, one of the most prominent architectures are Tor browser, I2P and Freenet, which collectively establish the backbone of anonymous communication systems.

2.1.1 Tor, I2P, and Freenet Overview

Initially, the Tor browser encodes data packets via multiple layers and sends the data records through selected random nodes (onion routing). Each of the nodes decrypts a layer in order and transmits it to the next destination to ensure that there is actually no single node that knows each other's or both the sender and receiver (Gharavi et al., 2024; Darzi & Yavuz, 2024). This method provides an efficient anonymity version model, based on centralized directory authorities capabilities, which introduces a potential vulnerability. Due to the similar context, I2P offers garlic routing, an advancement over onion routing in which numerous messages are bundled into one encrypted packet. Garlic routing design boosts the efficiency and resistance to traffic analysis by obscuring message correlation (Anbarkhan, 2024; Rustamova & Dutta, 2025). Moreover, the Freenet focuses on decentralized data storage and retrieval, utilizing distributed hash tables to store encrypted content across nodes (Suriya et al., 2026).

2.1.2 Onion Routing vs. Garlic Routing

Regarding routing, two types of routing have occurred nowadays, onion routing and garlic routing are both anonymity-preserving techniques as well as utilized in darknet and anonymous communication systems. Furthermore, utilizing both onion and garlic routing, it might be easy to differ in how cyber criminals encapsulate and transmit data (Anbarkhan, 2024)

I. **Onion Routing:** Refers to a type of routing which works by wrapping a single message in multiple layers of encryption, such as the layers of an onion. Where each layer relay a node decrypts one layer to reveal the next destination, to ensure that no single node knows both the sender and the receiver. This technique provides robust anonymity that can be vulnerable to traffic analysis if multiple messages are correlated (Rustamova & Dutta, 2025).

II. **Garlic Routing:** The following type is the second type of routing which is used in I2P as well as extending onion routing by merging multiple messages collectively into a single encrypted packet, such as the cloves in a garlic bulb. This aggregation renders traffic analysis tough, as it prevents the adversaries from rapidly correlating end-users messages. In addition, the garlic routing offers many robust and effective capabilities, including message bundling, behind-the-schedule shipping, and response-to-integration, which resistance design to timing attacks (Saleem et al., 2024).

In summary, encryption as performed within the tor browser encrypts messages in several layers, which are sequentially deleted via relay. Based on that, the encryption methods still preserve traffic patterns with cyber risk for correlation attacks as well as maximizing traffic control complexity, providing advanced functionality including time-supported transmission and content responses (Suriya et al., 2026; Collier, 2024; Abu Al-Haija et al., 2022, Saleem et al., 2022; El-Kady, 2025; Saleem et al., 2024). In addition, the comparison summary between onion and garlic routing is illustrated in Table 2.

Table 2. Comparison between onion and garlic routing

Features	*Routing*		*Ref.*
	Onion Routing	*Garlic Routing*	
Basic Concept	Single message wrapped in multiple encryption layers.	Multiple messages bundled into one encrypted packet.	(Anbarkhan, 2024; Rustamova & Dutta, 2025)
Primary Use	Tor network for anonymous browsing.	I2P network for anonymous services and communication.	(Suriya et al., 2026; Collier, 2024)
Encryption Layers	Each layer corresponds to one relay hop.	Each bundle contains multiple encrypted messages.	(Abu Al-Haija et al., 2022)
Traffic Analysis Resistance	**Moderate**; vulnerable to correlation attacks.	**Stronger**; bundling makes correlation more complex.	(Saleem et al., 2022)
Efficiency	Less efficient due to single-message encapsulation.	More efficiently by aggregating multiple messages.	(Suriya et al., 2026; El-Kady, 2025)

continued on following page

Table 2. Continued

Features	Routing		Ref.
	Onion Routing	*Garlic Routing*	
Flexibility	Focused on anonymous web browsing.	Supports delayed delivery, replies, and diverse applications.	(Saleem et al., 2024).
Analogy	Onion with layers.	Garlic bulb with multiple cloves.	(Anbarkhan, 2024; Suriya et al., 2026)

2.1.3 Darknet Tools

This subsection explores and identifies the real-world datasets as well as the recent tools for darknet research. Figure 3 identifies, discusses, and highlights the real-world datasets and tools for darknet research that are covered in this subsection. The organization of this subsection is as follows:

I. Darknet Crawlers & Monitoring Frameworks:
- **OnionScan:** widely Utilized for scanning and mapping Tor hidden services.
- **Ahmia Search Engine:** Indexes Tor sites and provides metadata for research.
- **Tor Metrics Portal:** Official Tor project statistics on relay counts, bandwidth, and usage trends.
- **I2P Network Database Tools:** Utilities for crawling and analyzing I2P peers and tunnels.
- **Freenet Node Monitors:** Community tools for measuring Freenet's distributed data-stored activity.

II. Blockchain Analytics Tools (for darknet marketplaces and crypto transactions):
- **Chainalysis, Elliptic, and CipherTrace:** Commercial platforms for tracing cryptocurrency flows linked to darknet services.
- **GraphSense:** Is an open source blockchain analytics framework for clustering addresses and visualizing transaction graphs purposes.
- **BlockSci:** Intelligent tool provides an academic toolkit for blockchain data analysis, which is often deployed in darknet marketplace studies.

III. Datasets for Traffic and Content Analysis:
- **CIC-Darknet2020:** Curated dataset integrating Tor and VPN traffic for ML research.
- **ISCX Tor & VPN datasets:** Widely used benchmarks for darknet traffic classification.
- **DARPA Intrusion Detection Evaluation datasets:** For historical, still referenced for anomaly detection baselines.
- **Darknet Market Archives:** Criminology and economics research utilize scraped datasets of marketplace listings, including drugs, malware, and stolen data.

IV. Forensic Investigation Platforms:
- **Recorded Future and Cybersixgill:** Intelligent digital threat platform for monitoring darknet forums and marketplaces.
- **Maltego with Darknet plugins:** Graph-based investigation tool that links darknet entities with blockchain addresses.

- **OSINT Frameworks:** Integrating darknet crawlers with social media and surface web intelligence for cross-domain analysis goals.

Figure 3. Real-world darknet datasets & tools

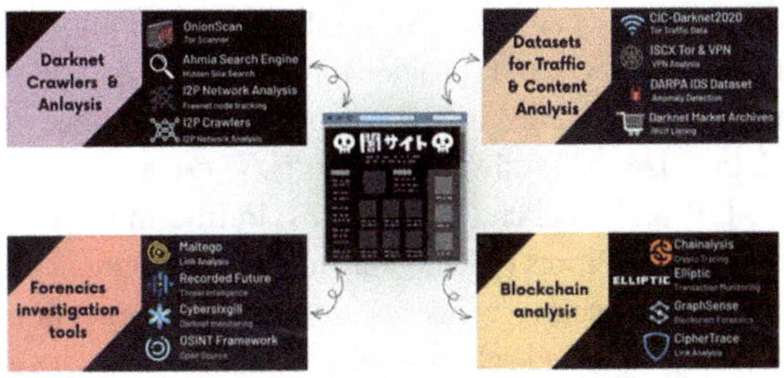

2.1.4 Limitations

Despite the dark web benefits, it might suffer from several limitations, including centralized control points in Tor's directory servers and reliance on volunteer nodes that are susceptible to traffic consistency and time behavior, as mentioned in the work. Moreover, the performance is also impacted by other issues and challenges, including scalability and latency and the novel cyber threat caused by emerging AI based network traffic analysis technologies aiming for a maximization of the anonymity threats to cyberspace (Saleem et al., 2022; Abu Al-Haija et al., 2022). Thus, these challenges reflect an insistent demand for decentralized and quantum-resistant networks.

2.2 Decentralized Systems and Web3 Foundations

The decentralized infrastructure of the darknet, which utilizes Blockchain technology, facilitates the integration of consensus with external mandatory governments to ensure transparency and immutability, as described in El-Kady (2025)

Although P2P overlay networks develop resistance after addressing single points of failure (SPoF) in negotiation zones, structures with the InterPlanetary File System (IPFS) and Filecoin extend this principle to distributed storage, which can stabilize and protect content-addressed fact sharing, as the author asserts within the work. On the other hand, smart contracts in the paradigm of Web3 should automate transactions and trigger proposals without an intermediary. These autonomous executor scripts are commonly used in blockchain epoch structures that have an Ethereum platform to provide settings that depend on clients, as discussed in the examination in Figueras-Martín et al. (2022). Decentralized Autonomous Organizations (DAOs), moreover, reflected games using more centralized manipulation. This integration of blockchain and P2P technology into the darknet architecture results in improved and increased anonymity, accountability, and scalability. Unlike traditional structures, decentralized platforms are scalable, hardware-monitored, and provide a robust foundation for privacy preservation applications (de-Marcos et al., 2026). In addition, exploring many unacceptable situations and obstacles in interoperability, power aggregate performance, and quantum pressure, the PQC chain and blockchain integration.

2.3 Foundation of Cryptographic

The context of cryptography provides anonymity for all insiders. where the necessary directive on all mechanisms of anonymity and decentralization. Public key encryption strategies, including RSA and Elliptic Curve Cryptography (ECC), that provides a secure key and an alternative authentication mechanism. However, the RSA rule set relies on the computational efficiency of factoring of large integers, while ECC (Merlec & In, 2024; AlTamimi et al., 2025). These algorithmic forms guarantee stable communication across Tor, I2P, and blockchain structures. Furthermore, the advanced cryptographic strategy developed Zero-Knowledge Proofs (ZKPs) that enabled the demonstration of a SPoF that holds records without disclosing it. Thus, privacy concerns are heavily dependent on ZKP, which facilitates verification and authentication without revealing touching data, as described within Hammoud et al. (2021). In a comparable context of the security of Multiparty Computing (MPC) .Also, as discussed in Pincheira et al. (2022). MPC is becoming increasingly common in decentralized networks for collaborative decision making while protecting confidentiality.

In short, the cryptographic algorithms are essential to guarantee confidentiality, integrity, and authenticity in dark web and decentralized ecosystems. Nevertheless, the reliance on classical mathematical hardness assumptions can also render users to be vulnerable to quantum cyber-attacks, promoting the search for post-quantum alternatives (Fan et al., 2024).

2.4 Quantum Computing Fundamentals

In recent years, QC introduced unprecedented computational capabilities that threaten classical cryptographic algorithms. As mentioned in Gentile et al. (2024), a famous two algorithms, Shor's and Grover's, pose the most significant cyber risks. Shor's algorithm can efficiently factor huge, large integers and compute discrete logarithms, rendering RSA and ECC insecure and raising various concerns regarding privacy. While Grover's algorithm accelerates brute-force searches, minimizing the effective security of symmetric encryption schemes such as AES by half. The breakthroughs threaten the foundation of current darknet and blockchain security models. Therefore, QC should potentially decrypt encrypted communications, compromise digital signatures, and undermine blockchain integrity. Consequently, PQC has emerged as a critical research area that focuses on lattice-based, hash-based, and multivariate polynomial schemes that are resistant to quantum attacks, as discussed in Gilbert and Gilbert (2024). As a result, the integration of PQC into decentralized infrastructures may ensure long-term resilience. However, the quantum-resistant algorithms which recently integrated with distributed architecture promise sustainable anonymity and security within the post-quantum era. The resulting convergence emphasizes the significant progression of the darknet architecture from traditional anonymity networks ecosystems.

Table 3 compares the traditional darknet architecture with emerging decentralized platforms. Table 3 additionally offers a comparison of certain essential factors such as architectural type, routing method, data storage, data trust models, vulnerabilities, and other crucial features. Moreover, Table 4 presents comparative analysis of PQC and PQS regarding the following aspects: scope, encryption, decryption, authentication, threat detection, blockchain integration, zero trust, governance and monitoring.

Table 3. Comparison of traditional darknet architectures & emerging decentralized platforms

Feature	Traditional Darknet Architectures (Tor, I2P, Freenet)	Emerging Decentralized Platforms (Blockchain, IPFS, Web3)	Ref.
Architecture Type	Centralized or semi-centralized anonymity networks.	Fully decentralized, P2P blockchain-based systems.	(Gharavi et al., 2024)
Routing Mechanism	Onion and garlic routing through volunteer nodes.	Distributed consensus and smart contract-based routing.	(Anbarkhan, 2024; Figueras-Martín et al., 2022)
Data Storage	Encrypted content stored on volunteer nodes.	Distributed storage via IPFS/Filecoin with content addressing.	(Saleem et al., 2024; de-Marcos et al., 2026).
Trust Model	Rely on directory authorities and node operators.	Trustless environment using cryptographic verification.	(Collier, 2024; Chen et al., 2026)
Security Basis	Classical cryptography (RSA, ECC).	PQC (lattice, hash-based).	(Merlec & In, 2024; Fan et al., 2024; Gilbert & Gilbert, 2024)
Scalability	Limited by bandwidth and latency.	Enhance distributed consensus and sharding.	(Abu Al-Haija et al., 2022; Avasthi et al., 2024)
Vulnerability	Susceptible to traffic correlation and quantum attacks.	Resistant to censorship and quantum decryption.	(Saleem et al., 2022; Gentile et al., 2024)
Governance	Centralized control via directory servers.	DAOs	(Avasthi et al., 2024)
Primary Goal	Anonymity and privacy.	Resilience, transparency, and quantum security.	(de-Marcos et al., 2026; Fan et al., 2024)
Strengths	• Mature, widely adopted. • strong anonymity through. onion/garlic routing. • low entry barrier for users.	• High resilience. • Censorship resistance. • Scalable. • Integrates smart contracts & DAOs. • Quantum-Resilient Cryptography.	(Fan et al., 2024)
Limitations	• Pivotal points of failure (directory servers). • Vulnerable to traffic correlation. • Scalability issues. • Classical cryptography exposed to quantum threats.	• High computational and energy costs. • interoperability challenges. • complexity of governance. • adoption barriers for PQC.	(Avasthi et al., 2024; Gentile et al., 2024)

Table 4. Comparison summary between PQC & PQS

Feature	PQC	PQS
Scope	Cryptography only.	Entire security architecture
Encryption	Core focus	Included
Decryption		
Authentication	Limited	Full
Threat Detection	Not supported	Supported
Blockchain Integration		

3. EMERGING DECENTRALIZED DARKNET PLATFORMS

The rapid growth of centralized network anonymity to decentralized infrastructures presents a significant evolution towards privacy, resilience, and autonomy in digital ecosystems. Even though the most recent generation of decentralized darknet sites utilizes blockchain, P2P, and distributed storage to generate censorship-resistant spaces without centralized authorities. This framework is the intersection of cryptographic innovation, distributed consensus, and autonomous protocols, as recognized and discussed to support strong markets, tokenized economies, and self-sustaining operations (Darzi & Yavuz, 2024), where modern phases introduce the ultramodern decentralized structures in the dark internet.

3.1 Blockchain-Based Darknet Infrastructures

In the field of technology, especially contemporary results of blockchain technology, mainly blockchain generation, which emerged as an inspiration for decentralized darknet architectures, provide new and specialized functions of immutable ledgers, transparent transactions, and trustworthy consensus mechanisms. This method renders it much more unusual than traditional darknet market systems such as the Tor browser, which rely on centralized artifact management. Also, the infrastructure mainly based on blockchain distributes the management among nodes and is fault tolerant and proof of control (Rustamova & Dutta, 2025).

3.1.1 Decentralized Marketplaces

Because decentralization allows anonymous exchange with external intermediaries and establishes blockchain generation. Various systems, which include OpenBazaar and Particl, which facilitate P2P trading through smart contracts and cryptocurrency payments, serve to illustrate the model discussed through illustrations (Suriya et al., 2026). Additionally, this marketplace eliminates escrow agents by embedding transaction logic directly into blockchain protocols to ensure that funds are released only when predefined conditions are met in Collier (2024). Although, using privacy-focused cryptocurrencies that include Monero and Zcash enhances transaction anonymity, decentralized identity structures save you from user profiling (Abu Al-Haija et al., 2022). Additionally, dark web markets that use blockchain and include geographic information from cryptographic certificate clients promise to keep users' identities secret. This decentralization offers the same clarity in sharp assessment as the traditional dark web market with its proven contrary figures, which often fall under central government or regulatory enforcement intervention.

3.1.2 Tokenized Ecosystems

Tokenization was recently introduced with a programmable asset gift with multiple values with access to rights, or governance rights, within the decentralized dark web ecosystem. These tokens allow microtransactions, encourage participation in the community, and help DAOs as authors who made the diagnosis within the observation (El-Kady, 2025). As an instance, Particl's PART token hit the market and is giving up customers via token bets for privacy-advancing elements of the government. Similarly, they have a look at Saleem et al. (2024). ZeroNet presents the integration of bitcoin-first and essentially based peer-to-peer authentication, translated by diskless alignment of incentives among sponsors. Auditors and developers are rewarded through the mechanisms of Decentralized Finance (DeFi) for the continued network growth. Furthermore, the discussions in both studies (Figueras-Martín et al., 2022; de-Marcos et al., 2026) often support tokenization privacy-preserving computation, where smart contracts execute cryptographic logic using ZKP static MPC . This integration of cryptographic primitives ensures that darknet activities remain verifiable and private domains are computed.

3.2 P2P and Distributed Storage Integration

P2P networks present the backbone of decentralized dark internet systems, enabling changes to be negotiated directly between nodes without an intermediary. Where the workflow in Chen et al. (2026) offers flexibility, scalability, and censorship resistance through data sharing and monitoring among multiple members are complements. This section categorizes as follows:

3.2.1 IPFS-based Hosting

IPFS revolutionizes darknet website hosting by transforming centralized servers with distributed content and located storage. Every document is verified with the help of a cryptographic hash that ensures its integrity and immutability (Avasthi et al., 2024). IPFS integration therefore enables decentralized hosting of web pages, storage of web pages, applications, and marketplaces across multiple nodes. This configuration prevents downloads and ensures continuous availability even in the event of network outages (Merlec & In, 2024). While platforms that include ZeroNet and Freenet followed similar concepts of using Distributed Hash Tables (DHTs) to discover and retrieve content that they operate differently. Moreover, IPFS is developed to boost these models via help to integrate version control and peer replication by allowing darknet websites to dynamically optimize even while maintaining pristine transparency to be able to monetize their work (Hammoud et al., 2021).

3.2.2 Resilience and Censorship Resistance

Distributed storage inherently resists censorship by eliminating SPoF. The data blocks are replicated across geographically dispersed nodes, preventing authorities or adversaries from completely removing content (Pincheira et al., 2022). Furthermore, encryption algorithms were used to ensure that the community securely continued its function even if some nodes were compromised. Decentralized routing protocols therefore increase security by dynamically routing traffic to protect it from surveillance or obstruction (Fan et al., 2024). As another illustration, quantum-resistant cryptography is becoming a part of newer darknet infrastructures for a more forward-thinking security approach; lattice- and hash-based fully encrypted designs make use of the provided space to secure information from quantum deciphering approaches, offering the most current possible anonymity inside pictures (Gentile et al., 2024). Thus, these enhancements have proved to make sure that centralized darknet designs are forward-looking solutions in the era of QC that are additionally lightweight.

3.3 Smart Contracts for Autonomous Operations

Smart contracts are also a package that automatically executes the agreements for the transactions and enforces business rules in the decentralized environments. Besides that, escorting services are automated without human supervision in monitoring, disputing, and governing the agreement (Maire, 2024).

3.3.1 Automated Transactions and Escrow Systems

Typical darknet exchanges employ human-managed escrow systems for payment, raising concerns about trustworthiness and susceptibility to attack, and the issue is resolved by making conditional judgments within coding with no delay at the blockchain epoch instead of using mediators in the prior years. Following, in Guizani et al. (2026), in some instances a payment from a customer for items held within a contract until the vendor confirms their transaction, and each fund delivered can be instantaneously released. These improvements lead to increased transparency and reduce scams and guarantee fairer dealings without surrendering anonymous benefits. Apart from that, some sophisticated smart contracts apply multi-sig authorization with ZKPs, which empower each user to prove their payment is correct and do not leave traces when touching anything without being seen or detected; on page (Magliocco, 2026) the authors demonstrated how those techniques have improved the static aspect to make exchanges auditable while preserving anonymity features needed on the dark net.

The next step involves sophisticated smart contracts that deal with decentralized arbitration mechanisms where payment disputes are resolved either by distributed voting or by the means of an automatic system rather than being referred to a higher government entity (Naz et al., 2026).

3.3.2 Based Governance Models

As a result of DAOs, a new governance level appears on darknet infrastructure whereby network governance based on DAOs enables the communities to coordinate and participate in decision-making on token weight votes, thereby developing guidelines at a network level under the common consensus. Also, DAOs could be applied in allocating network resources to maintain protocol upgrading and serve as community requirements, replacing conventional governing hierarchized structures by offering protocols as programmable order codes. In addition, darknet's structure of communities with DAOs enables maximal commitments to preserving its anonymity. The example is from Hammoud et al. (2021), whereby community members vote on all amendments, with any individual either voting or submitting a proposal on any adaptation without any type of identification or connection to other member by relating them with crypto- Credentials, whereby this adaptation also facilitates self-governance of the community such that it maintains the discipline with ethics and also enforce technical regulations in its networks as the darknet infrastructure would operate in a sustainable mechanism while relying on block chains and P2P technology in order to mitigate challenges related to scaling and protections including punishments protection.

3.4 Case Studies of Emerging Platforms

Case Study #1: OpenBazaar

The Open Bazaar is the main decentralized marketplace that works with external centralizers or intermediaries. Although it is P2P shaped miles and bitcoin-based payments, it enables users to exchange goods and offers instantly, as discussed in Gharavi et al. (2024). Also, smart contracts manipulate escrow and dispute resolution, while encrypted communication ensures privacy. Although OpenBazaar, in (Darzi & Yavuz, 2024), faces stressful situations of scalability, it shows that decentralized trading in darknet environments is applicable.

Case Study #2: The Particl

Particl extends the idea of decentralized operation through the integration of privacy-enhancing technologies with non-public transactions and RingCT. Its blockchain-based, fully token-based marketplace uses a portion of tokens for billing and governance. Particl's architecture allows for encryption, and it can encrypt escrow committees as an instance of how contract and escrow self-regulated darknet financial systems (Rustamova & Dutta, 2025).

Case Study #3: ZeroNet

ZeroNet marks the integration of the Bitcoin cryptocurrency with BitTorrent-style P2P networks to host websites and packages without a central server (Suriya et al., 2026). Each site is known using a public key, and updates are propagated through a P2P network. In addition, the integration of ZeroNet with IPFS includes storage to create certain resilience to censorship and takedown (Collier, 2024). Furthermore, its lightweight design and compatibility with Tor flexible design platform for decentralized darknet website hosting (Abu Al-Haija et al., 2022).

Case Study #4: Freenet

Freenet is one of the oldest periods in the distributed darknet structure. To maintain anonymity and availability, encrypted statistics use adaptive routing as identified (Saleem et al., 2022). Modern iterations of Freenet include blockchain-first primarily based identity verification and tokenized incentives to evaluate node participation (El-Kady, 2025). This hybridization of legacy P2P publishing with blockchain shows continuous improvement in the field of decentralized dark web infrastructure (Saleem et al., 2024). Figure 4 illustrates the structure of a decentralized dark web platform that integrates blockchain, P2P networks, and distributed garages. More decentralizing elements appear, such as distributed autonomous ecosystems (blockchain, P2P and parking spaces), but unlike cryptographic centralized networks, which provided the ultimate privacy, security, and flexibility, which is impossible with the current methods due to the nature of decision-making. DAO, Smart Contracts and DAOs could automate ways for making decisions, and the economy is there to increase contribution. Also, OpenBazaar, Particl, and ZeroNet provide examples of these standards-based standards where static decency with spatial endurance and distributed infrastructures are to be redefined in relation to QC and AI.

Figure 4. Architecture of decentralized darknet platform integrating blockchain, P2P networking, & distributed storage

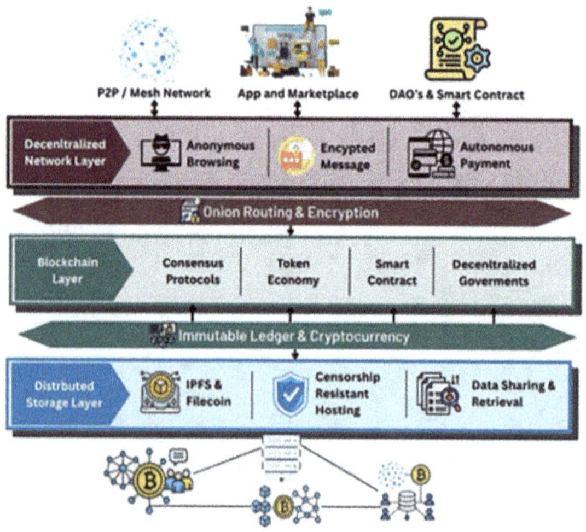

4. POST-QUANTUM THREAT LANDSCAPE

The emergence of Cryptographically Relevant Quantum Computers (CRQCs) represents a seismic transformation in the field of cybersecurity. CRQC's ability to execute algorithms, including Shor's and Grover's, threatens the mathematical foundations of modern encryption, anonymity, and privacy schemes that underlines botnet and darknet infrastructure. Evolving threat models in the quantum era are also analyzed This section discusses and presents the following:

4.1 Vulnerabilities of Current Cryptographic Systems

4.1.1 RSA and ECC Breakability Under QC

Public-key cryptography, especially RSA and ECC, is based on the computationally impossible to solve integer multiplication and discrete logarithm problems. Gharavi et al. (2024) identifies the assumption of Shor's rule set, added in 1994, that can solve those problems in a polynomial quantum computer.

4.1.1.1 RSA Vulnerability

The RSA-2048 bit would take and work on classical computers with thousands of years to factor. Also, it could be broken within hours once quantum computers reach the million-qubit threshold, as identified and discuss in Anbarkhan (2024). Furthermore, the key vulnerabilities of RSA are:

- **Key Length Dependency:** Requires extremely large keys (≥ 2048 bits) for modern security, improving the computational overhead.

- **Quantum Susceptibility:** Shor's algorithm can factor large integers efficiently, breaking RSA encryption.
- **Performance Bottlenecks:** Slow key technology and decryption in terms of elliptic curved structures.
- **Side Channel Attacks:** Vulnerability to the following: timing, lightning, and fault injection attacks targeting non-public key process.
- **Padding Oracle Exploits:** Implementations vulnerability of PKCS#1 that can leak plain text through error messages.
- **Poor Randomness:** Weak random generation number at specified phases of key arrival can lead to predictable key generation.

4.1.1.2 ECC Vulnerability

ECC, though more efficient than RSA in classical contexts, is paradoxically more vulnerable in the quantum era since it includes shorter key lengths which require for fewer qubits to break, approximately 2,300 for P256 curves, as discussed in Rustamova and Dutta (2025). Where the key vulnerabilities of ECC are:

- **Curve Selection Risks:** Insecure or poorly chosen curves, such as non-prime fields may lead to exploit the weaknesses by cyber criminals.
- **Implementation Flaws:** Incorrect parameter validation or point addition errors can expose private keys.
- **Side Channel Attacks:** Susceptible to timing and electromagnetic analysis during scalar multiplication.
- **Small Subgroup Attacks:** Occur when curve parameters allow points of low order.
- **Quantum Threat:** Shor's algorithm also breaks ECC by solving discrete logarithms efficiently.
- **Complexity in Validation:** This process requires careful checking of both curve parameters and public keys to prevent attacks that exploit invalid curves.

The discussions in the work (Suriya et al., 2026; Collier, 2024) highlights the critical consequences for structures relying on TLS, VPN, PKI, and virtual signatures. When CRQCs are enabled, attackers can forge certificates, impersonate servers, and decrypt historical communication harvested today. Thus, an algorithm, known as Harvest Now, Decrypt Later (HNDL) Figure 5 shows each RSA and ECC vulnerability, and highlights common weaknesses in RSA and ECC.

Figure 5. Overview of RSA & ECC with common vulnerabilities

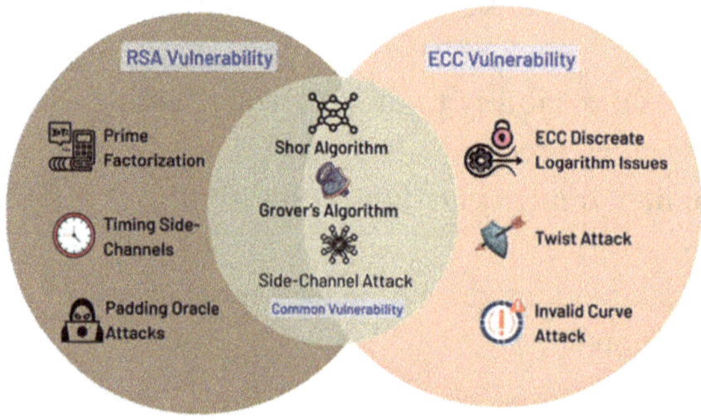

4.1.2 Cyber Risks to Anonymity and Encryption

QC undermines not only encryption but also framework anonymities.

- **Tor and I2P Networks:** As discussed in Abu Al-Haija et al. (2022), Tor and I2P networks rely on layered encryption (RSA/ECC) for onion routing. Therefore, quantum decryption could expose relay identities, compromising user anonymity.
- **Blockchain Systems:** Approximately 74 of the top 100 cryptocurrencies use ECDSA signatures which are vulnerable to Shor's algorithm (Saleem et al., 2022). Thus, quantum attackers could forge transactions, drain wallets, and redefine the blockchain histories.
- **Symmetric Encryption:** Grover's algorithm halves the effective key strength of symmetric ciphers (El-Kady, 2025). Furthermore, AES-128 drops to ~64-bit security, while AES-256 remains integration of the secure ~128-bit quantum for enhancement purposes (Saleem et al., 2024).

Overall, the convergence of those cyber threats disrupts confidentiality and integrity simultaneously. Although encrypted files, backups, and long-term data stores are at risk of tricky decryption as quantum capacity evolves (Figueras-Martín et al., 2022).

4.2 Impact on Darknet Security and Privacy

4.2.1 Deanonymization Cyber Risks

Darknet ecosystems are built on anonymity, where the decentralization, and cryptographic trust face existential threats in the post-quantum era. Therefore, decryption of onion-routed traffic could reveal user identities, server locations, and transaction metadata (de-Marcos et al., 2026).

- **Onion Routing Breakdown:** Encrypted Tor layer using RSA/ECDH, as mentioned in Chen et al. (2026), would be fully compromised under Shor's algorithm, exposing relay nodes and end-to-end communication paths.

- **Decentralized Marketplaces:** Platforms such as OpenBazaar and Particl that deploy blockchain-based smart contracts and privacy coins could suffer deanonymization through quantum signature forgery (Avasthi et al., 2024).
- **Pseudonymity Collapse:** Quantum-enhancement correlation attacks could link pseudonymous identities across darknet forums, cryptocurrency wallets, and messaging systems, as discussed in the work (Merlec & In, 2024).

4.2.2 Traffic Analysis with Quantum-Enhanced Capabilities

QC further amplifies traffic analysis through Quantum Machine Learning (QML) and Quantum-Assisted Pattern Recognition (QAPR) as identified in AlTamimi et al. (2025).

- **Quantum Accelerated Correlation:** QML models as provided in Hammoud et al. (2021) that can process massive traffic datasets exponentially rapidly, identifying timing patterns and relay behaviors than traditional systems.
- **Quantum Sensor Networks:** Future quantum communication infrastructures may enable passive interception of photonic signals deploying in encrypted tunnels and allow the adversaries to reconstruct routing paths (Pincheira et al., 2022).
- **Quantum-Enhanced Decryption of Metadata:** Even if payloads remain encrypted with post-quantum algorithms, metadata packet timing, size, and frequency can be exploited to infer user behavior (Fan et al., 2024).

In summary, these capabilities transform the traffic analysis from probabilistic inference into deterministic deanonymization, eroding the privacy guarantees that redefine darknet operations.

4.3 Threat Modeling in a Quantum Era

4.3.1 Adversarial Capabilities

Quantum adversaries have unprecedented computational and analytical power. Quantum countermeasure capabilities extend beyond brute-force decryption to the strategic exploitation of hybrid infrastructure.

A. **State Actor Dominance:** Nation states with quantum sources can engage in large-scale HNDL campaigns, collecting anonymous site visitors for message decryption as confirmed (Gentile et al., 2024).
B. **Quantum-Enabled Cyber Espionage:** In Gilbert and Gilbert (2024), intelligence agencies must retroactively decrypt diplomatic, financial, and military communications, undermining many years of secrecy.
C. **Quantum Malware:** Cyber attackers can also embed quantum resistant payloads capable of exploiting the vulnerabilities, including buffer overflow caused by large PQC key sizes (Maire, 2024).
D. **Quantum-Assisted AI Attacks:** The integration of QC with AI enables adaptive cryptanalysis, algorithms that undergoing real-time development to exploit new vulnerabilities and weaknesses (Guizani et al., 2026).

4.3.2 Attack Scenarios

A. **Retrospective Decryption such as (HNDL):** Adversaries intercept encrypted darknet traffic in the recent days and store it for future decryption. Once CRQCs mature, political users or forensics team can reconstruct entire communication histories, revealing identities, transactions, and operational structures (Magliocco, 2026).

Quantum-Forged Certificates: Using Shor's algorithm, attackers forge CA signatures, allowing Man-in-the-Middle (MITM) attacks on darknet gateways and marketplaces. This agreement is valid for chains that allow large-scale simulations (Naz et al., 2026).

B. **Blockchain Manipulation:** The most common ECDSA vulnerabilities involve quantum attackers forging transactions, manipulating ledger history, and undermining decentralized acceptance as truth. The financial impact could be destabilizing privacy-focused cryptocurrencies (Song et al., 2026).
C. **Quantum-Enhanced Surveillance:** Governments deploy quantum sensors and QML systems to monitor encrypted traffic across Tor, I2P, and Freenet, correlating end-user activity with real-world credential identities (Hammoud et al., 2021).
D. **Hybrid Exploitation During Migration:** During the transition of PQC within hybrid systems, integrated classical and PQC algorithms might be exposed to interoperability flaws. Attackers could exploit these weaknesses by bypassing the encryption or inject malicious certificates as discussed in (Gupta, 2026; Khan et al., 2025).
E. **Quantum-Resistant Subversion:** Even post-quantum algorithms are not immune to side-channel attacks. Quantum adversaries could be exploiting timing, power, or electromagnetic emissions to extract keys from PQC implementations (Sengupta & Bose, 2025; Baseri et al., 2026).
F. **Quantum-AI Social Engineering:** Quantum-accelerated AI models could simulate human behavior with extreme precision, enabling large-scale phishing and identity manipulation campaigns within darknet communities (Carruthers & Clincy, 2025, October).

Table 5 shows the impact of QC on cryptographic primitives used in darknet systems. Additionally, Table 5 outlines the effects of the primitive darknet use case, the implications of QC, the repercussions for darknet systems, and the strategies for migration and mitigation.

Table 5. Impact of QC on cryptographic primitives used in darknet systems

Ref.	Primitive	Darknet Use Case	Quantum Impact	Consequence for Darknet Systems.	Migration / Mitigation Direction
(Gharavi et al., 2024)	RSA	Marketplace authentication, escrow signatures, and onion service TLS handshakes.	Broken by Shor's algorithm. integer factorization in polynomial time.	Loss of transaction integrity and identity spoofing across hidden services.	• Replace with lattice-based signatures (ML-DSA / Dilithium). • Adopt hybrid TLS using ML KEM [5] KEM.
(Suriya et al., 2026)	ECC (ECDSA / ECDH)	Cryptocurrency wallets (Bitcoin, Monero), Tor relay certificates.	Shor's algorithm Solves discrete. algorithm problem.	Key forgery wallet Drain and fake node certificates.	• Transition to post quantum blockchain signatures. (FALCON, SPHINCS+). • Use quantum-secured address schemes.
(de-Marcos et al., 2026)	AES / SHA 2	Encrypted storage of darknet data and P2P document exchange.	Grover's algorithm halves bit security (256 to 128 bits).	Reduced confidentiality of bulk data and metadata hashes.	• Employ AES 256 and SHA 3 512. • increase key rotation frequency and entropy sources.
(Merlec & In, 2024	Blockchain Consensus & Smart Contracts	Decentralized market ledgers and autonomous DAOs.	PQC not yet integrated signature and key exchange vulnerable.	Tampering with ledger records and contract execution via forged keys.	• Embed Kyber KEM and Dilithium signatures in blockchain protocols. • Use quantum resistant hash chains
(Hammoud et al., 2021)	MPC Protocols (SSS, HE, OT)	Privacy-preserving data sharing in darknet analytics.	Classical MPC depends on RSA/ECC to Break quantum physics.	Exposure of shared inputs and loss of confidential computation.	• Integrate lattice-based PQC within MPC frameworks (QKD + Kyber). • Use quantum secure secret sharing.
(Guizani et al., 2026)	Quantum Key Distribution (QKD)	Secure channel setup between darknet nodes.	Resistant to quantum attacks but limited by distance and hardware.	Partial adoption in darknet networks due to infrastructure constraint.	Integrate QKD with PQC for hybrid key exchange; develop satellitebased QKD for global coverage.
(Gupta, 2026)	TLS / PKI Infrastructure	Hidden service authentication and encrypted traffic.	RSA / ECDHE broken by Shor; record now decrypt future cyber risk.	Retroactive decrypts of captured darknet traffic and identity spoofing.	• Deploy hybrid TLS (ML KEM + X25519). • Implement crypto agility and PQC certificate chains.
(Ishaque & Al-Anesi, 2025)	Lattice Based Cryptography (LWE, NTRU, Kyber)	Quantum safe darknet communication and storage.	Resistant to quantum attacks under current knowledge.	Enables secure darknet transactions and data exchange post quantum.	• Standardize Kyber for key encapsulation and Dilithium for signatures. • Integrate with Tor protocols.
(Okika et al., 2025)	Zero Trust Security + PQC Integration.	Access control and continuous authentication in darknet services.	Quantum threat to legacy auth tokens and certificates.	Compromise of user identity and session integrity.	• Implement ZeroTrust framework with PQC keys. • Continuous verification and micro-segmentation of nodes.

5. PQC FOR THE DARKNET

The darknet relies on anonymity networks (Tor, I2P) and cryptographic primitives for confidentiality, integrity, and authentication, making the Confidentiality, Integrity, and Availability (CIA) Triad particularly sensitive to the arrival of large-scale quantum computers. Therefore, PQC aims to either replace or improve classical public-key systems (like RSA, ECC, and Diffie–Hellman) with algorithms that are thought to be safe from quantum attacks. The following section summarizes the most relevant PQC families, explains how they can be integrated into Darknet protocols, and discusses the principal performance and deployment challenges that operators and researchers must address.

5.1 Overview of PQC Algorithms

To begin with, post-quantum computing can break RSA in polynomial time, as identified in Joshi et al. (2023), which is something conventional computers cannot achieve due to their processing power constraints. Moreover, quantum computers with more qubits, as provided in Shivarudraiah (2023) will crack factorization ciphers faster. Additionally, post-quantum proposals fall into several families; each family brings different security assumptions, message sizes, and computational costs. Three families are particularly relevant for darknet applications.

5.1.1 Hash-based Signatures (SPHINCS+)

Stateless hash-based signature schemes such as SPHINCS+ rely only on the security of hash functions; therefore, they are conceptually simple and conservative. Kaur et al. (2024) employ a survey to study the percentage awareness of end-users and society in the dark web and hashing algorithms. The results show that 38.4% used them for curiosity purposes, whereas 21.7% are deployed for research and academic reasons. The dark web is a growing asset, especially when it comes to illegal services and activities. The security mechanisms require awareness of these issues (4044) and the implementation of steps to eliminate them (Kavitha et al., 2023). Table 5 shows the impact of QC on cryptographic primitives used in darknet systems. Additionally, Table 5 outlines the effects of the primitive darknet use case, the implications of QC, the repercussions for darknet systems, and the strategies for migration and mitigation. Therefore (Tazi et al., 2022; abdulhamza Noor, 2025), these schemes produce relatively large signatures and public keys compared with lattice schemes, but they are attractive in scenarios where long-term security and conservative assumptions are paramount, such as when signing long-lived service descriptors or software updates for hidden services. The deterministic nature and reliance on well-known hash primitives render them a strong alternative whenever they don't cause the store size or bandwidth limitations to occur.

5.1.2 Lattice-based Schemes (Kyber, Dilithium)

Lattice structures, especially Learning with Errors (LWE) and Ring LWE variants, are associated with prime candidates for smart public key encryption and signatures. Key Encapsulation Mechanisms (KEMs) incorporating Kyber are the latest robust security protection exceptions to worst-case scenarios. Signal color green problems key statements provide relatively small public keys and fast verification (abdulhamza Noor, 2025). Regarding darknet protocols that require a routine of ephemeral key exchange (for instance, setting up onion tunnels or P2P encrypted channels), forged KEMs are attractive because they can be executed on state-of-the-art servers at moderate CPU costs and provide more privacy when utilizing ephemeral keys.

5.1.3 Code-Based and Multivariate Schemes

Code-based systems traditionally offer robust security mechanisms as well as rapid encryption/decryption, however, usually have large public keys in Megabytes size in some parameter units. Multivariable systems are preferably compact and fast for signatures than shared file in cryptanalysis. These families can be useful in particular darknet contexts where a service operator can tolerate large public keys once they are stored and reused or when limited smart keys need to be verified very rapidly, so as discussed in Al Tamimi (2025), weak code and repeated code will cause failures in structures.

In summary, each script has tradeoffs of lattice schemes that generally balanced in between key/signature size and speed well, hash-based schemes that are conservative but huge, code-based, and multivariate schemes can be efficient in some operations but impose storage or trust-model excessive costs. Selecting a PQC primitive for a darknet deployment therefore requires matching the algorithmic profile to the protocol role (for instance, ephemeral key exchange, long-term signing, or bulk encryption) and to the operational constraints of the nodes involved.

5.2 Integration into Darknet Protocols

Integrating PQC into darknet stacks must preserve the core properties darknet users expect unlikability, forward secrecy, and low-profile operation (Begum et al., 2025). This section recommends three practical integration patterns.

5.2.1 PQS Communication Channels

Replace classical key exchange primitives (such as RSA, classical Diffie-Hellman, or ECDH) with PQC KEMs for establishing session keys. In practice, this means embedding a KEM handshake protocol into the existing tunnel setup: the client and relay exchange KEM ciphertexts and derive symmetric session keys via a KDF (Azeez et al., 2024). To preserve forward secrecy, operators should use ephemeral KEM keys per session or combine ephemeral classical DH with PQC KEMs in a hybrid handshake. Although there is a demand for attention paid to message sizes, some PQC KEMs increase handshake packet length, so protocol framing must be adjusted to avoid fingerprinting or MTU fragmentation that could degrade anonymity.

5.2.2 PQC for long-term Credentials and Signatures

Long-lived artifacts, service descriptors, software update signatures, and public keys advertised in directories are especially vulnerable to "store now, decrypt later" attacks. For these artifacts, PQC signatures (or hash-based signatures) should be used (Al-Tameemi et al., 2025). Where signature size is a concern, operators can use a hybrid signing strategy: sign the long-term artifact with a PQC scheme and include a compact classical signature for backward compatibility; clients that understand PQC verify the PQC signature, while legacy clients fall back to the classical signature (with appropriate warnings). For software updates and package signing, deterministic hash-based signatures provide a conservative option that minimizes cryptanalytic risk.

5.2.3 Hybrid Cryptographic Approaches

A practical transfer strategy is hybridization: exchanging classical and PQC keys in parallel and deriving negotiation keys from the two contributions Al Tamimi, S. (2025, August). Hybrid handoffs provide immediate security against future quantum adversaries while maintaining consistency with legacy peers. For dark networks, hybridization additionally reduces the cyber risk of implementation errors in new PQC code being exploited to anonymize customers. Therefore, the hybrid handoff designs should be conservative, integrating the independent entropy sources, using robust KDFs, and ensure that failure of one primitive does not leak key material from the other (Vithalkar et al., 2024).

5.2.4 Key Management and Identity

Darknet structures often rely on self-authenticating identifiers that contain onion addresses derived from public keys. The transition to PQC requires defining how features are derived from new public keys without violating the agreement on semantics (Patel et al., 2025). One technique is to declare a versioned identity configuration that contains version bytes indicating meaningful object types (classical or PQC) and hashes of public keys. This might allow the integration with deployments and gradual migration while preserving the ability for key detection types and applying appropriate verification logic.

5.3 Performance and Deployment Challenges

To avoid undermining anonymity or availability, PQC should be implemented in dark web ecosystems to provide many operationally demanding scenarios that need to be solved.

5.3.1 Computational Overhead and Latency

Many PQC schemes impose higher CPU charging costs than classical counterparts, especially on constrained devices. Lattice systems are relatively green but do require more cycles of large-scale production and packaging than ECDH which can become intensely valuable to produce a hash-based signature in general (Vithalkar et al., 2024). For latency touch paths such as onion routing, where more than one hop performs cryptographic operations, extended latency corresponding to with-hop counting can expand to eventually fall Thus, mitigation may be to offload heavy workloads that require multiple successful relays .

5.3.2 Bandwidth and Packetization

PQC public keys, ciphertext, and signatures are regularly larger than classical equivalents. Although, large handshake packets can maximize the cyber threat of traffic estimation and fingerprinting, which specifies multifactor authentication types if not carefully normalized (Dwivedi et al., 2023). Thus, the protocol should adopt constant-length padding strategies for handshake protocol messages and remember multiplexing or compression in each appropriate. Where MTU fragmentation is unavoidable, implement robust reconnection to keep out leaky differentiating features (Patel et al., 2025).

5.3.3 Scalability and Storage

Some PQC families (notably code-based) require large public keys that must be stored and distributed. However, storage offerings and secret transport records must be tailored to handle large key content without revealing garage styles that can be exploited for context (Vithalkar et al., 2024). Operators need to remember content-coding garages, collection strategies, and rate restrictions to prevent misuse.

5.3.4 Interoperability and Gradual Migration

Darknet ecosystems are heterogeneous; nodes potentially change location at a certain speed. Hybrid handshakes and versionable introductions allow incremental deployment. Moreover, they can maximize the complexity and attack surface of the protocol (Anbarkhan, 2024). Carefully, the specification, contextual implementation, cross-platform efforts, and interoperability are essential. Although consistency must be balanced against promptness with quantum-gradient primitive replacement.

5.3.5 Implementation of Security and Side Channels

In addition, the PQC should not only be structured consistently but should also prevent side channel leaks, such as those that were more relevant in the network, especially if a single compromised relay or user can be anonymizing for several clients, as the author of this paper covered in Vithalkar et al. (2024). Therefore, it is important that administrators use well-documented libraries, economically friendly solutions, and a more formal framework of management and sub-coding for auditing and fuzzing by outsiders.

5.3.6 Usability and User Expectations

Large images as well as signatures might degrade user enjoyment, diminish connection availability, lower performance, prolong download time, and exacerbate multiple rounds of authentication (Anbarkhan, 2024). For example, they are likely to deter many low-friction, private dark web users from considering adopting them. Designers need to offer a clear path with little friction towards transition (history key upgrades or opportunistic hybrid handshakes) and make honest trade-offs explicit, detailing why they achieve the security advantages (Patel et al., 2025).

Figure 6 shows the architecture that is to utilize classical encryption schemes (RSA, AES) with PQC comprising mesh-primary based and hash-based completeness algorithm to secure the darknet communication. The version consists of QKE, cryptography to realize seamless swapping of all classics, and PQC keeping layers It also employs static IoT devices with anonymous network management techniques like Tor, Onion management for integrity, privacy, and to achieve resilience to the quantum decryption. The entire setup emphasizes maintaining privacy of data, integrity, and anonymity of distributed darknet servers. In more simplified terms; Table 6 describes all the terminology used in the entire architecture.

Figure 6. Hybrid post-quantum secure communication model for next-generation darknet systems

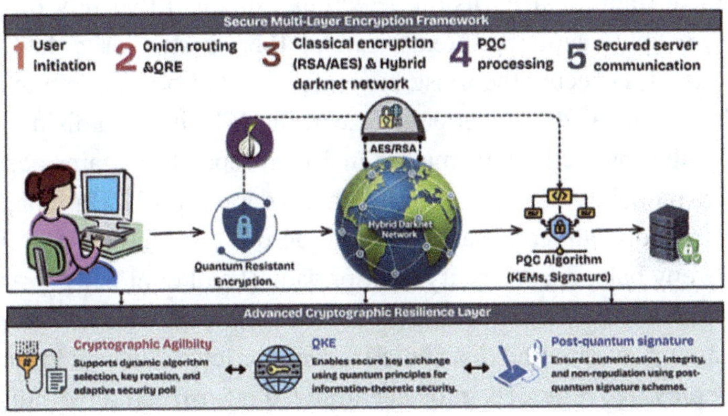

Table 6. Hybrid post-quantum secure communication framework to secure data transmission summary

Step #	Description
Step 1	User initiates communication through a secure client.
Step 2	Data is anonymized using onion routing (Tor browser) and protected with quantum-resistant encryption to conceal the sender's identity and communication path.
Step 3	Encrypted traffic transmitted throughout the hybrid darknet community through classical encryption mechanisms associated with AES and RSA algorithms using a higher degree of fact-privacy and secure routing.
Step 4	The communication is further strengthened utilizing PQC algorithms, including KEMs for secure key establishment and post-quantum digital signatures for authentication and integrity verification.
Step 5	The protected data reaches the secured destination server, where confidentiality, integrity, authentication, and resistance against future quantum attacks are maintained.

The proposed hybrid PQS conversation framework secures statistical communication through a multi-layer architecture that integrates anonymity, classical cryptography, and quantum-resistant security mechanisms. Thus, supporting the entire framework is an Advanced Cryptographic Resilience Layer (ACRL) that incorporates cryptographic agility, QKE, and post-quantum digital signatures, enabling adaptive, future-proof security for IoT environments, distributed systems, and anonymous communications.

6. AI AND INTELLIGENT THREAT DETECTION IN FUTURE DARKNET

6.1 Role of AI in Decentralized Environments

The future of the dark web could be a growing increase and relieve autonomous AI vendors that can track decentralized ecosystems without centralized oversight. These vendors can continuously scan P2P visitors, blockchain-based holistic transactions, and secret service advertisers to detect anomalies in real-world data. Unlike traditional intrusion detection structures that rely on static guidelines, AI agents can dynamically adapt to evolving threats, making them particularly ideal for decentralized environments where adversaries execute the most anonymous and allocated architecture (Bhushan et al., 2022; Altamimi & Abu Al-Haija, 2024). Federated Learning (FL) is a promising paradigm for darknet evaluation. Instead of gathering tactile information in a vital repository, gains access to more than one node to collaborate learn models even to preserve immature data near FL (Hammad & Abu-Zaid, 2024). For instance, federated models can learn traffic patterns across Tor relays or I2P nodes without exposing individual logs, thereby balancing security with privacy (Patel et al., 2025; Al Jasem et al., 2025). Furthermore, AI-powered decentralized tracking is consistent with broader trends in blockchain-enabled AI systems, where smarter contracts and distributed ledgers promote trust and transparency in collaborative intelligence in deploying AI models into decentralized infrastructure within dark web scalability, unreliability. Thus, it can achieve adaptive random detection.

6.2 Behavioral Analysis and Anomaly Detection

One of the most effective applications of AI in Darknet defense is transactional visitor profiling. ML models can classify anonymous traffic flows, identify suspicious management behaviors, and stumble upon hidden channels used for illicit activities. For instance, deep mastering classifiers trained on packet metadata can distinguish between benign anonymity-bearing site visitors and malicious site visitors that are indicative of ransomware system control or illicit markets (Al Tamimi, 2025; Altamimi & Abu Al-Haija, 2024). AI also enhances anomaly detection by identifying deviations from predicted network operations. Techniques, including clustering, autoencoders, and recurrent neural networks, can reveal unusual access to patterns, sudden surges in cryptocurrency transactions, or irregularities in hidden service descriptors These anomalies usually signal illicit activities involving drug trafficking, illegal arms sales, or child exploitation networks (Rasyid et al., 2025).

Additionally, AI-driven semantic analysis of darknet boards and marketplaces can detect hidden warnings of miscommunication. Natural language processing (NLP) models can examine multilingual terms, stumble upon coded language, and flag emerging threats. Integrated with blockchain analysis, AI can signal illicit financial flows on decentralized exchanges, strengthening forensic capability (Hammad & Abu-Zaid, 2024).

6.3 Challenges in AI Deployment

Despite its promise, deploying AI in the Darknet faces several challenges:

I. **Data scarcity and labelling:** Training robust AI models requires large, labeled datasets. However, darknet traffic is inherently encrypted and encrypted, making it difficult to sense bottom-line reality. Researchers usually rely on synthetic datasets or honeypots that do not fully capture real-world adversarial behavior (Altamimi & Abu Al-Haija, 2024).

II. **Adversarial AI threats:** Malicious actors can use the most adversarial ML to avoid detection. Techniques including traffic redirections, hostile perturbations, or toxic FL updates can mislead AI models (Vithalkar et al., 2024). This points out between defenders and attackers requires flexible AI architectures with adversarial training and robust authentication techniques (Patel et al., 2025).

III. **Privacy and governance concerns**. The integration of AI into decentralized ecosystems increases ethical and governance issues. While the federal investigation preserves privacy, questions remain largely about accountability, transparency, and abuse of AI surveillance in encryption networks.

IV. **Resource constraints**. Many darknet nodes operate on low-power devices. The deployment of computationally extensive AI models can also strain resources, requiring lightweight architecture or hardware acceleration (Altamimi & Abu Al-Haija, 2024).

Table 7 identify the summary evaluation of AI technologies for darknet threat detection: technologies, packages, and limitations. The play a significant role in reviewing each methodology and limitation which will assist in choosing the appropriate method which is utilized in threat detection.

Table 7. AI techniques for darknet threat detection: Methods, applications, and limitations

Detection Method	Applications	Limitations
Deep Learning Classifiers	Traffic profiling, encrypted packet analysis, hidden service fingerprinting.	• Requires large, labelled datasets (Altamimi & Abu Al-Haija, 2024) • vulnerable to adversarial evasion (Hui & Tucker, 2025)
Federated Learning *(FL)*	Collaborative Darknet monitoring, privacy-preserving model training.	• Susceptible to poisoning attacks (Patel et al., 2025) • Coordination overhead (Al Jasem et al., 2025)
Clustering & Autoencoders	Anomaly detection in traffic flows, cryptocurrency transaction analysis.	• High false positives (Vithalkar et al., 2024). • difficulty in interpreting anomalies (Rasyid et al., 2025).
NLP & Semantic Analysis	Darknet forum monitoring, detection of coded language, illicit coordination.	Multilingual complexity; obfuscation by adversaries (Hammad & Abu-Zaid, 2024; (Hui & Tucker, 2025)
Blockchain Analytics & AI	Tracing illicit financial flows, smart contract monitoring, decentralized exchanges.	Scalability challenges; requires integration with heterogeneous ledgers (Al Jasem et al., 2025)
Adversarial Training Models	Defense against adversarial AI attacks, robust classification.	Computationally expensive; evolving adversarial strategies (Vithalkar et al., 2024)

7. LEGAL, ETHICAL, AND POLICY CONSIDERATIONS

7.1 Ethical Concerns in Darknet Research

Due to ethical concern, research in darknet ecosystems poses unique ethical challenges and barriers. Scholars are required to navigate with issues of informed consent, dual-use cyber risks, and researcher safety. The Menlo Report and AoIR guidelines stress and respect for persons, beneficence, and contextual integrity, but applying these principles to darknet research is complex (Supe, 2025). It is impractical to obtain consent from anonymous participants and publishing granular data poses cyber risks that enable criminal replication (Ferreira et al., 2025). Therefore, ethical challenges also emerge when dealing with sensitive datasets. For example, the Ashley Madison breach (Davitaia, 2025) shows how leaked personal data, once analyzed, can inadvertently continue to be harmful. Researchers must also use minimization techniques such as de-identification, aggregation, and publication of synthetic data. However, the operational security is equally critical, as engagement with illicit content exposes scholars to legal and psychological cyber risks. The case studies further highlight best practices such as the use of archival datasets, traffic classification without payloads, and ethnographic observation with paraphrased quotations (Ferreira et al., 2025; Supe, 2025). Darknet investigations require, in the ultimate analysis, a lifecycle approach of planning, reviewing, collecting, analyzing, and responsibly publishing grounded in ethical oversight and legal compliance. This allows scientific inquiry to advance cybersecurity knowledge without compromising privacy, safety, or legality.

7.2 Jurisdictional Challenges in Decentralized Systems

Through decentralized systems such as the DeFi protocol and blockchain-mainly based darknet platforms, management does not have relevant rights to apply, which makes applying traditional sector rules difficult because they are not fully based on traditional financial institutions yet on distributed nodes in different countries (Uzougbo et al., 2024). For instance, the implementation of cryptocurrency is mysterious when an exchange is registered in one jurisdiction but in international service to users. This leads to regulatory speculating. The actors benefit from differences in nationwide legal guidelines to avoid compliance (Widiastuti & Saragih, 2025). International law has historically relied on territoriality, nationality, and protection principles, yet they are all under pressure in cyberspace, where behavior immediately crosses borders (Shami et al., 2025). The Budapest Convention on Cybercrime attempted to standardize definitions and detection strategies, approaches, and operations. But the low adoption in important powers such as Russia and China limits its generalizability (Khan, 2025). Therefore, the empirical studies show that treaty waivers do not meet the certainty of enforcement, yet its effectiveness depends on the strengthening of legal mechanisms highlight gaps in jurisdiction that necessitate new frameworks that blend international cooperation with technical tools for enforcement.

7.3 Privacy vs. Surveillance Trade-offs

Darknet and decentralized systems seem contradictory because they need to provide privacy and anonymity and furthermore facilitate illicit interest. Technologies that enhance user privacy, such as onion routing and garlic routing, also provide a protection of anonymity for rogue actors to stay out of surveillance (Supe, 2025; Davitaia, 2025). The use of surveillance by governments to combat cybercrime raises many ethical questions, especially when it breaks privacy rights. In this context, the General Data Protection Regulation (GDPR) emphasizes legal justification, reduction, and statistical subjectivity, but anonymity and impossibility of consent in dark web surveys tend to prevent compliance to prioritize security across the board (Supe, 2025). The trade-offs of surveillance might be observed in national led monitoring programs, such as the U.S. CLOUD Act or China's Cybersecurity Law, which prioritize national security above privacy (Khan, 2025). The measures raise concerns about proportionality and due process, especially when cross-border data flows are involved. Scholars also argue that excessive surveillance cyber risks eroding trust in digital ecosystems and undermining democratic values (Ferreira et al., 2025; Shami et al., 2025). On the other hand, minimal oversight permits anonymity to be exploited for terrorism financing, child exploitation, and ransomware (Uzougbo et al., 2024; Widiastuti & Saragih, 2025). Privacy and surveillance policies must be sophisticated, and integrated human rights principles with practical enforcement so that anonymity tools remain available for legitimate uses such as whistleblowing and political dissent (Davitaia, 2025).

7.4 International Cooperation and Cyber Law

Regarding the necessity of international cooperation to combat the borderless nature of cybercrime. Therefore, the cooperative entities such as the Financial Action Task Force and the Joint Chiefs of Global Tax Enforcement (J5), which had been discussed in Uzougbo et al. (2024), are instances of how information sharing and joint investigations are critical in overcoming jurisdictional hurdles. In similar context, the Budapest Convention provides a framework for harmonization of substantive and procedural laws, but this law effectiveness depends on the domestic rule of law and institutional capacity (Malikzada, 2026). The policy debates are centered on the tension between sovereignty and global governance. While some states promoting various cyber sovereignty and tight national control, others support multilateral frameworks that emphasize openness and interoperability (Shami et al., 2025). The Tallinn Manuals and UN GGE report also seek to apply existing international law to cyberspace, but their non-binding nature limits enforceability. Empirical data suggest that operational cooperation, including mutual legal assistance requests, carries more weight in the success of prosecution than the mere ratification of a treaty (Malikzada, 2026). Cross-border data privacy leads to additional complexities in cooperation. Multiple regulations, such as GDPR, CCPA and Brazil's LGPD lead to fragmentation, which introduces compliance costs for multinational corporations and restricts interoperability (Khan, 2025). Mutual Legal Assistance Treaties (MLATs) are still slow and administrative, and alternative mechanisms have been developed, such as the CLOUD Act (Khan, 2025). The lack of harmonization is exploited by cybercriminals to escape detection.

Effective international cooperation should therefore be multi-layered:

I. **Legal Harmonization**: through treaties and model laws (Widiastuti & Saragih, 2025; Shami et al., 2025).
II. **Operational Collaboration:** via joint investigations and intelligence sharing (Uzougbo et al., 2024; Malikzada, 2026).
III. **Technological Solutions:** such as blockchain analytics and AI-driven monitoring (Uzougbo et al., 2024).
IV. **Human Rights Safeguards:** to balance enforcement with privacy and civil liberties (Supe, 2025; Ferreira et al., 2025).

8. FUTURE RESEARCH DIRECTIONS

The rapid evolution of darknet technologies, cyber criminals techniques and decentralized infrastructures present a fertile ground for future research. Whereas the emerging paradigms such as quantum-resistant cryptography, integration with next-generation networks, and sustainable infrastructures demand rigorous exploration.

I. Quantum-resistant anonymity networks

With the advent of QC, traditional cryptographic primitives such as RSA and ECC face obsolescence. Future darknet systems must adopt PQC to preserve anonymity and resilience against quantum attacks (Shami et al., 2025). Research should focus on designing onion and garlic routing protocols fortified with lattice-based, hash-based, or code-based schemes (Supe, 2025). Additionally, hybrid models that combine classical and quantum-resistant algorithms could ensure backward compatibility while preparing for quantum threats (Malikzada, 2026).

II. Fully decentralized Darknet ecosystems

Current darknet platforms rely on partial centralization, such as directory authorities in Tor. Future ecosystems should eliminate SPoF by leveraging blockchain-based governance, DAOs, and distributed storage systems such as IPFS/Filecoin (Uzougbo et al., 2024). This would enable censorship-resistant infrastructures with transparent governance models. Research must address scalability, interoperability, and resilience against Sybil attacks (Widiastuti & Saragih, 2025).

III. Integration with IoT, CPS, and 6G networks

The convergence of darknet technologies with IoT and Cyber-Physical Systems (CPS) introduces new opportunities and cyber risks. IoT devices often lack robust security, making them vulnerable to exploitation in darknet-enabled botnets (Ferreira et al., 2025). Integrating darknet anonymity with 6G networks could provide secure machine-to-machine communication, but latency, bandwidth, and energy constraints must be addressed (Shami et al., 2025). Research should explore lightweight cryptographic protocols, edge computing integration, and zero-trust architectures for IoT-darknet convergence (Khan, 2025).

IV. XAI for Darknet intelligence

AI is increasingly used for darknet monitoring, traffic analysis, and anomaly detection. However, opaque models raise ethical and legal concerns (Ferreira et al., 2025). Future research should prioritize XAI frameworks that provide transparency in darknet intelligence operations. This includes interpretable ML models for detecting illicit activities while respecting privacy rights (Davitaia, 2025). Integration of XAI with blockchain audit trails could enhance accountability and trust in darknet monitoring systems (Shami et al., 2025).

V. Energy-efficient and green Darknet infrastructures

Darknet infrastructures, particularly blockchain-based systems, consume significant energy. Future research must explore sustainable architectures that minimize carbon footprints (Widiastuti & Saragih, 2025). Approaches include proof-of-stake consensus, energy-aware routing, and integration with renewable energy sources (Khan, 2025). Green darknet infrastructures would align with global sustainability goals while ensuring secure and anonymous communication.

Figure 7 shows a decentralized darknet environment that integrates the blockchain era, DAO-based perfect governance, allocated garages, anonymous transactions, and quantum-resistant cryptography for privacy-focused customers through a worldwide network of decentralized, interconnected encrypted communication without reliance on centralized authorities. Distributed storage mechanisms therefore enhance the availability and flexibility of records, while anonymous transaction options improve user privacy The DAO system provides a transparent and decentralized voting framework for community management and enforcement of coverage. To combat emerging threats from QC, the version features quantum-resistant cryptographic mechanisms that preserve confidentiality, integrity, and authentication, but the mentioned elements create a self-sustaining, privacy-focused infrastructure that supports the development of stable, decentralized, and quantum-resistant private technology systems. In short, destiny research pathways can emphasize resilience, decentralization, integration with emerging technologies, ethical AI, and sustainability in opposing quantum threats. Thus, those areas illuminate the path of dark web development in the next decade.

Figure 7. Future vision of a fully decentralized and quantum-resilient darknet ecosystem, depicting blockchain-based DAO governance, quantum-resistant cryptography, and privacy-focused decentralized nodes

9. OPEN CHALLENGES AND LIMITATIONS

Darknet technologies have definitely found their way in recent years, however, there are definite limitations that limit their mainstream use and stable operation.

I. Decentralized Darknet platforms Scalability

Decentralized infrastructure often struggles with scalability. While blockchain-first based governance and distributed storage structures face several obstacles that include latency issues and high usable resource consumption as acknowledged in (Uzougbo et al., 2024; Widiastuti & Saragih, 2025). Furthermore, to allow a large-scale darknet ecosystem, the research domain must cope with consensus screening and adaptive management.

II. PQC standardization and adoption barriers

While PQC algorithms are promising, standardization is still incompletely adopted without computational efficiency, interoperability with legacy structures, and worldwide adoption as mentioned in (Shami et al., 2025; Malikzada, 2026). Darknet structures without standardized PQC are still vulnerable to quantum adversaries.

III. Legal enforcement limitations

In the case of criminal enforcement, the ambiguity of jurisdiction continues to hinder the enforcement of the darknet-related cybercrimes. While international treaties, including the Budapest Convention, provide a framework, ratification and sovereignty are nevertheless heterogeneous with respect to the effectiveness of sanctions (Widiastuti & Saragih, 2025; Shami et al., 2025) and empirical evidence suggests that business cooperation, rather than treaty ratification, drives implementation success (Malikzada, 2026).

IV. Ethical and misuse concerns

There are dual-use dilemmas in darknet technology. While protecting free speech and privacy, they facilitate illicit gaming with drug trafficking, child abuse, and ransomware (Davitaia, 2025). Therefore, ethical concerns additionally rise within the investigative exercise, which includes the dangers of hiding records to preserve harm (Supe, 2025). The magnificent work maintains consistency from legitimate use and abuse.

10. CONCLUSIONS AND KEY INSIGHTS

To conclude, the current chapter discusses and identifies dark internet technologies in the context of decentralized infrastructure and global social governance, emphasizing the complex interplay between innovation, law, and ethics.

Key Insights

The most significant feature of Precis Darknet is its dual use. Therefore, the dark web offers anonymity and protection from touching relationships with journalists, activists, and dissidents' services. Also, firms may also interact with cybercriminals, illicit markets, and cyberattacks. This chapter emphasizes the urgent need for government-specified frameworks, algorithms, smart devices, and tools that do not undermine legitimate use, even when providing security services against cyber risk abuses resulting from technological advancements that significantly transform the landscape. The integration of darknet systems through IoT, cyber-physical infrastructure, and 6G networks might also introduce new and advanced vulnerabilities. In addition, numerous opportunities for static decentralized verbal exchange, such as AI and XAI offer a powerful equipment for darknet intelligence in terms of transparency and accountability improvement. Finally, increasing the carrying capacity to necessary limits, with robust untested infrastructure, may be crucial to align darknet technologies with worldwide environmental desires preferably limiting enforcement to all prisons and morally recognized legally decentralized organizational intelligence such as manual decentralization opacity. However, global treaties and cooperation frameworks offer a partial answer as problems with unequal restrictions and sovereignty limit their effectiveness. Ethical screening protocols are vital to reduce the harm of dark internet environments, limit counterfeiting, and prevent security abuses.

Importance of Proactive Adaptation

The proactive pace of technological improvement is a choice among policymakers, researchers, and business partners. where sanctions require a willingness to move beyond symbolic commitments to operational mechanisms that allow real-time collaboration and enforcement. Ethical studies should ensure that the collection and dissemination of information will not compromise privacy or security. Similarly, adoption of sustainable PQC infrastructure should be a priority in the face of emerging cyber threats to destiny-proof dark web ecosystems. Additionally, robust passwords and multifactor authentication are powerful mechanisms for certain cross-functional collaboration. In addition to cryptography, AI researchers, legal scholars, and ethicists may be using early visual designs to flesh out designs which can be reliable, transparent, and ethical. Dark web cybersecurity will be fragmented and contentious and thus ripe for subversion and proof to machines.

Remarks on Balancing Privacy, Security, and Governance

The union of Privacy security and Manipulation Privacy security is a very useful benefit to any commercial enterprise For privacy, the civil rights to defensibility have important privacy elements that should, therefore, come with some enforceable means for preventing yourself from an abuse that has also the need of solid cryptography base, multiple factors authentication, dynamic structures and worldwide collaboration of individuals as they could collaborate to build the harmonized global rule together with national laws, international and national criminal/civil laws; standard laws of nature, time politics and rights to defend individuals' privacy and security.

Finally, it could also change the future path of the dark web with its ability to reconcile the competing imperatives. By designing, implementing intelligent models, facilitating worldwide collaboration, and integrating sustainability into the layout, stakeholders can transform the dark internet from contested territory into virtual settings that respect the rights.

REFERENCES

abdulhamza Noor, M. (2025). Quantum Machine Learning for Cyber Threat Detection: Enhancing Security in the Quantum Era. *CyberSystem Journal, 2*(2), 79-81.

Abu Al-Haija, Q., Krichen, M., & Abu Elhaija, W. (2022). Machine-Learning-Based Darknet Traffic Detection System for IoT Applications. *Electronics (Basel), 11*(4), 556. DOI: 10.3390/electronics11040556

Al Jasem, M. S., De Clark, T., & Shrestha, A. K. (2025). Toward decentralized intelligence: A systematic literature review of blockchain-enabled AI systems. *Information (Basel), 16*(9), 765. DOI: 10.3390/info16090765

Al-Tameemi, H. A., Shayea, G. G., Al-Zubaidie, M., Khaleel, Y. L., Hussein, N. A. H. K., Homod, R. Z., & Albahri, A. S. (2025). A Systematic review of metaverse cybersecurity: Frameworks, challenges, and strategic approaches in a quantum-driven era. *Mesopotamian Journal of CyberSecurity, 5*(2), 770–803.

Al Tamimi, S. (2025, August). Towards Beyond Technology: Reviewing Human Error (HE) as the Primary Reason of Cyber Security Breaches. In *2025 International Conference on Artificial Intelligence, Computer, Data Sciences and Applications (ACDSA)* (pp. 1-6). IEEE. DOI: 10.1109/ACDSA65407.2025.11166279

Altamimi, S., & Abu Al-Haija, Q. (2024). Maximizing intrusion detection efficiency for IoT networks using extreme learning machine. *Discover Internet of Things, 4*(1), 5. DOI: 10.1007/s43926-024-00060-x

AlTamimi, S., Al-Haija, Q. A., & AlShuaibi, A. (2025, October). Securing Distributed IoT Systems: Blockchain-Based Protocol with Integrated Intrusion Response. In *2025 IEEE 22nd International Conference on Mobile Ad-Hoc and Smart Systems (MASS)* (pp. 700-704). IEEE.

Anbarkhan, S. H. (2024). Securing IoT Networks: A Post-Quantum Blockchain and Deep Learning Approach for Enhanced Cyber Defense. *International Journal of Safety and Security Engineering, 14*(6), 1689–1698. DOI: 10.18280/ijsse.140604

Avasthi, S., Jain, K., Prakash, A., & Sanwal, T. (2024, February). A blockchain architecture for secure decentralized system and computing. In *2024 3rd International conference on Power Electronics and IoT Applications in Renewable Energy and its Control (PARC)* (pp. 415-420). IEEE. DOI: 10.1109/PARC59193.2024.10486648

Azeez, M., Nenebi, C. T., Hammed, V., Asiam, L. K., & James, E. (2024). Developing intelligent cyber threat detection systems through quantum computing. *International Journal of Science and Research Archive, 12*(2), 1297–1307. DOI: 10.30574/ijsra.2024.12.2.1369

Baseri, Y., Chouhan, V., & Ghorbani, A. (2026). Cybersecurity in the quantum era: Assessing the impact of quantum computing on infrastructure. *Computers & Security, 167*, 104917. DOI: 10.1016/j.cose.2026.104917

Begum, S. H., Mohammed, I., Rahman, S., & Khan, M. O. W. (2025, December). Quantum Computing for Cyber Threat Detection. In *2025 4th International Conference on Applied Artificial Intelligence and Computing (ICAAIC)* (pp. 22-27). IEEE. DOI: 10.1109/ICAAIC64647.2025.11330692

Bhushan, S., Kumar, M., Kumar, P., Ravi, R. V., & Singh, A. K. (Eds.). (2022). *Holistic Approach to Quantum Cryptography in Cyber Security* (1st ed.). CRC Press., https://doi-org.eres.qnl.qa/10.1201/9781003296034 DOI: 10.1201/9781003296034

Carruthers, Z., & Clincy, V. (2025, October). How Effective are Classical Cryptographic Protocols Against Early Quantum Decryption Attempts? In *2025 5th International Conference on Electrical, Computer, Communications and Mechatronics Engineering (ICECCME)* (pp. 1-3). IEEE. DOI: 10.1109/ICECCME64568.2025.11277985

Chen, Q., Yang, M., Ling, Z., Liu, Z., Luo, L., Cao, C., & Fu, X. (2026). A Tor-based Anonymous Network Covert Channel. *IEEE Transactions on Dependable and Secure Computing*.

Collier, B. (2024). *Tor: From the dark web to the future of privacy.* MIT Press. DOI: 10.7551/mit-press/14907.001.0001

Darzi, S., & Yavuz, A. A. (2024, October). Counter denial of service for next-generation networks within the artificial intelligence and post-quantum era. In *2024 IEEE 6th International Conference on Trust, Privacy and Security in Intelligent Systems, and Applications (TPS-ISA)* (pp. 138-147). IEEE. DOI: 10.1109/TPS-ISA62245.2024.00025

Davitaia, A. (2025). Ethical Challenges of Crime and Content Hosting on the Dark Web. *Available at SSRN* 5367005. DOI: 10.2139/ssrn.5367005

de-Marcos, L., Domínguez-Díaz, A., & Stapic, Z. (2026). Mapping the Tor darkmarket ecosystem: A network analysis of topics, communication channels, and languages. *Forensic Science International Digital Investigation*, *56*, 302032. DOI: 10.1016/j.fsidi.2025.302032

Dwivedi, A., Saini, G. K., & Musa, U. I. (2023, March). Cybersecurity and prevention in the quantum era. In *2023 2nd International conference for innovation in technology (INOCON)* (pp. 1-6). IEEE. DOI: 10.1109/INOCON57975.2023.10101186

El-Kady, R. (2025). Decoding the dark: AI and ML in the dark web cybercrime and cryptocurrency forensics. *International Cybersecurity Law Review*, *6*(2), 107–143. DOI: 10.1365/s43439-025-00145-5

Fan, S., Ranly, P. M., Graner, L., Vogel, I., & Steinebach, M. (2024, July). Unveiling the Darkness: Analysing Organised Crime on the Wall Street Market Darknet Marketplace using PGP Public Keys. In *Proceedings of the 19th International Conference on Availability, Reliability and Security* (pp. 1-10). DOI: 10.1145/3664476.3670464

Ferreira, J. J., Fernandes, C., Veiga, P. M., & Rammal, H. G. (2025). Ethics and the dark side of online communities: Mapping the field and a research agenda. *Information Systems and e-Business Management*, *23*(1), 99–123. DOI: 10.1007/s10257-023-00653-z

Figueras-Martín, E., Magán-Carrión, R., & Boubeta-Puig, J. (2022). Drawing the web structure and content analysis beyond the Tor darknet: Freenet as a case of study. *Journal of Information Security and Applications*, *68*, 103229. DOI: 10.1016/j.jisa.2022.103229

Gentile, A. F., Macrì, D., Carnì, D. L., Greco, E., & Lamonaca, F. (2024). A network performance analysis of MQTT security protocols with constrained hardware in the dark net for DMS. *Applied Sciences (Basel, Switzerland)*, *14*(18), 8501. DOI: 10.3390/app14188501

Gharavi, H., Granjal, J., & Monteiro, E. (2024). Post-quantum blockchain security for the Internet of Things: Survey and research directions. *IEEE Communications Surveys and Tutorials*, *26*(3), 1748–1774. DOI: 10.1109/COMST.2024.3355222

Gilbert, C., & Gilbert, M. (2024). Unlocking privacy in blockchain: Exploring zero-knowledge proofs and secure multi-party computation techniques. *Available at SSRN* 5258791.

Guizani, S., Mazhar, T., & Hamam, H. (2026). Quantum Secure Multiparty Computation: Bridging Privacy, Security, and Scalability in the Post-Quantum Era. *Computers, Materials & Continua*, *87*(1), 1–10. DOI: 10.32604/cmc.2025.073883

Gupta, M. (2026). Security Risks for Enterprises in the Post-Quantum Computing World. *International Journal of Emerging Trends in Computer Science and Information Technology*, *7*(1), 328–337. DOI: 10.63282/3050-9246.IJETCSIT-V7I1P147

Hammad, A., & Abu-Zaid, R. (2024). Applications of AI in decentralized computing systems: Harnessing artificial intelligence for enhanced scalability, efficiency, and autonomous decision-making in distributed architectures. *Applied Research in Artificial Intelligence and Cloud Computing*, *7*(6), 161–187.

Hammoud, O., Tarkhanov, I., & Kosmarski, A. (2021). An Architecture for Distributed Electronic Documents Storage in Decentralized Blockchain B2B Applications. *Computers*, *10*(11), 142. DOI: 10.3390/computers10110142

Hui, X., & Tucker, C. (2025). Decentralization, blockchain, artificial intelligence (AI): Challenges and opportunities. *Journal of Product Innovation Management*, *42*(5), 947–957. DOI: 10.1111/jpim.12800

Ishaque, M., & Al-Anesi, B. (2025, February). Quantum cryptography and post-quantum security: Safeguarding cryptographic protocols against quantum threats. In *2025 2nd International Conference on Advanced Innovations in Smart Cities (ICAISC)* (pp. 1-7). IEEE.

Joshi, S., Bairwa, A. K., Pljonkin, A. P., Garg, P., & Agrawal, K. (2023, May). From pre-quantum to post-quantum RSA. In *Proceedings of the 6th international conference on networking, intelligent systems & security* (pp. 1-8).

Kaur, G., Mukherjee, D., Moza, B., Pahwa, V., Kaur, K., & Kaur, K. (2024). The dark web: A hidden menace or a tool for privacy protection. *IP International Journal of Forensic Medicine and Toxicological Sciences*, *8*(4), 160–167. DOI: 10.18231/j.ijfmts.2023.034

Kavitha, R., Kapilsurya, V., Shanmugam, R., & Kumar, S. (2023). The dark web: Privacy and anonymity. *International Journal for Research in Applied Science and Engineering Technology*, *11*(3), 1087–1093. DOI: 10.22214/ijraset.2023.49599

Khan, M. A., Noor, F., Javaid, S., & Żywiołek, J. (2025). Implementation and performance of post-quantum cryptography for resource constrained consumer electronics. *Discover Internet of Things*, *5*(1), 139. DOI: 10.1007/s43926-025-00238-x

. Khan, M. N. I. (2025). Cross-border data privacy and legal support: a systematic review of international compliance standards and cyber law practices.

. Magliocco, L. (2026). The mirage of honesty in cryptography: secure multi-party computation with untrusted devices.

Maire, J. (2024). *Zero-knowledge arguments from secure multiparty computation* (Doctoral dissertation, Sorbonne Université).

. Malikzada, T. (2026). Assessing the Role of International Law in Regulating the Fight Against Cybercrime in the Digital Environment. *Futurity Economics&Law, 6*(1).

Merlec, M. M., & In, H. P. (2024). Blockchain-based decentralized storage systems for sustainable data self-sovereignty: A comparative study. *Sustainability (Basel), 16*(17), 7671. DOI: 10.3390/su16177671

Naz, R., Howlader, J., & Ahmad, S. (2026). A secure expert system framework for private function evaluation using functional encryption and multi-party computation. *Computers & Electrical Engineering, 131*, 110930. DOI: 10.1016/j.compeleceng.2025.110930

Okika, N., Nwatuzie, G. A., Olarinoye, H. S., Nwaka, A. A., Igba, E., & Dunee, R. (2025). Assessing the vulnerability of traditional and post-quantum cryptographic systems through penetration testing and strengthening cyber defenses with zero trust security in the era of quantum computing. *International Journal of Innovative Science and Research Technology, 10*(2), 1240–1258.

Patel, J. C., Kaashvi, R., & Sarasvathi, V. (2025, July). Hybrid Authentication Model using Adaptive Authentication and Post Quantum Cryptographic Biometric Encryption. In *2025 8th International Conference on Computing Methodologies and Communication (ICCMC)* (pp. 746-751). IEEE. DOI: 10.1109/ICCMC65190.2025.11139930

Pincheira, M., Donini, E., Vecchio, M., & Kanhere, S. (2022). A Decentralized Architecture for Trusted Dataset Sharing Using Smart Contracts and Distributed Storage. *Sensors (Basel), 22*(23), 9118. DOI: 10.3390/s22239118 PMID: 36501820

Rasyid, A., Willim, A. P., & Khaeryyah, S. (2025). Cryptocurrency and the law: The challenges of regulating decentralized finance in global markets. *Impact: Multidisciplinary Journal, 1*(01), 1–10.

Rustamova, N., & Dutta, S. (2025). Securing the Future: A Comprehensive Review of Post-Quantum Cryptography in the Modern Threat Landscape. *Qubahan Techno Journal, 4*(2), 30–42. DOI: 10.48161/qtj.v4n2a58

Saleem, J., Islam, R., & Islam, M. Z. (2024). Darknet traffic analysis: A systematic literature review. *IEEE Access : Practical Innovations, Open Solutions, 12*, 42423–42452. DOI: 10.1109/ACCESS.2024.3373769

Saleem, J., Islam, R., & Kabir, M. A. (2022). The anonymity of the dark web: A survey. *IEEE Access : Practical Innovations, Open Solutions, 10*, 33628–33660. DOI: 10.1109/ACCESS.2022.3161547

Sengupta, S., & Bose, A. (2025). Securing the Quantum Era: A Comprehensive Review of Post-Quantum Cryptography, Threat Models, Algorithmic Foundations, and Standardization Pathways. *Qubahan Techno Journal, 4*(3), 1–10.

Shami, A. Z. A., Asghar, U., & Haider, A. (2025). The Role of International Law in Regulating Cybersecurity: A Critical Analysis of Existing Frameworks and Future Directions. *Liberal Journal of Language & Literature Review*, *3*(3), 224–242.

Shivarudraiah, A. (2023). Quantum Computing's Impact on Banking Encryption: Preparing for Post-Quantum Security. *International Journal of AI, BigData. Computational and Management Studies*, *4*(3), 40–49.

Song, Z., Long, L., Song, J., & Jiang, R. (2026). A Zero-Knowledge Proof-Driven Architecture for Privacy-Preserving Data Trading on Blockchain. *ACM Transactions on Internet Technology*, *26*(3), 1–34. DOI: 10.1145/3805044

Supe, A. (2025). *A Survey of Ethical and Legal Challenges in Dark-Web Research: Balancing Privacy*. Security, and Responsibility.

Suriya, P., Balamurugan, G., & Shabin, O. S. (2026, March). A Comprehensive Review on Cyber Investigation and Detection across Ontology-Driven Dark Web and Email Phishing. In *International Conference on Artificial Intelligence and Secure Data Analytics (ICAISDA 2025)* (pp. 1514-1530). Atlantis Press. DOI: 10.2991/978-94-6239-616-6_109

Tazi, F., Shrestha, S., De La Cruz, J., & Das, S. (2022). SoK: An Evaluation of the Secure End User Experience on the Dark Net through Systematic Literature Review. *Journal of Cybersecurity and Privacy*, *2*(2), 329–357. DOI: 10.3390/jcp2020018

. Uzougbo, N. S., Ikegwu, C. G., & Adewusi, A. O. (2024). International enforcement of cryptocurrency laws: Jurisdictional challenges and collaborative solutions. *Magna Scientia Advanced Research and Reviews, 11*(01), 068-083.

Uzougbo, N. S., Ikegwu, C. G., & Adewusi, A. O.Ngozi Samuel UzougboChinonso Gladys IkegwuAdefolake Olachi Adewusi. (2024). Regulatory frameworks for decentralized finance (DEFI): Challenges and opportunities. *GSC Advanced Research and Reviews*, *19*(02), 116–129. DOI: 10.30574/gscarr.2024.19.2.0170

Vithalkar, P. N., Prabhat, P., Satonkar, V. H., Sagar, M., Jangale, R. M. G., & Murab, S. A. (2024). Cryptographic protocols resilient to quantum attacks: Advancements in post-quantum cryptography. *CANA*, *31*, 805.

Widiastuti, A., & Saragih, Y. M.Yasmirah Mandasari Saragih. (2025). Transnational Cyber Crime: Challenges of International Cooperation in Combating Cybercrime. [IJCS]. *International Journal of Contemporary Sciences*, *3*(7), 109–122. DOI: 10.55927/9gazwn03

Compilation of References

Abdo, J. B., & Hossain, L. (2023, November). Modeling the invisible internet. In *International Conference on Complex Networks and Their Applications* (pp. 359–370). Springer Nature.

abdulhamza Noor, M. (2025). Quantum Machine Learning for Cyber Threat Detection: Enhancing Security in the Quantum Era. *CyberSystem Journal, 2*(2), 79-81.

Abu Al-Haija, Q., Krichen, M., & Abu Elhaija, W. (2022). Machine-Learning-Based Darknet Traffic Detection System for IoT Applications. *Electronics (Basel), 11*(4), 556. DOI: 10.3390/electronics11040556

Achuthan, K., Ramanathan, S., Srinivas, S., & Raman, R. (2024). Advancing cybersecurity and privacy with artificial intelligence: Emerging trends and challenges. *Journal of Cybersecurity and Privacy, 4*(1), 1–18.

Adel, A., & Norouzifard, M. (2024). Weaponization of the growing cybercrimes inside the dark net: The question of detection and application. *Big Data and Cognitive Computing, 8*(8), 91. DOI: 10.3390/bdcc8080091

Adewopo, V., Gonen, B., Varlioglu, S., & Ozer, M. (2019, December). Plunge into the underworld: A survey on the emergence of the darknet. In *2019 International Conference on Computational Science and Computational Intelligence (CSCI)* (pp. 155–159). IEEE. DOI: 10.1109/CSCI49370.2019.00033

Afroz, S., Brennan, M., & Greenstadt, R. (2012). Detecting hoaxes, frauds, and deception in writing style online. *Proceedings of the 2012 IEEE Symposium on Security and Privacy (SP)*, 461–475. DOI: 10.1109/SP.2012.34

Agarwal, U., Rishiwal, V., Tanwar, S., & Yadav, M. (2024). Blockchain and crypto forensics: Investigating crypto frauds. *International Journal of Network Management, 34*(2), e2255. DOI: 10.1002/nem.2255

Agbesi, J. S., Otchill, A. N., Tay, R. H., & Bamfo, N. K. (2026). Machine learning for network intrusion detection in USA critical infrastructure: Challenges and opportunities. *International Journal of Network Security & its Applications, 18*(1), 1–15.

Ahmed, A., Abdullah, S., Bukhsh, M., Ahmad, I., & Mushtaq, Z. (2022). An energy-efficient data aggregation mechanism for iot secured by blockchain. *IEEE Access : Practical Innovations, Open Solutions, 10*, 11404–11419. DOI: 10.1109/ACCESS.2022.3146295

Ahmed, M. A. M., Idris, S., Yunus, N. A. M., Ali, F. M., & Sofian, H. (2024). CyberShield framework: Attacks and defense modelling for cybersecurity in internet of things (IoT). *International Journal of Advanced Research in Computational Thinking and Data Science, 4*(1), 30–39. DOI: 10.37934/ctds.4.1.3039

Ahmed, T., & Chen, L. (2024). A comprehensive risk analysis method for adversarial attacks on biometric authentication systems. *IEEE Access : Practical Innovations, Open Solutions, 12*, 45678–45695.

Akour, I., Alauthman, M., Nahar, K. M. O., Al-Qerem, A., Aldweesh, A., Alauthman, M., & Khalifeh, A. (2024). Analyzing darknet traffic through machine learning and NeuCube spiking neural networks. *Intelligent and Converged Networks, 5*(4), 265–283. DOI: 10.23919/ICN.2024.0022

Al Jasem, M. S., De Clark, T., & Shrestha, A. K. (2025). Toward decentralized intelligence: A systematic literature review of blockchain-enabled AI systems. *Information (Basel), 16*(9), 765. DOI: 10.3390/info16090765

Al Nabki, M. W., Fidalgo, E., Alegre, E., & de Paz, I. (2017). Classifying Illegal Activities on Tor Network Based on Web Textual Contents. *Proceedings of the 15th Conference of the European Chapter of the Association for Computational Linguistics:* Volume 1, *Long Papers*, 35–43. DOI: 10.18653/v1/E17-1004

Al Tamimi, S. (2025, August). Towards Beyond Technology: Reviewing Human Error (HE) as the Primary Reason of Cyber Security Breaches. In *2025 International Conference on Artificial Intelligence, Computer, Data Sciences and Applications (ACDSA)* (pp. 1-6). IEEE. DOI: 10.1109/ACDSA65407.2025.11166279

Alam, M. H., Ryu, W.-J., & Lee, S. (2022). A survey on deep-learning-based focused crawling. *ACM Computing Surveys, 55*(3), 1–37. DOI: 10.1145/3507904

Alarfaj, F. K., & Khan, N. A. (2023). Enhancing the performance of SQL injection attack detection through probabilistic neural networks. *Applied Sciences (Basel, Switzerland), 13*(7), 4365. DOI: 10.3390/app13074365

Alcaraz, C., & Zeadally, S. (2015). Critical infrastructure protection: Requirements and challenges for the 21st century. *International Journal of Critical Infrastructure Protection, 8*, 53–66. DOI: 10.1016/j.ijcip.2014.12.002

Aldera, S., Emam, A., Al-Qurishi, M., Alrubaian, M., & Alothaim, A. (2021). Online extremism detection in textual content: A systematic literature review. *IEEE Access : Practical Innovations, Open Solutions, 9*, 42384–42396. DOI: 10.1109/ACCESS.2021.3064178

Aldridge, J., & Décary-Hétu, D. (2016). Hidden wholesale: The drug diffusing capacity of online drug cryptomarkets. *The International Journal on Drug Policy, 35*, 7–15. DOI: 10.1016/j.drugpo.2016.04.020 PMID: 27260863

Alfahaid, A., Alalwany, E., Almars, A. M., Alharbi, F., Atlam, E., & Mahgoub, I. (2025). Machine learning-based security solutions for IoT networks: A comprehensive survey. In *Proceedings of the Italian National Conference on Sensors*. DOI: 10.3390/s25113341

Alghawazi, M., Alghazzawi, D., & Alarifi, S. (2023). Deep learning architecture for detecting SQL injection attacks based on RNN autoencoder model. *Mathematics, 11*(15), 3286. DOI: 10.3390/math11153286

Alghuried, A., & Mohaisen, D. (2024). Simple perturbations subvert ethereum phishing transactions detection: An empirical analysis. In Lee, J., Emura, K., and Lee, S., editors, *Information Security Applications - 25th Interna-tional Conference, WISA 2024, Jeju Island, South Korea, August 21-23, 2024, Revised Selected Papers*, Lecture Notes in Computer Science, pages 123–137. Springer.

Alghuried, A., Alghamdi, A., Alkinoon, A., Choi, S., Mohaisen, M., and Mo-haisen, D. (2025a). Fishing for phishers: Learning-based phishing detection in ethereum transactions. *CoRR*, abs/2504.17953.

Alghuried, A., Alkinoon, A., Alghamdi, A., Choi, S., Mohaisen, M., and Mo-haisen, D. (2025b). Evaluating the vulnerability of ml-based ethereum phishing detectors to single-feature adversarial perturbations. *CoRR*, abs/2504.17684.

Alghuried, A., Alkinoon, M., Mohaisen, M., Wang, A., Zou, C. C., and Mohaisen, D. (2026). Blockchain security and privacy: Threats, challenges, applications, and tools. *Distributed Ledger Technol. Res. Pract.*, 5(1):8:1–8:61.

Ali, A., Husain, M., & Hans, P. (2025). *Privacy-Aware Cyberterrorism Network Analysis using Graph Neural Networks and Federated Learning.*

Ali, A., Ali, M., Mushtaq, U., & Akram, M. A. (2025). Secure software engineering for industrial IoT: A comprehensive review of threat modeling and defense mechanisms. *ICCK Journal of Software Engineering*, *5*(2), 33–45. DOI: 10.62762/JSE.2025.834259

Allaw, Z., Zein, O., & Ahmad, A.-M. (2025). Cross-layer security for 5G/6G network slices: An SDN, NFV, and AI-based hybrid framework. *Sensors (Basel)*, *25*(11), 3120. DOI: 10.3390/s25113335 PMID: 40968899

Almeida, F. (2023). Prospects of cybersecurity in smart cities. *Future Internet*, *15*(9), 285. DOI: 10.3390/fi15090285

Almomani, A. (2025). Darknet traffic analysis, and classification system based on modified stacking ensemble learning algorithms. *Information Systems and e-Business Management*, *23*(1), 209–240. DOI: 10.1007/s10257-023-00626-2

Al-Nabki, M. W., Fidalgo, E., Alegre, E., & Chaves, D. (2019). Content-based features to rank influential hidden services of the Tor Darknet. arXiv preprint arXiv:1910.02332.

Al-rimy, B. A. S., Maarof, M. A., & Shaid, S. Z. M. (2018). Ransomware threat success factors, taxonomy, and countermeasures: A survey and research directions. *Computers & Security*, *74*, 144–166. DOI: 10.1016/j.cose.2018.01.001

Alsalami, N., & Zhang, B. (2019). Sok: A systematic study of anonymity in cryptocurrencies. In *2019 IEEE Conference on Dependable and Secure Computing, DSC 2019,* Hangzhou, China, November 18-20, 2019, pages 1–9. IEEE. DOI: 10.1109/DSC47296.2019.8937681

Alsubaei, F. S. (2025). Smart deep learning model for enhanced IoT intrusion detection. *Scientific Reports*, *15*(1), 7890. Advance online publication. DOI: 10.1038/s41598-025-06363-5 PMID: 40596059

Al-Tameemi, H. A., Shayea, G. G., Al-Zubaidie, M., Khaleel, Y. L., Hussein, N. A. H. K., Homod, R. Z., & Albahri, A. S. (2025). A Systematic review of metaverse cybersecurity: Frameworks, challenges, and strategic approaches in a quantum-driven era. *Mesopotamian Journal of CyberSecurity*, *5*(2), 770–803.

AlTamimi, S., Al-Haija, Q. A., & AlShuaibi, A. (2025, October). Securing Distributed IoT Systems: Blockchain-Based Protocol with Integrated Intrusion Response. In *2025 IEEE 22nd International Conference on Mobile Ad-Hoc and Smart Systems (MASS)* (pp. 700-704). IEEE.

Altamimi, S., & Abu Al-Haija, Q. (2024). Maximizing intrusion detection efficiency for IoT networks using extreme learning machine. *Discover Internet of Things*, *4*(1), 5. DOI: 10.1007/s43926-024-00060-x

Amarasinghe, N., Boyen, X., & McKague, M. (2019). A survey of anonymity of cryptocurrencies. In *Proceedings of the Australasian Computer Science Week Multiconference, ACSW 2019, Sydney, NSW, Australia, January 29-31, 2019*, pages 2:1–2:10. ACM.

Ambudkar, B., Rahangdale, P., Abdullah, A., Thoutam, N., & Shelke, G. C. (2024). Developing cyber-security policies for smart cities: A case study approach. *Computer Fraud & Security*, *2024*(6), 12–20.

Anbarkhan, S. H. (2024). Securing IoT Networks: A Post-Quantum Blockchain and Deep Learning Approach for Enhanced Cyber Defense. *International Journal of Safety and Security Engineering*, *14*(6), 1689–1698. DOI: 10.18280/ijsse.140604

Anderson, R., Barton, C., Bölme, R., Clayton, R., Ganán, C., Grasso, T., ... Vasek, M. (2019). *Measuring the changing cost of cybercrime.*

Anderson, R. (2001). Why information security is hard: An economic perspective. In *Proceedings of the 17th Annual Computer Security Applications Conference (ACSAC)* (pp. 358–365). DOI: 10.1109/ACSAC.2001.991552

Anthropic. (2025a). *Detecting and countering misuse of AI: August 2025.* Anthropic Threat Research. https://www.anthropic.com/news/detecting-countering-misuse-aug-2025

Anthropic. (2025b). *Disrupting the first reported AI-orchestrated cyber espionage campaign.* Anthropic Threat Research. https://www.anthropic.com/news/disrupting-AI-espionage

Apurva, S., & Vetrithangam, D. (2025). Blockchain-integrated zero-trust architectures for cybersecurity in IoT ecosystems. In *Proceedings of the IEEE 6th Global Conference on Advancement Technologies (GCAT).* DOI: 10.1109/GCAT66372.2025.11368384

Aqeel, M., Ali, F., Iqbal, M. W., Rana, T. A., Arif, M., & Auwul, R. (2022). A review of security and privacy concerns in the internet of things (IoT). *Journal of Sensors*, *2022*, 5724168. Advance online publication. DOI: 10.1155/2022/5724168

Arasteh, B., Aghaei, B., Farzad, B., Arasteh, K., Kiani, F., & Torkamanian-Afshar, M. (2024). Detecting SQL injection attacks by binary gray wolf optimizer and machine learning algorithms. *Neural Computing & Applications*, *36*(12), 6771–6792. DOI: 10.1007/s00521-024-09429-z

Arazzi, M., Arikkat, D. R., Nicolazzo, S., Nocera, A., Rehiman, R., Vinod, P., & Conti, M. (2025). NLP-based techniques for cyber threat intelligence. *Computer Science Review*, *58*, 100765. DOI: 10.1016/j.cosrev.2025.100765

Arnold, N., Ebrahimi, M., Zhang, N., Lazarine, B., Patton, M., Chen, H., & Samtani, S. (2019). Dark-net ecosystem cyber-threat intelligence (CTI) tool. In *2019 IEEE International Conference on Intelligence and Security Informatics (ISI)* (pp. 92-97). IEEE. DOI: 10.1109/ISI.2019.8823501

Asghar, M. N., Raza, M. A., Murad, Z., & Alyahya, A. (2024). Detecting malicious botnets in IoT networks using machine learning techniques. *IPSI Transactions on Internet Research*, *20*(2), 33–45. DOI: 10.58245/ipsi.tir.2402.03

Ataullah, M., & Chauhan, N. (2024). Exploring security and privacy enhancement technologies in the internet of things: A comprehensive review. *Security and Privacy*, *7*(2), e341. DOI: 10.1002/spy2.448

Atlam, H. F., Ekuri, N., Azad, M. A., & Lallie, H. S. (2024). Blockchain forensics: A systematic literature review of techniques, applications, challenges, and future directions. *Electronics (Basel)*, *13*(17), 3568. DOI: 10.3390/electronics13173568

Avasthi, S., Jain, K., Prakash, A., & Sanwal, T. (2024, February). A blockchain architecture for secure decentralized system and computing. In *2024 3rd International conference on Power Electronics and IoT Applications in Renewable Energy and its Control (PARC)* (pp. 415-420). IEEE. DOI: 10.1109/PARC59193.2024.10486648

Ayub, M., Saleem, T., Janjua, M. U., and Ahmad, T. (2023). Storage state analysis and extraction of ethereum blockchain smart contracts. *ACM Trans. Softw. Eng. Methodol.*, 32(3):57:1–57:32. 25

Azeez, M., Nenebi, C. T., Hammed, V., Asiam, L. K., & James, E. (2024). Developing intelligent cyber threat detection systems through quantum computing. *International Journal of Science and Research Archive*, *12*(2), 1297–1307. DOI: 10.30574/ijsra.2024.12.2.1369

Bada, M., Sasse, M. A., & Nurse, J. R. C. (2019). Cyber security awareness campaigns: Why do they fail to change behaviour? *arXiv preprint arXiv:1901.02672*. https://arxiv.org/abs/1901.02672

Bahamazava, K., & Nanda, R. (2022). The shift of darknet illegal drug trade preferences in cryptocurrency: The question of traceability and deterrence. *Forensic Science International Digital Investigation*, *40*(Supplement), 301377. DOI: 10.1016/j.fsidi.2022.301377

Balasubramanian, P., Nazari, S., Khosh Kholgh, D., Mahmoodi, A., Seby, J., & Kostakos, P. (2025). A cognitive platform for collecting cyber threat intelligence and real-time detection using cloud computing. *Decision Analytics Journal*, *14*, 100545. DOI: 10.1016/j.dajour.2025.100545

Balta, E. C., Pease, M., Moyne, J., Barton, K., & Tilbury, D. (2024). Digital twin-based cyber-attack detection framework for cyber-physical manufacturing systems. *IEEE Transactions on Automation Science and Engineering*, *21*(3), 1802–1815. DOI: 10.1109/TASE.2023.3243147

Bancroft, A. (2019). Secrecy and anonymity online. In *The darknet and smarter crime.*

Bandara, E., Liang, X., Shetty, S., Mukkamala, R., Rahman, A., & Ng, W. K. (2022). Skunk — a blockchain and zero trust security enabled federated learning platform for 5G/6G network slicing. In *Proceedings of the IEEE SECON* (pp. 45–54). DOI: 10.1109/SECON55815.2022.9918536

Barbosa, L., & Freire, J. (2007). An adaptive crawler for locating hidden-web entry points. *Proceedings of the 16th International Conference on World Wide Web*, 441–450. DOI: 10.1145/1242572.1242632

Baseri, Y., Chouhan, V., & Ghorbani, A. (2026). Cybersecurity in the quantum era: Assessing the impact of quantum computing on infrastructure. *Computers & Security*, *167*, 104917. DOI: 10.1016/j.cose.2026.104917

Basheer, R., & Alkhatib, B. (2021). Threats from the Dark: A Review over Dark Web Investigation Research for Cyber Threat Intelligence. *Journal of Computer Networks and Communications*, *2021*, 1–21. DOI: 10.1155/2021/1302999

Basyoni, L., Fetais, N., Erbad, A., Mohamed, A., & Guizani, M. (2020, February). Traffic analysis attacks on Tor: A survey. In *2020 IEEE International Conference on Informatics, IoT, and Enabling Technologies (ICIoT)* (pp. 183–188). IEEE. DOI: 10.1109/ICIoT48696.2020.9089497

Begum, S. H., Mohammed, I., Rahman, S., & Khan, M. O. W. (2025, December). Quantum Computing for Cyber Threat Detection. In *2025 4th International Conference on Applied Artificial Intelligence and Computing (ICAAIC)* (pp. 22-27). IEEE. DOI: 10.1109/ICAAIC64647.2025.11330692

Behl, A., Behl, K., & Rao, V. (2021). *Cybersecurity and cyberwar: What everyone needs to know*. Oxford University Press.

Bellagarda, J. S., & Abu-Mahfouz, A. M. (2022). An updated survey on the convergence of distributed ledger technology and artificial intelligence: Current state, major challenges and future direction. *IEEE Access : Practical Innovations, Open Solutions*, *10*, 50774–50793. DOI: 10.1109/ACCESS.2022.3173297

Bergman, J., & Popov, O. B. (2023). Exploring Dark Web Crawlers: A Systematic Literature Review of Dark Web Crawlers and Their Implementation. *IEEE Access : Practical Innovations, Open Solutions*, *11*, 35914–35933. DOI: 10.1109/ACCESS.2023.3255165

Bernab'e, J. B., C'anovas, J. L., Hern'andez-Ramos, J. L., Moreno, R. T., & Skarmeta, A. F. (2019). Privacy-preserving solutions for blockchain: Review and challenges. *IEEE Access : Practical Innovations, Open Solutions*, *7*, 164908–164940. DOI: 10.1109/ACCESS.2019.2950872

Bhushan, S., Kumar, M., Kumar, P., Ravi, R. V., & Singh, A. K. (Eds.). (2022). *Holistic Approach to Quantum Cryptography in Cyber Security* (1st ed.). CRC Press., https://doi-org.eres.qnl.qa/10.1201/9781003296034 DOI: 10.1201/9781003296034

Bhuvaneswari, A., Kanmani, E. D., Lakshme Prabha, T. M., Helina, R., Suresh, R., & Saravanan, A. (2024). Efficiently listing URLs from active hidden servers in the onion routing network. In *2024 5th International Conference on Smart Electronics and Communication (ICOSEC)* (pp. 625–629). DOI: 10.1109/ICOSEC61587.2024.10722186

Bidv, V., & Waghmare, A. S. (2024). Beyond the onion routing: Unmasking illicit activities on the dark web. *International Journal of Innovative Science and Research Technology*.

Biryukov, A., Pustogarov, I., Thill, F., & Weinmann, R.-P. (2014). Content and popularity analysis of Tor hidden services. *Proceedings of the 2014 IEEE 34th International Conference on Distributed Computing Systems Workshops (ICDCSW)*, 188–193. DOI: 10.1109/ICDCSW.2014.20

Biryukov, A., Pustogarov, I., & Weinmann, R.-P. (2013). Trawling for Tor hidden services: Detection, measurement, deanonymization. In *Proceedings of the IEEE Symposium on Security and Privacy* (pp. 80–94). DOI: 10.1109/SP.2013.15

Biswas, R., Paudel, B., Karn, R. K., Ghimire, A., & Bikram, K. C. (2023). A systematic review of dark web research. *International Journal of Computing*, *22*(4), 537–548. DOI: 10.47839/ijc.22.4.3335

Blancaflor, E., Eugenio, E. J., Lucas, M., Paglinawan, C., & Villaluz, A. C. (2025). Mirai malware and its impact on IoT security: Security threats and defense mechanisms. In *Proceedings of the International Conference on Communication, Computing & Security*. DOI: 10.1109/ICCCS65393.2025.11069543

Blum, C., Puchinger, J., Raidl, G. R., & Roli, A. (2011). Hybrid metaheuristics in combinatorial optimization: A survey. *Applied Soft Computing*, *11*(6), 4135–4151. DOI: 10.1016/j.asoc.2011.02.032

Böhme, R., & Moore, T. (2012). The economics of cybersecurity: Principles and policy options. *International Journal of Critical Infrastructure Protection*, *5*(1), 1–10. DOI: 10.1016/j.ijcip.2012.02.002

Breiman, L. (2001). Random forests. *Machine Learning*, *45*(1), 5–32. DOI: 10.1023/A:1010933404324

Broadhurst, R., Grabosky, P., Alazab, M., & Chon, S. (2014). An analysis of the nature of groups engaged in cyber crime. *International Journal of Cyber Criminology*, *8*(1), 1–20.

Brown, T. B., Mann, B., Ryder, N., ... (2020). Language models are few-shot learners. In *Advances in Neural Information Processing Systems (NeurIPS 33)* (pp. 1877–1901).

Buczak, A. L., & Guven, E. (2016). A survey of data mining and machine learning methods for cyber security intrusion detection. *IEEE Communications Surveys and Tutorials*, *18*(2), 1153–1176. DOI: 10.1109/COMST.2015.2494502

Bugajewska, M. (2025). *A Survey of Challenges in Dark Web Crawling: Technical.* Security, and Ethical Perspective., DOI: 10.1007/978-3-031-79086-7_27

Buitinck, L., Louppe, G., Blondel, M., Pedregosa, F., Mueller, A., Grisel, O., Niculae, V., Prettenhofer, P., Gramfort, A., Grobler, J., Layton, R., VanderPlas, J., Joly, A., Holt, B., & Varoquaux, G. (2013). API design for machine learning software: Experiences from the scikit-learn project. In *ECML PKDD Workshop: Languages for Data Mining and Machine Learning* (pp. 108–122).

Buitrago López, A., Pastor-Galindo, J., & Gómez Mármol, F. (2024). Updated exploration of the Tor network: Advertising, availability and protocols of onion services. *Wireless Networks*, *30*(9), 7527–7541. DOI: 10.1007/s11276-024-03679-4

Carruthers, Z., & Clincy, V. (2025, October). How Effective are Classical Cryptographic Protocols Against Early Quantum Decryption Attempts? In *2025 5th International Conference on Electrical, Computer, Communications and Mechatronics Engineering (ICECCME)* (pp. 1-3). IEEE. DOI: 10.1109/ICECCME64568.2025.11277985

Carthy, S. L., Doody, C. B., Cox, K., O'Hora, D., & Sarma, K. M. (2020). Counter-narratives for the prevention of violent radicalisation: A systematic review of targeted interventions. *Campbell Systematic Reviews*, *16*(3), e1106. DOI: 10.1002/cl2.1106 PMID: 37131913

Cartwright, E., Hernandez Castro, J., & Cartwright, A. (2019). To pay or not: Game theoretic models of ransomware. *Journal of Cybersecurity*, *5*(1), tyz009. Advance online publication. DOI: 10.1093/cybsec/tyz009

Cascavilla, G., Catolino, G., & Sangiovanni, M. (2022). Illicit Darkweb classification via natural-language processing: Classifying illicit content of webpages based on textual information. In Proceedings of the 19th International Conference on Security and Cryptography (SECRYPT 2022), Vol. 1 (pp. 620–626). SciTePress. Extended version available as arXiv:2312.04944. DOI: 10.5220/0011298600003283

Casey, E. (2011). *Digital Evidence and Computer Crime: Forensic Science, Computers and the Internet* (3rd ed.). Academic Press.

Cato Networks CTRL Threat Research. (2025). *WormGPT variants powered by Grok and Mixtral.* Cato Networks Blog. https://www.catonetworks.com/blog/cato-ctrl-wormgpt-variants-powered-by-grok-and-mixtral/

Cecílio, J., & Souto, A. (2024). Security issues in industrial internet-of-things: Threats, attacks and solutions. In Proceedings of the IEEE International Workshop on Metrology for Industry 4.0 & IoT (MetroInd4.0 & IoT). DOI: 10.1109/MetroInd4.0IoT61288.2024.10584236

Celestini, A., Me, G., & Montinaro, M. (2017). *Tor marketplaces exploratory data analysis: The drugs case* (Vol. 10063). Lecture Notes in Computer Science. Springer., DOI: 10.1007/978-3-319-55966-3_18

Chainalysis. (2022). The 2022 crypto crime report. https://go.chainalysis.com/2022-Crypto-Crime-Report.html

Chainalysis. (2024). Money laundering and cryptocurrency: Trends and new techniques for detection and investigation. https://www.chainalysis.com/blog/money-laundering-cryptocurrency/

Chainalysis. (2024). *The 2024 crypto crime report.* Chainalysis. https://www.chainalysis.com/

Chainalysis. (2025). *2025 crypto crime report.* Chainalysis.

Chainalysis. (2026). *The 2026 crypto crime report introduction: $154 billion in illicit activity last year.* Chainalysis Blog. https://www.chainalysis.com/blog/2026-crypto-crime-report-introduction/

Chainalysis. (2026, February 26). *Crypto ransomware: 2026 crypto crime report.* Chainalysis Blog.

Chao, D., Xu, D., Gao, F., Zhang, C., Zhang, W., & Zhu, L. (2024). A systematic survey on security in anonymity networks: Vulnerabilities, attacks, defenses, and formalization. *IEEE Communications Surveys and Tutorials*, *26*(3), 1775–1829. DOI: 10.1109/COMST.2024.3350006

Chaudhuri, A., Basak, S., Kira'ly, C., Ryajov, D., & Bautista-Gomez, L. (2024). On the design of ethereum's data availability sampling: A comprehensive simulation study. In *6th Conference on Blockchain Research & Applications for Innovative Networks and Services, BRAINS 2024,* Berlin, Germany, October 9-11, 2024, pages 1–4. IEEE. DOI: 10.1109/BRAINS63024.2024.10732486

Chaudhuri, A., & Kahyaoğlu, S. B. (2023). Cybersecurity assurance in smart cities: A risk management perspective. *EDPACS*, *67*(3), 1–10. DOI: 10.1080/07366981.2023.2165293

Chauhan, M., & Singh, A. K., & Komal. (2019, December). Survey of onion routing approaches: Advantages, limitations and future scopes. In *International Conference on Computer Networks, Big Data and IoT* (pp. 686–697). Springer.

Chavan, S., Gundakaram, J., Vaishnavi, S. D., Prasad, S., & Deepa, K. (2024). Real-time data extraction and prediction of cryptocurrency. *IEEE Access : Practical Innovations, Open Solutions*, *12*, 186703–186709. DOI: 10.1109/ACCESS.2024.3513034

Chawla, N. V., Bowyer, K. W., Hall, L. O., & Kegelmeyer, W. P. (2002). SMOTE: Synthetic minority over-sampling technique. *Journal of Artificial Intelligence Research*, *16*, 321–357. DOI: 10.1613/jair.953

Chen, T., Kornblith, S., Norouzi, M., & Hinton, G. (2020). A simple framework for contrastive learning of visual representations. Proceedings of the 37th International Conference on Machine Learning (ICML), PMLR 119, 1597–1607. https://proceedings.mlr.press/v119/chen20j.html

Chen, Q., Yang, M., Ling, Z., Liu, Z., Luo, L., Cao, C., & Fu, X. (2026). A Tor-based Anonymous Network Covert Channel. *IEEE Transactions on Dependable and Secure Computing.*

Chen, T., & Guestrin, C. (2016). XGBoost: A scalable tree boosting system. In *Proceedings of the 22nd ACM SIGKDD International Conference on Knowledge Discovery and Data Mining* (pp. 785–794). ACM. DOI: 10.1145/2939672.2939785

Chen, Y., Liang, G., & Wang, Q. (2025). Research on SQL Injection Detection Technology Based on Content Matching and Deep Learning. *Computers, Materials & Continua*, *84*(1), 1145–1167. DOI: 10.32604/cmc.2025.063319

Chen, Z., Liu, Y., Beillahi, S. M., Li, Y., & Long, F. (2024). Opentracer: A dynamic transaction trace analyzer for smart contract invariant generation and beyond. In *Proceedings of the 39th IEEE/ACM International Conference on Automated Software Engineering, ASE 2024,* Sacramento, CA, USA, October 27 - November 1, 2024, pages 2399–2402. ACM. DOI: 10.1145/3691620.3695361

Choraś, M., Pawlicki, M., Kozik, R., & Hołubowicz, W. (2020). Cybersecurity as a pillar of sustainable digital development. *Sustainability*, *12*(17), 6973. DOI: 10.3390/su12176973

Christin, N. (2013). Traveling the Silk Road: A measurement analysis of a large anonymous online marketplace. *Proceedings of the 22nd International Conference on World Wide Web (WWW)*, 213–224. DOI: 10.1145/2488388.2488408

Clarke, I., Sandberg, O., Wiley, B., & Hong, T. W. (2001). Freenet: A distributed anonymous information storage and retrieval system. In *Designing Privacy Enhancing Technologies* (pp. 46–66). Springer. DOI: 10.1007/3-540-44702-4_4

Clifford, B., & Powell, H. (2019). Encrypted extremism: Inside the English-speaking Islamic state ecosystem on telegram. *The George Washington University Program on Extremism*, 27-53.

Coles-Kemp, L. (2009). Information security management and organisational behaviour: Exploring the social context of information security. *Computers & Security*, *28*(1–2), 28–39. DOI: 10.1016/j.cose.2008.08.004

Collier, B. (2024). *Tor: From the dark web to the future of privacy.* MIT Press. DOI: 10.7551/mitpress/14907.001.0001

Connolly, L. Y., & Wall, D. S. (2019). The rise of crypto-ransomware in a changing cybercrime landscape: Taxonomising countermeasures. *Computers & Security*, *87*, 101568. Advance online publication. DOI: 10.1016/j.cose.2019.101568

Conti, M., Dehghantanha, A., Franke, K., & Watson, S. (2018). Internet of Things security and forensics: Challenges and opportunities. *Future Generation Computer Systems*, *78*, 544–546. DOI: 10.1016/j.future.2017.07.060

Conti, M., Lal, C., Mohammadi, M., Rawat, D. B., & Sadeghi, A. (2020). Security and privacy for artificial intelligence: Opportunities and challenges. *IEEE Communications Surveys and Tutorials*, *22*(3), 1639–1667. DOI: 10.1109/COMST.2020.2987868

Contreras-Velasco, O., Jones, N. P., Argomedo, D. W., Sullivan, J. P., & Callaghan, C. (2025). Uncovering hidden alliances in organized crime networks with machine learning: From node similarity to graph neural networks. *Journal of Computational Social Science*, *8*(4), 101. DOI: 10.1007/s42001-025-00429-0

Conway, M. (2017). Determining the role of the internet in violent extremism and terrorism: Six suggestions for progressing research. *Studies in Conflict and Terrorism*, *40*(1), 77–98. DOI: 10.1080/1057610X.2016.1157408

Conway, M. (2021). Online extremism and terrorism research ethics: Researcher safety, informed consent, and the need for tailored guidelines. *Terrorism and Political Violence*, *33*(2), 367–380. DOI: 10.1080/09546553.2021.1880235

Costa-jussà, M. R., Cross, J., Çelebi, O., Elbayad, M., Heafield, K., Heffernan, K., Kalbassi, E., Lam, J., Licht, D., Maillard, J., Sun, A., Wang, S., Wenzek, G., Youngblood, A., Bhosale, S., Nayak, N., Ropers, A., Sidorov, S., Wang, C., & Zettlemoyer, L. (2022). No language left behind: Scaling human-centered machine translation. arXiv. https://doi.org//arXiv.2207.04672DOI: 10.48550

Council of Europe. (2001). Convention on Cybercrime (ETS No. 185). Budapest, 23 November 2001. https://www.coe.int/en/web/conventions/full-list/-/conventions/treaty/185

Council of Europe. (2022). Second Additional Protocol to the Convention on Cybercrime on enhanced co-operation and disclosure of electronic evidence (ETS No. 224). https://www.coe.int/en/web/conventions/full-list/-/conventions/treaty/224

Coutinho Marim, M., Ramos, P. V. B., Vieira, A. B., Galletta, A., Villari, M., de Oliveira, R. M., & Silva, E. F. (2023). Darknet traffic detection and characterization with models based on decision trees and neural networks. *Intelligent Systems with Applications*, *18*, 200199. DOI: 10.1016/j.iswa.2023.200199

Creese, S., Hodges, D., Jamison-Powell, S., & Whitty, M. (2013). Relationships between cybersecurity and societal resilience. *Computers & Security*, *36*, 57–66. DOI: 10.1016/j.cose.2013.02.008

Crespo-Martínez, I. S., Campazas-Vega, A., Guerrero-Higueras, Á. M., Riego-DelCastillo, V., Álvarez-Aparicio, C., & Fernández-Llamas, C. (2023). SQL injection attack detection in network flow data. *Computers & Security*, *127*, 103093. DOI: 10.1016/j.cose.2023.103093

Cuddy, A. (2024). Ferrari executive foiled deepfake attempt by asking about a book. *Fortune*. https://fortune.com/2024/07/27/ferrari-deepfake-attempt-scammer-security-question-ceo-benedetto-vigna-cybersecurity-ai/

Cunha, J., Ferreira, P., Castro, E. M., Oliveira, P. C., Nicolau, M. J., Núñez, I., Sousa, X. R., & Serôdio, C. (2024). Enhancing network slicing security: Machine learning, software-defined networking, and network functions virtualization-driven strategies. *Future Internet*, *16*(7), 226. DOI: 10.3390/fi16070226

Cyber, K. E. L. A. (2025). *2025 AI threat report: How cybercriminals are weaponizing AI technology*. https://info.ke-la.com/hubfs/Reports/KELA%20Report%20-%202025%20AI%20Threat%20Report.pdf

Cybersecurity and Infrastructure Security Agency, Federal Bureau of Investigation, & Partners. (2023). *StopRansomware: LockBit 3.0.* U.S. Cybersecurity and Infrastructure Security Agency.

Cybersecurity and Infrastructure Security Agency, Federal Bureau of Investigation. MS-ISAC, & Partners. (2024). *StopRansomware: RansomHub ransomware.* U.S. Cybersecurity and Infrastructure Security Agency.

Cybersecurity Ventures. (2023). *2023 official cybercrime report.* Cybersecurity Ventures. https://cybersecurityventures.com/

Darzi, S., & Yavuz, A. A. (2024, October). Counter denial of service for next-generation networks within the artificial intelligence and post-quantum era. In *2024 IEEE 6th International Conference on Trust, Privacy and Security in Intelligent Systems, and Applications (TPS-ISA)* (pp. 138-147). IEEE. DOI: 10.1109/TPS-ISA62245.2024.00025

Dasari, N. S., Badii, A., Moin, A., & Ashlam, A. (2025). Enhancing SQL Injection Detection and Prevention Using Generative Models. *arXiv preprint arXiv:2502.04786.*

Davis, S., & Arrigo, B. A. (2021). The dark web and anonymizing technologies: Legal pitfalls, ethical prospects, and policy directions from radical criminology. *Crime, Law, and Social Change*, *76*(4), 367–386. DOI: 10.1007/s10611-021-09972-z

Davitaia, A. (2025). Ethical Challenges of Crime and Content Hosting on the Dark Web. *Available at SSRN* 5367005. DOI: 10.2139/ssrn.5367005

de Marcos, L., Medina-Merodio, J.-A., & Stapic, Z. (2025). Methodologies for dark web data collection. *Electronics (Basel)*, *14*(21), 4191. DOI: 10.3390/electronics14214191

Dearden, T. E., & Tucker, S. E. (2023). Follow the money: Analyzing dark-net activity using cryptocurrency and the bitcoin blockchain. *Journal of Contemporary Criminal Justice*, *39*(2), 257–275. DOI: 10.1177/10439862231157521

Décary-Hétu, D., & Giommoni, L. (2017). Do police crackdowns disrupt drug cryptomarkets? A longitudinal analysis of the effects of Operation Onymous. *Crime, Law, and Social Change*, *67*(1), 55–75. DOI: 10.1007/s10611-016-9644-4

de-Marcos, L., Domínguez-Díaz, A., & Stapic, Z. (2026). Mapping the Tor darkmarket ecosystem: A network analysis of topics, communication channels, and languages. *Forensic Science International Digital Investigation*, *56*, 302032. DOI: 10.1016/j.fsidi.2025.302032

Demertzis, K., Tsiknas, K., Takezis, D., Skianis, C., & Iliadis, L. (2021). Darknet Traffic Big-Data Analysis and Network Management for Real-Time Automating of the Malicious Intent Detection Process by a Weight Agnostic Neural Networks Framework. *Electronics (Basel)*, *10*(7), 781. DOI: 10.3390/electronics10070781

Dér, A. (2025). Cybersecurity in smart city energy systems. *Interdisciplinary Description of Complex Systems*, *23*(2), 145–160. DOI: 10.7906/indecs.23.2.4

Derrac, J., García, S., Molina, D., & Herrera, F. (2011). Nonparametric statistical tests tutorial. *Swarm and Evolutionary Computation*, *1*(1), 3–18. DOI: 10.1016/j.swevo.2011.02.002

Devine, M., Ardakani, S. P., Al-khafajiy, M., & James, Y. (2025). Federated machine learning to enable intrusion detection systems in IoT networks. *Electronics (Basel)*, *14*(12), 2210. DOI: 10.3390/electronics14061176

Devlin, J., Chang, M.-W., Lee, K., & Toutanova, K. (2019). BERT: Pre-training of deep bidirectional transformers for language understanding. *Proceedings of the 2019 Conference of the North American Chapter of the Association for Computational Linguistics: Human Language Technologies (NAACL-HLT)*, 1, 4171–4186. DOI: 10.18653/v1/N19-1423

Dhande, Y. H., & Zade, A. V. (2026). Multi-modal classification for dark web. *Soft Computing*. Advance online publication. DOI: 10.1007/s00500-025-11059-z

Dinev, T., & Hu, Q. (2007). The centrality of awareness in the formation of user behavioral intention toward protective information technologies. *Journal of the Association for Information Systems*, *8*(7), 386–408. DOI: 10.17705/1jais.00133

Dingledine, R., Mathewson, N., & Syverson, P. (2004). *Tor: The Second-Generation Onion Router*. DOI: 10.21236/ADA465464

Dingledine, R., Mathewson, N., & Syverson, P. (2004). Tor: The second-generation onion router. In *Proceedings of the 13th USENIX Security Symposium* (pp. 303–320). USENIX Association.

Dokeroglu, T., Sevinc, E., Kucukyilmaz, T., & Cosar, A. (2019). New generation metaheuristics survey. *Computers & Industrial Engineering*, *137*, 106040. DOI: 10.1016/j.cie.2019.106040

Doolan, M., Cox, K., & Sarma, K. M. (2025). Protocol: Understanding the content, context, and impact of far-right extremist propaganda disseminated online: A systematic review. *Campbell Systematic Reviews*, *21*(4), e70076. DOI: 10.1002/cl2.70076 PMID: 41245379

Döpmann, C. (2025). *On the evolution of onion routing networks* (Doctoral dissertation, Technische Universität Berlin).

Dorigo, M., & Gambardella, L. M. (1997). Ant colony system. *IEEE Transactions on Evolutionary Computation*, *1*(1), 53–66. DOI: 10.1109/4235.585892

Dos Reis, E. F., Teytelboym, A., ElBahrawy, A., De Loizaga, I., & Baronchelli, A. (2024). Identifying key players in dark web marketplaces through Bitcoin transaction networks. *Scientific Reports*, *14*(1), 2385. DOI: 10.1038/s41598-023-50409-5 PMID: 38286798

Draper-Gil, G., Lashkari, A. H., Mamun, M. S. I., & Ghorbani, A. A. (2016). Characterization of encrypted and VPN traffic using time-related features. In *Proceedings of the 2nd International Conference on Information Systems Security and Privacy (ICISSP)* (pp. 407–414). SciTePress. DOI: 10.5220/0005740700001242

Dudani, S., Baggili, I., Raymond, D. R., & Marchany, R. (2023). The current state of cryptocurrency forensics. *Forensic Science International Digital Investigation*, *46*, 301576. DOI: 10.1016/j.fsidi.2023.301576

Dunaiev, S. (2025). An integrated approach to data confidentiality in 5G/6G based on LDPC codes and post-quantum cryptography. *Terra Security*, *12*(2), 45–56.

Dutta, N., Jadav, N., Tanwar, S., Sarma, H. K. D., & Pricop, E. (2021). Being hidden and anonymous. In *Cyber security: Issues and current trends* (pp. 17–36). Springer.

Dwedar, M., Bayram, F. S., Eberhard, J., & Jesser, A. (2024). Dynamic anomaly detection in 5G-connected IoT devices using transfer learning. In *Proceedings of the International Conference on Multimodal Interaction (ICMI)*. DOI: 10.1109/ICMI60790.2024.10585712

Dwivedi, A., Saini, G. K., & Musa, U. I. (2023, March). Cybersecurity and prevention in the quantum era. In *2023 2nd International conference for innovation in technology (INOCON)* (pp. 1-6). IEEE. DOI: 10.1109/INOCON57975.2023.10101186

Dwork, C., & Roth, A. (2014). The algorithmic foundations of differential privacy. Foundations and Trends® in Theoretical Computer Science, 9(3–4), 211–407. DOI: 10.1561/0400000042

Ebrahimi, M., Nunamaker, J. F.Jr, & Chen, H. (2020). Semi-supervised cyber threat identification in dark net markets: A transductive and deep learning approach. *Journal of Management Information Systems*, *37*(3), 694–722. DOI: 10.1080/07421222.2020.1790186

Ejeofobiri, C. K., Victor-Igun, O. O., & Okoye, C. (2024). AI-driven secure intrusion detection for internet of things (IoT) networks. *Asian Journal of Mathematics and Computer Research*, *31*(4), 40–55. DOI: 10.56557/ajomcor/2024/v31i48971

ElBahrawy, A., Alessandretti, L., Rusnac, L., Goldsmith, D., Teytelboym, A., & Baronchelli, A. (2020). Collective dynamics of dark web marketplaces. *Scientific Reports*, *10*(1), 18827. Advance online publication. DOI: 10.1038/s41598-020-74416-y PMID: 33139743

Elijah, T., Samuel, A. A., & Familusi, O. B. (2025). AI-powered intrusion detection and prevention systems for the next generation network. *Traektoriâ Nauki*, *11*(2), 45–56. DOI: 10.22178/pos.123-3

El-Kady, R. (2025). Decoding the dark: AI and ML in the dark web cybercrime and cryptocurrency forensics. *International Cybersecurity Law Review*, *6*(2), 107–143. DOI: 10.1365/s43439-025-00145-5

Elkhodr, M. (2025). An AI-driven framework for integrated security and privacy in internet of things using quantum-resistant blockchain. *Future Internet*, *17*(1), 83. DOI: 10.3390/fi17060246

EMCDDA & Europol. (2019). EU Drug Markets Report 2019. European Monitoring Centre for Drugs and Drug Addiction and Europol. https://www.emcdda.europa.eu

ENISA. (2021). *ENISA threat landscape 2021*. European Union Agency for Cybersecurity. https://www.enisa.europa.eu

ENISA. (2023). *ENISA threat landscape 2023*. European Union Agency for Cybersecurity. https://www.enisa.europa.eu

European Commission. (2023). E-evidence: Cross-border access to electronic evidence. https://commission.europa.eu/law/cross-border-cases/judicial-cooperation/types-judicial-cooperation/e-evidence-cross-border-access-electronic-evidence_en

European Union Agency for Cybersecurity (ENISA). (2025). *ENISA threat landscape 2025*. https://www.enisa.europa.eu/sites/default/files/2025-11/ENISA%20Threat%20Landscape%202025.pdf

European Union Agency for Cybersecurity. (2024a). *2024 report on the state of cybersecurity in the Union.*

European Union Agency for Cybersecurity. (2024b). *ENISA threat landscape 2024.*

Europol. (2017, July 20). Massive blow to criminal dark web activities after globally coordinated operation: Takedown of AlphaBay and Hansa will lead to hundreds of new investigations in Europe. https://www.europol.europa.eu/media-press/newsroom/news/massive-blow-to-criminal-dark-web-activities-after-globally-coordinated-operation

Europol. (2020). Internet organised crime threat assessment (IOCTA) 2020. Europol. https://www.europol.europa.eu

Europol. (2021). Cryptocurrencies: Tracing the evolution of criminal finances. Technical report.

Europol. (2023). Internet organised crime threat assessment (IOCTA) 2023. https://www.europol.europa.eu/iocta-report

Europol. (2024). *Internet organised crime threat assessment (IOCTA) 2024.* European Union Agency for Law Enforcement Cooperation. https://www.europol.europa.eu/

Europol. (2024). Internet Organised Crime Threat Assessment (IOCTA) 2024. European Union Agency for Law Enforcement Cooperation. https://www.europol.europa.eu/publication-events/main-reports/internet-organised-crime-threat-assessment-iocta-2024

Europol. (2024a). *Internet organised crime threat assessment (IOCTA) 2024.*

Europol. (2024b, February 20). *Law enforcement disrupt world's biggest ransomware operation.*

Europol. (2025a). *EU serious and organised crime threat assessment (EU-SOCTA) 2025: The changing DNA of serious and organised crime.*

Europol. (2025b). *Steal, deal and repeat: IOCTA 2025.*

Fachkha, C., & Debbabi, M. (2016). Darknet as a source of cyber intelligence: Survey, taxonomy, and characterization. *IEEE Communications Surveys and Tutorials, 18*(2), 1197–1227. DOI: 10.1109/COMST.2015.2497690

Faizan, M., & Khan, R. A. (2019). Exploring and analyzing the dark Web: A new alchemy. *First Monday, 24*(5). Advance online publication. DOI: 10.5210/fm.v24i5.9473

Fakhouri, H. N., Alhadidi, B., Omar, K., Makhadmeh, S. N., Hamad, F., & Halalsheh, N. Z. (2024). AI-driven solutions for social engineering attacks: Detection, prevention, and response. In *2nd International Conference on Cyber Resilience (ICCR 2024).* IEEE. DOI: 10.1109/ICCR61006.2024.10533010

Fan, S., Ranly, P. M., Graner, L., Vogel, I., & Steinebach, M. (2024, July). Unveiling the Darkness: Analysing Organised Crime on the Wall Street Market Darknet Marketplace using PGP Public Keys. In *Proceedings of the 19th International Conference on Availability, Reliability and Security* (pp. 1-10). DOI: 10.1145/3664476.3670464

Faryad, S., Shoukat, I. A., Arif, E., Faheem, M. R., Kashif, M., & Nawaz, A. (2024). A review: Performance and security based comparative analysis of well-known stealth services. *Journal of Computing & Biomedical Informatics*.

Federal Bureau of Investigation, Internet Crime Complaint Center. (2025). *2024 IC3 annual report*. U.S. Department of Justice. https://www.ic3.gov/AnnualReport/Reports/2024_IC3Report.pdf

Federal Bureau of Investigation. (2017). AlphaBay takedown. https://www.fbi.gov/news/stories/alphabay-takedown

Federal Reserve Bank of Boston. (2025). *Gen AI is ramping up the threat of synthetic identity fraud*. https://www.bostonfed.org/news-and-events/news/2025/04/synthetic-identity-fraud-financial-fraud-expanding-because-of-generative-artificial-intelligence.aspx

Feng, X. (2025). Web crawling with TF-IDF and Word2Vec. *Journal of Web Engineering*, *24*(5), 713–738. DOI: 10.13052/jwe1540-9589.2452

Ferrag, M. A., Maglaras, L., Argyriou, A., Kosmanos, D., & Janicke, H. (2019). Security for 4G and 5G cellular networks: A survey of existing authentication and privacy-preserving schemes. *Journal of Network and Computer Applications*, *101*, 55–82. DOI: 10.1016/j.jnca.2017.10.017

Ferrag, M. A., Maglaras, L., Moschoyiannis, S., & Janicke, H. (2020). Deep learning for cyber security intrusion detection: Approaches, datasets, and comparative study. *Journal of Information Security and Applications*, *50*, 102419. DOI: 10.1016/j.jisa.2019.102419

Ferreira, J. J., Fernandes, C., Veiga, P. M., & Rammal, H. G. (2025). Ethics and the dark side of online communities: Mapping the field and a research agenda. *Information Systems and e-Business Management*, *23*(1), 99–123. DOI: 10.1007/s10257-023-00653-z

Figueras-Martín, E., Magán-Carrión, R., & Boubeta-Puig, J. (2022). Drawing the web structure and content analysis beyond the Tor darknet: Freenet as a case study. *Journal of Information Security and Applications*, *68*, 103229. DOI: 10.1016/j.jisa.2022.103229

Finn, C., Abbeel, P., & Levine, S. (2017). Model-agnostic meta-learning. *Proceedings of ICML*, 1126–1135. DOI: 10.48550/arXiv.1703.03400

Flashpoint. (2026). *2026 global threat intelligence report*. https://flashpoint.io/blog/global-threat-intelligence-report-2026/

Foley, S., & Jonathan, R. (2019, May). Karlsen, Tālis J Putniņš, Sex, Drugs, and Bitcoin: How Much Illegal Activity Is Financed through Cryptocurrencies? *Review of Financial Studies*, *32*(5), 1798–1853. DOI: 10.1093/rfs/hhz015

G. K. S., Ranjani, M., Nithiyanandam, N., Rajasekaran, A. S., Karthick, M. K., & Kumar, T. P. (2025). Cybersecurity: The part played by artificial intelligence. In D. Darwish & K. Charan (Eds.), *Analyzing privacy and security difficulties in social media: New challenges and solutions* (pp. 213–246). IGI Global. DOI: 10.4018/979-8-3693-9491-5.ch010

Gama, J., Žliobaitė, I., Bifet, A., Pechenizkiy, M., & Bouchachia, A. (2014). A survey on concept drift adaptation. *ACM Computing Surveys*, *46*(4), 44. Advance online publication. DOI: 10.1145/2523813

Gannon, C., Blokland, A. A. J., Huikuri, S., Babchishin, K. M., & Lehmann, R. J. B. (2023). Child sexual abuse material on the darknet. *Forensische Psychiatrie, Psychologie, Kriminologie, 17*(4), 353–365. DOI: 10.1007/s11757-023-00790-8

Gao, W., Hatcher, W. G., & Yu, W. (2018). A survey of blockchain: Techniques, applications, and challenges. In *27th International Conference on Computer Communication and Networks, ICCCN 2018,* Hangzhou, China, July 30 - August 2, 2018, pages 1–11. IEEE. DOI: 10.1109/ICCCN.2018.8487348

Garcia-Teodoro, P., Díaz-Verdejo, J., Maciá-Fernández, G., & Vázquez, E. (2009). Anomaly-based network intrusion detection: Techniques, systems and challenges. *Computers & Security, 28*(1–2), 18–28. DOI: 10.1016/j.cose.2008.08.003

Gehl, R. W. (2018). *Weaving the dark web: Legitimacy on Freenet, Tor, and I2P.* MIT Press. DOI: 10.7551/mitpress/11266.001.0001

Gentile, A. F., Macrì, D., Carnì, D. L., Greco, E., & Lamonaca, F. (2024). A network performance analysis of MQTT security protocols with constrained hardware in the dark net for DMS. *Applied Sciences (Basel, Switzerland), 14*(18), 8501. DOI: 10.3390/app14188501

Gharavi, H., Granjal, J., & Monteiro, E. (2024). Post-quantum blockchain security for the Internet of Things: Survey and research directions. *IEEE Communications Surveys and Tutorials, 26*(3), 1748–1774. DOI: 10.1109/COMST.2024.3355222

Ghosh, S., Das, A., Porras, P., Yegneswaran, V., & Gehani, A. (2017). Automated Categorization of Onion Sites for Analyzing the Darkweb Ecosystem. *Proceedings of the 23rd ACM SIGKDD International Conference on Knowledge Discovery and Data Mining*, 1793–1802. DOI: 10.1145/3097983.3098193

Giannilias, T., Papadakis, A., Nikolaou, N., & Zahariadis, T. (2025). Classification of Hacker's Posts Based on Zero-Shot, Few-Shot, and Fine-Tuned LLMs in Environments with Constrained Resources. *Future Internet, 17*(5), 207. DOI: 10.3390/fi17050207

Gilbert, C., & Gilbert, M. (2024). Unlocking privacy in blockchain: Exploring zero-knowledge proofs and secure multi-party computation techniques. *Available at SSRN* 5258791.

Gjorgjev, J., Ramadhan, M. F., & Dhamayana, S. (2025). Blockchain forensics—Unmasking anonymity in dark web transactions. *International Journal of Criminology and Sociology, 14*, 7. DOI: 10.6000/1929-4409.2025.14.07

Goldberg, D. E. (1989). *Genetic algorithms in search, optimization, and machine learning*. Addison-Wesley.

Gond, A. K. (2025). Hidden side of the internet: Between crime and freedom on the dark-web. *Journal of Communication Management (London), 4*(3), 55–61.

Goodfellow, I. J., Pouget-Abadie, J., Mirza, M., ... (2014). Generative adversarial nets. In *Advances in Neural Information Processing Systems (NeurIPS 27)* (pp. 2672–2680).

Goodfellow, I., Pouget-Abadie, J., Mirza, M., Xu, B., Warde-Farley, D., Ozair, S., Courville, A., & Bengio, Y. (2014). Generative adversarial nets. In Vol. 27, pp. 2672–2680). Advances in Neural Information Processing Systems. Curran Associates.

Google Cloud. (2026). *Bringing dark web intelligence into the AI era.* https://cloud.google.com/blog/products/identity-security/bringing-dark-web-intelligence-into-the-ai-era

Google Threat Intelligence Group. (2025a). *Adversarial misuse of generative AI.* https://cloud.google.com/blog/topics/threat-intelligence/adversarial-misuse-generative-ai

Google Threat Intelligence Group. (2025b). *GTIG AI threat tracker: Advances in threat actor usage of AI tools.* https://cloud.google.com/blog/topics/threat-intelligence/threat-actor-usage-of-ai-tools

Gordon, L. A., & Loeb, M. P. (2002). The economics of information security investment. *ACM Transactions on Information and System Security, 5*(4), 438–457. DOI: 10.1145/581271.581274

Gospodinov, G., Gotsev, L., Ristovska, T., Syarova, S., & Angelova, V. (2025). Cybersecurity in smart cities: A review of theoretical models, emerging threats, and defence strategies. In *Proceedings of the Environment Technology Resources International Scientific Practice Conference.* DOI: 10.1109/TELSIKS65061.2025.11240797

Graham, R., & Pitman, B. (2020). Freedom in the wilderness: A study of a darknet space. *Convergence (London), 26*(3), 593–619. DOI: 10.1177/1354856518806636

Greitzer, F. L., & Frincke, D. A. (2010). Combining traditional cyber security audit data with psychosocial data: Towards predictive modeling for insider threat mitigation. In *Insider Threats in Cyber Security* (pp. 85–113). https://doi.org/DOI: 10.1007/978-1-4419-7133-3_5

Grossklags, J., Christin, N., & Chuang, J. (2008). Secure or insure? A game-theoretic analysis of information security games. In *Proceedings of the 17th International World Wide Web Conference* (pp. 209–218). https://doi.org/DOI: 10.1145/1367497.1367526

Group-IB. (2025). *High-tech crime trends report 2025.* https://www.group-ib.com/media-center/press-releases/high-tech-crime-trends-report-2025/

Guan, Y., He, J., Li, T., Zhao, H., & Ma, B. (2023). Ssqli: A black-box adversarial attack method for sql injection based on reinforcement learning. *Future Internet, 15*(4), 133. DOI: 10.3390/fi15040133

Guizani, S., Mazhar, T., & Hamam, H. (2026). Quantum Secure Multiparty Computation: Bridging Privacy, Security, and Scalability in the Post-Quantum Era. *Computers, Materials & Continua, 87*(1), 1–10. DOI: 10.32604/cmc.2025.073883

Guo, C., Wang, S., Yu, K., Zhu, Y., & Tao, X. (2025). A differential game method against DDoS attacks in IoT botnets: Holistic and dynamic perspectives. *IEEE Internet of Things Journal, 12*(9), 7450–7463. DOI: 10.1109/JIOT.2025.3541852

Guoqiang ZHANG, M. X. (2024). *Push and pull Tor users' guards through optimized resource portfolios. 64*(8), 1293–1305. DOI: 10.16511/j.cnki.qhdxxb.2024.27.013

Gupta, M. (2026). Security Risks for Enterprises in the Post-Quantum Computing World. *International Journal of Emerging Trends in Computer Science and Information Technology, 7*(1), 328–337. DOI: 10.63282/3050-9246.IJETCSIT-V7I1P147

Gupta, S., & Patel, N. (2024). Decentralized biometric authentication based on fuzzy commitments and blockchain. *International Journal of Information Security*, *23*(4), 765–781.

Habibi Lashkari, A., Draper-Gil, G., Mamun, M. S. I., & Ghorbani, A. A. (2017). Characterization of Tor traffic using time-based features. In *Proceedings of the 3rd International Conference on Information Systems Security and Privacy (ICISSP)* (pp. 253–262). SciTePress. DOI: 10.5220/0006105602530262

Habibi Lashkari, A., Kaur, G., & Rahali, A. (2020). DIDarknet: A contemporary approach to detect and characterize the darknet traffic using deep image learning. In *Proceedings of the 10th International Conference on Communication and Network Security* (pp. 1–13). ACM. DOI: 10.1145/3442520.3442521

HaddadPajouh, H., Dehghantanha, A., Parizi, R., Aledhari, M., & Karimipour, H. (2021). IoT security survey. *Internet of Things : Engineering Cyber Physical Human Systems*, *14*, 100129. DOI: 10.1016/j.iot.2019.100129

Hadlington, L. (2017). Human factors in cybersecurity: Examining the link between internet addiction, impulsivity, attitudes towards cybersecurity, and risky cybersecurity behaviours. *Heliyon*, *3*(7), e00346. DOI: 10.1016/j.heliyon.2017.e00346 PMID: 28725870

Hamilton, W., Ying, Z., & Leskovec, J. (2017). Inductive representation learning on large graphs. Advances in Neural Information Processing Systems, 30. https://proceedings.neurips.cc/paper/2017/hash/5dd9db5e033da9c6fb5ba83c7a7ebea9-Abstract.html

Hammad, A., & Abu-Zaid, R. (2024). Applications of AI in decentralized computing systems: Harnessing artificial intelligence for enhanced scalability, efficiency, and autonomous decision-making in distributed architectures. *Applied Research in Artificial Intelligence and Cloud Computing*, *7*(6), 161–187.

Hammood, B. A. K., & Sadiq, A. T. (2023). Ensemble machine learning approach for IoT intrusion detection systems. *Iraqi Journal of Computers and Informatics*, *49*(2), 123–130. DOI: 10.25195/ijci.v49i2.424

Hammoud, O., Tarkhanov, I., & Kosmarski, A. (2021). An Architecture for Distributed Electronic Documents Storage in Decentralized Blockchain B2B Applications. *Computers*, *10*(11), 142. DOI: 10.3390/computers10110142

Hancock, P. J., van Hardeveld, G. J., Jakubcek, J., Akhgar, B., Davey, S., & Amann, P. (2024). Design of Cryptopol: A serious game for teaching cryptocurrency tracing techniques to law enforcement. *Games : Research & Practice*, *2*(4), 32. Advance online publication. DOI: 10.1145/3697845

Hatta, M. (2020). Deep web, dark web, dark net: A taxonomy of "hidden" internet. *Annals of Business Administrative Science*, *19*(6), 277–292. DOI: 10.7880/abas.0200908a

Haughey, H., Epiphaniou, G., & Al-Khateeb, H. M. (2016). Anonymity networks and the fragile cyber ecosystem. *Network Security*, *2016*(3), 10–18. DOI: 10.1016/S1353-4858(16)30028-9

He, H., Bai, Y., Garcia, E. A., & Li, S. (2008). ADASYN: Adaptive synthetic sampling approach for imbalanced learning. In *2008 IEEE International Joint Conference on Neural Networks (IJCNN)* (pp. 1322–1328). IEEE. DOI: 10.1109/IJCNN.2008.4633969

Hinton, G. E., & Salakhutdinov, R. R. (2006). Reducing the dimensionality of data with neural networks. *Science*, *313*(5786), 504–507. DOI: 10.1126/science.1127647 PMID: 16873662

Ho, J., Jain, A., & Abbeel, P. (2020). Denoising diffusion probabilistic models. In *Advances in Neural Information Processing Systems (NeurIPS 33)*.

Holland, J. H. (1992). Genetic algorithms. *Scientific American, 267*(1), 66–73. DOI: 10.1038/scientificamerican0792-66

Holt, T. J., Lee, J. R., & Griffith, E. (2023). An Assessment of Cryptomixing Services in Online Illicit Markets. *Journal of Contemporary Criminal Justice, 39*(2), 222–238. DOI: 10.1177/10439862231158004 PMID: 40822574

Homeland Security Investigations, I. C. E. (2025, May 22). ICE, Europol, law enforcement partners dismantle major illicit drug networks in global darknet crackdown: Operation RapTOR. U.S. Immigration and Customs Enforcement. https://www.ice.gov/news/releases/ice-europol-law-enforcement-partners-dismantle-major-illicit-drug-networks-global

Hossain, M. I., & Hasan, R. (2025). Analyzing smart cities: Cybersecurity architecture, threats, mitigation, challenges, and open problems. In *Proceedings of the IEEE World Forum on Public Safety Technologies (WF-PST)*. DOI: 10.1109/WF-PST65083.2025.00044

Hossain, M. M., Kayas, G., Hasan, R., Skjellum, A., Noor, S., & Islam, S. M. R. (2024). A holistic analysis of internet of things (IoT) security: Principles, practices, and new perspectives. *Future Internet, 16*(2), 40. DOI: 10.3390/fi16020040

Houichi, M., Jaidi, F., & Bouhoula, A. (2025). Enhancing cybersecurity in smart cities: A blockchain-based framework for securing IoT data. *Journal of Infrastructure Policy and Development, 5*(2), 123–134. DOI: 10.24294/jipd11733

Howell, C. J., Maimon, D., Perkins, R. C., Burruss, G. W., Ouellet, M., & Wu, Y. (2024). Risk Avoidance Behavior on Darknet Marketplaces. *Crime and Delinquency, 70*(2), 519–538. DOI: 10.1177/00111287221092713

Hu, E. J., Shen, Y., Wallis, P., ... (2021). LoRA: Low-rank adaptation of large language models. *arXiv preprint arXiv:2106.09685*. https://arxiv.org/abs/2106.09685

Hu, Y., Zou, F., Li, L., & Yi, P. (2020). Traffic classification of user behaviors in Tor, I2P, ZeroNet, Freenet. In *2020 IEEE 19th International Conference on Trust, Security and Privacy in Computing and Communications (TrustCom)* (pp. 418–424). IEEE. DOI: 10.1109/TrustCom50675.2020.00064

Huang, D. Y., Aliapoulios, M. M., Li, V. G., Invernizzi, L., Bursztein, E., McRoberts, K., Levin, J., Levchenko, K., Snoeren, A. C., & McCoy, D. (2018). Tracking ransomware end-to-end. In *2018 IEEE Symposium on Security and Privacy, SP 2018, Proceedings, 21-23 May 2018, San Francisco, California, USA*, pages 618–631. IEEE Computer Society.

Huang, K., Siegel, M., & Madnick, S. (2018). Systematically understanding the cyber attack business: A survey. *ACM Computing Surveys, 51*(4), 70. Advance online publication. DOI: 10.1145/3199674

Huete Trujillo, D. L., & Ruiz-Martínez, A. (2021). Tor hidden services: A systematic literature review. *Journal of Cybersecurity and Privacy, 1*(3), 496–518. DOI: 10.3390/jcp1030025

Hughes, J., Collier, B., & Hutchings, A. (2024). The art of cybercrime community research. *Communications of the ACM.*

Hui, X., & Tucker, C. (2025). Decentralization, blockchain, artificial intelligence (AI): Challenges and opportunities. *Journal of Product Innovation Management, 42*(5), 947–957. DOI: 10.1111/jpim.12800

Hutchings, A., & Holt, T. J. (2015). A crime script analysis of the online stolen data market. *British Journal of Criminology, 55*(3), 596–614. DOI: 10.1093/bjc/azu106

Hutchings, A., & Holt, T. J. (2017). The online stolen data market: Disruption and intervention approaches. *Global Crime, 18*(1), 11–30. DOI: 10.1080/17440572.2016.1197123

Hwang, S., & Kim, J. (2021). A malware distribution simulator for the verification of network threat prevention tools. *Sensors (Basel), 21*(21), 6983. DOI: 10.3390/s21216983 PMID: 34770290

Hwang, Y., Kurt, F., Curebal, F., Keskin, O., & Subasi, A. (2026). ContextualGraph-LLM: A multimodal framework for enhanced Darknet traffic analysis. *Expert Systems with Applications, 297*, 129298. DOI: 10.1016/j.eswa.2025.129298

Ige, A. B. (2024). Aligning sustainable development goals with cybersecurity frameworks: Strategies for secure digital societies. *Global Scientific Conference on Applied Research and Reviews, 6*(2), 45–53.

Igonor, O. S., Amin, M. B., and Garg, S. (2025). The application of blockchain technology in the field of digital forensics: A literature review. *Blockchains*, 3(1).

Ikram, H., Habib, R., Ali, M., & Uzmi, Z. A. (2024). *VaulTor: Putting the TEE in Tor* (arXiv Preprint No. arXiv:2412.16064). arXiv. https://arxiv.org/abs/2412.16064

Internet Watch Foundation. (2025). *How AI is being abused to create child sexual abuse imagery.* https://www.iwf.org.uk/about-us/why-we-exist/our-research/how-ai-is-being-abused-to-create-child-sexual-abuse-imagery/

Ishaque, M., & Al-Anesi, B. (2025, February). Quantum cryptography and post-quantum security: Safeguarding cryptographic protocols against quantum threats. In *2025 2nd International Conference on Advanced Innovations in Smart Cities (ICAISC)* (pp. 1-7). IEEE.

Islam, R., Bose, R., Roy, S., Khan, A. A., Sutradhar, S., Das, S., Ali, F., & AlZubi, A. A. (2025). Decentralized trust framework for smart cities: A blockchain-enabled cybersecurity and data integrity model. *Scientific Reports, 15*(1), 4321. Advance online publication. DOI: 10.1038/s41598-025-06405-y PMID: 40603417

ISO/IEC. (2022). *ISO/IEC 27001: Information security management systems—Requirements.* International Organization for Standardization.

Jadav, N. K., Kakkar, R., Mankodiya, H., Gupta, R., Tanwar, S., Agrawal, S., & Sharma, R. (2023). GRADE: Deep learning and garlic routing-based secure data sharing framework for IIoT beyond 5G. *Digital Communications and Networks, 9*(2), 422–435. DOI: 10.1016/j.dcan.2022.11.004

Jamshidi, S., Nikanjam, A., Nafi, K. W., Khomh, F., & Rasta, R. (2025). Application of deep reinforcement learning for intrusion detection in internet of things: A systematic review. *Internet of Things : Engineering Cyber Physical Human Systems*, *15*, 100410. DOI: 10.1016/j.iot.2025.101531

Jangale, M. D. (2025). *The convergence of shadow and silicon: Advanced forensic methodologies for decentralized webs, generative AI, and darknet infrastructure*. Research Hub International Multidisciplinary Research Journal.

Jaradat, M., Rattrout, A., & Jayousi, R. (2023). Improving ML Accuracy in SQL Injection Detection using NLP and Feature Engineering.

Jardine, E. (2018). Privacy, censorship, data breaches and internet freedom: The drivers of support and opposition to dark web technologies. *New Media & Society*, *20*(8), 2824–2843. DOI: 10.1177/1461444817733134

Jardine, E. (2019). Online content moderation and the Dark Web: Policy responses to radicalizing hate speech and malicious content on the Darknet. *First Monday*, *24*(12). Advance online publication. DOI: 10.5210/fm.v24i12.10266

Jardine, E. (2021). Policing the Cybercrime Script of Darknet Drug Markets: Methods of Effective Law Enforcement Intervention. *American Journal of Criminal Justice*, *46*(6), 980–1005. DOI: 10.1007/s12103-021-09656-3

Jayapradha, J., Prakash, M., Alotaibi, Y. A., Khalaf, O. I., & Alghamdi, S. A. (2022). Heap bucketization anonymity—An efficient privacy-preserving data publishing model for multiple sensitive attributes. *IEEE Access : Practical Innovations, Open Solutions*, *10*, 28773–28791. DOI: 10.1109/ACCESS.2022.3158312

Jha, A., & Jha, A. (2024). Securing tomorrow's urban frontiers: A holistic approach to cybersecurity in smart cities. *Information Systems for Smart City*, *5*(2), 33–45. DOI: 10.59400/issc.v3i1.418

Jin, Y., Jang, E., Cui, J., Chung, J.-W., Lee, Y., & Shin, S. (2023). DarkBERT: A language model for the dark side of the internet. *Proceedings of the 61st Annual Meeting of the Association for Computational Linguistics (ACL)*, 1, 7515–7533. DOI: 10.18653/v1/2023.acl-long.415

Joshi, S., Bairwa, A. K., Pljonkin, A. P., Garg, P., & Agrawal, K. (2023, May). From pre-quantum to post-quantum RSA. In *Proceedings of the 6th international conference on networking, intelligent systems & security* (pp. 1-8).

Kakisim, A. G. (2024). A deep learning approach based on multi-view consensus for SQL injection detection. *International Journal of Information Security*, *23*(2), 1541–1556. DOI: 10.1007/s10207-023-00791-y

Kang, D.-W., & Kim, J. (2026). Identification of criminal networks on dark web. *IEEE Access : Practical Innovations, Open Solutions*, *14*, 15394–15413. DOI: 10.1109/ACCESS.2026.3658951

Kareem, K. M. (2024). Guardians of anonymity: Exploring tactics to combat cyber threats in onion routing environments. *arXiv*. https://arxiv.org/abs/2406.07563

Karras, T., Laine, S., & Aila, T. (2019). A style-based generator architecture for generative adversarial networks. In *Proceedings of the IEEE/CVF Conference on Computer Vision and Pattern Recognition (CVPR)* (pp. 4401–4410). DOI: 10.1109/CVPR.2019.00453

Karunanayake, I., AlSabah, M., Ahmed, N., Jourjon, G., Seneviratne, S., & Seneviratne, A. (2024). Examining the rat in the tunnel: Interpretable multi-label classification of Tor-based malware. *arXiv preprint arXiv:2409.16639*. https://arxiv.org/abs/2409.16639

Kashyap, A., & Jana, A. (2025). A survey: On detection and prevention techniques of SQL injection attacks. *International Journal of Information and Computer Security*, *26*(4), 332–371. DOI: 10.1504/IJICS.2025.146528

Kate, A., & Goldberg, I. (2010, January). Using sphinx to improve onion routing circuit construction. In *Financial Cryptography and Data Security* (pp. 359–366). Springer. DOI: 10.1007/978-3-642-14577-3_30

Katiyar, N., Tripathi, S., Kumar, P., Verma, S., Sahu, A. K., & Saxena, S. (2024). AI and Cyber-Security: Enhancing threat detection and response with machine learning. *Educational Administration: Theory and Practice*, *30*(4), 6273–6282. DOI: 10.53555/kuey.v30i4.2377

Kaur, G., Mukherjee, D., Moza, B., Pahwa, V., Kaur, K., & Kaur, K. (2024). The dark web: A hidden menace or a tool for privacy protection. *IP International Journal of Forensic Medicine and Toxicological Sciences*, *8*(4), 160–167. DOI: 10.18231/j.ijfmts.2023.034

Kavitha, R. J., Kapilsurya, R., Shanmugam, V., & Kumar, R. (2023). The dark web: Privacy and anonymity. *International Journal for Research in Applied Science and Engineering Technology*, *11*(3), 1087–1093. DOI: 10.22214/ijraset.2023.49599

Kayser, F., Mayer, T., & Bücker, M. (2025). OSINT research framework. HICSS Proceedings, 5375–5384. DOI: 10.24251/HICSS.2025.646

Ke, G., Meng, Q., Finley, T., Wang, T., Chen, W., Ma, W., Ye, Q., & Liu, T.-Y. (2017). LightGBM: A highly efficient gradient boosting decision tree. In Vol. 30, pp. 3146–3154). Advances in Neural Information Processing Systems. Curran Associates.

Kennedy, J., & Eberhart, R. (1995). Particle swarm optimization. *IEEE International Conference on Neural Networks*, 1942–1948. DOI: 10.1109/ICNN.1995.488968

Khalilov, M. C. K., & Levi, A. (2018). A survey on anonymity and privacy in bitcoin-like digital cash systems. *IEEE Communications Surveys and Tutorials*, *20*(3), 2543–2585. DOI: 10.1109/COMST.2018.2818623

Khan, A., Jhanjhi, N. Z., Hamid, D. H., Omar, H. A., Amsaad, F., & Wassan, S. (2025). Future trends and challenges in cybersecurity and generative AI. In Jhanjhi, N. (Ed.), *Reshaping cybersecurity with generative AI techniques* (pp. 491–522). IGI Global., DOI: 10.4018/979-8-3693-5415-5.ch014

Khan, A., & Rehman, M. (2024). Deep convolutional generative adversarial networks for biometric authentication: A survey. *Artificial Intelligence Review*, *57*(3), 1–29.

Khan, M. A., Noor, F., Javaid, S., & Żywiołek, J. (2025). Implementation and performance of post-quantum cryptography for resource constrained consumer electronics. *Discover Internet of Things*, *5*(1), 139. DOI: 10.1007/s43926-025-00238-x

Khan, M. A., & Salah, K. (2018). IoT security: Review, blockchain solutions, and open challenges. *Future Generation Computer Systems*, *82*, 395–411. DOI: 10.1016/j.future.2017.11.022

Kharraz, A., Arshad, S., Mulliner, C., Robertson, W., & Kirda, E. (2015). Cutting the Gordian knot: A look under the hood of ransomware attacks. In *Detection of Intrusions and Malware, and Vulnerability Assessment* (Vol. 9148, pp. 3–24). Springer. DOI: 10.1007/978-3-319-20550-2_1

Kikissagbe, B. R., & Adda, M. (2024). Machine learning-based intrusion detection methods in IoT systems: A comprehensive review. *Electronics (Basel), 13*(12), 2314. DOI: 10.3390/electronics13183601

Kili¸c, B., Özturan, C., & Sen, A. (2022). Parallel analysis of ethereum blockchain transaction data using cluster computing. *Cluster Computing*, *25*(3), 1885–1898. DOI: 10.1007/s10586-021-03511-0

Kilic, Y., Destek, M. A., Cevik, E. I., Bugan, M. F., Korkmaz, O., & Dibooglu, S. (2022). Return and risk spillovers between the ESG global index and stock markets: Evidence from time and frequency analysis. *Borsa Istanbul Review*, *22*, S141–S156. DOI: 10.1016/j.bir.2022.11.015

Kim, M., Lee, J., Kwon, H., & Hur, J. (2022). Get off of chain: Unveiling dark web using multilayer bitcoin address clustering. *IEEE Access : Practical Innovations, Open Solutions*, *10*, 70078–70091. DOI: 10.1109/ACCESS.2022.3187210

Kingma, D. P., & Ba, J. (2015). Adam: A method for stochastic optimization. In *Proceedings of the 3rd International Conference on Learning Representations (ICLR).* https://arxiv.org/abs/1412.6980

Kipf, T. N., & Welling, M. (2017). Semi-supervised classification with graph convolutional networks. Proceedings of the 5th International Conference on Learning Representations (ICLR). https://openreview.net/forum?id=SJU4ayYgl

Kirkpatrick, S., Gelatt, C. D.Jr, & Vecchi, M. P. (1983). Optimization by simulated annealing. *Science*, *220*(4598), 671–680. DOI: 10.1126/science.220.4598.671 PMID: 17813860

Kotzias, P., Bilge, L., & Caballero, J. (2016). Measuring PUP prevalence and PUP distribution through pay-per-install services. Proceedings of the 25th USENIX Security Symposium, 739–756. https://www.usenix.org/conference/usenixsecurity16/technical-sessions/presentation/kotzias

Kravchenko, A. A., & Permyakov, R. A. (2025). Internet of things (IoT): Security threats in automated systems. *Digital Technology Security*, *5*(2), 12–20. DOI: 10.17212/2782-2230-2025-2-52-75

Krishnaveni, S., Sivamohan, S., Jothi, B., Chen, T. M., & Sathiyanarayanan, M. (2024). TwinSec-IDS: An enhanced intrusion detection system in SDN-digital-twin-based industrial cyber-physical systems. *Concurrency and Computation*, *36*(12), e8120. DOI: 10.1002/cpe.8120

Krotov, V., & Silva, L. (2020). Legality and ethics of web scraping. *Communications of the Association for Information Systems*, *47*, 539–563. DOI: 10.17705/1CAIS.04724

Kruger, H. A., & Kearney, W. D. (2006). A prototype for assessing information security awareness. *Computers & Security*, *25*(4), 289–296. DOI: 10.1016/j.cose.2006.02.008

Kshetri, N. (2019). Cybersecurity and development: The role of cybersecurity in supporting sustainable development goals. *Telecommunications Policy*, *43*(10), 101825. DOI: 10.1016/j.telpol.2019.101825

Kukkadapu, G. (2025). AI-driven security architecture in smart cities: Balancing safety and privacy. *European Journal of Computer Science and Information Technology*, *7*(2), 45–56. DOI: 10.37745/ejcsit.2013/vol13n478694

Kumar, G., Shelke, N. M., Pimpalkar, A., & Saini, D. K. J., N., P., & Kumar, Y. D. (2025). Zero trust-enabled digital twins for real-time anomaly detection in industrial cyber physical systems. In *Proceedings of the 3rd International Conference on Networking, Multimedia & Information Technology (NMITCON).* DOI: 10.1109/NMITCON65824.2025.11188236

Kumar, N. M., & Mallick, P. K. (2018). Blockchain technology for security issues and challenges in IoT. *Procedia Computer Science*, *132*, 1815–1823. DOI: 10.1016/j.procs.2018.05.140

Kumar, R., & Iyer, S. (2024). AI-powered cybersecurity framework for safeguarding biometric systems from deepfake attacks. *International Journal of Intelligent Systems and Applications in Engineering*, *12*(5), 334–349.

Kushwaha, S. S., Joshi, S., Singh, D., Kaur, M., & Lee, H. (2022). Ethereum smart contract analysis tools: A systematic review. *IEEE Access : Practical Innovations, Open Solutions*, *10*, 57037–57062. DOI: 10.1109/ACCESS.2022.3169902

Kuzuno, H., & Karam, C. (2017). Blockchain explorer: An analytical process and investigation environment for bitcoin. In *2017 APWG Symposium on Electronic Crime Research, eCrime 2017, Phoenix, AZ, USA, April 25-27, 2017*, pages 9–16. IEEE.

Labs, T. R. M. (2025). Europol and German authorities lead global takedown of darknet child exploitation platform Kidflix. TRM Blog. https://www.trmlabs.com/resources/blog/europol-and-german-authorities-lead-global-takedown-of-darknet-child-exploitation-platform-kidflix

Lakhal, H., Zegrari, M., & Bahnasse, A. (2025). Next-generation smart grid cybersecurity: A systematic review of OT cyber threats, AI-driven defense, cyber deception techniques, and emerging security strategies. *IEEE Access : Practical Innovations, Open Solutions*, *13*, 181519–181552. DOI: 10.1109/ACCESS.2025.3623834

Lakhani, R. (2023). Cybersecurity threats in internet of things (IoT) networks: Vulnerabilities and defense mechanisms. *International Journal of Engineering and Computer Science*, *12*(11), 25965–25981. DOI: 10.18535/ijecs/v12i11.4779

LastPass. (2024). *Attempted audio deepfake call targets LastPass employee.* https://blog.lastpass.com/posts/attempted-audio-deepfake-call-targets-lastpass-employee

Lawelai, H., Purnomo, E. P., Nurmandi, A., Jovita, H. D., & Baulete, E. (2025). Cybersecurity policy on smart city infrastructure: A mapping of new threats and protections. *Journal of Science and Technology Policy Management*, *16*(3), 233–245. DOI: 10.1108/JSTPM-09-2024-0359

Lee, H.-E., Ermakova, T., Ververis, V., & Fabian, B. (2020). Detecting child sexual abuse material: A comprehensive survey. *Forensic Science International Digital Investigation*, *34*, 301022. DOI: 10.1016/j.fsidi.2020.301022

Lelarge, M., & Bolot, J. (2008). Network externalities and the deployment of security features and protocols in the Internet. *Performance Evaluation Review*, *36*(1), 37–48. DOI: 10.1145/1384529.1375463

Lemaître, G., Nogueira, F., & Aridas, C. K. (2017). Imbalanced-learn: A Python toolbox to tackle the curse of imbalanced datasets in machine learning. *Journal of Machine Learning Research*, *18*(17), 1–5.

Lewinsky, D., Te'eni, D., Yahav-Shenberger, I. G., Schwartz, D., Silverman, G., & Mann, Y. (2024). Detecting terrorist influencers using reciprocal human-machine learning: The case of militant Jihadist Da'wa on the Darknet. *Humanities & Social Sciences Communications*, *11*(1), 1–11. DOI: 10.1057/s41599-024-03920-7

Li, F. (2025). Information security risk assessment in the digital economy and its impact on sustainable development. *Sustainability*, *17*(14), 6428. DOI: 10.3390/su17146428

Li, K., Li, C., Yuan, X., Li, S., Zou, S., Sohail Ahmed, S., Ni, W., Niyato, D., Jamalipour, A., Dressler, F., & Akan, Ö. B. (2025). Zero-trust foundation models: A new paradigm for secure and collaborative artificial intelligence for internet of things. *IEEE Internet of Things Journal*, *12*(5), 3890–3905. DOI: 10.1109/JIOT.2025.3603957

Li, M., Shen, Y., Ye, G., He, J., Zheng, X., Zhang, Z., Zhu, L., & Conti, M. (2024). Anonymous, secure, traceable, and efficient decentralized digital forensics. *IEEE Transactions on Knowledge and Data Engineering*, *36*(5), 1874–1888. DOI: 10.1109/TKDE.2023.3321712

Lin, X., Xiong, G., Gou, G., Li, Z., Shi, J., & Yu, J. (2022). ET-BERT: A contextualized datagram representation with pre-training transformers for encrypted traffic classification. In *Proceedings of the ACM Web Conference (WWW)* (pp. 633–642). DOI: 10.1145/3485447.3512217

Lin, Z., Cui, J., Liao, X., & Wang, X. (2024). Malla: Demystifying real-world large language model integrated malicious services. In *USENIX Security Symposium 33*.

Liu, Y., Ott, M., Goyal, N., ... (2019). RoBERTa: A robustly optimized BERT pretraining approach. *arXiv preprint arXiv:1907.11692*. https://arxiv.org/abs/1907.11692

Liu, F. T., Ting, K. M., & Zhou, Z.-H. (2008). Isolation forest. *Proceedings of the 2008 Eighth IEEE International Conference on Data Mining (ICDM)*, 413–422. DOI: 10.1109/ICDM.2008.17

Liu, L., Zhang, H., Shi, J., Yu, X., & Xu, H. (2019, October). I2P anonymous communication network measurement and analysis. In *International Conference on Smart Computing and Communication* (pp. 105–115). Springer. DOI: 10.1007/978-3-030-34139-8_11

Liu, X. F., Jiang, X., Liu, S., & Tse, C. K. (2021). Knowledge discovery in cryptocurrency transactions: A survey. *IEEE Access : Practical Innovations, Open Solutions*, *9*, 37229–37254. DOI: 10.1109/ACCESS.2021.3062652

Li, Y., & Liu, Q. (2021). A comprehensive review study of cyber-attacks and cybersecurity trends. *International Journal of Intelligent Systems and Applications in Engineering*, *9*(2), 122–131.

Li, Y., & Wang, Z. (2024). Blockchain-based CNN verification model for secure biometric authentication. *Journal of Big Data*, *11*(1), 1–19.

Lone, A. H., & Mir, R. N. (2019). Forensic-chain: Blockchain based digital forensics chain of custody with poc in hyperledger composer. *Digital Investigation, 28*(Supplement), 44–55. DOI: 10.1016/j.diin.2019.01.002

Lu, D., Fei, J., & Liu, L. (2023). A semantic learning-based SQL injection attack detection technology. *Electronics (Basel), 12*(6), 1344. DOI: 10.3390/electronics12061344

Lundberg, S. M., & Lee, S.-I. (2017). A unified approach to interpreting model predictions. Advances in Neural Information Processing Systems, 30. https://proceedings.neurips.cc/paper/2017/hash/8a20a8621978632d76c43dfd28b67767-Abstract.html

Lundberg, S. M., & Lee, S.-I. (2017). A unified approach to interpreting model predictions. In Vol. 30, pp. 4765–4774). Advances in Neural Information Processing Systems. Curran Associates.

Maalavika, S., Thangavel, G., & Basheer, S. (2023, October). A review on garlic routing and artificial intelligence applications in public network. In *2023 International Conference on Computer Science and Emerging Technologies (CSET)* (pp. 1–6). IEEE.

Macdonald, S., Correia, S. G., & Watkin, A.-L. (2019). Regulating terrorist content on social media: Automation and the rule of law. International Journal of Law in Context, 15(Special Issue 2), 183–197. DOI: 10.1017/S1744552319000119

Macdonald, S., & Whittaker, J. (2019). Online radicalization: Contested terms and conceptual clarity. In Vacca, J. R. (Ed.), *Online terrorist propaganda, recruitment, and radicalization* (pp. 33–46). CRC Press. DOI: 10.1201/9781315170251-2

Magramo, K. (2024). Finance worker pays out $25 million after video call with deepfake "chief financial officer". *CNN Business.* https://www.cnn.com/2024/05/16/tech/arup-deepfake-scam-loss-hong-kong-intl-hnk

Maimon, D., & Louderback, E. R. (2019). Cyber-dependent crimes: An interdisciplinary review. *Annual Review of Criminology, 2*(1), 191–216. DOI: 10.1146/annurev-criminol-032317-092057

Maire, J. (2024). *Zero-knowledge arguments from secure multiparty computation* (Doctoral dissertation, Sorbonne Université).

Maiwada, U., Imran, S. A., Danyaro, K. U., Janisar, A., Salameh, A. A., & Sarlan, A. (2024). Security concerns of IoT against DDoS in 5G systems. *International Journal of Electrical Engineering and Computer Science, 6*(11), 232–240. DOI: 10.37394/232027.2024.6.11

Malatji, M. (2024). A strategic overview of 5G/6G networks: Implications for 6G security. In *Proceedings of the International Conference on Engineering and Emerging Technologies (ICEET).* DOI: 10.1109/ICEET65156.2024.10913531

Manakhari, S. S., Jadhav, A. P., Paraye, T., and Gate, A. (2024). Improving data accessibility with distributed file system: A blockchain ethereum approach. *European Journal of Computer Science and Information Technology.*

Ma, R., Cao, J., He, S., Zhang, Y., Niu, B., & Li, H. (2024). A UAV-assisted UE access authentication scheme for 5G/6G network. *IEEE Transactions on Network and Service Management, 21*(2), 1430–1445. DOI: 10.1109/TNSM.2023.3341829

Marhoon, H. M., Basil, N., & Ma'arif, A. (2023). Exploring blockchain data analysis and its communications architecture: achievements, challenges, and future directions: a review article. *International Journal of Robotics and Control Systems, 3*(3), 609–626. DOI: 10.31763/ijrcs.v3i3.1100

Matencio-Escolar, A., Bernabé, J. B., Alcaraz, J. M., Wang, Q., & Gómez-Skarmeta, A. (2024). Network slicing as 6G security mechanism to mitigate cyber-attacks: The RIGOUROUS approach. In *Proceedings of the IEEE Conference on Network Softwarization (NetSoft)*. DOI: 10.1109/NetSoft60951.2024.10588939

McMahan, B., Moore, E., Ramage, D., Hampson, S., & Arcas, B. A. (2017). Communication-efficient learning of deep networks from decentralized data. Proceedings of the 20th International Conference on Artificial Intelligence and Statistics (AISTATS), PMLR 54, 1273–1282. https://proceedings.mlr.press/v54/mcmahan17a.html

McMahan, B., Moore, E., Ramage, D., Hampson, S., & Arcas, B. A. (2017). Communication-efficient learning of deep networks from decentralized data. In *Proceedings of the 20th International Conference on Artificial Intelligence and Statistics (AISTATS)* (pp. 1273–1282). PMLR.

McNulty, L., & Vassilakis, V. (2022). IoT botnets: Characteristics, exploits, attack capabilities, and targets. In *Proceedings of the International Symposium on Communication Systems, Networks & Digital Signal Processing (CSNDSP)*. DOI: 10.1109/CSNDSP54353.2022.9908039

Meiklejohn, S., Pomarole, M., Jordan, G., Levchenko, K., McCoy, D., Voelker, G. M., & Savage, S. (2016). A fistful of bitcoins: Characterizing payments among men with no names. *Communications of the ACM, 59*(4), 86–93. DOI: 10.1145/2896384

Meneghello, F., Calore, M., Zucchetto, D., Polese, M., & Zanella, A. (2019). IoT: Internet of threats? A survey of practical security vulnerabilities in real IoT devices. *IEEE Internet of Things Journal, 6*(5), 8182–8201. DOI: 10.1109/JIOT.2019.2935189

Merlec, M. M., & In, H. P. (2024). Blockchain-based decentralized storage systems for sustainable data self-sovereignty: A comparative study. *Sustainability (Basel), 16*(17), 7671. DOI: 10.3390/su16177671

Meurs, T., ... (2025). *An empirical study of the six stages of ransomware negotiation* (Tinbergen Institute Discussion Paper No. 25-052). Tinbergen Institute.

Microsoft. (2025a). *Microsoft digital defense report 2025*. https://www.microsoft.com/en-us/security/security-insider/threat-landscape/microsoft-digital-defense-report-2025

Microsoft. (2025b). *Security Copilot for SOC: Bringing agentic AI to every defender*. https://techcommunity.microsoft.com/blog/microsoftthreatprotectionblog/security-copilot-for-soc-bringing-agentic-ai-to-every-defender/4470187

Mireille, H., & Rueda Blanco, J. (2022). SoK: Cross-border criminal investigations and digital evidence. *Journal of Cybersecurity, 8*(1), tyac014. Advance online publication. DOI: 10.1093/cybsec/tyac014

Mirjalili, S. (2016). Sine cosine algorithm. *Knowledge-Based Systems, 96*, 120–133. DOI: 10.1016/j.knosys.2015.12.022

Mirjalili, S., Mirjalili, S. M., & Lewis, A. (2014). Grey wolf optimizer. *Advances in Engineering Software, 69*, 46–61. DOI: 10.1016/j.advengsoft.2013.12.007

Mirji, B. H., & S., S. (2026). Cyber security threats in the internet of things (IoT) ecosystem: A review. International Journal of Advanced Research in Science. *Tongxin Jishu, 6*(3), 1–10.

Mirsky, Y., & Lee, W. (2021). The creation and detection of deepfakes: A survey. *ACM Computing Surveys, 54*(1), 7. Advance online publication. DOI: 10.1145/3425780

Mo¨ser, M., Bo¨hme, R., & Breuker, D. (2013). An inquiry into money laundering tools in the bitcoin ecosystem. In *2013 APWG eCrime Researchers Summit, eCrime 2013, San Francisco, CA, USA, September 17-18, 2013*, pages 1–14. IEEE. DOI: 10.1109/eCRS.2013.6805780

Mo¨ser, M., Soska, K., Heilman, E., Lee, K., Heffan, H., Srivastava, S., Hogan, K., Hennessey, J., Miller, A., Narayanan, A., & Christin, N. (2018). An empirical analysis of traceability in the monero blockchain. *Proceedings on Privacy Enhancing Technologies. Privacy Enhancing Technologies Symposium, 2018*(3), 143–163. DOI: 10.1515/popets-2018-0025

Modi, D., Bhatt, B., Gambhava, B., & Baxi, J. (2026). *Behavioral Biometrics: A Comparison of Keystroke Dynamics and Mouse Trajectories for Bot Detection.*, DOI: 10.1007/978-3-032-16038-6_17

Mohan, J. P., Sugunaraj, N., & Ranganathan, P. (2022). Cyber security threats for 5G networks. In *Proceedings of the IEEE International Conference on Electro/Information Technology*. DOI: 10.1109/EIT53891.2022.9813982

Moore, D., & Rid, T. (2016). Cryptopolitik and the darknet. *Survival, 58*(1), 7–38. DOI: 10.1080/00396338.2016.1142085

Motoyama, M., McCoy, D., Levchenko, K., Savage, S., & Voelker, G. M. (2011). An analysis of underground forums. In *Proceedings of the 2011 ACM SIGCOMM Internet Measurement Conference* (pp. 71–80). DOI: 10.1145/2068816.2068824

Moustafa, N., & Slay, J. (2016). The evaluation of network anomaly detection systems: Statistical analysis of the UNSW-NB15 dataset and comparison with the KDD99 dataset. *Information Security Journal. Global Perspectives, 25*(1–3), 18–31. DOI: 10.1080/19393555.2015.1125974

Muntaka, S. A., & Bou Abdo, J. (2026). *Fifty shades of darknet.*

Muntaka, S. A., & Bou Abdo, J. (2025). Resilience of the invisible internet project: A computational analysis. *Internet Technology Letters, 8*(5), e70119. DOI: 10.1002/itl2.70119

Murty, C. A., Rana, H., Verma, R., Pathak, R., & Rughani, P. H. (2022). Building an AI/ML-based classification framework for dark web text data. In *Proceedings of International Conference on Computing and Communication Networks: ICCCN 2021* (pp. 93–111). Springer Nature. DOI: 10.1007/978-981-19-0604-6_9

Nagabhooshanam, N., & Murthy, C. R. (2023). Neural network based single index evaluation for SQL injection attack detection in health care data. *Measurement. Sensors, 27*, 100779. DOI: 10.1016/j.measen.2023.100779

Nalini, M. (2024). Securing smart cities: A cybersecurity perspective on integrating IoT, AI, and machine learning for digital twin creation. *Journal of Electrical Systems, 20*(4), 3548–3560. DOI: 10.52783/jes.2049

Narsing, A., & Srinivasan, S. (2025). Create AI-powered anomaly detection to stop intrusions in SCADA and critical infrastructure networks: Industrial IoT through cybersecurity. In *Proceedings of the International Conference on Future Technologies (ICFT)*. DOI: 10.1109/ICFT66708.2025.11336547

Nasr, M., Bahramali, A., & Houmansadr, A. (2018, October). DeepCorr: Strong flow correlation attacks on Tor using deep learning. In *Proceedings of the 2018 ACM SIGSAC Conference on Computer and Communications Security* (pp. 1962–1976). DOI: 10.1145/3243734.3243824

National Cyber Security Centre. (2023). *Ransomware, extortion and the cyber crime ecosystem* (White paper).

National Institute of Standards and Technology. (2024a). *FIPS 203: Module-lattice-based key-encapsulation mechanism standard*. https://csrc.nist.gov/pubs/fips/203/final

National Institute of Standards and Technology. (2024b). *FIPS 204: Module-lattice-based digital signature standard*. https://csrc.nist.gov/pubs/fips/204/final

Nazah, S., Huda, S., Abawajy, J., & Hassan, M. M. (2020). Dark web threat analysis. *IEEE Access : Practical Innovations, Open Solutions, 8*, 171796–171819. DOI: 10.1109/ACCESS.2020.3024198

Naz, R., Howlader, J., & Ahmad, S. (2026). A secure expert system framework for private function evaluation using functional encryption and multi-party computation. *Computers & Electrical Engineering, 131*, 110930. DOI: 10.1016/j.compeleceng.2025.110930

Negi, N. (2017). Comparison of anonymous communication networks—Tor, I2P, Freenet. *International Research Journal of Engineering and Technology, 4*(7).

Neha, & Bhatia, T. (2025). Adaptive intrusion detection system leveraging dynamic neural models with adversarial learning for 5G/6G networks. In Proceedings of the 4th International Conference on Computing Technologies (ICCTech). DOI: 10.1109/ICCTech63508.2025.10947861

Nguyen, D. C., Ding, M., Pathirana, P. N., Seneviratne, A., Li, J., Niyato, D., & Poor, H. V. (2021). Federated learning for Internet of Things: A comprehensive survey. *IEEE Communications Surveys and Tutorials, 23*(3), 1622–1658. DOI: 10.1109/COMST.2021.3075439

NIST. (2018). *Framework for improving critical infrastructure cybersecurity (Version 1.1)*. National Institute of Standards and Technology., DOI: 10.6028/NIST.CSWP.04162018

Noury, Z., & Rezaei, M. (2020). *Deep-CAPTCHA: a deep learning based CAPTCHA solver for vulnerability assessment.*

Ntayagabiri, J. P., Bentaleb, Y., Ndikumagenge, J., & El Makhtoum, H. (2025). A comprehensive approach to protocols and security in internet of things technology. *Journal of Computer Theories and Applications*, *2*(3), 324–341. DOI: 10.62411/jcta.11660

Nunes, E., Diab, A., Gunn, A., Marin, E., Mishra, V., Pacey, K., & Shakarian, P. (2018). Darknet and deepnet mining for proactive cybersecurity threat intelligence. *IEEE Intelligence and Security Informatics Conference*, 7–12. https://doi.org/DOI: 10.1109/ISI.2018.8587365

Nurse, J. R. C., Creese, S., & De Roure, D. (2017). Security risk assessment in Internet of Things systems. *IT Professional*, *19*(5), 20–26. DOI: 10.1109/MITP.2017.3680959

Obaidat, M. J., Al-Syouf, I. A., Awawdeh, Y. F., Masa'deh, A. E., & Abu Al-Haija, Q. (2025). Darknet threats and detection strategies: A concise overview. In *2025 16th International Conference on Information and Communication Systems (ICICS)* (pp. 1–6). DOI: 10.1109/ICICS65354.2025.11073091

Obaidat, M. J., Al-Syouf, I. A., Awawdeh, Y. F., & Masa'deh, A. E. (2025). SafeSurf Darknet 2025: A novel dataset for darknet traffic detection and analysis. *Preprints.org*. https://doi.org/DOI: 10.20944/preprints202507.1926

Okika, N., Nwatuzie, G. A., Olarinoye, H. S., Nwaka, A. A., Igba, E., & Dunee, R. (2025). Assessing the vulnerability of traditional and post-quantum cryptographic systems through penetration testing and strengthening cyber defenses with zero trust security in the era of quantum computing. *International Journal of Innovative Science and Research Technology*, *10*(2), 1240–1258.

Omar, K. O., Zraqou, J., & Gómez, J. M. (2025c). From synthetic text to real threats: Unraveling the security risks of generative AI. In *Examining cybersecurity risks produced by generative AI*. IGI Global., DOI: 10.4018/979-8-3373-0832-6.ch001

Omar, K., Zraqou, J., Alkhadour, W., & Gómez, J. M. (2025a). AI-driven transformation of cybersecurity insurance: The Cyber Risk Intelligence Platform (CRIP). In *Cybersecurity insurance frameworks and innovations in the AI era*. IGI Global., DOI: 10.4018/979-8-3373-1977-3.ch008

Omar, K., Zraqou, J., Alkhadour, W., & Gómez, J. M. (2025b). Evolving sentinels: How autonomous defense systems self-learn and adapt to dynamic threat environments. In *AI-driven security systems and intelligent threat response using autonomous cyber defense*. IGI Global., DOI: 10.4018/979-8-3373-0954-5.ch009

Onyagu, C., Obikwelu, O., Godspower, A., & John, J. (2024). Enhancing security in internet of things (IoT) architecture through defense-in-depth mechanism: A comprehensive study. *Newport International Journal of Engineering and Physical Sciences*, *4*(1), 110–120. DOI: 10.59298/NIJEP/2024/411722.1.1100

Oosthoek, K., Cable, J., & Smaragdakis, G. (2022). Investigating the ransomware payments economy. *Communications of the ACM*, *65*(7), 38–41. DOI: 10.1145/3524102

Open, A. I. (2024–2026). *Disrupting malicious uses of AI*. https://openai.com/index/disrupting-malicious-ai-uses/

OpenAI. (2025). *Disrupting malicious uses of AI: June 2025* (Threat Intelligence Report).

Osaba, E., Villar-Rodriguez, E., Del Ser, J., Nebro, A. J., Molina, D., LaTorre, A., Suganthan, P. N., Coello Coello, C. A., & Herrera, F. (2021). Metaheuristic design tutorial. *Swarm and Evolutionary Computation*, *64*, 100888. DOI: 10.1016/j.swevo.2021.100888

Otoom, S. (2025). Risk auditing for digital twins in cyber physical systems: A systematic review. *Journal of Cyber Security and Risk Auditing*, *2025*(1), 22–35. DOI: 10.63180/jcsra.thestap.2025.1.3

Owenson, G., Cortes, S., & Lewman, A. (2018). The darknet's smaller than we thought: The life cycle of Tor Hidden Services. *Digital Investigation*, *27*, 17–22. DOI: 10.1016/j.diin.2018.09.005

Pahuja, S., & Goel, N. (2024). Multimodal biometric authentication systems: A review. *Advances in Intelligent Systems and Computing*, 115–128.

Panchal, G., & Samanta, D. (2018). A novel approach to fingerprint biometric-based cryptographic key generation and its applications to storage security. *Computers & Electrical Engineering*, *69*, 461–478. DOI: 10.1016/j.compeleceng.2018.01.028

Panchenko, A., & Renner, J. (2009, July). Path selection metrics for performance-improved onion routing. In *2009 Ninth Annual International Symposium on Applications and the Internet* (pp. 114–120). IEEE. DOI: 10.1109/SAINT.2009.26

Panovyk, U. (2025). Information protection in automated systems based on a conceptual model with formalized efficiency evaluation. Cybersecurity: Education, Science. *Technology*, *3*(1), 55–66. DOI: 10.28925/2663-4023.2025.27.5566

Paquet-Clouston, M., Haslhofer, B., & Dupont, B. (2019). Ransomware payments in the bitcoin ecosystem. *Journal of Cybersecurity*, *5*(1), tyz003. DOI: 10.1093/cybsec/tyz003

Parihar, A., Kumar, A., & Kumar, A. (2024). Tracing transaction across bitcoin address behaviour for pattern analysis. In *2024 First International Conference on Technological Innovations and Advance Computing (TIACOMP)*, pages 244–249. IEEE. DOI: 10.1109/TIACOMP64125.2024.00049

Parisi, G. I., Kemker, R., Part, J. L., Kanan, C., & Wermter, S. (2019). Continual lifelong learning with neural networks: A review. *Neural Networks : The Official Journal of the International Neural Network Society*, *113*, 54–71. DOI: 10.1016/j.neunet.2019.01.012 PMID: 30780045

Parmar, P., Rangwala, H., & Parmar, P. (2026). Cyber physical security framework for smart cities using AI and quantum encryption. *Journal of Critical Infrastructure Policy*, *6*(1), 55–66. DOI: 10.1002/jci3.70020

Parsons, K., McCormac, A., Butavicius, M., Pattinson, M., & Jerram, C. (2014). Determining employee awareness using the human aspects of information security questionnaire (HAIS-Q). *Computers & Security*, *42*, 165–176. DOI: 10.1016/j.cose.2013.12.003

Pasdar, A., Lee, Y. C., and Dong, Z. (2023). Connect API with blockchain: A survey on blockchain oracle implementation. *ACM Comput. Surv.*, 55(10):208:1–208:39.

Pastor-Galindo, J., Gómez Mármol, F., & Martínez Pérez, G. (2023). On the gathering of Tor onion addresses. *Future Generation Computer Systems*, *145*, 12–26. DOI: 10.1016/j.future.2023.02.024

Pastor-Galindo, J., Nespoli, P., Mármol, F. G., & Pérez, G. M. (2020). The not yet exploited goldmine of OSINT: Opportunities, open challenges and future trends. *IEEE Access : Practical Innovations, Open Solutions*, *8*, 10282–10304. DOI: 10.1109/ACCESS.2020.2965257

Pastor-Galindo, J., Sandlin, H.-Â., Mármol, F. G., Bovet, G., & Pérez, G. M. (2024). A Big Data architecture for early identification and categorization of dark web sites. *Future Generation Computer Systems*, *157*, 67–81. DOI: 10.1016/j.future.2024.03.025

Pastrana, S., Thomas, D. R., Hutchings, A., Clayton, R., & Beresford, A. R. (2018). CrimeBB: Enabling cybercrime research on underground forums at scale. In *Proceedings of the 2018 World Wide Web Conference*. DOI: 10.1145/3178876.3186178

Patel, J. C., Kaashvi, R., & Sarasvathi, V. (2025, July). Hybrid Authentication Model using Adaptive Authentication and Post Quantum Cryptographic Biometric Encryption. In *2025 8th International Conference on Computing Methodologies and Communication (ICCMC)* (pp. 746-751). IEEE. DOI: 10.1109/ICCMC65190.2025.11139930

Paul, A., Sharma, V., & Olukoya, O. (2024). SQL injection attack: Detection, prioritization & prevention. Journal of Information Security and Applications, 85, 103871.

Paul, S., Mitra, A., Shambhavi, S., Ghosh, S., & Bandyopadhyay, A. (2025). Cybersecurity framework for deep web. *Procedia Computer Science*, *258*, 2405–2414. DOI: 10.1016/j.procs.2025.04.503

Pawlicki, M., Kozik, R., & Choraś, M. (2021). The role of cybersecurity in the sustainable development of smart cities. *Sustainable Cities and Society*, *67*, 102778. DOI: 10.1016/j.scs.2021.102778

Pedregosa, F., Varoquaux, G., Gramfort, A., Michel, V., Thirion, B., Grisel, O., Blondel, M., Prettenhofer, P., Weiss, R., Dubourg, V., Vanderplas, J., Passos, A., Cournapeau, D., Brucher, M., Perrot, M., & Duchesnay, É. (2011). Scikit-learn: Machine learning in Python. *Journal of Machine Learning Research*, *12*, 2825–2830.

Pei, G., Zhang, J., Hu, M., ... (2024). Deepfake generation and detection: A benchmark and survey. *arXiv preprint arXiv:2403.17881*

Pham, Q.-V., & Liyanage, M.. (2022). Intelligent crawling with reinforcement learning. *Information Sciences*, *605*, 258–273. DOI: 10.1016/j.ins.2022.05.035

Pincheira, M., Donini, E., Vecchio, M., & Kanhere, S. (2022). A Decentralized Architecture for Trusted Dataset Sharing Using Smart Contracts and Distributed Storage. *Sensors (Basel)*, *22*(23), 9118. DOI: 10.3390/s22239118 PMID: 36501820

Pocher, N. (2025). Obfuscation and traceability. In *Crypto-Asset Ecosystems and the EU Anti-Money Laundering Framework: Law and Technology Perspectives*, pages 95–134. Springer. DOI: 10.1007/978-3-031-94698-1_4

Powers, D. M. W. (2011). Evaluation: From precision, recall and F-measure to ROC, informedness, markedness and correlation. *Journal of Machine Learning Technologies*, *2*(1), 37–63.

Princewill, O. O., Eyo, E., & Ele, B. (2026). Federated learning based anomaly detection for privacy-preserving in IoT-enabled industrial control systems. *Journal of Statistical Sciences and Computational Intelligence*, *5*(2), 77–88. DOI: 10.64497/jssci.203

Qin, Q., Li, Y., Mi, Y., Shen, J., Wu, K., & Wang, Z. (2025). Sql injection detection algorithm based on Bi-LSTM and integrated feature selection. *The Journal of Supercomputing*, *81*(4), 1–32. DOI: 10.1007/s11227-025-07109-w

Qu, Z., Ling, X., Wang, T., Chen, X., Ji, S., & Wu, C. (2024). AdvSQLi: Generating Adversarial SQL Injections against Real-world WAF-as-a-service. *IEEE Transactions on Information Forensics and Security*, *19*, 2623–2638. DOI: 10.1109/TIFS.2024.3350911

Radanliev, P., De Roure, D., Nurse, J. R. C., Montalvo, R. M., Cannady, S., Santos, O., Maddox, L., & Burnap, P. (2020). Cyber risk at the edge: Current and future trends in IoT and edge computing security. *Future Internet*, *12*(3), 45. DOI: 10.3390/fi12030045

Radford, A., Narasimhan, K., Salimans, T., & Sutskever, I. (2018). Improving language understanding by generative pre-training. OpenAI Technical Report. https://cdn.openai.com/research-covers/language-unsupervised/language_understanding_paper.pdf

Rahman, A., Khan, M. S. I., Montieri, A., Islam, M. J., Karim, M. R., Hasan, M., Kundu, D., Nasir, M. K., & Pescapè, A. (2024). BlockSD-5GNet: Enhancing security of 5G network through blockchain-SDN with ML-based bandwidth prediction. *Transactions on Emerging Telecommunications Technologies*, *35*(4), e4950. DOI: 10.1002/ett.4965

Rahman, M. A., Hossain, M. S., & Muhammad, G. (2020). Blockchain-enabled cybersecurity for smart cities. *IEEE Internet of Things Journal*, *7*(8), 7467–7475. DOI: 10.1109/JIOT.2020.2975934

Rahmoune, I., Al-Ghaili, A. M., Ibrahim, Z., Ismail, S., & Rahim, F. A. (2025). Comparative study of machine learning and deep learning models for IoT botnet detection. In *Proceedings of the IEEE International Conference on Computing (ICOCO)*. DOI: 10.1109/ICOCO67189.2025.11334162

Rao, R. V., Savsani, V. J., & Vakharia, D. P. (2011). Teaching–learning-based optimization. *Computer Aided Design*, *43*(3), 303–315. DOI: 10.1016/j.cad.2010.12.015

Rasyid, A., Willim, A. P., & Khaeryyah, S. (2025). Cryptocurrency and the law: The challenges of regulating decentralized finance in global markets. *Impact: Multidisciplinary Journal*, *1*(01), 1–10.

Ribeiro, M. T., Singh, S., & Guestrin, C. (2016). "Why should I trust you?": Explaining the predictions of any classifier. Proceedings of the 22nd ACM SIGKDD International Conference on Knowledge Discovery and Data Mining (KDD), 1135–1144. DOI: 10.1145/2939672.2939778

Ricaldi, R., Schafer, M., Zech, P., Allodi, L., Groner, R., & Pekaric, I. (2026). *Topical Shifts in the Dark Web: A Longitudinal Analysis of Content from the Cybercrime Ecosystem.*

Ricaldi, R., Marjanov, T., Allodi, L., & Hutchings, A. (2025, November). Uncovering the Trust Signals Supporting Telegram's Cybercrime Economy. In *2025 APWG Symposium on Electronic Crime Research (eCrime)* (pp. 1-17). IEEE. DOI: 10.1109/eCrime66972.2025.11327769

Rid, T., & Buchanan, B. (2015). Attributing cyber attacks. *The Journal of Strategic Studies*, *38*(1–2), 4–37. DOI: 10.1080/01402390.2014.977382

Rodriguez Barredo-Valenzuela, A., Pastrana, S., & Suarez-Tangil, G. (2025). Snorkeling in Dark Waters: A Longitudinal Surface Exploration of Unique Tor Hidden Services. *IEEE Transactions on Information Forensics and Security*, *20*, 5386–5395. DOI: 10.1109/TIFS.2025.3573662

Rodriguez Barredo-Valenzuela, A., Pastrana, S., & Suarez-Tangil, G. (2025). Snorkeling in dark waters: A longitudinal surface exploration of unique Tor hidden services. IEEE Transactions on Information Forensics and Security, 20, 5386–5395. Extended version available as arXiv:2504.16836.

Rodriguez, M., & Singh, H. (2024). Passwordless authentication using biometrics, cryptography, and steganography. *Cryptography*, *4*(2), 14–28.

Rogers, R. (2020). Deplatforming: Following extreme Internet celebrities to Telegram and alternative social media. *European Journal of Communication*, *35*(3), 213–229. DOI: 10.1177/0267323120922066

Roman, R., López, J., & Mambo, M. (2018). Mobile edge computing, fog computing and IoT: A survey and analysis of security threats and challenges. *Future Generation Computer Systems*, *78*, 680–698. DOI: 10.1016/j.future.2016.11.009

Roy, S., Ellis, C., Shiva, S., Dasgupta, D., Shandilya, V., & Wu, Q. (2010). A survey of game theory as applied to network security. In *Proceedings of the 43rd Hawaii International Conference on System Sciences* (pp. 1–10). https://doi.org/DOI: 10.1109/HICSS.2010.35

Ruiz Ródenas, J. M., Pastor-Galindo, J., & Gómez Mármol, F. (2024). A general and modular framework for dark web analysis. *Cluster Computing*, *27*(4), 4687–4703. DOI: 10.1007/s10586-023-04189-2

Rupanetti, D., & Kaabouch, N. (2024). Combining edge computing-assisted internet of things security with artificial intelligence: Applications, challenges, and opportunities. *Applied Sciences (Basel, Switzerland)*, *14*(16), 7104. DOI: 10.3390/app14167104

Rustamova, N., & Dutta, S. (2025). Securing the Future: A Comprehensive Review of Post-Quantum Cryptography in the Modern Threat Landscape. *Qubahan Techno Journal*, *4*(2), 30–42. DOI: 10.48161/qtj.v4n2a58

Rust-Nguyen, N., Sharma, S., & Stamp, M. (2023). Darknet traffic classification and adversarial attacks using machine learning. *Computers & Security*, *127*, 103098. DOI: 10.1016/j.cose.2023.103098

Ryder, N. (2012). *Money laundering: An endless cycle? A comparative analysis of the anti-money laundering policies in the United States of America*. Routledge. DOI: 10.4324/9780203126783

Sabillon, R., Cano, J., Cavaller, V., & Serra, J. (2017). Cybercrime and cyberwar: What everyone needs to know. *International Journal of Information Security Science*, *6*(2), 45–56.

Sahu, S. K., & Mazumdar, K. (2024). Exploring security threats and solutions techniques for internet of things (IoT): From vulnerabilities to vigilance. *Frontiers in Artificial Intelligence*, *7*, 1397480. Advance online publication. DOI: 10.3389/frai.2024.1397480 PMID: 38845684

Saleem, J., Islam, R., & Islam, M. Z. (2024). Darknet traffic analysis: A systematic literature review. *IEEE Access : Practical Innovations, Open Solutions*, *12*, 42423–42452. DOI: 10.1109/ACCESS.2024.3373769

Saleem, J., Islam, R., & Kabir, M. A. (2022). The anonymity of the dark web: A survey. *IEEE Access : Practical Innovations, Open Solutions*, *10*, 33628–33660. DOI: 10.1109/ACCESS.2022.3161547

Salturk, S., & Kahraman, N. (2024). A deep learning-based multimodal biometric authentication system for secure online applications. *Neural Computing & Applications*, *36*(12), 8451–8468.

Samtani, S., Chinn, R., Chen, H., & Nunamaker, J. F.Jr. (2017). Cyber threat intelligence. *Journal of Management Information Systems*, *34*(4), 1023–1053. DOI: 10.1080/07421222.2017.1394049

Santos, P., Abreu, R., Reis, M. J. C. S., Serôdio, C., & Branco, F. (2025). A Systematic Review of Cyber Threat Intelligence: The Effectiveness of Technologies, Strategies, and Collaborations in Combating Modern Threats. *Sensors (Basel)*, *25*(14), 4272. DOI: 10.3390/s25144272 PMID: 40732398

Sarabi, A., Huang, Z., Wang, C., Karir, T., & Liu, M. (2025). The Ransomware Decade: The Creation of a {Fine-Grained} Dataset and a Longitudinal Study. In *34th USENIX Security Symposium (USENIX Security 25)* (pp. 4799-4818).

Sarker, I. H., Khan, A. I., Abushark, Y. B., & Alsolami, F. (2022). Internet of things (IoT) security intelligence: A comprehensive overview, machine learning solutions and research directions. *Mobile Networks and Applications*, *28*(1), 296–312. DOI: 10.1007/s11036-022-01937-3

Sarker, S. P. K., & Khan, R. (2024). Cybersecurity considerations for smart Bangladesh: Challenges and solutions. *Asian Journal of Research in Computer Science*, *12*(3), 33–45. DOI: 10.9734/ajrcos/2024/v17i6464

Sayyed, H., & Paul, S. R. (2025). Exploring the role of encryption and the dark web in cyber terrorism: Legal challenges and countermeasures in India. *Cogent Social Sciences*, *11*(1), 2479654. DOI: 10.1080/23311886.2025.2479654

Scalise, P., Boeding, M., Hempel, M., Sharif, H., Delloiacovo, J., & Reed, J. (2024). A systematic survey on 5G and 6G security considerations, challenges, trends, and research areas. *Future Internet*, *16*(3), 67. DOI: 10.3390/fi16030067

Scarfone, K., & Mell, P. (2007). *Guide to intrusion detection and prevention systems (IDPS)* (NIST Special Publication 800-94). National Institute of Standards and Technology.

Schaal, M., & Spagnuolo, M. (2023). Dark web ecosystem. *ACM Computing Surveys*, *55*(13s), 1–38. DOI: 10.1145/3579821

Schäfer, M., Fuchs, M., & Strufe, T. (2019). Dark web survey. *IEEE Access : Practical Innovations, Open Solutions*, *7*, 173070–173080. DOI: 10.1109/ACCESS.2019.2955979

Schlegel, L., Wiegold, L., Winkler, C., & Junk, J. (2025). Exploring the digital extremist ecosystem: A preliminary analysis of hateful posts on Mod DB. *Frontiers in Psychology*, *15*, 1502098. DOI: 10.3389/fpsyg.2024.1502098 PMID: 40013258

Security, I. B. M. (2024). *Cost of a data breach report 2024*. IBM. https://www.ibm.com/reports/data-breach

Şen, E., & Dash, E. A. (2023). Unveiling the shadows: Exploring the security challenges of the internet of things (IoT). *International Journal of Scientific Research and Engineering Management*, *8*(3), 45–56. DOI: 10.55041/IJSREM23970

Sengupta, S., & Bose, A. (2025). Securing the Quantum Era: A Comprehensive Review of Post-Quantum Cryptography, Threat Models, Algorithmic Foundations, and Standardization Pathways. *Qubahan Techno Journal*, *4*(3), 1–10.

Shackelford, S. J. (2016). Toward cyberpeace: Managing cyberattacks through polycentric governance. *The American University Law Review*, *62*(5), 1273–1344.

Shaikh, M., Wiil, U. K., Ebrahimi, A., & Memon, Y. (2026). An overview and comparison of blockchain consensus mechanisms. *Int. J. Networked Distributed Comput.*, *14*(1), 4. DOI: 10.1007/s44227-025-00087-8

Shakarian, P., Gunn, A., & Shakarian, J. (2017). Malicious hacker forums. In *Cyber Deception* (pp. 259–282). Springer., DOI: 10.1007/978-3-319-44270-0_11

Shameli-Sendi, A., Aghababaei-Barzegar, R., & Cheriet, M. (2016). Taxonomy of information security risk assessment methods. *Computers & Security*, *57*, 14–30. DOI: 10.1016/j.cose.2015.11.001

Shami, A. Z. A., Asghar, U., & Haider, A. (2025). The Role of International Law in Regulating Cybersecurity: A Critical Analysis of Existing Frameworks and Future Directions. *Liberal Journal of Language & Literature Review*, *3*(3), 224–242.

Sharma, R., & Verma, P. (2024). Blockchain-based multimodal biometric authentication using decentralized fuzzy vault scheme. *Journal of Information Security and Applications*, *78*, 103512. DOI: 10.1016/j.jisa.2024.103740

Sharma, S. B., & Bairwa, A. K. (2025). Leveraging AI for intrusion detection in IoT ecosystems: A comprehensive study. *IEEE Access : Practical Innovations, Open Solutions*, *13*, 36419–36438. DOI: 10.1109/ACCESS.2025.3550392

Shivarudraiah, A. (2023). Quantum Computing's Impact on Banking Encryption: Preparing for Post-Quantum Security. *International Journal of AI, BigData. Computational and Management Studies*, *4*(3), 40–49.

Sicari, S., Rizzardi, A., Grieco, L. A., & Coen-Porisini, A. (2015). Security, privacy and trust in Internet of Things: The road ahead. *Computer Networks*, *76*, 146–164. DOI: 10.1016/j.comnet.2014.11.008

Sindiramutty, S. R., Tan, C. E., Lau, S. P., Thangaveloo, R., Gharib, A. H., Manchuri, A. R., Bhardwaj, K., & Almaiah, M. A. (2024). Explainable AI for cybersecurity. In Ghonge, M., Pradeep, N., Jhanjhi, N., & Kulkarni, P. (Eds.), *Advances in explainable AI applications for smart cities* (pp. 31–97). IGI Global., DOI: 10.4018/978-1-6684-6361-1.ch002

Singh, I., Narayan, Y., Hazara, K., & Dubey, P. Yashita, Sharma, D., & Kumar, S. (2025). *Design and Implementation of a Secure Dark Web Crawler* (pp. 639–651). DOI: 10.1007/978-981-96-7131-1_45

Sohail, M.. (2025). Real-time detection of IoT botnet attacks on wireless routers using an open-source SIEM framework. In *Proceedings of the International Conference on Engineering & Computing Technologies (ICECT)*. DOI: 10.1109/ICECT66235.2025.11381696

Sommer, R., & Paxson, V. (2010). Outside the closed world: On using machine learning for network intrusion detection. In *2010 IEEE Symposium on Security and Privacy* (pp. 305–316). IEEE. https://doi.org/DOI: 10.1109/SP.2010.25

Song, Z., Long, L., Song, J., & Jiang, R. (2026). A Zero-Knowledge Proof-Driven Architecture for Privacy-Preserving Data Trading on Blockchain. *ACM Transactions on Internet Technology*, *26*(3), 1–34. DOI: 10.1145/3805044

Soska, K., & Christin, N. (2015). Measuring the longitudinal evolution of the online anonymous marketplace ecosystem. In Jung, J. and Holz, T., editors, *24th USENIX Security Symposium, USENIX Security 15, Washington, D.C., USA, August 12-14, 2015*, pages 33–48. USENIX Association.

Soska, K., & Christin, N. (2015). Measuring the longitudinal evolution of the online anonymous marketplace ecosystem. Proceedings of the 24th USENIX Security Symposium, 33–48. https://www.usenix.org/conference/usenixsecurity15/technical-sessions/presentation/soska

Soska, K., & Christin, N. (2015). Measuring the longitudinal evolution of the online anonymous marketplace ecosystem. In *Proceedings of the 24th USENIX Security Symposium* (pp. 33–48).

Spyros, A., Koritsas, I., Papoutsis, A., Panagiotou, P., Chatzakou, D., Kavallieros, D., Tsikrika, T., Vrochidis, S., & Kompatsiaris, I. (2025). AI-based cyber threat intelligence framework. *IEEE Access : Practical Innovations, Open Solutions*, *13*, 20820–20846. DOI: 10.1109/ACCESS.2025.3533084

Stockhammer, N. (2025). *From TikTok to terrorism? The online radicalization of European lone attackers since October 7, 2023. CTC Sentinel, 18(7).* Combating Terrorism Center at West Point.

Sulich, A. (2025). Cybersecurity and sustainable development: Bibliometric analysis and future research directions. *Sustainability*, *17*(3), 1085. DOI: 10.3390/su17031085

Sun, H., Du, Y., & Li, Q. (2023). Deep learning-based detection technology for SQL injection research and implementation. *Applied Sciences (Basel, Switzerland)*, *13*(16), 9466. DOI: 10.3390/app13169466

Supe, A. (2025). *A Survey of Ethical and Legal Challenges in Dark-Web Research: Balancing Privacy.* Security, and Responsibility.

Suriya, P., Balamurugan, G., & Shabin, O. S. (2026, March). A Comprehensive Review on Cyber Investigation and Detection across Ontology-Driven Dark Web and Email Phishing. In *International Conference on Artificial Intelligence and Secure Data Analytics (ICAISDA 2025)* (pp. 1514-1530). Atlantis Press. DOI: 10.2991/978-94-6239-616-6_109

Suryotrisongko, H., Musashi, Y., Tsuneda, A., & Sugitani, K. (2022). Robust botnet DGA detection: Blending XAI and OSINT for cyber threat intelligence sharing. *IEEE Access : Practical Innovations, Open Solutions*, *10*, 34613–34624. DOI: 10.1109/ACCESS.2022.3162588

Su, V. H., Gupta, S. S., & Khan, A. (2022). Automating ETL and mining of ethereum blockchain network. In *WSDM '22: The Fifteenth ACM Interna-tional Conference on Web Search and Data Mining, Virtual Event* / Tempe, AZ, USA, February 21 - 25, 2022, pages 1581–1584. ACM. DOI: 10.1145/3488560.3502187

Swan, K. (2016). Onion routing and Tor. *Georgetown Law Technology Review*, *1*, 110–125.

Syed, S., Iqbal, A., Mehmood, W., Syed, Z., Khan, M., & Pau, G. (2023). Split-second cryptocurrency forecast using prognostic deep learning algorithms: Data curation by deephaven. *IEEE Access : Practical Innovations, Open Solutions*, *11*, 128644–128654. DOI: 10.1109/ACCESS.2023.3331652

T., V. N. R., G., H. V., A., N., K., S., & Sangers, B. (2025). Future trends and trials in cybersecurity and generative AI. In N. Jhanjhi (Ed.), *Reshaping cybersecurity with generative AI techniques* (pp. 465–490). IGI Global. DOI: 10.4018/979-8-3693-5415-5.ch013

Taddeo, M., & Floridi, L. (2018). Cybersecurity capacity building and international development. *Global Policy*, *9*(3), 353–364. DOI: 10.1111/1758-5899.12550

Talbi, E.-G. (2002). Hybrid metaheuristics taxonomy. *Journal of Heuristics*, *8*(5), 541–564. DOI: 10.1023/A:1016540724870

Tarade, R., & Das, S. (2025). Cybersecurity in the age of AI: Enhancing defences for today's threats. In Gupta, B. B. (Ed.), *Critical phishing defense strategies and digital asset protection* (pp. 309–340). IGI Global., DOI: 10.4018/979-8-3693-8784-9.ch015

Tavabi, N., Bartley, N., Abeliuk, A., Soni, S., Ferrara, E., & Lerman, K. (2019). Characterizing activity on the deep and dark web. Companion Proceedings of the 2019 World Wide Web Conference (WWW), 206–213. DOI: 10.1145/3308560.3316502

Tavabi, N., Goyal, P., Almukaynizi, M., Shakarian, P., & Lerman, K. (2018). DarkEmbed. *AAAI Conference Proceedings*. DOI: 10.1609/aaai.v32i1.11428

Tazi, F., Shrestha, S., De La Cruz, J., & Das, S. (2022). SoK: An Evaluation of the Secure End User Experience on the Dark Net through Systematic Literature Review. *Journal of Cybersecurity and Privacy*, *2*(2), 329–357. DOI: 10.3390/jcp2020018

Temu, R., & Louca, S. (2025). Evaluation of crypto assets investigation techniques: Bitcoin address clustering. In da Cunha, P. R. and Themistocleous, M., editors, *Information Systems - 22nd European, Mediterranean, and Middle Eastern Conference, EMCIS 2025, Paphos, Cyprus, September 11-12, 2025, Proceedings, Part I*, Lecture Notes in Business Information Processing, pages 187–204. Springer.

Thalji, N., Raza, A., Islam, M. S., Samee, N. A., & Jamjoom, M. M. (2023). Ae-net: Novel autoencoder-based deep features for sql injection attack detection. *IEEE Access : Practical Innovations, Open Solutions*, *11*, 135507–135516. DOI: 10.1109/ACCESS.2023.3337645

Touvron, H., Martin, L., Stone, K., Albert, P., Almahairi, A., Babaei, Y., Bashlykov, N., Batra, S., Bhargava, P., Bhosale, S., Bikel, D., Blecher, L., Ferrer, C. C., Chen, M., Cucurull, G., Esiobu, D., Fernandes, J., Fu, J., Fu, W., . . . Scialom, T. (2023). Llama 2: Open foundation and fine-tuned chat models. *arXiv preprint arXiv:2307.09288*. https://arxiv.org/abs/2307.09288

Trend Micro Research. (2024). *Deepfake it 'til you make it: A comprehensive view of the new AI criminal toolset*. https://www.trendmicro.com/vinfo/us/security/news/cybercrime-and-digital-threats/deepfake-it-til-you-make-it-a-comprehensive-view-of-the-new-ai-criminal-toolset

Trend Micro Research. (2025). *The devil reviews Xanthorox: A criminal-focused analysis of the latest malicious LLM offering*. https://www.trendmicro.com/vinfo/us/security/news/cybercrime-and-digital-threats/the-devil-reviews-xanthorox-a-criminal-focused-analysis-of-the-latest-malicious-llm-offering

U., R., P., R., Chandrasekaran, G., & K., M. (2024). Assessment of cybersecurity risks in digital twin deployments in smart cities. International Journal of Computer and Experimental Science and Engineering, 12(4), 233–240. DOI: 10.55524/ijcesen.1566738

Unit 42, Palo Alto Networks. (2026). *Can AI attack the cloud? Lessons from building an autonomous cloud offensive multi-agent system*. https://unit42.paloaltonetworks.com/autonomous-ai-cloud-attacks/

United Nations. (2015). *Transforming our world: The 2030 agenda for sustainable development.* United Nations. https://sdgs.un.org/2030agenda

UNODC. (2023). Comprehensive study on cybercrime: Draft. United Nations Office on Drugs and Crime. https://www.unodc.org/unodc/en/cybercrime/comprehensive-study-on-cybercrime.html

Urman, A., & Katz, S. (2022). What they do in the shadows: Examining the far-right networks on Telegram. *Information Communication and Society*, *25*(7), 904–923. DOI: 10.1080/1369118X.2020.1803946

Uzougbo, N. S., Ikegwu, C. G., & Adewusi, A. O.Ngozi Samuel UzougboChinonso Gladys IkegwuAdefolake Olachi Adewusi. (2024). Regulatory frameworks for decentralized finance (DEFI): Challenges and opportunities. *GSC Advanced Research and Reviews*, *19*(02), 116–129. DOI: 10.30574/gscarr.2024.19.2.0170

Van der Bruggen, M., & Blokland, A. (2021). A crime script analysis of child sexual exploitation material fora on the darkweb. *Sexual Abuse : A Journal of Research and Treatment*, *33*(8), 950–974. DOI: 10.1177/1079063220981063 PMID: 33353483

Van Wegberg, R., Oerlemans, J. J., & Van Deventer, O. (2018). Bitcoin money laundering: Mixed results? An explorative study on money laundering of cybercrime proceeds using bitcoin. *Journal of Financial Crime*, *25*(2), 419–435. DOI: 10.1108/JFC-11-2016-0067

Van Wegberg, R., Oerlemans, J.-J., & Van Deventer, O. (2018). Plug and prey? Measuring the commoditization of cybercrime via online anonymous markets. In *Proceedings of the 27th USENIX Security Symposium* (pp. 1009–1026).

Vaswani, A., Shazeer, N., Parmar, N., ... (2017). Attention is all you need. In *Advances in Neural Information Processing Systems (NeurIPS 30)* (pp. 5998–6020).

Vaswani, A., Shazeer, N., Parmar, N., Uszkoreit, J., Jones, L., Gomez, A. N., Kaiser, Ł., & Polosukhin, I. (2017). Attention is all you need. Advances in Neural Information Processing Systems, 30. https://proceedings.neurips.cc/paper/2017/hash/3f5ee243547dee91fbd053c1c4a845aa-Abstract.html

Vaswani, A., Shazeer, N., Parmar, N., Uszkoreit, J., Jones, L., Gomez, A. N., Kaiser, Ł., & Polosukhin, I. (2017). Attention is all you need. In Vol. 30, pp. 5998–6008). Advances in Neural Information Processing Systems. Curran Associates.

Verizon Business. (2025). *2025 data breach investigations report.*

Verizon. (2024). *2024 data breach investigations report.* Verizon Business. https://www.verizon.com/business/resources/reports/dbir/

Vithalkar, P. N., Prabhat, P., Satonkar, V. H., Sagar, M., Jangale, R. M. G., & Murab, S. A. (2024). Cryptographic protocols resilient to quantum attacks: Advancements in post-quantum cryptography. *CANA*, *31*, 805.

Von Solms, R., & Van Niekerk, J. (2013). From information security to cybersecurity. *Computers & Security*, *38*, 97–102. DOI: 10.1016/j.cose.2013.04.004

Wang, K. (2022). Research on the effectiveness of cybersecurity awareness on incident response. *Electronics (Basel)*, *11*(10), 1659. DOI: 10.3390/electronics11101659

Wang, N., Shi, S., Chen, Y., Lou, W., & Hou, Y. T. (2025). FeCo: Boosting intrusion detection capability in IoT networks via contrastive learning. *IEEE Transactions on Dependable and Secure Computing*, *22*(4), 1120–1135. DOI: 10.1109/TDSC.2025.3544106

Wang, X., Wang, Y., Yu, B., & Gao, Y. (2024). Multi-identity recognition of darknet vendors based on metric learning. *Applied Sciences (Basel, Switzerland)*, *14*(4), 1–22. DOI: 10.3390/app14041619

Wang, Y., Arief, B., & Hernandez-Castro, J. C. (2023). Dark ending: What happens when a dark web market closes down. In *Proceedings of the 9th International Conference on Information Systems Security and Privacy (ICISSP 2023)* (pp. 106-117). SciTePress. DOI: 10.5220/0011681600003405

Weber, M., Domeniconi, G., Chen, J., Weidele, D. K. I., Bellei, C., Robinson, T., & Leiserson, C. E. (2019). Anti-money laundering in Bitcoin: Experimenting with graph convolutional networks for financial forensics. arXiv. https://arxiv.org/abs/1908.02591

Wei, Q., Li, B., Chang, W., Jia, Z., Shen, Z., and Shao, Z. (2022). A survey of blockchain data management systems. *ACM Trans. Embed. Comput. Syst.*, 21(3):25:1–25:28.

Widiastuti, A., & Saragih, Y. M.Yasmirah Mandasari Saragih. (2025). Transnational Cyber Crime: Challenges of International Cooperation in Combating Cybercrime. [IJCS]. *International Journal of Contemporary Sciences*, *3*(7), 109–122. DOI: 10.55927/9gazwn03

William, P., Jawale, M. A., Pawar, A. B., Bibave, R. R., & Narode, P. (2022). Systematic approach for detection and assessment of dark web threat evolution. In Rawat, R., Kaur, U., Khan, S., Sikarwar, R., & Sankaran, K. (Eds.), *Using computational intelligence for the dark web and illicit behavior detection* (pp. 230–256). IGI Global., DOI: 10.4018/978-1-6684-6444-1.ch013

Wolpert, D. H., & Macready, W. G. (1997). No free lunch theorem. *IEEE Transactions on Evolutionary Computation*, *1*(1), 67–82. DOI: 10.1109/4235.585893

Workman, M. (2008). Wisecrackers: A theory-grounded investigation of phishing and pretext social engineering threats to information security. *Journal of the American Society for Information Science and Technology*, *59*(4), 662–674. DOI: 10.1002/asi.20779

World Economic Forum. (2024). *Disrupting cybercrime networks: A collaboration framework*. World Economic Forum.

Wu, Y., Luo, A., & Xu, D. (2019). Forensic analysis of bitcoin transactions. In *2019 IEEE International Conference on Intelligence and Security Informatics, ISI 2019,* Shenzhen, China, July 1-3, 2019, pages 167–169. IEEE.

Xiao, N., Wang, Z., Sun, X., & Miao, J. (2024). A novel blockchain-based digital forensics framework for preserving evidence and enabling investigation in industrial internet of things. *Alexandria Engineering Journal*, *86*, 631–643. DOI: 10.1016/j.aej.2023.12.021

Xu, Y., Chen, G., Wu, J., Xu, W., & Liu, Q. (2021). Research on Dark Web Monitoring Crawler Based on TOR. *2021 IEEE 2nd International Conference on Information Technology, Big Data and Artificial Intelligence (ICIBA)*, 197–202. DOI: 10.1109/ICIBA52610.2021.9687954

Xu, S. (2014). Cybersecurity dynamics: A foundation for the science of cybersecurity. In *Proceedings of the ACM Workshop on New Security Paradigms* (pp. 1–6). https://doi.org/DOI: 10.1145/2683467.2683470

Yang, M., Qu, Y., Ranbaduge, T., Thapa, C., Sultan, N., Ding, M., Suzuki, H., Ni, W., Abuadbba, S., Smith, D., Tyler, P., Pieprzyk, J., Rakotoarivelo, T., Guan, X., & M'rabet, S. (2024). From 5G to 6G: A survey on security, privacy, and standardization pathways. *ACM Computing Surveys*. Advance online publication. DOI: 10.1145/3785467

Yang, X.-S. (2010). *Bat-inspired algorithm. Studies in Computational Intelligence* (Vol. 284). Springer., DOI: 10.1007/978-3-642-12538-6_6

You, I., Kim, J., Pawana, I. W. A. J., & Ko, Y. (2024). Mitigating security vulnerabilities in 6G networks: A comprehensive analysis of the DMRN protocol using SVO logic and ProVerif. *Applied Sciences (Basel, Switzerland)*, *14*(12), 5122. DOI: 10.3390/app14219726

Yusuf, R., & Abdulrahman, I. A. (2025). Towards quantum-resilient log integrity in 5G/6G mobile network protocol analysis. *Global Journal of Engineering and Technology Advances*, *7*(2), 33–45. DOI: 10.30574/gjeta.2025.23.2.0076

Zabihimayvan, M., Sadeghi, R., Rude, H. N., & Doran, D. (2019). Tor ecosystem evaluation. Proceedings of WebSci, 333–342. DOI: 10.1145/3292522.3326053

Zaman, S., Alhazmi, K., Aseeri, M. A., Ahmed, M. R., Khan, R. T., Kaiser, M. S., & Mahmud, M. (2021). Security threats and artificial intelligence based countermeasures for internet of things networks: A comprehensive survey. *IEEE Access : Practical Innovations, Open Solutions*, *9*, 94668–94690. DOI: 10.1109/ACCESS.2021.3089681

Zambiasi, D., & Coull, S. (2022). Exploring the privacy implications of stylometric analysis for cyber-crime investigation. *Digital Investigation*, *40*, 301349. DOI: 10.1016/j.fsidi.2022.301349

Zangana, H. M., Omar, M., & Mohammed, D. (2025). Introduction to artificial intelligence in cybersecurity and forensic science. In Omar, M., Zangana, H., & Mohammed, D. (Eds.), *Integrating artificial intelligence in cybersecurity and forensic practices* (pp. 1–24). IGI Global., DOI: 10.4018/979-8-3373-0588-2.ch001

Zhang, B., Ren, R., Liu, J., Jiang, M., Ren, J., & Li, J. (2024). Sqlpsdem: A proxy-based mechanism towards detecting, locating and preventing second-order sql injections. IEEE Transactions on Software Engineering.

Zhang, R., Xue, R., and Liu, L. (2019). Security and privacy on blockchain. 52(3).

Zhang, Q., Chen, M., Li, L., & Tang, Y. (2022). Artificial intelligence and cybersecurity: Future research directions. *IEEE Access : Practical Innovations, Open Solutions*, *10*, 74216–74230. DOI: 10.1109/ACCESS.2022.3192515

Zhang, X., & Chow, K. P. (2020). A framework for dark web threat intelligence analysis. In *Cyber Warfare and Terrorism: Concepts, methodologies, tools, and applications* (pp. 266–276). IGI Global., DOI: 10.4018/978-1-7998-2466-4.ch017

Zhang, X., Li, P., Tong, X., Chow, K. P., Yuan, D., Chen, S., & Jin, B. (2025). Decoding the shadows: Multi-modal identity profiling in darknet markets using latent behavior feature fusion. *Discover Applied Sciences*, *7*(7), 656. DOI: 10.1007/s42452-025-07217-5

Zhang, Y., Liu, W., & Zhu, T. (2026). MOAT: Federated learning-based method for improved detection of IoT botnets. *IEEE Internet of Things Journal*, *13*(2), 1120–1132. DOI: 10.1109/JIOT.2025.3631450

Zhang, Y., & Liu, Y. (2010). A quantitative risk assessment model for cyber security. *International Journal of Information Security Science*, *2*(4), 45–53.

Zhang, Y., Wang, J., & Luo, J. (2020). Heuristic-based address clustering in bitcoin. *IEEE Access : Practical Innovations, Open Solutions*, *8*, 210582–210591. DOI: 10.1109/ACCESS.2020.3039570

Zhao, Y., Qu, Y., Xiang, Y., Uddin, M. P., Peng, D., and Gao, L. (2025). A comprehensive survey on edge data integrity verification: Fundamentals and future trends. *ACM Comput. Surv.*, 57(1):8:1–8:34.

Zhao, Z., Wang, J., Shi, K., & Zhang, H. (2022). Improving address clustering in bitcoin by proposing heuristics. *IEEE Transactions on Network and Service Management*, *19*(4), 3737–3749. DOI: 10.1109/TNSM.2022.3186466

Zhou, C., Zhao, X., Qiu, Q., & Zhu, C. (2025). Transformer-based intelligent processing techniques for IPv6 internet of things security data. In *Proceedings of the 6th International Conference on Big Data, Artificial Intelligence and Internet of Things Engineering (ICBAIE)*. DOI: 10.1109/ICBAIE66852.2025.11326648

Zhou, Y. (2025). Network security threats and defense mechanisms for 6G multi-virtual network scenarios. *International Journal of Network Management*, *35*(4), e2240. DOI: 10.1002/nem.70003

About the Contributors

Qasem Abu Al-Haija is Chair of the Cybersecurity Department at Jordan University of Science & Technology (JUST), Irbid, with a Ph.D. in Computer Engineering from Tennessee State University (USA). Recognized in Stanford/Elsevier's top 2% scientists list (2023–2025), he has 200+ publications spanning cybersecurity, AI, IoT, CPS, & cryptography.

***

Abdullah S. Alshraa is an Assistant Professor of Cybersecurity at Jordan University of Science and Technology (JUST), He earned his Ph.D. in 2022 from Technische Universität Ilmenau (Germany), researching Software-Defined Networking (SDN) security. Dr. Abdullah later served as an Assistant Professor at FAU University (Germany) and AUM University (Jordan). Dr. Abdullah's current research advances cybersecurity in intrusion detection/prevention systems (IDS/IPS), SDN, smart grids, and related areas in Cyber-Security.

Mohammad Bany Taha is an Associate Professor and Acting Vice Dean at the American University of Madaba, Jordan, specializing in machine learning, cybersecurity, and IoT. He holds a PhD from the University of Quebec (ETS) and has published extensively in IEEE journals and conferences. He also leads the Department of Data Science and AI, where he developed both undergraduate and graduate programs in cybersecurity and AI.

Susanta Das is a seasoned educator with a proven record of teaching and mentoring diverse student populations, working at multiple institutions, and contributing to various organizational initiatives. He received his Ph.D. and M.A. degrees in Physics from Western Michigan University (WMU), USA, and his M.Sc. degree in Physics from Banaras Hindu University (BHU), India. He continued his research as a Marie Curie Postdoctoral Fellow at Stockholm University, Sweden, working on beam diagnostics for DESIREE (Double ElectroStatic Ion Ring ExpEriment) under the DITANET project (Diagnostic Techniques for Particle Accelerators – a Marie Curie Initial Training Network). He also conducted research at the Indian Institute of Science Education and Research (IISER), Kolkata, India, on high-pressure physics as a Project Scientist-B, and at the University of Electro-Communications, Tokyo, Japan, on ion–surface interactions as a Postdoctoral Fellow. Throughout his career, Dr. Das has worked and collaborated with numerous researchers, Ph.D. scholars, master's students, and visiting scholars from different countries. He has visited several countries to present and discuss his research and has participated in international conferences in the UK, Italy, Germany, Greece, Belgium, Bulgaria, Romania, Brazil, and other countries. He worked at several institutions before assuming his current role at Ajeenkya D Y Patil University. He has received several prestigious awards and fellowships, including the Marie Curie

Postdoctoral Fellowship (Sweden), the Science Academies' Summer Research Fellowship (India), the Gowen Frostic Doctoral Fellowship, the Department Graduate Research and Creative Scholar Award from WMU, and the Leo R. Parpart Doctoral Fellowship from the Department of Physics, WMU, among many others. Dr. Das has co-authored several research articles in WoS- and Scopus-indexed international journals, conference proceedings, and scholarly book chapters. He has also co-edited multiple books published by renowned international publishing houses, including IGI Global, Springer Nature, Wiley, Scrivener-Wiley, and Notion Press. Currently, Dr. Das is actively engaged in cutting-edge research with a keen interest in nanotechnology, the United Nations Sustainable Development Goals (UN SDGs), and data science. His multifaceted contributions in teaching, research, and academic leadership reflect a dedicated professional who significantly advances the vision and mission of the institutions he serves.

Hussam N. Fakhouri is an Assistant Professor of Data Science at Al-Balqa Applied University (BAU) in Jordan, a position he has held since 2025. He earned his Ph.D. in Computer Science from the University of Jordan in 2020, where his doctoral research focused on data science. Dr. Fakhouri's research interests span multiple domains within artificial intelligence and data science, including metaheuristic algorithms, optimization, data analysis, data exploration, data engineering, machine learning, and deep learning. He has authored approximately 100 research papers in reputable international journals and conference proceedings. In addition, Dr. Fakhouri contributes to the scholarly community as an academic editor and reviewer. Dr. Fakhouri has also undertaken significant academic leadership roles. He has also participated in Erasmus Programs such as doctoral schools hosted by universities in Denmark, Germany, and Russia.

Faten F. Hamad is an Associate Professor in the Department of Information Studies at Sultan Qaboos University (Oman), where she has served since September 2021. She earned her Ph.D. in Information Science from Aberystwyth University (UK) in 2013, following an M.Sc. in Computer Science from the University of Jordan (2006) and a B.Sc. in Computer Science from Yarmouk University (2004). Her research interests span advanced metaheuristic optimization and AI-driven data analytics, applied to engineering design, cybersecurity, and intelligent systems, and extend to digital transformation, accessibility, and resilience in academic libraries and education.

Abdelraouf M. Ishtaiwi is an Associate Professor of Artificial Intelligence and Data Science at the University of Petra, Jordan, with over 22 years of academic and research experience in AI. He earned his Master's and Ph.D. degrees in Artificial Intelligence from Griffith University, Australia, where he focused on heuristic optimization techniques for satisfiability problems. His research expertise spans machine learning, hybrid metaheuristic optimization, associative classification, and AI applications in cybersecurity and emerging technologies like the metaverse. Dr. Ishtaiwi has developed innovative AI algorithms, such as ACRIPPER and hybrid crayfish-DE models, and contributed significantly to areas like phishing detection, blockchain security, and smart IoT defense. As a former Head of the Department of Data Science and AI at Petra University, he led academic reforms and accreditation initiatives. He has also been a visiting scholar at Griffith University and Universitat Pompeu Fabra, reflecting his international academic engagement.

Fawaz A. Khasawneh is currently an assistant professor in the cybersecurity department at Jordan University of Science and Technology. My research interest in Malware analysis, Network security and Machine Learning.

Tanishka Prashant Madke is currently pursuing her B.Tech. in Computer Engineering at the School of Engineering, Ajeenkya D Y Patil University, Pune, Maharashtra, India. She has a strong passion for research and has authored multiple articles in NOVA Science Publishers and IGI-Global, USA. Her research interests encompass AI (Artificial Intelligence), Big Data, climate change, and environmental sustainability. She is particularly focused on contributing to the United Nations Sustainable Development Goals (SDGs), especially those related to climate action, innovation in technology, and sustainable cities. Through her work, she aims to explore how AI and emerging technologies can drive sustainable solutions, bridging the gap between innovation and global challenges.

Surya Prakash Nalluri is a cybersecurity innovator, researcher, and executive leader with 20+ years of experience in cybersecurity, privacy, DevSecOps, and security architecture, specializing in banking and finance. He holds a Bachelor's in Computer Science and a Master's in Information Systems Security. Surya is the inventor of an integrated security testing framework and has pioneered methodologies for web and thick client application security. His work spans AI-driven security, intrusion detection, threat intelligence, IoT, and blockchain. He also developed a supply chain defense framework to counter protestware threats. Surya leads global security operations, promotes secure SDLC practices, and mentors cybersecurity professionals through public sessions and expert panels. Widely regarded as a top-tier cybersecurity expert, he continues to shape security innovation and policy through research and industry collaboration.

Khalil Omar is an assistant professor at the University of Petra in Jordan. He received his Ph.D. degree in computer science from the University of Oldenburg, Germany, in 2018. His academic focus is on distance learning and e-learning in combination with software engineering, mobile applications, usability design, adaptive interfaces, and ERP systems. Users can reach him through his email address: komar@uop.edu.jo.

Yaakulya Sabbani is an aspiring Cybersecurity & Machine Learning Researcher, passionate about threat detection, AI-driven security, and digital resilience. As a student at NYU, I specialize in cyber defense, cloud security, and adversarial AI. Recognized as India's youngest ethical hacker (CEH at 18) and recipient of the Best Intern Award for identifying critical vulnerabilities. My work includes ML-powered phishing detection (92% accuracy), cloud security enhancements, and adversarial testing on LLMs.

Amisha Shaikh is currently doing her B.Tech. in Computer Engineering at the School of Engineering, Ajeenkya D Y Patil University, Pune, Maharashtra, India. She has broad research interests from understanding the properties of biogenic gold nanoparticles to their application in various fields. In addition to nanoparticles, her interests extend into AI (Artificial Intelligence), Biotechnology, and Cybersecurity. She strives to contribute significantly in the possibilities of nanoparticles and AI, focusing on their vast applications. She aims to conduct research in these domains and make them more applied.

K. Muthamil Sudar received his Ph.D. in Computer Science and Engineering and currently serves as an Assistant Professor in the Department of Computer Science and Engineering at Mepco Schlenk Engineering College, Sivakasi, Tamil Nadu, India. He has published extensively in the domains of network security, Software Defined Networking (SDN), and machine learning, with a strong emphasis on DDoS attack detection, adversarial defense, and secure network architectures.

Index

Symbols

A

B

C

D

E

F

G

H

I

L

M

N

O

P

R

S

T

W

www.ingramcontent.com/pod-product-compliance
Lightning Source LLC
LaVergne TN
LVHW080532300926
849162LV00007B/1587